LAND REGISTRATION MANUAL

FOURTH EDITION

LAND REGISTRATION MANUAL

FOURTH EDITION

Ash Jones

LLB (Hons)
Land Registrar, HM Land Registry

WS &H

Wildy, Simmonds & Hill Publishing

ISBN: 9780854903115

British Library Cataloguing in Publication Data

A catalogue record for this book is available from the British Library

Second edition 2014
Third edition 2018

This edition published in 2026 by

Wildy, Simmonds & Hill Publishing
Wildy & Sons Ltd
Lincoln's Inn Archway
Carey Street
London WC2A 2JD
www.wildy.com

Printed in Great Britain by CPI Group (UK) Ltd, Croydon CR0 4YY.

Contents

Glossary of Terms

ANLA 1992	Access to Neighbouring Land Act 1992
CA 2006	Commons Act 2006
CCBSA 2014	Co-operative and Community Benefit Societies Act 2014
CILEX	Chartered Institute of Legal Executives
CIO	charitable incorporated organisation
CNBC	Civil National Business Centre
Commissioners	Commissioners of HM Revenue and Customs
conveyancer	definition set out in LRR 2003, r 217(A)(1)
CRA 1965	Commons Registration Act 1965
developing estate	registered title consisting of land being developed for residential and/or commercial purposes and disposed of in individual plots or flats
DRS	Digital Registration Service
DX	document exchange
ED	electronic discharge
EDMO	empty dwelling management order
EEIG	European Economic Interest Grouping
EEIG Regulations 1989	European Economic Interest Grouping Regulations 1989 (SI 1989/638)
FCA	Financial Conduct Authority
Fee Order	Land Registration Fee Order 2024 (SI 2024/931) or (where appropriate) the current Land Registration Fee Order for the time being in force
FLA 1996	Family Law Act 1996
HA 1985	Housing Act 1985
HA 1988	Housing Act 1988
HA 1996	Housing Act 1996
HA 2004	Housing Act 2004
HMLR	HM Land Registry and (where the context so admits) the Chief Land Registrar of HM Land Registry
HMRC	HM Revenue and Customs
IA 1986	Insolvency Act 1986

IHT	inheritance tax
IR 2016	Insolvency (England and Wales) Rules 2016 (SI 2016/1024)
IVA	individual voluntary arrangement
LA 1980	Limitation Act 1980
LFRA 2024	Leasehold and Freehold Reform Act 2024
LHA	local housing authority
LLP	limited liability partnership
LPA 1925	Law of Property Act 1925
LPA receiver	LPA 1925 receiver
LRA 1925	Land Registration Act 1925
LRA 2002	Land Registration Act 2002
LRA (TP) Order 2003	Land Registration Act 2002 (Transitional Provisions) Order 2003 (SI 2003/1953)
LRHUDA 1993	Leasehold Reform, Housing and Urban Development Act 1993
LRR 2003	Land Registration Rules 2003 (SI 2003/1417)
LSST	Large Scale Services Team for HMLR
LTT	land transaction tax
LURA 2023	Levelling-up and Regeneration Act 2023
Model Law	United Nations Commission on International Trade Law Model Law on Cross-Border Insolvency
OS	Ordnance Survey
PAA 1971	Powers of Attorney Act 1971
PHSO	Parliamentary and Health Service Ombudsman
PPP	public-private partnership
proper office	office designated under LRA 2002, s 100(3) and the current Land Registration (Proper Office) Order for the receipt of applications or a specified description of application or, if no such order subsists, under the provisions of any relevant direction by the registrar under LRA 2002, s 100(4) as to the address to be used for the delivery of applications
Referral Rules	Land Registration (Referral to the Adjudicator to HM Land Registry) Rules 2003 (SI 2003/2114)
relevant enactments	(in relation to rights of reverter) School Sites Acts of 1841, 1844, 1849, 1851 and 1852, Literary and Scientific Institutions Act 1854 and Places of Worship Sites Act 1873
RH(W)A 2016	Renting Homes (Wales) Act 2016
RPT	Residential Property Tribunal

RTE company	right to enfranchise company, i.e. a private company limited by guarantee, of which all qualifying tenants are entitled to be members, and having as an object the exercise of the right to collective enfranchisement
RTM	right to manage
Sch 1 form	form contained within LRR 2003, Sch 1
Sch 3 form	form contained within LRR 2003, Sch 3
SDLT	stamp duty land tax
SLA 1925	Settled Land Act 1925
standard form restriction	restriction in one of the standard forms set out in LRR 2003, Sch 4; references to a particular form (for example Form A, etc) are to the relevant standard form of restriction set out in Sch 4
statement of truth	statement of truth which complies with the requirements set out in LRR 2003, r 215A
the 1986 Measure	Patronage (Benefices) Measure 1986 (1986/3)
the 2018 Measure	Church Property Measure 2018 (2018/8)
the 2021 Measure	Cathedrals Measure 2021 (2021/2)
TLATA	Trusts of Land and Appointment of Trustees Act 1996
Tribunal	Land Registration Division of the Property Chamber, First-tier Tribunal
Tribunal Rules	Tribunal Procedure (First-tier Tribunal) (Property Chamber) Rules 2013 (SI 2013/1169)
UKEIG	United Kingdom Economic Interest Grouping
UK GDPR	United Kingdom General Data Protection Regulation
WRA	Welsh Revenue Authority

References to an Act or Statutory Instrument are (if applicable) to that Act or Statutory Instrument as amended.

The commentary in this book is that of the author and not of HMLR.

The law is stated as at 31 May 2025, although subsequent changes have been taken into account where possible.

For brevity throughout the book, masculine references are used to represent both masculine and feminine.

1 ACCESS TO NEIGHBOURING LAND ORDERS

Someone who:

(a) wishes to enter onto adjoining or adjacent land, for the purpose of carrying out works to land, and
(b) needs, but does not have, the consent of some other person to that entry,

may apply to the court for an access order.[1]

'Land' for this purpose:

(a) does not include a highway;[2]
(b) does include a party wall;[3] and
(c) is otherwise as defined in Interpretation Act 1978, Sch 1.

The applicant must commence the application in the county court.[4] Once issued it is a pending land action. The applicant should protect the priority of the application by entry of an agreed notice or a unilateral notice in the register for the land to be accessed. Usually, an application for an agreed notice will be appropriate. The application cannot comprise an overriding interest.[5]

The High Court set out the questions the court should consider when deciding whether to make an access order in *Prime London Holdings 11 Ltd v Thurloe Lodge Ltd*.[6]

Where the court makes an access order, the beneficiary should protect it by entry of an agreed notice in the register for the land to be accessed. It is not possible to protect such an access order by a unilateral notice.[7] Further, it cannot comprise an overriding interest.[8]

Subject, where necessary, to its priority being protected by a notice in the register, an access order binds:

(a) the original respondent to the application;
(b) his successors in title; and
(c) all persons who subsequently obtain an estate, right or interest in or over the servient land which is derived under that respondent.[9]

The court may, on the application of the parties to the proceedings or any other person bound by the access order, make an order varying the access order.[10] The variation should also be protected by entry of an agreed notice. The entry made in the register will give details of the variation. It is not possible to protect such a variation by entry of a unilateral notice.[11]

Where a licence allows access to neighbouring land, it is not possible to note this in the register. Even a contractual licence does not bind successors in title.[12] If the registered proprietor consents, the licensee may enter a restriction in the register of the servient title. A restriction does not confer any priority. However, it prevents an entry being made in the register relating to any disposition, or a disposition of a specified kind, unless the terms of the restriction have (where applicable) been complied with.

It is also possible to have an easement to enter on another's land for the purpose of carrying out work on a person's own land.[13]

1.1 Notice of a pending land action

1.1.1 Agreed notice

In addition to the usual documents required,[14] an applicant should deliver to HM Land Registry (HMLR) the claim form sealed by the court showing the court reference number, or a certified copy of it. This should satisfy HMLR of the validity of the applicant's claim in accordance with LRA 2002, s 34(3)(c).

The agreed notice in the register will give details of the interest protected.

1.1.2 Unilateral notice

In addition to delivering the usual documents required,[15] an applicant should ensure the statement in panel 11 or conveyancer's certificate in panel 12 of form UN1 is completed to show the applicant's interest. An example might be:

> applicant in an application under section 1 of the Access to Neighbouring Land Act 1992 in the [*name*] County Court [*set out full court reference and parties*].

The unilateral notice will give brief details of the interest protected and identify the beneficiary of the notice.

1.2 Agreed notice in respect of an access order

In addition to the usual documents required,[16] an applicant should deliver to HMLR the access order or a certified copy of it. This should satisfy HMLR of the validity of the applicant's claim in accordance with LRA 2002, s 34(3)(c).

The agreed notice in the register will give details of the interest protected.

1.3 Agreed notice in respect of an order varying the access order

In addition to the usual documents required,[17] an applicant should deliver to HMLR the order varying the access order or a certified copy of it. This should satisfy HMLR as to the validity of the applicant's claim in accordance with LRA 2002, s 34(3)(c).

The agreed notice in the register will give details of the interest protected.

1.4 Restriction in respect of a licence

An applicant should deliver to HMLR the usual documents required.[18]

Panel 9 of form RX1 should set out the required restriction(s). Assuming the licence contains an express obligation on the licensor to ensure any disponee grants the licensee a new licence, a possible form of restriction based on Form L is:

> No disposition of the registered estate (other than a charge) by the proprietor of the registered estate is to be registered without a written consent signed by [*licensee*] of [*address*] or their conveyancer that the provisions of [*specify clause imposing obligation to procure new licence*] of the licence agreement dated [*date*] made between [*licensor*] and [*licensee*] have been complied with.

The wording of Form L is set out in Appendix IV.

A restriction in a standard form contained in LRR 2003, Sch 4 does not require the approval of HMLR to the terms of the restriction under LRA 2002, s 43(3).

1 Access to Neighbouring Land Act 1992 (ANLA 1992), s 1.
2 ANLA 1992, s 8(3).
3 *Dean v Walker* [1996] EWCA Civ 505.
4 ANLA 1992, s 5(6).
5 Land Registration Act 2002 (LRA 2002), s 87(3).
6 [2022] EWHC 303 (Ch).
7 Land Registration Rules 2003 (LRR 2003), r 80.
8 ANLA 1992, s 5(5) as substituted by LRA 2002, Sch 11, para 26(4).
9 ANLA 1992, s 4.
10 ANLA 1992, s 6.
11 LRR 2003, r 80.
12 *Ashburn Anstalt v W J Arnold and Co* [1988] EWCA Civ 14.
13 See 62 Equitable Easements, and 101 Legal Easements.
14 See 119.1 Agreed notice.

[15] See 119.3 Unilateral notice.
[16] See 119.1 Agreed notice.
[17] See 119.1 Agreed notice.
[18] See 153.1 Application for entry of restriction.

2 ACCRETION AND DILUVION

The doctrine of accretion and diluvion recognises that where land is bounded by water, the forces of nature are likely to cause changes in the boundary between the land and the water. Consequently, where land has a boundary with water, title of the owner of the land normally extends to any land added by accretion. Equally, where there is erosion, or diluvion, title to the land affected is lost.

This doctrine applies only where the changes are gradual and imperceptible[1] and where they are natural, not man-made. The doctrine can be excluded if this is the intention of the parties concerned.

If the doctrine applies, the boundary between registered titles abutting a natural non-tidal river or stream will change if the course of the river or stream alters naturally over time. The fact that a registered estate in land is shown in the register as having a particular boundary does not affect the operation of accretion or diluvion.[2] This applies whether the registered title has a general boundary or a determined boundary.[3]

An agreement about the operation of accretion or diluvion in relation to registered land has effect only if registered. An application to register such an agreement must be made by, or accompanied by the consent of, the registered proprietor of the land and of any registered charge, but no such consent is required from a person who is party to the agreement.[4]

2.1 Registration of agreement

An applicant should deliver to HMLR:

(a) an application in form AP1;
(b) the agreement about the operation of accretion or diluvion or a certified copy of it;
(c) the consent of the registered proprietor of the land and of any registered charge, where such person or persons is/are not party/parties to the agreement; and
(d) the fee payable.[5]

On registration of the agreement, HMLR makes a note in the property register that the agreement is registered for the purposes of LRA 2002, s 61(2).[6]

---

1 *Southern Centre of Theosophy Inc v State of South Australia* [1982] AC 706.
2 LRA 2002, s 61(1).
3 See 22 Boundaries.
4 LRR 2003, r 123(1).
5 See 67 Fees.
6 See also 72 Foreshore.

3 ADDRESS FOR SERVICE

The register contains an address for service (including any postcode) of each proprietor of the registered estate and any registered charge. Such an address is also required for certain other persons, including:

(a) the beneficiary of a unilateral notice;
(b) the cautioner under a caution against first registration;
(c) the person named in a restriction which requires his consent or certificate or the service of notice upon him; and
(d) a person entitled to be notified of an application for adverse possession under LRR 2003, r 194.

A person's address for service must be kept up to date. Otherwise, there is a risk official notices sent by HMLR might not reach him.

Where the proprietor lives at the registered property, the address for service will usually be the full postal address of the property. However, in other cases, such as where the property is acquired for rental purposes, this is not likely to be appropriate and an alternative address should be provided.

A person may have up to three addresses, including the address of his conveyancer, entered in the register.[1] One address for service must be a postal address inside or outside the United Kingdom. HMLR will enter an address for service in a format that conforms with official sources such as Royal Mail. Where HMLR sends a notice, the period for responding to it is determined by reference to the date of issue of the notice, not the date it is deemed to have been received. A person providing an overseas address should bear in mind that notice periods are not extended for overseas addresses and there is a risk that he may not receive the notice in time to respond. Up to two additional addresses for service may be provided, which can include a document exchange (DX) box number and/or an electronic address. To mitigate the risks of post going missing or being intercepted, a proprietor should consider having an electronic address for service in addition to the mandatory postal address.

An application to change to an address for service in the register should be made in form AP1. Registered proprietors may also use form COG1 to update their address(es) for service. No fee is currently payable. Unless a conveyancer lodges the application, HMLR will require evidence of identity.[2] As a security measure, HMLR will enter a note in the register whenever an address for service is changed.

---

1 LRR 2003, r 198.
2 See 84 Identity Evidence.

4 ADMINISTRATIVE RECEIVERS

An administrative receiver is either:

(a) a receiver or manager of the whole (or substantially the whole) of a company's property appointed by or on behalf of the holders of any debentures of the company secured by a charge which, as created, was a floating charge, or by such a charge and one or more other securities; or
(b) a person who would be such a receiver or manager but for the appointment of some other person as the receiver of part of the company's property.[1]

An administrative receiver must be an insolvency practitioner. He can be appointed either by the court or under powers contained in a debenture. Subject to certain limited exceptions, an administrative receiver cannot be appointed by the holder of a debenture dated on or after 15 September 2003, notwithstanding any provision contained in the debenture.[2] The exceptions are set out in Insolvency Act 1986 (IA 1986), ss 72B to 72GA and include, for example, where the company is a registered social landlord or is a project company of a project which is a public-private partnership (PPP).

There should already be an entry relating to the debenture under which the receiver is appointed in the register of the company's title, either because it has been:

(a) registered as a registered charge; or
(b) protected by entry of a notice.

As the property remains vested in the company:

(a) HMLR cannot register the administrative receiver as proprietor of the title; and
(b) his appointment cannot be noted in the register.

The administrative receiver may, however, make an application for any necessary changes to the company's address for service in the register.

4.1 Amendment to address for service

The administrative receiver should ensure he will receive any notices sent to the company's address for service shown in the register.[3] If he requires an amended address or additional address for service (up to three are permitted), he should deliver to HMLR:

(a) an application in form AP1;
(b) a certified copy of the appointment of the receiver; and
(c) a certified copy of the debenture (if not already registered or the subject of a notice in the register with a copy filed at HMLR).

No fee is currently payable.

4.2 Sale or other disposition by an administrative receiver

The powers given by the debenture to an administrative receiver are deemed to include the powers specified in IA 1986, Sch 1, except insofar as they are inconsistent with the provisions of the debenture. The powers in Sch 1 include power to sell and to grant, or accept a surrender of, a lease. An administrative receiver has a statutory power to use the company's seal and to execute any deed or other document in the name and on behalf of the company.[4]

Although the administrative receiver will usually use the statutory power, the debenture will also usually give the administrative receiver the right to sell or otherwise dispose of the company's property. Such a power includes the power to execute in the name and on behalf of the company and will survive liquidation of the company.[5]

Alternatively, the debenture may grant a power of attorney in favour of the administrative receiver; such a power is not a security power and will not survive liquidation of the company. If the administrative receiver executes as attorney, even if the power is under 12 months old, the application for registration of the disposition will need to be accompanied by a statutory declaration or statement of truth confirming that the applicant did not, at the time of the completion of the transaction, know of any revocation of the power or know of the occurrence of any event (such as the liquidation of the company) which had the effect of revoking the power. The applicant may provide a conveyancer's certificate to the same effect instead.

An administrative receiver is agent of the company. On liquidation this agency comes to an end, but the receiver continues to have power to act for the purposes of holding and disposing of the company's property and may use the company's name for that purpose.[6]

Any person dealing with the administrative receiver for value and in good faith does not need to verify whether he is acting within his powers.[7]

An administrative receiver, being the agent of the company not of the debenture holder, has no power to discharge the company's property from any mortgage or charge (including the debenture under which he was appointed), whether or not the mortgage or charge was created after the debenture. Consequently, on a sale of a property by an administrative receiver, the transferee must, where appropriate, ensure he obtains a discharge for all mortgages and charges, including the debenture itself.

However, an administrative receiver may apply to the court for an order authorising him to dispose of the property free from charges that have priority to the debenture under which he was appointed.[8] The administrative receiver would need to satisfy the court that the property could be more advantageously disposed of free from the charges.

When registering a transfer of a registered title by an administrative receiver, the transferee should deliver to HMLR:

(a) an application in form AP1;
(b) the transfer by the company;
(c) evidence that the power of appointment of an administrative receiver under the debenture has arisen. This may be in the form of a certificate by, or on behalf of, the chargee that the power has arisen. If the debenture is dated on or after 15 September 2003 and the appointment is not made by the court, the applicant must supply evidence that one of the exceptions in IA 1986, ss 72A to 72GA applies;
(d) the instrument of appointment of the administrative receiver or a certified copy of it. If joint administrative receivers are appointed, the appointment must state whether they can act jointly and severally;[9]
(e) the debenture, or a certified copy of it, under which the receiver was appointed (unless already registered or the subject of a notice in the register with a copy filed at HMLR);

(f) releases or discharges in respect of any charges appearing in the registered title (including the debenture under which the administrative receiver was appointed) and not dealt with under (g) below;
(g) where the court has made an order allowing the administrative receiver to dispose of the registered title free from charges, an office copy or certified copy of that order;
(h) evidence of non-revocation, where the administrative receiver executes as attorney of the company;
(i) details of any challenge to the validity of the debenture by a liquidator of the company, including the name and address of the liquidator;
(j) any new mortgage or charge entered into by the transferee;
(k) form DI, giving the information as to overriding interests required by LRR 2003, r 57, including any documentary evidence of the interests;[10]
(l) the appropriate confirmation or evidence as to identity;[11]
(m) the appropriate stamp duty land tax (SDLT) and/or land transaction tax (LTT) certificate(s) or other evidence;[12] and
(n) the fee payable.[13]

---

1 Insolvency Act 1986 (IA 1986), s 29(2).
2 IA 1986, s 72A.
3 See 3 Address for Service.
4 IA 1986, s 42(1) and Sch 1.
5 *Barrows v Chief Land Registrar*, *The Times*, 20 October 1977.
6 *Sowman v David Samuel Trust Ltd* [1978] 1 All ER 616.
7 IA 1986, s 42(3).
8 IA 1986, s 43.
9 IA 1986, s 231(2).
10 See 128.4 Duty to Disclose Overriding Interests.
11 See 84 Identity Evidence.
12 See 168 Stamp Duty Land Tax and/or 94 Land Transaction Tax.
13 See 67 Fees.

5 ADMINISTRATORS OF A COMPANY

An administrator is a person appointed under IA 1986, s 8 and Sch B1 to manage the affairs, business and property of a company. An administrator must be an insolvency practitioner and can be appointed by either:

(a) an administration order made by the court;[1]
(b) the holder of a qualifying floating charge;[2] or
(c) the company or its directors.[3]

The administrator must perform his functions with the objective of rescuing the company as a going concern or, failing that, achieving a better result for the company's creditors as a whole than would be likely if it were wound up. If neither objective is reasonably practicable, he may realise property to make a distribution to one or more secured or preferential creditors provided he does no unnecessary harm to the interests of the creditors of the company as a whole.[4]

The administrator can apply for the administration order and his appointment to be noted in the register.[5]

5.1 Entry of appointment of an administrator in the register

The administrator should deliver to HMLR:

(a) an application in form AP1;
(b) either:

    (i) an office copy or certified copy of the order of the court appointing the administrator, or
    (ii) a sealed copy of the prescribed notice of appointment completed in accordance with Insolvency (England and Wales) Rules 2016 (SI 2016/1024) (IR 2016), r 3.17, r 3.24 or r 3.25,[6]

    as the case may be; and
(c) the fee payable.[7]

A similar application will be needed where a new or additional administrator is appointed.

HMLR will enter the following note of the appointment in the proprietorship register:

> (*Date*) By [an order of the court made on] [or a notice of appointment filed on] (*date*) [*name of administrator*] of [*administrator's address*] was appointed administrator of [*name of company*].

Although administration normally terminates automatically after one year, this period can be extended. Consequently, HMLR will not automatically remove the entries without an application supported by evidence. Where the administration has come to an end, the administrator or registered proprietor should apply to cancel the note of the administrator's appointment. The applicant should deliver to HMLR:

(a) an application in form AP1; and
(b) either:

   (i) an office copy or certified copy of a court order; or
   (ii) a certified copy of the prescribed notice registered with Companies House.

There is currently no fee payable.

5.2 Sale or other disposition by an administrator

While a company is in administration its property remains vested in it. The administrator acts as agent of the company and has powers to do anything necessary or expedient for the management of the affairs, business and property of the company. This includes the powers specified in IA 1986, Sch 1, which include power to sell and to grant or accept a surrender of a lease. The administrator can use the company seal and execute any deed, receipt or document in the name of and on behalf of the company.

Any person dealing with the administrator for value and in good faith does not need to verify whether he is acting within his powers.[8]

An administrator's appointment ceases to have effect after one year unless it has been expressly extended. It can be extended only:

(a) for a specific time; and
(b) by either:

   (i) an order of the court; or
   (ii) (once only and for not more than 6 months) the consent of all the secured creditors and a majority of the unsecured creditors of the company.

If an administrator makes a disposition more than one year after the company went into administration, HMLR will require evidence that the administrator's appointment has been extended.

An administrator may dispose of the company's property free from any floating charge to which it is subject.[9] This extends to any charge which, as created, was a floating charge. It is irrelevant that the charge has, under its terms, crystallised on the service of notice by the administrator.[10]

An administrator may also apply to the court for an order authorising him to dispose of the property free from a charge which, as created, was not a floating charge.[11]

Where the disposition by an administrator is a transfer, the transferee of a registered title from the administrator should deliver to HMLR:

(a) an application in form AP1;
(b) the transfer by the company;
(c) either:

  (i) an office copy or certified copy of the order of the court appointing the administrator, or
  (ii) a sealed copy of the prescribed notice of appointment completed in accordance with IR 2016, r 3.17, r 3.24 or r 3.25,[12]

  as the case may be (where this has not previously been noted in the register);
(d) if the transfer is made more than one year after the company went into administration, evidence that the administrator's appointment has been extended, in the form of either:

  (i) an office copy or certified copy of an order of the court; or
  (ii) a certified copy of a prescribed notice of extension;

(e) releases or discharges in respect of any charges appearing in the title and not dealt with under (f), (g) or (h) below;[13]
(f) where a floating charge is noted in the register (other than by way of unilateral notice), form CN1 signed by the administrator with panel 11 stating that the registered title has been transferred pursuant to IA 1986, Sch B1, para 70;
(g) where a floating charge is noted in the register by way of unilateral notice, form UN2 to remove it or form UN4 to cancel it;[14]
(h) where the court has made an order allowing the administrator to dispose of the registered title free from a fixed charge, an office copy or certified copy of that order;
(i) form DI giving the information as to overriding interests required by LRR 2003, r 57, including any documentary evidence of the interests;[15]
(j) the appropriate confirmation or evidence as to identity;[16]
(k) the appropriate SDLT or LTT certificate(s) or other evidence;[17] and
(l) the fee payable.[18]

5.3 Acquisition by company subject to an administration order

Where a company's property has with the authorisation of the court been disposed of free from a charge, the chargee is entitled to his original security in respect of any new property the company acquires with the proceeds.[19] Accordingly, where a company subject to an administration order is being registered as proprietor of a registered estate, HMLR will make the following entry in the charges register:

> The registered estate is subject to such security or securities as may exist and affect the same by virtue of the provisions of paragraph 70(2) of Schedule B1 to the Insolvency Act 1986.

HMLR does not make this entry if the administrator certifies there are no such securities or that such securities as are affected have been discharged.

---

1 IA 1986, Sch B1, para 10.
2 IA 1986, Sch B1, para 14.
3 IA 1986, Sch B1, para 22.
4 IA 1986, Sch B1, para 3.
5 LRR 2003, r 184(2).
6 Or, where the appointment was made before 6 April 2017 or under the transitional provisions contained in the 2016 rules, in form 2.6B, 2.7B, 2.9B or 2.10B prescribed under the Insolvency Rules 1986 (SI 1986/1925).
7 See 67 Fees.
8 IA 1986, s 14(6).
9 IA 1986, Sch B1, para 70.
10 IA 1986, s 251; *Re Brightlife Ltd* [1987] Ch 200.
11 IA 1986, Sch B1, para 71.
12 Or, where the appointment was made before 6 April 2017 or under the transitional provisions contained in the 2016 rules, in form 2.6B, 2.7B, 2.9B or 2.10B prescribed under the Insolvency Rules 1986 (SI 1986/1925).
13 See 100.11 Discharge of registered charge.
14 See 119.5 Removal of a unilateral notice and 119.6 Cancellation of a unilateral notice.
15 See 128.4 Duty to disclose overriding interests.
16 See 84 Identity Evidence.
17 See 168 Stamp Duty Land Tax and/or 94 Land Transaction Tax.
18 See 67 Fees.
19 IA 1986, Sch B1, para 70(2).

6 ADVERSE POSSESSION

Adverse possession is the mechanism by which a person 'squatting' on land may:

(a) in the case of unregistered land, acquire an unregistered legal estate in that land and extinguish that of the documentary title owner; or
(b) in the case of registered land, become entitled to be registered as proprietor of the land in place of the existing proprietor.

There are different principles and procedures applicable to an application for registration based upon adverse possession, depending upon whether the application:

(a) is for first registration; or
(b) relates to registered land and is made under the transitional provisions of LRA 2002, Sch 12, para 18; or
(c) relates to registered land and is made under the provisions of LRA 2002, Sch 6.

The different types of application are discussed below. However, the underlying principles of adverse possession will apply to each of them. Essentially, an application based upon adverse possession must be supported by evidence to satisfy HMLR that:

(a) the squatter has factual possession of the land;
(b) the squatter has the necessary intention to possess the land;
(c) the squatter's possession is without the owner's consent; and
(d) all of the above have been true of the squatter (and any predecessors through whom he claims) for at least the minimum required period.

For adverse possession in relation to rentcharges, see 151 Rentcharges.

Special considerations apply where the application relates to leasehold land or where the squatter has encroached from their own leasehold land onto other land.[1]

Where a person has been in adverse possession of unregistered land for the appropriate period of limitation, the documentary title owner's paper title is extinguished.[2] The normal period of limitation for recovery of land is 12 years but this period may be extended in certain circumstances.

The LRA 2002 introduced new provisions to obtain title to registered land by adverse possession. The position relating to registered land now differs significantly from that relating to unregistered land. The LRA 2002 provides that no period of limitation under LA 1980, s 15 (time limits in relation to recovery of land) runs against any person, other than a chargee, in relation to an estate in land or rentcharge the title to which is registered. No period of limitation under LA 1980, s 16 (time limits in relation to redemption of land) is to run against any person in relation to such an estate in land or rentcharge. Accordingly, LA 1980, s 17 (extinction of title on expiry of time limit) does not operate to extinguish the title of any person where, by virtue of this, a period of limitation does not run against him.[3]

Instead, under LRA 2002, Sch 6, para 1, a person may apply to be registered as proprietor of a registered estate in land if he has been in adverse possession of the estate for the period of 10 years ending on the date of the application. The estate need not have been registered throughout the period of adverse possession.[4]

A person may also apply for registration if:

(a) he has, in the period of 6 months before the application, ceased to be in adverse possession of the estate because of eviction by the registered proprietor or a person claiming under the registered proprietor;
(b) on the day before his eviction he had been in adverse possession for the period of 10 years; and
(c) the eviction was not pursuant to a judgment for possession.

A person may not make such an application if he is a defendant in proceedings which involve asserting a right to possession of the land, or if judgment for possession of the land has been given against him in the last 2 years.

HMLR must give notice of the application to the proprietor of the registered estate and certain other specified persons. In addition, any person who can satisfy HMLR that he has an interest in a registered estate in land which would be prejudiced by the registration of any other person as proprietor consequent upon an adverse possession application may apply to be registered as a person to be notified of such application.[5]

Those people given notice may then either:

(a) consent to the application;
(b) give counter-notice to HMLR;
(c) object to the application; or
(d) give counter-notice and object.

If HMLR receives a counter-notice, HMLR will reject the application unless:

(a) the applicant has stated in his application that he intends to rely on one or more of the three conditions set out in Sch 6, para 5; and
(b) HMLR is satisfied the applicant has shown an arguable case for relying on at least one of the specified conditions.

If HMLR rejects the application, then the registered proprietor is likely either to bring an action to recover the land or to agree with the applicant that he may remain in possession as a tenant or licensee. If, however, the applicant remains in adverse possession for a further 2 years after his first application was rejected, then he may apply again to HMLR under Sch 6, para 6 and will be entitled to be registered as the new proprietor of the registered estate.

If the applicant is registered as proprietor following a successful application under either Sch 6, para 1 or para 6, he becomes in effect the successor in title of the former proprietor. Consequently, he will take subject to interests affecting the registered estate, other than (in most cases) registered charges. The unregistered possessory title by virtue of adverse possession which he had at the time of the application is extinguished.[6] The registered estate is normally vested in him free of any registered charge affecting the estate immediately before registration, but otherwise his registration does not affect the priority of any interest affecting the registered estate.

6.1 Meaning of 'adverse possession'

In the leading case of *J A Pye (Oxford) Ltd v Graham*,[7] the House of Lords reviewed the law relating to adverse possession and Lord Hope of Craighead said:

> At first sight, it might be thought that the word 'adverse' describes the nature of the possession that the squatter needs to demonstrate. It suggests that an element of aggression, hostility or subterfuge is required. But an examination of the context makes it clear that this is not so. It is used as a convenient label only, in recognition simply of the fact that the possession is adverse to the interests of the paper owner or, in the case of registered land, of the registered proprietor.

As regards the meaning of 'factual possession', in *Powell v McFarlane*,[8] Slade J said:

> Factual possession signifies an appropriate degree of physical control. It must be a single and [exclusive] possession, though there can be a single possession exercised by or on behalf of several persons jointly. Thus an owner of land and a person intruding on that land without his consent cannot both be in possession of the land at the same time. The question what acts constitute a sufficient degree of exclusive physical control must depend on the circumstances, in particular the nature of the land and the manner in which land of that nature is commonly used or enjoyed. … Everything must depend on the particular circumstances, but broadly, I think what must be shown as constituting factual possession is that the alleged possessor has been dealing with the land in question as an occupying owner might have been expected to deal with it and that no-one else has done so.

The House of Lords approved this statement in *Pye*.

As regards the meaning of 'intention to possess', in *Buckinghamshire County Council v Moran*,[9] Hoffmann J stated that what is required is:

> not an intention to own or even an intention to acquire ownership but an intention to possess.

In *Pye*, the House of Lords also approved the following statement by Slade J in *Powell v McFarlane* that 'intention to possess' requires an:

> intention, in one's own name and on one's own behalf, to exclude the world at large, including the owner with the paper title if he be not himself the possessor, so far as is reasonably practicable and so far as the processes of the law will allow.

As regards the meaning of 'possession without the owner's consent', the squatter must not be in possession of the land with the owner's consent. In *Buckinghamshire County Council v Moran*,[10] Slade LJ stated that:

> Possession is never 'adverse' within the meaning of the [LA] 1980 … if it is enjoyed under a lawful title. If, therefore, a person occupies or uses land by licence of the owner with the paper title and his licence has not been duly determined, he cannot be treated as having been in 'adverse possession' as against the owner of the paper title.

This remains the case under the LRA 2002. In *Healey v Fraine*,[11] Nugee LJ confirmed:

> [A]dverse possession under the LRA 2002 continues to mean what it has always meant such that one cannot be in adverse possession of a property if one occupies it under a licence.

The House of Lords' decision in *Pye* was the subject of an application to the European Court of Human Rights. Ultimately, the Grand Chamber of that court found that English law on adverse possession is not contrary to the European Convention for the Protection of Human Rights and Fundamental Freedoms 1950.[12] That decision related to the law applicable before 13 October 2003; the new regime relating specifically to registered land introduced by LRA 2002, Sch 6 was drafted to be compliant with the human rights legislation.

The effect of illegality of the possession by the squatter in relation to adverse possession is unclear. This will be of particular relevance where the land in question comprises a residential building[13] or part of a highway.[14] In *R (Best) v The Secretary of State for Justice*,[15] the Court of Appeal held that the fact that the Legal Aid, Sentencing and Punishment of Offenders Act 2012 made squatting in a residential building a criminal offence would not preclude the right to make an application under LRA 2002, Sch 6 once the squatter had accrued the requisite period of adverse possession.

The fact that the squatter's original entry onto the land constituted a criminal offence would not appear to preclude a relevant period of adverse possession subsequently accruing in favour of the squatter.[16]

A person may be in adverse possession of land even if it has been included within his existing registered title in error.[17]

6.2 Registration as a person entitled to be notified of an adverse possession application

An applicant should deliver to HMLR:

(a) an application in form ADV2; and
(b) the fee payable.[18]

The applicant must set out his interest in the statement of truth in panel 10 of form ADV2. If successful, HMLR will typically make an entry in the proprietorship register in the following wording:

> [*Name*] of [*address*] is a person entitled to be notified of an application for registration based on Adverse Possession under paragraph 2 of Schedule 6 to the Land Registration Act 2002.

6.3 Application under Land Registration Act 2002, Sch 6, para 1 for registration by person in adverse possession of registered land

An applicant should deliver to HMLR:

(a) an application in form ADV1;
(b) a statutory declaration or statement of truth made by the applicant not more than one month before the application, together with any necessary supporting statutory declarations or statements of truth, to provide evidence of adverse possession of the land against which the application is made for a period of not less than 10 years ending on the date of application;[19]
(c) if the application relates to part only of the land in a registered title, a plan enabling the extent of the land to be fully identified on the Ordnance Survey (OS) map, unless that part is referred to in the statutory declaration or statement of truth by reference to the title plan and this enables that part to be so identified; this plan (if required) should be an exhibit to the applicant's statutory declaration or statement of truth;

(d) any additional evidence which the applicant considers necessary to support the claim;
(e) a list in duplicate in form DL of all the documents delivered;
(f) the appropriate confirmation or evidence of identity;[20] and
(g) the fee payable (which includes the cost of a survey).[21]

The statutory declaration or statement of truth by the applicant must also contain:[22]

(a) if the applicant is relying on LRA 2002, Sch 6, para 1(2), the facts relied upon with any appropriate exhibits. Paragraph 1(2) allows a person to apply for registration if he has, in the period of 6 months before the application, ceased to be in adverse possession of the estate because of eviction by the registered proprietor or a person claiming under the registered proprietor, and on the day before his eviction he had been in adverse possession for the period of 10 years and the eviction was not pursuant to a judgment for possession;
(b) confirmation that LRA 2002, Sch 6, para 1(3) does not apply. Paragraph 1(3) provides that a person may not make an application under Sch 6, para 1 if he is a defendant in proceedings which involve asserting a right to possession of the land, or if judgment for possession of the land has been given against him in the last 2 years;
(c) confirmation that to the best of his knowledge the restriction on applications in LRA 2002, Sch 6, para 8 does not apply. Paragraph 8 provides that no one who has been in adverse possession of a registered estate may apply to be registered as proprietor of that estate during, or before the end of 12 months after the end of, any period in which the existing registered proprietor is for the purposes of the Limitation (Enemies and War Prisoners) Act 1945 an enemy or detained in enemy territory. Paragraph 8 also provides that no one who has been in adverse possession of a registered estate may apply to be registered as proprietor of that estate during any period in which the existing registered proprietor is unable, because of mental disability, to make decisions about issues of the kind to which such an application would give rise, or unable to communicate such decisions because of mental disability or physical impairment. For these purposes 'mental disability' means a disability or disorder of the mind or brain, whether permanent or temporary, which results in an impairment or disturbance of mental functioning;[23]
(d) confirmation that to the best of his knowledge the estate is not, and has not been during any of the period of alleged adverse possession, subject to a trust (other than one where the interest of each of the beneficiaries is an interest in possession); and
(e) if, should a person given notice of the application require that it be dealt with under LRA 2002, Sch 6, para 5, it is intended to rely on one or more of the

conditions set out in that paragraph, the facts supporting such reliance. Paragraph 5 and its three conditions are dealt with under 6.4 Notice of an application based on adverse possession under Land Registration Act 2002, Sch 6, para 1.

The applicant must also supply such additional evidence as HMLR may require after it has considered the application.[24]

HMLR will normally arrange for OS to inspect the land.

Although LRA 2002, s 96 provides that no period of limitation under LA 1980, s 15 is to run against any person, other than a chargee, in relation to an estate in registered land, a person is treated as being in adverse possession of an estate in registered land if, but for s 96, a period of limitation under LA 1980, s 15 would run in his favour in relation to the estate.[25] In determining whether for these purposes a period of limitation would run under LA 1980, s 15, the commencement of any legal proceedings is disregarded.

LA 1980, Sch 1, para 6 provides that:

(a) where a person is in possession under a lease in writing that reserves a rent of at least £10, and
(b) the rent is wrongfully received by some person claiming to be entitled to the immediate reversion,

the right of action to recover the land is deemed to have accrued on the date when the rent was first wrongfully received, not on the date of the determination of the lease. In determining whether, for the purposes of LRA 2002, Sch 6, para 11, a period of limitation would run under the LA 1980, s 15, however, LA 1980, Sch 1, para 6 is disregarded.

A person is also to be regarded as having been in adverse possession of an estate in land where he is the successor in title during any period of adverse possession by a predecessor in title to that estate. When relying on any period of adverse possession by a predecessor in title, HMLR will need evidence of a conveyance of the unregistered estate created by the incomplete period of adverse possession. Such a conveyance may be express or implied. For example, where there is a conveyance of a house and the land in question forms part of the garden, HMLR may be prepared to infer a conveyance of the garden land also.

A person is also regarded as having been in adverse possession during any period of adverse possession by another person which comes between, and is continuous with, periods of adverse possession of his own.

When an estate in registered land is subject to a trust, a person is not to be regarded as being in adverse possession of that estate unless the interest of each of the beneficiaries is an interest in possession. However, there must be identifiable beneficiaries holding the equitable title. A trust will not arise for these purposes where the registered proprietor (or person in whom their interest has vested) is acing in a fiduciary capacity with no identifiable beneficiaries. For example, there is no trust for these purposes where the registered proprietor has died and their estate is in the course of administration.[26]

Where the registered land consists of foreshore belonging to the King in right of the Crown or the Duchy of Lancaster or to the Duchy of Cornwall, the period of adverse possession required before an application may be made is 60 years rather than 10 years.[27]

If the application is in order, HMLR will serve notice of the application upon the registered proprietor and any other relevant persons in accordance with LRA 2002, Sch 6, para 2.

6.4 Notice of an application based on adverse possession under Land Registration Act 2002, Sch 6, para 1

HMLR must serve notice of an application under Sch 6, para 1 on:

(a) the registered proprietor of the land;
(b) any registered chargee;
(c) (where the estate is leasehold) the registered proprietor of any superior registered estate;
(d) any person who is registered as a person to be notified of such an application; and
(e) (where the registered proprietor is a dissolved company) the Treasury Solicitor (or the Solicitor for the affairs of the Duchy of Lancaster or the Duke of Cornwall, where appropriate).

The notice HMLR serves includes notice that, if the application is not required to be dealt with under LRA 2002, Sch 6, para 5, the applicant is entitled to be entered in the register as the new proprietor of the estate. The period allowed for reply is the period ending at 12 noon on the 65th working day after the date of issue of the notice. A working day is any day from Monday to Friday (inclusive) which is not Christmas Day, Good Friday or any other day either specified or declared by proclamation under Banking and Financial Dealings Act 1971, s 1 or appointed by the Secretary of State or certified by HMLR as being an 'interrupted day' due to delay or failure of a communication service or to some other event or circumstance causing substantial interruption in the normal operation of HMLR.

A person given notice of such an application may require that it is dealt with under LRA 2002, Sch 6, para 5. He must do this by giving notice to HMLR in form NAP, a copy of which will have accompanied the notice of the application. When notice in form NAP has been given to HMLR requiring that the application be dealt with under para 5, the applicant is entitled to be registered as the new proprietor only if one of the following three conditions is met.

The first condition is that it would be unconscionable, because of an equity by estoppel, for the registered proprietor to seek to dispossess the applicant and the circumstances are such that the applicant ought to be registered as the proprietor. An example might be where a person built on the registered land under the mistaken belief that he was the owner and the registered proprietor acquiesced in that belief, and the person in possession applied for registration after 10 years, having then learnt the true position.

The second condition is that the applicant is for some other reason entitled to be registered as the proprietor of the estate; for example, where a person entered into a valid contract to purchase and paid the purchase money over 10 years before, but the registered title has never been transferred to him.

The third condition (commonly known as the 'mistaken boundary' condition) is the one most likely to be met with in practice. It is that:

(a) the land to which the application relates is adjacent to land belonging to the applicant;
(b) the exact line of the boundary between the two has not been determined under LRR 2003, rr 118 to 122;[28]
(c) for at least 10 years of the period of adverse possession ending on the date of the application, the applicant (or any predecessor in title) reasonably believed that the land to which the application relates belonged to him; and
(d) the estate to which the application relates was registered more than one year before the date of the application.

The whole of the land in question must be in the vicinity of the applicant's property.[29] Accordingly, an applicant cannot rely on the third condition if only a small part of the overall area claimed adjoins his existing title.

The applicant's 10-year period of reasonable belief may be at any time while he is in adverse possession; it need not be the 10 years ending on the application date.[30]

Where an application is made after the applicant has been evicted by the registered proprietor or a person claiming under him, the period referred to in (c) of the third condition is to be treated as the period ending on the day before the date of the applicant's eviction.

If HMLR is required to deal with the matter under Sch 6, para 5 and none of the three conditions is met, HMLR will reject the application.

It is also possible for the registered proprietor or other recipient of the notice to use form NAP to object to the registration on grounds set out in panel 6 of that form; for example, that the alleged acts of adverse possession had not happened or that those acts did not constitute adverse possession. Such an objection would be dealt with in accordance with LRA 2002, s 73.[31] In addition to objecting on form NAP, the registered proprietor or other recipient of the notice may also require within that form that the application is dealt with under Sch 6, para 5. By doing so, he retains the option of proceeding under para 5 if his objection (which would need to be determined first) is not successful.

6.5 Application under Land Registration Act 2002, Sch 6, para 6 for registration by person in adverse possession of registered land

If a person has an application for registration rejected on the basis of adverse possession of a registered estate pursuant to LRA 2002, Sch 6, para 5, he may apply again to be registered as the proprietor of the estate if he is in adverse possession of the estate from the date of the application until the last day of the period of 2 years beginning with the date of its rejection. A person may not, however, make such an application if:

(a) he is a defendant in proceedings which involve asserting a right to possession of the land;
(b) judgment for possession of the land has been given against him in the last 2 years; or
(c) he has been evicted from the land pursuant to a judgment for possession.

The special form of notice required by Sch 6, para 2 and the right to require the application to be dealt with under Sch 6, para 5 do not apply to such applications. Instead, under LRR 2003, r 17, 15 working days' notice of the application will be served by HMLR on:

(a) the registered proprietor of the land;
(b) any registered chargee;
(c) (where the estate is leasehold) the registered proprietor of any superior registered estate;

(d) any person who is registered as a person to be notified of such an application; and
(e) any other person HMLR considers it appropriate to notify.

If a person makes such an application, he is entitled to be entered in the register as the new proprietor of the estate. This is, however, subject to no valid objection being made by the registered proprietor or other person; for example on the grounds that the alleged acts of adverse possession had not happened or that those acts did not constitute adverse possession. Such an objection would be dealt with in accordance with LRA 2002, s 73.[32]

The applicant should deliver to HMLR:

(a) an application in form ADV1;
(b) a statutory declaration or statement of truth made by the applicant not more than one month before the application (or a certified copy of it), together with any necessary supporting statutory declarations, to provide evidence of adverse possession of the land against which the application is made for a period of not less than 2 years beginning with the date of rejection of the original application and ending on the date of application;[33]
(c) if the application relates to part only of the land in a registered title, a plan enabling the extent of the land to be fully identified on the OS map; this plan should be an exhibit to the applicant's statutory declaration or statement of truth. A plan is not needed if the previous rejected application related only to that part, or that part is referred to in the statutory declaration or statement of truth by reference to the title plan and this enables that part to be so identified;
(d) any additional evidence which the applicant considers necessary to support the claim; and
(e) the fee payable.[34]

The statutory declaration or statement of truth by the applicant must also contain:

(a) full details of the previous rejected application;
(b) confirmation that to the best of his knowledge the restriction on applications in LRA 2002, Sch 6, para 8 does not apply. The restrictions imposed by para 8 are discussed under 6.3 Application under Land Registration Act 2002, Sch 6, para 1 for registration by person in adverse possession of registered land;
(c) confirmation that to the best of his knowledge the estate is not, and has not been during any of the period of alleged adverse possession, subject to a trust (other than one where the interest of each of the beneficiaries is an interest in possession); and

(d) confirmation that LRA 2002, Sch 6, para 6(2) does not apply. Paragraph 6(2) provides that a person may not make an application under para 6 if:

   (i) he is a defendant in proceedings which involve asserting a right to possession of the land;
   (ii) judgment for possession of the land has been given against him in the last 2 years; or
   (iii) he has been evicted from the land pursuant to a judgment for possession.

The applicant must also supply such additional evidence as HMLR may require after it has considered the application.[35]

6.6 Registered charges

HMLR will register a successful applicant under LRA 2002, Sch 6, para 1 or para 6 free of any registered charge affecting the estate immediately before his registration unless the application proceeded only because one of the three conditions in Sch 6, para 5 was met.

If the application proceeded only because one of the three conditions in Sch 6, para 5 was met, the estate remains subject to any registered charges. Where such a charge affects other property as well as the registered estate, the proprietor of the estate may require the chargee to apportion the amount secured by the charge at that time between the estate and the other property based on their respective values. The person requiring the apportionment is entitled to a discharge of his estate from the charge on payment of the amount apportioned to the estate and the costs incurred by the chargee as a result of the apportionment. LRR 2003, rr 194A to 194G contain procedures relating to apportionment.

Where an application is made under LRA 2002, Sch 12, para 18(1), the applicant takes subject to any registered charge in existence when he commenced adverse possession.[36] The same applies where an application is made for first registration.[37]

6.7 Additional defences to actions for possession

LRA 2002, s 98 contains various defences to an action for possession of land. These are additional to any other defences a person may have. That section also sets out when a judgment for possession of land ceases to be enforceable. Where in any proceedings a court determines that a person is entitled to a defence under that section, or that a judgment for possession has ceased to be enforceable against a person by virtue of s 98(4), the court must order HMLR to register that person as the proprietor of the registered estate in respect of which he is entitled to make an application based on adverse possession.

A person has a defence to an action for possession of land if, on the day immediately preceding that on which the action was brought, he was entitled to make an application to be registered as the proprietor of registered land having been in adverse possession for 10 years and, had he made such an application on that day, the third condition in LRA 2002, Sch 6, para 5 would have been satisfied.[38] The court made such an order in *Pollock v Burnett*.[39]

A judgment for possession of land ceases to be enforceable at the end of the period of 2 years beginning with the date of the judgment if the proceedings in which the judgment is given were commenced against a person who at that time had been in adverse possession for 10 years.[40]

A person has a defence to an action for possession of land if, on the day immediately preceding that on which the action was brought, he was entitled to make a further application to be registered as proprietor having been in adverse possession for a period of 2 years from the date of the rejection of his prior application.[41]

A judgment for possession of land ceases to be enforceable at the end of the period of 2 years beginning with the date of the judgment if, at the end of that period, the person against whom the judgment was given is entitled to make a further application to be registered as proprietor having been in adverse possession for a period of 2 years from the date of the rejection of his prior application.[42]

6.8 Transitional provisions

The position under the Land Registration Act 1925 (LRA 1925) was that where a registered proprietor's title had been extinguished by adverse possession, it was open to the squatter to apply for the closure of the registered proprietor's title which was deemed, in the meantime, to be held on trust for the squatter by the registered proprietor.[43] The LRA 2002 contains transitional provisions, so that where a registered estate in land was held in trust for a person by virtue of LRA 1925, s 75(1) immediately before the coming into force of the LRA 2002, he is entitled to be registered as the proprietor of the estate.[44]

A person has a defence to any action for the possession of land (in addition to any other defence he may have) if he is entitled to be registered as the proprietor of an estate in the land under LRA 2002, Sch 12, para 18. Where in an action for possession of land a court determines that a person is entitled to such a defence, the court must order HMLR to register him as the proprietor of the estate in question.[45]

An application to be registered as proprietor under these transitional provisions should be made using application form AP1, not form ADV1. The applicant should deliver to HMLR:

(a) an application in form AP1, specifying that the applicant is applying to be registered as proprietor in accordance with LRA 2002, Sch 12, para 18(1);
(b) evidence of adverse possession, by way of statutory declaration(s) or statement(s) of truth (a statement of truth may be in form ST1 in LRR 2003, Sch 4, although its use is not compulsory);
(c) sufficient details, by plan or otherwise, so that the land can be clearly identified on the OS map;
(d) a list in duplicate in form DL of all the documents delivered; and
(e) the fee payable (which includes the cost of a survey).[46]

Similar limitation periods to those which apply to unregistered land apply, but the evidence lodged must *also* demonstrate that the minimum limitation period had expired before 13 October 2003 so that a trust under LRA 1925, s 75 had arisen by that date. In addition, the title to the land must have been registered before that date, although not necessarily for the entire period of the adverse possession.

Where the requisite limitation period had expired before 13 October 2003 but the land only became registered on or after that date, no application can be made under the transitional provisions. Instead, application may be made in form AP1 (accompanied by supporting evidence as above) for alteration of the register to reflect the fact that the documentary owner's title had already been extinguished at the time of first registration of the estate. If the first registered proprietor had notice of the squatter's title or the squatter remained in actual occupation throughout, the registered estate will have vested in that proprietor subject to the squatter's title.[47] The applicant may wish to accompany the AP1 with an application in form FR1 for first registration of the estate created by his adverse possession.

HMLR will normally arrange for OS to inspect the land. If the application is in order, HMLR will serve notice of it upon the registered proprietor of the land, any registered chargee, and any other person HMLR considers it appropriate to notify. The registered proprietor or other recipient of the notice may object to the registration; for example, on the grounds that the alleged acts of adverse possession had not happened or that those acts did not constitute adverse possession. Such an objection would be dealt with in accordance with LRA 2002, s 73.[48]

If the application succeeds, HMLR will register the applicant as proprietor of the land in place of the existing proprietor, with the same class of title.

6.9 Application for first registration

Where a person has been in adverse possession of unregistered land for the appropriate limitation period, the documentary title owner's paper title is extinguished.[49] The normal period of limitation for recovery of land is 12 years, but this period is extended to:

(a) 30 years for the Crown and any spiritual or eleemosynary corporation sole; and
(b) 60 years for foreshore owned by the Crown.

The normal period may also be extended where:

(a) there has been fraud or deliberate concealment of a cause or action, or mistake;[50] or
(b) the person entitled to recover the land is under the age of 18 or is of unsound mind.[51]

Where the land is held on trust or is settled land, the legal estate is not extinguished until the rights of action of all the beneficiaries to recover the land have been barred.[52]

A squatter usually cannot apply for a caution against first registration relying on his adverse possession; he will be a person entitled to an unregistered possessory estate in land which will preclude him from making such an application.[53] However, he may apply for such a caution where he:

(a) is a successor in title to an earlier squatter who transferred the possessory estate to the squatter; and
(b) does not apply for first registration within 2 months of the transfer or does so but the application is cancelled.

In that situation, the title to the estate would revert to the transferor, who would then hold it on a bare trust for the squatter. The squatter, having a beneficial interest in this estate and therefore being entitled to an interest affecting a legal freehold estate in land (rather than being the owner of such an estate) may therefore be entitled to apply for a caution. This will apply equally whether or not the documentary title has been extinguished by the time of the transfer of the possessory estate.[54]

An applicant who has been in adverse possession of unregistered land for the appropriate limitation period may apply for first registration of his title. In addition to the usual documents required,[55] an applicant should deliver to HMLR:

(a) evidence of the adverse possession by way of statutory declaration(s) or statement(s) of truth (a statement of truth may be in form ST1 in LRR 2003, Sch 4, although its use is not compulsory);
(b) a certified copy of each such declaration or statement, if the applicant wishes for the original to be returned;
(c) Land Charges searches against the names of the applicant and any known owners of the paper title (with any entries accounted for and, where applicable, certified by a conveyancer as not affecting the estate); and
(d) any other relevant searches such as a company search or commons registration search where appropriate.

The applicant may be required to pay an additional fee to meet the cost of a survey or special enquiries.

HMLR will normally arrange for OS to inspect the land. If the application is in order, HMLR may serve notice of it upon (if known) the owner and any mortgagee of the paper title, and such adjoining owners and others as it considers appropriate. The recipient of the notice may object to the registration; for example, on the grounds that the alleged acts of adverse possession had not happened or that those acts did not constitute adverse possession. Such an objection would be dealt with in accordance with LRA 2002, s 73.[56]

If the application succeeds, HMLR will register the applicant as proprietor of the land. However, HMLR will normally only grant a possessory title because it will not be able to be certain that the applicant's adverse possession has extinguished the documentary owner's title. HMLR will usually make a protective entry in the register to guard against the risk that the land may be subject to undisclosed restrictive covenants, easements or rentcharges.

HMLR may register an applicant with possessory title if it is of the opinion that the applicant is in actual possession of the land, or in receipt of the rents and profits of the land, by virtue of the estate, and that there is no other class of title with which he may be registered.[57] HMLR's policy of normally granting a possessory title, rather than an absolute title, on first registration of a title based upon adverse possession has been upheld on judicial review by the High Court as being neither unlawful nor irrational.[58] This was on the basis that it struck a balance between the economic and social interest in having absolute titles which could be readily marketed, on the one hand, and the need to protect the public purse against claims for indemnity, on the other hand.

6.10 Adverse possession and leasehold land

6.10.1 Adverse possession of leasehold land

If a squatter takes possession of leasehold land, time runs against the tenant, but does not run against the landlord until the lease expires. The exception would be where the adverse possession commenced before the grant of the lease, in which case time will continue to run against the landlord during the term of the lease. Non-payment of rent before the lease expires is of no effect. However, if a third party wrongfully receives the rent from leasehold land for the requisite period, and provided:

(a) the title to the reversion is unregistered,
(b) the lease is in writing,
(c) the rent is at least £10 a year, and
(d) the lease is not granted by the Crown,

the third party becomes entitled to make an appropriate application to HMLR.[59] The position will be similar where the title to the reversion was registered before 13 October 2003 and by that date the period of limitation in favour of the third party wrongfully receiving the rent had accrued; in such a case the third party would be entitled to make an application to the registrar for registration as proprietor of the registered reversionary title under the transitional provisions of LRA 2002, Sch 12, para 18(1). However, where the title to the reversion is registered and the third party wrongfully receiving the rent has no entitlement under the transitional provisions, he cannot apply for registration as proprietor of the registered reversionary title under the Sch 6 procedure. This is because, for the purposes of determining whether a person is in adverse possession of an estate in land for the purposes of the Sch 6 procedure, LA 1980, Sch 1, para 6 is to be disregarded.[60]

In the case of adverse possession of an unregistered leasehold estate the House of Lords, in *Fairweather v St Marylebone Property Co Ltd*,[61] held that when the tenant has been ousted by a squatter for the full period of limitation, the tenant may still surrender to the landlord who can then take action to recover possession from the squatter. Accordingly, HMLR will generally only accept an application for first registration of such an estate where:

(a) there is no registered reversionary title; and
(b) the registrar is satisfied the possibility of there being a surrender to a reversioner who may claim possession against the applicant is sufficiently remote to be discounted.

If HMLR accepts such an application, the applicant will usually receive a qualified freehold title. The title will be freehold because that is always the estate acquired by adverse possession of an unregistered estate. However, where the squatter is a tenant encroaching from leasehold land and the presumption discussed below[62] had not been rebutted, HMLR will award a qualified leasehold title. In such circumstances, the qualification will usually be:

> QUALIFICATION: This title arises from the adverse possession of the leasehold estate under a lease dated [*date*] and made between [*parties*]. There is excepted from the effect of registration any estate, right or interest adverse to, or in derogation of, the proprietor's title subsisting at the time of the registration or then capable of arising and any right of the person for the time being entitled to the reversion expectant on the term of the lease to take possession following a surrender of the lease.

Where the application does not meet the above requirements, HMLR will reject it. This is not the case where the lease is registered and the application is made either under LRA 2002, Sch 6 or (where the limitation period expired before 13 October 2003) under the transitional provisions of LRA 2002, Sch 12, para 18(1).[63]

6.10.2 Encroachment from leasehold land onto other land

There is a legal presumption that a tenant who encroaches onto other land does so for the benefit of his landlord.[64]

In relation to LRA 2002, Sch 6, one view of the effect of this presumption is that it means that there can be no adverse possession by the tenant and that any application under Sch 6 should be by the landlord. However, the presumption can be rebutted by evidence that the tenant intended the encroachment to be for his own benefit. In practice, HMLR will treat the fact that the application has been made as sufficient evidence of such an intention. A different view of the effect of the presumption is that it is only concerned with who might have acquired title at common law to the estate concerned and does not alter the fact that the tenant is in adverse possession, so it is irrelevant where the application is being made under Sch 6. If a tenant applicant applies under Sch 6 and it is not clear he is aware of the presumption, HMLR will contact him to explain the position and request confirmation he wishes to proceed with the application. If he does so, HMLR will, in addition to the other relevant notices, also serve notice on the tenant's landlord, referring to the presumption and to the above points.

In relation to encroachment onto unregistered freehold land, where the squatter accepts that the presumption applies, he may make an application for first registration on the basis that the land is to be treated as an accretion to his existing lease, provided there is more than 7 years of the term of the existing lease unexpired.[65] Evidence of the squatter's title to that lease, if unregistered, should accompany the application. Any notice served by HMLR will confirm the application is being made on this basis. If HMLR completes the application, it will enter a note in the property register to the effect that, although not originally within the extent demised by the existing lease, the land encroached on is now held for the term of, and as an accretion to, that lease.

Where the squatter does not accept that the presumption applies, he may instead make an application for first registration of a freehold estate, subject to providing evidence of rebuttal of the presumption. In addition to any other notices served, HMLR will serve notice on the landlord of the applicant, confirming that the application is being made on this basis. If the landlord cannot be identified, HMLR will only be able to consider registering with a qualified title. The qualification will be on the lines that the enforcement of any estate, right or interest adverse to, or in derogation of, the proprietor's title subsisting at the time of first registration or then capable of arising is excepted from the effect of registration.

In relation to encroachment by a squatter from leasehold land onto other land which was registered before 13 October 2003 and 12 years' adverse possession had accrued by that date, the tenant squatter cannot be the beneficiary under a trust under LRA 1925, s 75(1) and cannot therefore apply for registration under the transitional provisions of LRA 2002, Sch 12, para 18. However, where the squatter accepts that the presumption applies, he may make an application for first registration on the basis that the land is to be treated as an accretion to his existing lease, provided:

(a) there are more than 7 years of the term of the existing lease unexpired;[66] and
(b) the title has not been subsequently lost through registration of a registrable disposition of the registered estate for valuable consideration at any time when the leasehold estate was not an overriding interest.[67]

Evidence of the squatter's title to his existing lease, if unregistered, should accompany the application. Any notice served by HMLR will confirm the application is being made on this basis. If HMLR completes the application, it will enter a note in the property register to the effect that, although not originally within the extent demised by the existing lease, the land encroached on is now held for the term of, and as an accretion to, that lease. Where the encroachment has been onto registered leasehold land and the squatter's existing lease is for a longer term than that of that registered lease, the note will also make it clear that

the land is held as an accretion to the squatter's existing lease, but only for the term of years demised by that registered lease.
Where the squatter does not accept that the presumption applies, he may instead make an application under the transitional provisions of LRA 2002, Sch 12, para 18, accompanied by evidence of rebuttal of the presumption. In addition to any other notices served, HMLR will also usually serve notice of the application on the applicant's landlord, confirming that the application is being made on this basis.

6.11 Overriding interests

Before the coming into force of the LRA 2002, rights acquired, or in the course of being acquired, under the Limitation Acts were overriding interests.[68] Although this particular category of overriding interest is not reproduced in the LRA 2002, for the period of 3 years from 13 October 2003 there was included in the list of unregistered interests which override first registration a right acquired under the Limitation Act 1980 (LA 1980) before the coming into force of the LRA 2002. For this period therefore, a person who had acquired title by adverse possession continued to have an interest which overrode first registration.[69] This would be the case even if he was no longer in actual occupation and gave him a protected period within which he could seek to register his rights. That period of 3 years has now expired, but if such a person *is* in actual occupation of the land then his interest may instead now be an interest which overrides under para 2 of either LRA 2002, Sch 1 or Sch 3.

For the overriding status of the right to be registered as proprietor where a registered estate in land was held in trust for a person by virtue of LRA 1925, s 75(1) immediately before the coming into force of the LRA 2002, see 6.8 Transitional provisions.

---

1 See 6.10 Adverse possession and leasehold land.

2 LA 1980, s 17.

3 LRA 2002, s 96.

4 Although see the comments below about when the applicant claims to have barred title before first registration and the estate has been registered less than 10 years.

5 LRR 2003, r 194.

6 LRA 2002, Sch 6, para 9(1).

7 [2002] UKHL 30.

8 (1979) 38 P & CR 452.

9 [1988] 2 WLUK 208. Endorsed by the Court of Appeal in *Buckinghamshire County Council v Moran* [1989] EWCA Civ 11.

10 [1989] EWCA Civ 11.

11 [2023] EWCA Civ 549.

12 *J A Pye (Oxford) Limited v The United Kingdom* (App No 44302/02) [2007] ECHR 700.
13 See Legal Aid, Sentencing and Punishment of Offenders Act 2012, s 144 and Criminal Law Act 1977, s 7.
14 See Highways Act 1980, s 137 and *R v Smith* [2009] EWHC 328 (Admin).
15 [2015] EWCA Civ 17.
16 *Lambeth LBC v Blackburn* [2001] EWCA Civ 912.
17 *Rashid v Nasrullah* [2018] EWCA Civ 2685.
18 See 67 Fees.
19 An applicant may make a statement of truth may using form ST1 in LRR 2003, Sch 1. However, its use is not compulsory.
20 See 84 Identity Evidence.
21 See 67 Fees.
22 LRR 2003, r 188(2).
23 LRA 2002, Sch 6, para 6(3).
24 LRR 2003, r 17.
25 LRA 2002, Sch 6, para 11.
26 *Nazir v Begum* [2025] EWCA Civ 587.
27 LRA 2002, Sch 6, para 13.
28 See 22 Boundaries.
29 *Dowse v Bradford Metropolitan District Council* [2020] UKUT 0202 (LC).
30 *Brown v Ridley and Another* [2025] UKSC 7.
31 See 54 Disputes.
32 See 54 Disputes.
33 An applicant may make a statement of truth may using form ST1 in LRR 2003, Sch 1. However, its use is not compulsory.
34 See 67 Fees.
35 LRR 2003, r 17.
36 See 6.8 Transitional provisions.
37 See 6.9 Application for first registration.
38 LRA 2002, s 98(1).
39 [2023] 4 WLUK 204.
40 LRA 2002, s 98(2).
41 LRA 2002, s 98(3).
42 LRA 2002, s 98(4).
43 LRA 1925, s 75(1).
44 LRA 2002, Sch 12, para 18(1).
45 LRA 2002, Sch 12, para 18(2) and (3).
46 See 67 Fees.
47 LRA 2002, s 11 and Sch 1, para 2.
48 See 54 Disputes.
49 LA 1980, s 17.
50 LA 1980, s 32.
51 LA 1980, ss 28 and 38.
52 LA 1980, s 18.
53 LRA 2002, s 15(3) and *Turner v Chief Land Registrar* [2013] EWHC 1382 (Ch).

54 See 25 Cautions Against First Registration.
55 See 68.4 Application for first registration.
56 See 54 Disputes.
57 LRA 2002, s 9(5).
58 *R (Diep) v Chief Land Registrar* [2010] EWHC 3315 (Admin).
59 LA 1980, Sch 1, Pt 1, para 6.
60 LRA 2002, Sch 6, para 11(3)(b).
61 [1962] UKHL 1.
62 See, 6.10.2 Encroachment from leasehold land onto other land.
63 *Spectrum Investment Co v Holmes* [1981] 1 All ER 6 and *Central London Commercial Estates Ltd v Kato Kagaku Co Ltd* [1998] EWHC Ch 314.
64 *Smirk v Lyndale Developments Ltd* [1975] Ch 317 and *Tower Hamlets v Barrett* [2005] EWCA Civ 923.
65 LRA 2002, s 3(3).
66 LRA 2002, s 3(3).
67 LRA 2002, s 29.
68 LRA 1925, s 70(1)(f).
69 LRA 2002, Sch 12, para 7.

7 ADVOWSONS

An advowson is a right to appoint a vicar or rector to a church of the Church of England. It is a property right and was, for the purposes of the LRA 1925, included in the definition of 'land'. Consequently, it was possible to register an advowson. HMLR allocated it a title number and issued a land certificate.

To identify existing advowsons and their owners or 'patrons', the General Synod of the Church of England passed the Patronage (Benefices) Measure 1986 (1986/3) (the 1986 Measure). This required the compilation of a new register of rights of advowson to be held by the diocesan registrar in each diocese. Patrons were given a period of 15 months from 1 October 1987 (i.e. until 1 January 1989) to register their advowson with the appropriate diocesan registrar.

The 1986 Measure did not amend the law of real property. Consequently, an advowson remains an interest in land for most purposes. However, the 1986 Measure, s 6(2) amended LRA 1925, s 3 to remove the words 'an advowson' from the definition of 'land'. The definition of land in the LRA 2002 does not include an advowson, nor is an advowson a registrable legal estate under the LRA 2002.

As a result of the 1986 Measure, after 1 October 1987 no advowson can be registered at HMLR; and on 1 January 1989 any existing registered title to an advowson was deemed to have been closed and removed from the register. Any transfer of an advowson for valuable consideration was rendered void.

In Wales and Monmouthshire, advowsons were abolished on 31 March 1920. Any parishes that straddled the boundary between England and Wales could opt to remain under the jurisdiction of the Church of England and if they did so, they subsequently became subject to the 1986 Measure.

8 AGREEMENT FOR LEASE

An applicant may protect an agreement for lease of registered land by the entry of an agreed notice or a unilateral notice, and possibly also (depending on the terms of the agreement) a restriction. The fact that it is the subject of a notice does not necessarily mean that the agreement for lease is valid but does protect the priority of the agreement on any registered disposition for valuable consideration.[1] A restriction does not confer any priority. However, it prevents an entry being made in the register relating to any disposition, or a disposition of a specified kind, unless the terms of the restriction have (where applicable) been complied with.

LRA 2002, s 72(6)(a) provides rules may make provision for priority periods in connection with the noting in the register of a contract for the making of a registrable disposition of a registered estate or charge. No such rules have currently been made.

A leasehold estate in land granted for a term not exceeding 7 years from the date of the grant is usually an interest falling within LRA 2002, Sch 3, para 1 and therefore overrides registered dispositions. However, an agreement to create such a lease is not itself an interest which overrides. Consequently, its priority should be protected by entry of a notice in the register.

Even where an agreement for lease of registered land is not protected by a notice, it may still override a later registered disposition for valuable consideration if, at the time of that later disposition, the person having the benefit of the agreement for lease is in actual occupation of the land to which the agreement relates. If he is in actual occupation of only part of the land to which the agreement relates, he has an overriding interest only in respect of the part he is occupying.[2]

The interest of the person in actual possession does not override a registered disposition if:

(a) enquiry was made of him before the disposition and he failed to disclose the agreement for lease when he could reasonably have been expected to do so; or
(b) the interest:

(i) belongs to a person whose occupation would not have been obvious on a reasonably careful inspection of the land at the time of the disposition; and

(ii) the person to whom the disposition is made does not have actual knowledge of the agreement for lease at the time of the disposition.[3]

The agreement for lease should be made and signed by the proprietor of the registered estate, or a satisfactory chain of title shown between the person making the agreement and that registered proprietor. For example, if the registered proprietor has contracted to sell a registered freehold title to A, and A then agrees to lease the land in the title to B, B's agreement for lease can be protected by a notice, whether or not A's contract is also protected by a notice.

A mortgage of an agreement for lease is a general equitable charge and therefore creates a new interest in land which can be protected by a notice independently of the agreement for lease itself, and whether or not the agreement for lease has itself been protected by a notice. The notice can be entered in the prospective landlord's title, providing a satisfactory chain of title is shown.[4]

8.1 Agreed notice

In addition to the usual documents required,[5] an applicant should deliver to HMLR the agreement for lease or a certified copy of it.

Where the consent of the registered proprietor is not available but, for example, the agreement for lease is signed by him, this is likely to be sufficient to satisfy HMLR as to the validity of the applicant's claim in accordance with LRA 2002, s 34(3)(c).

The agreed notice in the register will give details of the interest protected.

The applicant may prefer to apply for entry of a unilateral notice, where he does not wish the terms of the agreement for lease to be open to public inspection and copying.

8.2 Unilateral notice

In addition to delivering the usual documents required,[6] an applicant should ensure that the statement in panel 11 or conveyancer's certificate in panel 12 of form UN1 is completed on the following lines to show the interest of the applicant:

> intending lessee under an agreement for lease dated [*date*] made between [*parties*].

The unilateral notice in the register will give brief details of the interest protected and identify the beneficiary of that notice.

8.3 Restriction

HMLR may not enter any restriction for the purpose of protecting the priority of an interest which is, or could be, the subject of a notice.[7] However, this does not prevent a restriction being entered in addition to a notice in respect of the agreement for lease. Although the notice protects the priority of the agreement, a restriction may be used to ensure the registered proprietor complies with any conditions in relation to another disposition.

In addition to delivering the usual documents required,[8] an applicant should deliver to HMLR (if the application is without the consent of the registered proprietor) a certified copy of the agreement for lease.

The statement in panel 12 of form RX1 signed by the applicant, or a certificate by his conveyancer in panel 13 of form RX1, must give details of the nature of the agreement and of the provision in the agreement limiting the registered proprietor's powers to enter into a disposition.

Panel 9 of form RX1 should set out the required restriction(s). A restriction in a standard form contained in LRR 2003, Sch 4 does not require the approval of HMLR to the terms of the restriction under LRA 2002, s 43(3). A possible form of restriction based on Form L is:

> No disposition of the registered estate by the proprietor of the registered estate is to be registered without a certificate signed by [*intending lessee*] of [*address*] or their conveyancer that the provisions of [*clause, paragraph or other particulars*] of the agreement for lease dated [*date*] made between [*parties*] have been complied with or that they do not apply to the disposition.

The wording of Form L is set out in Appendix IV.

HMLR must give notice of the application for a restriction to the proprietor of the registered estate or charge concerned, if it has not been made by or with the consent of such proprietor or a person entitled to be registered as such proprietor.[9]

---

1 LRA 2002, ss 29 and 32.

2 LRA 2002, ss 29 and 30 and Sch 3, para 2.

3 LRA 2002, Sch 3, para 2.

4 See 9 Agreement for Mortgage.

5 See 119.1 Agreed notice.

6 See 119.3 Unilateral notice.
7 LRA 2002, s 42(2).
8 See 153.1 Application for entry of restriction.
9 LRA 2002, s 45.

9 AGREEMENT FOR MORTGAGE

An applicant may protect an agreement for mortgage of registered land by the entry of an agreed notice or a unilateral notice, and possibly also (depending on the terms of the agreement) a restriction. The fact that it is the subject of a notice does not necessarily mean that the agreement for mortgage is valid but does protect the priority of that agreement on any registered disposition.[1] A restriction does not confer any priority. However, it prevents an entry being made in the register relating to any disposition, or a disposition of a specified kind, unless the terms of the restriction have (where applicable) been complied with.

LRA 2002, s 72(6)(a) provides rules may make provision for priority periods in connection with the noting in the register of a contract for the making of a registrable disposition of a registered estate or charge. No such rules have currently been made.

The agreement for mortgage should be made and signed by the proprietor of the registered estate, or a satisfactory chain of title shown between the person making the agreement and the registered proprietor. For example, if the registered proprietor has contracted to sell a registered freehold title to A, and A then agrees to mortgage the land in the title to B, B's agreement for mortgage can be protected by a notice, whether or not A's contract is also protected by a notice.

9.1 Agreed notice

In addition to the usual documents required,[2] an applicant should deliver to HMLR the agreement for mortgage or a certified copy of it.

Where the consent of the registered proprietor is not available but, for example, the agreement for mortgage is signed by him, this is likely to be sufficient to satisfy HMLR as to the validity of the applicant's claim in accordance with LRA 2002, s 34(3)(c).

Where the agreement is by an intending purchaser or lessee who has the benefit of a contract for sale or agreement for lease, that contract or agreement, or a certified copy of it, should be lodged with the application. This is not necessary if there is already a notice in the register in respect of that contract or agreement.

The agreed notice in the register will give details of the interest protected.

The applicant may prefer to apply for entry of a unilateral notice where he does not wish the terms of the agreement to be open to public inspection and copying.

9.2 Unilateral notice

In addition to delivering the usual documents required,[3] an applicant should ensure that the statement in panel 11 or conveyancer's certificate in panel 12 of form UN1 is completed on the following lines to show the interest of the applicant:

> intending mortgagee under an agreement for mortgage dated [*date*] made between [*parties*].

In the case of an agreement for mortgage given by an intending purchaser who has the benefit of a contract for sale, the statement in panel 11 or conveyancer's certificate in panel 12 of form UN1 should be completed on the following lines:

> intending mortgagee under an agreement for mortgage dated [*date*] made between [*purchaser*] and [*prospective mortgagee*], [*purchaser*] being the purchaser under a contract for sale dated [*date*] made between [*parties*].

The wording must establish the link between the registered proprietor and the person who is to be shown as the beneficiary of the notice. It must also confirm that an agreement for mortgage exists – a simple statement that monies have been advanced is insufficient, as this does not prove the existence of an interest which affects a registered estate, only the existence of a debt. The position is similar in relation to an agreement for mortgage given by an intending lessee who has the benefit of an agreement for lease.

The unilateral notice in the register will give brief details of the interest protected and identify the beneficiary of that notice.

9.3 Restriction

HMLR may not enter any restriction for the purpose of protecting the priority of an interest which is, or could be, the subject of a notice.[4] However, this does not prevent a restriction being entered in addition to a notice in respect of the agreement for mortgage. Although the notice protects the priority of the agreement for mortgage, a restriction may be used to ensure the registered proprietor complies with any conditions in relation to another disposition.

In addition to delivering the usual documents required,[5] an applicant should deliver to HMLR (if the application is made without the consent of the registered proprietor) a certified copy of the agreement for mortgage.

The statement in panel 12 of form RX1 signed by the applicant, or a certificate by his conveyancer in panel 13 of form RX1, must give details of the nature of the agreement and of the provision in the agreement limiting the registered proprietor's powers to enter into a disposition.

Panel 9 of form RX1 should set out the required restriction(s). A restriction in a standard form contained in LRR 2003, Sch 4 does not require the approval of HMLR to the terms of the restriction under LRA 2002, s 43(3). A possible form of restriction based on Form L is:

> No disposition of the registered estate by the proprietor of the registered estate is to be registered without a certificate signed by [*prospective mortgagee*] of [*address*] or their conveyancer that the provisions of [*clause, paragraph or other particulars*] of the agreement for mortgage dated [*date*] made between [*parties*] have been complied with or that they do not apply to the disposition.

HMLR must give notice of the application for a restriction to the proprietor of the registered estate or charge concerned, if it has not been made by or with the consent of such proprietor or a person entitled to be registered as such proprietor.[6]

---

1 LRA 2002, ss 29, 30 and 32.
2 See 119.1 Agreed notice.
3 See 119.3 Unilateral notice.
4 LRA 2002, s 42(2).
5 See 153.1 Application for entry of restriction.
6 LRA 2002, s 45.

10 AGREEMENT TO PAY FURTHER CONSIDERATION

A vendor may impose a covenant or provision requiring the purchaser to pay a further sum or sums. This is sometimes referred to as 'overage'. A common example is where a vendor of undeveloped land is to be paid further sums if planning permission is granted in the future. Another example is where a payment will become due if the use of the land changes in the future.

Such sums may be secured by a legal charge or an equitable charge.[1] Where the vendor does not take some form of charge to secure payment, the question arises whether he can claim that a vendor's lien has arisen. This depends on the particular facts. However, usually the requirement to pay overage does not give rise to a vendor's lien.[2] For the situation where a vendor's lien has arisen, see 182 Vendor's Liens.

Generally, covenants to pay further sums will be personal covenants because they benefit the vendor personally rather than other neighbouring land owned by the vendor. If the obligation is in the form of a positive covenant, HMLR will make an appropriate entry in the register.[3]

If the agreement contains a provision which limits the registered proprietor's powers to enter into any further disposition, the vendor may apply to enter a restriction in the register. A restriction does not confer any priority. However, it prevents an entry being made in the register relating to any disposition, or a disposition of a specified kind, unless the terms of the restriction have (where applicable) been complied with.

10.1 Restriction

In addition to the usual documents required,[4] an applicant should deliver to HMLR (if the application is made without the consent of the registered proprietor) a certified copy of the agreement to pay further consideration.

The statement in panel 12 of form RX1 must be signed by the applicant, or a certificate by his conveyancer in panel 13 of form RX1, giving details of the nature of the agreement and of the provision in the agreement limiting the registered proprietor's powers to enter into a disposition.

Panel 9 of form RX1 should set out the required restriction(s). A restriction in a standard form contained in LRR 2003, Sch 4 does not require the approval of HMLR to the terms of the restriction under LRA 2002, s 43(3). A possible form of restriction based on Form L is:

> No disposition of the registered estate by the proprietor of the registered estate is to be registered without a certificate signed by [*beneficiary*] of [*address*] or their conveyancer that the provisions of [*clause, paragraph or other particulars*] of [*details of document containing agreement to pay further consideration*] have been complied with or that they do not apply to the disposition.

The wording of Form L is set out in Appendix IV.

Alternatively, where the certificate of the registered proprietor of a specified title number is required, a similar restriction based upon Form M may be appropriate. The wording of Form M is set out in Appendix IV.

HMLR must give notice of the application for a restriction to the proprietor of the registered estate or charge concerned, if it has not been made by or with the consent of such proprietor or a person entitled to be registered as such proprietor.[5]

---

1 See 61 Equitable Charges and 100 Legal Charges.

2 *Woolf Project Management v Woodtrek Limited* (1988) 56 P & CR 134.

3 See 135 Positive Covenants.

4 See 153.1 Application for entry of restriction.

5 LRA 2002, s 45.

11 AIRSPACE

Unless an entry to the contrary appears in the property register of a registered title, that title includes the airspace above the land identified on the title plan.

In an application for first registration, unless all the land above the surface is included in that application, the applicant must provide a plan of the surface on, under or over which the land to be registered lies. He must also provide sufficient information to define the vertical and horizontal extents of the land.[1] On completion of the registration HMLR will reflect this information by an appropriate entry in the property register. Where the registration is of a leasehold estate, the description in the register must be read in conjunction with the lease.[2]

Registrations of airspace, although unusual, are increasing. They can relate to a freehold or leasehold estate, and may be registrations in their own right or form part of the registration of another structure: typically, commercial premises such as an office block, an industrial unit or a unit within a shopping complex. Leases of airspace to accommodate solar panels or vertical extensions to existing buildings are also becoming increasingly common.

A register of title relating to freehold or leasehold land may describe the land by reference to:

- the Newlyn Datum;
- Ordnance Datum Newlyn; or
- OS Datum.

These are one and the same. OS Datum is mean sea level. The level was based on hourly readings taken by OS on the south pier at Newlyn in Cornwall between 1915 and 1921. OS Datum may also be used in transfers, leases and other deeds as a means of defining the levels or strata within a transfer, demise or grant.

---

1 LRR 2003, r 26.

2 *R (HCP Hendon) Ltd v Chief Land Registrar* [2020] EWHC 1278 (Admin).

12 ALTERATION OF THE REGISTER

The LRA 2002 provides for alteration of the register for several purposes, either by HMLR of its own volition, or in pursuance of an application for alteration, or in pursuance of a court order for alteration.[1]

In considering applications for alteration of the register, one must distinguish between those applications that involve 'rectification' and those that do not. It is also necessary to distinguish alterations made pursuant to a court order for alteration from those which are not made pursuant to such an order.

The LRA 2002 makes a clear distinction between 'alteration' generally and 'rectification' as a specific type of alteration, unlike the LRA 1925 where those two terms were used interchangeably. The distinction between the two is important in relation to both alteration of the register itself (where the power to *rectify* against a 'proprietor in possession' of an estate in land is limited) and entitlement to indemnity (which arises, in relation to alteration for the purposes of correcting a mistake in the register, where the register is rectified or there is a mistake whose correction would involve rectification).

Rectification in this context is an alteration which:

(a) involves the correction of a mistake; and
(b) prejudicially affects the title of a registered proprietor.[2]

Therefore, rectification is a type of alteration, but not all alterations amount to rectification. For applications involving rectification, see 148 Rectification. For applications relating to payment of indemnity in rectification cases, see 86 Indemnity.

LRA 2002, Sch 4 para 9 provides for the discretionary payment of costs and expenses in connection with an alteration of the register in non-rectification cases.

12.1 Alteration pursuant to a court order

Where in any proceedings the court decides that:

(a) there is a mistake in the register,
(b) the register is not up to date, or
(c) there is an estate, right or interest excepted from the effect of registration that should be given effect to,

it must order alteration of the register.[3] However, where the alteration is not rectification, the court is not obliged to make an order if there are exceptional circumstances that justify not doing so.[4]

NRAM Ltd v Evans[5] confirmed an entry on the register made pursuant to a voidable transaction will not be a mistake if the transaction is later rescinded. Any alteration to the register to give effect to the rescission will be an update to the register. *Antoine v Barclays Bank UK PLC*[6] took a similar approach where a vesting order was later set aside by the court. Classifying such alterations as updates rather than the correction of a mistake means indemnity is not payable in such circumstances.[7]

An estate, right or interest may be excepted from the effect of registration by virtue of the registration of a registered title with qualified, possessory or good leasehold title.[8] Such an estate, right or interest could be the subject of a court order for alteration of the register even though the class of title was not itself changed.

The court order for alteration of the register must:

(a) state the title number of the title affected and the alteration that is to be made; and
(b) direct HMLR to make the alteration.[9]

If the court makes an order for alteration, HMLR must give effect to the order when it is served on it. Service of the order must be made by making an application to HMLR, accompanied by the order.[10]

An applicant should deliver to HMLR:

(a) an application in form AP1;
(b) the court order for alteration of the register or a sealed copy of the order; and
(c) the fee (if applicable).[11]

12.2 Alteration not pursuant to a court order

HMLR may alter the register for the purpose of:

(a) correcting a mistake;
(b) bringing the register up to date;
(c) giving effect to any estate, right or interest excepted from the effect of registration; or
(d) removing a superfluous entry.

HMLR may make the alteration following an application or of its own volition without an application having been made. HMLR may make such enquiries as it thinks fit and must give notice of the proposed alteration to any person who would be affected by it, unless it is satisfied that such notice is unnecessary.[12] However, this does not apply to alteration of the register in the specific circumstances covered by any other rule. An application for alteration by HMLR (otherwise than under a court order) must be supported by evidence to justify the alteration.[13]

An applicant for an alteration of the register not pursuant to a court order should deliver to HMLR:

(a) an application in form AP1;
(b) a statement of the alteration being applied for;
(c) all evidence held by the applicant which is relevant to the application to alter the register; and
(d) the fee (if applicable).[14]

12.3 Costs and expenses in non-rectification cases

If HMLR alters the register under LRA 2002, Sch 4 in a case *not* involving rectification, HMLR may pay such amount as it thinks fit in respect of any costs or expenses reasonably incurred by a person in connection with the alteration which have been incurred with the consent of HMLR.[15] Even where HMLR has not consented to the costs or expenses being incurred, it may still make a payment if it appears to HMLR that:

(a) the costs or expenses had to be incurred urgently; and
(b) it was not reasonably practicable to apply for HMLR's consent.

HMLR may also still make a payment if it has subsequently approved the incurring of the costs or expenses.

HMLR has discretion whether to pay costs and expenses are payable under Sch 4, para 9. Further, HMLR may only make such a payment when the register is actually altered. For costs and expenses in connection with the payment of indemnity in rectification cases, see 86 Indemnity.

---

1 LRA 2002, s 65 and Sch 4.
2 LRA 2002, Sch 4, para 1.
3 LRA 2002, Sch 4, para 2(1) and LRR 2003, r 126(1).
4 LRR 2003, r 126(2).
5 [2017] EWCA Civ 1013.
6 [2018] EWCA Civ 2846.
7 Because the alteration does not meet the statutory definition of rectification. See 86 Indemnity.
8 LRA 2002, ss 11 and 12. See 32 Classes of Title.
9 LRR 2003, r 127(1).
10 LRR 2003, r 127(2).
11 See 67 Fees.
12 LRR 2003, r 128.
13 LRR 2003, r 129.
14 See 67 Fees.
15 LRA 2002, Sch 4, para 9.

13 AMALGAMATION OF REGISTERED TITLES

Amalgamation is the joining of two or more registered or unregistered estates affecting different extents of land, under a single registered title. HMLR may amalgamate two or more registered titles to form one registered title. It may also add an unregistered estate which is being registered for the first time to an existing registered title. In either case the estates must be of the same kind and vested in the same proprietor.[1] Consequently, the titles to be amalgamated must be:

(a) of the same estate and tenure; and
(b) held by the same proprietor in the same capacity.

Accordingly, a freehold title cannot be amalgamated with a leasehold title, nor can a possessory title be amalgamated with an absolute title. Nor can amalgamation be effected where the same proprietor holds all the titles, but in a differing capacity; one as beneficial owner and one as trustee, for example.

Amalgamation will most commonly be considered for estates in land. However, it is possible to amalgamate other estates where the estates are of the same kind and are vested in the same proprietor. For example, a proprietor can hold more than one profit à prendre in gross and these can be registered under one title number and set out in a schedule within the property register.

It is possible to amalgamate a title that is subject to a registered charge with one that is not. However, if this is done it will not be possible for the registered chargee to discharge the charge electronically later.

Amalgamation can occur either as the result of an application by the proprietor of the registered estate or of any registered charge over it, or because HMLR considers it desirable for the keeping of the register of title. An application by the proprietor should be made in form AP1, listing the relevant title numbers in panel 2. For the fee (if any) payable, see 67 Fees.

HMLR has a discretion as to whether to amalgamate titles. It will consider each request on its merits, taking into account the current office work situation; the amount of work and cost involved in amalgamating; and the likely future benefit to the applicant/proprietor and to HMLR in amalgamating.

Where the proprietor has not applied but amalgamation is effected because HMLR considers it desirable for the keeping of the register of title, it must notify the proprietor of the registered estate and any registered charge, unless they have agreed to the amalgamation. In these circumstances, HMLR may make a new edition of any individual register or make entries on any individual register to reflect the amalgamation.[2]

LRR 2003, r 70 applies on amalgamation where a registered estate in land includes any mines or minerals but there is no note in the register that they are included, and it is appropriate when describing the amalgamated registered estate to do so by reference to the land where the mines or minerals are or may be situated. In such circumstances HMLR may make an entry in the property register to the effect that such description is an entry made under LRR 2003, r 5(a), and is not a note that the registered estate includes the mines or minerals for the purposes of extending the payment of indemnity to such mines or minerals. LRR 2003, r 5(a) provides that the property register must contain a description of the registered estate.[3]

---

1 LRR 2003, r 3(4).

2 LRR 2003, r 3(5).

3 See also 115 Mines and Minerals.

14 ANNUITIES

Strictly, an annuity is not secured on land and so does not require protection at HMLR. However, the term 'annuity' is sometimes used to describe a rentcharge for life, which is an interest under a trust of land or a settlement under the Settled Land Act 1925 (SLA 1925). No notice may be entered in the register in respect of any such interest.[1]

In the case of settled land, restrictions are entered in the register to protect people interested in the settled land. The proprietor, or (if there is no proprietor) the personal representatives of a deceased proprietor, must apply for the entry of such restrictions (in addition to a restriction in Forms G, H or I) as may be appropriate. The applicant must state that the restrictions applied for are required for the protection of the beneficial interests and powers under the settlement. HMLR must enter such restrictions without enquiry as to the terms of the settlement.[2] Even so, if it does not appear to HMLR that the terms of the proposed restriction are reasonable and that applying the proposed restriction would be straightforward and not place an unreasonable burden on it, it may not approve the application for the restriction.[3] For the various restrictions appropriate to settled land, see 162.1 Settled land forms of restriction.

Where the annuity is an interest under a trust of land, the proprietor of the registered land must apply for entry of a restriction in Form A in LRR 2003, Sch 4, unless one already appears in the register.[4] The wording of Form A is set out in Appendix IV.

Where a restriction in Form A is required but the proprietor of the registered land has not applied for it, any person who has an interest in a registered estate held under a trust of land has a sufficient interest for the purposes of LRA 2002, s 43(1)(c) to apply for that restriction to be entered in the register of that registered estate.[5]

An annuity which is a rentcharge for life or lives, or determinable on the dropping of a life, and not arising under a settlement or trust of land, can be overreached by a disposition under SLA 1925, s 72(3) or Law of Property Act 1925 (LPA 1925), s 2(2) and (3). A settled land restriction or Form A restriction would again be appropriate, depending on the circumstances.

14.1 Restriction

The applicant should deliver to HMLR the usual documents required.[6]

Panel 9 of form RX1 should set out the required restriction(s). A restriction in a standard form contained in LRR 2003, Sch 4 does not require the approval of HMLR to the terms of the restriction under LRA 2002, s 43(3).

HMLR must give notice of the application for a restriction to the proprietor of the registered estate or charge concerned, if it has not been made by or with the consent of such proprietor or a person entitled to be registered as such proprietor.[7]

---

1 LRA 2002, s 33.
2 LRR 2003, Sch 7, para 7.
3 LRA 2002, s 43(3).
4 LRR 2003, r 94.
5 LRR 2003, r 93(a).
6 See 153.1 Application for entry of restriction.
7 LRA 2002, s 45.

15 APPLICATION MANAGEMENT SERVICE

The application management service gives those dealing with complex commercial transactions direct access to the HMLR staff who will deal with the application throughout its lifecycle. The applicant may discuss the matter from before it is lodged through to its completion and beyond, if required.

An applicant wishing to use the application management service must apply using form AMS1. No fee is payable.

The HMLR website[1] provides further details of the service, including details of what HMLR considers comprises a complex commercial transaction.

---

1 www.gov.uk/guidance/submit-complex-commercial-or-infrastructure-development-enquiries-and-transactions-to-hm-land-registry.

16 APPLICATIONS TO HM LAND REGISTRY

Applications to HMLR must be made in accordance with the provisions of the LRA 2002 and the LRR 2003 and related practice and procedures as laid down by HMLR from time to time.

Many applications are now lodged digitally.[1] Applicants using HMLR's Digital Registration Service (known as DRS) can only send electronic certified copies of documents.

Under LRR 2003, r 214, applicants do not need to lodge the originals of scheduled forms and documents which comprise registrable dispositions with an application. Instead, certified copies of deeds or documents need to be provided. This applies to postal and digital applications.

Although originals of documents will still be acceptable in the case of postal applications, it is important to bear in mind that these will be destroyed once HMLR has made a scanned copy of them for registration purposes.[2]

For HMLR purposes, a 'certified copy' is a copy of a document which has been certified on its face as a true copy of the original document by a conveyancer or such other person as the registrar may permit.[3] In each case, the person certifying the document should endorse it with his name and address.

This practice applies only to postal applications relating to existing registered titles. It does not apply to applications for first registration.[4]

---

1 See 56 Electronic Services.

2 See 155 Retention, Destruction and Return of Documents.

3 LRR 2003, r 217.

4 See 68 First Registration.

17 ASSENTS

Where a beneficiary is entitled to registered or unregistered land under the will or intestacy of a deceased owner, the personal representative may execute an assent in favour of the beneficiary to vest the legal estate in him, whether or not the personal representative has (in the case of registered land) first been registered as proprietor in place of the deceased proprietor. Although the assent must be in writing and signed by all the personal representatives (if more than one), it does not have to be drawn as a deed.

Where an assent relates only to the beneficial share of a deceased proprietor, this does not effect a transfer of the legal estate. Such an assent should not be lodged for registration and, if a transfer of the legal estate is required, this should be effected in the appropriate form and an appropriate application for registration made.

17.1 Unregistered land

When the title to land is unregistered, the assentee must apply for first registration if the assent has transferred:

(a) a legal freehold estate in the land; or
(b) a legal leasehold estate in the land for a term which, at the time of the assent, has more than 7 years to run.[1]

The requirement to apply for first registration does not apply to mines and minerals held apart from the surface.

The assentee must apply for first registration within 2 months of the assent.[2] If necessary, he may apply to HMLR for an order that the period for registration ends on a later date, which date will be specified in the order. HMLR will make such an order if it is satisfied that there is good reason for doing so.[3]

If the assentee does not comply with the requirement to register, the legal estate reverts to the personal representative who holds it on a bare trust for the assentee.[4] Where an order is made under LRA 2002, s 6(5), this reverter of the legal estate is treated as not having occurred.[5]

If there must be a further assent because of the failure to apply for first registration following the original assent, the assentee is liable for the proper costs of the personal representative in respect of the new assent.[6]

In addition to delivering the usual documents required,[7] an applicant for first registration should deliver to HMLR evidence of the appointment of the personal representative, being the original or an office copy or certified copy of the grant of probate, or letters of administration, or order of the court appointing the personal representative.

HMLR will enter a restriction in Form A, where necessary, if the assent is in favour of two or more assentees.[8] The assentee should apply for any other restrictions required, as appropriate. The wording of Form A is set out in Appendix IV.

17.2 Registered land

Where a sole proprietor or the last surviving joint proprietor has died, his personal representative may transfer the deceased's registered estate or registered charge without himself becoming registered as proprietor. LRR 2003, r 162(2) places responsibility on the personal representative in relation to registered land forming part of the deceased's estate. It provides HMLR is not under a duty to investigate the reasons why any transfer by such a personal representative is made, nor to consider the contents of the will. Provided the terms of any restriction in the register are complied with, HMLR must assume, whether or not it knows the terms of the will, that the personal representative is acting correctly and within his powers.

The assent must be in the appropriate prescribed form, being form AS1 (assent of whole of land in a registered title), form AS2 (assent of registered charge), or form AS3 (assent of part of land in a registered title). Until the assent of the registered estate or registered charge is completed by registration, it does not operate at law.[9]

The assentee (not being a 'purchaser') cannot apply for an official search with priority using form OS1 or form OS2, but may apply for an official search without priority.[10]

A person applying to register an assent of registered land should deliver to HMLR:

(a) an application in form AP1;
(b) forms AS1, AS2 or AS3 as appropriate;
(c) evidence of the appointment of the personal representative (unless the personal representative is already registered as proprietor), being the original or an office copy or certified copy of the grant of probate, or letters of administration, or order of the court appointing the personal representative. Alternatively, the applicant's conveyancer may provide a certificate that he holds the original or an office copy of the grant, letters of administration or court order;[11]
(d) form DI giving the information as to overriding interests required by LRR 2003, r 57, including any documentary evidence of the interests;[12]
(e) the appropriate confirmation or evidence of identity;[13]
(f) the appropriate SDLT or LTT certificate(s) or other evidence;[14] and
(g) the fee payable.[15]

HMLR will register the applicant subject to any existing entries in the register which are not cancelled or withdrawn, including any existing restrictions. The terms of any such restrictions will, where necessary, need to be complied with before the assent can be completed by registration. Where a restriction in Form C[16] appears in the register, the assent will not be caught by it and it will be automatically cancelled on registration of the assent. The wording of Form C is set out in Appendix IV.

HMLR will enter a restriction in Form A, where necessary, if the assent is in favour of two or more assentees.[17] The assentee should apply for any other restrictions required, as appropriate. The wording of Form A is set out in Appendix IV.

---

1 LRA 2002, s 4.
2 LRA 2002, s 6(4).
3 LRA 2002, s 6(5).

4 LRA 2002, s 7.
5 LRA 2002, s 7(3).
6 LRA 2002, s 8.
7 See 68.4 Application for first registration.
8 See 92.1 Entry of Form A restriction.
9 LRA 2002, s 27(1).
10 See 123 Official Searches.
11 LRR 2003, r 163(2).
12 See 128.4 Duty to disclose overriding interests.
13 See 84 Identity Evidence.
14 See 168 Stamp Duty Land Tax and/or 94 Land Transaction Tax.
15 See 67 Fees.
16 See 133 Personal Representatives.
17 See 92.1 Entry of Form A restriction.

18 ASSETS OF COMMUNITY VALUE

Chapter 3 of Localism Act 2011, Pt 5, which deals with 'assets of community value', came into force in England on 21 September 2012, but is not yet in force in Wales. Under s 87 of this Act, local authorities in England must maintain a list of assets of community value, such as a village shop, a pub or a community centre, which further the social well-being or social interests of the local community. The listing of an asset of community value will constitute a local land charge.[1] Unless removed sooner, the listing will last for 5 years.

Under Localism Act 2011, s 95(1), the owner of listed land is prohibited from entering into a 'relevant disposal' of it unless specified conditions are satisfied. These provide for the owner to give notification to the local authority of his intention to make a relevant disposal, and for a moratorium during which a community interest group may bid for the land, although the owner does not have to accept any such bid.

A 'relevant disposal' is defined as a disposal with vacant possession of a freehold estate or the grant or assignment with vacant possession of a lease granted for a term of at least 25 years. Certain types of relevant disposals are exempted from the right to bid: these include:

(a) gifts and transfers at nil value;
(b) transfers between family members;
(c) business-to-business going concern exemptions; and
(d) disposals where only part of the land is listed.

LRR 2003, Sch 4 includes a standard form of restriction for use in existing registered titles and on first registration. This is Form QQ, the wording of which is set out in Appendix IV.

Where the listed land is registered, the relevant local authority is under a duty to apply for the registration of a restriction in Form QQ against the registered estate.[2] The local authority must apply as soon as practicable after listing unless there is an existing Form QQ restriction in respect of the same registered estate.

Where the listed land is currently unregistered, an applicant for first registration of title to the land must at the same time apply for entry of a Form QQ restriction in respect of that land.[3] This includes an applicant who is making the application as mortgagee under a first legal mortgage, the creation of which has triggered compulsory first registration.

Where a person applies for first registration of title to such land and any of the deeds and documents accompanying the application includes a conveyance or lease to the applicant (or to a predecessor in title) made at any time when the land was listed land, the applicant must, in respect of each conveyance or lease, provide a certificate by a conveyancer that the conveyance or lease did not contravene Localism Act 2011, s 95(1).[4]

A transfer or lease in breach of s 95(1) will be ineffective from the outset, unless the owner who made it did not know that the land was listed despite making all reasonable efforts.[5] A Form QQ restriction only 'catches' transfers and leases, including those taking effect by operation of law. On registration of a transfer or lease, HMLR will not normally cancel the restriction without a specific application in form RX3 by or with the consent of the relevant local authority.

A local authority must apply to the registrar to cancel any Form QQ restriction in the register as soon as practicable after removing a property from the list of assets of community value.[6]

---

1 Localism Act 2011, s 100.
2 LRR 2003, r 94(11).
3 LRR 2003, r 27A(1).
4 LRR 2003, r 27A(2).
5 Assets of Community Value (England) Regulations 2012 (SI 2012/2421), reg 21.
6 Assets of Community Value (England) Regulations 2012 (SI 2012/2421), reg 18.

19 BANKRUPTCY

The proprietor of a registered estate or charge may become bankrupt. The LRA 2002 contains provisions to cover this situation when it occurs. The main statutory provisions relating to insolvency are contained in the IA 1986 and the IR 2016. These are supplemented by specific provisions in the LRA 2002 and the LRR 2003 relating to bankruptcy. The bankruptcy process, where initiated by a creditor, involves two stages:

(a) the presentation by a creditor of a bankruptcy petition to the court for a bankruptcy order; and
(b) the making of a bankruptcy order by the court.

Alternatively, since 1 April 2016 a debtor may apply for his own bankruptcy to an adjudicator within the Insolvency Service under IA 1986, s 263H. After the bankruptcy order is made, whether by the court or by an adjudicator, a trustee in bankruptcy is appointed who will be either an authorised insolvency practitioner or the Official Receiver.

As an alternative to bankruptcy, a debtor may enter into an individual voluntary arrangement (IVA) with his creditors.[1]

19.1 Petition in bankruptcy

The adjudicator or court must apply to the Land Charges Department for registration of the application or petition in the register of pending actions immediately after the bankruptcy application or petition has been filed.[2] As soon as practicable after registration under the Land Charges Act 1972, HMLR must enter in the register, in relation to any registered estate or charge which appears to it to be affected, a notice in respect of the pending action.[3] This notice is designated a 'bankruptcy notice'.[4] No fee is payable.

A bankruptcy notice in relation to a registered estate is entered in the proprietorship register and a bankruptcy notice in relation to a registered charge is entered in the charges register. The notice will be in the following form:

> BANKRUPTCY NOTICE entered under section 86(2) of the Land Registration Act 2002 in respect of a pending action, as the title of the [proprietor of the registered estate] or [proprietor of the charge dated … referred to above] appears to be affected by a [petition in bankruptcy against [*name of debtor*], presented in the [*name*] Court (Court Reference Number …)] *or* [bankruptcy application made by [*name of debtor*] (reference …)] (Land Charges Reference Number PA …).

HMLR must give notice of the entry of a bankruptcy notice to the proprietor of the registered estate or charge to which it relates.

Unless HMLR cancels the bankruptcy notice, it continues in force until HMLR enters a bankruptcy restriction in the register or the trustee in bankruptcy is entered as proprietor.[5] As to cancellation, see 19.10 Cancellation of bankruptcy notice or bankruptcy restriction.

Where a bankruptcy notice appears in the register, an application to register a disposition by the registered proprietor after the entry of a bankruptcy notice, such as a transfer, can still be made but, unless it is clear the interest of the disponee has priority over the bankruptcy proceedings, the registration will be made subject to the bankruptcy notice by the entry of a note in the register along the following lines:

> The registration of the proprietor is subject to the rights of all creditors of [*transferor's name*] (a former proprietor) protected by the Bankruptcy Notice(s) referred to above.

This reflects the fact that the priority of the bankruptcy proceedings has been protected by the bankruptcy notice.

19.2 Bankruptcy order

Immediately after the adjudicator or court has made a bankruptcy order they must send at least two sealed copies to the Official Receiver. On receipt, the Official Receiver must send notice of the making of the order to the Land Charges Department for registration in the register of writs and orders affecting land.[6] As soon as practicable after registration of a bankruptcy order under the Land Charges Act 1972, HMLR must enter in the register, in relation to any registered estate or charge which appears to it to be affected, a restriction reflecting the effect of the IA 1986.[7] This restriction is designated a 'bankruptcy restriction'.[8] No fee is payable.

A bankruptcy restriction in relation to a registered estate is entered in the proprietorship register and a bankruptcy restriction in relation to a registered charge is entered in the charges register. The restriction will be in the following form:

> BANKRUPTCY RESTRICTION entered under section 86(4) of the Land Registration Act 2002, as the title of [the proprietor of the registered estate] or [the proprietor of the charge dated ... referred to above] appears to be affected by a bankruptcy order made by the [[*name*] Court (Court Reference Number ...)] *or*

> [adjudicator (reference ...) against [*name of debtor*] (Land Charges Reference Number WO ...).
>
> No disposition of the registered estate is to be registered until the trustee in bankruptcy of the property of the bankrupt is registered as proprietor of the [registered estate] *or* [charge].

HMLR must give notice of the entry of a bankruptcy restriction to the proprietor of the registered estate or registered charge to which it relates.

The bankruptcy restriction reflects the position under the IA 1986, s 284 which provides where a person is adjudged bankrupt, any disposition of property made by him between the making of the bankruptcy application or presentation of the petition and the time at which the property vests in the trustee in bankruptcy is void, except to the extent that it is or was made with the consent of the court, or is or was subsequently ratified by the court.

Where a bankruptcy restriction appears in the register, no disposition (other than the registration of the trustee in bankruptcy) affecting the registered estate or charge can be completed by registration until the restriction is cancelled. The restriction may additionally have the effect of precluding the entry of notices to protect certain third-party interests which consist of a disposition by the debtor.

The bankruptcy restriction does not prejudice dealings with, or in right of, interests or charges having priority over the registered estate or registered charge. Thus, the proprietor of a registered charge which was registered before a bankruptcy restriction (and any bankruptcy notice) was entered could exercise his power of sale, notwithstanding the entry of the bankruptcy restriction in the proprietorship register. However, the restriction would need to be considered on a disposition by a receiver appointed by the chargee as he would be acting as agent for the debtor/chargor, not the chargee.

19.3 Bankruptcy entries under the Land Registration Act 1925

The position before 13 October 2003 was that HMLR entered a creditors' notice in the register, under LRA 1925, s 61, following the petition in bankruptcy, in a similar way to that in which a bankruptcy notice is now entered. Following the making of the bankruptcy order, HMLR entered a bankruptcy inhibition in the register, in a similar way to that in which a bankruptcy restriction is now entered.

Where a creditors' notice still appears in a registered title, it has the same effect as a bankruptcy notice. A bankruptcy inhibition still appearing in a registered title has the same effect as a bankruptcy restriction.[9]

The form of entry of a creditors' notice in the register in respect of the proprietor of a registered estate was:

> Creditors' Notice entered under section 61(1) of the Land Registration Act 1925 to protect the rights of all creditors, as the title of the proprietor of the land appears to be affected by a petition in bankruptcy against [*name of debtor*], presented in the [*name*] Court (Court Reference Number ...) (Land Charges Reference Number PA ...).

Where it appeared that the title of the proprietor of a registered charge was affected, the creditors' notice, in a similar form, was entered in the charges register.

The form of entry of a bankruptcy inhibition in the register in respect of the proprietor of a registered estate was:

> BANKRUPTCY INHIBITION entered under section 61(3) of the Land Registration Act 1925, as the title of the proprietor of the land appears to be affected by a bankruptcy order made by the [*name*] Court (Court Reference Number ...) against [*name of debtor*] (Land Charges Reference Number WO ...).
>
> No disposition by the proprietor of the land or transmission is to be registered until the trustee in bankruptcy of the property of the bankrupt is registered.

Where it appeared that the title of the proprietor of a registered charge was affected, the bankruptcy inhibition, in a similar form, was entered in the charges register.

19.4 Registration of the trustee in bankruptcy

All the property, including any registered estate or registered charge, owned by the bankrupt for his own benefit at the date of the bankruptcy order automatically vests without any formal transfer in the trustee in bankruptcy when his appointment takes effect.[10] Property held by the bankrupt on trust for any other person is excluded, whether or not he also holds it on trust for himself.[11]

Although the usual rule is that the disposition of a registered estate (even where it occurs by operation of law) does not operate at law until the relevant registration requirements are met, this does not apply to a transfer by operation of law on the bankruptcy of an individual proprietor.[12] LRR 2003, r 168 provides for registration of the trustee in bankruptcy as proprietor in place of the bankrupt.

A trustee in bankruptcy may apply for the register to be altered by the registration of the trustee in place of the bankrupt proprietor where a sole proprietor has had a bankruptcy order made against him and the bankrupt's registered estate or registered charge has vested in the trustee in bankruptcy.

Where joint trustees in bankruptcy are appointed:

(a) if appointed jointly and severally, HMLR will accept an application for one or some of them to be registered as proprietor in place of the bankrupt proprietor; and
(b) if appointed jointly, HMLR will not accept an application for one or some of them to be registered as proprietor in place of the bankrupt proprietor. All appointed trustees must apply (subject to the limit permitting only four registered proprietors on the register).

An applicant should deliver to HMLR:

(a) an application in form AP1;
(b) an office copy of the bankruptcy order relating to the bankrupt;
(c) a certificate signed by the trustee that the registered estate or registered charge is comprised in the bankrupt's estate;
(d)
    (i) where the Official Receiver is the trustee, a certificate by him to that effect; or (where the trustee is another person)
    (ii) the trustee's certificate of appointment as trustee by the meeting of the bankrupt's creditors; or
    (iii) the trustee's certificate of appointment as trustee by the Secretary of State; or
    (iv) an office copy of the order of the court appointing the trustee; and
(e) the fee payable, based upon a certificate as to the value of the registered estate or charge which should accompany the application.[13]

On completion of the application, HMLR will alter the relevant entry to read:

> [*Name of Official Receiver or Trustee in Bankruptcy*] of [*address*], the [Official Receiver and Trustee in Bankruptcy] *or* [Trustee in Bankruptcy] of [*name of bankrupt proprietor*].

On registration of the trustee in bankruptcy, HMLR will cancel any bankruptcy notice or bankruptcy restriction appearing in the register.

19.5 Vacating of office by trustee in bankruptcy

Where a trustee in bankruptcy, who has been registered as proprietor, vacates his office and the Official Receiver or some other person has been appointed as trustee in bankruptcy, the Official Receiver or that person may apply to be registered as proprietor in place of the former trustee.[14]

An applicant should deliver to HMLR:

(a) an application in form AP1:

(b)

  (i) where the Official Receiver is the new trustee, a certificate by him to that effect; or (where the trustee is another person)
  (ii) the new trustee's certificate of appointment as trustee by the meeting of the bankrupt's creditors; or
  (iii) the new trustee's certificate of appointment as trustee by the Secretary of State; or
  (iv) an office copy of the order of the court appointing the new trustee;

(c) the fee payable, based upon a certificate as to the value of the registered estate or charge which should accompany the application.[15]

On completion of the application, HMLR will alter the relevant entry to read:

> [*Name of Official Receiver or Trustee in Bankruptcy*] of [*address*], the [Official Receiver and Trustee in Bankruptcy] *or* [Trustee in Bankruptcy] of [*name of bankrupt proprietor*].

19.6 Sale by trustee in bankruptcy

A trustee in bankruptcy may sell the registered estate or charge either as registered proprietor or without having himself been entered in the register as proprietor.

Where joint trustees have been appointed:

(a) where any trustees have been registered as proprietor(s) all registered trustees must be named as transferor and execute the transfer; and

(b) where no trustee has been registered as proprietor:

  (i) if the trustees have been appointed jointly, all trustees must be named as disponor and execute the transfer; and
  (ii) if the trustees have been appointed jointly and severally, either a single trustee or any or all of them can be named as disponor and execute the transfer.

In addition to delivering the usual documents required,[16] the transferee should deliver to HMLR:

(a) (if appropriate) any new mortgage or charge entered into by the applicant;
(b) releases or discharges in respect of any charges appearing in the registered title;
(c) an office copy of the bankruptcy order relating to the bankrupt proprietor;
(d) a certificate signed by the trustee that the registered estate or registered charge was comprised in the bankrupt's estate;
(e)

  (i) where the Official Receiver is the trustee, a certificate by him to that effect; or (where the trustee is another person)
  (ii) the trustee's certificate of appointment as trustee by the meeting of the bankrupt's creditors; or
  (iii) the trustee's certificate of appointment as trustee by the Secretary of State; or
  (iv) an office copy of the order of the court appointing the trustee.

The applicant may omit the documents listed in (c), (d) and (e) where the trustee has been registered as proprietor in place of the bankrupt former proprietor.

On registration of the transfer, HMLR will cancel any bankruptcy notice or bankruptcy restriction.

19.7 Protection of purchaser from bankrupt

For the purposes of the LRA 2002, references to an interest affecting an estate or charge do not include a bankruptcy application or petition in bankruptcy or a bankruptcy order.[17] Instead, LRA 2002, s 86(5) provides a degree of protection for purchasers in relation to such applications, petitions and orders. This follows the scheme of the IA 1986, even though this brings in the concept of notice in relation to registered land. A person to whom a registrable disposition is made is not required to make any search under the Land Charges Act 1972.[18]

Where the proprietor of a registered estate or charge is adjudged bankrupt, the title of his trustee in bankruptcy is void against a person to whom a registrable disposition of the estate or charge is made if:

(a) the disposition is made for valuable consideration;
(b) the person to whom the disposition is made acts in good faith; and
(c) at the time of the disposition:

  (i) no bankruptcy notice or bankruptcy restriction is entered in relation to the registered estate or charge; and

(ii) the person to whom the disposition is made has no notice of the bankruptcy application or petition or the adjudication.

Although this protection applies only if the relevant registration requirements are met in relation to the disposition, as and when they are met it has effect from the date of the disposition.

The fact that a bankruptcy restriction has been entered in the register after the date of the disposition but before application has been made to register it will not prevent the disposition being completed by registration when application has been made, as the provisions of s 86(5)(c) will nevertheless apply in relation to the disposition.[19]

19.8 Bankruptcy of a joint proprietor

Where one of two or more joint registered proprietors becomes bankrupt, the registrar does not enter any bankruptcy notice or bankruptcy restriction in the register. This is because, as the bankrupt is holding the legal estate as trustee, the legal estate does not automatically vest in the trustee in bankruptcy. Consequently, all the joint proprietors will need to execute any subsequent transfer of the property in the usual way. The bankrupt proprietor's trustee in bankruptcy does not need to be a party to such transfer. However, the bankruptcy order does sever any beneficial joint tenancy, and the bankrupt's beneficial share vests in the trustee in bankruptcy.

If there is no restriction in Form A already in the register, the trustee in bankruptcy has a sufficient interest to apply for entry of a restriction in Form A to ensure that a survivor of the joint proprietors (unless a trust corporation) is not able to give a valid receipt for capital money.[20] The wording of Form A is set out in Appendix IV.

The trustee in bankruptcy also has a sufficient interest to apply for entry of a restriction in Form J, to ensure that he receives notice of a disposition.[21] The wording of Form J is set out in Appendix IV.

A Form J restriction does not prevent a disposition, provided it is complied with. This is because the interest of the trustee in bankruptcy will be overreached where the requirements of the Form A restriction have been met.[22] However, entry of the restriction does ensure the trustee is given notice of the disposition so he can pursue his share of any proceeds of a sale.

HMLR must give notice of an application for entry of a restriction to the proprietor of the registered estate or charge concerned.[23]

If applying for entry of a restriction in Form A, the trustee in bankruptcy should deliver to HMLR an application in form RX1. No fee is currently payable where the application is in respect of a restriction in Form A only.

The statement in panel 12 or the conveyancer's certificate in panel 13 of form RX1 should be completed on the following lines:

> The interest is that specified in rule 93(a) of the Land Registration Rules 2003 (SI 2003/1417), the applicant being the trustee in bankruptcy of [*name of bankrupt joint proprietor*] who is the subject of a bankruptcy order made by the [*name*] Court (Court Reference Number [*number*]) (Land Charges Reference Number WO [*reference*]) and has a beneficial interest in the property.

Panel 9 of form RX1 should set out the wording of Form A.

If applying for a restriction in Form J, the trustee in bankruptcy should deliver to HMLR the usual documents required.[24]

The statement in panel 12 or the conveyancer's certificate in panel 13 of form RX1 should be completed on the following lines:

> The interest is that specified in rule 93(j) of the Land Registration Rules 2003 (SI 2003/1417), the applicant being the trustee in bankruptcy of [*name of bankrupt joint proprietor*] who is the subject of a bankruptcy order made by the [*name*] Court (Court Reference Number [*number*]) (Land Charges Reference Number WO [*reference*]) and has a beneficial interest in the property.

Panel 9 of form RX1 should set out the wording of Form J.

A restriction in standard Form A or J in LRR 2003, Sch 4 does not require the approval of HMLR to the terms of the restriction under LRA 2002, s 43(3).

19.9 Administration of an insolvent estate

If a debtor dies after a bankruptcy application has been made by him or a bankruptcy petition has been presented against him, the proceedings will, unless the court orders otherwise (in the case of a bankruptcy petition), be continued – subject to certain modifications to reflect the death of the debtor – as if he was alive.[25]

Where a person dies before the making of a bankruptcy application or presentation of a bankruptcy petition, his estate, if insolvent, may be administered in bankruptcy. The relevant provisions of the IA 1986 will (subject to certain modifications to reflect the death of the debtor) apply to the administration of an insolvent estate in bankruptcy.[26]

When an insolvency administration petition is made by creditors or the personal representatives of the deceased debtor, the petition will be registered in the name of the debtor in the Land Charges Department as a pending action under the Land Charges Act 1972, and HMLR will enter a bankruptcy notice in the register of any title where the deceased appears as proprietor of the land or of a registered charge. Following registration of the insolvency administration order in the register of writs and orders under the Land Charges Act 1972, HMLR will enter a bankruptcy restriction in the proprietorship register or charges register as appropriate.

Where, because of an insolvency administration order, the deceased's registered estate or registered charge has vested in the trustee in bankruptcy, the trustee may apply for the alteration of the register by registering the trustee in place of the deceased proprietor.

An applicant should deliver to HMLR:

(a) an application in form AP1;
(b) an office copy of the insolvency administration order relating to the deceased debtor's estate;
(c) a certificate signed by the trustee that the registered estate or registered charge is comprised in the deceased debtor's estate;
(d)
    (i) where the Official Receiver is the trustee, a certificate by him to that effect; or (where the trustee is another person)
    (ii) the trustee's certificate of appointment as trustee by the meeting of the deceased debtor's creditors; or
    (iii) the trustee's certificate of appointment as trustee by the Secretary of State; or
    (iv) an office copy of the order of the court appointing the trustee; and
(e) the fee payable, based upon a certificate as to the value of the registered estate or charge which should accompany the application.[27]

On completion of the application, HMLR will alter the relevant entry to read:

> [*Name of Official Receiver or Trustee in Bankruptcy*] of [*address*], the [Official Receiver and Trustee in Bankruptcy] *or* [Trustee in Bankruptcy] of [*name of bankrupt proprietor*].

On registration of the trustee in bankruptcy, HMLR will cancel any bankruptcy notice or bankruptcy restriction appearing in the register.

19.10 Cancellation of bankruptcy notice or bankruptcy restriction

As mentioned above, HMLR will cancel a bankruptcy notice (or creditors' notice) and a bankruptcy restriction (or bankruptcy inhibition) on the registration of the trustee in bankruptcy as proprietor or (if he has not become the registered proprietor) on registration of a transfer on sale by him.

HMLR will not cancel a bankruptcy notice (or creditors' notice) on the production of a court order which simply authorises the cancellation of the registration of the bankruptcy application or petition as a pending action in the Land Charges Department. Similarly, HMLR will not cancel a bankruptcy restriction (or bankruptcy inhibition) on the production of a court order which simply authorises the cancellation of the registration of the bankruptcy order at the Land Charges Department. Such an order does not re-vest property in a bankrupt which has automatically vested in his trustee in bankruptcy. Such property will remain vested in the trustee in bankruptcy, subject to the provisions discussed in 19.12 Re-vesting of bankrupt's home.

LRR 2003, r 167(1) provides HMLR must cancel a bankruptcy notice or bankruptcy restriction if it is satisfied that:

(a) the bankruptcy order has been annulled; or
(b) the adjudicator has refused to make a bankruptcy order; or
(c) the bankruptcy petition has been dismissed or withdrawn with the court's permission; or
(d) the bankruptcy proceedings do not affect or have ceased to affect the registered estate or registered charge in relation to which the bankruptcy notice or restriction has been entered in the register.

Neither an automatic discharge under the provisions of IA 1986, s 279 nor an order for discharge by the court under IA 1986, s 280 re-vest the bankrupt's property. Consequently, production of evidence of discharge is not enough to enable HMLR to cancel a bankruptcy notice or bankruptcy restriction (even if accompanied by the consent of the trustee or an order of the court under Land Charges Act 1972, s 1(6) ordering cancellation of Land Charges bankruptcy entries).

The application for cancellation should be made in form AP1. Where made in the circumstances referred to at (a) and (c) above, it must be accompanied by an office copy of the relevant court order which must expressly authorise the cancellation of the Land Charges bankruptcy entries under the reference number set out in the bankruptcy notice and/or bankruptcy restriction.

Where application for cancellation is made in the circumstances referred to at (b) above, it must be accompanied by a copy of the adjudicator's letter of refusal which contains the debtor's name, the adjudicator's unique reference number for the bankruptcy application and the Land Charges registration reference number for the bankruptcy application. The Land Charges registration reference number in the letter must match that shown in the bankruptcy notice in the register.

Where application for cancellation is made in the circumstances referred to at (c) above, and the proprietor of a registered estate or registered charge is not affected by the bankruptcy proceedings and the entry was made recently, HMLR will normally remove it if the applicant provides a signed disclaimer (as supplied by HMLR) that he was not the subject of the bankruptcy proceedings. In some cases, particularly where the entry was made some years ago, HMLR may require the applicant to supply a statutory declaration or statement of truth to similar effect. Production of a clear Land Charges search showing that the registration of the relevant bankruptcy application or petition and/or bankruptcy order is no longer subsisting is not enough without further evidence.

No fee is currently payable for the cancellation of a bankruptcy notice or bankruptcy restriction.

19.11 Discharge from bankruptcy

A discharge from bankruptcy releases the bankrupt from his bankruptcy debts, but does not have the effect of re-vesting in him any property which has vested in the trustee in bankruptcy. A certificate of discharge does not allow HMLR to cancel any bankruptcy notice or bankruptcy restriction.

Special provisions apply in relation to the re-vesting of the bankrupt's home,[28] but these do not apply to a registered estate or registered charge in general.

If, unusually, the trustee in bankruptcy is prepared to re-vest registered land in the discharged bankrupt, this should be carried out by a formal transfer.

Where the trustee in bankruptcy has not been registered as proprietor, the applicant should, in addition to the usual documents required,[29] deliver to HMLR:

(a) a transfer in form TR1 or other prescribed form of transfer, as appropriate;
(b) an office copy of the bankruptcy order relating to the discharged bankrupt;
(c) a certificate signed by the trustee that the registered estate or registered charge was comprised in the discharged bankrupt's estate;

(d)

(i) where the Official Receiver is the trustee, a certificate by him to that effect; or (where the trustee is another person)
(ii) the trustee's certificate of appointment as trustee by the meeting of the bankrupt's creditors; or
(iii) the trustee's certificate of appointment as trustee by the Secretary of State; or
(iv) an office copy of the order of the court appointing the trustee.

The applicant may omit the documentation listed in (b), (c) and (d) omitted where the trustee has been registered as proprietor in place of the bankrupt former proprietor.

On registration of the transfer, HMLR will cancel any bankruptcy notice or bankruptcy restriction in the register relating to the bankruptcy.

19.12 Re-vesting of bankrupt's home

Enterprise Act 2002, s 261 introduced a new s 283A into the IA 1986, with effect from 1 April 2004. This applies where the bankrupt's estate includes an interest in a dwelling house which, at the date of the bankruptcy order, was the sole or principal residence of either:

(a) the bankrupt;
(b) the bankrupt's spouse or civil partner; or
(c) a former spouse or former civil partner of the bankrupt.

The interest will automatically re-vest in the bankrupt (without any transfer, assignment or conveyance) 3 years after the date of the bankruptcy order, unless the trustee in bankruptcy takes action to deal with the interest in the meantime, for instance by selling it or applying for a possession order. If the bankruptcy order was made before 1 April 2004, the period is 3 years from 1 April 2004.

The 3-year period can be extended by order of the court, or if the debtor fails to inform the trustee in bankruptcy or the Official Receiver of his interest in the property. The 3-year period can also be reduced in certain circumstances. If the trustee in bankruptcy considers the continuing vesting of the property in the bankrupt's estate is of no benefit to the creditors; or the re-vesting to the bankrupt will facilitate a more efficient administration of the bankrupt's estate, the trustee can send the bankrupt a notice to that effect. The property will then re-vest in the bankrupt one month after the date of the notice.

Where re-vesting occurs where the debtor was a sole proprietor, the trustee in bankruptcy must, within 5 business days, make whatever application to HMLR is necessary to reflect the re-vesting in the register.[30] Such application must be in form:

(a) AP1 where the trustee has been registered in place of the bankrupt,
(b) RX3 where there is a bankruptcy restriction or inhibition in the register,
(c) RX4 where the trustee has registered a restriction in Form J, or
(d) WCT where the trustee had registered a caution against dealings under the LRA 1925,

and be accompanied by:

(a) evidence of the trustee in bankruptcy's appointment (where not previously provided to HMLR); and
(b) a certificate from the trustee in bankruptcy stating that the interest has re-vested in the bankrupt under IA 1986, s 283A(2) or s 283A(4) or Enterprise Act 2002, s 261(8) (as appropriate).

No fee is currently payable.

As soon as reasonably practicable after making the application, the trustee in bankruptcy must deliver notice of it to:

(a) the bankrupt; and
(b) the bankrupt's spouse, former spouse, civil partner or former civil partner, if the dwelling house was the sole or principal residence of that person.

HMLR will cancel any bankruptcy notice (or creditors' notice) which relates to the application or petition under which the bankruptcy order was made, but not any other bankruptcy notice (or creditors' notice) without the evidence specified in 19.10 Cancellation of bankruptcy notice or bankruptcy restriction.

The re-vesting will not undo any severance of a beneficial joint tenancy effected by the bankruptcy. Therefore, HMLR will not automatically cancel any restriction in Form A appearing in the register.

19.13 Annulment of bankruptcy order

A court may annul the bankruptcy order on a number of grounds; for example, where the bankruptcy debts and the expenses of the bankruptcy have all been paid or secured.[31] Where HMLR is satisfied that the bankruptcy order has been annulled, it must cancel any bankruptcy notice or bankruptcy restriction which relates to that bankruptcy order as soon as practicable.

An applicant for cancellation of such entries should deliver to HMLR:

(a) an application in form AP1; and
(b) an office copy of the court order of annulment, which must expressly authorise the cancellation of the Land Charges bankruptcy entries under the reference number set out in the bankruptcy notice and/or bankruptcy restriction.[32]

No fee is currently payable.

On annulment, any of the bankrupt's estate which is vested in the Official Receiver or trustee in bankruptcy vests in such person as the court appoints. If no other person is appointed, it will vest in the former bankrupt on such terms as the court may direct.[33] Where the Official Receiver or trustee in bankruptcy has been registered as proprietor, an applicant for the former bankrupt to be re-registered should deliver to HMLR:

(a) an application in form AP1;
(b) an office copy of the court order of annulment, which must expressly authorise the cancellation of the Land Charges bankruptcy entries under the reference number set out in the bankruptcy notice and/or bankruptcy restriction;[34] and
(c) the fee payable, based upon a certificate as to the value of the registered estate or charge which should accompany the application.[35]

19.14 After-acquired property

A trustee in bankruptcy may claim property which has been acquired by, or devolved on, the bankrupt after the commencement of the bankruptcy and before his discharge. The trustee does this by the service of notice within 42 days beginning on the day when it came to his knowledge that the property had been acquired by, or had devolved on, the bankrupt; this period may be extended by the court.[36]

Where, before or after service of such a notice by the trustee in bankruptcy, a person acquires the property in good faith for value and without notice of the bankruptcy, the trustee has no remedy against the purchaser.[37]

When the trustee has served notice on the bankrupt, he may apply to be registered as proprietor of the after-acquired property in place of the bankrupt. The trustee should deliver to HMLR:

(a) an application in form AP1;
(b) an office copy of the bankruptcy order relating to the bankrupt;
(c) a certified copy of the notice served by the trustee under the IA 1986, s 307(1);
(d) an office copy of any order for extension of time for service of notice made under IA 1986, s 309;
(e) a certificate signed by the trustee that the registered estate or registered charge is comprised in the bankrupt's estate and that the notice under IA 1986, s 307(1) was served within the period prescribed by s 309;
(f)
    (i) where the Official Receiver is the trustee, a certificate by him to that effect; or (where the trustee is another person)
    (ii) the trustee's certificate of appointment as trustee by the meeting of the bankrupt's creditors; or
    (iii) the trustee's certificate of appointment as trustee by the Secretary of State; or
    (iv) an office copy of the order of the court appointing the trustee; and
(g) the fee payable, based upon a certificate as to the value of the registered estate or charge which should accompany the application.[38]

Where the Official Receiver is registered as proprietor, the words 'Official Receiver and trustee in bankruptcy of [*name*]' are added to the register. Where another trustee in bankruptcy is registered as proprietor, the words 'Trustee in bankruptcy of [*name*]' are added to the register.

Where the bankrupt holds the after-acquired property as joint proprietor and the trustee in bankruptcy has served the notice under IA 1986, s 307(1), the trustee in bankruptcy may apply for a restriction in Form J and, where it does not already appear in the register, in Form A.[39]

19.15 Voidable dispositions

The IA 1986 contains provisions to prevent the bankrupt from putting his assets beyond the reach of his creditors after a bankruptcy petition has been presented. It makes certain dispositions of property by the bankrupt void.

The general rule is that when a person has been adjudged bankrupt, any disposition of property made by him between the date of the making of the bankruptcy application or presentation of the bankruptcy petition and the vesting of his estate in the trustee in bankruptcy or in the Official Receiver as trustee is void.[40] It remains subject to the claim of the trustee in bankruptcy, who may assert his title to it for the benefit of the bankrupt's estate. However, the rule does not apply where the disposition is made with the consent of, or is subsequently ratified by, the court.

The general rule does not apply to property held on trust.[41] Nor does it apply where a person takes a disposition of property in good faith and without notice that the bankruptcy application has been made or the bankruptcy petition has been presented or the bankruptcy order made.[42]

If a void disposition has been completed by registration, the trustee in bankruptcy may apply for alteration of the register so that he is registered as proprietor of the registered estate or charge, as trustee in bankruptcy for the bankrupt former proprietor. The ground of alteration would be to correct the mistaken registration of the void disposition.[43]

The IA 1986 also contains anti-avoidance provisions by which the title of the trustee in bankruptcy can extend to property which was no longer vested in the bankrupt when his bankruptcy commenced, because of a voidable disposition by the bankrupt.

Where there has been a transaction at an undervalue for the purposes of IA 1986, s 339, or a preference for the purposes of s 340 of that Act within the relevant timeframe, the trustee in bankruptcy may apply to the court for an order. The court may make such order as it thinks fit for restoring the position to what it would have been had the relevant transaction not taken place. Where the court is satisfied that a transaction at an undervalue constitutes a transaction defrauding creditors for the purposes of IA 1986, s 423, it may make such order as it thinks fit for restoring the position to what it would have been if the transaction had not been entered into and protecting the interests of victims of the transaction.

If the bankrupt has entered an extortionate credit transaction within the 3 years before the commencement of the bankruptcy, the trustee in bankruptcy may apply to the court for an order.[44] The court has wide powers to vary or set aside the transaction.

Where a court order under ss 339, 340, 343 or 423 requires the register to be altered, the applicant should deliver to HMLR:

(a) an application in form AP1;
(b) the court order or a sealed copy of the court order; and
(c) the fee payable.[45]

On first registration where the title deduced revealed a possible transaction at undervalue, HMLR previously made an entry in the register referring to the IA 1986. HMLR discontinued that practice in 2000. When next updating a register, HMLR will cancel automatically any such entries relating to IA 1986, s 339 (or to Bankruptcy Act 1914, s 42).

19.16 Bankruptcy and home rights

Nothing occurring in the period between the making of the bankruptcy application or presentation of the petition for the bankruptcy order and the vesting of the bankrupt's estate in the trustee is to be taken as having given rise to any home rights under the Family Law Act 1996 (FLA 1996) in relation to a dwelling house comprised in the bankrupt's estate.[46]

Where the home rights of a spouse or civil partner under the FLA 1996 are a charge on the estate or interest of the other spouse or civil partner and the other spouse or civil partner is adjudged bankrupt, the charge continues and binds the trustee in bankruptcy.[47]

The trustee in bankruptcy may apply to the court at any time for an order to restrict or terminate the home rights; any application must be made to the court having jurisdiction in relation to the bankruptcy. On such application the court may make such order as it thinks just and reasonable having regard to the matters set out in IA 1986, s 336(4). However, where such an application is made more than a year after the property vested in the trustee in bankruptcy, the court must assume, unless the circumstances of the case are exceptional, that the interests of the bankrupt's creditors outweigh all other considerations.[48] Any application for cancellation of a home rights notice[49] should be accompanied by an office copy of the court order.

Whether or not the bankrupt's spouse or civil partner has any rights of occupation, a bankrupt may himself have rights equivalent to home rights under the FLA 1996 against the trustee in bankruptcy if he was entitled to occupy a dwelling house, and any persons under the age of 18 with whom he occupied the house had their home with him when the bankruptcy application was made or bankruptcy petition was presented and at the commencement of the bankruptcy.[50] If the bankrupt is in occupation, he has a right not to be evicted or excluded without leave of the bankruptcy court. If he is not in occupation, he has a right, with leave of the bankruptcy court, to enter into occupation.

Such rights are a charge having the same priority as an equitable interest created immediately before the commencement of the bankruptcy, on so much of his estate or interest in the dwelling house as vests in the trustee in bankruptcy. That charge is treated as if it were a charge under the FLA 1996 on the estate or interest of a spouse or civil partner.[51] To restrict or terminate these rights, the trustee in bankruptcy must apply to the bankruptcy court, which must have regard to the same matters mentioned above.

Where a bankrupt has such rights, these may be protected by entry of an agreed notice notwithstanding the fact that the bankrupt is shown in the register as the registered proprietor.

A bankrupt applying to register an agreed notice should deliver to HMLR an application in form HR1 (rather than in form AN1), together with the fee payable.[52] In form HR1 the applicant should state that he is applying pursuant to the provisions of IA 1986, s 337 and that the property is vested in his (named) trustee in bankruptcy.

19.17 Charging order in favour of trustee in bankruptcy

Where the trustee in bankruptcy cannot realise an interest in a dwelling house which forms part of the bankrupt's estate and which is occupied by the bankrupt or his spouse, civil partner, former spouse or former civil partner, the trustee may apply to the court for a charging order on that dwelling house.[53] Any such order should also provide for the re-vesting of the interest in the bankrupt, subject to the charging order and any prior charges.[54] Such an order enables HMLR to cancel any bankruptcy notice or bankruptcy restriction appearing in the register.

Where the bankrupt is the sole proprietor and does not hold as trustee, the trustee in bankruptcy may apply for the entry in the register of an agreed notice or a unilateral notice in respect of the charging order, as it will take effect as an equitable charge on the legal estate. The application should be accompanied by a request for cancellation of any bankruptcy notice and bankruptcy restriction in the register.

Where the debtor's interest was a beneficial interest in a trust of land, the charging order will take effect as an equitable charge over the debtor's beneficial interest. In this case, the trustee in bankruptcy may apply for entry of a restriction in Form K (and a restriction in Form A if there is not already one in the register). The wording of Form K is set out in Appendix IV.

19.17.1 Agreed notice of the charging order

In addition to the usual documents required,[55] an applicant should deliver to HMLR the charging order or a certified copy of it. This should satisfy HMLR of the validity of the applicant's claim in accordance with LRA 2002, s 34(3)(c).

The agreed notice in the register will give details of the interest protected.

19.17.2 Unilateral notice of the charging order

An applicant should deliver to HMLR the usual documents required.[56] The statement in panel 11 or conveyancer's certificate in panel 12 of form UN1 should be completed on the following lines to show the interest of the applicant:

> chargee under an equitable charge created by an [*interim/final*] charging order of the [*name*] Court dated [*date*] in proceedings between [*parties*] (Court reference: [*reference*]).

The unilateral notice in the register will give brief details of the interest protected and identify the beneficiary of that notice.

19.17.3 Restriction where the charging order is over a beneficial interest

The trustee in bankruptcy will have a sufficient interest to apply for entry of a restriction in Form K, to ensure that he receives notice of a disposition.[57]

This restriction does not prevent a disposition, provided it is complied with. However, entry of the restriction helps to ensure the trustee is given notice of the disposition so he can pursue a share of any proceeds of a sale. The restriction will not prevent the interest of the trustee in bankruptcy being overreached where the requirements of LPA 1925, ss 2 and 27 have been fulfilled.

If applying for a restriction in Form K, the trustee in bankruptcy should deliver to HMLR the usual documents required.[58] The statement in panel 12 or the conveyancer's certificate in panel 13 of form RX1 should be completed on the following lines:

> The interest is that specified in rule 93(k) of the Land Registration Rules 2003 (SI 2003/1417). The applicant is the trustee in bankruptcy of [*name of bankrupt joint proprietor*] who is the subject of a bankruptcy order made by the [*name*] Court (Court Reference Number …) (Land Charges Reference Number WO …). [*Name of bankrupt joint proprietor*]'s beneficial interest in the property has been charged

by [an interim/a final] charging order dated [*date*] made by the [*name*] Court in proceedings between [*parties*] (Court reference: [*reference*]).

Panel 9 of form RX1 should set out the wording of Form K.

19.18 Disclaimer by trustee in bankruptcy

A trustee in bankruptcy may disclaim any onerous property comprised in the bankrupt's estate. In the case of land, it is normally a leasehold estate which is disclaimed, although a trustee may also disclaim a freehold estate, in which case the ownership of the land will revert to the Crown (or relevant royal duchy) by escheat. The effect of a disclaimer is to determine the rights, interests and liabilities of the bankrupt and his estate in respect of the disclaimed property. It also discharges the trustee from all personal liability for it.[59]

The trustee disclaims property by authenticating and dating the prescribed form of notice and filing it at the court. Where the disclaimer is of registered land, the trustee must send a copy of the notice to HMLR.[60] Within 7 business days after the date of the notice of disclaimer, the trustee must serve a copy of the notice upon specified categories of person, including those who claim an interest in the disclaimed property or are under any liability in respect of it which will not be discharged by the disclaimer.[61]

Special rules apply to the disclaimer of a leasehold property. The disclaimer is not effective unless a copy of it has been served on any underlessee or mortgagee claiming under the bankrupt within 7 business days of the disclaimer.[62] In the case of a dwelling house a copy of the disclaimer must also be served within 7 business days of the disclaimer on every person who is in occupation or claims a right to occupy.[63]

Any of the above people served with notice may apply to the court for a vesting order vesting the property in him or in a trustee on his behalf.[64] The disclaimer will not take effect unless no person has applied to the court within 14 days of the last notice being served to have the property vested in him, or despite any such application, the court has directed that the disclaimer should take effect.[65]

If no vesting order is made in respect of a leasehold estate, a lease which has been disclaimed vests in the landlord and so will determine. If no vesting order is made in respect of a freehold estate, a freehold which has been disclaimed vests in the Crown (or relevant royal duchy) by escheat.[66]

Where the trustee in bankruptcy has disclaimed a registered lease, an applicant should deliver to HMLR:

(a) an application in form AP1 quoting the title numbers for the leasehold and any reversionary titles and showing the application as 'Disclaimer of lease';
(b) the lease;
(c) a certificate signed by the trustee in bankruptcy that:

  (i) he has power to make the disclaimer;
  (ii) all notices required to be served under the IA 1986 have been served; and
  (iii) he is not aware of any application to the court for a vesting order under IA 1986, s 320;

(d) an office copy of the notice of disclaimer;
(e) (if applicable) a certified copy of any court order directing that the disclaimer should take effect; and
(f) the fee payable.[67]

Where the trustee in bankruptcy has not been registered as proprietor of the leasehold title, the applicant should also deliver to HMLR:

(a) an office copy of the bankruptcy order relating to the bankrupt;
(b) a certificate signed by the trustee that the registered lease is comprised in the bankrupt's estate; and
(c)

  (i) where the Official Receiver is the trustee, a certificate by him to that effect; or (where the trustee is another person)
  (ii) the trustee's certificate of appointment as trustee by the meeting of the bankrupt's creditors; or
  (iii) the trustee's certificate of appointment as trustee by the Secretary of State; or
  (iv) an office copy of the order of the court appointing the trustee.

The disclaimer does not affect the rights and liabilities of other persons acquired before the disclaimer. Consequently, HMLR will not close the disclaimed leasehold title if there is a registered or noted charge in that title, unless the applicant also lodges:

(a) an application to discharge the registered charge or to cancel the entry of the noted charge;
(b) evidence that the chargee's application for a vesting order has been dismissed; or
(c) evidence of forfeiture of the lease.

If the disclaimed leasehold title cannot be closed because there is evidence of a continuing registered or noted charge, HMLR will make:

(a) appropriate entries in the title for the disclaimed lease and in the landlord's registered title, to refer to the disclaimer; and
(b) a restriction preventing registration of any disposition of the registered estate in the disclaimed leasehold title.

HMLR may close the disclaimed leasehold title if there is no registered or noted charge, but if there is a registered sub-lease or other third-party rights which are the subject of a notice in that title, HMLR will make appropriate entries in the landlord's title and any sub-leasehold title, referring to the disclaimer and to the rights in question.

Where the disclaimed lease has not been registered but is the subject of a notice against a registered superior title, an applicant should deliver to HMLR:

(a) an application in form CN1, panel 9 being completed by entering details of the lease and placing an 'X' against 'disclaimer';
(b) the lease;
(c) evidence of devolution of title, if the bankrupt is not the original tenant;
(d) a certificate signed by the trustee in bankruptcy that:

    (i) he has power to make the disclaimer;
    (ii) all notices required to be served under the IA 1986 have been served; and
    (iii) he is not aware of any application to the court for a vesting order under IA 1986, s 320;

(e) an office copy of the notice of disclaimer;
(f) (if applicable) a certified copy of any court order directing that the disclaimer should take effect;
(g) an office copy of the bankruptcy order relating to the bankrupt;
(h) a certificate signed by the trustee that the registered lease is comprised in the bankrupt's estate;
(i)

    (i) where the Official Receiver is the trustee, a certificate by him to that effect; or (where the trustee is another person)
    (ii) the trustee's certificate of appointment as trustee by the meeting of the bankrupt's creditors; or
    (iii) the trustee's certificate of appointment as trustee by the Secretary of State; or
    (iv) an office copy of the order of the court appointing the trustee; and

(j) the fee payable.[68]

Where there is no evidence of any charge, sub-lease or other third-party rights affecting the disclaimed lease, HMLR may cancel the notice of the lease in the landlord's title. Otherwise, HMLR cannot cancel the notice of the lease, but will make appropriate entries in the landlord's title and any sub-leasehold title, referring to the disclaimer and to the rights in question.

Where the property has been disclaimed and an order has been made by the court vesting the property in some other person, an applicant should deliver to HMLR:

(a) an application in form AP1;
(b) an office copy of the court order; and
(c) the fee payable.[69]

Where a property has been disclaimed and HMLR has received notice of the disclaimer but no formal application, HMLR may alter the register itself to reflect the disclaimer, for the purposes of bringing the register up to date.[70] In the case of a disclaimer of a leasehold estate, HMLR will enter a note of the disclaimer in the register of the disclaimed leasehold title. In the case of a disclaimer of a freehold estate, HMLR will enter a note of the disclaimer in the register to reflect the determination by escheat.

19.19 Insolvency proceedings commenced in another part of the United Kingdom

IA 1986, s 426(1) provides an order made by a court in any part of the United Kingdom in the exercise of jurisdiction in relation to insolvency law shall be enforced in any other part of the United Kingdom as if it were made by a court exercising the corresponding jurisdiction in that other part. The courts in England and Wales may not therefore question the jurisdiction of the Scottish or Northern Irish courts to adjudicate a debtor bankrupt. However, nothing in IA 1986, s 426(1) requires a court in any part of the United Kingdom to enforce, in relation to property situated in that part, any order made by a court in any other part of the United Kingdom.[71] This preserves the principle that the law governing the transfer of land on bankruptcy is the *lex situs*. Thus, for example, registered land in England and Wales owned by a person adjudged bankrupt under the law of Northern Ireland will not vest in the Northern Irish trustee in bankruptcy since the *lex situs* does not have that effect.

Under IA 1986, s 426(4), the courts having jurisdiction in relation to insolvency law in any part of the United Kingdom shall assist the courts having the corresponding jurisdiction in any other part of the United Kingdom. Thus the court in England and Wales may, for example, make an order vesting the bankrupt's legal or equitable estate in land in the trustee in bankruptcy of the other jurisdiction. In practice, the court in England and Wales will generally reseal a bankruptcy order made in Scotland or Northern Ireland. It then becomes an order of the bankruptcy court in England and Wales from the date of the resealing.

For overseas insolvency proceedings, see 129 Overseas Insolvency Proceedings.

---

1 See 88 Individual Voluntary Arrangements.
2 Insolvency (England and Wales) Rules 2016 (SI 2016/1024) (IR 2016), rr 10.13 and 10.37.
3 LRA 2002, s 86(2).
4 LRR 2003, r 165.
5 LRA 2002, s 86(3).
6 IR 2016, rr 10.32(3)(a)(i) and 10.45(3)(a)(i).
7 LRA 2002, s 86(4).
8 LRR 2003, r 166.
9 LRA 2002, Sch 12, para 2(1) and (2).
10 IA 1986, s 306.
11 IA 1986, s 283(3). See 19.8 Bankruptcy of a joint proprietor.
12 LRA 2002, s 27(5)(a).
13 See 67 Fees.
14 LRR 2003, r 169.
15 See 67 Fees.
16 See 176.1 Registration of transfer.
17 LRA 2002, s 86(1).
18 LRA 2002, s 86(7).
19 *Pick v Chief Land Registrar* [2011] EWHC 206 (Ch).
20 LRR 2003, 93(a).
21 LRR 2003, r 93(j).
22 Law of Property Act 1925 (LPA 1925), ss 2 and 27.
23 LRA 2002, s 45.
24 See 153.1 Application for entry of restriction.
25 Administration of Insolvent Estates of Deceased Persons Order 1986 (SI 1986/1999), r 5, Sch 2.
26 Administration of Insolvent Estates of Deceased Persons Order 1986 (SI 1986/1999), r 3, Sch 1.
27 See 67 Fees.
28 See 19.12 Re-vesting of bankrupt's home.
29 See 176.1 Registration of transfer.
30 IR 2016, r 10.168(2).
31 IA 1986, s 282.
32 IR 2016, rr 8.34(1) and 10.137(4).
33 IA 1986, s 282(4)(b).
34 IR 2016 rr 8.34(1) and 10.137(4).
35 See 67 Fees.

36 IA 1986, ss 307(1) and 309.
37 IA 1986, s 307(4)).
38 See 67 Fees.
39 See 19.8 Bankruptcy of a joint proprietor.
40 IA 1986, s 284(1).
41 See 19.8 Bankruptcy of a joint proprietor.
42 See 19.7 Protection of purchaser from bankrupt.
43 LRA 2002, Sch 4, paras 2(1)(a) and 5(a).
44 IA 1986, s 343.
45 See 67 Fees.
46 IA 1986, s 336(1).
47 IA 1986, s 336(2).
48 IA 1986, s 336(5).
49 See 81.3 Cancellation of home rights notice.
50 IA 1986, s 337.
51 IA 1986, s 337(3).
52 See 67 Fees.
53 IA 1986, s 313(1).
54 IA 1986, s 313(3).
55 See 119.1 Agreed notice.
56 See 119.3 Unilateral notice.
57 LRR 2003, r 93(k).
58 See 153.1 Application for entry of restriction.
59 IA 1986, s 315(3).
60 IR 2016, r 19.2(3)(b).
61 IR 2016, r 19.3(1).
62 IR 2016, r 19.4.
63 IR 2016, r 19.5.
64 IA 1986, s 320.
65 IA 1986, s 318.
66 See 21 Bona Vacantia and Escheat.
67 See 67 Fees.
68 See 67 Fees.
69 See 67 Fees.
70 LRA 2002, Sch 4, para 5(b).
71 IA 1986, s 426(2).

20 BARE TRUSTS

A bare trust arises where a trustee holds property for a single beneficiary who is of full age and under no legal disability. Where the property consists of or includes land, the trust is a trust of land for the purposes of the Trusts of Land and Appointment of Trustees Act 1996 (TLATA). HMLR may not enter any notice in the register in respect of an interest under a trust of land.[1]

Where the trustee is, or becomes, the registered proprietor of property held on a bare trust, he must apply for entry of a restriction in Form A.[2] The wording of Form A is set out in Appendix IV. Where the declaration of trust imposes limitations on the powers of the trustee under TLATA, s 8, the trustee must also apply for entry of a restriction in Form B.[3] The wording of Form B is set out in Appendix IV. For example, the declaration of trust may require the trustees to obtain consent to any sale of the property.

If the trustee does not apply for the necessary restriction(s), the beneficiary has a sufficient interest to do so.[4] HMLR must give notice of the application to the proprietor of the registered estate or charge concerned if it has not been made by or with his consent or the consent of a person entitled to be registered as such proprietor.[5]

A bare trustee must act only on the instructions of the beneficiary. Consequently, HMLR will accept an application for a restriction in Form N to protect the beneficiary's interest. The wording of Form N is set out in Appendix IV.

A restriction in Form B does not prevent a disposition, provided it is complied with. This is because the interest of the beneficiary will be overreached where the requirements of the Form A restriction have been met.[6]

An applicant for entry of a restriction should deliver to HMLR the usual documents required.[7]

Panel 9 of form RX1 should set out the required restriction(s). A restriction in standard Forms A, B or N in LRR 2003, Sch 4 does not require the approval of HMLR to the terms of the restriction under LRA 2002, s 43(3).

Form RX1 does not need to be used if the application is for a standard form restriction and is contained in either the 'additional provisions' panel of a prescribed form of transfer or assent, or in clause LR13 of a prescribed clauses lease (or any other lease containing clauses LR1 to LR14 of LRR 2003, Sch 1A).[8]

---

1 LRA 2002, s 33(a).
2 LRR 2003, r 94(1) and (2).
3 LRR 2003, r 94(4).
4 LRR 2003, r 93(a) and (c).
5 LRA 2002, s 45.
6 LPA 1925, ss 2 and 27.
7 See 153.1 Application for entry of restriction.
8 LRR 2003, r 92(7).

21 BONA VACANTIA AND ESCHEAT

Where a company is dissolved, its property (other than that held on trust for another person) vests as bona vacantia in the Crown, under the jurisdiction of the Treasury Solicitor, or in the Duchy of Lancaster or Duchy of Cornwall, under the jurisdiction of the solicitor of the relevant Duchy.[1] This transfer by operation of law does not constitute a disposition requiring to be completed by registration under LRA 2002, s 27. Pursuant to LRA 2002, s 85, the LRR 2003 contain provisions relating to bona vacantia.

Where a corporation shown as the proprietor of a registered estate or registered charge has been dissolved, HMLR may enter a note of that fact in the proprietorship register or charges register, as appropriate.[2] The Crown (or relevant Duchy) may apply for registration as proprietor in place of the dissolved company; HMLR will enter the Treasury Solicitor or the Solicitor to the Duchy of Lancaster or the Duke of Cornwall (as the case may be) in the register as proprietor. Where an estate that has vested as bona vacantia is subsequently disposed of, a later order reviving the dissolved company will have no effect on the disposition; the revived company may be entitled to compensation.[3]

The Treasury Solicitor and the Solicitors to the Duchies of Lancaster and Cornwall may disclaim property that has vested as bona vacantia.[4] The disclaimer is effected by a notice in writing signed by the appropriate solicitor. The effect of the disclaimer is to terminate the rights, interests and liabilities of the company in respect of the disclaimed property. It does not affect the rights and liabilities of other persons acquired before the disclaimer.[5]

Although they are not formally required to do so, the Treasury Solicitor or either of the Royal Duchies may send a copy of the notice of disclaimer to HMLR, without making a formal application for closure of the relevant title or cancellation of an entry relating to the disclaimed estate or interest. Provided the dissolved company named in the notice is the same as the company registered as proprietor and there is only one proprietor, HMLR will make an entry in the register to reflect the disclaimer. A formal application can, however, be made to close the disclaimed title where appropriate or cancel an entry relating to the disclaimed estate or interest.

As the disclaimer does not affect the rights and liabilities of other persons acquired before the disclaimer, HMLR will not close a disclaimed leasehold title if there is a registered or noted charge in that title, unless the applicant also lodges:

(a) an application to discharge the registered charge or to cancel the entry of the noted charge;
(b) evidence that the chargee's application for a vesting order has been dismissed; or
(c) evidence of forfeiture of the lease.

If the disclaimed leasehold title cannot be closed because there is evidence of a continuing registered or noted charge, HMLR will make appropriate entries in the title for the disclaimed lease and in the landlord's registered title, to refer to the disclaimer. HMLR will also enter a restriction preventing registration of any disposition of the registered estate in the disclaimed leasehold title. HMLR may close the leasehold title for a disclaimed lease if there is no registered or noted charge but there is a registered sub-lease or other third-party rights noted in the title. In such instances, HMLR will make appropriate entries referring to the disclaimer in the landlord's title and any registered sub-leasehold title.

Escheat occurs when a freehold estate determines. An escheated estate is usually onerous property of little or no (or even negative) value which is difficult to dispose of because, for example, the land is contaminated. Escheat can arise in different ways, but the most common is where the Treasury Solicitor disclaims a freehold estate passing as bona vacantia, or where the estate is disclaimed by a liquidator or trustee in bankruptcy following insolvency. The freehold estate escheats either to the Crown as demesne land or to one of the Royal Duchies of Cornwall or Lancaster by virtue of their own superior freehold estate. In time, the Crown may re-grant the estate or a Royal Duchy may transfer its freehold estate. The escheat does not constitute a disposition requiring to be completed by registration under LRA 2002, s 27. Pursuant to LRA 2002, s 82, the LRR 2003 contain provisions relating to escheat.

Escheat is based on the feudal principle that land itself is held by the Crown in demesne. Other landowners own a right to possess the land, known as an estate in land. When a leasehold estate determines it merges into the superior estate. When a freehold estate determines, because there is no superior estate, the land reverts to the Crown. For the purposes of the LRA 2002, 'demesne land' is defined as land belonging to His Majesty in right of the Crown which is not held for an estate in fee simple absolute in possession. This does not include land in relation to which a freehold estate in land has determined, but in relation to which there has been no act of entry or management by the Crown.[6]

If in the past the Crown has granted a fee simple to one of the Royal Duchies, the determined freehold estate reverts to that Duchy. The Royal Duchies cannot grant a new freehold estate; instead they can transfer their freehold estate in the land to a new owner.

There are various formalities to which the Duchies must adhere when drawing up deeds. For the Duchy of Cornwall, the purchase price or premium needs to be paid into the Bank of England; the Duchy Auditor then endorses a memorandum of the payment on the conveyance or lease. To be effective against the Duke of Cornwall, a conveyance or lease should be enrolled with the Keeper of the Duchy Records who endorses a certificate of enrolment on the deed.[7] Similar arrangements exist for the Duchy of Lancaster. However, none of the requirements relating to formalities or enrolment contained in any enactment relating to the Duchy of Lancaster or the Duchy of Cornwall now apply to dispositions by a registered proprietor.[8]

The LRA 2002, s 83 provides for an 'appropriate authority' to represent, make applications and receive notice on behalf of, His Majesty and the Duchies of Lancaster and Cornwall. For land vested in His Majesty in right of the Crown, this may be the Crown Estate Commissioners; or a government department; or such person as His Majesty may appoint in writing under the Royal Sign Manual. For an interest belonging to His Majesty in right of the Duchy of Lancaster, the appropriate authority is the Chancellor of the Duchy. For an interest belonging to the Duchy of Cornwall, the appropriate authority is such person as the Duke of Cornwall, or the possessor for the time being of the Duchy of Cornwall, appoints.

On escheat, the Crown and the Royal Duchies take the land subject to all existing incumbrances affecting the determined estate. Where the Crown grants a new estate or a Royal Duchy transfers its estate, the new owner is similarly bound by the incumbrances that affected the escheated estate. An application for registration by the new owner would be one for first registration, as opposed to one for registration of a disposition of an existing registered title. Where a registered freehold estate in land has determined on escheat, HMLR may enter a note of that fact in the property register and in the property register of any inferior registered title. If HMLR considers that there is doubt whether a registered freehold estate in land has determined, it must modify the entry by a statement to that effect.[9] Where HMLR makes such an entry, it need not close that registered title until a new freehold estate has been registered in respect of the land in which the former estate subsisted.

Under Companies Act 2006, s 1013(2), the Crown or relevant duchy may lose the ability to disclaim bona vacantia by express waiver, taking possession or any act clearly showing the intention to do so. If application was made to register the Treasury Solicitor, the Solicitor to the Duchy of Lancaster or the Duke of Cornwall as proprietor, that could amount to such a waiver. Therefore, if HMLR has already entered the vesting as bona vacantia in the register, it will modify the escheat entry to refer to this possibility.

Application may be made in form AP1 to cancel the escheat entry, if accompanied by either a letter from the Crown Estate Commissioners or the Solicitor for one of the Royal Duchies confirming that escheat has not in fact taken place; or an office copy court order reviving a dissolved company; or an office copy court order reinstating the original freehold estate.

---

1 Companies Act 2006, s 1012; previously Companies Act 1985, s 654.
2 LRR 2003, r 185.
3 Companies Act 2006, s 1034(2).
4 Companies Act 2006, s 1013.
5 Companies Act 2006, s 1015.
6 LRA 2002, s 132(1) and (2).
7 Duchy of Cornwall Management Act 1863, s 30.
8 LRA 2002, s 84.
9 LRR 2003, r 173.

22 BOUNDARIES

Every property, whether or not it is registered, has exact legal boundaries. That is, lines separating the property owned by one person from that owned by his neighbour. But deeds rarely identify these legal boundaries precisely and often the owners themselves do not know exactly where they are. Trying to fix the boundaries precisely at the time of registration of title would involve a great deal of expense and could cause a dispute that would not otherwise have occurred. For that reason, the boundary of a registered estate as shown for the purposes of the register on the title plan, or otherwise in the register, is a general boundary unless it is shown as determined under LRA 2002, s 60. A general boundary does not determine the exact line of the boundary.[1]

There is no definition of a general boundary in the LRA 2002. The Law Commission Report, *Land Registration for the Twenty-First Century: A Conveyancing Revolution* (Law Com No 271) (2001) indicated that it was intended to retain the so-called 'general boundaries rule', then contained in Land Registration Rules 1925, r 278,[2] which stated:

> (1) Except in cases in which it is noted in the Property Register that the boundaries have been fixed, the filed plan shall be deemed to indicate the general boundaries only.
>
> (2) In such cases the exact line of the boundary will be left undetermined – as, for instance, whether it includes a hedge or wall and ditch, or runs along the centre of a wall or fence, or its inner or outer face, or how far it runs within or beyond it; or whether or not the land registered includes the whole or any portion of an adjoining road or stream.

(3) When a general boundary only is desired to be entered in the register, notice to the owners of the adjoining lands need not be given.
(4) This rule shall apply notwithstanding that a part or the whole of a ditch, wall, fence, road, stream, or other boundary is expressly included in or excluded from the title or that it forms the whole of the land comprised in the title.

Under the LRR 2003, all registered estates in land, registered rentcharges and registered franchises which are affecting franchises have a title plan. That title plan is based on the OS map.[3] A registered franchise is an affecting franchise if it relates to a defined area of land and is an adverse right affecting, or capable of affecting, the title to an estate or charge.[4]

Before 13 October 2003, the title plan was known as the 'filed plan'.

The title plan usually shows the extent of the registered estate by red edging, although HMLR may use other means in particular circumstances. Sometimes the verbal description of the estate in the property register will contain information clarifying the extent. For example, if the title relates to a first floor flat there will be a note in the property register to explain this. HMLR sometimes uses enlargement plans as part of a title plan, to clarify detail beyond the scope of the normal OS scales; for example, to show small juts in boundary walls and different floor levels. Supplementary plans can be annexed to title plans where appropriate; for example, to show parts of buildings at different floor levels or to carry complicated reference markings that would cause confusion if shown on the title plan itself.

Where the boundary shown is a general boundary, the legal boundary of the land does not necessarily follow the red edging on the title plan. For example, the so-called 'hedge and ditch rule' may apply. This is a rebuttable presumption that arises when a boundary comprises a hedge and a man-made ditch. It is presumed that the owner of the hedge also owns the ditch beyond it, although this may be rebutted on the facts. The House of Lords applied this presumption in *Alan Wibberley Building Ltd v Insley*,[5] where Lord Hope of Craighead said:

> Any boundary dispute which leads to litigation as protracted as the dispute has been in this case is regrettable. But no workable system of conveyancing can be expected to eliminate entirely the opportunity for disputes to arise about boundaries. In most cases neighbours are content to accept that absolute precision is unattainable. They recognise that a certain amount of latitude must be given to whatever method has been used to fix the boundaries of their land. That also is the view which has been taken by the legislature. The original system of precise guaranteed boundaries under the Land Registry Act 1862 gave rise to considerable difficulty. It had to be abandoned in view of the expense which was involved in a survey of the precise boundaries and the many disputes which arose between neighbours who had been content until then to accept a certain amount of vagueness as to the precise line of

> their common boundary. The result … was the introduction of the general boundaries rule now contained in rule 278 of the Land Registration Rules 1925.
>
> The use of maps or plans such as those published by the Ordnance Survey is now widespread and has obvious advantages. Ordnance Survey maps are prepared to a high standard of accuracy *and are frequently and appropriately used to fix boundaries by reference, for example, to Ordnance Survey field numbers. But* like all maps they are subject to limitations. The most obvious are those imposed by scale. No map can reproduce to anything like the same scale of detail every feature which is found on the ground. Furthermore … the Ordnance Survey does not fix private boundaries. The purpose of the survey is topographical, not taxative. Even the most detailed Ordnance Survey map may not show every feature on the ground which can be used to identify the extent of the owner's land. In the present case the Ordnance Survey map shows the hedge, but it does not show the ditch. So there is no reason in principle *in this case* for preferring *the* line on the map to other evidence which may be relevant to identify the boundary. (original emphasis)

As title plans are based on the OS map, they are limited by the precision with which OS prepares such maps. As with any map, OS maps are subject to some limitations which depend upon the scale of the map and the accuracy of the surveying techniques used. These limitations may result in some variation between what is shown on the map and what exists on the ground. Consequently, title plans cannot be used to establish the precise position of features on the ground simply by scaling from the title plan. In some cases, the nature of particular features on the ground can add to the uncertainty. For example, a mature hedge can be several metres wide, so that it can be difficult to relate it to the single line representing it on the map.

General boundaries therefore allow flexibility in the relationship between the legal boundaries and any physical features on the OS map that HMLR refers to when making a reasonable interpretation of the estate comprised within the title deeds.

The nature and effect of registration with general boundaries was considered by the court in *Lee v Barrey*.[6] More recent cases, such as *Derbyshire County Council v Fallon*,[7] *Strachey v Ramage*[8] and *Drake and Another v Fripp*,[9] have further emphasised the importance of this point.

Where, on first registration or on the registration of a disposition of a registered estate (such as a transfer of part), an agreement or declaration about the ownership of boundary structures appears in the relevant deeds, HMLR may make an entry in the register reflecting this. Commonly, for example, this may be an agreement that a particular wall is a party wall. But neither a party wall notice, nor a party wall award under the Party Wall etc Act 1996, may be the subject of a notice in the register. Other matters arising under the Party Wall etc Act 1996 may give rise to an entry in the register.[10]

LRA 2002, s 61 and LRR 2003, r 123 make provision for accretion or diluvion.[11]

Under the LRA 1925, application could be made for a title to be registered with 'fixed boundaries'. The applicant had to bear the cost of this expensive process, and there was no guarantee that it would be possible, as a result of the investigations made, to fix the boundaries. In practice such applications were extremely rare. The LRA 2002 instead contains provision for the exact line of a boundary to be 'determined' instead of it being a general boundary.

Except in those rare cases where the boundary has been fixed or determined, HMLR cannot decide or confirm where the exact legal boundary between two properties lies. Therefore, if the exact legal line of the boundary must be otherwise established, this can only be done either by the adjoining owners reaching an agreement or by judicial determination.

If the parties agree the exact line of a boundary and the terms of the agreement are recorded in a formal document, they may apply to HMLR in form AP1 for the agreement to be 'noted' in the register of any registered titles affected.[12] However, such an agreement can only *clarify* the position of an existing boundary; it cannot be used to effect a transfer of property (instead, the parties would need to complete a transfer in the prescribed form). Also, such an agreement does not 'determine' a boundary for land registration purposes; it would remain a general boundary in the register.

If the exact line of a boundary is established by an order of the court, application may be made to HMLR in form AP1 for such an order to be 'noted' in the register of any registered titles affected. Such an order does not 'determine' a boundary for land registration purposes and it would therefore remain a general boundary in the register.

22.1 Determination of the exact line of a boundary

A proprietor of a registered estate may apply to HMLR for the exact line of the boundary of that registered estate to be determined. The application may be in respect of part only of such a boundary.[13]

A person applying for the exact line of a boundary to be determined should deliver to HMLR:

(a) an application in form DB;
(b) a plan, or a plan and a verbal description, identifying the exact line of the boundary claimed and showing sufficient surrounding physical features to allow the general position of the boundary to be drawn on the OS map;
(c) the documents and other evidence on which the applicant relies to establish the exact line of the boundary; and
(d) the fee payable.[14]

Where HMLR is satisfied that:

(1) the plan, or plan and verbal description, supplied identifies the exact line of the boundary claimed;
(2) the applicant has shown an arguable case that the exact line of the boundary is in the position shown on that plan, or plan and verbal description; and
(3) it can identify all the owners of the land adjoining the boundary to be determined and has an address at which each owner may be given notice,

it must give such adjoining owners notice of the application.[15] For these purposes 'owner' means:

(a) the proprietor of any registered estate or charge affecting land;
(b) a person who holds an unregistered legal estate in land which he could apply to register; and
(c) if the land is demesne land, His Majesty.

Where the evidence supplied in support includes an agreement in writing about the exact line of the boundary with an owner of the land adjoining the boundary, or a court order determining the line of that boundary, HMLR need not give notice of the application to that owner.

Where HMLR is not satisfied about (1), (2) and (3) above, it must cancel the application.[16]

If no recipient of a notice of the application objects within the relevant period, HMLR must complete the application.[17] The time for objection fixed by the notice is the period ending at 12 noon on the 20th working day after the date of issue of the notice, or such longer period as HMLR may decide before the issue of the notice.[18] A working day is any day from Monday to Friday (inclusive) which is not Christmas Day, Good Friday or any other day either specified or declared by proclamation under Banking and Financial Dealings Act 1971, s 1, or appointed by the Secretary of State, or certified by HMLR as being an 'interrupted day' due to delay or failure of a communication service or to some other event or circumstance causing substantial interruption in the normal operation of HMLR.

Before the period specified in the notice has expired, a recipient of the notice may apply to HMLR for an extension of the period, setting out why an extension should be allowed.[19] On receipt of such a request, HMLR may, if it considers it appropriate, seek the views of the applicant. If, after considering any such views and all other relevant matters, HMLR is satisfied that a longer period should be allowed, it may allow such period as it considers appropriate, whether or not the period is the same as any period requested by the recipient of the notice.[20]

If HMLR receives a valid objection to the application which cannot be disposed of by agreement, the matter will have to be dealt with in accordance with LRA 2002, s 73.[21]

If an objector objects to an application for determination of the exact line of a boundary and the dispute reaches the Tribunal, the Tribunal:

(a) must direct HMLR to cancel the application if it concludes the applicant's plan does not meet the technical requirements of LRR 2003, r 118(2)(a);[22] but
(b) may determine part of the exact boundary is not as claimed by the applicant and direct HMLR to make an entry dealing with that inaccuracy.[23]

On completion of an application to determine a boundary, HMLR will:

(a) make any necessary updates to the applicant's title plan; and
(b) make an entry referring to the determination in the property register for the applicant's title.

HMLR will do likewise on any neighbouring title and, where appropriate, on any superior or inferior registered title.

Instead of, or as well as, updating the title plan(s), HMLR may make an entry in the relevant title(s) referring to any other plan showing the exact line of the boundary.

Typically, such an entry might read:

> The exact line of the boundaries of the land in this title between the points lettered A–B in blue on the title plan is determined under section 60 of the Land Registration Act 2002 as shown on the plan lodged with the application to determine the boundaries dated [*date*].
> NOTE: Plan filed.

Where the exact line of only part of the boundary of a registered estate has been determined, the ends of that part of the boundary are not to be treated as determined for the purposes of adjoining parts of the boundary the exact line of which has not been determined.[24] By way of example, Figure 1 (below) shows a rectangular piece of land, where A–B is the northern boundary. The part of the boundary between points C and D has been determined but not the rest of the boundary. The determined position for points C and D shown on the title plan determines those points for the boundary C–D but not for the boundaries A–C and B–D. HMLR will have served notice of the application on the owners of the land adjoining on the south of C–D, but not the owners of the land adjoining on the east of B–D nor the owners of the land adjoining on the west of A–C:

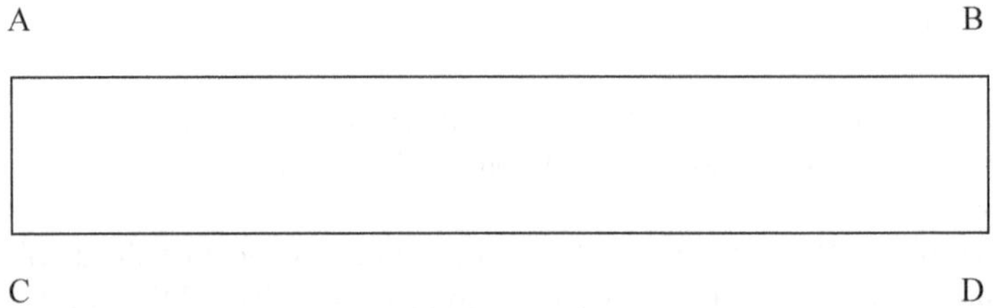

Figure 1

HMLR may determine the exact line of a common boundary without an application where there is a transfer of part of a registered estate in land and there is sufficient information in the transfer to enable it to do so. The same applies on a grant of a lease which is a registrable disposition of part of a registered estate in land. A 'common boundary' in this context is any boundary of the land disposed of by the transfer of part or lease of part which adjoins land in which the transferor or landlord, at the date of the transfer or lease, had a registered estate in land or of which such transferor or landlord was entitled to be registered as proprietor.[25]

Where HMLR determines the exact line of the common boundary without an application, it must:

(a) make an entry in the property registers of the affected registered titles stating that the exact line of the common boundary is determined under LRA 2002, s 60; and
(b) add to the title plan of the transferor's or landlord's affected registered title (whether or not the transferor or landlord is still the proprietor of that title, or still entitled to be registered as proprietor of that title), and to the title plan of the registered title under which the transfer or lease is being registered, such particulars of the exact line of the common boundary as it considers appropriate.

Instead of, or as well as, adding such particulars to the title plans, HMLR may make an entry in the property register of the affected registered titles referring to the description of the common boundary in the transfer or lease.

22.2 Party Wall etc Act 1996

As to the effect of the Party Wall etc Act 1996, see 131 Party Wall etc Act 1996.

---

1 LRA 2002, s 60(2).

2 Land Transfer Rules 1898, r 213 and Land Transfer Rules 1903, r 274 also provided for general boundaries.

3 LRR 2003, r 5.

4 See 74 Franchises.

5 [1999] UKHL 15.

6 [1957] Ch 251, CA.

7 [2007] EWHC 1326 (Ch).

8 [2008] EWCA Civ 384.

9 [2011] EWCA Civ 1279.

10 See 22.2 Party Wall etc Act 1996.

11 See 2 Accretion and Diluvion.

12 Although the agreement will be binding on the parties and their successors even if they are unaware of it (*White v Alder* [2025] EWCA Civ 392), it is recommended it be noted in the registers for the relevant properties to avoid future disputes.

13 LRR 2003, rr 117 and 118(1).

14 See 67 Fees.

15 LRR 2003, r 119(1).

16 LRR 2003, r 119(7).

17 LRR 2003, r 119(6).

18 LRR 2003, r 119(3).

19 LRR 2003, r 119(4).

20 LRR 2003, r 119(5).

21 See 54 Disputes.

22 *Murdoch v Amesbury* [2016] UKUT 3 (TCC).

23 *Bean v Katz* [2016] UKUT 168 (TCC).

24 LRR 2003, r 121.

25 LRR 2003, r 122.

23 CAUTIONS AGAINST CONVERSION

Where a proprietor was registered with possessory, qualified or good leasehold title, it was possible to enter a caution against conversion in the register.[1] This had the effect of preventing the title being converted to qualified, good leasehold or absolute (as appropriate) until notice of the application had been served on the cautioner, allowing him an opportunity to object to the conversion. It has not been possible to register a caution against conversion since 13 October 2003, but there are transitional provisions which apply to pre-existing cautions. Under the LRA 2002 and the LRR 2003, 'conversion' of title is now referred to as 'upgrade' of title.[2]

If a caution against conversion remains in the register and HMLR receives an application to upgrade the title, HMLR must give notice of it to the person named in the caution before determining the application. Where the cautioner responds to the notice by claiming any estate, right or interest in the land in the title, then, to the extent such estate right or interest subsists and is otherwise enforceable, the claim is treated for the purposes of LRA 2002, s 62(6) as one for an estate, right or interest whose enforceability is preserved by virtue of the existing entry about the class of title.[3]

LRA 2002, s 62(6) provides that HMLR cannot exercise any of the powers to upgrade the title contained in s 62 if there is outstanding any claim adverse to the title of the registered proprietor which is made by virtue of an estate, right or interest whose enforceability is preserved by virtue of the existing entry about the class of title.

---

1 Land Registration Rules 1925, r 215(2).
2 See 181 Upgrade of Class of Title.
3 Land Registration Act 2002 (Transitional Provisions) Order 2003 (SI 2003/1953) (LRA (TP) Order 2003), art 15.

24 CAUTIONS AGAINST DEALINGS

LRA 1925, s 54 provided that any person interested in any land or charge registered in the name of any person might lodge a caution to the effect that no dealing with such land or charge is to be registered until notice has been served upon the cautioner.

It has not been possible to register a caution against dealings since 13 October 2003. However, any pre-existing caution against dealings in the register continues to have effect.[1]

Where a caution has been registered, no registration of any dealing will be completed until notice of it has been served on the cautioner by HMLR.[2] The notice may be served:

(a) by post to the address for service (whether within or outside the United Kingdom);
(b) by leaving the notice at the address for service in the United Kingdom;
(c) by directing the notice to a DX number entered as the address for service; or
(d) by electronic transmission to an electronic address for service.[3]

HMLR may also serve the notice by post to an address, other than an address for service, where it believes the addressee is likely to receive it. The same applies to delivery by DX to, or leaving the notice at, an address other than an address for service.

Whatever method of service is used, the notice period is the period ending at 12 noon on the 15th working day or ending at 12 noon on such later working day as HMLR may allow, after the date of issue of the notice.[4] A working day is any day from Monday to Friday (inclusive) which is not Christmas Day, Good Friday or any other day either specified or declared by proclamation under Banking and Financial Dealings Act 1971, s 1 or appointed by the Secretary of State, or certified by HMLR as being an 'interrupted day' due to delay or failure of a communication service or to some other event or circumstance causing substantial interruption in the normal operation of HMLR.[5]

The notice warns the cautioner that the caution will cease to have effect at the expiry of the notice period (or such longer period as HMLR may allow) unless HMLR makes an order to the contrary. That is the only effect of a caution. It does not provide any form of priority or confer validity upon any claim.[6]

A cautioner may at any time apply for a replacement or additional address, subject to there being, after the application, no more than three addresses, at least one of which is a postal address.[7] No fee is currently payable for such an application, which should be made in form AP1.

Where the caution is registered against the proprietor of the land, this does not allow the cautioner to prevent a registered chargee selling under his power of sale.[8] The cautioner will therefore be informed that his caution has been cancelled. The cautioner should remember this when consenting to the registration of a charge.

An interest under a trust of land may have been protected by a caution against dealings.[9] However, a disposition by two or more trustees or a trust corporation which overreaches that interest under LPA 1925, ss 2 and 27 will mean any objection by the cautioner will be groundless (although he will have received notice of the application to register the dealing).

If a cautioner lodged a caution without reasonable cause, they are liable to pay such compensation as may be just, to any person who may have sustained damage by the lodging of the caution. Such compensation is recoverable as a debt by the person who has sustained damage from the person who lodged the caution.[10] In practice, the prospects of a successful claim may be more limited than would appear at first sight. In *Clearbrook Property Holdings v Verrier*,[11] Templeman J said:

> It is at least arguable that a person who genuinely believes he is entitled to specific performance and issues a writ for that purpose under legal advice may say that he lodged his caution with reasonable cause.

Where a cautioner has died, his personal representative may proceed in the same manner as the cautioner.[12] The LRR 2003 define 'cautioner' as including his personal representative.[13] The personal representative should always consider the need to amend the cautioner's address for service in the register.[14]

The cautioner may apply at any time for the cancellation of the caution.[15] The application must be in form WCT and signed by the cautioner or his conveyancer. If the cautioner has died, the application should be made by his personal representative and a copy of the grant enclosed. Where the cautioner is applying to withdraw the caution as to part only, a plan defining the relevant land should be attached to form WCT. No fee is currently payable.

A cautioner may only make an application for the entry of:

(a) a notice under LRA 2002, s 34, or
(b) a restriction under LRA 2002, s 43,

in relation to the estate, right, interest or claim in respect of which the caution was lodged if he also applies for the withdrawal of the caution.[16]

The proprietor of the registered estate or charge to which the caution relates may apply for the cancellation of the caution at any time.[17] A person who, but for the existence of the caution, would be entitled to be registered as the proprietor of that estate or charge, may also apply to cancel the caution. The application must be in form CCD. No fee is currently payable. HMLR must give the cautioner notice of the application.[18] The notice period is the period ending at 12 noon on the 15th working day, or ending at 12 noon on such later working day as HMLR may allow, after the date of issue of the notice.[19]

24.1 Cautioner showing cause

When the cautioner has received a notice (whether under LRA 1925, s 55 because of an application to register a dealing, or under LRR 2003, r 223 because of an application to cancel the caution), he may at any time before the expiry of the notice period 'show cause' why HMLR should not give effect to that application. If he does not reply to the notice, or consents unconditionally to the cancellation of the caution, HMLR will cancel the caution.

To show cause, the cautioner must deliver to HMLR a written statement setting out the grounds relied upon and show that he has a fairly arguable case for HMLR not to give effect to the application in question.[20] The written statement must be signed by the cautioner or his conveyancer.

If, after reading the written statement, and making any enquiries it thinks necessary, HMLR is satisfied the cautioner has shown cause, it must order that the caution is to continue until withdrawn or otherwise disposed of under the LRA 2002 or the LRR 2003. HMLR must then give notice to the applicant and the cautioner that it has made the order and that the cautioner is to be treated as having objected under LRA 2002, s 73 to the application that resulted in notice being served.[21] The notice given by HMLR under r 221(5) is treated as notice under LRA 2002, s 73(5)(a).

The cautioner and the applicant may still resolve their dispute by agreement. However, if they cannot, the matter will have to be dealt with in accordance with LRA 2002, s 73(7).[22]

Potential agreed solutions might be that:

(a) the dealing be registered but with the caution remaining in the register; or
(b) the caution be cancelled and the dealing completed but with the interest to which the caution related being protected by entry of a notice in priority to the dealing.

The latter course of action is possible only where the interest is one capable of being protected by a notice and an appropriate application would need to be made.

Where a cautioner is considering agreeing to the registration of a charge on condition that his caution remains in the proprietorship register, he should remember that his caution could subsequently be overreached if the chargee sells under his power of sale.

If after service of the notice under LRA 1925, s 55(1) or LRR 2003, r 223(3) the application that resulted in the notice being served is cancelled, withdrawn or otherwise does not proceed, HMLR must make an order that the caution will continue to have effect, unless it has already done so or the caution has been cancelled.[23]

Where the notice is served on the cautioner under LRA 1925, s 55 as a result of an application to register a dealing and the cautioner objects but is unable to show cause, or consents to the registration of the dealing but not to cancellation of his caution, HMLR will complete the application but will normally make an order under s 55 that the caution is to continue until withdrawn or otherwise disposed of under the LRA 2002 or the LRR 2003. However, HMLR will not make any such order where it is clear the interest protected by the caution has been defeated as a result of the dealing.

---

1 LRA 2002, Sch 12, para 2(3) and LRR 2003, rr 218 to 223.
2 LRA 1925, s 55.
3 LRR 2003, r 220(1).
4 LRR 2003, rr 218 and 220(2).
5 LRR 2003, r 217(1).
6 LRA 1925, s 56(2)). See also *Barclays Bank v Taylor* [1974] Ch 137 and *Clark v Chief Land Registrar* [1994] EWCA Civ 12.
7 LRR 2003, r 198(6).
8 *Chancery plc v Ketteringham* [1994] EWCA Civ 12.
9 *Elias v Mitchell* [1972] Ch 652.
10 LRA 1925, s 56(3).
11 [1973] 3 All ER 614.
12 LRA 1925, s 56(4).
13 LRR 2003, r 218.
14 LRR 2003, r 198(6A). See 3 Address for Service.
15 LRR 2003, r 222.
16 LRA 2002, Sch 12, para 17.
17 LRR 2003, r 223.
18 LRR 2003, r 223(3).
19 LRR 2003, rr 218 and 220(2).
20 LRR 2003, r 221(3).
21 LRR 2003, r 221(5).
22 See 54 Disputes.
23 LRR 2003, r 221(6).

25 CAUTIONS AGAINST FIRST REGISTRATION

A person claiming to be the owner of a qualifying estate or entitled to an interest affecting a qualifying estate may lodge an application for a caution against first registration. For these purposes, a 'qualifying estate' is a legal estate which relates to land to which the caution relates and is an estate in land, a rentcharge, a franchise, or a profit à prendre in gross.[1] However, HMLR cannot register a caution against first registration in the cautions register where the applicant is the owner of a freehold estate in land or of a leasehold estate in land where more than 7 years of the term are unexpired.[2] The limitation on a leaseholder applies equally to a caution in respect of his leasehold estate and a caution in respect of the landlord's estate. The purpose of the limitation is to encourage the owner of a such an estate to protect it by applying for substantive registration of his title.

LRA 1925, s 53 contained no limitation equivalent to that in LRA 2002, s 15(3). For the period of 2 years from 13 October 2003 the limitation in s 15(3) did not have effect.[3] However, any caution lodged during that transitional period ceased to have effect on 13 October 2005 except in relation to applications for first registration made before then.

Different rules apply to cautions against first registration lodged by the King where the land is demesne land.[4]

A caution against first registration which was lodged under the LRA 1925, s 53 continues to have effect, and the provisions of LRA 2002, other than the limitation in s 15(3) on an owner applying for a caution against first registration, apply to such a caution.

HMLR must keep a register of cautions against first registration, comprising an individual caution register for each such caution. Each individual caution register has its own caution title number and is divided into two parts: the caution property register and the cautioner's register.

A person applying for a caution against first registration should deliver to HMLR:

(a) an application in form CT1;
(b) a plan allowing the extent of the land to which the caution relates to be identified clearly on the OS map, unless this can be clearly identified from the description in panel 2 on form CT1;
(c) (if applicable) any consent in writing of a third party to the lodging of the caution (which may be provided in panel 12 of form CT1); and
(d) the fee payable.[5]

Either the cautioner (or at least one of them, if there is more than one cautioner), or someone authorised by the cautioner, or the cautioner's conveyancer must make the statement of truth in panel 10 of form CT1. The cautioner should not exhibit any documents, as the statement should be self-contained.

The interest stated in the form CT1 will appear in the caution property register of the individual caution register, together with a description of the legal estate to which the caution relates. The description of the legal estate will refer to a caution plan based on the OS map, unless the legal estate is a relating franchise.[6]

The other part of an individual caution register is the cautioner's register. This contains the name of the cautioner, an address for service and, where appropriate, details of any person consenting to the lodging of the caution. A person consents to the lodging of a caution if, before the caution is entered in the cautions register, he has confirmed in writing that he consents to the lodging of the caution and that consent is produced to HMLR.[7]

Where the cautioner is a company registered under the Companies Acts, or a limited liability partnership (LLP) incorporated under the Limited Liability Partnerships Act 2000, HMLR will enter its registered number in the cautioner's register.

The cautioner must supply at least one and not more than three addresses for service to which all notices are to be sent. One address must be a postal address, whether or not in the United Kingdom. The other one or two additional addresses may be postal addresses, but may also be a box number at a UK DX or an email address. The box number referred to must be at a UK DX to which delivery can be made on behalf of HMLR under arrangements already in existence between HMLR and a service provider at the time the box number details are provided to HMLR.[8] A cautioner may at any time apply for a replacement or additional address, subject to there being, after the application, no more than three addresses, at least one of which is a postal address. No fee is currently payable for such an application, which should be made in form AP1.

If a cautioner lodged a caution against first registration without reasonable cause, they are liable to pay such compensation as may be just to any person who may have sustained damage by the lodging of the caution. Such compensation is recoverable as a debt by the person who has sustained damage from the person who lodged the caution.[9]

A person must not exercise the right to lodge a caution against first registration under LRA 2002, s 15 without reasonable cause.[10] This duty to act reasonably is owed to any person who suffers damage in consequence of its breach.[11]

For the purposes of the LRA 2002 and the LRR 2003, the 'cautioner' in relation to a caution against first registration means the person who lodged the caution or the person for the time being shown in the cautioner's register, where that person is not the person who lodged the caution.[12]

25.1 Effect of a caution against first registration

Where an application for first registration relates to a legal estate which is subject to a caution against first registration, HMLR must give the cautioner notice of the application and of his right to object to it.[13]

The period in which the cautioner can object is a period ending at 12 noon on the 15th working day after the date of issue of the notice or such longer period as HMLR may allow following a request by the cautioner.[14] Any request for further time must:

(a) set out why HMLR should allow the longer period; and
(b) be made before expiry of the original notice period.

After receiving such a request HMLR may, if it considers it appropriate, seek the views of the applicant for first registration. If, after considering any such views and all other relevant matters, HMLR is satisfied that a longer period should be allowed, it may allow such period. However, this may not be later than 12 noon on the 30th working day after the date of issue of the notice. Subject to that limit HMLR may allow a longer or shorter period than that requested by the cautioner.[15] A working day is any day from Monday to Friday (inclusive) which is not Christmas Day, Good Friday or any other day either specified or declared by proclamation under Banking and Financial Dealings Act 1971, s 1 or appointed by the Secretary of State or certified by HMLR as being an 'interrupted day' due to delay or failure of a communication service or to some other event or circumstance causing substantial interruption in the normal operation of HMLR.[16]

The application for first registration cannot be completed within the notice period unless the cautioner has:

(a) given notice to HMLR that he does not intend to object; or
(b) objected and the objection has been disposed of within the notice period.

An example of the latter is where the cautioner objects on the grounds that he had an easement over the land sought to be registered and, still within the notice period, the applicant consents to the making of an entry in the register in respect of the easement.

The above is the only effect of a caution against first registration. In particular, a caution against first registration has no effect on the validity or priority of any interest of the cautioner in the legal estate to which the caution relates.[17] The legal estate remains unregistered and registration of a caution against first registration can therefore never supersede the need to register a land charge under the Land Charges Act 1972 in appropriate cases.

25.2 Objection by cautioner

Where the cautioner objects to the application for first registration, he must deliver to HMLR, at the address indicated in the notice, a written statement signed by himself or his conveyancer:

(a) giving the full name of the cautioner;
(b) stating that he objects;
(c) setting out the grounds for the objection; and
(d) specifying a postal address to which HMLR should send correspondence about the objection.[18]

Unless HMLR is satisfied that the objection is groundless, it must give notice of the objection to the applicant for first registration and may not complete the application for first registration until the objection has been disposed of. The cautioner and the applicant may still resolve their dispute by agreement. However, if, they cannot, the matter will have to be dealt with in accordance with LRA 2002, s 73.[19]

25.3 Withdrawal of a caution against first registration

The cautioner may withdraw the caution against first registration at any time.[20] The cautioner should deliver to HMLR:

(a) an application in form WCT; and
(b) if the withdrawal relates to part only of the land to which the caution relates, a plan or other sufficient details to allow the extent in question to be clearly identified on the OS map.

No fee is currently payable.

25.4 Cancellation of a caution against first registration

Subject to the limitations discussed below, the owner of:

(a) the legal estate affected by a caution against first registration relates, and
(b) a legal estate which derives out of the legal estate affected by the caution against first registration,

may also apply to cancel the caution.[21] However, if the owner of the legal estate affected by the caution against first registration consented to the lodging of the caution in accordance with LRR 2003, r 47, he may only apply for cancellation if:

(a) the interest claimed by the cautioner has come to an end; or
(b) he claims that the consent was induced by fraud, misrepresentation, mistake or undue influence or given under duress.[22]

The applicant for cancellation of a caution against first registration should deliver to HMLR:

(a) an application in form CCT;
(b) if the application relates to part only of the land affected by the caution, a plan or other sufficient details to allow the extent in question to be clearly identified on the OS map;
(c) evidence that the applicant is the owner of the legal estate affected by the caution, where he is applying as such owner;
(d) evidence that the applicant is the owner of a legal estate derived out of the legal estate affected by the caution, where he is applying as such owner; and
(e) where the applicant, or a person from whom the applicant derives title to the legal estate by operation of law, has consented to the lodging of the caution, evidence that the interest claimed by the cautioner has come to an end or that the consent was induced by fraud, misrepresentation, mistake or undue influence or given under duress.

No fee is currently payable.

When HMLR receives such an application, it must give the cautioner notice of the application and notice that if he does not object to the application within the prescribed period, HMLR must cancel the caution.[23] The cautioner has until 12 noon on the 15th working day after the date of issue of the notice to object. If it receives a request from the cautioner, HMLR may extend that period. Any request for additional time by the cautioner must set out why the longer period should be allowed. The cautioner must make any request for additional time before the period ending at 12 noon on the 15th working day after the date of issue of the notice has expired. After receiving such a request HMLR may, if it considers it appropriate, seek the views of the applicant for cancellation; if, after considering any such views and all other relevant matters, HMLR is satisfied a longer period should be allowed, it may allow such period (not exceeding a period ending at 12 noon on the 30th working day after the issue of the notice) as it considers appropriate, whether or not the period is the same as any period requested by the cautioner.[24] A working day is any day from Monday to Friday (inclusive) which is not Christmas Day, Good Friday or any other day either specified or declared by proclamation under Banking and Financial Dealings Act 1971, s 1 or appointed by the Secretary of State or certified by HMLR as being an 'interrupted day' due to delay or failure of a communication service or to some other event or circumstance causing substantial interruption in the normal operation of HMLR.[25]

Only the cautioner, being the person who lodged the caution or the person for the time being shown in the cautioner's register, where that person is not the person who lodged the caution, can object to the cancellation of the caution.[26] Where the cautioner shown in the cautioner's register comprises more than one person, each such person has a separate right to object to the cancellation of the caution.[27]

Where the cautioner objects to the application for cancellation, he must deliver to HMLR, at the address indicated in the notice, a written statement signed by himself or his conveyancer:

(a) giving the full name of the cautioner;
(b) stating that he objects;
(c) setting out the grounds for the objection; and
(d) specifying a postal address to which HMLR should send correspondence about the objection.[28]

Unless HMLR is satisfied that the objection is groundless, it must give notice of the objection to the applicant for cancellation and may not complete the application for cancellation until the objection has been disposed of.[29] The cautioner and the applicant may still resolve their dispute by agreement. However, if they cannot, the matter will have to be dealt with in accordance with LRA 2002, s 73.[30]

25.5 Alteration of the cautions register

The LRA 2002 provides for alteration of the cautions register. HMLR may alter the cautions register[31] or the court may order for alteration of the cautions register.[32] In either case, the alteration must be for the purpose of correcting a mistake or bringing the register up to date.

A person may apply to HMLR to alter the cautions register provided the requested alteration is to correct a mistake in the register or bring the register up to date. Where the requested alteration is to reflect a transfer of the whole of the relevant interest to the applicant by operation of law, provided HMLR does not receive any objection to any notice of the application, HMLR must complete the application.[33] Further, if HMLR is satisfied that the cautioner does not own the relevant interest, or owns only part, or that such interest did not exist or has come to an end wholly or in part, it must on application alter the cautions register under LRA 2002, s 21(1).[34] HMLR may also alter the cautions register for the purpose of bringing it up to date in some other manner, or for the purpose of correcting a mistake. However, HMLR is not obliged to alter the cautions register in such circumstances.[35]

A person who wishes to apply for an alteration under LRA 2002, s 21 should deliver to HMLR the usual documents required[36] along with any supporting documents.

Before HMLR alters the cautions register it must serve a notice on the cautioner giving details of the application, unless it is satisfied that service of the notice is unnecessary.[37]

Where HMLR alters the caution register under LRA 2002, s 21, HMLR may pay such amount as it thinks fit in respect of any costs reasonably incurred by a person in connection with the alteration.[38] This is most likely to arise where there has been a mistake in the cautions register.

The court may make an order for alteration of the cautions register for the purpose of bringing it up to date in some other manner, or for the purpose of correcting a mistake.[39] If, in any proceedings, the High Court or a county court decides that a cautioner does not own the interest claimed by the cautioner, or owns only part, or that such interest either wholly or in part did not exist or has come to an end, the court must order alteration of the cautions register.[40] If the court orders alteration of the cautions register, the order must state the caution title number of the individual cautions register affected, describe the alteration that is to be made and direct HMLR to make the alteration.[41] The order must be served on HMLR by making an application for it to give effect to the order.[42]

In addition to delivering the usual documents required,[43] the applicant should provide HMLR with the court order or a certified copy of it.

---

1 LRA 2002, s 15.
2 LRA 2002, s 15(3).
3 LRA 2002, Sch 12, para 14(1).
4 See 51 Demesne Land.
5 See 67 Fees.
6 See 74 Franchises.
7 LRR 2003, r 47.
8 LRR 2003, r 198.
9 LRA 1925, s 56(3), which continues to have effect in relation to cautions against first registration lodged under that Act because of the transitional provisions of LRA 2002, Sch 12, para 4.
10 LRA 2002, s 77(1)(a).
11 LRA 2002, s 77(2).
12 LRA 2002, s 22 and LRR 2003, r 52(1).
13 LRA 2002, s 16(1).
14 LRR 2003, r 53.
15 LRR 2003, r 53(3).
16 LRR 2003, r 217(1).
17 LRA 2002, s 16(3).
18 LRR 2003, r 19.
19 See 54 Disputes.

20 LRA 2002, s 17.
21 LRA 2002, s 18 and LRR 2003, r 45.
22 LRR 2003, r 46.
23 LRA 2002, s 18(3).
24 LRR 2003, r 53.
25 LRR 2003, r 217(1).
26 LRA 2002, s 73(2).
27 LRR 2003, r 52(2).
28 LRR 2003, r 19.
29 LRA 2002, s 73(5) and (6).
30 See 54 Disputes.
31 LRA 2002, s 21.
32 LRA 2002, s 20.
33 LRR 2003, r 51.
34 LRR 2003, r 49(1).
35 LRR 2003, r 49(2).
36 See 12 Alteration of the Register.
37 LRR 2003, r 50(2).
38 LRA 2002, s 21(3).
39 LRA 2002, s 20.
40 LRR 2003, r 48(1).
41 LRR 2003, r 48(2).
42 LRA 2002, s 20(2) and LRR 2003, r 48(3).
43 See 12 Alteration of the Register.

26 CHANCEL REPAIR

Chancel repair liability is a liability of the owner of land to pay for the repair of the chancel of a parish church. The liability is mediaeval in origin and arises in relation to certain churches of the Church of England and the Church in Wales, so that there may be a liability where land was formerly attached to a rectory. Such former rectorial land is not necessarily close to a church building or situated within a rural area. In England, the parochial church council and, in Wales, the Representative Body of the Church in Wales, have the right to enforce the liability.

In most cases the liability is joint and several between the respective owners of the parts of the land burdened by the right, so that each owner is potentially liable for the whole cost of the repairs to the chancel, subject to a right of contribution from others similarly liable.[1] In rare cases the liability may be limited to only a proportion of the cost of repair of the chancel; this would be the case where, in particular, the title to a parcel of land is one in which a tithe rentcharge has previously redeemed pursuant to the Tithe Act 1936. Further details as to the background to chancel repair liability are contained in a report by the Law Commission, *Property Law – Liability for Chancel Repairs* (Law Com No 152) (1985).

In certain cases, it may be possible to obtain a release from any further liability for chancel repair; for example, by means of a 'composition' under Ecclesiastical Dilapidations Measure 1923 (1923/3), s 52. Also, if a parish church of the Church of England is declared redundant, any liability of a parochial church council or rector (including a lay rector) ceases upon a declaration of redundancy taking effect.[2]

The benefit of a right in respect of the repair of a church chancel cannot be registered; it is not a legal estate which can be registered as appurtenant to a registered estate. Until 12 October 2013, the burden of such a right was an unregistered interest which overrode first registration and registered dispositions.[3] Such a right was therefore protected notwithstanding that there was no entry in the register in respect of it.[4] After 12 October 2013, the protection of the burden of the right as an overriding interest ceased.

On first registration of title, HMLR will enter a notice in the register of the burden of such a liability, if it appears from its examination of the title to affect the land.

Until 13 October 2013, there was a duty to disclose a liability for chancel repair.[5] Since then, such liability no longer takes effect as an interest which overrides.

The person having the benefit of the right (if its priority has not already been previously defeated and it continues to subsist) should where necessary protect it. If he does not do so, the priority of the right may be defeated on a subsequent first registration of unregistered burdened land or on a subsequent registration of a registrable disposition of registered burdened land for valuable consideration, as the case may be.[6] If the burdened land is unregistered, he should apply for a caution against first registration. If the burdened land is registered, he should apply for the entry of a notice if one does not already appear in the register. The normal fee will apply.[7]

26.1 Caution against first registration

An applicant should deliver to HMLR the usual documents required.[8]

The statement of truth in panel 10 of form CT1 should be completed on the following lines to show the interest of the applicant:

> the person entitled to enforce a liability [to repair] or [to contribute towards the cost of repair] of the chancel of [*specify the church in question*] arising by reason of

[*summarise the basis on which the interest arises*] and payable by [*name of registered proprietor*].

The interest stated in the form CT1 will appear in the caution register, together with a description of the legal estate to which the caution relates. For the effect of a caution against first registration, see 25 Cautions Against First Registration.

26.2 Agreed notice

An applicant should deliver to HMLR the usual documents required.[9]

Documentary evidence of the creation or existence of the right in respect of the repair of a church chancel will normally be in the form of a statutory declaration or statement of truth containing details of how the right arose and how it has devolved to the applicant.

The agreed notice in the register will give details of the interest protected.

Where the registered proprietor does not consent to the entry in the register of an agreed notice and the applicant cannot supply HMLR with evidence to satisfy it of the validity of the applicant's claim, the applicant may still apply for entry of a unilateral notice.

26.3 Unilateral notice

An applicant should deliver to HMLR the usual documents required.[10]

The statement in panel 11 or conveyancer's certificate in panel 12 of form UN1 should be completed on the following lines to show the interest of the applicant:

> the person entitled to enforce a liability [to repair] or [to contribute towards the cost of repair] of the chancel of [*specify the church in question*] arising by reason of [*summarise the basis on which the interest arises*] and payable by [*name of registered proprietor*].

The unilateral notice in the register will give brief details of the interest protected and identify the beneficiary of that notice.

---

1 *Wickhambrook PCC v Croxford* [1935] 2 KB 417.

2 Mission and Pastoral Measure 2011 (2011/3), s 61(3)

3 LRA 2002, Sch 1, para 16 and Sch 3, para 16.

4 LRA 2002, ss 11, 12, 29 and 30.

5 LRR 2003, r 28 or r 57. See also 128.4 Duty to disclose overriding interests.
6 LRA 2002, ss 11, 12, 29 and 30.
7 See 67 Fees.
8 See 25 Cautions Against First Registration.
9 See 119.1 Agreed notice.
10 See 119.3 Unilateral notice.

27 CHANGE OF GENDER RESULTING IN A CHANGE OF NAME

An applicant should deliver to HMLR:

(a) an application in form CNG;
(b) evidence of change of gender, in the form of a gender recognition certificate, a new birth certificate or a UK medical practitioner's letter.

No fee is currently payable.

28 CHANGE OF NAME

It is important the registered proprietor of a registered estate or charge keeps his name, as well as his address for service, up to date. Where necessary, the proprietor should apply to update the register to reflect any change in name. Such a change may be effected by a private individual or by a corporate body.

28.1 Change of name of private individuals

An applicant should deliver to HMLR:

(a) an application in form AP1;
(b) evidence of change of name, which may be in the form of:

    (i) an original or official copy of a marriage certificate or civil partnership certificate or (unless the certificate was from outside the United Kingdom, in which case a certified copy is required) a conveyancer's certificate confirming the names of the couple (including their former name(s)) and the date and place of the marriage or civil partnership;
    (ii) an original or certified copy of a marriage or civil partnership certificate and either the decree absolute or dissolution (as the case may

be) provided the person is reverting to their original name or a certificate by a conveyancer that the person formerly known by the name on the register is now known by the new name;

(iii) a deed poll or a certified copy of it; or

(iv) a statutory declaration or statement of truth (and a certified copy, if the applicant wishes the original to be returned); and

(c) where the evidence provided is a deed poll, statutory declaration or statement of truth the appropriate confirmation or evidence of identity.[1]

No fee is currently payable.

28.2 Change of name of corporate bodies

An applicant should deliver to HMLR:

(a) an application in form AP1; and

(b) evidence of change of name, in the form of:

 (i) the original or a certified copy of the certificate of incorporation of change of name; or

 (ii) a copy of a Companies House printout showing the change of name.

No fee is currently payable. Satisfactory alternative evidence may be required where the proprietor is an overseas company, Credit Union or LLP.

---

1 See 84 Identity Evidence.

29 CHARGING ORDERS

A charging order is an order, usually of the court, imposing a charge upon a person's property to secure the payment of money that is due. Most charging orders are made under the Charging Orders Act 1979. However, charging orders can arise under other statutes. For example, in certain circumstances the court can make a charging order on a bankrupt's home in favour of a trustee in bankruptcy under the provisions of the IA 1986.[1] A charging order takes effect as an equitable charge.

Although the process under the Charging Orders Act 1979 involves two separate orders, it appears there is only one equitable charge. At the interim charging order stage, the charge is conditional and if the charging order is made absolute then the charge becomes unconditional.

A person who has obtained a charging order against the legal estate in registered land may apply to enter a notice of the charging order. This is so whether it is an interim or final charging order. Such a charging order will arise where it is one made against a sole proprietor who is the sole legal and beneficial owner, or against joint proprietors expressly as 'trustees'. The applicant cannot apply for an official search with priority using form OS1 or form OS2, as the making of the charging order is not a protectable disposition.

Where the charging order is over a beneficial interest in registered land held under a trust of land, HMLR cannot enter a notice in the register.[2] Such a charging order will arise, for example, where it is made against the beneficial interest of one of two or more registered proprietors. In this situation, the beneficiary of the order may apply for the entry of a restriction in Form K.[3] The wording of Form K is set out in Appendix IV. This is an exception to the general principle that a person with the benefit of an equitable charge upon such a beneficial interest does not have a right or claim which would give him a sufficient interest to apply for entry of any restriction, other than one in Form A (if one does not already appear in the register) to reflect the severance of any beneficial joint tenancy which such a charge will normally effect. The wording of Form A is set out in Appendix IV.

Separate charging orders made against joint proprietors in the same court proceedings will not be treated as charging the legal estate. In such circumstances, the beneficiary would need to make separate applications for restrictions in Form K. The applications may be made within a single form RX1.

An application for entry of a notice may be for an agreed notice or a unilateral notice. In the case of an agreed notice, HMLR may approve the application without the consent of the proprietor where it is satisfied of the validity of the applicant's claim.[4] Normally, production of the charging order enables HMLR to be so satisfied.

Where an application for a charging order against the legal estate is pending before the court, this will represent a 'pending land action' within the meaning of Land Charges Act 1972, s 17(1). A pending land action is treated as an interest affecting an estate or charge for the purposes of the LRA 2002.[5] However, it cannot be an interest belonging to a person in actual occupation falling within LRA 2002, Sch 1, para 2 or Sch 3, para 2 which will override first registration or registered dispositions.[6] The priority of the pending land action should be protected by application for entry of an agreed notice or a unilateral notice.[7]

An application for a charging order over a beneficial interest in land held under a trust of land would not be a pending land action. Consequently, it is not protectable by entry of a notice. Nor is it protectable by entry of a restriction, as at this stage the applicant for the charging order has no interest in the beneficial interest in question.

29.1 Notice in respect of a pending land action

29.1.1 Agreed notice

In addition to the usual documents required,[8] an applicant should deliver to HMLR:

(a) where the application has been made to the Civil National Business Centre (CNBC):

  (i) a copy of the application form of the charging order;
  (ii) any covering letter to the CNBC; and
  (iii) an assurance from the applicant that this has been submitted; and

(b) where the application is to another court, a certified copy of the application bearing the court's seal and court reference number.

This should satisfy HMLR of the validity of the applicant's claim in accordance with LRA 2002, s 34(3)(c).

The agreed notice in the register will give details of the interest protected.

29.1.2 Unilateral notice

An applicant should deliver to HMLR the usual documents required.[9]

The statement in panel 11 or conveyancer's certificate in panel 12 of form UN1 should be completed on the following lines to show the interest of the applicant:

> applicant in an application for a charging order in the [*name of court*] Court [*set out full court reference and parties*].

The unilateral notice in the register will give brief details of the interest protected and identify the beneficiary of that notice.

29.2 Agreed notice in respect of the charging order

In addition to the usual documents required,[10] an applicant should deliver to HMLR the charging order or a certified copy of it. This should satisfy HMLR of the validity of the applicant's claim in accordance with LRA 2002, s 34(3)(c).

The agreed notice in the register will give details of the interest protected.

29.3 Unilateral notice in respect of the charging order

An applicant should deliver to HMLR the usual documents required.[11]

The statement in panel 11 or conveyancer's certificate in panel 12 of form UN1 should be completed on the following lines to show the interest of the applicant:

> chargee under a charging order of the [*name of court*] Court dated [*date*] [*set out full court reference and parties*].

The unilateral notice in the register will give brief details of the interest protected and identify the beneficiary of that notice.

29.4 Restriction where the charging order is over a beneficial interest

If there is no restriction in Form A already in the register, the beneficiary of a charging order over a beneficial interest under a trust of land has a sufficient interest to apply for entry of a restriction in Form A, to ensure that a survivor of the joint proprietors (unless a trust corporation) will not be able to give a valid receipt for capital money.[12]

The person having the benefit of a charging order over a beneficial interest under a trust of land also has a sufficient interest to apply for entry of a restriction in Form K to ensure he receives notice of a disposition.[13]

A Form K restriction does not of itself prevent a disposition, provided its terms are complied with. This is because the interest of the beneficiary of a charging order will be overreached where the requirements of Form A have been met.[14] Because of this, some applicants ask the court to make an order for entry of a non-standard restriction under LRA 2002, s 46 requiring prior notice of any disposition or the consent of the beneficiary to any disposition.

Except where the court has ordered HMLR to enter a particular restriction under LRA 2002, s 46, HMLR must give notice of an application for a restriction to the proprietor of the registered estate or charge concerned, if it has not been made by or with the consent of such proprietor or a person entitled to be registered as such proprietor.[15]

A restriction does not confer any priority. However, it prevents an entry being made in the register relating to any disposition, or a disposition of a specified kind, unless the terms of the restriction have (where applicable) been complied with.

If applying for entry of a restriction in Form A, an applicant should deliver to HMLR an application in form RX1, accompanied by the charging order or a certified copy of it. No fee is currently payable where the application is in respect of a restriction in Form A only.

As the application is unlikely to be made by or with the consent of the registered proprietor, the statement in panel 12 or conveyancer's certificate in panel 13 of form RX1 should be completed on the following lines:

> The interest is that specified in rule 93(a) of the Land Registration Rules 2003 (SI 2003/1417), the applicant being the person with the benefit of [an interim *or* a final] charging order on the beneficial interest of [*name of judgment debtor*] made by the [*name of court*] on [*date*] (Court reference [*insert reference*]).

Panel 9 of form RX1 should set out the wording of Form A.

If applying for a restriction in Form K, an applicant should deliver to HMLR the usual documents required[16] accompanied by the charging order or a certified copy of it.

As the application is unlikely to be made by or with the consent of the registered proprietor, the statement in panel 12 or conveyancer's certificate in panel 13 of form RX1 should be completed on the following lines:

> The interest is that specified in rule 93(k) of the Land Registration Rules 2003 (SI 2003/1417), the applicant being the person with the benefit of [an interim *or* a final] charging order on the beneficial interest of [*name of judgment debtor*] made by the [*name of court*] on [*date*] (Court reference [*insert reference*]).

Panel 9 of form RX1 should set out the wording of Form K.

If applying for a non-standard restriction in a form ordered by the court, an applicant should deliver to HMLR an application in form AP1[17] together with the court order or a certified copy of it.

29.5 Assignment of a charging order

A money judgment is a legal chose in action which is capable of assignment. If the creditor has begun enforcement proceedings, assignment of the judgment will assign the benefit of any steps taken to enforce it. This includes the benefit of any charging order obtained to secure the debt.[18]

The action required to reflect an assignment of a charging order will depend upon the entry on the register protecting that interest.

29.5.1 Agreed notice

An agreed notice identifies only the original beneficiary of the interest protected. It is not possible to apply to update the entry following an assignment.

29.5.2 Unilateral notice

If there is a unilateral notice relating to:

(a) a pending land action, or
(b) a charging order,

the assignee may apply to amend the beneficiary of the unilateral notice.

Any such application must be in form UN3. If a conveyancer provides details of the assignment in panel 11 of that form. HMLR will not usually require further evidence of the assignment. Otherwise, the applicant must provide evidence of the assignment with the application, for example, a certified copy of any deed of assignment.

29.5.3 Form K restriction

The assignee of the charging order should apply to update the restriction to include his name and address for service. In addition to the usual documents required,[19] the applicant must deliver to HMLR evidence of the assignment, for example a certified copy of any deed of assignment.

29.5.4 Non-standard restriction to protect a charging order

As explained above,[20] in exceptional circumstances, the court may direct HMLR to enter a non-standard form of restriction to protect a charging order. HMLR will not accept an application to update such a restriction to refer to the assignee or enter a new restriction in similar wording unless accompanied by a court order ordering HMLR to:

(a) update the existing restriction; or
(b) register a new restriction in the wording applied for.

This is because HMLR cannot be sure that the exceptional circumstances which led the court to make the original order apply to the assignee.

If the applicant has such an order, he should:

(a) apply to update the restriction;[21]
(b) apply to cancel the existing restriction using form RX3 and enter the new restriction using form RX1;[22] or
(c) procure that the assignor withdraw the existing restriction using form RX4 and apply to enter the new restriction using form RX1.[23]

In each case, the applicant must include a certified copy of the court order with his application.

If the applicant does not have such an order, he should either:

(a) apply to cancel the existing restriction using form RX3 and enter the new restriction using form RX1;[24] or
(b) procure that the assignor withdraw the existing restriction using form RX4 and apply to enter the new restriction using form RX1[25]

In addition to the usual documents required, the applicant must deliver to HMLR a certified copy of the charging order and evidence of the assignment, for example a certified copy of any deed of assignment.

29.6 Removal of charging order entries

The action required to remove entries protecting a charging order will depend upon the nature of those entries.

29.6.1 Agreed notice

Where the agreed notice protects a pending land action, in addition to the usual documents required,[26] the applicant must deliver to HMLR evidence that the action is no longer pending. This will usually be a certified copy of the order disposing of the application.

Where the agreed notice protects a charging order, in addition to the usual documents required,[27] the applicant must deliver to HMLR:

(a) a court order discharging the charging order;
(b) a statement in form CN1 signed by the applicant or their solicitor stating that all moneys secured have been paid to the applicant;
(c) a receipt for the money secured endorsed on a copy of the charging order;
(d) a discharge in form DS1 suitably amended; or
(e) a receipt for payment of the money secured.

If the applicant is the original beneficiary of the charging order, he should also provide written confirmation that, at the date of repayment, the benefit of the order had not vested in anybody else.

If the applicant is not the original beneficiary of the charging order, he should provide appropriate evidence of assignment to him, for example, a certified copy of any assignment deed.

Depending on the circumstances, HMLR may serve notice of the application on the original beneficiary of the charging order.

29.6.2 Unilateral notice

A unilateral notice protecting an application for a charging order or a charging order is no different to any other unilateral notice. For further details, see 119.5 Removal of a unilateral notice and 119.6 Cancellation of a unilateral notice.

29.6.3 Form A restriction

A charging order severs any beneficial joint tenancy. Repayment of the sums owed under the charging order will not undo that. Accordingly, if the parties wish to remove a Form A restriction entered following the making of a charging order, they must re-settle the land and apply to cancel the Form A restriction.[28]

29.6.4 Form K restriction

29.6.4.1 Automatic removal

HMLR will usually automatically remove a Form K restriction following a transfer of the affected estate for value provided the applicant provides the certificate required by the restriction.

HMLR will not automatically remove a Form K restriction if it appears the transfer is of a beneficial share. An example might be a transfer from A and B to B alone. If an applicant wishes to apply for cancellation of the Form K restriction in such circumstances, he must apply using form RX3 with either:

(a) evidence that the consideration was paid for the entire legal and beneficial interest in the property; or
(b) other evidence to satisfy HMLR the Form K restriction is no longer required.

HMLR will usually serve notice of the application on the beneficiary of the restriction.

29.6.4.2 Withdrawal of Form K restriction

The beneficiary named in a Form K restriction may apply to withdraw it in the normal way.[29]

29.6.4.3 Cancellation of Form K restriction

If the charging order has been discharged, an applicant may apply to cancel the Form K restriction relating to it. In addition to the usual documents required,[30] the applicant must deliver to HMLR:

(a) a court order discharging the charging order;
(b) a statement in form RX3 signed by the applicant or their solicitor stating that all moneys secured have been paid to the applicant;
(c) a receipt for the money secured endorsed on a copy of the charging order;
(d) a discharge in form DS1 suitably amended; or
(e) a receipt for payment of the money secured.

HMLR will usually serve notice of the application on the beneficiary of the restriction.

29.6.4.4 Cancellation of other restrictions

HMLR will not usually automatically cancel any other form of restriction entered to protect a charging order. An applicant wishing to remove such a restriction must apply to do so. In addition to the usual documents required,[31] the applicant must deliver to HMLR:

(a) a court order discharging the charging order;
(b) a statement in form RX3 signed by the applicant or their solicitor stating that all moneys secured have been paid to the applicant;
(c) a receipt for the money secured endorsed on a copy of the charging order;
(d) a discharge in form DS1 suitably amended; or
(e) a receipt for payment of the money secured.

HMLR will usually serve notice of the application on the beneficiary of the restriction.

---

1 See 19.17 Charging order in favour of trustee in bankruptcy.
2 LRA 2002, s 33(a).
3 LRA 2002, s 42(4) and LRR 2003, r 93(k).
4 LRA 2002, s 34(3).
5 LRA 2002, s 87(1).
6 LRA 2002, s 87(3).
7 LRA 2002, s 87(1) and LRR 2003, r 172.
8 See 119.1 Agreed notice.
9 See 119.3 Unilateral notice.
10 See 119.1 Agreed notice.
11 See 119.3 Unilateral notice.
12 LRR 2003, r 93(a).
13 LRR 2003, r 93(k).
14 LPA 1925, ss 2 and 27.
15 LRA 2002, s 45.
16 See 153.1 Application for entry of restriction.
17 LRR 2003, r 127.
18 *Adedeji v Pathania* [2015] EWHC 1434 (Ch).
19 See 12.2 Alteration not pursuant to a court order.
20 See 29.4 Restriction where the charging order is over a beneficial interest.
21 For further details of the procedure, see 29.5.3 Form K restriction.
22 For further details, see 153.8 Cancellation of a restriction and 153.1 Application for entry of restriction.
23 For further details, see 153.9 Withdrawal of a restriction and 153.1 Application for entry of restriction.
24 For further details, see 153.8 Cancellation of a restriction and 153.1 Application for entry of restriction.

25 For further details, see 153.9 Withdrawal of a restriction and 153.1 Application for entry of restriction.
26 See 119.2 Cancellation of a notice other than a unilateral notice or a home rights notice.
27 See 119.2 Cancellation of a notice other than a unilateral notice or a home rights notice.
28 See 92.3 Cancellation of Form A restriction.
29 See 153.9 Withdrawal of a restriction.
30 See 153.8 Cancellation of a restriction.
31 See 153.8 Cancellation of a restriction.

30 CHARITIES

In addition to the requirements of the LRA 2002 and the LRR 2003, the requirements of the Charities Act 2011 need to be borne in mind when making applications to register dispositions by or in favour of charities.

For the purposes of the Charities Act 2011:

(a) a 'charity' is any institution, corporate or not, which is established for charitable purposes only and is subject to the control of the High Court in the exercise of the court's jurisdiction with respect to charities;[1]
(b) 'Charitable purposes' is defined as a purpose which falls within Charities Act 2011, s 3(1) (which lists 13 descriptions of purposes) and is for the public benefit; and
(c) 'Charity trustees' is defined as being the persons having the general control and management of the administration of a charity.[2]

'Charity' and 'charity trustees' have the same meanings in the LRR 2003.[3]

Most charities are subject to the jurisdiction of the Charity Commission and are referred to as 'non-exempt' charities. A minority of charities, referred to as 'exempt charities', are covered by the Charities Act 2011 for some purposes, but are largely exempted from the jurisdiction of the Charity Commission. Exempt charities are those which are listed in Charities Act 2011, Sch 3 (or which are an exempt charity by virtue of any other enactment) and include the board of trustees of certain museums, for example.

The trustees of non-exempt charities are generally allowed to sell, mortgage or otherwise dispose of the charity's land without an order of the court or of the Charity Commission, if they follow the correct procedures. These procedures are not binding on exempt charities, nor do they apply to certain specific transactions.

All dispositions of an estate *in favour of a charity* or contracts for such dispositions must contain an appropriate statement as to whether the charity is exempt or non-exempt and, if the latter, as to the restrictions on dispositions imposed by the Charities Act 2011.

All dispositions of a registered estate *by a charity* or contracts for such dispositions must contain an appropriate statement.[4]

The statements enable HMLR, when registering a non-exempt charity or its trustees as proprietors of land, to enter an appropriate restriction; and when registering a disposition by a non-exempt charity, to be satisfied that the restriction has been complied with.

A transfer of a registered or unregistered estate on or in consequence of the appointment of a new charity trustee is not a 'disposition' for the purposes of the Charities Act 2011. Therefore, none of the statements or the certificate need to be included in a deed that appoints a new trustee or is made in consequence of the appointment of a new charity trustee. In the case of an unregistered estate, the appointment of a new charity trustee may 'trigger' compulsory first registration.[5]

The Charities Act 2011 does not apply to land held by corporations in the Church of England in cases where they hold the land as part of their corporate property for ecclesiastical purposes, or where a diocesan board of finance is holding glebe land of the diocese.[6]

The Charity Commission has a sufficient interest to apply for a restriction in relation to registered land held on charitable trusts[7]

30.1 Dispositions in favour of charities

Any disposition of registered land in favour of a charity which must be registered, and any disposition in favour of a charity which 'triggers' first registration, must contain a statement in one of the following forms,[8] depending upon whether it is an exempt or a non-exempt charity:

(a) The land transferred (*or as the case may be*) will, as a result of this transfer (*or as the case may be*) be held by (or in trust for) (*name of charity*), an exempt charity.

(b) The land transferred (*or as the case may be*) will, as a result of this transfer (*or as the case may be*) be held by (or in trust for) (*name of charity*), a non-exempt charity, and the restrictions on disposition imposed by sections 117 to 121 of the Charities Act 2011 will apply to the land (subject to section 117(3) of that Act).

The appropriate statement should be made in the contract as well as in the document effecting the disposition.

None of the above applies to a mortgage in favour of a charity, nor do any of the restrictions discussed below need to be entered where a charity is registered as proprietor of a charge.[9]

The application to register the disposition is not required to be in any special form merely because the applicants are charity trustees. In the case of an exempt charity HMLR is not under an obligation to enter a restriction. If such a restriction is required because of limitations on the powers of the charity, the trustees should apply for its entry.[10]

In the case of a non-exempt charity, HMLR must enter a restriction that reflects the powers of the charity as registered proprietor.[11]

If a non-exempt charity is voluntarily applying for first registration of an estate, the conveyance or other instrument may not contain one of the above statements. Consequently, the application must be accompanied by an application for entry of a restriction in Form E.[12] The wording of Form E is set out in Appendix IV.

An application to register:

(a) a transfer in favour of a non-exempt charity which does not contain the necessary statement, or
(b) a transfer by operation of law in favour of a non-exempt charity,

must be accompanied by an application for a restriction in Form E.[13]

A restriction in Form E in LRR 2003, Sch 4 does not require the approval of HMLR to the wording of the restriction under LRA 2002, s 43(3).

Where the disposition is in favour of an exempt charity, the application must be accompanied by the document creating the trust or a certified copy of it.[14] This requirement does not apply in the case of a disposition to a non-exempt charity.[15] However, where the charity is incorporated otherwise than under the Charities Acts 2011 or 1993 or under the Companies Acts, the applicant should lodge evidence of the charity's constitution or trusts.[16]

If the disposition is in favour of a charitable incorporated organisation (CIO), the disposition must show the CIO's status, that is describe it as a CIO. The disposition or the application form (AP1 or FR1, or panel LR3 for a prescribed clauses lease) should also state the CIO's registered number.

If the disposition is in favour of charity trustees incorporated under Charities Act 2011, Pt 12 or Charities Act 1993, Pt VII, they must be described as 'a body corporate under Part 12 of the Charities Act 2011 (*or* Part VII of the Charities Act 1993)' and the application to register the disposition must be accompanied by the certificate granted by the Charity Commission under Charities Act 2011, s 251 or Charities Act 1993, s 50.[17] These requirements apply equally to a disposition of a registered charge in favour of charity trustees.

Where the application is to register the Official Custodian for Charities as proprietor of a registered estate or registered charge, the application must be accompanied by:

(a) an order of the court made under Charities Act 2011, s 90(1) or Charities Act 1993, s 21(1); or
(b) an order of the Charity Commission made under Charities Act 2011, s 9(1)(c) or s 76(3) or Charities Act 1993, ss 16 or 18; and
(c) (in cases where the land is vested in the Official Custodian by virtue of a vesting order under Charities Act 2011, s 76 or Charities Act 1993, s 18) an application in form RX1 for entry of a restriction in Form F. This situation may arise where, for example, the Charity Commission has intervened because of misconduct or mismanagement in the administration of the charity. The wording of Form F is set out in Appendix IV.

Where the Official Custodian for Charities is registered as proprietor of a registered estate or a registered charge, the address of the charity trustees or, where the registered estate or charge is held on behalf of a charity which is a corporation, the address of the charity, must be entered in the register as his address for service.[18] However, this does not apply where the estate or charge is vested in him by virtue of an order under Charities Act 2011, s 76 or Charities Act 1993, s 18, in which case the address of the Official Custodian will be entered as the address for service.

Where the Official Custodian is not being registered as proprietor, there is no limit to the number of trustees of a charity who can be registered as proprietors.[19] Where charity trustees are individuals HMLR will, if requested, enter the names of the trustees in the proprietorship register followed by an appropriate description such as:

> the trustees of the charity known as [*name of charity*].

If the charity trustees have been incorporated under Charities Act 2011, Pt 12 or Charities Act 1993, Pt VII, this fact will be stated in the proprietorship entry.

Where the charity is a corporation, HMLR will enter its name and address in the register, together with the company registration number, if applicable.

Where the charity being registered as proprietor is an exempt charity, it is not compulsory for HMLR to enter any restriction in the register. In the case of an application to register a non-exempt charity, or trustees of a non-exempt charity, as proprietor(s), it must be accompanied by an application for the appropriate restriction.[20] The application may be made in form RX1 or set out in the additional provisions panel of forms TP1, TP2, TR1, TR2, TR4, TR5, AS1, AS2 or AS3 or in clause LR13 of a prescribed clauses lease (or any other lease containing clauses LR1 to LR14 of LRR 2003, Sch 1A). No additional fee is currently payable for the application for the restriction.

The appropriate restriction is Form E.

Where the estate is vested in the Official Custodian for Charities under Charities Act 2011, s 76 or Charities Act 1993, s 18, in addition to a restriction in Form E, a restriction in Form F is required for the reasons explained above.

In all cases where two or more trustees of the charity are registered as proprietors, HMLR will enter a restriction in Form A in the register.[21] Where a sole or last surviving trustee or custodian trustee of the charity applies to be registered as proprietor of the land held on a trust of land, he must apply for entry of a restriction in Form A in addition to any charity restriction.[22] The wording of Form A is set out in Appendix IV.

30.2 Dispositions by charities

A disposition by a charity of registered land, or of unregistered land which 'triggers' first registration, must contain a statement about the land and the charity.[23] The type of statement to be included depends upon whether the charity is exempt or non-exempt and whether or not the disposition is a mortgage. The deed effecting the disposition and the contract for such disposition must contain any appropriate statement. Any disposition of registered land by a charity which must be registered must also comply with any restrictions which appear in the register, including any restriction in Form E. In the case of a disposition by a non-exempt charity, this may require the disposition to also contain an appropriate certificate.

The disposition will need to be executed by the charity. Where the charity is a body corporate incorporated under the Companies Acts, it should execute a disposition in the form appropriate for a company. Where the charity consists of individual trustees, a disposition must normally be executed by them all.

However, subject to the trusts of the charity, charity trustees may confer on two or more of their number authority to execute deeds and instruments in the names and on behalf of the trustees.[24] This also allows execution on behalf of the Official Custodian for Charities, unless a contrary intention appears. Where a deed is expressed to be executed under Charities Act 2011, s 333 and the disposition is in favour of a person acquiring in good faith for money or money's worth an interest in or charge on land, it is not necessary to deliver to HMLR evidence of the authority to execute under that section.

Where the registered proprietor is a charitable company and its name does not include the words 'charity' or 'charitable', the deed effecting the disposition must contain a statement that the company is a charity.[25]

Where the charity is an incorporated body under Charities Act 2011, Pt 12 or Charities Act 1993, Pt VII, it can execute deeds using its common seal, if it has one,[26] in the presence of appropriate officers of the charity. If the charity chooses not to use or does not have a common seal, Charities Act 2011, s 260(3) provides two other methods of execution:

(a) by being signed by a majority of the trustees of the charity and expressed to be executed by the incorporated body; or
(b) by being executed by two or more of the trustees authorised[27] to execute in the name and on behalf of the incorporated body.

This also allows execution on behalf of the Official Custodian for Charities unless a contrary intention appears.[28] In favour of a purchaser (including a lessee or mortgagee) in good faith and for valuable consideration, a document is deemed to be duly executed by an incorporated body which is a charity if it purports to be executed by either of the two methods mentioned above.[29] Where this applies, no evidence that the trustees are a majority, or of their authority, needs to be delivered to HMLR.

Where the Official Custodian for Charities is the registered proprietor, he will no longer execute deeds in person. Instead, the charity trustees have full power to execute the disposition, except where the estate has been vested in the Official Custodian under Charities Act 2011, s 76 or Charities Act 1993, s 18 and a restriction in Form F appears in the register. A deed may be executed by the charity trustees, either by all of them, or under the provisions of Charities Act 2011, s 260 or s 333 referred to above.

If the Charity Commission has appointed a receiver and manager under Charities Act 2011, s 76, a certified copy of the order must accompany any application in respect of a deed executed by him.

30.3 Transfers on sale or leases by non-exempt charities

Under Charities Act 2011, ss 117 to 121, a non-exempt charity must go through certain procedural steps before disposing of land, such as taking advice from a designated adviser[30] (or, in the case of a lease for a term of 7 years or less, from a person reasonably believed by the trustees to have the requisite ability and practical experience to provide them with competent advice on the proposed disposition[31]). Once these steps have been taken then, provided that it has power under the trusts of the charity to make the disposal and the transaction is not in favour of a connected person,[32] the charity can dispose of the land without an order of the Charity Commission or the court. In all other cases such an order is required.

However, dispositions falling within Charities Act 2011, s 117(3) are not subject to those restrictions and so these will not need to be complied with nor will the consent of the Charity Commission or the court be required. The categories of disposition covered by s 117(3) are:

(a) any disposition for which general or special authority is expressly given by a statutory provision or a legally established scheme;
(b) any disposition by a liquidator, provisional liquidator, receiver, mortgagee or an administrator;
(c) any disposition of land held by or in trust for a charity which is made to another charity otherwise than as:

  (i) a disposition made with a view to achieving the best price that can reasonably be obtained; or
  (ii) a disposition which is a social investment for the purposes of Charites Act 2011, part 14A;

(d) any disposition by way of lease to a beneficiary under the trusts of the charity which:

  (i) is granted for less than the best rent that can be obtained; and
  (ii) is intended to enable the demised premises to be occupied for the purposes of the charity.

Where the charity's land is registered, the requirements of the Charities Act 2011, which apply notwithstanding anything in the trusts of the charity, are reflected in the register by the restriction in Form E. Providing any disposition by a non-exempt charity contains the relevant statement confirming whether or not the restrictions imposed by the Charities Act 2011 apply and, if they do apply, also contains a certificate confirming that those restrictions have been complied with, the requirements of the restriction in Form E will be met and HMLR can register the disposition.

LRR 2003, r 180 specifies the alternative forms of statement to be included. The statements for dispositions other than mortgages are:

(a) The land transferred (*or as the case may be*) is held by [(*proprietors*) in trust for] (*charity*), a non-exempt charity, and this transfer (*or as the case may be*) is not one falling within paragraph (a), (aa), (c) or (d) of section 117(3) of the Charities Act 2011, but the disposition has been sanctioned by an order of the court or of the Charity Commission;
(b) The land transferred (*or as the case may be*) is held by [(*proprietors*) in trust for] (*charity*), a non-exempt charity, and this transfer (*or as the case may be*) is not one falling within paragraph (a), (aa), (c) or (d) of section 117(3) of the Charities Act 2011, but there is power under the trusts of the charity to effect the disposition and sections 117 to 121 of that Act have been complied with.
(c) The land transferred (*or as the case may be*) is held by [(*proprietors*) in trust for] (*charity*), a non-exempt charity, but this transfer (*or as the case may be*) is one falling within paragraph (a), (aa), (c) or (d) (*as the case may be*) of section 117(3) of the Charities Act 2011.

Where a disposition contains any such statement, when a person acquires an interest in land for money or money's worth it shall be conclusively presumed that the facts are as stated in the certificate.[33] If the disposition does not contain such a statement, a disposition in favour of a person who in good faith acquires an interest in the land for money or money's worth it will still be valid even if:

(a) the disposition has not been sanctioned by an order of the court or of the Charity Commission; or
(b) there is no power under the trusts of the charity to effect the disposition and/or Charities Act 2011 ss 117 to 121 have not been complied with in relation to it.[34]

Where charity land is unregistered, the restrictions on dispositions apply in much the same way as they would do if the title were registered. Therefore, when examining a title on first registration, HMLR will apply the principles outlined above as if the appropriate restriction in Form E had applied. The requirement that the disposition contains statements about the land, the charity and the nature of the disposition also applies to dispositions of unregistered land.

Any other restrictions appearing in the register, including a restriction in Form A, will need to be complied with as necessary.[35] If a restriction in Form F appears in the register and the disposition has been executed in the name of and on behalf of the Official Custodian by the charity trustees, an order of the Charity Commission will be required to authorise the disposition.[36] If this is the case, the disposition should include the statement confirming that it has been sanctioned by an order of the Charity Commission or of the court, as appropriate. The restriction does not apply to dispositions executed by the Official Custodian.

HMLR will cancel a restriction in the register in Form A, Form E or Form F where an application is made to register a transfer of the title by the charity provided the restriction has been complied with and the application is otherwise in order. If the charity will remain as proprietor following registration of a disposition, such as a lease or a charge, the restrictions will remain in the register.

30.4 Mortgages by non-exempt charities

Generally, non-exempt charities are subject to the restrictions on mortgaging under Charities Act 2011, s 124, which requires the charity to go through certain procedural steps before mortgaging its land, such as taking advice on whether the loan is necessary and its terms are reasonable. However, mortgages falling within Charities Act 2011, s 124(9) are not subject to those restrictions and so these will not need to be complied with. The categories of mortgage covered by s 124(9) are:

(a) any disposition for which general or special authority is expressly given by a statutory provision or a legally established scheme; and
(b) any charge granted by a liquidator, provisional liquidator, receiver, mortgagee or an administrator.

Where the charity's land is registered, the requirements of the Charities Act 2011, which apply notwithstanding anything in the trusts of the charity, are reflected in the register by the restriction in Form E. Providing any mortgage by a non-exempt charity contains the relevant statement confirming whether or not the restrictions imposed by the Charities Act 2011 apply and, if they do that those restrictions have been complied with, the requirements of the restriction in Form E will be met and HMLR can register the mortgage.

LRR 2003, r 180(2) specifies the alternative forms of statement to be included. The statements for mortgages are:

> (a) The land charged is held by (*or* in trust for) (*charity*), a non-exempt charity, but this charge (*or* mortgage) is one falling within section 124(9) of the Charities Act 2011;

(b) The land charged is held by (*or* in trust for) (*charity*), a non-exempt charity, and this charge (*or* mortgage) is not one falling within section 124(9) of the Charities Act 2011, but the charge (*or* mortgage) has been sanctioned by an order of the court or of the Charity Commission; or
(c) The land charged is held by (*or* in trust for) (*charity*), a non-exempt charity, and this charge (*or* mortgage) is not one falling within section 124(9) of the Charities Act 2011, but there is power under the trusts of the charity to grant the charge (*or* mortgage) and the requirements of section 124(2) of that Act have been complied with.

In addition, a mortgage by a non-exempt charity that 'triggers' compulsory first registration should also contain the following statement:

> The restrictions on disposition imposed by sections 117–121 of the Charities Act 2011 also apply to the land (subject to section 117(3) of that Act).

Where a mortgage contains any such statement, when a person acquires an interest in land for money or money's worth (whether under the mortgage or afterwards), it shall be conclusively presumed that the facts are as stated in the certificate.[37] If the mortgage does not contain such a statement, a mortgage in favour of a person who in good faith acquires an interest in the land for money or money's worth will still be valid even if:

(a) the mortgage has not been sanctioned by an order of the court or of the Charity Commission; or
(b) there is no power under the trusts of the charity to effect the mortgage and/or Charities Act 2011 s 124(2) has not been complied with in relation to it.[38]

Where charity land is unregistered, the restrictions on mortgages apply in much the same way as they would be if the title were registered. Therefore, when examining a title on first registration, HMLR will apply the principles outlined above as if the appropriate restriction in Form E had applied. The requirement that the mortgage contains statements about the land, the charity and the nature of the mortgage also applies to mortgages of unregistered land.

Any other restrictions appearing in the register, including a restriction in Form A, will need to be complied with as necessary.[39] If a restriction in Form F appears in the register and the mortgage has been executed in the name of and on behalf of the Official Custodian by the charity trustees, an order of the Charity Commission will be required to authorise the mortgage.[40] If this is the case, the mortgage should include the statement confirming that it has been sanctioned by an order of the Charity Commission or of the court, as appropriate. The restriction does not apply to mortgages executed by the Official Custodian.

30.5 Dispositions by exempt charities

HMLR will not have been obliged to enter a charity restriction on the registration of a disposition to an exempt charity. However, an application may have been made to enter an appropriate restriction to reflect any limitation on the powers of disposition of the charity. Any restriction which does appear in the proprietorship register must be complied with.

Even where there is no restriction in the register, an appropriate statement must be included in any disposition of registered land,[41] or of unregistered land which 'triggers' compulsory first registration, by the exempt charity.

The statement required in the case of a disposition which is not a charge is:[42]

> The land transferred (*or as the case may be*) is held by [(*proprietors*) in trust for] (*charity*), an exempt charity.

The statement required in the case of a charge is:[43]

> The land charged is held by (*or* in trust for) (*charity*), an exempt charity.

30.6 Merger of charities

Typically, charities merge in one of two ways, either:

(a) one charity (or more) transfers/transfer all its/their property to another existing charity. The transferring charity/charities is/are then wound up; or
(b) two charities (or more) create a new charity. Each then transfers all its property to that new charity and are then wound up.

The Charity Commission maintains a register of such mergers.[44]

A CIO cannot merge without the consent of the Charity Commission. Charities Act 2011, ss 235–244 deal with the merger of CIOs.

30.6.1 Dealing with property on merger

A charity which is not a CIO which is merging may simply transfer any registered or unregistered property using one or more appropriate forms of transfer.[45] Alternatively, the charity trustees may make a vesting declaration before the merger takes place. Subject to exceptions and the requirement to register the deed, the effect of such a deed is to vest the property in the transferee charity.[46]

A vesting declaration must:

(a) be made by deed by the charity trustees of the transferor;
(b) be made in connection with a charity merger; and
(c) provide for the transferor's property to vest in the transferee on the date specified in the declaration.

A vesting declaration will not vest title to any land held by the transferor under a lease or agreement if, had the transferor assigned its interest in the land on the specified sate to the transferee, that assignment would have given rise to:

(a) an actionable breach of covenant or condition against alienation; or
(b) a forfeiture.

Accordingly, where there is an entry in the register reflecting a restriction or prohibition on alienation of a leasehold title, HMLR will not register a transfer by vesting declaration without any consent required by the lease.

Any transfers or declaration must contain the relevant Charities Act 2011 statement(s) for both the transferor and transferee charities.[47] Any restrictions affecting the relevant title(s) must also be complied with.

30.6.2 Registering gifts post-merger

Subject to limited exceptions, any gift to a charity which has merged with another will take effect as a gift to the new merged charity.[48] The principal exception to the rule is where:

(a) the transferor had both permanent endowment and other property; and
(b) the gift is intended to be held subject to the trusts on which the whole or part of the charity's permanent endowment is held.[49]

Assuming the exception does not apply, the new charity may apply to register a transfer to the transferor charity. As well as the usual documents required to register the transfer,[50] the applicant should deliver to HMLR:

(a) evidence of the merger; and
(b) confirmation that Charities Act 2011, s 311(3) does not apply to the transfer.

30.7 Rentcharge titles

Where there is a release of a registered rentcharge falling within the Charities Act 2011, s 127, which provides that the restrictions on dispositions do not apply to the release of a rentcharge given in consideration of a sum which is not less than ten times the annual amount of the rentcharge or to a redemption of a registered rentcharge under Rentcharges Act 1977, ss 8 to 10, no certificate of compliance with the Charities Act 2011 is required. In either of these situations the statement required in the instrument effecting the release of the registered rentcharge is:[51]

(a) in the case of an exempt charity:

> The rentcharge released is held by [*(proprietors)* in trust for] (*charity*), an exempt charity.

(b) in the case of a non-exempt charity:

> The rentcharge released is held by [*(proprietors)* in trust for] (*charity*), a non-exempt charity, but this release is one falling within paragraph (a) of section 117(3) of the Charities Act 2011.

Any other disposition of a rentcharge title should be dealt with in the same way as a disposition of registered land, as set out above.

30.8 Appointment of new trustees

Where a charity is registered as proprietor, application should be made to reflect any relevant changes to the charity in the register, as appropriate. For example, if there is a change in the individual charity trustees following an appointment and/or discharge, or a change in the name of the charity. The general law relating to the appointment and discharge of trustees also applies to charities. In addition, Charities Act 2011, s 334 provides that where under the trusts of a charity its trustees may be appointed or discharged by resolution of a meeting of the charity trustees, members or other persons, a memorandum declaring a trustee to have been so appointed or discharged operates as a vesting declaration under Trustee Act 1925, s 40, provided:

(a) the memorandum is executed as a deed;
(b) the execution is effected either at the meeting by the person presiding or in some other manner directed by the meeting;
(c) the memorandum is attested by two persons present at the meeting; and
(d) the memorandum relates to land to which Trustee Act 1925, s 40 applies.

The exclusions relating to charges and leases referred to in Trustee Act 1925, s 40 also apply to this procedure under Charities Act 2011, s 334.

Where an application is made to register the new trustees as proprietors and this procedure has been used, the applicant should deliver to HMLR:

(a) an application in form AP1;
(b) the memorandum;
(c) a certificate from the charity's conveyancer that it has power to use the procedure set out in Charities Act 2011, s 334;
(d) evidence of the death of any deceased trustee; and
(e) the fee payable.[52]

Where the appropriate restriction does not appear in the register, this should be applied for using form RX1.[53]

A transfer merely vesting the estate in new trustees does not need to contain a statement or certificate under the Charities Act 2011 as it is not a 'disposition' for the purposes of that Act.

The Charity Commission has the same powers as the High Court of appointing, discharging or removing a trustee of a charity.[54] Where such powers are exercised and affect the registered proprietors, the applicant should deliver to HMLR:

(a) an application in form AP1;
(b) a certified copy of the order of the Charity Commission; and
(c) the fee payable.[55]

Where the appropriate restriction does not appear in the register, this should be applied for using form RX1.[56]

30.9 Incorporation of trustees of a charity

Where the Charity Commission grants a certificate of incorporation to the trustees of a charity under Charities Act 2011, s 251, the property of the charity, other than any vested in the Official Custodian for Charities, vests in the new body corporate.[57] An application should be made to amend the register of all affected titles. The applicant should deliver to HMLR:

(a) an application in form AP1;
(b) a certified copy of the certificate of incorporation; and
(c) the fee payable.[58]

Where the appropriate restriction does not appear in the register, this should be applied for using form RX1.[59]

Where an incorporated body is dissolved under Charities Act 2011, s 263, the order has the effect of vesting the land in the trustees of the charity where it has up to then been held by the body corporate or by any other person (apart from the

Official Custodian) on trust for the charity. The order may also direct that particular land be vested in a specified person as trustee for, or nominee of, the charity or in such persons other than the charity trustees as the Charity Commission may specify.

An application should be made to amend the register of all affected titles. The applicant should deliver to HMLR:

(a) an application in form AP1;
(b) a certified copy of the order of the Charity Commission;
(c) where the order does not state in whom the land is vested, a certificate by the charity's conveyancer as to who are the trustees of the charity; and
(d) the fee payable.[60]

Where the appropriate restriction does not appear in the register, this should be applied for using form RX1.[61]

30.10 Corporation becoming a non-exempt charity

Where a registered estate is held by or in trust for a corporation and the corporation becomes a non-exempt charity, the charity trustees must apply for a restriction in Form E.[62]

The charity trustees should deliver to HMLR:

(a) an application in form RX1; and
(b) the fee payable.[63]

Panel 9 of form RX1 should set out the required restriction. A restriction in standard Form E in LRR 2003, Sch 4 does not require the approval of HMLR to the terms of the restriction under LRA 2002, s 43(3).

30.11 Change of status of charity

Where an exempt charity ceases to be exempt, or registered land not previously so held becomes held in trust for a non-exempt charity as a result of a declaration of trust by the proprietor, an application must be made using form RX1 (as above) to ensure the appropriate restriction is entered in the register.[64] Where a non-exempt charity becomes exempt, an application to cancel any Form E restriction should be made in form RX3 accompanied by evidence of the change of status.[65]

30.12 Change of name of charity

Where a charity changes its name, whether of its own volition or at the direction of the Charity Commission, an application to change the name of the charity or its description in the register should be made. The applicant should deliver to HMLR:

(a) an application in form AP1; and
(b) a new certificate of incorporation (where the charity is incorporated), or (if not incorporated) a certificate by the charity or its conveyancer as to its new name.

No fee is currently payable for reflecting a change in the name, address or description of a registered proprietor.

---

1 Charities Act 2011, s 1.
2 Charities Act 2011, s 177.
3 LRR 2003, r 217(1) and Charities Act 2011, Sch 8, para 3.
4 Charities Act 2011, s 122(2).
5 See 68 First Registration.
6 See 31 Church of England.
7 LRA 2002, s 43(1)(c) and LRR 2003, r 93(f).
8 Charities Act 2011, s 122(8) and LRR 2003, r 179.
9 Charities Act 2011, s 122(9).
10 See 153.1 Application for entry of restriction.
11 Charities Act 2011, s 123 and LRR 2003, r 176.
12 LRR 2003, r 176(2)(a).
13 See 153.1 Application for entry of restriction.
14 LRR 2003, r 182(1).
15 LRR 2003, r 182(2).
16 Or a conveyancer's certificate in the appropriate form specified in LRR 2003, r 183, being Form 7 or Form 8 in Sch 3, as the case may be. See Appendix V.
17 LRR 2003, r 177.
18 LRR 2003, r 178(3).
19 Trustee Act 1925, s 34(3).
20 LRR 2003, r 176.
21 LRA 2002, s 44(1).
22 LRR 2003, r 94.
23 Charities Act 2011, ss 122 and 125.
24 Charities Act 2011, s 333.
25 Charities Act 2011, s 194.
26 Charities Act 2011, s 260(2).
27 Under Charities Act 2011, s 261.
28 Charities Act 2011, s 261(3).
29 Charities Act 2011, s 260(5).

30 As defined in Charities Act 2011 s 119(3) and Charities (Dispositions of Land: Designated Advisors and Reports) Regulations 2023 (SI 2023/467), reg 3 and who may be a charity trustee or an officer or employee of the charity or of the charity trustees (Charities Act 2011, s 128A).
31 Charities Act 2011, s 120(2).
32 As defined in Charities Act 2011, s 118.
33 Charities Act 2011, s 122(4A).
34 Charities Act 2011, s 122(5A).
35 Although Charities Act 2011, s 334A confirms a trustee of or for a charitable trust which is a body corporate and a charity is a trust corporation for these purposes.
36 Charities Act 2011, s 91(4).
37 Charities Act 2011, s 125(3).
38 Charities Act 2011, s 125(5).
39 Although Charities Act 2011, s 334A confirms a trustee of or for a charitable trust which is a body corporate and a charity is a trust corporation for these purposes.
40 Charities Act 2011, s 91(4).
41 Charities Act 2011, ss 122(2) and 125(1).
42 LRR 2003, r 180(1).
43 LRR 2003, r 180(2).
44 Charities Act 2011, s 305.
45 See 176 Transfers.
46 Charities Act 2011, s 310.
47 See 30.1 Dispositions in favour of charities, 30.2 Dispositions by charities, 30.3 Transfers on sale or leases by non-exempt charities and/or 30.5 Dispositions by exempt charities.
48 Charities Act 2011, s 311(2A).
49 Charities Act 2011, s 311(3).
50 See 176.1 Registration of transfer.
51 LRR 2003, r 180(1).
52 See 67 Fees.
53 See 153.1 Application for entry of restriction.
54 Charities Act 2011, s 69(1)(b).
55 See 67 Fees.
56 See 153.1 Application for entry of restriction.
57 Charities Act 2011, s 252.
58 See 67 Fees.
59 See 153.1 Application for entry of restriction.
60 See 67 Fees.
61 See 153.1 Application for entry of restriction.
62 LRR 2003, r 176(3).
63 See 67 Fees.
64 Charities Act 2011, s 123(5).
65 See 153.8 Cancellation of a restriction.

31 CHURCH OF ENGLAND

The Church of England owns a significant of amount of land, which may be vested in one of several ecclesiastical bodies and is subject to various ecclesiastical statutes and measures governing its acquisition and disposal. In addition, the restrictions upon disposition contained in the Charities Act 2011 apply to some, but not all, of such land.

Some of the statutes relating to the acquisition of church land contain rights of reverter; for example, the Consecration of Churchyards Act 1867. A right of reverter allowed individuals to donate land for certain purposes on the basis that, if the land ever ceased to be used for the stated purpose, it would revert to the donor or his successor.[1]

31.1 Application of the Charities Act 2011

The Charities Act 2011 contains restrictions upon mortgages and other dispositions of charity land.[2] However, the Charities Act 2011 does not in general apply to:

(a) any ecclesiastical corporation sole or corporation aggregate in the Church of England which is established for spiritual purposes in respect of its corporate property, except:

- (i) a corporation aggregate having some purposes which are not ecclesiastical in respect of its corporate property held for those purposes; or
- (ii) once Cathedrals Measure 2021 (2021/2) (the 2021 Measure), s 8 is in effect, the Chapter of a cathedral to which the 2021 Measure applies. Consequently, this does not include a diocesan board of finance, nor does it include a parochial church council, as these are not established for spiritual purposes;

(b) a diocesan board of finance (or any subsidiary thereof) in respect of the diocesan glebe land of the diocese; or

(c) any trust of property for purposes for which the property has been consecrated.[3]

Land in this category includes land held by:

(a) the incumbent of a benefice in respect of the parsonage house and grounds and the church and churchyard vested in him;

(b) the bishop of a diocese in respect of parsonage land vested in him during a vacancy in the benefice;
(c) the diocesan board of finance of a diocese in respect of diocesan glebe land vested in it.

Therefore, when registering one of the above bodies as proprietor of a registered estate in such land, a restriction in Form E will not be entered in the register. The wording of Form E is set out in Appendix IV. However, dispositions by the above corporations are subject to the requirements of ecclesiastical law as discussed below.

Where a corporation aggregate in the Church of England other than the Chapter of a Cathedral to which the 2021 Measure applies has some purposes which are ecclesiastical and some which are not, the Charities Act 2011 applies in respect of its corporate property held for non-ecclesiastical purposes. For example, where land is vested in the incumbent and churchwardens of a parish for the purposes of an educational trust, the Charities Act 2011 applies. Equally, where an ecclesiastical corporation such as a bishop is an *ex officio* trustee of a charity, the trust property is not corporate property of the ecclesiastical corporation and the Charities Act 2011 applies. The Church of England Pensions Board is a charity to which the Charities Act 2011 applies, as was the Central Board of Finance of the Church of England until it was dissolved in 2008. That Act also applies where land which is not glebe land is vested in a diocesan board of finance and where a diocesan authority (which may be the diocesan board of finance or, in some dioceses, a separate diocesan trust) is holding land on behalf of the parochial church council or the incumbent and churchwardens of a parish. The appropriate statement and certificate should therefore be included in any disposition, whether in favour of or by the ecclesiastical corporation. HMLR will enter a restriction in Form E on registration of such a corporation as proprietor of a registered estate or charge in these circumstances.

The Church Commissioners was formerly an exempt charity but the Church Commissioners and any institution that is administered by it became non-exempt on 1 June 2010 when Charities Act 2006, s 11(7) came into force. Consequently, the restrictions on dispositions and on mortgaging contained in the Charities Act 2011 apply to dispositions on or after 1 June 2010. The appropriate statement and certificate should therefore be included in any disposition, whether in favour of or by the Church Commissioners or any institution administered by it. HMLR will enter a restriction in Form E on registration of the Church Commissioners or such an institution as proprietor of a registered estate or charge.

Where a corporation or body of trustees holding on charitable, ecclesiastical or public trusts applies to be registered as proprietor of a registered estate or registered charge, the application must be accompanied by the document creating the trust or a certified copy of it.[4] It may be necessary to make an application to enter an appropriate restriction to reflect any limitations on the power of disposition contained in that trust document. The requirement to provide the document creating the trust or a certified copy of it does not apply in the case of an estate or a charge held by or in trust for a non-exempt charity.[5]

For details of the relevant statements and certificates required under the Charities Act 2011 and the LRR 2003, and of the relevant forms of restriction, see 30 Charities.

31.2 Incumbent of a benefice

The incumbent of a benefice (who may be a vicar or a rector, depending upon whether the benefice is a vicarage or a rectory) is an ecclesiastical corporation sole and usually has the parsonage house and grounds, and the church and churchyard, vested in him. Land may be transferred directly to an incumbent or it may become vested in him in his corporate capacity by virtue of the operation of a particular statute or measure.

Church Property Measure 2018 (2018/8) (the 2018 Measure), s 28(1) allows a diocesan board of finance to acquire land for various purposes. The diocesan board of finance will require the consent of the Church Commissioners to such an acquisition unless:

(a) no person who is a party to the proposed transaction is a connected person (as defined in the 2018 Measure, s 49(6)) or a trustee for or nominee of a connected person; and
(b) the person in whom the property will be vested has obtained a written report on the proposed transaction from a qualified surveyor instructed by and acting exclusively for that person and having considered the report, is satisfied that the terms of the proposed transaction are the best that can be reasonably obtained for that person.[6]

Most property acquired by a diocesan board of finance for use as or in association with a church, churchyard, burial ground or parsonage house automatically vests in the incumbent of the benefice on a transfer to the diocesan board of finance.[7]

In any transfer of the land, the diocesan board of finance will be shown as transferee. However, the 'additional provisions' panel of the transfer (for example panel 11 of form TR1) should include an appropriate statement to explain the statutory authority for the transfer and a request that the land be registered in the name of the incumbent. A certificate in Form 4 in LRR 2003, Sch 3 should either accompany, or be included in, the transfer.[8] The wording of Form 4 is set out in Appendix V.

The diocesan board of finance may also appropriate land it already holds for one of the purposes mentioned above. If it does, it should execute a declaration to this effect. The declaration should be sufficient evidence of vesting for HMLR.

In each of the above cases, the incumbent will be registered as proprietor in the following form:

> The incumbent of the benefice of (*name of benefice*) in the county of (*county*) in the diocese of (*name of diocese*) and the incumbent's successors of (*address for service*).

When making an application to register the incumbent of a benefice as proprietor, the applicant should also make an application to enter a restriction in Form D. The wording of Form D is set out in Appendix IV. LRR 2003, r 93(g) provides that the Church Commissioners, the parsonages board and the diocesan board of finance have a sufficient interest under LRA 2002, s 43(1)(c) to apply for such a restriction.

If, as a result of a pastoral scheme, a church, churchyard or burial ground is subsequently included in a new parish, it will automatically transfer to the incumbent of that new parish unless the scheme provides otherwise.[9] Application should be made to bring the register up to date to reflect this by registering the new incumbent in place of the existing incumbent. The diocesan board of finance or diocesan registrar should certify the facts and confirm that the land is vested in the incumbent of the new parish.

Under the 2018 Measure the incumbent (or the bishop during a vacancy) may sell or exchange parsonage land, subject to the consent of:

(a) the Church Commissioners;
(b) the diocesan parsonages board (or where designated as such, the diocesan board of finance);
(c) the bishop of the diocese (unless the bishop is selling during a vacancy);
(d) the Crown Estate Commissioners (where the property is held under a grant made by the Crown); and
(e) any member of the ministry team who is occupying the property.[10]

However, the consent of the Church Commissioners is not required where:

(a) the sale is not to a connected person (as defined in the 2018 Measure, s 49(6)); and
(b) the person entitled to sell the property has obtained a written report on the proposed transaction from a qualified surveyor instructed by and acting exclusively for that person and:

(i) having considered the report, is satisfied that the terms of the proposed transaction are the best that can be reasonably obtained for the benefice; and
(ii) has advertised the proposed transaction for the period and in the manner advised by the surveyor in the report, unless the surveyor has advised in the report that advertising the proposed transaction would not be in the best interests of the benefice.

If the consent of the Church Commissioners is required, the transfer should state that it has been obtained. If it is not, the transfer should say so and give the provision of the 2018 Measure which means it is not required.

Any consent required by the 2018 Measure must be in writing and signed by a person duly authorised by the relevant body.

Provided the transfer contains any certificates required by the 2018 Measure, it will comply with the terms of any Form D restriction appearing in the register. HMLR will cancel the restriction if registration of the disposition will mean that the incumbent will no longer be the registered proprietor. If, however, the incumbent is to remain in the register after completion of the application (for example following registration of a transfer of part of the land in the title), HMLR will not cancel the restriction.

Before 13 October 2003 HMLR entered an inhibition in the proprietorship register when registering an incumbent.[11] The wording of the inhibition was:

> No disposition of the land shall be registered except on production of a certificate from the Church Commissioners in accordance with section 99 of the Land Registration Act 1925.

Where this appears, HMLR will accept evidence of compliance with the 2018 Measure as sufficient to meet the requirements of such an inhibition. HMLR will cancel such an inhibition if registration of the disposition will mean the incumbent will no longer be the registered proprietor. If, however, the incumbent is to remain on the register after completion of the application, HMLR will not cancel the inhibition.

31.3 The Church Commissioners

By the Church Commissioners Measure 1947 (1947/2), the Ecclesiastical Commissioners and Queen Anne's Bounty were dissolved on 1 April 1948 and all property vested in either of them was transferred to and vested in the

Church Commissioners for England without the need for any deed. The Church Commissioners and any institution which is administered by them are now non-exempt charities.[12] See 31.1 Application of the Charities Act 2011.

An application to register the Church Commissioners as proprietors by virtue of:

(a) a scheme of the Church Commissioners, or
(b) an instrument taking effect on publication in the *London Gazette* made pursuant to any Act or Measure relating to or administered by the Church Commissioners, or
(c) any transfer authorised by any such Act or Measure,

should include a certificate in Form 5 in LRR 2003, Sch 3.[13] The wording of Form 5 is set out in Appendix V. The certificate may be given either in a transfer or in a separate document.

In addition, the applicant should lodge one of the following, as appropriate:

(a) a sealed copy of the scheme of the Church Commissioners;
(b) a copy of the *London Gazette* publishing the instrument; or
(c) the transfer.

In other respects the application should be dealt with as in 30 Charities. Similarly, in respect of an application to register a disposition by the Church Commissioners.

31.4 Cathedrals

The 2021 Measure created a new structure for cathedral governance. This includes the co-regulation of all 42 cathedrals in England (other than Oxford, which is part of Christ Church) by the Church Commissioners and Charity Commission. Cathedrals are no longer exempt charities and are bound by the Charities Act 2011.[14]

Each cathedral continues to have a body corporate that will hold property for the cathedral. That body corporate consists of the members for the time being of the Chapter of the cathedral who will be charity trustees for the purposes of the Charities Act 2011.

By virtue of the 2021 Measure, s 47, certain property held by the Church Commissioners automatically vested in the Chapter of the specified cathedral. Any application to register the Chapter of a cathedral as proprietor relying on the

2021 Measure, s 47 should be accompanied by a statutory declaration confirming that the property formed part of the specified trust at the relevant date.

The Chapter may not dispose of the cathedral church building and certain other property.[15]

Subject to certain exceptions, the 2021 Measure, ss 21 and 22 provide that any acquisition or disposal requires the consent of the Church Commissioners. In each case:

(a) a written statement by the Church Commissioners that the formalities have been complied with will be conclusive evidence of compliance; and
(b) a statement in a document sealed by the Chapter that the Church Commissioners' consent is not required will be conclusive evidence of that fact.

The 2021 Measure, s 22(2) includes additional restrictions on disposals of a house of residence.

These restrictions are in addition to any imposed by the Charities Act 2011.[16] However, where the consent of the Church Commissioners is required, this will be a disposition for which general or special authority is given for the purposes of Charities Act 2011, s 117(3). Consequently, it will comply with any Form E restriction.

31.5 Diocesan boards of finance

A diocesan board of finance is a limited company empowered to hold real and personal property for purposes connected to the Church of England. It is a non-exempt charity and therefore, apart from glebe land, the restrictions on dispositions contained in the Charities Act 2011 normally apply to all land vested in such a board.[17] Such land may, for example, consist of its own corporate property held in accordance with its memorandum and articles of association; property held as trustee for all purposes on specific charitable trusts; and property vested for disposal under schemes made under the Mission and Pastoral Measure 2011 (2011/3). For property held as custodian trustee under Parochial Church Councils (Powers) Measure 1956 (1956/3), s 6 and property held under the Incumbents and Churchwardens (Trusts) Measure 1964 (1964/2), see 31.6 Diocesan authorities.

Glebe land is land owned by the diocesan board of finance as an investment. Historically, its function was to provide an income for the benefice to which it was attached and its incumbent. Much of such glebe land consisted of small parcels of agricultural land and was vested in the incumbent. Since 1 April 1978, glebe land has been vested in the diocesan board of finance of the relevant diocese.[18] The board has power to acquire or appropriate land as glebe land.[19] The power to appropriate is subject to the board obtaining the consent of the Charity Commission.[20]

A diocesan board of finance may sell, exchange, lease, mortgage or otherwise deal with the diocesan glebe land of the diocese. The board must give notice of most transactions to the 'relevant persons' as defined in the 2018 Measure, s 22.

A diocesan board of finance cannot make any of the dispositions specified in the 2018 Measure, s 21(1) without the consent of the Church Commissioners. However, such consent is not required if the disposition is not to a connected person (or a trustee for, or nominee of, a connected person), and various requirements (including as to the obtaining and considering of advice) are complied with. The document giving effect to the disposition must state that either:

(a) the board has obtained the necessary consent; or
(b) the Church Commissioners' consent is not required. If this is the case, the document must also specify the provision of the 2018 Measure which states such consent is not required.[21]

If the consent of the Church Commissioners is required, it must be in writing and signed by a duly authorised person on behalf of the Church Commissioners.[22]

The above restrictions do not apply to grants or appropriation of land for the various church purposes specified in the 2018 Measure, s 23(1).[23]

Where a diocesan board of finance is to be registered as proprietor of land, it may apply to enter a restriction in Form D, the wording of which in this case will be:

> No disposition by the proprietor of the registered estate is to be registered unless the instrument giving effect to the disposition contains either certificate (a) or certificate (b):
>
> (a) the disposition is made in accordance with Part 2 of the Church Property Measure 2018;
> (b) the Church Commissioners are a party to the instrument and have applied their seal to it.

When glebe land previously vested in an incumbent became vested in a diocesan board of finance under Endowments and Glebe Measure 1976 (1976/4), s 15, it was vested subject to all such rights in the nature of easements as were necessary for the reasonable enjoyment of any parsonage land belonging to the benefice or any church land which had been previously exercisable by the incumbent in right of his benefice.[24] Such rights became legal easements appurtenant to the parsonage or church land.[25] This remains the case despite the repeal of s 15 by the 2018 Measure.[26] Consequently, where title devolved to the diocesan board of finance under s 15, HMLR will on first registration of title to the land make the following entry in the charges register:

> The land is subject to such easements as affect the same by virtue of section 15(1)(b) of the Endowments and Glebe Measure 1976 and section 16(3) of the Church Property Measure 2018.

Mission and Pastoral Measure 2011 (2011/3), s 75 confers power, when selling a redundant church or the site of a redundant church, to impose such covenants as to the use of the building or land as it thinks necessary. Covenants imposed under this section[27] are enforceable as if the vendors were the owners of adjacent land and, in the case of covenants of a positive character, as if they were negative and will therefore bind future owners. The Mission and Pastoral Measure 2011 (2011/3) expressly provides that, unlike other restrictive covenants relating to land, such covenants cannot be varied or released on application to the Upper Tribunal (Lands Chamber).

31.6 Diocesan authorities

A diocesan authority may be the diocesan board of finance of the diocese, although in some dioceses, it will be a separate body. A diocesan authority may, as custodian trustee under Parochial Church Councils (Powers) Measure 1956 (1956/3), s 6, hold land on behalf of a parochial church council of a parish. It may also hold land as custodian trustee under the Incumbents and Churchwardens (Trusts) Measure 1964, on behalf of the incumbent and churchwardens of a parish. In either case such land may consist, for example, of a church hall or a house of residence for a curate. Under the provisions of each of those Measures, any such land (other than a lease of less than one year or from year to year) must be vested in the diocesan authority, with the parochial church council or the incumbent and churchwardens (as the case may be) acting as the managing trustees. Neither the parochial church council nor the incumbent and churchwardens may acquire or dispose of any property held or to be held on permanent trusts without the consent of the diocesan authority.

The restrictions on dispositions contained in the Charities Act 2011 would appear to apply to all land vested in a diocesan authority.[28]

Where a diocesan authority is to be registered as proprietor of land, it should apply for entry of an appropriate form of restriction. For example, a restriction in Form A would appear to be appropriate given that the diocesan authority will be holding the land as custodian trustee. The diocesan authority should also consider applying for a restriction in Form E.

Where a diocesan board of finance holds property as diocesan authority, it may appropriate such property to be glebe land. However, as well as obtaining the consent of the Charity Commission discussed in 31.5 Diocesan boards of finance:

(a) if the land is vested in it under Parochial Church Councils (Powers) Measure 1956 (1956/3), s 6(2), it must also obtain the consent of the relevant Parochial Church Council;[29] and
(b) if the land is vested in it under Incumbents and Churchwardens (Trusts) Measure 1964 (1964/2), s 3, it must obtain the consent of the managing trustees of the land.[30]

---

1 See 160 Rights of Reverter.
2 See 30 Charities.
3 Charities Act 2011, s 10(2).
4 LRR 2003, r 182(1).
5 LRR 2003, r 182(2).
6 Church Property Measure 2018 (SI 2018/8) (the 2018 Measure), s 28.
7 The 2018 Measure, s 32(1).
8 See Appendix V. LRR 2003, r 174.
9 The 2018 Measure, s 32(2).
10 The 2018 Measure, s 3(1).
11 Land Registration Rules 1925, r 232.
12 Charities Act 2006, s 11(7).
13 LRR 2003, r 178. See Appendix V.
14 See 31.1 Application of the Charities Act 2011 and 30 Charities.
15 Cathedrals Measure 2021 (SI 2021/2), s 20(1).
16 See 30 Charities.
17 See 31.1 Application of the Charities Act 2011.
18 Endowments and Glebe Measure 1976 (1976/4), s 15.
19 The 2018 Measure, s 19.
20 See also 31.6 Diocesan authorities where the land is vested in the board as diocesan authority.
21 The 2018 Measure, s 46(5).
22 The 2018 Measure, s 46(1).
23 The 2018 Measure, s 23(2).
24 Endowments and Glebe Measure 1976 (1976/4), s 15(1)(b).
25 Endowments and Glebe Measure 1976 (1976/4), s 15(2).
26 The 2018 Measure, s 16(3).
27 Which re-enacts Pastoral Measure 1983 (1983/1), s 62.
28 See 31.1 Application of the Charities Act 2011.
29 The 2018 Measure, s 19(2)(a).
30 The 2018 Measure, s 19(2)(b).

32 CLASSES OF TITLE

The LRA 2002 provides that, on first registration, HMLR may grant one of several different classes of title. The best class of title is absolute title, but HMLR has a discretion to grant a lesser class of title if appropriate. Under the LRA 1925, the court had no jurisdiction to overrule HMLR if it was not prepared to register a title as absolute, or indeed to register it with any class of title.[1] Similarly, there is no provision under the LRA 2002 for an appeal to either a court or the Tribunal in respect of such a decision of HMLR.

In judicial review proceedings, the High Court upheld HMLR's policy of normally granting a possessory title, rather than an absolute title, on first registration of a title based upon adverse possession.[2] The court stated the policy was neither unlawful nor irrational. This was on the basis that it struck a balance between the economic and social interest in having absolute titles which could be readily marketed, on the one hand, and the need to protect the public purse against claims for indemnity, on the other hand.

32.1 Titles to freehold estates

HMLR may register a proprietor of a freehold estate with one of three classes of title: absolute title, qualified title and possessory title.

32.1.1 Absolute title

HMLR may register a person with absolute title if HMLR is of the opinion that the person's title to the freehold estate is such as a willing buyer could properly be advised by a competent professional adviser to accept.[3] In assessing this, HMLR may disregard the fact that a person's title appears to it to be open to objection if it is of the opinion that the defect will not cause the holding under the title to be disturbed.[4]

First registration of a proprietor with absolute title vests the estate in the proprietor:

(a) together with all interests subsisting for the benefit of the estate;[5] and
(b) subject to the following interests affecting the estate at the time of registration:

    (i) interests which are the subject of an entry in the register in relation to the estate;
    (ii) unregistered interests falling within LRA 2002, Sch 1;[6] and
    (iii) interests acquired under the LA 1980 of which the proprietor has notice.[7]

If, on first registration, the proprietor is not entitled to the estate for his own benefit, or not entitled solely for his own benefit, then, as between himself and the persons beneficially entitled to the estate, the estate is vested in him subject to such of their interests as he has notice of.[8]

32.1.2 Qualified title

HMLR may register a person with qualified title if HMLR is of the opinion that the person's title to the estate has been established for a limited period only, or is subject to certain reservations which cannot be disregarded as defects which will not cause the holding under the title to be disturbed.[9] Qualified titles are rarely met with in practice. A qualified title might be given, for example, where the conveyance to the applicant for first registration constituted a breach of trust.

Registration with qualified title has the same effect as registration with absolute title, except that it does not affect the enforcement of any estate, right or interest which appears from the register to be excepted from the effect of registration.[10]

HMLR may upgrade a qualified title to absolute, if HMLR is satisfied as to the title to the estate.[11]

32.1.3 Possessory title

HMLR may register a person with possessory title if HMLR is of the opinion:

(a) that the person is in actual possession of the land, or in receipt of the rents and profits of the land, by virtue of the estate; and
(b) that there is no other class of title with which he may be registered.[12]

The most common situations where HMLR grants possessory title on first registration are where the applicant has been in adverse possession for 12 years or more; and where the applicant has lost the deeds and documents to prove his title. For further details as to such applications, see 6 Adverse Possession and 110 Lost or Destroyed Title Deeds.

Registration with possessory title has the same effect as registration with absolute title, except that it does not affect the enforcement of any estate, right or interest adverse to, or in derogation of, the proprietor's title subsisting at the time of registration or then capable of arising.[13]

HMLR may upgrade a possessory title to absolute if HMLR is satisfied as to the title to the estate.[14]

32.2 Titles to leasehold estates

HMLR may register a proprietor of a leasehold estate with one of four classes of title: absolute title, good leasehold title, qualified title and possessory title.

32.2.1 Absolute title

HMLR may register a person with absolute title if HMLR is of the opinion that the person's title to the leasehold estate is such as a willing buyer could properly be advised by a competent professional adviser to accept and HMLR approves the landlord's title to grant the lease.[15] In assessing this, HMLR may disregard the fact that a person's title appears to it to be open to objection if it is of the opinion that the defect will not cause the holding under the title to be disturbed.[16]

First registration of a proprietor with absolute title vests the estate in the proprietor:

(a) together with all interests subsisting for the benefit of the estate;[17] and
(b) subject only to the following interests affecting the estate at the time of registration:

  (i) implied and express covenants, obligations and liabilities incident to the estate;
  (ii) interests which are the subject of an entry in the register in relation to the estate;
  (iii) unregistered interests falling within LRA 2002, Sch 1;[18] and
  (iv) interests acquired under the LA 1980 of which the proprietor has notice.[19]

If, on first registration, the proprietor is not entitled to the estate for his own benefit, or not entitled solely for his own benefit, then, as between himself and the persons beneficially entitled to the estate, the estate is vested in him subject to such of their interests as he has notice of.[20]

32.2.2 Good leasehold title

HMLR may register a person with good leasehold title if HMLR is of the opinion that the person's title to the leasehold estate is such as a willing buyer could properly be advised by a competent professional adviser to accept.[21] In assessing this, HMLR may disregard the fact that a person's title appears to it to be open to objection if it is of the opinion that the defect will not cause the holding under the title to be disturbed.[22]

Registration with good leasehold title has the same effect as registration with absolute title, except that it does not affect the enforcement of any estate, right or interest affecting, or in derogation of, the title of the landlord to grant the lease.[23]

It is possible to upgrade a good leasehold title to absolute under LRA 2002, s 62(2), if HMLR is satisfied as to the superior title.[24]

32.2.3 Qualified title

HMLR may register a person with qualified title if HMLR is of the opinion that the person's title to the estate, or the landlord's title to the reversion, has been established only for a limited period or subject to certain reservations which cannot be disregarded as defects which will not cause the holding under the title to be disturbed.[25] Qualified titles are rarely met with in practice. A qualified title might be given, for example, where the assignment to the applicant for first registration constituted a breach of trust or in the circumstances set out in 6.10 Adverse possession and leasehold land.

Registration with qualified title has the same effect as registration with absolute title, except that it does not affect the enforcement of any estate, right or interest which appears from the register to be excepted from the effect of registration.[26]

It is possible to upgrade a qualified title to good leasehold if HMLR is satisfied as to the title to the estate; and to absolute if it is satisfied both as to the title to the estate and as to the superior title.[27]

32.2.4 Possessory title

HMLR may register a person with possessory title if HMLR is of the opinion that:

(a) the person is in actual possession of the land, or in receipt of the rents and profits of the land, by virtue of the estate; and
(b) there is no other class of title with which he may be registered.[28]

The most common example of a situation where HMLR may grant a possessory title is where the applicant has lost the deeds and documents to prove his title.

Registration with possessory title has the same effect as registration with absolute title, except that it does not affect the enforcement of any estate, right or interest adverse to, or in derogation of, the proprietor's title subsisting at the time of registration or then capable of arising.[29]

It is possible to upgrade a possessory title to good leasehold, if HMLR is satisfied as to the title to the estate; and to absolute if it is satisfied both as to the title to the estate and as to the superior title.[30]

---

1 *Dennis v Malcolm* [1934] Ch 244.
2 *R (Diep) v Chief Land Registrar* [2010] EWHC 3315 (Admin).
3 LRA 2002, s 9(2).
4 LRA 2002, s 9(3).
5 LRA 2002, s 11(3).
6 For further details, see 128.1 Unregistered interests which override first registration.
7 LRA 2002, s 11(4).
8 LRA 2002, s 11(5).
9 LRA 2002, s 9(4).
10 LRA 2002, s 11(6).
11 LRA 2002, s 62(1). See 181.1 Upgrading possessory or qualified freehold to absolute.
12 LRA 2002, s 9(5).
13 LRA 2002, s 11(7).
14 LRA 2002, s 62(1). See 181.1 Upgrading possessory or qualified freehold to absolute.
15 LRA 2002, s 10(2).
16 LRA 2002, s 10(4).
17 LRA 2002, s 12(3).
18 For further details, see 128.1 Unregistered interests which override first registration.
19 LRA 2002, s 12(4).
20 LRA 2002, s 12(5).
21 LRA 2002, s 10(3).
22 LRA 2002, s 10(4).
23 LRA 2002, s 12(6).
24 LRA 2002, s 62(2). See 181.3 Upgrading good leasehold to absolute.
25 LRA 2002, s 10(5).
26 LRA 2002, s 12(7).
27 LRA 2002, s 62(3). See 181 Upgrade of Class of Title.
28 LRA 2002, s 10(6).
29 LRA 2002, s 12(8).
30 LRA 2002, s 62(3). See 181 Upgrade of Class of Title.

33 COAL

Following the privatisation of the coal industry in 1994, the ownership of almost all coal is now vested in the Mining Remediation Authority, which is a non-departmental public body. The main functions of the Mining Remediation Authority are to manage the coal resources under its control and grant licences for coal exploration and extraction; to provide effective management of subsidence damage claims; and to provide information on past, present and proposed future coal mining activities.

An interest in any coal or coal mine, the rights attached to any such interest and the rights of any person under Coal Industry Act 1994, ss 38, 49 or 51 are unregistered interests which override both first registration and registered dispositions.[1] Accordingly, such interests are protected notwithstanding that there is no entry in the register in respect of them.[2] Coal Industry Act 1994, s 38 deals with rights to withdraw support after the service of notices, s 49 with rights to work coal in land that was formerly copyhold land after the service of notices, and s 51 with rights attaching to underground land. These interests were similarly overriding interests under LRA 1925.[3]

It is not possible to enter a notice in the register in respect of an interest in any coal or coal mine, the rights attached to any such interest and the rights of any person under Coal Industry Act 1994, ss 38, 49 or 51.[4] It was similarly not possible to register or lodge any notice or caution relating to such interests under the LRA 1925. Consequently, such interests are not subject to the duty to disclose overriding interests under LRR 2003, rr 28 and 57.[5]

See also 115 Mines and Minerals.

1 LRA 2002, Sch 1, para 7 and Sch 3, para 7.
2 LRA 2002, ss 11, 12, 29 and 30.
3 LRA 1925, s 70(1)(m) and Coal Industry Act 1994, Sch 9, para 1(1).
4 LRA 2002, s 33(e).
5 See 128.4 Duty to disclose overriding interests.

34 COLLECTIVE ENFRANCHISEMENT

The Leasehold Reform, Housing and Urban Development Act 1993 (LRHUDA 1993) confers on qualifying tenants of flats the right to have the freehold of the building containing the flats acquired on their behalf by their nominee. This right applies whether or not the landlord wishes to sell. The nominee may be a right to enfranchise (RTE) company,[1] for the purposes of that Act, of which the tenants are the members. A person is a 'qualifying tenant' if he is a tenant under a long lease for a term exceeding 21 years whether or not it is determinable by notice or re-entry. LRHUDA 1993 also lays down a framework within which negotiations take place with the aim of entering into a contract for sale in the normal way. Where tenants acquire the premises outside the legislation, by independent negotiation, the provisions of LRHUDA 1993 do not apply.

The Landlord and Tenant Act 1987 confers certain rights on tenants of flats as against their landlord that continue to exist in addition to the provisions of LRHUDA 1993. These include provision for compulsory acquisition by tenants of their landlord's interest in certain circumstances. Where a landlord of a building containing flats is in breach of his obligations to his tenants regarding the maintenance or management of the premises, the court may, on the application of the tenants, make an acquisition order.[2] If granted, the order will provide for the tenant's nominee to be entitled to acquire the landlord's interest in the premises on such terms as may be agreed, or, failing agreement, on such terms as the appropriate tribunal may determine.[3]

34.1 Notice served under Leasehold Reform, Housing and Urban Development Act 1993, s 13

Any right of a tenant arising from a notice served under LRHUDA 1993, s 13 claiming to exercise the right of collective enfranchisement is not capable of being an interest within LRA 2002, Sch 1, para 2 or Sch 3, para 2, which overrides first registration or registered dispositions.[4] However, it may be protected by the entry of a notice as if it were an estate contract. Where the freehold is registered, application may be made for the entry of an agreed notice or a unilateral notice.

34.1.1 Agreed notice

In addition to the usual documents required,[5] an applicant should deliver to HMLR a certified copy of the notice under LRHUDA 1993, s 13. This should satisfy HMLR of the validity of the applicant's claim in accordance with LRA 2002, s 34(3)(c).

The agreed notice in the register will give details of the interest protected.

34.1.2 Unilateral notice

An applicant should deliver to HMLR the usual documents required.[6]

The statement in panel 11 or conveyancer's certificate in panel 12 of form UN1 should be completed on the following lines to show the interest of the applicant:

> [nominee] or [RTE company], notice of collective enfranchisement under section 13 of the Leasehold Reform, Housing and Urban Development Act 1993 having been served by [*tenants*] on [*date*] to [*name and address of landlord*].

The unilateral notice in the register will give brief details of the interest protected and identify the beneficiary of that notice.

34.2 Application for vesting order under Leasehold Reform, Housing and Urban Development Act 1993, s 26(1)

If the qualifying tenants wish to exercise their right to collective enfranchisement but the landlord cannot be found or his identity cannot be ascertained, the court may make a vesting order.[7] An application for such a vesting order is treated as a pending land action[8] and cannot therefore be an interest within LRA 2002, Sch 1, para 2 or Sch 3, para 2, which overrides first registration or registered dispositions.[9] However, such an application may be protected by entry of an agreed notice or a unilateral notice, and a restriction.

34.2.1 Agreed notice

In addition to the usual documents required,[10] the applicants should deliver to HMLR the application to the court for the vesting order or a certified copy of it. This should satisfy HMLR of the validity of the applicants' claim in accordance with LRA 2002, s 34(3)(c).

The agreed notice in the register will give details of the interest protected.

34.2.2 Unilateral notice

The applicants should deliver to HMLR the usual documents required.[11]

The statement in panel 11 or conveyancer's certificate in panel 12 of form UN1 should be completed on the following lines to show the interest of the applicants:

> qualifying tenants in an application under section 26(1) of the Leasehold Reform, Housing and Urban Development Act 1993 in the [*name* County Court] *or* [*name* Division of the High Court of Justice] [*state full court reference and parties*].

The unilateral notice in the register will give brief details of the interest protected and identify the beneficiaries of that notice.

34.2.3 Restriction

The applicants for a vesting order under LRHUDA 1993, s 26(1) are to be regarded as having a sufficient interest in relation to a registered estate or charge if they are applying for a restriction in Form N.[12] The wording of Form N is set out in Appendix IV. HMLR must give notice of the application for a restriction to the proprietor of the registered estate concerned, if it has not been made by or with his consent or a person entitled to be registered as such proprietor.[13] A restriction does not confer any priority. However, it prevents an entry being made in the register relating to any disposition, or a disposition of a specified kind, unless the terms of the restriction have (where applicable) been complied with.

In addition to delivering the usual documents required,[14] the applicants should deliver to HMLR the application to the court for the vesting order or a certified copy of it.

As the application is unlikely to be made by or with the consent of the registered proprietor, the statement in panel 12 or conveyancer's certificate in panel 13 of form RX1 must be completed, confirming that the applicants' interest is that specified in LRR 2003, r 93(q) and setting out details of the application to the court. Any supporting documents should be listed in panel 5 of form RX1 or in a separate form DL.

Panel 9 of form RX1 should set out the appropriate restriction. A possible form of restriction based on the wording of Form N is:

> No [disposition *or specify type of disposition*] of the registered estate by the proprietor of the registered estate [or by the proprietor of any registered charge, not being a charge registered before the entry of this restriction] is to be registered without a written consent signed by [*name*] of [*address*] [or [their conveyancer *or specify appropriate details*]].

A restriction in standard Form N in LRR 2003, Sch 4 does not require the approval of HMLR to the wording of the restriction under LRA 2002, s 43(3).

34.3 Vesting order under Leasehold Reform, Housing and Urban Development Act 1993, s 26(1)

Where the court makes a vesting order under LRHUDA 1993, s 26(1), the LRA 2002 applies in relation to that order as it applies in relation to an order affecting land which is made by the court for the purpose of enforcing a judgment or recognisance.[15] Such a vesting order cannot be an interest within LRA 2002, Sch 1, para 2 or Sch 3, para 2, which overrides first registration or registered dispositions,[16] but it may be protected by an entry of an agreed notice or a unilateral notice, and a restriction.

34.3.1 Agreed notice

In addition to the usual documents required,[17] an applicant should deliver to HMLR the vesting order or a certified copy of it. This should satisfy HMLR of the validity of the applicants' claim in accordance with LRA 2002, s 34(3)(c).

The agreed notice in the register will give details of the interest protected.

34.3.2 Unilateral notice

An applicant should deliver to HMLR the usual documents required.[18]

The statement in panel 11 or conveyancer's certificate in panel 12 of form UN1 should be completed on the following lines to show the interest of the applicants:

> [qualifying tenants] or [nominee] or [RTE company] having the benefit of an order under section 26(1) of the Leasehold Reform, Housing and Urban Development Act 1993 made by the [*name* County Court] *or* [*name* Division of the High Court of Justice] [*state full court reference and parties*].

The unilateral notice in the register will give brief details of the interest protected and identify the beneficiaries of that notice.

34.3.3 Restriction

A person who has obtained a vesting order under LRHUDA 1993, s 26(1) is to be regarded as having a sufficient interest in relation to a registered estate or charge if he is applying for a restriction in Form L or Form N.[19] The wording of Form L is set out in Appendix IV. HMLR must give notice of the application for a restriction to the proprietor of the registered estate concerned if it has not been made by or with his consent or a person entitled to be registered as such proprietor.[20] A restriction does not confer any priority. However, it prevents an entry being made in the register relating to any disposition, or a disposition of a specified kind, unless the terms of the restriction have (where applicable) been complied with.

In addition to delivering the usual documents required,[21] an applicant should deliver to HMLR the vesting order or a certified copy of it.

As the application is unlikely to be made by or with the consent of the registered proprietor, the statement in panel 12 or conveyancer's certificate in panel 13 of form RX1 must be completed, confirming that the applicants' interest is that specified in LRR 2003, r 93(p) and setting out details of the vesting order made by the court. Any supporting documents should be listed in panel 5 of form RX1 or in a separate form DL.

Panel 9 of form RX1 should set out the appropriate restriction(s). A possible form of restriction based on the wording of Form L is:

> No [disposition *or specify type of disposition*] of the registered estate by the proprietor of the registered estate [or by the proprietor of any registered charge, not being a charge registered before the entry of this restriction] is to be registered without a certificate signed by [*name*] of [*address*] [or [their conveyancer *or specify appropriate details*]] that the provisions of [*specify clause, paragraph or other particulars*] of [*specify details*] have been complied with [or that they do not apply to the disposition].

A possible form of restriction based on the wording of Form N is:

> No [disposition *or specify type of disposition*] of the registered estate by the proprietor of the registered estate [or by the proprietor of any registered charge, not being a charge registered before the entry of this restriction] is to be registered without a written consent signed by [*name*] of [*address*] [or [their conveyancer *or specify appropriate details*]].

A restriction in standard Form L or Form N in LRR 2003, Sch 4 does not require the approval of HMLR to the wording of the restriction under LRA 2002, s 43(3).

34.4 Vesting order under Leasehold Reform, Housing and Urban Development Act 1993, s 24(4) or s 25(6)

Although there is no provision in the LRHUDA 1993 relating to the protection of vesting orders made under s 24(4) or s 25(6) in circumstances where there is a dispute between the parties, such orders may be capable of being protected in a manner similar to that relating to vesting orders under s 26(1) as described above.

34.5 Transfer or conveyance to nominee or right to enfranchise company

Once the nominee or RTE company has taken a transfer or conveyance of the freehold estate, an application for registration should be made in the normal way.[22] Where the acquisition is made under the provisions of the LRHUDA 1993, the transfer or conveyance must contain a statement in the following terms:[23]

> This conveyance (or transfer) is executed for the purposes of Chapter 1 of Part 1 of the Leasehold Reform, Housing and Urban Development Act 1993.

The LRHUDA 1993 does not contain any provision for the grant or reservation of statutory easements (unlike the Leasehold Reform Act 1967), and so the parties must include any necessary easements in the conveyance or transfer.

Where the court has made a vesting order under LRHUDA 1993, ss 24(4), 25(6) or 26(1), a certified copy of the order should accompany the application for registration.

Unless there is a contrary agreement, the transfer or conveyance is effective to discharge the property from any mortgage and from the operation of any order made by a court for the enforcement of the mortgage, and to extinguish any term of years created for the purpose of the mortgage.[24] It is the duty of the nominee or RTE company to apply the consideration payable, in the first instance, in or towards the redemption of any such mortgage or charge and, if there are more than one, then according to their priorities.[25] The application for registration must be accompanied by the normal evidence of discharge (for example in form DS1) or by a statutory declaration or statement of truth establishing that the nominee or RTE company has applied a sufficient part of the purchase money in discharge of the mortgage or charge direct to the chargee or into court. HMLR may serve notice of the application upon the chargee, if it considers it necessary. If such evidence is not lodged, HMLR will assume that the mortgage or charge is subsisting.

The transfer or conveyance will normally take effect subject to any existing rentcharge affecting the freehold estate. The landlord may either procure a release of the rentcharge from the rentcharge owner, or require, subject to the reasonable consent of the tenant, that the land be exonerated or the rentcharge apportioned.

HMLR will not automatically cancel notices where an application is received to register a transfer of the freehold and so the applicant for registration should at the same time apply for cancellation or removal of notices previously entered to protect the interest under the LRHUDA 1993, using either form CN1 or form UN2 as appropriate.[26]

34.6 Vendor's lien

A vendor's lien can arise on the transfer to the nominee or RTE company where an amount remains outstanding. The vendor's lien for the price payable extends to amounts which, at the time of the transfer or conveyance, are due to him from his tenants in respect of their leases or any collateral agreements. Presently, the lien also extends to sums payable to the vendor under LRHUDA 1993, s 18(2) (relating to increases in the price where the RTE company has not disclosed the existence of agreements in accordance with s 18(1)) and to any costs of the enfranchisement payable to him under LRHUDA 1993, s 33.[27] However, if/when

Leasehold and Freehold Reform Act 2024 (LFRA 2024), Pt 2 comes into effect such costs will no longer be payable.

For the protection of a vendor's lien by entry of an agreed notice, see 182 Vendor's Liens. Since the items referred to in the previous paragraph (other than the price payable) do not arise under the contract as such, it would appear that the vendor could apply for a notice in respect of the lien in respect of those items after the transfer had been completed.

34.7 Lease back by nominee or right to enfranchise company

Under certain circumstances as set out in LRHUDA 1993, Sch 9, the nominee or RTE company must grant a lease back to the person from whom the freehold has been acquired.[28] For example, a lease back is required where the former freeholder was the immediate landlord of a tenant of a flat let under a secure tenancy.[29] The lease back will be for 999 years at a peppercorn rent,[30] unless the nominee or RTE company and the freeholder have agreed otherwise with the approval of the appropriate tribunal.[31] Such a lease itself requires registration.[32]

34.8 Application for acquisition order under Landlord and Tenant Act 1987, s 28

An application for an acquisition order under Landlord and Tenant Act 1987, s 28 is treated as a pending land action[33] and cannot therefore be an interest within LRA 2002, Sch 1, para 2 or Sch 3, para 2, which overrides first registration or registered dispositions.[34] Such an application may be protected by entry of an agreed notice or a unilateral notice, and a restriction.

34.8.1 Agreed notice

In addition to the usual documents required,[35] the applicants should deliver to HMLR the application to the court for the acquisition order or a certified copy of it. This should satisfy HMLR of the validity of the applicants' claim in accordance with LRA 2002, s 34(3)(c).

The agreed notice in the register will give details of the interest protected.

34.8.2 Unilateral notice

The applicants should deliver to HMLR the usual documents required.[36]

The statement in panel 11 or conveyancer's certificate in panel 12 of form UN1 should be completed on the following lines to show the interest of the applicant:

> qualifying tenants in an application under section 28 of the Landlord and Tenant Act 1987 in the [*name*] Court [*state full court reference and parties*].

The unilateral notice in the register will give brief details of the interest protected and identify the beneficiaries of that notice.

34.8.3 Restriction

The applicants for an acquisition order under Landlord and Tenant Act 1987, s 28 are to be regarded as having a sufficient interest in relation to a registered estate or charge if they are applying for a restriction in Form N.[37] HMLR must give notice of the application for a restriction to the proprietor of the registered estate concerned if it has not been made by or with his consent or a person entitled to be registered as such proprietor.[38] A restriction does not confer any priority. However, it prevents an entry being made in the register relating to any disposition, or a disposition of a specified kind, unless the terms of the restriction have (where applicable) been complied with.

In addition to delivering the usual documents required,[39] the applicants should deliver to HMLR the application to the court for the acquisition order or a certified copy of it.

As the application for a restriction is unlikely to be made by or with the consent of the registered proprietor, the statement in panel 12 or conveyancer's certificate in panel 13 of form RX1 must be completed, confirming that the applicants' interest is that specified in LRR 2003, r 93(o) and setting out details of the application to the court. Any supporting documents should be listed in panel 5 of form RX1 or in a separate form DL.

Panel 9 of form RX1 should set out the appropriate restriction. A possible form of restriction based on the wording of Form N is:

> No [disposition *or specify type of disposition*] of the registered estate by the proprietor of the registered estate [or by the proprietor of any registered charge, not being a charge registered before the entry of this restriction] is to be registered without a written consent signed by [*name*] of [*address*] [or [their conveyancer *or specify appropriate details*]].

A restriction in standard Form N in LRR 2003, Sch 4 does not require the approval of HMLR to the wording of the restriction under LRA 2002, s 43(3).

34.9 Acquisition order under Landlord and Tenant Act 1987, s 28

Where the court makes an acquisition order under Landlord and Tenant Act 1987, s 28, the LRA 2002 applies in relation to that order as it applies in relation to an order affecting land which is made by the court for the purpose of enforcing a judgment or recognisance.[40] Such an order cannot be an interest within LRA 2002, Sch 1, para 2 or Sch 3, para 2 which overrides first registration or registered dispositions,[41] but it may be protected by entry of an agreed notice or a unilateral notice, and a restriction.

34.9.1 Agreed notice

In addition to the usual documents required,[42] the applicants should deliver to HMLR the acquisition order or a certified copy of it. This should satisfy HMLR of the validity of the applicants' claim in accordance with LRA 2002, s 34(3)(c).

The agreed notice in the register will give details of the interest protected.

34.9.2 Unilateral notice

The applicants should deliver to HMLR the usual documents required.[43]

The statement in panel 11 or conveyancer's certificate in panel 12 of form UN1 should be completed on the following lines to show the interest of the applicant:

> qualifying tenants having the benefit of an acquisition order under section 28 of the Landlord and Tenant Act 1987 made by the [*name*] Court [*state full court reference and parties*].

The unilateral notice in the register will give brief details of the interest protected and identify the beneficiaries of that notice.

34.9.3 Restriction

A person who has obtained an acquisition order under Landlord and Tenant Act 1987, s 28 is to be regarded as having a sufficient interest in relation to a registered estate or charge if he is applying for entry of a restriction in Form L or Form N.[44] HMLR must give notice of the application for a restriction to the proprietor of the registered estate concerned if it has not been made by or with his consent or a person entitled to be registered as such proprietor.[45] A restriction does not confer any priority. However, it prevents an entry being made in the register relating to any disposition, or a disposition of a specified kind, unless the terms of the restriction have (where applicable) been complied with.

In addition to delivering the usual documents required,[46] an applicant should deliver to HMLR the acquisition order or a certified copy of it.

As the application is unlikely to be made by or with the consent of the registered proprietor, the statement in panel 12 or conveyancer's certificate in panel 13 of form RX1 must be completed, confirming that the applicants' interest is that specified in LRR 2003, r 93(n) and setting out details of the acquisition order made by the court. Any supporting documents should be listed in panel 5 of form RX1 or in a separate form DL.

Panel 9 of form RX1 should set out the appropriate restriction(s). A possible form of restriction based on the wording of Form L is:

> No [disposition *or specify type of disposition*] of the registered estate by the proprietor of the registered estate [or by the proprietor of any registered charge, not being a charge registered before the entry of this restriction] is to be registered without a certificate signed by [*name*] of [*address*] [*or* [their conveyancer *or specify appropriate details*]] that the provisions of [*specify clause, paragraph or other particulars*] of [*specify details*] have been complied with [or that they do not apply to the disposition].

A possible form of restriction based on the wording of Form N is:

> No [disposition *or specify type of disposition*] of the registered estate by the proprietor of the registered estate [or by the proprietor of any registered charge, not being a charge registered before the entry of this restriction] is to be registered without a written consent signed by [*name*] of [*address*] [*or* [their conveyancer *or specify appropriate details*]].

A restriction in standard Form L or N in LRR 2003, Sch 4 does not require the approval of HMLR to the wording of the restriction under LRA 2002, s 43(3).

34.9.4 Registering the change of ownership

Following a transfer or conveyance of the freehold estate pursuant to the acquisition order, an application for registration should be made in the normal way.[47]

Where the landlord cannot be found, Landlord and Tenant Act 1987, s 33 enables the court to order the vesting of the landlord's interest in a nominated person and for the payment of the purchase money into court. Following the vesting, the appropriate application to register the vesting may be made as above, accompanied by the court order and court receipt for the purchase money.

34.10 Tenants' right of first refusal to purchase the reversion under the Landlord and Tenant Act 1987

A landlord of a building containing flats must not dispose or contract to dispose of an interest in those premises unless he has served a notice of his intention on the tenants giving them collectively a right of first refusal.[48] The Landlord and Tenant Act 1987 contains detailed definitions and prescribed procedures in this regard.

As any offer and any acceptance are deemed to be 'subject to contract', there is at that stage no interest capable of being protected in the register. However, once a contract has been entered into, the tenants can protect their interest by applying for entry in the landlord's title of an agreed notice, using form AN1 or a unilateral notice, using form UN1.[49]

Where a landlord has disposed of an interest in the premises in contravention of the tenants' right of first refusal, the tenants have additional rights such as, where applicable, the right to take the benefit of the contract or to compel the purchaser to sell to them. The notice by which the right is exercised does not itself give an interest that can be protected in the register, but when a binding contract has been entered into in pursuance of the tenants' rights, their interest may, in the case of registered land, be protected by application for entry in the landlord's title of an agreed notice, using form AN1 or a unilateral notice, using form UN1.[50]

34.11 Appointment of manager under the Landlord and Tenant Act 1987

A tenant of a building containing flats or a special measures manager appointed under Building Safety Act 2022, Sch 7, para 4 may apply to the appropriate tribunal for the appointment of a manager if the landlord has failed to manage the premises in accordance with his obligations[51] or the service charges are unreasonable.[52] It may, in the case of registered land, be possible to protect such an application as a pending land action by application for entry in the landlord's title of an agreed notice, using form AN1 or a unilateral notice, using form UN1.[53]

The appropriate tribunal may then, if it thinks fit, make an order appointing a manager to carry out functions in connection with management or functions of a receiver. Any such order may, in the case of registered land, be protected by entry of a suitable non-standard restriction in the register of the landlord's title.[54]

---

1 A private company limited by guarantee, of which all qualifying tenants are entitled to be members, and having as an object the exercise of the right to collective enfranchisement.
2 Landlord and Tenant Act 1987, ss 25, 28 and 29.
3 Landlord and Tenant Act 1987, ss 30 and 31.
4 Leasehold Reform, Housing and Urban Development Act 1993 (LRHUDA 1993), s 97(1).
5 See 119.1 Agreed notice.
6 See 119.3 Unilateral notice.
7 LRHUDA 1993, s 26(1).
8 LRHUDA 1993, s 97(2)(b).
9 LRA 2002, s 87(3).
10 See 119.1 Agreed notice.
11 See 119.3 Unilateral notice.
12 LRR 2003, r 93(q).
13 LRA 2002, s 45.
14 See 153.1 Application for entry of restriction.
15 LRHUDA 1993, s 97(2)(a).
16 LRA 2002, s 87(3).
17 See 119.1 Agreed notice.
18 See 119.3 Unilateral notice.
19 LRR 2003, r 93(p).
20 LRA 2002, s 45.
21 See 153.1 Application for entry of restriction.
22 See 176.1 Registration of transfer or 68 First Registration, as appropriate.
23 LRHUDA 1993, s 34(10) and LRR 2003, r 196(1)).
24 LRHUDA 1993, s 35.
25 LRHUDA 1993, s 35 and Sch 8, para 2.
26 See 119.2 Cancellation of a notice other than a unilateral notice or a home rights notice or 119.5 Removal of a unilateral notice, as appropriate.
27 LRHUDA 1993, s 32(2).
28 LRHUDA 1993, s 36. Once Leasehold and Freehold Reform Act 2024 (LFRA 2024), s 32 is in force, they must also accept such a lease in the circumstances to be set out in LRHUDA 1993, Sch 9, para 3A.
29 LRHUDA 1993, Sch 9, para 2.
30 LRHUDA 1993, Sch 9, para 8.
31 LRHUDA 1993, Sch 9, para 4(1).
32 See 98.2 Leases which are registrable dispositions.
33 Landlord and Tenant Act 1987, s 28(5).
34 LRA 2002, s 87(1) and (3).
35 See 119.1 Agreed notice.
36 See 119.3 Unilateral notice.
37 LRR 2003, r 93(o).
38 LRA 2002, s 45.

39 See 153.1 Application for entry of restriction.
40 Landlord and Tenant Act 1987, s 30(6).
41 LRA 2002, s 87(3).
42 See 119.1 Agreed notice.
43 See 119.3 Unilateral notice.
44 LRR 2003, r 93(n).
45 LRA 2002, s 45.
46 See 153.1 Application for entry of restriction.
47 See 176.1 Registration of transfer or 68 First Registration, as appropriate.
48 Landlord and Tenant Act 1987, ss 1(1) and 5(1).
49 See 119.1 Agreed notice and 119.3 Unilateral notice.
50 See 119.1 Agreed notice and 119.3 Unilateral notice.
51 Including any obligations owed to the special measures manager by virtue of a special measures order.
52 Landlord and Tenant Act 1987, ss 21 and 24ZA.
53 See 119.1 Agreed notice and 119.3 Unilateral notice.
54 See 153 Restrictions.

35 COMMONHOLD

Commonhold is a form of freehold ownership of properties which share common parts. It was introduced by Commonhold and Leasehold Reform Act 2002, Pt 1, which came into force on 27 September 2004. Until it was introduced, such properties were normally held as leasehold because positive covenants to maintain common parts were enforceable under a lease, but not where the land was owned freehold.

Commonhold must be registered at HMLR in accordance with the Commonhold (Land Registration) Rules 2004 (SI 2004/1830) and can only be created out of a freehold estate in land registered with absolute title. It must consist of a minimum of two residential, commercial or industrial units which share common parts. It cannot be a flying freehold, agricultural land or a title which could in certain circumstances revert to someone other than the registered proprietor.[1]

Unit-holders in a commonhold development own the freehold of their own unit and are members of a commonhold association, which owns and manages the common parts. A commonhold unit is each property in the commonhold, as defined in the commonhold community statement. Common parts are all parts of the commonhold which are not a unit.

A commonhold can be created either where there are no unit-holders and a new development is planned or where freeholders or leaseholders agree to convert an existing development into a commonhold. If the title is not yet registered, an application for first registration can accompany an application to register the commonhold.

35.1 The commonhold association

A commonhold association is a private company limited by guarantee incorporated under the Companies Act 1985 or the Companies Act 2006. The members of the company are the unit-holders with each unit being represented by one member.

The two documents which govern a commonhold are the memorandum and articles of association (or, as from 1 October 2009, the articles of association) of the commonhold association and the commonhold community statement. The form and contents of those two documents are prescribed by the Commonhold Regulations 2004 (SI 2004/1829). The memorandum and articles (or articles) define the powers of the association and contain the rules, for example as to voting rights and meetings, under which it operates. Neither document can be designated as an exempt information document.[2]

35.2 The commonhold community statement

The commonhold community statement defines the extent of the commonhold and the extent of the units by reference to a plan; sets out the framework for the commonhold including the regulations for the use and maintenance of the units and the rights and duties of the association and the unit-holders; and describes how management decisions will be taken.

35.3 Applying to register a commonhold

An application to register a freehold estate in commonhold land must be made in form CM1.[3] Application can be for registration either without unit-holders, when it is a new development, or with unit-holders when an existing leasehold or freehold development is being converted to commonhold. The application must be accompanied by the relevant documentation, including consent to registration in form CON1 from relevant interest holders (including the registered proprietor of the freehold estate in the land) or, in appropriate circumstances, a court order dispensing with consent.[4]

35.4 Winding up or dissolution of a community association

If a community association is the subject of a voluntary winding up, or a winding-up order by the court and no successor community association has been appointed, application may be made to HMLR to remove the commonhold entries from the common parts and all the unit titles. The titles will then be ordinary freehold titles and unit-holders will not be able to rely on the rights contained in the commonhold community statement and will need to make arrangements with the liquidator, or whoever the common parts are transferred to, to ensure that new deeds are completed granting them any necessary rights, etc.

---

1 Commonhold and Leasehold Reform Act 2002, Sch 2.
2 Commonhold (Land Registration) Rules 2004 (SI 2004/1830), r 3(3)(c).
3 Commonhold (Land Registration) Rules 2004 (SI 2004/1830), r 5(1).
4 Commonhold and Leasehold Reform Act 2002, s 3.

36 COMMONS

The Commons Registration Act 1965 (CRA 1965) defines common land as land subject to rights of common and waste land of a manor not subject to rights of common. There are more than 500,000 hectares of common land in England and Wales.

The purpose of the CRA 1965 was to establish a record of:

(a) land in England and Wales which was either:

  (i) common land;
  (ii) a town green; or
  (iii) a village green;

(b) the rights of common existing over such land; and
(c) the ownership of the land.

The Commons Act 2006 (CA 2006) is not fully in force yet. When it is, it will repeal the CRA 1965 and the regulations passed under its authority. Currently, s 6 of the CA 2006 applies only in certain pilot areas. In those areas (and elsewhere when its scope is extended), a right of common:

(a) cannot be created by prescription; and
(b) is capable of creation by express grant only if the benefit is attached to identifiable land, so that it will not be a profit à prendre in gross.

The Planning (Wales) Act 2015 has amended the CA 2006 in relation to common land in Wales.

As to town and village greens, see 175 Town or Village Greens.

As a result of the CRA 1965, all common land in England and Wales was required to be registered with the appropriate council by 31 July 1970.[1] After that date no land capable of being registered under the CRA 1965 is deemed to be common land unless so registered.

Registration under the CRA 1965 was of land which is common land, the rights of common over that land, and of the persons claiming to be or found to be owners of that land. No person was to be registered as owner of any land the freehold estate to which was already registered at HMLR.

Where a town or village green was registered under the CRA 1965 and the Commons Commissioner, following enquiry, was not satisfied that any person was the owner of the land, he could direct the registration authority to register as owner the parish council or other appropriate local authority.[2] On registration under that section, the land vested in that local authority. Any such direction should be revealed on a subsequent application for first registration of the land.

Once common land is registered at HMLR, HMLR notifies the appropriate council accordingly. The council then deletes the registration of ownership and indicates that the land is registered at HMLR.[3]

Rights of common, subject to the exceptions stated below, ceased to exist if they were not registered under the CRA 1965. CRA 1965, s 1(1) and CA 2006, s 3(7) provide that no rights of common over land which is capable of being registered under those Acts may be registered in the register of title at HMLR. The express grant or reservation of a right which is capable of being registered under the CRA 1965 is not required to be completed by registration at HMLR.[4] No notice may be entered in the register at HMLR in respect of any interest which is capable of being registered under the CRA 1965.[5] Accordingly, it is not possible to register or enter a notice in respect of any right of common at HMLR. This applies whether the right is in gross or appurtenant to land[6] and whether the right was registered under the CRA 1965 or the Commons Registration (New Land) Regulations 1969 (SI 1969/1843). However, as rights held for a term of years or from year to year are not registrable under the CRA 1965, it follows that leasehold profits à prendre can be registered under the LRA 2002, even if they are of a kind that could otherwise be registered under the CRA 1965. The limitation under the LRA 2002 does not prejudice the effect of registration of any rights of common under the LRA 1925.

Common rights can broadly be described as rights that a person has to take part of the natural produce of another person's land and are in general a kind of profit à prendre which may exist in gross or as appurtenant for the benefit of another parcel of land.[7] However, land affected by cattlegates is sometimes vested in the cattlegate owners as tenants in common.[8]

There are six principal categories of common rights which may be encountered:

(a) rights of common of pasture (rights to turn out cattle to graze);
(b) rights of pannage (rights to turn out pigs to eat acorns and beechmast);
(c) rights of turbary (rights to dig turf or peat for fuel);
(d) rights of estovers (rights to take timber for limited purposes);
(e) rights of piscary (rights to fish); and
(f) rights of common in the soil (rights to dig for sand, stone, coals and minerals).

CRA 1965, s 11 exempts from the effect of that Act the New Forest, Epping Forest and the Forest of Dean and any land exempted by an order of the Minister. Such orders were made in respect of the following areas:

> Austenwood Common (Amersham), Brooks Hill Common (Esher), Cassiobury Common (Watford), Cippenham Village Green Common (Slough), Coleshill Common (Amersham), Coulsdon Common (Croydon), Downside Common (Esher), Farthing Down Common (Croydon), Gold Hill Common (Amersham), Gosford Green (Coventry), Greyfriars Green (Coventry), Hearsall Common (Coventry), Hyde Heath (Amersham), Kenley Common (Croydon), Keresley Common (Coventry), Leigh Hill Common (Esher), Ley Hill Common (Amersham), Little Heath Common (Esher), Lower Tilt Common (Esher), Micklegate Stray (York), Mitcham Common (Merton), Old Common (Esher), Otterbourne Hill Common (Hampshire), Oxshott Heath (Esher), Radford Common (Coventry), Riddlesdown Common (Croydon), Shenfield Common (Brentwood), Sowe Common (Coventry), Spring Park (Bromley), Stivichall Common (Coventry), Stoke Commons (Coventry), The Links Common (Whitley Bay), The Stray (Harrogate), Thorpe Green (Egham), Top Green (Coventry), Upper Tilt Common (Esher), Victoria Gardens (Portland), West End Road Recreation Ground (Southampton), West Wickham Common (Bromley) and Whitley Common (Coventry).

Where a profit affects land exempted from the CRA 1965, it should be dealt with in the usual way.[9]

The Common Land (Rectification of Registers) Act 1989 made provision for removal from the register of common land, on application by the owner, of dwelling houses and land ancillary to dwelling houses. Any such application had to be made by 22 July 1992. A copy of any order made under that Act should be lodged with any application for first registration of the land in question.

36.1 First registration of common land

In addition to the usual documents required,[10] an applicant should deliver to HMLR a copy of the entries in the commons register.

If there are any rights, interests or claims affecting the estate which are known to the applicant, other than those disclosed in the title deeds or form DI, these should be disclosed in form FR1. This would include, for example, any rights in the course of being acquired over the estate by adverse possession, or a disputed third-party claim relating to the estate.

In examining the title, HMLR may have regard to any examination by a conveyancer before the application and to the nature of the property. It may make searches and enquiries and give notice to other persons, direct that searches and enquiries be made by the applicant, and advertise the application.[11]

Any discrepancy between the commons registration ownership register and the deeds must be accounted for. Registration as owner under the CRA 1965 is not conclusive proof of ownership; evidence of the applicant's title must be produced to HMLR in the normal way.

36.2 Dispositions of registered common land

Once common land has been registered, any subsequent registrable disposition of it should be completed by registration in the normal way.[12]

---

1 Commons Registration Act (CRA 1965), s 1(2) and Commons Registration (Time Limits) Order 1966 (SI 1966/1470).

2 CRA 1965, s 8.

3 CRA 1965, s 12 and Commons Registration (England) Regulations 2014 (SI 2014/3038), reg 47.

4 LRA 2002, s 27(2)(d).

5 LRA 2002, s 33(d).

6 Including where an appurtenant right of pasture is severable, as in *Bettison v Langton* [2001] UKHL 24.

7 See 139 Profits à Prendre.

8 *R v Whixley Inhabitants* (1786) 1 Term Rep 137.

9 See 139 Profits à Prendre.
10 See 68 First Registration.
11 LRR 2003, r 30.
12 See 176 Transfers, 98 Leases and 100 Legal Charges.

37 COMPANIES

Certain special provisions apply to registration of and dispositions by a company. The effect of those provisions in relation to a particular company depends upon the type of company concerned and whether or not it is a UK company.

37.1 Registering UK companies as proprietor

Where a UK company (i.e. one registered in England, Wales, Scotland or Northern Ireland under the Companies Acts or in Northern Ireland under the Companies (Northern Ireland) Order 1986 (SI 1986/1032)) applies to be registered as proprietor of a registered estate or registered charge, the application must state its registered number including any prefix. This number will appear in the entry of the company as proprietor in the register. No evidence of the company's powers to hold, sell or otherwise deal with land will normally be required. The same applies to a UK LLP (i.e. one incorporated in the United Kingdom under the Limited Liability Partnerships Act 2000 or the Limited Liability Partnerships Act (Northern Ireland) 2002).[1]

Where a corporation or body of trustees holding on charitable, ecclesiastical or public trusts (other than a non-exempt charity) applies to be registered as proprietor of a registered estate or charge, the application must be accompanied by the document creating the trust.[2]

If the company is, or holds on trust for, a registered social landlord within the meaning of the Housing Act 1996 (HA 1996), the application must include a certificate to that effect.[3] Similarly, if the company is, or holds on trust for, a private registered provider of social housing, the application must include a certificate to that effect.[4]

If the company is, or holds on trust for, an unregistered housing association within the meaning of the Housing Associations Act 1985 and the application relates to grant-aided land as defined in Sch 1 to that Act, the application must include a certificate to that effect.[5]

37.2 Registering entities which are not a UK company as proprietor

Where a corporate body, which is not either:

(a) a UK company,
(b) a UK LLP, or
(c) the trustee of a public, ecclesiastical or charitable trust (other than a non-exempt charity),

applies to be registered as proprietor of a registered estate or registered charge, the applicant for registration must provide evidence of the extent of its powers to hold and sell, mortgage, lease and otherwise deal with land, and, in the case of a charge, to lend money on mortgage.[6] The evidence must include the document(s) constituting the corporation, or a certified copy, and any further evidence HMLR may require.[7] If the evidence is in a language other than English or Welsh, the applicant must also provide a certified translation.

Alternatively, an applicant may provide a certificate:

(a) in Form 7 (for a corporation incorporated outside the United Kingdom) from a qualified lawyer practising in the territory of incorporation; or
(b) in Form 8 (for a corporation incorporated within the United Kingdom) from the applicant's conveyancer.

LRR 2003, Sch 3 contains Forms 7 and 8, the wording of which is set out in Appendix V.[8]

These provisions enable HMLR to be satisfied the applicant has the necessary power to hold, sell and otherwise deal with the registered estate (or to lend money on mortgage, in the case of a registered charge) and to enter any appropriate restrictions in the register.

An application for registration of an overseas company (i.e. one incorporated outside the United Kingdom) must be accompanied by:

(a) details of its territory of incorporation;
(b) its registered number in the United Kingdom; and
(c) an Overseas Entity ID issued by Companies House where it is applying to be registered as proprietor of a qualifying estate.

For these purposes, a qualifying estate is:

(a) a freehold estate in land; and
(b) a leasehold estate in land granted for a term of more than 7 years from the date of grant.[9]

Consequently, no Overseas Entity ID is required when dealing with an interest which is not an estate in land, such as a rentcharge, franchise or profit à prendre in gross.

The Overseas Entity ID must be valid at the date HMLR receives the relevant application.

An overseas company does not need to provide an Overseas Entity ID when applying to be registered as proprietor of a qualifying estate if it is exempted from the requirement by regulations made by the Secretary of State. At the time of writing, no such regulations have been made.

On registering an overseas company as proprietor of a qualifying estate, HMLR must enter a restriction in the register.[10] The current wording of that restriction is:

> No disposition within section 27(2)(a), (b)(i) or (f) of the Land Registration Act 2002 is to be completed by registration unless one of the provisions in paragraph 3(2)(a)–(f) of Schedule 4A to that Act applies.

HMLR must also enter that restriction in the register of any existing qualifying estate owned by an overseas company where HMLR registered that company as proprietor pursuant to an application made on or after 1 January 1999.

If more than one non-UK company is applying to be registered, HMLR will require this information for each of them.

If the corporation is, or holds on trust for, a registered social landlord within the meaning of the HA 1996, the application must include a certificate to that effect.[11] Similarly, if the corporation is, or holds on trust for, a private registered provider of social housing, the application must include a certificate to that effect.[12]

If the corporation is, or holds on trust for, an unregistered housing association within the meaning of the Housing Associations Act 1985 and the application relates to grant-aided land as defined in Sch 1 to that Act, the application must include a certificate to that effect.[13]

37.3 Dispositions by UK companies

In the absence of any restriction in the register, HMLR does not require any evidence of a UK company's power to transfer or otherwise deal with land of which it is the registered proprietor. Although a search of Companies House records is not normally necessary in relation to a registered estate, a purchaser of registered land from a UK company may wish to consider making such a search for the purposes of checking that the company which is shown as the registered proprietor has not been dissolved, or that the company purporting to sell the property is that shown in the register (i.e. that the company registration number and/or other details correspond).

37.4 Dispositions by non-UK companies

Absent any restriction, HMLR does not require any additional evidence of non-UK companies' ability to deal with land. However, many registers for estates held by non-UK companies will now include the restriction referred to in 37.2 Registering entities which are not a UK company.

Where such a restriction applies in the register, any application to register a:

(a) transfer,
(b) lease for a term of more than 7 years from the date of grant, and/or
(c) legal charge,

by the non-UK company must be accompanied by either:

(a) an Overseas Entity ID issued by Companies House which is valid at the date of the application to register the disposition; or
(b) a certificate in form OE1 or OE2 (as the case may be).

Where two or more non-UK companies are registered as proprietor, HMLR will require such evidence for each of them.

Where the non-UK company is registered proprietor, a restriction appears on its register and it claims that one of the exceptions in LRA 2002, Sch 4A, para 3(2) applies, it should include a certificate in form OE1 by a conveyancer with its application. The exceptions are:

(a) that the disposition:

    (i) was made pursuant to a statutory obligation;
    (ii) was made pursuant to a court order;
    (iii) occurred by operation of law;
    (iv) was made pursuant to a contract made before HMLR entered the restriction on the register;

   (v) was made in exercise of a power of sale or leasing conferred on the proprietor of a registered charge or a receiver appointed by the proprietor of such a charge;

(b) that the Secretary of State has consented to the disposition; or
(c) that the disposition is made by a specified insolvency practitioner in specified circumstances. At the time of writing, no secondary legislation setting out who comprises a specified insolvency practitioner and what the specified circumstances are has been passed.

Where a non-UK company is entitled to be registered as proprietor of a qualifying estate, has not yet been so registered but is exercising owner's powers under LRA 2002, s 24(b), HMLR will also require evidence of compliance with the restriction (albeit it has not yet been entered on the register). An applicant wishing to rely on any relevant exception should provide a certificate from their conveyancer in form OE2 rather than form OE1. LRA 2002, Sch 4A, para 4(2) sets out the exceptions which apply in these circumstances. These are:

(a) that the disposition:

   (i) was made pursuant to a statutory obligation;
   (ii) was made pursuant to a court order;
   (iii) occurred by operation of law;
   (iv) was made pursuant to a contract made before the non-UK company became entitled to be registered as proprietor;
   (v) was made in exercise of a power of sale or leasing conferred on the proprietor of a registered charge or a receiver appointed by the proprietor of such a charge;

(b) that the Secretary of State has consented to the disposition; or
(c) that the disposition is made by a specified insolvency practitioner in specified circumstances. At the time of writing no secondary legislation setting out who comprises a specified insolvency practitioner and what the specified circumstances are has been passed.

The non-UK company and every officer of the company commits an offence if they dispose of a qualifying estate without complying with the restriction (unless any exception applies).[14]

Certificates OE1 and OE2 are set out in Appendix VII.

37.5 Registration of a charge created by a UK company

In the case of a UK company, registration of the charge at Companies House should precede an application for registration to HMLR. Registration of a charge of registered land at Companies House alone is insufficient – it should also be completed by registration in accordance with LRA 2002, s 27, to take effect at law and be protected in the register. Likewise, registration of a charge in a debenture at HMLR does not remove the need for it to be registered under the Companies Act 2006.

LRA 2002, s 121 allows the Secretary of State to make rules for HMLR to transmit applications to register charges to Companies House. However, no such rules have yet been made. An applicant must, therefore, apply to Companies House separately. Since 6 April 2013, such application may be made electronically, in which case the certificate of registration will be issued electronically. It is still possible to apply in paper form and the certificate of registration will be issued in paper form; the charge itself will no longer be stamped with Companies House stamp.

When making an application for registration of a charge created by a UK company, the applicant must produce to HMLR the certificate issued under Companies Act 2006, s 859I that the charge has been registered at Companies House under s 859A of that Act,[15] together with a Companies House official copy of the charge or a certificate or confirmation in writing by the lender or a conveyancer that the charge lodged for registration is identical to the copy charge filed at Companies House and is the charge to which the certificate of registration relates.

If the certificate is not produced, HMLR must enter a note in the register stating that no evidence of registration of the charge in accordance with Companies Act 2006, s 859A has been lodged.[16] Similar provisions applied before 6 April 2013 in relation to Companies Act 2006, s 860 or s 878 and, before 1 October 2009, in relation to Companies Act 1985, s 395 or s 410 or the Companies (Northern Ireland) Order 1986 (SI 1986/1032), with any necessary note in the register referring to the relevant provision. The note reflects the fact that where the charge was not registered with Companies House within the prescribed period, it is void against the liquidator or administrator of the company and any creditor of the company.

A fixed legal charge or mortgage of registered land in a debenture can be registered as a registered charge.[17] A fixed equitable charge or floating charge in a debenture may be capable of protection by entry of a notice in the register.[18]

37.6 Execution of deeds by UK companies

Companies Act 2006, s 44 applies to deeds executed by a UK company. The formalities for execution depend upon whether a company executes a deed using a company seal. A deed which has been executed by a company must also be delivered to be effective. In practice, HMLR will assume that a document has been delivered as a deed unless there is some indication to the contrary.

37.6.1 Execution by a company under its common seal

Where a company adopts this form of execution, the common seal will normally be affixed to the deed in the presence of the company secretary and one director, or two directors, who attest the sealing by countersigning the deed and describing themselves by their respective offices. If this is done, a purchaser is protected by LPA 1925, s 74(1) which provides that, in favour of a 'purchaser',[19] an instrument executed in this manner shall be deemed to have been duly executed.

Because Companies Act 2006, s 45 appears to envisage affixing a physical seal to a document, HMLR will not accept documents electronically sealed by a company.

In transfers of registered land and other deeds whose form is prescribed, the attestation clause in Form C in LRR 2003, Sch 9 should be used when a company executes a deed under its common seal.[20]

Most companies have articles of association that authorise the affixing of the company seal to a deed in the presence of people other than a director and the secretary. The protection provided by LPA 1925, s 74(1) is limited to cases where the seal is affixed in the presence of a director and the secretary or two directors. Where a deed is executed by a company affixing its seal in the presence of persons other than a director and the secretary or two directors, HMLR may call for evidence that the persons attesting the affixing of the seal are duly authorised by the company's articles to do so. Where their authority also depends upon a decision by the directors of the company, HMLR may require a certified copy of the board resolution

37.6.2 Execution by a company other than under a common seal

Companies Act 2006, s 44(2)(a) and (3) provides that a document is validly executed by a company if it is signed on its behalf by two 'authorised signatories', being every director of the company and (in the case of a private company with a secretary or a public company) the secretary, or any joint secretary, of the company. In transfers of registered land and other deeds whose form is prescribed, the attestation clause in Form D(i) in LRR 2003, Sch 9 should be used when a company executes a deed in this way.[21]

Companies Act 2006, s 44(2)(b) provides that a company may execute a document by a single director if that signature is witnessed and attested. In transfers of registered land and other deeds whose form is prescribed, the attestation clause in Form D(ii) in LRR 2003, Sch 9 should be used when a company executes the deed in this way.[22]

Authorised signatories may execute a deed on behalf of a company using an electronic signature.[23] The usual requirements for electronic signatures apply in such situations with some modifications. These modifications are set out fully in HMLR's *Practice guide 82: electronic signatures accepted by HM Land Registry*. This is available to view and download at the HMLR website.[24]

Companies Act 2006, s 44(4) and (5) provides that:

(a) a document signed in accordance with s 44(2) of that Act and expressed, in whatever words, to be executed by the company has the same effect as if executed under the common seal of the company; and
(b) in favour of a 'purchaser',[25] a document is deemed to have been duly executed by a company if it purports to be signed in accordance with s 44(2) of that Act.

37.7 Execution of deeds by overseas companies

The Overseas Companies (Execution of Documents and Registration of Charges) Regulations 2009 (SI 2009/1917) provide that a foreign corporation can execute a deed using one of the following three methods.

37.7.1 Execution under common seal

An overseas company possessing a common seal may execute a deed using that seal. The points made above in relation to a UK company apply if a deed is executed in this way.

37.7.2 Execution in a manner permitted by the local law

An overseas company can execute a deed in any manner permitted by the laws of the territory in which the company is incorporated. If the overseas company uses this method, HMLR will require evidence to establish that the manner of execution used is effective according to the laws of the territory of incorporation.

Usually, a letter from a qualified lawyer practising in, or familiar with, the laws of that territory to this effect will suffice. Any such letter should be addressed to HMLR and be unqualified Any documentation in a language other than English or Welsh will need to be accompanied by a certified translation.

37.7.3 Execution by signature of authorised person(s)

A deed may be signed by a person who, in accordance with laws of the territory in which the company is incorporated, is acting under the express or implied authority of the company and expressed (in whatever form of words) to be executed by the company. A deed executed in this way has the same effect as it would have in relation to a company incorporated in England and Wales or Northern Ireland if executed under the common seal of a company so incorporated. In transfers of registered land and other deeds whose form is prescribed, the attestation clause in Form E in LRR 2003, Sch 9 should be used when a foreign corporation executes a deed in this way.[26]

Authorised signatories may execute a deed on behalf of a company using an electronic signature.[27] The usual requirements for electronic signatures apply in such situations with some modifications. These modifications are set out fully in HMLR's *Practice guide 82: electronic signatures accepted by HM Land Registry*. This is available to view and download at the HMLR website.[28]

37.8 Merger of non-UK companies

A merger occurs when a new or existing non-UK company acquires one or more other such companies with the effect that:

(a) the acquiring company absorbs the other companies; and
(b) the existing companies are dissolved without going into liquidation, their assets passing to the remaining company.

Where the existing company is registered proprietor of a legal estate or charge, the acquiring company must apply to HMLR to update the register. The evidence required to do so will depend on whether the merging companies are in a single or multiple jurisdictions.

37.8.1 Merger within a single jurisdiction

In addition to the documents listed in 37.2 Registering entities which are not a UK company, the applicant for registration should provide a letter from a qualified lawyer practising in the relevant jurisdiction confirming:

(a) the registered proprietor has merged with the applicant;
(b) the law of that jurisdiction recognises the applicant as the universal successor and continuing legal personality of the registered proprietor; and
(c) the law of that jurisdiction recognises that all property of the registered proprietor as belonging to the applicant without the need for transfer or other action to vest the property in the applicant.

37.8.2 Cross-border merger

In addition to the documents listed in 37.2 Registering entities which are not a UK company, the applicant for registration should provide:

(a) a letter from qualified lawyers practising in the registered proprietor's former place of incorporation (territory 1) confirming:

  (i) the registerer proprietor has merged with the applicant, the law of territory 1 recognises the applicant as universal successor and continuing legal personality of the registered proprietor; and
  (iii) the law of territory 1 recognises all property of the registered proprietor as belonging to the applicant without the need for transfer or other action to be taken to vest the property in the applicant; and

(b) a letter from qualified lawyers practising in the applicant's place of incorporation (territory 2) confirming:

  (i) the registered proprietor has merged with the applicant;
  (ii) the law of territory 2 recognises the applicant as universal successor and continuing legal personality of the registered proprietor; and
  (iii) the law of territory 2 recognises all property of the registered proprietor as belonging to the applicant without the need for transfer or other action to be taken to vest the property in the applicant.

37.9 Related topics

In addition to the matters discussed above in respect of companies, reference should be made, as appropriate, to 4 Administrative Receivers, 5 Administrators of a Company, 21 Bona Vacantia and Escheat, 49 Debentures, 69 Floating Charges, 108 Liquidators and 146 Receivers Appointed under the Law of Property Act 1925.

---

1 See 105 Limited Liability Partnerships.
2 LRR 2003, r 182. See also 30 Charities.

3 LRR 2003, r 183A(1).
4 LRR 2003, r 183A(1A).
5 LRR 2003, r 183A(2).
6 LRR 2003, r 183(1).
7 LRR 2003, r 183(2).
8 See Appendix V.
9 LRA 2002, Sch 4A, para 1.
10 LRA 2002, Sch 4A, para 3(1).
11 LRR 2003, r 183A(1).
12 LRR 2003, r 183A(1A).
13 LRR 2003, r 183A(2).
14 LRA 2002, Sch 4A, para 6.
15 LRR 2003, r 111(1).
16 LRR 2003, r 111(2).
17 See 100 Legal Charges.
18 See 48 Debentures.
19 As defined in LPA 1925, s 205(1)(xxi).
20 See Appendix VI.
21 See Appendix VI.
22 See Appendix VI.
23 See 57 Electronic Signatures.
24 www.gov.uk/government/collections/land-registration-practice-guides.
25 As defined in Companies Act 2006, s 44(5).
26 See Appendix VI.
27 See 57 Electronic Signatures.
28 www.gov.uk/government/collections/land-registration-practice-guides.

38 COMPULSORY PURCHASE

Public bodies often need to acquire land to carry out their functions, even if the owner does not agree to sell. Consequently, certain statutes provide some public bodies[1] with power to acquire land compulsorily. Such powers may be of general application[2] or to facilitate a particular project.[3] Unless expressly authorised by statute, private companies or persons cannot compulsorily acquire land.

The Acquisition of Land Act 1981 deals with the making and confirmation of compulsory purchase orders. The Compulsory Purchase Act 1965 deals with the process following the confirmation; in particular, the service of notice to treat (i.e. negotiate) and the payment of compensation. Under the Compulsory Purchase Act 1965 there is provision for the vesting of title by deed poll if the owner fails to convey the land. Alternatively, an acquiring authority can rely on the Compulsory Purchase (Vesting Declarations) Act 1981 and make a general vesting declaration. The Housing and Planning Act 2016 made wide-ranging changes to the compulsory purchase regime, including to compensation provisions and access arrangements for acquiring authorities.

38.1 Notice of the compulsory purchase order

Once confirmed, a compulsory purchase order takes effect as a local land charge and the acquiring authority must serve a confirmation notice to HMLR.[4]

Where HMLR is responsible for registration of local land charges in the local authority affected by the compulsory purchase order, such notification will not trigger notification. Instead, the relevant authority must apply for registration under Local Land Charges Rules 2018 (SI 2018/273), r 3. Where HMLR is not the registration authority, it will acknowledge receipt of the notification and advise the notifier to contact the local authority to register the local land charge.

For further details about local land charges, see 109 Local Land Charges.

38.2 Deed poll

Where an owner:

(a) refuses to accept the compensation,
(b) does not show a good title,
(c) refuses to convey or release the land,
(d) is absent from the United Kingdom, or
(e) cannot be found after diligent enquiry,[5]

the acquiring authority may execute a deed poll to vest the land in itself. The acquiring authority must pay compensation into court for the benefit of the owners.

The deed poll must:

(a) contain a description of the land in respect of which the payment into court was made; and
(b) declare the circumstances under which, and the names of the parties to whose credit, the payment into court was made.[6]

The effect of the deed poll is to vest absolutely in the acquiring authority all the estate and interest in the land of the parties for whose use the compensation was paid into court.[7] However, the acquiring authority does not acquire the interests of others; the deed poll does not extinguish any existing easements or restrictive covenants.

38.2.1 Registered land

Where land is registered and the recitals in the deed poll show that the statutory procedures have been followed correctly, this will be sufficient evidence of the disposition for the purpose of LRR 2003, r 161. The deed poll is a registrable disposition under LRA 2002, s 27. In addition to the usual documents required in the case of a transfer,[8] the acquiring authority should deliver to HMLR the deed poll or a certified copy of it.

38.2.2 Unregistered land

Execution of a deed poll does not trigger compulsory first registration, as the vesting of the land takes effect by operation of law. However, an acquiring authority may voluntarily apply for first registration. In addition to the usual documents required,[9] the acquiring authority should deliver to HMLR the deed poll and all other deeds and documents relating to the title that are in the control of the applicant, including relevant Land Charges searches (with any entries accounted for and, where applicable, certified by a conveyancer as not affecting the estate).

If the applicant knows of any rights, interests or claims affecting the estate other than those disclosed in the title deeds or form DI, they should disclose these in form FR1. If the applicant does not produce the title deeds this may not preclude the grant of an absolute title. However, HMLR will normally make a 'protective' entry in the register in respect of the possible existence of undisclosed incumbrances; the entry will state that the land is subject to such easements and restrictive covenants as may have been created or imposed before the date of the deed poll and are still subsisting and enforceable.

A 'certificate of title' under an arrangement with a local authority will not normally be appropriate in relation to a vesting by deed poll, because of the absence of a full investigation of title.

38.3 General vesting declaration

When authorised to acquire land under a compulsory purchase order, an acquiring authority can vest the land in itself by way of a general vesting declaration.[10] The acquiring authority must follow the relevant provisions laid down in the Compulsory Purchase (Vesting Declarations) Act 1981 and in the relevant Regulations. This enables the authority to obtain title to the land more quickly, as vesting is not dependent on the payment or deposit of the compensation money. The effect of the declaration is that the land vests in the acquiring authority at the end of the period specified in the declaration, as if the authority had on that date executed a deed poll. However, the acquiring authority does not acquire the interests of others; the general vesting declaration does not extinguish any existing easements or restrictive covenants.

Before 3 February 2017 (in the case of land situated in England) and 6 April 2017 (in the case of land situated in Wales), the form of declaration was as set out in the Schedule to the Compulsory Purchase of Land (Vesting Declarations) Regulations 1990 (SI 1990/497). That form may still be relevant where a compulsory purchase order was 'authorised' before certain dates.

On 3 February 2017 (in the case of land situated in England) the Compulsory Purchase of Land (Vesting Declarations) (England) Regulations 2017 (SI 2017/3) came into force. The form of declaration in respect of such land, for compulsory purchase orders which are 'authorised' on or after 3 February 2017, is prescribed within those Regulations. The question of whether a compulsory purchase order was 'authorised' on or after that date is set out in those Regulations.

On 6 April 2017 (in the case of land situated in Wales) the Compulsory Purchase of Land (Vesting Declarations) (Wales) Regulations 2017 (SI 2017/362) came into force. The form of declaration in respect of such land, for compulsory purchase orders which are 'authorised' on or after 6 April 2017, is prescribed within those Regulations. The question of whether a compulsory purchase order was 'authorised' on or after that date is set out in those Regulations.

As soon after the execution of the declaration as is possible the acquiring body must serve notices in the prescribed form on every occupier of the land and anyone else who has given information to the acquiring body of any entitlement to compensation.[11] The period stated in the declaration after which the land will vest in the acquiring body must be at least 3 months from the service of such notices.

Unlike a notice to treat, a declaration cannot be withdrawn. Once made, the acquiring authority must proceed with the purchase of the land.[12] A declaration must be made within 3 years of the service of the preliminary notice or such longer period as may be specified in the order.[13] It is possible to challenge the making of a declaration and serving statutory notice of it by way of judicial review.

If the declaration comprises part only of a house, building or factory, or of a park or garden belonging to a house, any person who is able to sell the whole of the property in question may serve a 'counter notice' upon the acquiring authority requiring the authority to purchase the whole. If this notice is served, the part concerned will not vest until the notice has been disposed of. This means, in effect, that the acquiring authority must decide whether to give up its acquisition of the part, acquire the whole, or refer the matter to the Upper Tribunal (Lands Chamber). A 'counter-notice' requiring the acquiring authority to purchase an owner's interest in the whole of his land must normally be served within 28 days of the date on which the acquiring authority serves notice of the execution of the declaration on him.

38.3.1 Registered land

Where the title to the land is registered, the acquiring authority cannot apply for an official search with priority using form OS1 or form OS2 as it is not a 'purchaser' for that purpose.

Where land is registered, the declaration will be sufficient evidence of the disposition for the purpose of LRR 2003, r 161. The declaration is a registrable disposition under the LRA 2002, s 27. In addition to the usual documents required in the case of a transfer,[14] the acquiring authority should deliver to HMLR:

(a) the general vesting declaration or a certified copy of it in the relevant prescribed form and including a plan if only part of the land in the title is affected;
(b) a certificate by the authority's chief executive officer or conveyancer that the service of notice required by Compulsory Purchase (Vesting Declarations) Act 1981, s 6 was completed on a specified date;
(c) confirmation by the chief executive officer or conveyancer that:

    (i) the acquiring authority has not served any notice to treat relating to any land within the declaration that has not been withdrawn; and
    (ii) (where appropriate) that no counter-notice has been served in respect of any land in the declaration; and

(d) where it is not clear from the documents, a covering letter giving details of the statute containing the relevant enabling powers.

If compensation has been fixed or the value of the land agreed so that the HMLR fee can be assessed, it must be paid on delivery of the application. If compensation has not been fixed so that the HMLR fee cannot be assessed, a minimum sum towards the fee must be paid on delivery of the application and an undertaking lodged at the same time to pay the balance, if any, on demand.

38.3.2 Unregistered land

Execution of a general vesting declaration does not 'trigger' compulsory first registration, as the vesting of the land takes effect by operation of law. However, an acquiring authority may voluntarily apply for first registration. In addition to the usual documents required,[15] the acquiring authority should deliver to HMLR:

(a) the general vesting declaration in the relevant prescribed form;
(b) a certificate by the authority's chief executive officer or conveyancer that the service of notice required by Compulsory Purchase (Vesting Declarations) Act 1981, s 6 was completed on a specified date;
(c) confirmation by the chief executive officer or conveyancer that:

    (i) the acquiring authority has not served any notice to treat relating to any land within the declaration that has not been withdrawn; and
    (ii) (where appropriate) that no counter-notice has been served in respect of any land in the declaration; and

(d) where it is not clear from the documents, a covering letter giving details of the statute containing the relevant enabling powers.

If compensation has been fixed or the value of the land agreed so that the HMLR fee can be assessed, it must be paid on delivery of the application. If compensation has not been fixed so that the HMLR fee cannot be assessed, a minimum sum towards the fee must be paid on delivery of the application and an undertaking lodged at the same time to pay the balance, if any, on demand.

If the applicant knows of any rights, interests or claims affecting the estate, other than those disclosed in the title deeds or form DI, they should disclose these in form FR1. If the applicant does not produce the title deeds, this may not preclude the grant of an absolute title. However, HMLR will normally make a 'protective' entry in the register in respect of the possible existence of undisclosed incumbrances; the entry will state that the land is subject to such easements and restrictive covenants as may have been created or imposed before the date of the general vesting declaration and are still subsisting and enforceable.

A 'certificate of title' under an arrangement with a local authority will not normally be appropriate in relation to a vesting under a general vesting declaration, because of the absence of a full investigation of title.

---

1 Defined as acquiring authorities in Acquisition of Land Act 1981, s 7(1).

2 Such as the power conferred on local authorities by Town and Country Planning Act 1990, s 226.

3 For example, the power conferred by High Speed Rail (London – West Midlands) Act 2017, s 4.

4 Acquisition of Land Act 1981, s 15(6) and Transport and Works Act 1992, s 14A(6). If/when the Levelling-up and Regeneration Act 2023 (LURA 2003), s 183 comes into force, it will be possible for compulsory purchase orders to be confirmed conditionally. Then the acquiring authority must serve notice on confirmation of the order and fulfilment of the conditions.

5 Land Clauses Consolidation Act 1845, s 76 and Compulsory Purchase Act 1965, s 9.

6 Land Clauses Consolidation Act 1845, s 77 and Compulsory Purchase Act 1965, s 9(3).

7 Land Clauses Consolidation Act 1845, s 77 and Compulsory Purchase Act 1965, s 9(4).

8 See 176.1 Registration of transfer.

9 See 68.4 Application for first registration.

10 Compulsory Purchase (Vesting Declarations) Act 1981, s 1.

11 Compulsory Purchase (Vesting Declarations) Act 1981, s 6.

12 Although Compulsory Purchase (Vesting Declarations) Act 1981, s 8A does permit the parties to agree to defer the vesting.

13 Compulsory Purchase (Vesting Declarations) Act 1981, s 5A.

14 See 176.1 Registration of transfer.

15 See 68.4 Application for first registration.

39 CONSTRUCTIVE AND RESULTING TRUSTS

Constructive and resulting trusts arise by operation of law in circumstances where equity deems it would be unfair not to recognise the beneficiary's interest in the property. Consequently, they are not required to be in writing.[1]

Any constructive or resulting trust which consists of or includes land is a trust of land.[2]

A resulting trust can arise where a payment was made in or towards the purchase price at the time of acquisition of the land; in equity it will then be presumed that the legal estate will be held on a trust of land, with the contributing person or persons having a beneficial interest proportionate to their contribution to the purchase price. This presumption is rebuttable on evidence to the contrary; for example, where it is shown that the contribution was made by way of gift.

A constructive trust is another form of implied trust and can arise where, for example, a person has acted to his detriment in reliance upon a common intention that he will acquire an interest in the land.

The case law in this area continues to develop and has been the subject of leading decisions by senior courts; in particular the decisions of the House of Lords in *Stack v Dowden*[3] and the Supreme Court in *Jones v Kernott*.[4]

HMLR cannot enter any notice in the register relating to any interest under a trust of land.[5] Where a constructive or resulting trust has arisen, it may be protected by entry of a restriction. A restriction does not confer any priority. However, it prevents an entry being made in the register relating to any disposition, or a disposition of a specified kind, unless the terms of the restriction have (where applicable) been complied with.

39.1 Entry of restrictions

Where:

(a) a registered estate becomes subject to a trust of land, other than on a registrable disposition, or
(b) where the estate is held on a trust of land and there is a change in the trusts,

and a sole or last surviving trustee will not be able to give a valid receipt for capital money, the registered proprietor must apply for entry of a restriction in Form A.[6] The wording of Form A is set out in Appendix IV. Where there are two or more people registered as proprietor of the estate, an application by one or more of them satisfies the obligation. If the registered proprietor(s) do not apply, a person having a beneficial interest under a trust of land has a sufficient interest to apply for entry of a restriction in Form A.[7]

The person having a beneficial interest under a trust of land also has a sufficient interest to apply for entry of a restriction in Form II to ensure that he receives notice of a disposition. The wording of Form II is set out in Appendix IV. This restriction does not prevent a disposition, provided its terms are complied with. This is because the interest of the beneficiary will be overreached where the requirements of Form A have been met.[8]

Unless the application is made by or with the consent of the registered proprietor or a person entitled to be registered as proprietor, HMLR must give notice of an application for a restriction to the proprietor of the registered estate or charge concerned.[9]

Ordinarily, an application for a restriction in Form N, requiring the consent of the beneficiary, will not be appropriate; it would effectively confer upon the beneficiary a right to which he was not entitled and could undermine the principle of overreaching pursuant to the LRA 2002, ss 42(1)(b) and 44(1) and the LPA 1925, ss 2 and 27. The wording of Form N is set out in Appendix IV. However, if the applicant claims the registered proprietor holds on bare trust for him, the applicant may have sufficient interest to justify HMLR entering a Form N restriction

An applicant for a restriction should deliver to HMLR the usual documents required.[10]

The applicant must complete panel 9 of form RX1 with the required restriction(s). A restriction in standard Form A or Form II in LRR 2003, Sch 4 does not require the approval of HMLR to the terms of the restriction under LRA 2002, s 43(3).

If the application is made by a person who claims that he has a sufficient interest in the making of the entry, form RX1 should include either:

(a) a statement in panel 12 of form RX1 signed by the applicant, or
(b) a certificate by his conveyancer in panel 13,

giving details of the nature of the applicant's interest in the entry of the required restriction(s) (or, if the interest is one of those specified in LRR 2003, r 93, stating which of them) and details of how the applicant's interest arose, including details of how the beneficiary's interest under the constructive, resulting or other implied trust of land arose. Any supporting documents should be listed in panel 5 of form RX1 or in a separate form DL.

No fee is currently payable where the application is in respect of a restriction in Form A only.

An applicant does not need to use form RX1 if the application is for a standard form restriction and is contained in either the 'additional provisions' panel of a prescribed form of transfer or assent, or in clause LR13 of a prescribed clauses lease (or any other lease containing clauses LR1 to LR14 of LRR 2003, Sch 1A).[11]

---

1 LPA 1925, s 53(2) and Law of Property (Miscellaneous Provisions) Act 1989, s 2(5).
2 Trusts of Land and Appointment of Trustees Act 1996 (TLATA), s 1.
3 [2007] UKHL 17.
4 [2011] UKSC 53.
5 LRA 2002, s 33(a).
6 LRR 2003, r 94(1) and (2).
7 LRR 2003, r 93(a).
8 LPA 1925, ss 2 and 27.
9 LRA 2002, s 45.
10 See 153.1 Application for entry of restriction.
11 LRR 2003, r 92(7).

40 CONTRACTS FOR SALE (INCLUDING SUB-SALE)

A contract for sale of registered land may be protected by the entry in the register by an agreed notice or a unilateral notice and possibly also (depending on the terms of the contract) a restriction. A notice does not necessarily mean that the contract is valid but does protect the priority of the contract on any registered disposition.[1] A restriction does not confer any priority. However, it prevents an entry being made in the register relating to any disposition, or a disposition of a specified kind, unless the terms of the restriction have (where applicable) been complied with.

LRA 2002, s 72(6)(a) provides that rules may make provision for priority periods in connection with the noting in the register of a contract for the making of a registrable disposition of a registered estate or charge. No such rules have currently been made.

A contract for sale is not itself an interest which overrides either first registration or a registered disposition. A purchaser should protect its priority by entry of a notice in the register. However, even where a contract for sale of registered land is not noted in the register, it may still override a later registered disposition for valuable consideration if, at the time of that later disposition, the person having the benefit of the contract is in actual occupation of the land to which the contract relates. If he is in actual occupation of only part of the land to which the contract relates, he has an overriding interest only in respect of the part he is occupying.[2]

The interest of the person in actual possession does not override a registered disposition if enquiry was made of him before the disposition and he failed to disclose the contract for sale when he could reasonably have been expected to do so. Nor does the contract for sale override a registered disposition if it belongs to a person whose occupation would not have been obvious on a reasonably careful inspection of the land at the time of the disposition, and if the person to whom the disposition is made does not have actual knowledge of the contract for sale at the time of the disposition.[3]

The contract for sale should be made and signed by the proprietor of the registered estate, or a satisfactory chain of title between the person making the contract and the registered proprietor shown. For example, if the registered proprietor has contracted to sell a registered title to A, and A then agrees to sell the land in the title to B by way of sub-sale, B's contract for sub-sale can be protected by a notice, whether or not A's contract is also protected by a notice.

A mortgage of a contract for sale is a general equitable charge. It creates a new interest in land which can be protected by a notice independently of the contract for sale itself, and whether or not the contract for sale has itself been protected by a notice. The notice can be entered in the current proprietor's title, providing a satisfactory chain of title is shown.[4]

40.1 Agreed notice

In addition to the usual documents required,[5] an applicant should deliver to HMLR the contract or a certified copy of it.

Where the consent of the registered proprietor is not available but, for example, the original agreement is signed by him, this is likely to be sufficient to satisfy HMLR as to the validity of the applicant's claim for the purposes of LRA 2002, s 34(3)(c).

Where the contract is in respect of a sub-sale, the earlier contract or a certified copy of it should be included with the application. This is not necessary if there is already a notice of the earlier contract in the register.

The agreed notice in the register will give details of the interest protected.

The applicant may prefer to apply for entry of a unilateral notice, where he does not wish the terms of the contract to be open to public inspection and copying.

40.2 Unilateral notice

An applicant should deliver to HMLR the usual documents required.[6]

The statement in panel 11 or conveyancer's certificate in panel 12 of form UN1 should be completed on the following lines to show the interest of the applicant:

> purchaser under a contract for sale dated [*date*] made between [*registered proprietor*] and [*purchaser*].

In the case of a sub-sale both contracts should be referred to:

> purchaser under a contract for sale dated [*date*] made between [*purchaser*] and [*sub-purchaser*], [*purchaser*] being the purchaser under a contract for sale dated [*date*] made between [*registered proprietor*] and [*purchaser*].

The wording must establish the link between the registered proprietor and the person who is to be shown as the beneficiary of the notice.

The unilateral notice will give brief details of the interest protected and identify the beneficiary of that notice.

40.3 Restriction

HMLR may not enter any restriction to protect the priority of an interest which is, or could be, the subject of a notice.[7] However, this does not prevent HMLR entering a restriction in addition to a notice of the contract. Although the notice protects the priority of the contract, a restriction may be used to ensure that any conditions in relation to another disposition by the registered proprietor are complied with.

The consent of the registered proprietor to the entry of the restriction is required, unless the contract for sale contains a provision which limits the registered proprietor's powers to enter into any further disposition. HMLR must give notice of the application for a restriction to the proprietor of the registered estate or charge concerned, if it has not been made by or with the consent of such proprietor or a person entitled to be registered as such proprietor.[8]

In addition to the usual documents required,[9] an applicant should deliver to HMLR (if the application is made by a person who claims that he has a sufficient interest in the making of the entry) a certified copy of the contract for sale.

The statement in panel 12 or conveyancer's certificate in panel 13 of form RX1 must be completed, setting out details of the contract and of the provision in the contract limiting the registered proprietor's powers to enter into a disposition.

Panel 9 of form RX1 should set out the required restriction(s). A restriction in a standard form contained in LRR 2003, Sch 4 does not require the approval of HMLR to the terms of the restriction under LRA 2002, s 43(3). A possible form of restriction based on Form L in LRR 2003, Sch 4 is:

> No disposition of the registered estate by the proprietor of the registered estate is to be registered without a written certificate signed by [*purchaser*] of [*address*] or their conveyancer that the provisions of [*clause, paragraph or other particulars*] of [*details of contract for sale*] have been complied with or that they do not apply to the disposition.

The wording of Form L is set out in Appendix IV.

---

1 LRA 2002 ss 29, 30 and 32.

2 LRA 2002, ss 29 and 30 and Sch 3, para 2.

3 LRA 2002, Sch 3, para 2.

4 See 9 Agreement for Mortgage.

5 See 119.1 Agreed notice.

6 See 119.3 Unilateral notice.

7 LRA 2002, s 42(2).
8 LRA 2002, s 45.
9 See 153.1 Application for entry of restriction.

41 CONVEYANCERS

The LRR 2003 refer in various contexts to 'conveyancer', including provision for a conveyancer's certificate to be given in relation to certain matters. The definition of 'conveyancer' in LRR 2003, r 217A(1) effectively includes:

(a) solicitors and firms of solicitors;
(b) licensed conveyancers;
(c) barristers;
(d) duly certificated notaries public;
(e) Chartered Institute of Legal Executives (CILEX) conveyancing practitioners;
(f) alternative business structures (licensed bodies);
(g) organisations which employ a person who is a conveyancer and will undertake or direct or supervise conveyancing activities;
(h) local authorities;
(i) the Homes and Communities Agency (trading as Homes England);
(j) the Legal Aid Agency; and
(k) a person carrying out conveyancing activities in the course of his duties as a public officer.

Where a rule, form or restriction does not specify that a form or a certificate must be signed by an individual conveyancer, it can be signed in the name of the conveyancer by an employee. However, r 217A(2) limits the definition of 'conveyancer' in certain contexts.

42 COPYHOLD

Copyhold was an ancient form of tenure, where the owner was the tenant of the lord of the manor. A copyholder would take his grant of land at the manor court of the lord of the manor and the steward would record the admittance on the court roll and give the tenant a copy of the entry – hence the name 'copyhold'. A copyholder was not allowed to transfer his land by conveyance. Instead, if he wanted to sell the land, he had to return to the manor court and surrender the land back into the hands of the lord of the manor on condition that he grant it to the purchaser.

Copyholds could always be enfranchised (i.e. turned into a freehold) by a conveyance of the freehold from the lord of the manor to the copyholder. Various 19th-century statutes allowed for compulsory enfranchisement and the Law of Property Act 1922 abolished copyhold and converted all existing copyholds into freehold land. Any copyhold land then remaining in existence was enfranchised on 1 January 1926.[1] Such enfranchisement did not affect any rights of the lord or tenant in any mines and minerals or ancillary rights, or any rights of the lord in respect of fairs, markets or sporting rights.[2]

On first registration, where the title deduced reveals that the rights of the lord have been preserved under the Law of Property Act 1922 or the earlier Copyhold Acts, HMLR will enter a notice to that effect in the property register. However, the absence of such a notice is not conclusive that the land was not formerly copyhold. Applications are sometimes made to HMLR to have such a notice cancelled on the grounds that Law of Property Act 1922, s 128 and Sch 12 have been repealed by the Statute Law (Repeals) Act 1969. Such applications are misconceived because the repeal of an enactment does not, unless the contrary intention appears, affect any right, privilege, obligation or liability acquired, accrued or incurred under that enactment.[3] No contrary intention appears in the Statute Law (Repeals) Act 1969.

Any unregistered manorial rights were interests which overrode both first registration or a registered disposition.[4] Such interests were therefore protected notwithstanding that there was no entry in the register in respect of them.[5] Consequently, there was a duty to disclose the burden of such rights under LRR 2003, r 28 or r 57.[6] However, such rights ceased to have overriding status at the end of 10 years from 13 October 2003.[7]

The person having the benefit of a manorial right (if its priority has not already been previously defeated and it continues to subsist) should protect it in the register. If he does not do so, the priority of the right may be defeated in favour of a subsequent registrable disposition for valuable consideration which is completed by registration.[8] If the burdened land is unregistered, he should apply for a caution against first registration. If the burdened land is registered, he should apply for the entry of a notice if one does not already appear in the register.

42.1 Caution against first registration

A person applying for a caution against first registration should deliver to HMLR the usual documents required.[9]

No documents should be exhibited, as the statement should be self-contained. The statement of truth in panel 10 of form CT1 should be completed on the following lines to show the interest of the applicant:

> the person entitled to a manorial right affecting that estate being [*set out nature of the manorial right*].

The interest stated in the form CT1 will appear in the caution register, together with a description of the legal estate to which the caution relates. For the effect of a caution against first registration, see 25 Cautions Against First Registration.

42.2 Agreed notice

An applicant should deliver to HMLR the usual documents required.[10]

To establish the validity of his claim for the purposes of entry of an agreed notice, the applicant will normally need to produce evidence:

(a) that the land in question was previously copyhold of the manor in question (usually in the form of a copy of the deed of enfranchisement or compensation agreement);
(b) that it was the custom of the manor in question that the lord had the rights claimed (for example by evidence from the court rolls);
(c) that the rights in question survived enfranchisement (usually in the form of a copy of the deed of enfranchisement or compensation agreement); and
(d) of the applicant's title to the particular manorial rights claimed (usually in the form of an abstract or epitome of title showing the applicant's title to the lordship of the manor and that the rights have not been severed from the lordship).

The agreed notice in the register will give details of the interest protected.

Where the registered proprietor does not consent to the entry in the register of an agreed notice and the applicant cannot provide evidence to satisfy HMLR as to the validity of his claim, they may still apply for entry of a unilateral notice.

42.3 Unilateral notice

An applicant should deliver to HMLR the usual documents required.[11]

The statement in panel 11 or conveyancer's certificate in panel 12 of form UN1 should be completed on the following lines to show the interest of the applicant:

the person having the benefit of a manorial right being [*set out nature of the manorial right*].

The unilateral notice will give brief details of the manorial right protected and identify the beneficiary of that notice.

---

1 Law of Property Act 1922, s 128.
2 Law of Property Act 1922, Sch 12. Copyhold Act 1852, s 48 and Copyhold Act 1894, s 23 excepted similar rights in respect of enfranchisements made under those Acts.
3 Interpretation Act 1978, s 16.
4 LRA 2002, Sch 1, para 11 and Sch 3, para 11.
5 LRA 2002, ss 11, 12, 29 and 30.
6 See 128.4 Duty to disclose overriding interests.
7 LRA 2002, s 117.
8 LRA 2002, s 29.
9 See 25 Cautions Against First Registration.
10 See 119.1 Agreed notice.
11 See 119.3 Unilateral notice.

43 CORRECTION OF MISTAKES IN AN APPLICATION OR ACCOMPANYING DOCUMENT

Where an application or an accompanying document contains a mistake, HMLR may, if it thinks fit, make an alteration to correct the mistake.[1] Where the mistake is of a clerical or like nature, the alteration has effect in all circumstances as if made by the applicant or other interested party or parties. In the case of any other mistake, the alteration has effect as if made by the applicant or other interested party or parties only if the applicant and any other interested party has requested, or consented to, the alteration.[2]

If an applicant discovers such a mistake either during the course of an application or after it has been completed, he should draw it to the attention of HMLR. He may ask HMLR to correct the mistake. However, an applicant cannot insist that HMLR alter a document pursuant to LRR 2003, r 130 – it is entirely at the discretion of HMLR. Further, HMLR's practice is not to make such alterations unless it is not practicable or proportionate for the parties to alter it themselves.

When requesting that HMLR exercise the power under LRR 2003, r 130, an applicant should provide:

(a) evidence to show there is a mistake in the original document. The evidence required will depend on the nature of the alteration sought but might include a statutory declaration or statement of truth by the applicant annexing other supporting evidence;
(b) an explanation of why it is not practicable or proportionate for the parties to correct the mistake themselves;
(c) the consent of all relevant parties to the proposed alteration (where the alteration is not clerical);
(d) an application in form AP1 if any consequential amendments are required to the register; and
(e) the relevant fee for any update to the register.

In deciding whether to alter the document, HMLR will consider the potential effects both on HMLR (for example if the change might give rise to a statutory indemnity claim) and third parties (for example somebody who had already relied on a copy of the unaltered document). In assessing such effects, HMLR may require additional evidence. As a rule of thumb, the older a document is, the less likely HMLR is to exercise the discretion to alter. This is because the number of people who may have relied on the unaltered document is likely to increase over time.

Alterations to documents under LRR 2003, r 130 can only be made if the original deed is lodged at HMLR or if HMLR holds the original of the deed in its file or as a scanned image.

Where an alteration is made under LRR 2003, r 130, it may be necessary to consider whether consequential amendments to the register are required. If such alterations are necessary, an application in form AP1 will be required accompanied by the appropriate fee.[3]

If a proposed alteration does not fall within the scope of LRR 2003, r 130 or HMLR refuses to exercise the statutory discretion, a deed of rectification or corrective disposition may be necessary.[4] Alternatively, a party may be able to apply to the Tribunal for an order rectifying the relevant document under LRA 2002, s 108(2).[5]

---

1 LRR 2003, r 130.
2 LRR 2003, r 130(2).
3 See 67 Fees.
4 See 50 Deeds Amending Dispositions of Registered Titles.
5 See 177 Tribunal.

44 COSTS

The LRA 2002 provides for the payment of costs, both by HMLR and by a third party. In the case of costs payable by HMLR, these may involve costs arising in connection with indemnity, or alternatively the payment of 'non-rectification' costs which do not involve indemnity. In addition, HMLR may pay compensation for maladministration. This may include reimbursement of additional costs occasioned by HMLR's actions.

44.1 Costs payable by HM Land Registry under the Land Registration Act 2002

If HMLR alters the register under LRA 2002, Sch 4 in a case *not* involving rectification, it has discretion to reimburse or contribute towards a party's costs or expenses in connection with the alteration.[1] Where a person is entitled to be indemnified by HMLR under LRA 2002, Sch 8 (including cases involving rectification), an indemnity under that Schedule is payable in respect of loss consisting of costs or expenses incurred by the claimant in relation to the matter.[2] Further, if no indemnity is payable to a claimant under LRA 2002, Sch 8, HMLR has discretion to reimburse or contribute towards the claimant's costs and expenses.[3]

In all the above cases the costs or expenses must be reasonably incurred with HMLR's consent. The requirement of reasonableness applies both to:

(a) the need to incur the cost or expense; and
(b) the amount of the cost or expense.

Accordingly, when applying for HMLR's consent to incur costs, an applicant should set out:

(a) the steps he proposes to take;
(b) the purpose of each step;
(c) the estimated cost of each step; and
(d) how that estimated cost has been calculated.

A person need not obtain HMLR's consent where the costs or expenses must be incurred by the claimant urgently and it is not reasonably practicable to apply for HMLR's consent. However, it would be advisable for that person to notify HMLR of the costs or expenses as soon as practicable to minimise the chance of that person incurring irrecoverable costs. In all cases HMLR may, but is not obliged to, give retrospective consent to incur costs or expenses. HMLR's consent to the incurring of costs or expenses does not mean that it will necessarily pay all, or indeed any, of those costs or expenses.

HMLR must pay interest on indemnity for costs or expenses at the applicable rate for the period from the date when the claimant pays them to the date of payment.[4] In calculating the exact period in respect of which interest is payable, the date when the claimant pays the costs or expenses is excluded, but the date of payment by HMLR is included.

Where a claim to indemnity for costs or expenses under LRA 2002, Sch 8 cannot be resolved by agreement with HMLR, a person may apply to the High Court or a county court for the determination of:

(a) whether he is entitled to such indemnity; and/or
(b) the amount of the indemnity.

The requirement that HMLR consents to the incurring of costs or expenses does not apply to the costs of such an application to the court or of any legal proceedings arising out of such an application.

44.2 Costs payable by HM Land Registry in connection with maladministration

In its 'Principles for Remedy',[5] the Parliamentary and Health Service Ombudsman (PHSO) states:

> Where maladministration or poor service has led to injustice or hardship, public bodies should try to offer a remedy that returns the complainant to the position they would have been in otherwise. If that is not possible, the remedy should compensate them appropriately.

Accordingly, if a person reasonably incurs costs or expenses he would not otherwise have incurred because of HMLR's maladministration, HMLR should reimburse that person. As with statutory payments, it will be incumbent on the claimant to show it was reasonable for him to incur the costs and they were reasonable in amount. Further, the applicant will need to provide evidence that HMLR's maladministration caused him to incur the costs or expenses in question and receipts for those costs or expenses. For further details on maladministration, see 111 Maladministration.

44.3 Costs payable by a third party

Any person who has incurred costs in relation to proceedings before the registrar may request HMLR make an order requiring a party to those proceedings to pay the whole or part of those costs.[6] HMLR may make such an order only where those costs were occasioned by the unreasonable conduct of the party in question in relation to the proceedings.[7] This power relates only to proceedings before the registrar, not to proceedings before the Tribunal.[8]

The request for the payment of costs must be made by delivering to HMLR a written statement by 12 noon on the 20th working day after the completion of the proceedings to which the request relates.[9] A working day is any day from Monday to Friday (inclusive) which is not Christmas Day, Good Friday or any other day either specified or declared by proclamation under Banking and Financial Dealings Act 1971, s 1 or appointed by the Secretary of State, or certified by HMLR as being an 'interrupted day' due to delay or failure of a communication service or to some other event or circumstance causing substantial interruption in the normal operation of HMLR.

The statement must:

(a) identify the party against whom the order is sought;
(b) include an address where notice may be served on that party;
(c) state in full the grounds for the request;
(d) give an address to which communications may be sent; and
(e) be signed by the person making the request or his conveyancer.[10]

HMLR must give notice of the request to the party against whom the order is sought at the address stated and also at any address for service for him stated in a registered title that relates to the proceedings.[11] The notice gives the recipient a period ending at 12 noon on the 20th working day after the issue of the notice, or such other period as HMLR thinks appropriate, to deliver a written response to HMLR by the method and to the address stated in the notice.[12]

The response must:

(a) state whether the recipient opposes the request;
(b) if he does, he must state in full the grounds for that opposition;
(c) give an address to which communications may be sent; and
(d) be signed by the recipient or his conveyancer.[13]

HMLR must determine the matter based on:

(a) the written request and any response submitted to it;
(b) all the circumstances including the conduct of the parties; and
(c) the result of any enquiries HMLR considers it necessary to make.[14]

HMLR may make an order requiring the party against whom it is made to pay to the requesting party the whole, or such part as HMLR thinks fit, of the costs incurred in the proceedings by the person who made the request. The order may specify the sum to be paid or require the costs to be assessed by the court (if not otherwise agreed) and specify the basis of the assessment to be used by the court.[15]

HMLR must send all parties its written reasons for any such order it makes.[16] Such an order is enforceable as an order of the court.[17] A person aggrieved by the order may appeal to a county court, which may make any order which appears appropriate.[18]

---

1 LRA 2002, Sch 4, para 9. For further details about alteration, see 12 Alteration of the Register.
2 LRA 2002, Sch 8, para 3. For further details of when a person is entitled to indemnity, see 86 Indemnity.
3 LRA 2002, Sch 8, para 4.
4 LRR 2003, r 195.
5 www.ombudsman.org.uk/about-us/our-principles/principles-remedy/putting-things-right.
6 LRA 2002, s 76 and LRR 2003, r 202.
7 LRR 2003, r 202(2).
8 For which the Tribunal has power to make an order as to costs (see 54 Disputes).
9 LRR 2003, r 202(3).
10 LRR 2003, r 202(4).
11 LRR 2003, r 202(6).
12 LRR 2003, r 202(8).
13 LRR 2003, r 202(9).
14 LRR 2003, r 202(10).
15 LRR 2003, r 202(12).
16 LRR 2003, r 202(11).
17 LRA 2002, s 76(4).
18 LRA 2002, s 76(5)

45 CREDIT UNIONS

Provided it meets certain requirements set out in the Credit Unions Act 1979, a society may register as a credit union under the Co-Operative and Community Benefits Act 2014. Such a credit union is a body corporate with limited liability.[1] The name of a credit union must include the words 'credit union' or, provided its registered office is in Wales, 'undeb credyd'.[2]

A credit union may hold, purchase or take on lease in its own name any land for the purpose of conducting its business thereon but for no other purpose; it may sell, exchange, mortgage or lease any such land, and erect, alter or pull down buildings on it.[3] It can also hold an interest in land as a mortgagee.

As credit unions have statutory powers to deal with and hold land that does not depend upon their rules, it will not normally be necessary to lodge a copy of the rules when application is made to register such a body as proprietor of registered land.

By virtue of Credit Unions Act 1979, s 11, a credit union has the power, under its rules, to make a loan to a member or another credit union with or without security. Section 11 also imposes limits on the rate of interest the credit union can charge on its loans. Consequently, any application to register a charge in favour of a credit union must be supported by a certificate by its secretary or conveyancer, confirming that the charge is in accordance with the provisions of the Credit Unions Act 1979. HMLR will accept this certificate as evidence of compliance not only with the Act, but also with the rules of the credit union.

A credit union may by special resolution amalgamate with, transfer its engagements to, or accept a transfer of engagements from, another credit union.[4] When applying to register such a disposition, the applicant must provide evidence of such amalgamation in the form of a certified copy of the Acknowledgement of Registration of copy of Special Resolution issued by the Financial Conduct Authority (FCA).[5]

1 Co-operative and Community Benefit Societies Act 2014 (CCBSA 2014), s 3(3).
2 Credit Unions Act 1979, s 3(1).
3 Credit Unions Act 1979, s 12.
4 Credit Unions Act 1979, s 21.
5 See 150 Registered Societies.

46 DAY LIST

The day list is a record of the date and time at which every pending application is made and of every application for an official search with priority.[1] For this purpose 'pending application' does not include an application under LRR 2003, Pt 13 (which covers 'Information etc' such as applications for official copies), except an application to designate a document an exempt information document under LRR 2003, r 136.[2] Notice of an application for an official search with priority remains on the day list until the priority period allowed by the search comes to an end.[3] If HMLR proposes to alter the register without having received an application, it must enter its proposal on the day list and, when so entered, it will have the same effect as if it were an application made at the date and time of its entry.[4]

46.1 Delivery and priority of applications

Unless lodged electronically or in accordance with a written arrangement about delivery made between HMLR and the applicant or his conveyancer, all applications and correspondence should be delivered to:

(a) the 'proper office', as designated by an order of the Secretary of State as the proper office for the receipt of applications;[5] or
(b) if no such order subsists, to HMLR under the provisions of any relevant direction by the registrar under LRA 2002, s 100(4) as to the address to be used for the delivery of applications.[6]

An application is 'received' by HMLR when it is delivered:

(a) to the proper office;
(b) in accordance with a written arrangement as to delivery made between HMLR and the applicant or his conveyancer; or
(c) electronically where that is authorised.[7]

This does not apply to an application under LRR 2003, Pt 13 other than an application to designate a document an exempt information document under LRR 2003, r 136.

An application received *on* a business day is taken as made at the earlier of:

(a) the time of the day that notice of it is entered in the day list; or
(b) midnight marking the end of:

    (i) the day it was received if the application was received before 12 noon; or
    (ii) the next business day after the day it was received if the application was received at or after 12 noon.[8]

An application received on a day which is *not* a business day is taken as made at the earlier of:

(a) the time of the day that notice of it is entered in the day list; or
(b) midnight marking the end of the next business day after the day it was received.[9]

A business day is a day when HMLR is open to the public, that is every day except Saturdays, Sundays, Christmas Day, Good Friday or any other day either specified or declared by proclamation under Banking and Financial Dealings Act 1971, s 1 or appointed by the Secretary of State or certified by HMLR as being an 'interrupted day' due to delay or failure of a communication service or to some other event or circumstance causing substantial interruption in the normal operation of HMLR.[10] If the registrar is satisfied that adequate arrangements have been made or will be in place for opening HMLR for business on any or all of the days referred to above, he may, in such manner as he considers appropriate, give notice to that effect.[11] Following such notice those days will also be business days for the purposes of the LRR 2003.[12]

Entries made in the register on first registration, or on the registration of a disposition required to be completed by registration or entries made, removed or altered as a result of any other application have effect from the time the application is made.[13]

Where two or more applications relating to the same registered title are taken as having been made at the same time, the order in which they should rank in priority as between each other is determined in accordance with the provisions of LRR 2003, r 55.

46.2 Day list information

LRR 2003, r 141 provides for applications for day list information. This includes historic day list information to be provided as well as current day list information. Historic day list information is information that was, but is no longer, kept on the day list. Such applications may be made only during the currency of a relevant notice given under LRR 2003, Sch 2, and subject to and in accordance with the limitations contained in the notice. HMLR must provide the historic day list information in the manner specified in the relevant notice.

---

1 LRR 2003, r 12.
2 LRR 2003, r 12(4).
3 LRR 2003, r 12(2).
4 LRR 2003, r 12(3).
5 LRA 2002, s 100(3).
6 LRR 2003, r 15(3)(a). See 140 Proper Office.
7 LRR 2003, r 15(3).
8 LRR 2003, r 15(1)
9 LRR 2003, r 15(2)
10 LRR 2003, rr 217(1) and 216(1).

11 LRR 2003, r 216(2).
12 LRR 2003, r 216(3).
13 LRA 2002, s 74 and LRR 2003, r 20

47 DEATH OF APPLICANT FOR REGISTRATION

If an applicant dies before HMLR has completed his application, his personal representative may continue the application.[1] The personal representative should lodge a copy of the probate or letters of administration to show that he is the person to whom the applicant's interest has devolved by operation of law and thus entitled to continue the application.

In relation to registered land, where the deceased applicant was applying to be registered as proprietor, the personal representative should consider whether to be registered as proprietor himself or whether to deal with the registered estate or registered charge without being registered as proprietor.[2]

In relation to unregistered land, it is not possible to make an application for first registration in the name of a deceased estate owner (including a deceased mortgagor), as the deceased is not a 'person' for the purpose of LRA 2002, s 9(2), (4) or (5) or s 10(2), (3) or (5); a deceased owner cannot therefore be entered in the register as proprietor. The vesting of the legal estate in a deceased owner's personal representative by operation of law does not trigger compulsory first registration. The personal representative should consider whether to apply for voluntary first registration of title and be registered as proprietor himself or whether to deal with the unregistered estate or charge without making such an application.[3]

Where unregistered land is subject to a mortgage, LRR 2003, r 21 allows a mortgagee under any protected first legal mortgage of a qualifying estate (as defined in LRA 2002, s 4) to apply for registration of the estate charged, whether or not the estate owner consents. This applies only where the mortgage itself is the trigger for compulsory first registration. The mortgagee must apply to register either the executors as proprietor (if the deceased left a will, whether or not a grant has been issued) or the Public Trustee (where the deceased died intestate but no grant of letters of representation has been issued) or the administrators (where the deceased died intestate and a grant has been issued). In the case of any other charge, the mortgagee cannot apply for registration without an estate owner's consent, unless authorised to apply under the mortgage terms or conditions.

---

1 LRR 2003, r 18.

[2] See 133.1 Registration of personal representative and 133.3 Dispositions by personal representatives.
[3] See 133.4 First registration.

48 DEATH OF A REGISTERED PROPRIETOR

The effect of the death of a registered proprietor of a registered estate, and the steps which should be taken to reflect the death, will depend upon whether the deceased was a sole proprietor or one of two or more joint registered proprietors.

48.1 Death of a sole proprietor

On the death of the proprietor, the legal estate will vest in his personal representative by operation of law. As an interim measure, before any further action is taken in relation to the title, an application may be made to note the death in the proprietorship register. This is not obligatory, but it helps to keep the register up to date and reduce the possibility of fraud, particularly if there is likely to be some delay in obtaining a grant of representation.

The application should be made in form AP1, citing 'death of sole proprietor'. There is currently no fee payable. The application must be accompanied by evidence of the death in the form of the original or an office copy of:

(a) the death certificate;
(b) a coroner's certificate of the fact of death;
(c) a grant of probate;
(d) the letters of administration;
(e) a court order appointing the applicant as the deceased's personal representative; or
(f) a certificate of presumed death.

Alternatively, where the registered proprietor died in the United Kingdom, a conveyancer may provide a written confirmation of the fact of death. Such a certificate must include:

(a) the full name of the deceased;
(b) the date of death; and
(c) either the deceased's:

    (i) date of birth; or
    (ii) age at death.

On completion of the application, HMLR will enter a simple note of the death in the register. Where HMLR receives notification from a conveyancer, it will include the conveyancer's name and address in the note. HMLR will not change the address for service, even if requested, unless the personal representative applies to be registered as proprietor at the same time.

Once a grant of representation has been obtained, the personal representative may either apply to register himself as proprietor, execute an assent of the registered estate in favour of the beneficiaries or transfer the property to a third party.[1]

48.2 Death of a joint proprietor

See 92.2 Death of a joint proprietor.

1 See 133.1 Registration of personal representative and 133.3 Dispositions by personal representatives.

49 DEBENTURES

A debenture is used by companies and usually contains one or more charges by way of security by the company to secure money raised by way of loan. If the debenture does not in fact charge land it cannot be protected at HMLR. If a debenture does contain a charge, this may comprise a legal charge, a fixed equitable charge and/or a floating charge.

If a company has created a debenture containing a fixed equitable or a floating charge on its assets, the existence of the charge must be disclosed when the company makes an application for the first registration of its title to an estate affected by the debenture. HMLR will enter a notice of the charge in the register and retain a copy of the debenture.[1]

Where a company that has created a debenture acquires a registered estate or a registered charge, or where a company that is already the proprietor of a registered estate or a registered charge creates a debenture, HMLR will not make any entry in the register to protect any charge created by the debenture (whether registered at Companies House or not) in the absence of a specific application.

For:

(a) registration of a legal charge created by a debenture given by a UK company, see 37.5 Registration of a charge created by a UK company;

(b) registration of a legal created by a debenture by a non-UK company, see 37.4 Dispositions by non-UK companies;
(c) noting of an equitable charge created by a debenture, see 61 Equitable Charges; or
(d) noting of a floating charge created by a debenture, see 69 Floating Charges.

A purchaser taking a transfer of registered land from a company registered with absolute title or good leasehold title need not search that company's file at Companies House for debentures. If any had been created before the company became registered proprietor of the estate, a notice should appear in the register. Further, if the company had created a debenture and then acquired a registered estate, or had become proprietor of a registered estate and then created a debenture, a purchaser of the registered land would not be concerned with any charge created by the debenture unless it was registered or protected in the register.[2]

Where a company is the proprietor of a registered estate and a notice of a fixed equitable charge under a debenture by the company appears in the register, any application to register a lease by the company must be accompanied by the consent of the chargee if the tenant wishes to have absolute leasehold title. Otherwise, HMLR may make a protective entry in the register.[3]

Where a notice of a floating charge under a debenture by a company appears in the register:

(a) any transferee from that company will usually need to lodge a certificate of non-crystallisation;[4] and
(b) the tenant of any lease from that company will need to lodge the consent of the chargee under the floating charge if the tenant wishes to be registered with absolute leasehold title. Otherwise, HMLR may make a protective entry in the register.[5]

---

1 LRR 2003, r 35.
2 LRA 2002, s 29.
3 See 32.2 Titles to leasehold estates.
4 See 69 Floating Charges.
5 See 32.2 Titles to leasehold estates.

50 DEEDS AMENDING DISPOSITIONS OF REGISTERED TITLES

Sometimes it is necessary, due to a clerical error or change of circumstances for example, to correct or otherwise amend a deed which has effected a disposition of a registered estate or charge. The need for correction or amendment may arise before the deed has been completed by registration, or after such registration.

50.1 Amendment before application for registration

If the need to amend an original deed is discovered after it has been executed but before any application to register it has been made, the original deed should be altered to give effect to the parties' true intentions before it is lodged for registration. All alterations to the deed must be authenticated by the signatures of all the parties against each amendment made. If a plan to the original deed is amended or substituted, all the parties should sign the plan. Priority for any additional land added to a disposition effected by the deed should, where necessary, be protected by an official search.

50.2 Amendment after application for registration but before completion of registration

It may be that the need for the amendment of an original deed is not discovered until after the application to register it has been lodged at HMLR. This may result in the application being rejected, or the subject of a requisition, by HMLR and an amendment to the deed is made (as above) in consequence. In other cases, the applicant may request the temporary return of the original deed for amendment, provided the request is made before completion of the application and the intended variation is compatible with keeping the application on the day list.

50.3 Amendment after registration

Where the original deed has been registered, different considerations apply. This is because once the register has been changed to give legal effect to a registrable disposition and reflect the information contained in the deed, it records the existence of the relevant registered estates, charges and legal interests that subsist and the identity of the persons in whom, as registered proprietors, the estates and charges are vested. Consequently, if a further disposition of a registered title is needed, this must be effected by means of a further registrable deed. This must, where necessary, be in the appropriate prescribed form[1] and be completed by registration to take effect at law.[2]

50.3.1 Transfers

If an original transfer transferred the incorrect extent of a registered estate, the correction must be effected by one or more transfers in the prescribed form. Appropriate adjusting provisions may, where necessary, be included in those transfer(s) in relation to easements or covenants, etc contained in the original transfer. If the extent transferred by the original transfer was correct so that no adjusting transfer is required, but other provisions within it require amendment, this may be effected by a deed of variation. There is no prescribed form for such a deed. It must, however, be completed by registration where necessary – for example, if it grants or reserves an easement. In other cases, the appropriate form of application to reflect the deed in the register should be made. The parties will need to take appropriate steps in relation to any existing registered charges and other existing register entries, including compliance with any restriction(s) where necessary.

50.3.2 Leases

If a registered lease has demised the incorrect extent or term, see 98.10 Variation of a lease. In other cases, where certain terms in a registered lease require amendment, this may be effected by a deed of variation. There is no prescribed form for such a deed. It must, however, be completed by registration. The parties will need to take appropriate steps in relation to any existing registered charges and other existing register entries, including compliance with any restriction(s) where necessary.

50.3.3 Charges

Where a registered charge should have included additional registered land that was not referred to in the original charge, the parties may either:

(a) execute a further deed creating a legal charge over the additional land as additional security for the borrowing secured by the original charge; or
(b) replace the existing registered charge with a fresh legal charge that charges both the land charged by the original deed and the additional land as security. The lender would also need to discharge the existing charge.

In either case, the charge would need to be completed by registration.

Where a registered charge includes registered land that should not have been included, the parties should apply to cancel the registration of the charge against the land in question. This should be a discharge of the whole, or the relevant part of the registered charge, as appropriate.

Where the extent charged by a registered charge is correct but certain terms within it require amendment, the parties may either:

(a) replace the existing registered charge with a fresh legal charge that incorporates the revised terms. The lender would also need to discharge the existing charge; or
(b) execute a deed of variation by which they agree to amend the original charge. There is no prescribed form for a deed of variation.

The fresh charge or deed of variation would need to be completed by registration.

50.4 Related topics

For:

(a) amendments to electronically signed documents, see 57.4 Amendment of documents signed using conveyancer-certified electronic signatures;
(b) the correction of mistakes in applications, see 43 Correction of Mistakes in an Application or Accompanying Document;
(c) leases, see 98 Leases;
(d) transfers, see 176 Transfers;
(e) registered charges, see 100 Legal Charges; and
(f) the rectification or setting aside of a document by an order of the Tribunal, see 177 Tribunal.

---

1 LRA 2002, s 25 and LRR 2003, r 206(1).
2 LRA 2002, s 27.

51 DEMESNE LAND

For the purposes of the LRA 2002 'demesne land' is defined as land belonging to His Majesty in right of the Crown which is not held for an estate in fee simple absolute in possession.[1] This does not include land in relation to which a freehold estate in land has determined, but in relation to which there has been no act of entry or management by the Crown.[2] The demesne land of the Crown includes:

(a) the foreshore around England and Wales, except where it has been granted away or it has vested in a private owner;
(b) land which has escheated to the Crown;[3] and
(c) the ancient lands of the Crown which it has never granted away.

Demesne land held by the Crown is not land held for an estate in fee simple. Consequently, it was not capable of registration under the LRA 1925. LRA 2002, s 79(1) provides that His Majesty may grant an estate in fee simple out of demesne land to himself. Such a grant must be followed by an application for first registration. If it is not, the grant is to be regarded as not having been made[4] and the land will continue to be held as demesne land.

The period in which the application for first registration must be made is 2 months beginning with the date of the grant. If, on the application of His Majesty, HMLR is satisfied that there is a good reason for doing so, it may by order extend the period for registration. If HMLR makes an order extending the period for registration where LRA 2002, s 79(2) has already applied, that application of s 79(2) is treated as not having occurred.[5]

Grants of legal estates in land by the King out of demesne land to other parties are normally subject to compulsory registration.[6] Compulsory registration applies to:

(a) a grant by His Majesty out of demesne land of a freehold estate (otherwise than to himself under s 79); and
(b) leases out of demesne land for more than 7 years from the date of the grant which are for valuable or other consideration; by way of gift (including a grant for the purpose of constituting a trust under which His Majesty does not retain the whole of the beneficial interest); or in pursuance of an order of the court.

Compulsory registration does not apply to a grant of an estate in mines and minerals held apart from the surface.

See further 68 First Registration.

LRA 2002, s 83 provides for an 'appropriate authority' to represent, make applications and receive notice on behalf of, His Majesty and the Duchies of Lancaster and Cornwall. For land vested in His Majesty in right of the Crown, this may be the Crown Estate Commissioners; or a government department; or such person as His Majesty may appoint in writing under the Royal Sign Manual.

The LRA 2002 also includes provision for registration of cautions against first registration in respect of demesne land, so that LRA 2002, s 15 (which confers a right to lodge a caution) shall apply as if demesne land were held by His Majesty for an unregistered estate in fee simple absolute in possession.[7]

The LRA 2002 binds the Crown.[8] Consequently, on any application relating to a registered estate the Crown must comply with its provisions.

51.1 First registration

Applications for first registration should be made using form FR1 with such modifications as are appropriate and have been approved by HMLR.[9] The King will be entered as the registered proprietor in the following form:

> THE KING'S MOST EXCELLENT MAJESTY IN RIGHT OF HIS CROWN of the Crown Estate Commissioners, 1 St James's Market, London SW1Y 4AH.

51.2 Cautions against first registration

For the period of 10 years from 13 October 2003, the Queen could lodge a caution against first registration of demesne land as if she held the demesne land for an unregistered estate in fee simple absolute in possession.[10] Any such caution ceased to have effect on 13 October 2013, except in relation to applications for first registration made before the end of that period.[11]

Otherwise, cautions against first registration of demesne land operate in the same way as other cautions against first registrations.[12]

---

1 LRA 2002, s 132(1).
2 LRA 2002, s 132(2).
3 See 21 Bona Vacantia and Escheat.
4 LRA 2002, s 79(2).
5 LRA 2002, s 79(5).
6 LRA 2002, s 80.
7 LRA 2002, s 81.
8 LRA 2002, s 129.
9 LRR 2003, r 23(2).
10 LRA 2002, s 81 and Sch 12, para 15(1).
11 LRA 2002, Sch 12, para 15(2).
12 See 25 Cautions Against First Registration.

52 DEVELOPING ESTATES

A registered title may consist of land which is intended to be developed for residential and/or commercial purposes and divided into plots or units which will be individually transferred or leased. HMLR provides several services relating to such 'developing estate' titles. HMLR encourages developers to utilise these, both to minimise the scope for problems as the estate is being developed and to facilitate registration of subsequent transfers and leases. Those services are:

(a) estate boundary approval;
(b) estate plan approval;
(c) approval of draft transfers and leases; and
(d) pre- and post-registration services on plot sales.

These services are designed to complement each other, but may be used independently if preferred. There are currently no fees for any of these services.

52.1 Estate boundary approval

This service is for use *before* design of the estate layout. It ensures that the developer's initial site survey plan corresponds with the extent of his registered title. Any discrepancies can then be identified and resolved. HMLR can also provide advice on easements intended to be granted.

The developer or his conveyancer should send the initial site survey plan showing the extent of the land included in the development either:

(a) using the form on GOV.UK;[1] or
(b) if the developer or his conveyancer is a HMLR portal user, through the Specialist Support Services area in the HMLR portal.

If it is satisfied that the external boundaries shown on the site survey plan agree with those shown on the title plan and the latest OS map, HMLR will give estate boundary approval. HMLR cannot give such approval until the developer's title has been registered.

If HMLR cannot approve the plan supplied, it will write to the developer or his conveyancer outlining the reasons for this. In appropriate cases, HMLR may provide an illustrative plan showing the extent of the land it considers falls outside the developer's title and details of any title number(s) it falls within.

52.2 Estate plan approval

As early as possible before the first transfer or lease of part is likely to be lodged for registration, the developer or his conveyancer should send the estate plan to HMLR for approval of its use in connection with official searches of the register and official certificates of inspection of the title plan. The developer or his conveyancer should submit the plan to HMLR either:

(a) using the form on GOV.UK;[2] or
(b) if the developer or his conveyancer is a HMLR portal user, through the Specialist Support Services area in the HMLR portal.

The person making the submission must confirm that he is either:

(a) the registered proprietor of the land;
(b) entitled to be registered as the proprietor; or
(c) acting with the consent of the registered proprietor or a person entitled to be registered as proprietor.

Where the developer has used the estate boundary approval service, the estate plan should be based upon the same plan.

The estate plan should show the final layout of the proposed development and must show sufficient detail to enable it to be accurately related to the title plan of the developer's title and the surrounding boundary features. It must be drawn to a suitable scale, usually 1:500; its true scale and orientation must be shown and it must clearly and precisely define each plot or property and identify it by a plot number or other reference. Plot numbers or references must not be duplicated. Plans marked 'For identification only' or with some similar phrase are not acceptable, nor are those bearing a statement of disclaimer intended to comply with the Property Misdescriptions Act 1991.

Where a property comprises more than one parcel (for example a house and separate garage) each parcel must be distinguished on the estate plan by a separate number. If two or more floors of a purpose-built block of flats are co-extensive and the layout of the flats on each floor is identical, it is usually sufficient to lodge the plan of a single floor, but this plan must show the reference numbers distinguishing each flat on each floor. Common areas should be identified. All buildings, drives and pathways should be shown in their correct positions.

HMLR will notify the developer or his conveyancer whether it approves the estate plan in whole or part. HMLR may refuse to approve an estate plan where it believes doing so may mislead members of the public into believing a future development is likely.

The advantages of obtaining estate plan approval are that:

(a) negotiations for the sale of individual plots can proceed without an official copy of the title plan;
(b) applications for official searches of the register and for official certificates of inspection of the title plan may describe the land being purchased by reference to the plot number(s) on the approved plan, so avoiding the need to provide separate plans; and
(c) the approved plan, or extracts from it, can form the basis of transfer or lease plans, ensuring consistency throughout the transaction.

Problems can be avoided if, before contract, the developer checks the position of plot fences on the ground against the approved estate plan. The developer should notify HMLR immediately of any change in the layout of the estate and apply for approval of a new estate plan. Failure to do this may lead to HMLR withdrawing approval of the obsolete part of the plan and in turn to the cancellation of applications for official searches against individual plots. It may also lead to difficulties in the registration of transfers or leases based on the obsolete part of the estate plan.

The developer or his conveyancer should keep HMLR informed of the progress of the development periodically so that new surveys can be undertaken, as necessary.

52.3 Approval of draft transfers and leases

The appropriate form of transfer in LRR 2003, Sch 1, such as form TP1 or form TP2, must be used for transfers of individual plots. In the case of leases of individual plots, the lease will normally need to be in the form of a prescribed clauses lease and contain the prescribed clauses set out in LRR 2003, Sch 1A. A developer or his conveyancer may send HMLR a draft of the proposed form of transfer or lease (with plan) for approval either:

(a) using the form on GOV.UK;[3] or
(b) if the developer or his conveyancer is a HMLR portal user, through the Specialist Support Services area in the HMLR portal.

Approval of the draft transfers and leases ensures consistency and helps avoid difficulties in connection with easements and the development generally. If the draft is approved, it should be used as the basis for all plot transfers or leases on the development.

If the developer intends for an attorney to execute the plot transfers and/or leases on its behalf, it may submit a copy of the relevant attorney with the drafts for approval. HMLR will retain the copy attorney on file and will not require each plot purchaser to supply a copy with their application for registration.

52.4 Pre- and post-registration services on plot sales

HMLR plans are based on the OS map. OS frequently surveys developing estates so HMLR's plans can be revised to show all new buildings, fences, roads and other physical features.

If a draft transfer or lease for the estate has been approved, HMLR will, where appropriate, supply a letter to the developer, which may be passed to purchasers, confirming that if easements are granted in the approved form they will be registered as appurtenant to the purchaser's title. This avoids the need for each purchaser to inspect the title plan to ensure that the developer has power to grant the easements.

Although a developer may have been under a duty to disclose any existing overriding interests when he was registered as proprietor of the land, further overriding interests may subsequently arise or come to light. If these affect more than one plot, they will have to be disclosed with each application to register a transfer or lease of an individual plot. There may therefore be an advantage in a developer applying voluntarily to enter a notice of the burden of any such overriding interests in the register where appropriate, before the development of the estate and sales of individual plots or flats commences.[4]

For details of official copies and certificate of official inspection of the title plan, see 122 Official Copies and Inspection.

---

1 https://customerhelp.landregistry.gov.uk/EPA-start/.

2 https://customerhelp.landregistry.gov.uk/EPA-start/.

3 https://customerhelp.landregistry.gov.uk/EPA-start/.

4 See 128 Overriding Interests.

53 DEVELOPING SCHEMES

Where a local authority or company or similar purchaser acquires a large extent of land in a piecemeal manner over a period of time, they may request that each parcel of land be incorporated into a single registered title as and when it is acquired. This is known as a 'developing scheme title'. It avoids the applicant becoming the proprietor of lots of individual registered titles and subsequently having to request amalgamation. A developing scheme title may be appropriate where, for example, a local authority is in the process of acquiring several individual properties by compulsory purchase, as part of a redevelopment scheme.

The applicant will need to contact HMLR with all the relevant facts before a decision can be made as to whether a development scheme will be appropriate and what extent it will cover. The title to the land to be acquired may be wholly registered, wholly unregistered or a mixture of both.

On receipt of the first application to register a parcel of land within the proposed development, HMLR will allocate a title number. Subsequent additions will be made by amalgamation with this title. HMLR will register leasehold interests and rentcharges within the development scheme separately. When all the land has been acquired and added to the scheme, the applicant should inform HMLR that the scheme is complete, and whether or not the land within the scheme has been redeveloped, so that HMLR has the opportunity (if necessary) to request a survey.

If the development scheme will constitute a large-scale application, the applicant should initially contact the Large Scale Services Team for HMLR (LSST).[1]

---

1 See 96 Large Scale Applications.

54 DISPUTES

Most applications to HMLR are uncontentious. However, some are disputed and the LRA 2002 provides a mechanism to resolve such disputes. If the parties cannot resolve the matter between themselves, it must be determined judicially either by the court or the Tribunal.[1]

54.1 Objections

Generally, anyone may object to an application to HMLR.[2] The exceptions to this general rule are:

(a) only:

(i) the person who lodged the caution against first registration; or
(ii) the current beneficiary of a caution against first registration,

may object to its cancellation;[3] and

(b) only:

(i) the beneficiary of a unilateral notice; or
(ii) a person entitled to be registered as the beneficiary of a unilateral notice,

may object to its cancellation.[4]

In either case, where there are two or more people of the class mentioned above, each such person may object to the cancellation.[5]

Any objection must comply with LRR 2003, r 19. This provides an objection must:

(a) be in writing (but may be delivered by email);
(b) be delivered to the correct office;
(c) be signed by the objector or their conveyancer;
(d) state that the objector objects to the application;
(e) state the grounds for the objection; and
(f) give the full name of the objector and a postal address for service.

The email address for delivery of objections is:

noticeresponse@landregistry.gov.uk.[6]

When HMLR receives a valid objection it:

(a) must give notice of it to the applicant; and
(b) cannot determine the application until the objection has been disposed of.[7]

However, this does not apply where HMLR is satisfied the objection is groundless.[8] If it is so satisfied, HMLR may disregard the objection and continue with the application. Accordingly, when HMLR receives an objection, it will first consider it to determine whether it is groundless.

The LRA 2002 does not define what comprises a groundless objection. HMLR's view is that it is one which cannot possibly succeed either on the facts or law.

This has been described as a 'very low threshold'.[9] If the objection relies on statement of fact, that fact must be credible. Equally, if the objector's claims would not prevent HMLR either making the entry applied for or making it in the form proposed, the objection will be groundless.

In some instances, HMLR may write to the objector to clarify his grounds of objection or provide further information before deciding whether his objection is groundless.

If HMLR determines the objection is groundless, it will write to the objector to explain this and give reasons for that decision. The objector may request a review of that decision in accordance with HMLR's complaints policy. The objector may also be able to seek a judicial review of the decision.

If HMLR decides the objection is not groundless, it will send notice to the applicant with a copy of the objection. The notice will ask the applicant:

(a) if he wishes to proceed with his application notwithstanding the objection; and
(b) if so, whether he wants to have an opportunity to seek a negotiated settlement with the objector.

At the same time as writing to the applicant, HMLR will write to the objector to ask if he would be willing to negotiate.

If the applicant does not respond by the deadline in the notice, HMLR will cancel his application and inform the objector of this. The notification to the objector will include the date of cancellation. If the objector wishes to seek an order for costs, he must apply by 12 noon on the 20th working day after that date.[10]

If all parties wish to negotiate, HMLR will allow them up to 6 months to reach a settlement. HMLR lawyers can exercise a discretion to extend this period in exceptional and unavoidable circumstances when cogent reasons have been given for the need for additional time. During the 6-month period HMLR will only contact the parties twice: once after 3 months of the 6-month period have elapsed, and again after 5 months have elapsed. On each occasion, it will ask if negotiations are continuing. If any party says they are not, HMLR must refer the matter to the Tribunal.[11]

At the 5-month stage HMLR will also provide a draft case summary to the parties for comment in advance of the referral to the Tribunal being made at the end of the 6-month period. The case summary provides brief details of the disputed application, which will be sent to the Tribunal as part of the referral process.

If either party indicates they do not wish to negotiate, HMLR will begin preparation of the draft case summary immediately.

The right to object to an application must not be exercised without reasonable cause. This duty to act reasonably is owed to any person who suffers damage in consequence of its breach.[12] A person in breach of such duty is therefore liable in damages to a person who suffers loss in consequence.

54.2 Referral to the Tribunal

HMLR must refer matters to the Tribunal in accordance with the Land Registration (Referral to the Adjudicator to HM Land Registry) Rules 2003 (SI 2003/2114) (the Referral Rules). HMLR must send the Tribunal a written notice informing it that the matter is being referred under LRA 2002, s 73(7), accompanied by a case summary and copies of the documents listed in that case summary.[13]

HMLR prepares the case summary which is sent to the Tribunal. This must contain:

(a) the names and addresses of the parties;
(b) details of the parties' legal or other representatives;
(c) a summary of the core facts;
(d) details of the disputed application;
(e) details of the objection;
(f) a list of any documents that will be copied to the Tribunal; and
(g) any other information HMLR considers appropriate.[14]

Before sending the case summary to the Tribunal, HMLR must send a copy of it and a list of the accompanying documents to the parties, who may comment on anything in it. HMLR may amend the summary in the light of any comments, but is not required to do so. The case summary does not form part of the pleadings in the proceedings before the Tribunal and does not set out the parties' detailed arguments or deal with their evidence. However, it may be used by the Tribunal to assist in the identification of the matter referred to it for determination.

When the case summary has been finalised HMLR will send it, with copies of the documents listed in it, to the Tribunal under cover of the written notice informing it that the matter is being referred to the Tribunal under s 73(7).

Once HMLR has referred a matter to the Tribunal, an objector cannot bring the proceedings to an end by simply withdrawing his objection. From then on, the matter is within the jurisdiction of the Tribunal, not HMLR.[15] It would appear that a similar principle would apply in relation to a withdrawal of the application itself.

54.3 Determination by the Tribunal

The Tribunal will deal with the matter in accordance with the Tribunal Procedure (First-tier Tribunal) (Property Chamber) Rules 2013 (SI 2013/1169) (the Tribunal Rules). The overriding objective of the Tribunal Rules is to enable the Tribunal to deal with matters fairly and justly.

54.3.1 Should the Tribunal hear the dispute?

The first decision the Tribunal must make is whether to hear the dispute itself or direct a party to commence court proceedings. LRA 2002, s 110(1) provides the Tribunal may direct a party to commence proceedings in court, within a specified period, for the purpose of obtaining the court's decision on the matter.[16] Examples of when the Tribunal may make such a direction are either where it does not have jurisdiction to resolve a key issue between the parties[17] or where the remedies available to it are likely to be insufficient.[18]

Before the Tribunal decides whether to make such a direction, the parties may make representations on:

(a) whether the Tribunal should make a direction;
(b) which party it should direct to commence court proceedings;
(c) the time within which court proceedings must commence; and
(d) the questions the court should determine.[19]

If the Tribunal directs a party to commence court proceedings or a party otherwise commences proceedings, that party must give written notice to the Tribunal and all other parties stating:

(a) that court proceedings have been issued,
(b) the date of issue of the court proceedings,
(c) the names and any known addresses of the parties to the court proceedings,
(d) the name of the court at which the proceedings are pending,
(e) the case number allocated to the court proceedings, and
(f) the way and the extent to which the court proceedings concern or relate to the matter before the Tribunal,

within the time limit specified in the Tribunal Rules, r 38(3) or (4). The party must also advise the parties of the other matters specified in that rule.

If the Tribunal makes a direction to commence court proceedings, the proceedings before the Tribunal are automatically stayed pending the outcome of the court proceedings.[20] Following a final decision by the court, the Tribunal proceedings are to be regarded as stayed (except in relation to any question of costs), although the Tribunal may make a decision, including to lift the stay, if such a decision is necessary to implement the final court order.[21]

54.3.2 Case management

The Tribunal has broad case management powers and may give directions relating to the conduct or disposal of proceedings at any time.[22] The Tribunal may impose a sanction upon a party who fails to comply with a direction, including a sanction that the application be cancelled in whole or part or that HMLR should give effect to the application as if the objection had not been made, as the case may be.[23] Also, the Tribunal may stay proceedings.

The Tribunal must decide which party is the applicant for the purpose of the proceedings before it and which party is the respondent.[24] The parties must each provide the Tribunal with a statement of case and copies of the documents referred to in it.[25] The Tribunal has power to strike out a party's case in certain circumstances, including where the Tribunal considers that the applicant or respondent has no reasonable prospect of succeeding in the proceedings.[26]

54.3.3 Withdrawal

Any party may give notice of withdrawal of his case or any part of it, either orally at a hearing or by lodging with the Tribunal a written notice of withdrawal.[27] However, the notice will not take effect unless the Tribunal consents to the withdrawal.[28] The Tribunal may make such directions or impose such conditions on withdrawal as it considers appropriate.[29] A party may apply to re-instate a case, or part of it, subject to certain time limits as set out in the Tribunal Rules, r 22.

54.3.4 Hearings before the Tribunal

The Tribunal will normally hold a hearing. However, it can determine a dispute without holding a hearing in some circumstances.[30] Any hearings before the Tribunal must be held in public, except where the Tribunal gives a direction that a hearing (or part of it) is to be held in private.[31]

54.3.5 Tribunal decisions

As soon as reasonably practicable after making a decision which finally disposes of all issues in the proceedings (or of a preliminary issue), the Tribunal must provide each party with:

(a) a decision notice stating the Tribunal's decision;
(b) written reasons for the decision; and
(c) notification of any right of appeal against the decision and the time within which, and the manner in which, such right of appeal may be exercised.[32]

The Tribunal must send written notice to HMLR of any direction which requires HMLR to take action.[33] Where the Tribunal has made a decision, that decision may include a direction to HMLR to:

(a) give effect to the original application in whole or in part as if the objection to that original application had not been made; or
(b) cancel the original application in whole or in part.[34]

Such a direction must be in writing, must be sent or delivered to HMLR and may include:

(a) a condition that a specified entry be made on the register of any title affected; or
(b) a direction to reject any future application of a specified kind by a named party to the proceedings either unconditionally or unless that party satisfies specified conditions.[35]

If the Tribunal does not need to serve a decision on HMLR then the parties should send a copy of the decision to HMLR so it can take any appropriate action in the light of it.

A requirement of the Tribunal is enforceable as an order of the court.[36]

Where, in determining a dispute relating to an application under LRA 2002, Sch 6, para 1 for the registration of a person who has been in adverse possession of registered land, the Tribunal determines that it would be unconscionable because of an equity by estoppel for the registered proprietor to seek to dispossess the applicant, but that the circumstances are not such that the applicant ought to be registered as proprietor, the Tribunal must determine how the equity due to the applicant is to be satisfied. It may for that purpose make any order that the High Court could make in the exercise of its equitable jurisdiction.[37]

The Tribunal may make an order for costs in proceedings before it.[38]

The Tribunal may, at the request of the parties but only if it considers it appropriate, make a consent order disposing of the proceedings and making such other appropriate provision as the parties have agreed.[39]

The Tribunal Rules, r 50 provides a conventional 'slip rule'. Rule 51 allows the Tribunal to set aside a decision (or part of a decision) which disposes of proceedings if it is in the interests of justice to do so and one or more of the conditions specified in that rule is fulfilled, such as a document not being received by the Tribunal at the appropriate time or other procedural irregularity.

54.3.6 Appeals

A person aggrieved by a decision of the Tribunal may appeal to the Upper Tribunal, subject to permission to appeal being granted by the Tribunal or the Upper Tribunal. When applying for permission to appeal, a party may at the same time apply for a stay of the implementation of the decision:

(a) appeals on a point of law arise under Tribunals, Courts and Enforcement Act 2007; and
(b) other appeals arise under LRA 2002, s 111.

If, on an appeal to the High Court relating to an application under LRA 2002, Sch 6, para 1 for the registration of a person who has been in adverse possession of registered land, the court determines that it would be unconscionable because of an equity by estoppel for the registered proprietor to seek to dispossess the applicant, but that the circumstances are not such that the applicant ought to be registered as proprietor, the court must determine how the equity due to the applicant is to be satisfied.[40]

54.4 Rectification of documents

The Tribunal may also, on application, make any order which the High Court could make for the rectification or setting aside of a document which:

(a) effects a registrable disposition of a registered estate or registered charge;
(b) effects a disposition in respect of a registered estate or registered charge which creates an interest which may be the subject of a notice in the register;
(c) is a contract to make a disposition falling within (a) or (b) above; or
(d) effects a transfer of an interest which is the subject of a notice in the register.[41]

Any such application must be made direct to the Tribunal and not to HMLR. The general law about the effect of an order of the High Court for the rectification or setting aside of a document applies to any such order of the Tribunal.[42]

---

1 See 177 Tribunal.

2 LRA 2002, s 73(1).

3 LRA 2002, s 73(2) and LRR 2003, r 52(1).

4 LRA 2002, s 73(3) and LRR 2003, r 86(7).

5 LRR 2002, rr 52(2) and 86(8).

6 Direction 4: Electronic address for the delivery of objections under section 73 of the Land Registration Act 2002 (effective 20 March 2022) (www.gov.uk/government/publications/directions-under-the-land-registration-act-2002/direction-4-electronic-address-for-the-delivery-of-objections-under-section-73-of-the-land-registration-act-2002).

7 LRA 2002, s 73(5). Where an objection relates to part only of the land subject to the application and that objection is not groundless, HM Land Registry (HMLR) cannot complete the application in relation to any other land until the dispute is resolved (*R (Sensar Ltd) v Chief Land Registrar* [2021] EWHC 13 (Admin)).

8 LRA 2002, s 73(6).

9 *Silkstone v Tatnall* [2010] EWHC 1627 (Ch) at [17] per Floyd J.

10 See 43.3 Costs payable by a third party.

11 LRA 2002, s 73(7).

12 LRA 2002, s 77.

13 Land Registration (Referral to the Adjudicator to HM Land Registry) Rules 2003 (SI 2003/2114) (the Referral Rules), r 5(2)(a) and (3).

14 The Referral Rules, r 3(2).

15 *Chief Land Registrar and Silkstone v Tatnall* [2011] EWCA Civ 801.

16 LRA 2002, s 110(1).

17 For example, in *Hallman v Harkins* [2019] UKUT 245 (LC) the Upper Tribunal concluded the Tribunal had power to determine whether a party had a beneficial interest in the subject property, but no jurisdiction to quantify that interest.

18 For example, in *Cowie v Ashworth* [2021] UKUT 32 (LC) the Upper Tribunal recognised the Tribunal could not grant the declarative relief sought.

19 Tribunal Procedure (First-tier Tribunal) (Property Chamber) Rules 2013 (SI 2013/1169) (the Tribunal Rules), r 37.

20 The Tribunal Rules, r 39(2).

21 The Tribunal Rules, r 39(3) and (4).

22 The Tribunal Rules, r 6.

23 The Tribunal Rules, r 8.

24 The Tribunal Rules, r 28(3)(c).

25 The Tribunal Rules, rr 28(4) and 30(1).

26 The Tribunal Rules, r 9.

27 The Tribunal Rules, r 22(1).

28 The Tribunal Rules, r 22(3).

29 The Tribunal Rules, r 22(4).

30 The Tribunal Rules, r 31.

31 The Tribunal Rules, r 33.
32 The Tribunal Rules, r 36(2).
33 The Tribunal Rules, r 40(1).
34 The Tribunal Rules, r 40(2).
35 The Tribunal Rules, r 40(3).
36 LRA 2002, s 112.
37 LRA 2002, s 110(4).
38 The Tribunal Rules, r 13. For costs in proceedings before the registrar, see 44.3 Costs payable by a third party.
39 The Tribunal Rules, r 35(1).
40 LRA 2002, s 111(3).
41 LRA 2002, s 108(2) and (3).
42 LRA 2002, s 108(4).

55 DIVISION OF REGISTERED TITLES

Sometimes it is necessary or desirable to divide a registered title. On first registration, HMLR may open an individual register for each separate area of land affected by the proprietor's registered estate as it designates.[1] Subsequently, HMLR may open an individual register for part of the registered estate in a registered title and retain the existing register for the remainder. Such a subsequent division of a registered title may be as the result of an application by the proprietor of the registered estate and of any registered charge over it; or because HMLR considers it desirable for the keeping of the register of title; or on the registration of a charge of part of the registered title.[2] HMLR's power to divide a title is always discretionary.

An application by the proprietor which does not relate to a charge of part should be made in form AP1. It should be accompanied by a plan identifying the division sought. For the position where the application is for a charge of part, see 100 Legal Charges.

Where the proprietor has not made an application but division is effected because HMLR considers it desirable for the keeping of the register of title, HMLR must notify the proprietor of the registered estate and of any registered charge, unless they have agreed to the division. In these circumstances HMLR may make a new edition of any individual register or make entries on any individual register to reflect the division.[3]

LRR 2003, r 70 will apply on division where a registered estate in land includes any mines or minerals but there is no note in the register that they are included, and it is appropriate, when describing any of the registered estates created on division, to do so by reference to the land where the mines or minerals are or may be situated. In such circumstances, HMLR may make an entry in the property register to the effect that such description is an entry made under LRR 2003, r 5(a) and is not a note that the registered estate includes the mines or minerals for the purposes of extending the provision for payment of indemnity under LRA 2002, Sch 8, para 2 to such mines or minerals. LRR 2003, rule 5(a) provides that the property register must contain a description of the registered estate.[4]

---

1 LRR 2003, r 3.

2 LRR 2003, r 3(3).

3 LRR 2003, r 3(5).

4 See 115 Mines and Minerals.

56 ELECTRONIC SERVICES

The LRA 2002 contains provisions which authorise the establishment of an HMLR network to facilitate a system of e-conveyancing.[1] Various consultation exercises on such a system have been carried out by HMLR in recent years, as a result of which HMLR has concluded that the system should be introduced in stages over a period of time rather than in one major change.

HMLR's 'Business e-services' are accessed through the HMLR portal, which is HMLR's web-based electronic channel, and are divided into three service groups each governed by an agreement between HMLR and the user:

(a) 'Information Services' provide online access to information about the register, title plan and day list. These can be used to lodge searches of the index map with supporting plans, official searches of whole or part, and to conduct land charges and bankruptcy searches in the Land Charges Department. There is no interaction with the register.
(b) 'Network Services' are available to users who have applied for and been granted a network access agreement. These permit the creation and lodgement of e-documents and electronic substantive applications directly with HMLR. This includes the facility to use e-signatures, where appropriate and for the electronic attachment of supporting documents and certificates of compliance, if necessary. A subscriber to Network Services also has access to Information Services. Network access agreements are dealt with in LRA 2002, s 92 and Sch 5 and the Land Registration (Network Access) Rules 2008 (SI 2008/1748).
(c) 'Lender Services' provides an automated discharge service that allows mortgage lenders, or their appointed agents, to lodge electronic applications to discharge registered charges (see 100.11 Discharge of registered charge).

HMLR's DRS is available through its portal and also through its 'business to business' channel called 'Business Gateway'. DRS dispenses with the need for a form AP1 and certain other application forms and allows applicants to supply the necessary information to HMLR in a digital format. This allows some of the data to be checked against the register and for some fields to be automatically completed, resulting in fewer requisitions. If any requisitions do arise, HMLR will deliver them to the applicant electronically. Replies to requisitions and further documents must be lodged using the Reply to Requisition function in the portal.

Business e-services have been developed for business users and are not available to individual members of the public. Instead, HMLR provides a free service for use by the general public known as 'Search for land and property information'. This allows users to search by:

(a) postcode;
(b) street and town;
(c) map;
(d) title number; and
(e) INSPIRE ID.

It displays:

(a) the postal address;
(b) property description from the register;
(c) tenure type;
(d) last price paid and date of sale;
(e) whether the property is subject to restrictive covenants (although not the details of those covenants); and
(f) whether the property enjoys the benefit of or is subject to any easements (although not the details of those easements).

Users can also register for an account and purchase copies of the register and title plan for the property.

Due to the increasing demand for electronic services, to enable conveyancing and registration to be carried out entirely online, the LRR 2003 were amended with effect from 6 April 2018 to provide more flexibility for the introduction of new electronic conveyancing and registration services. LRR 2003, rr 54A to 54D specify that all transactions of registered land that have to be registered can be carried out using electronic documents with electronic signatures, once the registrar is satisfied that adequate arrangements are in place and publishes a notice to that effect. This allows for the incremental introduction of new digital conveyancing and registration services (such as a new digital mortgage service), without rule changes for each new service.

The latest information on HMLR's Business e-services is available on the Government website.[2]

---

[1] LRA 2002, ss 91 to 95 and Sch 5.

[2] www.gov.uk/guidance/apply-for-hm-land-registry-business-e-services.

57 ELECTRONIC SIGNATURES

Previously, HMLR would not accept deeds which had been signed electronically. However, with the COVID-19 pandemic and resultant lockdowns, HMLR began to accept such documents, buoyed by the Law Commission's conclusion that electronically signed deeds could be validly executed for the purposes of Law of Property (Miscellaneous Provisions) Act 1989, s 2.[1]

HMLR currently accepts three forms of electronically signed documents:

(a) Mercury signed documents;
(b) conveyancer-certified electronic signatures; and
(c) qualified electronic signatures.

57.1 Mercury signed documents

Mercury signing requires parties to print out and execute the signature page of a document before returning the final document and a copy of their signature to their conveyancer. The High Court accepted the validity of Mercury signatures when executing a deed in *R (Mercury Tax Group Ltd) v HMRC*.[2]

HMLR will only accept some documents signed using Mercury signing. HMLR's *Practice Guide 82: electronic signatures accepted by HM Land Registry* contains a list of those documents. This is available to view and download at the HMLR website.[3] Where HMLR will accept a document signed using the Mercury signing method, all parties must be represented by a conveyancer (even those who are not signing the document). However:

(a) only a lender must have a conveyancer when dealing with a mortgage, discharge or release;

(b) only the personal representatives must have a conveyancer when dealing with an assent; and

(c) only the donor of a power of attorney must have a conveyancer acting for him.

All conveyancers must agree to Mercury signing.

Assuming those conditions are met, HMLR requires the parties to complete the following steps:

(1) final agreed copies of the deed (including any plans) are emailed to each signing party by their conveyancer;

(2) each party prints the signature page only;

(3) each party signs the signature page in the presence of a witness;

(4) the witness signs the signature page;

(5) each party sends a single email to their conveyancer attaching the final agreed copy of the deed and a scanned copy of the signature page;

(6) the conveyancers complete the transaction; and

(7) the conveyancer applying for registration includes with the application the final agreed copy of the deed and the signed signature page(s) as a single document. The conveyancer must certify the copy is a true copy of the original deed.

Any plan to the deed must be signed by the disponor.[4] HMLR suggests that the disponor's conveyancer sign the plan (perhaps by a typed signature) as agent for the disponor before sending it to the parties. If a conveyancer proposes to do this, he must be sure he has sufficient authority to sign the plan as agent.

Where the document being executed is an assent of unregistered land, there is no need for the personal representative(s) to sign in front of a witness or for the witness to sign the signature page.

Practice guide 82: Electronic signatures accepted by HM Land Registry contains variations to the above process where the party signing is a company.

57.2 Conveyancer-certified electronic signatures

Conveyancer-certified electronic signatures require a conveyancer to certify to HMLR that certain steps have been performed.

HMLR will only accept some documents signed using conveyancer-certified electronic signatures. *Practice Guide 82: electronic signatures accepted by HM Land Registry* contains a list of those documents. Where HMLR will accept a document signed using the conveyancer-certified electronic signature, all parties must be represented by a conveyancer (even those who are not signing the document). However:

(a) only a lender must have a conveyancer when dealing with a mortgage, discharge or release;
(b) only the personal representatives must have a conveyancer when dealing with an assent; and
(c) only the donor of a power of attorney must have a conveyancer acting for him.

All conveyancers must agree to use conveyancer-certified electronic signing and a conveyancer must set up and administer the signing process through the relevant platform.

Assuming those conditions are met, HMLR requires the parties to complete the following steps:

(1) the conveyancer controlling the signing process must ensure:

    (a) the final copy of the document (including any plans) is uploaded to the signing platform;
    (b) the platform is populated with the name, email address and mobile phone number of the signatories and the witnesses. Where the platform allows, witness details can be inserted later provided this is done before step 5; and
    (c) the fields are completed within the document (including signature fields on any plans that must be signed), highlighted and indicate who is to complete them as well as in what order, so that the signatory is followed by their witness. A conveyancer must date the document in the platform. Consequently, the controlling conveyancer may wish to highlight the date field as one that requires completing in the signing flow and assign it to the conveyancer dating the document;

(2) the platform emails the signatories to give them access to the document;
(3) the platform texts the signatories a one-time password of at least 6 numbers;
(4) the signatories enter the one-time password and then sign the document in the physical presence of the witness, with the date and time being automatically recorded within the platform's audit trail;
(5) once the signatory has signed the document, the witness will receive an email from the platform inviting them to sign and add their details in the space provided in the attestation clause. The witness inputs a one-time password sent to them by text message by the platform, signs and adds their address in the space provided, with the date and time being automatically recorded again;

(6) once the signing process has been concluded, the conveyancer controlling the signing process or another conveyancer acting for one of the parties dates the document within the platform with the date it took effect;
(7) the conveyancer who lodges the application does so by electronic means and includes with the application:

   (a) a PDF of the completed document. Where the application is for first registration, a print-out of the PDF, certified to be a true copy of the original deed, can be lodged; and
   (b) a certificate (not necessarily signed by the conveyancer: see below) in the following form:

   > I certify that, to the best of my knowledge and belief, the applicable requirements set out in practice guide 82 for the use of conveyancer-certified electronic signatures have been satisfied.

   The certificate needs to be dated and signed by an individual conveyancer (not somebody working in a conveyancing firm). His full name and firm or employer must be added and the deed or deeds for which the certificate is given must be specified.

Where the document being executed is an assent of unregistered land, there is no need for the personal representative(s) to sign in front of a witness or for the witness to electronically sign the document.

Practice guide 82: Electronic signatures accepted by HM Land Registry contains variations to the above process where the party signing is a company.

57.3 Mixed signing

HMLR will allow parties to mix the methods by which they sign. For example, one party may sign in wet ink and another using a conveyancer-certified electronic signature or they may each sign using different platforms.

In such cases all parties must follow the formalities applicable to their chosen method. Where a party is signing a counterpart which will not be submitted to HMLR, he need only ensure he is represented by a conveyancer.

HMLR does not permit a signatory and his witness to sign using different methods. For example, it would not be possible for a party to sign in wet ink and his witness use a conveyancer-certified electronic signature.

57.4 Amendment of documents signed using conveyancer-certified electronic signatures

Occasionally, it is necessary to amend a deed which has been electronically signed using a conveyancer-certified signature. There are currently two options available to deal with this.

First, the parties may print out the deed and endorse it as follows:

> The electronic deed of which this is a print-out is amended this day [*date*] as follows.

If the amendment is material, all parties should countersign the change. An amendment is material if it is 'potentially prejudicial to a party's legal rights or obligations under the instrument'.[5]

If a mistake is not material, a conveyancer acting for one of the parties may sign and add his full name and the name of his employer and endorse the print-out.

A material change made without consent may not be enforceable against the non-consenting party Accordingly, in case of doubt, the parties should proceed on the assumption the change is material.

Once the amendments have been made, the electronic deed and the amended print-out should be submitted to HMLR. If the applicant has already lodged his application, he should attach the amended print-out to his application using the Reply to Requisition function in the portal.

Alternatively, the parties may complete a deed of variation or rectification of the deed. However, if the amendment is to include additional land in a transfer, the parties must complete a new transfer of the additional land in the relevant prescribed form. Similarly, if the parties wish to add land to the area demised by a lease or extend its term, they should remember that this will effect a surrender and re-grant of the lease.[6]

57.5 Qualified electronic signatures

Qualified electronic signatures are a form of electronic signature which is:

(a) uniquely linked to the signatory and capable of identifying him;
(b) linked to the signed data in a manner which means any later change in the data is detectable;

(c) supported by a 'qualified certificate' issued by a 'qualified service provider'; and
(d) created by a qualified signature-creation device.

Pursuant to LRA 2002, s 91(5) and because of these additional security features, a document signed using a qualified electronic signature may be treated as a deed even if it is not witnessed.

57.6 Further information

HMLR has only comparatively recently started to accept electronically signed documents. Further, technology continues to advance at pace. Consequently, HMLR's practice on electronic signatures is rapidly evolving. For details of the latest practice, see *Practice guide 82: electronic signatures accepted by HM Land Registry*.

---

1 Law Commission, *Electronic execution of documents* (Law Com No 386) (2019).
2 [2008] EWHC 2721 (Admin).
3 www.gov.uk/government/collections/land-registration-practice-guides.
4 LRR 2003, r 213(2).
5 *Raiffeisen Zentralbank v Crossseas Shipping* [2000] 1 WLR 1135 at 1148 per Potter LJ.
6 See 98.10.1 Deeds of variation varying the term and 98.10.2 Deeds of variation varying the extent.

58 EMBANKMENTS OR SEA OR RIVER WALLS

Liabilities in respect of embankments or sea or river walls include, but are not limited to, the liabilities of owners whose properties front the sea or a river to repair and maintain sea walls and river banks. Until 12 October 2013, the benefit of a non-statutory right in respect of an embankment or sea or river wall was an unregistered interest which overrode first registration and registered dispositions.[1] To take effect as interests which overrode, liabilities in respect of embankments and sea and river walls must have arisen by proprietary means; that is, by virtue of custom, prescription, grant, a covenant supported by a rentcharge, or tenure.[2]

A contractual obligation, not being proprietary,[3] was not an interest which overrode. Nor was a liability imposed by statute; for example, one arising under the Coast Protection Act 1949, the Land Drainage Act 1991 or Water Resources Act 1991, Pt VI.

On first registration of title, HMLR will enter a notice in the register as to the burden of such a right if it appears from its examination of the title to affect the land.

After 12 October 2013, the automatic protection as an overriding interest ceased.[4] Consequently, the person having the benefit of the right (if its priority has not already been previously defeated and it continues to subsist) should protect it in the register. If he does not do so, the priority of the right is liable to be defeated on a subsequent first registration of unregistered burdened land or on a subsequent registration of a registrable disposition of registered burdened land for valuable consideration,[5] as the case may be. If the burdened land is unregistered, he should apply for a caution against first registration. If the burdened land is registered, he should apply for the entry in the register of a notice. The normal fee will apply.[6]

58.1 Caution against first registration

An applicant should deliver to HMLR the usual documents required.[7]

The statement of truth in panel 10 of form CT1 should be completed on the following lines to show the interest of the applicant:

> the person entitled to enforce a liability [to repair] or [to contribute towards the cost of repair] of [*specify the embankment or wall in question*] arising by reason of [*summarise the basis on which the interest arises*] and payable by [*specify relevant details*].

The interest stated in form CT1 will appear in the caution register, together with a description of the legal estate to which the caution relates. For the effect of the caution against first registration, see 25 Cautions Against First Registration.

58.2 Agreed notice

An applicant should deliver to HMLR the usual documents required.[8]

Documentary evidence of the creation or existence of the non-statutory right in respect of an embankment or sea or river wall will normally be in the form of a statutory declaration or statement of truth containing details of how the right arose and how it has devolved to the applicant.

The agreed notice in the register will give details of the interest protected.

Where the registered proprietor does not consent to the entry in the register of an agreed notice and the applicant cannot lodge evidence to satisfy HMLR of the validity of the applicant's claim, the applicant can still apply to enter a unilateral notice.

58.3 Unilateral notice

An applicant should deliver to HMLR the usual documents required.[9]

The statement in panel 11 or conveyancer's certificate in panel 12 of form UN1 should be completed on the following lines to show the interest of the applicant:

> the person entitled to enforce a liability [to repair] or [to contribute towards the cost of repair] of [*specify the embankment or wall in question*] arising by reason of [*summarise the basis on which the interest arises*] and payable by [*specify relevant details*].

The unilateral notice in the register will give brief details of the interest protected and identify the beneficiary of that notice.

---

1 LRA 2002, ss 11, 12, 29 and 30, Sch 1, para 13 and Sch 3, para 13.
2 See *London & North-Western Railway Co v Fobbing Sewers Commissioners* [1896] 75 LT 629.
3 See *Eton Rural District Council v Thames Conservators* [1950] Ch 540.
4 LRA 2002, s 117(1).
5 LRA 2002, ss 11, 12, 29 and 30.
6 See 67 Fees.
7 See 25 Cautions Against First Registration.
8 See 119.1 Agreed notice.
9 See 119.3 Unilateral notice.

59 EMPTY DWELLING MANAGEMENT ORDERS

Housing Act 2004 (HA 2004), Part 4, Chapter 2 introduced empty dwelling management orders (EDMOs). The aim of EDMOs is to give giving local housing authorities (LHAs) powers to bring back into occupation certain private sector dwellings that have remained unoccupied for at least 6 months where the owners are unwilling or unable to do so themselves.

While an EDMO is in place the LHA has the right to possession of a dwelling and the right to do in relation to the management and use of the dwelling anything that all the relevant proprietors would normally be entitled to do.[1] However, there is no transfer of ownership and the relevant proprietor(s) remains/remain the owner(s) of the property. The LHA does not acquire any estate or interest in the property and cannot sell or create a charge over it. Under an EDMO, the LHA may also apply to a Residential Property Tribunal (RPT) for an order determining an existing lease or licence of the dwelling.[2]

An EDMO is made against all the 'relevant proprietors'. Where the dwelling is freehold only, this would be the freeholder.[3] Where the dwelling is subject to a lease, all the relevant proprietors would be the leaseholders with the shortest unexpired term, provided it still has more than 7 years to run.[4]

There are two types of EDMO:

(a) an interim EDMO; and
(b) a final EDMO.

An interim EDMO must be approved by an RPT before it can take effect.[5] Once approved, it will usually last for a maximum period of 12 months.[6] Under an interim EDMO, the LHA cannot arrange occupation of the dwelling without seeking the consent of the owner.[7] Where an agreement cannot be reached, an interim EDMO can be revoked and replaced with a final EDMO made by the LHA.

The making of a final EDMO does not require approval from an RPT.[8] Once in force, it lasts for a fixed period of no more than 7 years.[9] The LHA does not in most cases require the consent of the owner to grant occupation rights under a final EDMO.[10] Before making a final EDMO, the LHA must consider whether any compensation should be paid to any third party whose rights will be interfered with as a result of making the EDMO.[11]

59.1 Restrictions

While an EDMO is in force, the registered proprietor may not grant a lease, tenancy or licence to occupy the property. Accordingly, the LHA may apply for a restriction to prevent registration of any such disposition during the existence of the EDMO.

In addition to the usual documents required,[12] the LHA should deliver to HMLR:

(a) a certified copy of the interim or final EDMO;
(b) in the case of an interim EDMO, a certificate from the LHA that the RPT has given the authorisation required by HA 2004, s 134; and

(c) in the case of a final EDMO, a certificate from the LHA that the final EDMO has come into force and the LHA has complied with its obligations under HA 2004, s 136.

There is no standard form of restriction. Suitable wording for a restriction protecting an interim EDMO might be:

> No lease of the registered estate (other than a lease of the reversion) by the proprietor of the registered estate is to be completed by registration unless authorised by an order of the court, the property being subject to an interim Empty Dwelling Management Order dated [*date*] made by [*the RPT*] pursuant to section 133 and Schedule 7 to the Housing Act 2004.

Suitable wording for a restriction protecting a final EDMO might be:

> No lease of the registered estate (other than a lease of the reversion) by the proprietor of the registered estate is to be completed by registration unless authorised by an order of the court, the property being subject to a final Empty Dwelling Management Order dated [*date*] made by [*LHA*] pursuant to section 136 and Schedule 7 to the Housing Act 2004.

As a non-standard restriction, the suggested wording will require the approval of HMLR under LRA 2002, s 43(3).

The statement in panel 12 or conveyancer's certificate in panel 13 of form RX1 should be completed on the following lines:

> The applicant is the local housing authority for the area in which the property is situated and the property is subject to [an interim] or [a final] empty dwelling management order dated [*date*] made by [the Residential Property Tribunal *or insert details of the local housing authority*] under section [133 *or* 136] of the Housing Act 2004.

HMLR must give notice of an application for a restriction to the proprietor of the registered estate concerned if it has not been made by or with his consent or the consent of a person entitled to be registered as such proprietor.[13]

59.2 Registration of leases granted by a local housing authority under an empty dwelling management order

An LHA cannot:

(a) grant a lease of the property under an interim EDMO,[14] or
(b) grant a lease with a fixed term expiring after the date on which a final EDMO is due to expire,[15]

without all relevant proprietors' consent. Accordingly, applications to register a lease granted by an LHA under an EDMO are rare.

In addition to the usual documents required,[16] an applicant should deliver to HMLR:

(a) a certified copy of the EDMO under which the LHA granted the lease;
(b) in the case of a lease granted under an interim EDMO, a certificate from the LHA that the RPT has given the authorisation required by HA 2004, s 134;
(c) the consent of all relevant proprietors to the grant of the lease (unless the lease was made under a final EDMO, the term of the lease expires before the EDMO and the lease is terminable by notice to quit of no more than 4 weeks); and
(d) in the case of a lease granted under a final EDMO, a certificate from the LHA that the final EDMO has come into force and the LHA has complied with its obligations under HA 2004, s 136.

HMLR may serve notice of the application to all relevant proprietors and any registered chargee.

When completing the application, HMLR will add a note to:

(a) the register for the new lease, and
(b) the notice of the new lease in the reversionary title(s),

to explain it was made by the LHA under an EDMO.

59.3 Noting leases granted by a local housing authority under an empty dwelling management order

If an LHA grants a lease under an EDMO which is not capable of substantive registration but is for a term of more than 3 years, a tenant may apply to note it against the relevant title.

59.3.1 Agreed notice

In addition to the usual documents required,[17] an applicant should deliver to HMLR:

(a) a certified copy of the EDMO under which the LHA granted the lease;
(b) in the case of a lease granted under an interim EDMO, a certificate from the LHA that the RPT has given the authorisation required by HA 2004, s 134;
(c) in the case of a lease granted under an interim EDMO, the consent of all relevant proprietors to the grant of the lease;

(d) in the case of a lease granted under a final EDMO for a term which expires after the EDMO and/or the lease is terminable by notice to quit of more than 4 weeks, the consent of all relevant proprietors to the grant of the lease;
(e) in the case of a lease granted under a final EDMO, a certificate from the LHA that the final EDMO has come into force and the LHA has complied with its obligations under HA 2004, s 136.

This is likely to be sufficient to satisfy HMLR as to the validity of the applicant's claim for the purposes of LRA 2002, s 34(3)(c).

HMLR may serve notice of the application to all relevant proprietors and any registered chargee.

When completing the application, HMLR will add a note to the notice of the new lease to explain it was made by the LHA under an EDMO.

59.3.2 Unilateral notice

An applicant should deliver to HMLR the usual documents required.[18]

The statement in panel 11 or conveyancer's certificate in panel 12 of form UN1 should be completed on the following lines to show the interest of the applicant:

> tenant of a lease for a term of [*number*] years from and including [*commencement date*] to and including [*expiry date*] dated [*date*] made between (1) [*LHA*] and (2) [*tenant*] made pursuant to [an interim] or [a final] Empty Dwelling Management Order dated [*date of EDMO*] made under section [133 *or* 136] and Schedule 7 to the Housing Act 2004.

The unilateral notice in the register will give brief details of the interest protected and identify the beneficiary of that notice.

59.4 Determination of leases

An LHA may apply to determine certain leases affecting a property subject to a EDMO.[19] If the RPT makes such an order, the LHA may apply to close the relevant registered leasehold title and/or remove any notice of it from the register.

59.4.1 Closure of registered leases

In addition to the usual documents required,[20] an applicant should deliver to HMLR:

(a) a certified copy of the EDMO;
(b) a certified copy of the order of the RPT which determines the lease;
(c) in the case of interim EDMO, a certificate from the LHA that the RPT has given the authorisation required by HA 2004, s 134; and
(d) in the case of a final EDMO, a certificate from the LHA that the final EDMO has come into force and the LHA has complied with its obligations under HA 2004, s 136.

The applicant will also need to account for any incumbrances affecting the registered leasehold title (unless the order from the RPT operated to determine the lease free of incumbrances).

HMLR would serve notice of the application on the registered proprietor and any registered chargee.

59.4.2 Cancellation of agreed notice of lease

In addition to the usual documents required,[21] an applicant should deliver to HMLR:

(a) a certified copy of the EDMO;
(b) a certified copy of the order of the RPT which determines the lease;
(c) in the case of interim EDMO, a certificate from the LHA that the RPT has given the authorisation required by HA 2004, s 134; and
(d) in the case of a final EDMO, a certificate from the LHA that the final EDMO has come into force and the LHA has complied with its obligations under HA 2004, s 136.

HMLR would serve notice of the application on the tenant, freeholder and any registered chargee.

---

1 Housing Act 2004 (HA 2004), Sch 7, paras 2(3)(a) and (b) and 10(3)(a) and (b).
2 HA 2004, Sch 7, paras 2(3)(d) and 10(3)(d).
3 HA 2004, s 132(1)(c)(ii).
4 HA 2004, s 132(1)(c)(i).
5 HA 2004, s 133(1)(b).
6 HA 2004, Sch 7, para 1(3).
7 HA 2004, Sch 7, para 2(4).
8 HA 2004, s 136(1).
9 HA 2004, Sch 7, para 9(3).
10 HA 2004, Sch 7, para 10(4).

[11] HA 2004, s 136(4).
[12] See 153.1 Application for entry of restriction.
[13] LRA 2002, s 45.
[14] HA 2004, Sch 7, para 2(4).
[15] HA 2004, Sch 7, para 10(4)(a)(i).
[16] See 98 Leases.
[17] See 119.1 Agreed notice.
[18] See 119.3 Unilateral notice.
[19] HA 2004, s 133(6) and Sch 7, paras 2(3)(d), 10(3)(d) and 22.
[20] See 98.18 Determination of registered leases.
[21] See 119.2 Cancellation of a notice other than a unilateral notice or a home rights notice.

60 ENLARGEMENT OF LONG LEASES

A tenant may enlarge a lease originally created for a term of not less than 300 years, of which at least 200 years remain unexpired, into a fee simple if it meets the other requirements in LPA 1925, s 153. The other requirements in s 153 are:

(a) there must not be any trust or right of redemption affecting the term in favour of the owner of the reversionary estate;
(b) there must not be any rent payable other than a peppercorn or other rent having no monetary value; or, a rent having been payable (not being a peppercorn rent or other rent having no monetary value), the rent has been released or become barred by lapse of time, or has in any other way ceased to be payable; and
(c) there must not be any right of re-entry affecting the leasehold estate or any superior leasehold estate out of which it was created.

A tenant cannot enlarge where their lease is an underlease and the headlease is incapable of enlargement.[1] A yearly rent not exceeding £1 that has not been collected or paid for 20 years or more is deemed to have ceased to be payable.[2]

In most cases, leases which are capable of enlargement tend to be of relatively ancient origin. This reflects the fact that many such leases were deliberately granted in certain areas to avoid extending the voting franchise, as formerly only freeholders were entitled to vote. However, some modern leases may also be capable of enlargement; in these cases, the landlord may have granted a long lease instead of conveying the freehold, to ensure that positive covenants, which do not normally bind successors in title of a freehold estate, continue to run with the land.

The enlargement is usually effected by either the execution of a deed poll or endorsement on one of the unregistered title deeds. On enlargement, the land remains subject to the same trusts and covenants that affected the original lease.[3] Where the conditions for enlargement are not met, it may still be possible to acquire the freehold under the Leasehold Reform Act 1967.[4]

60.1 Leasehold title unregistered

Where the existing leasehold title is unregistered (regardless of whether or not the freehold estate is registered), in addition to the usual documents required,[5] an applicant should deliver to HMLR:

(a) the lease or a certified copy or examined abstract of it;
(b) (where applicable) a statutory declaration or statement of truth confirming non-payment of the rent over a period of 20 years, where it is necessary to show that a rent not exceeding £1 is deemed to have ceased to be payable; and
(c) the original deed poll or the document from the unregistered title deeds that bears the endorsement.

Where the freehold title is registered, whether or not the lease is the subject of a notice in the register, HMLR will not close that freehold title. Instead, HMLR will leave the existing freehold title open and enter a note in the property register confirming that if the effect of the enlargement is to determine the former landlord's estate, then the estate has determined. This practice reflects the fact that the effect of enlargement under s 153 upon the landlord's legal estate is uncertain and in particular as to whether it extinguishes the landlord's estate or whether the landlord's estate continues alongside the tenant's new freehold estate. Previously, HMLR's practice had been to close the former landlord's title.

On completion of the application for registration, HMLR makes an entry in the property register of the new freehold title to show that the fee simple has been acquired by enlargement and is therefore subject to the matters set out in LPA 1925, s 153(8). The entry will instead refer to Conveyancing and Law of Property Act 1881, s 65(4), if the date of the deed of enlargement is before 1 January 1926. HMLR will reflect any charges or other relevant entries affecting the leasehold title in the charges register of the new freehold title.

Where the applicant cannot produce full details of the lease so that it is not certain that the conditions for enlargement have been met, HMLR may refuse an application for enlargement; for example, where it is not clear whether the lease was originally created for a term of not less than 300 years of which at least 200 years remain unexpired. In some cases, HMLR will accept the application for enlargement but will only grant a qualified class of title.[6] In such a case, the qualification shown in the proprietorship register will be on the following lines:

> As neither the Lease dated [*date*] referred to in the Property Register nor full evidence of its contents was produced on first registration it is possible that the term was not capable of being enlarged. There are excepted from the effect of registration all estates rights and interests vested in any other person or persons if and so far as the enlargement was ineffective.

This entry (which will be in addition to that referring to the matters set out in LPA 1925, s 153(8) specified above) makes clear that the registered title is subject to all estates rights and interests vested in any other person or persons if and so far as the enlargement was ineffective.

60.2 Leasehold title registered

Where the existing leasehold title is registered (regardless of whether or not the freehold estate is registered), an applicant should deliver to HMLR:

(a) an application in form AP1;
(b) the deed of enlargement or a certified copy of it;
(c) the lease or a certified copy or examined abstract of it;
(d) (if applicable) a statutory declaration or statement of truth confirming non-payment of the rent over a period of 20 years, where it is necessary to show that a rent not exceeding £1 is deemed to have ceased to be payable; and
(e) the fee payable.[7]

Where the freehold title is registered, whether or not the lease is the subject of a notice in the register, HMLR will not close that freehold title. Instead, HMLR will leave the existing freehold title open and enter a note in the property register confirming that if the effect of the enlargement is to determine the former landlord's estate, then the estate has determined. This practice reflects the fact that the effect of enlargement under s 153 upon the landlord's legal estate is uncertain as to whether it extinguishes the landlord's estate or whether the landlord's estate continues alongside the tenant's new freehold estate. Previously, HMLR's practice was to close the former landlord's title.

If the leasehold title is already registered, HMLR will close it on completion of the application. An entry is made in the property register of the new freehold title to show that the fee simple has been acquired by enlargement and is therefore subject to the matters set out in LPA 1925, s 153(8). The entry will instead refer to Conveyancing and Law of Property Act 1881, s 65(4), if (unusually) the date of the deed of enlargement is before 1 January 1926. HMLR will reflect any charges or other relevant incumbrances affecting the leasehold title in the charges register of the new freehold title.

1 LPA 1925, s 153(2)(ii).
2 LPA 1925, s 153(4).
3 LPA 1925, s 153(8).
4 See 97 Leasehold Enfranchisement.
5 See 68.4 Application for first registration.
6 See 32 Classes of Title.
7 See 67 Fees.

61 EQUITABLE CHARGES

An equitable charge (or mortgage) may arise where, for example, the charge is created in writing other than by deed; or if it charges only an equitable interest; or if it takes effect as a contract to create a legal mortgage. Where the land is registered, the creation of such a charge on the land is not a registrable disposition required to be completed by registration. Where an equitable charge on land is created and the charged land is unregistered, that charge should be protected by way of a land charge (normally Class C(iii)).[1] An equitable charge can also arise in relation to registered land where, although it is created by deed and is capable of registration as a legal charge, it cannot be completed by registration. This could occur where, for example, there is a restriction in the register requiring the consent of a prior chargee to the registration and that consent is not forthcoming. The grant of a legal charge of registered land must be completed by registration[2] and until then it takes effect as an equitable charge of the legal estate. On registration it becomes a legal charge and the chargee is entered in the register as proprietor of the registered charge.[3]

A charge which takes effect in equity only cannot be substantively registered as a registered charge. A person who has obtained an equitable charge against the legal estate in registered land may apply for the entry in the register of a notice in respect of the equitable charge. The equitable chargee cannot apply for an official search with priority using form OS1 or form OS2.

Where an equitable charge is in respect only of a beneficial interest in registered land held under a trust of land, HMLR cannot enter a notice in the register.[4] In that case, the chargee can apply for the entry of a restriction. A restriction does not confer any priority. However, it prevents an entry being made in the register relating to any disposition, or a disposition of a specified kind, unless the terms of the restriction have (where applicable) been complied with.

An application for a notice may be for an agreed notice or a unilateral notice. In the case of an application for an agreed notice, HMLR may approve the application without the consent of the proprietor where it is satisfied of the validity of the applicant's claim. An applicant may prefer a unilateral notice where the applicant does not wish the terms of the charge to be open to public inspection and copying.

61.1 Agreed notice

In addition to the usual documents required,[5] an applicant should deliver to HMLR the equitable charge or a certified copy of it.

Where the consent of the registered proprietor is not available but, for example, he has signed the equitable charge, this is likely to be sufficient to satisfy HMLR of the validity of the applicant's claim in accordance with LRA 2002, s 34(3)(c).

The agreed notice in the register will give details of the interest protected.

If the chargee subsequently discharges the equitable charge, a party should apply to cancel the agreed notice using form CN1, accompanied by an appropriate form of receipt or other evidence of the discharge. This may consist of either:

(a) a form DS1 or form DS3;
(b) an endorsed receipt on the instrument of charge; or
(c) a letter from the chargee addressed to HMLR, confirming that the charge has been satisfied.

The applicant should also include either:

(a) confirmation that there has been no assignment of the benefit of the charge; or
(b) the normal conveyancing evidence of devolution of title to the person giving the discharge.

61.2 Unilateral notice

An applicant should deliver to HMLR the usual documents required.[6]

The statement in panel 11 or conveyancer's certificate in panel 12 of form UN1 should be completed on the following lines to show the interest of the applicant:

equitable chargee under [*specify the document creating the equitable charge*] dated [*date*] and made between [*registered proprietor*] and [*beneficiary of the unilateral notice*].

The unilateral notice in the register will give brief details of the interest protected and identify the beneficiary of that notice.

If the chargee subsequently discharges the equitable charge, the beneficiary of the notice may apply to cancel the unilateral notice using form UN2.[7] If the beneficiary fails to do so, the registered proprietor of the land may apply in form UN4 for cancellation of the unilateral notice.[8]

61.3 Restriction where the equitable charge is over a beneficial interest

The chargee in an equitable charge over a beneficial interest under a trust of land may apply for entry of a restriction in Form A if there is not already one in the register.[9] The wording of Form A is set out in Appendix IV. Such a restriction does not prevent a disposition of the property provided it is complied with. However, it should ensure the beneficial interest to which the equitable charge attaches will be overreached.[10]

HMLR must give notice of an application for a restriction to the proprietor of the registered estate concerned, if it has not been made by or with his consent or the consent of a person entitled to be registered as such proprietor.[11]

The chargee cannot apply for any other form of restriction. This is because such a charge is not a right or claim in relation to a registered estate within LRA 2002, s 42(1)(c); it is a right or claim in relation to the beneficial interest under a trust of land and not in relation to the registered estate. Such a charge does not fall within the exception applicable to charging orders, which may be protected by entry of a restriction in Form K.[12] The wording of Form K is set out in Appendix IV.

In addition to the usual documents required,[13] if applying for a restriction in Form A, the applicant should deliver to HMLR the equitable charge or a certified copy of it.

No fee is payable where the application is for entry of a restriction in Form A only.

The statement in panel 12 or conveyancer's certificate in panel 13 of form RX1 should be completed on the following lines:

> The interest is that specified in rule 93(a) of the Land Registration Rules 2003 (SI 2003/1417), the applicant having the benefit of a charge over a beneficial interest in the registered estate.

Panel 9 of form RX1 should set out the wording of Form A, as set out above. A restriction in a standard Form A in LRR 2003, Sch 4 does not require the approval of HMLR to the terms of the restriction under LRA 2002, s 43(3).

61.4 Priority of equitable charges

There are no specific provisions in the LRA 2002 dealing with the priority of competing equitable charges. Consequently, the priority of such charges accords with the dates when they were created, the first in time having priority.[14] The priority of such charges in relation to registered dispositions (including the grant of a legal charge) for valuable consideration will be governed by the special rule of priority set out in LRA 2002, s 29.[15]

61.5 Orders under Law of Property Act 1925, s 90

Where the court makes an order for sale relating to an equitable mortgage on land, the court may:

(a) in favour of a purchaser, make a vesting order conveying the land;
(b) appoint a person to convey the land; or
(c) create and vest in the mortgagee a legal term of years absolute to enable him to carry out the sale.[16]

If the court has made a vesting order transferring registered land, this must be completed by registration.[17] In addition to the usual documents required in the case of a transfer,[18] the applicant should deliver to HMLR the court order, a sealed copy of it or a certified copy of it.

If the court has made an order appointing a person to convey the land, the applicant should lodge that order, a sealed copy of it or a certified copy of it in support of the application to register a transfer executed by that person.

Where the court has made an order vesting in the equitable mortgagee a legal term of years absolute to enable him to carry out a sale, the charge takes the form of a demise. The demise is usually for 3,000 years if a freehold estate has been charged or, if a leasehold estate has been charged, for one day less than the original term granted by the lease. If a leasehold estate is being charged, care should therefore be taken that the term of the demise does not extend beyond the term granted in the lease.

Although LRA 2002, s 23(1)(a) removed the power of the owner of a registered estate to create a mortgage by demise or sub-demise, this does not affect the ability of the courts to do so. Such a charge created by the court order would appear to be a registrable disposition which is required to be completed by registration;[19] it must therefore be substantively registered if it is to take effect at law.

The mortgagee should deliver to HMLR:

(a) an application in form AP1;
(b) the court order or a sealed copy of that order or a certified copy of it; and
(c) the fee payable.[20]

However, as LPA 1925, s 90 provides that the mortgage will take effect 'as if the mortgage had been created by deed by way of legal mortgage', the registered estate can effectively be transferred under the power of sale without the mortgage created under s 90 being registered. This reflects the decision in *Swift 1st Ltd v Colin*,[21] which provides that if a charge of the registered estate is by deed expressed to be by way of legal mortgage but is not completed by registration, the chargee still has a statutory power of sale. The sale will override all rights over which the charge has priority and the transfer will be of the registered estate. A copy of the order of the court under s 90 must accompany an application to register a transfer made under the chargee's power of sale in such circumstances. As to the exercise of a power of sale, see 100.10.1 Power of sale.

In determining the priority of a mortgage created under LPA 1925, s 90, account would need to be taken of the wording in s 90(1) which states that the creation of the mortgage is 'without prejudice to any encumbrance having priority to the equitable mortgage' and also the effect of LRA 2002, ss 28 and 29. In some circumstances, the mortgage may have priority over an existing registered charge shown in the register. For example, if the mortgage under s 90 was created in respect of a charging order which pre-dated the registered charge and its priority had been protected by a notice in the register for the purposes of LRA 2002, s 29 when the registered charge was registered, the mortgage under s 90 would appear to have priority over the existing registered charge. That priority would need to be reflected by an entry in the register.[22] Before making such an entry, HMLR would serve notice on the registered proprietor of the existing registered charge unless he had consented to the making of the entry.[23]

1 The beneficiary of the charge may also wish to register a caution against first registration against the affected land. See 25 Cautions Against First Registration.

2 LRA 2002, s 27(2)(f).
3 LRA 2002, Sch 2, para 8.
4 LRA 2002, s 33(a).
5 See 119.1 Agreed notice.
6 See 119.3 Unilateral notice.
7 See 119.5 Removal of a unilateral notice.
8 See 119.6 Cancellation of a unilateral notice.
9 LRR 2003, r 93(a).
10 LPA 1925, ss 2 and 27.
11 LRA 2002, s 45.
12 See 29.4 Restriction where the charging order is over a beneficial interest.
13 See 153.1 Application for entry of restriction.
14 LRA 2002, s 28.
15 See 138 Priorities.
16 LPA 1925, s 90(1).
17 LRA 2002, s 27.
18 See 176.1 Registration of transfer.
19 LRA 2002, s 27(2)(f) and(5).
20 See 67 Fees.
21 [2011] EWHC 2410 (Ch).
22 LRA 2002, s 48 and LRR 2003, r 101.
23 LRR 2003, r 128.

62 EQUITABLE EASEMENTS

If an easement is granted or reserved in writing other than by deed, or other than for a period equivalent to a fee simple absolute in possession or a term of years absolute, it will be equitable. Where the burdened land is registered, the grant or reservation of such an easement is not a registrable disposition required to be completed by registration. Where an easement is granted or reserved and the burdened land is unregistered, that easement should be protected by way of a Class D(iii) land charge. Equitable easements can arise in relation to leases as well as freehold land; if the lease is merely in writing but not by deed, any easement granted or reserved within it can only be equitable. The express grant or reservation of a legal easement out of registered land must be completed by registration[1] and until then it takes effect as an equitable easement. On registration it becomes a legal easement and a notice of it is entered in the register of the servient land.[2]

The LRA 2002 provides only for the registration of legal interests.[3] Consequently, HMLR will not enter the benefit of an equitable interest in the register of the benefiting estate, either on first registration or subsequently.

The burden of equitable easements will, if disclosed within the application, be the subject of a notice in the register on first registration of the burdened estate.[4] If the burdened estate is already registered, a person may apply to enter an agreed notice or a unilateral notice in respect of the burden of the equitable easement.

Where an equitable easement is granted in a transfer, lease or other disposition of registered land, HMLR will enter a notice of the burden of the easement in the register of a registered burdened estate, providing the title number is entered in panel 2 of form AP1, clause LR2.2 in the case of a prescribed clauses lease or in the data transmitted to HMLR via the portal; otherwise, a separate application must be made.[5]

Before 13 October 2003, equitable easements that were openly exercised and enjoyed as appurtenant to the dominant tenement could take effect as overriding interests on the registered servient title under Land Registration Rules 1925, r 258.[6] Any such equitable easement which was an overriding interest in relation to a registered estate immediately before 13 October 2003 is treated as an unregistered interest which overrides registered dispositions within LRA 2002, Sch 3, para 3.[7]

All other equitable easements are not interests which override either first registration under LRA 2002, Sch 1 or registered dispositions under LRA 2002, Sch 3. Accordingly, they must be protected by way of notice in the register. The overriding status conferred by LRA 2002, Sch 1, para 3 and Sch 3, para 3 relates only to legal easements.

62.1 Agreed notice

In addition to the usual documents required,[8] an applicant should deliver to HMLR the document creating the equitable easement or a certified copy of it.

Where the consent of the registered proprietor is not available but, for example, the document creating the easement is signed by him, this is likely to be sufficient to satisfy HMLR of the validity of the applicant's claim in accordance with LRA 2002, s 34(3)(c).

The agreed notice in the register will give details of the interest protected.

62.2 Unilateral notice

An applicant should deliver to HMLR the usual documents required.[9]

The statement in panel 11 or conveyancer's certificate in panel 12 of form UN1 should be completed on the following lines to show the interest of the applicant:

> the person having the benefit of an equitable right of [*specify the easement*] created by a [*description of document*] dated [*date*] and made between [*parties*].

The unilateral notice in the register will give brief details of the interest protected and identify the beneficiary of that notice.

---

1 LRA 2002, s 27(2)(d).
2 LRA 2002, Sch 2, para 7.
3 LRA 2002, s 2.
4 LRR 2003, r 35
5 LRR 2003, rr 72(4) and (5), 72A(4) and 72C(2) and (3) and Notices 19 and 25 given under LRR 2003, Sch 2.
6 *Celsteel Ltd v Alton House Holdings Ltd* [1985] 2 All ER 562.
7 LRA 2002, Sch 12, para 9.
8 See 119.1 Agreed notice.
9 See 119.3 Unilateral notice.

63 EQUITABLE INTERESTS

Any interest in land that does not qualify as a legal estate or interest is an equitable interest.[1] Equitable interests include, for example:

(a) the interest of a beneficiary under a trust;
(b) interests arising under a contract for sale;
(c) interests that do not meet the formal requirements for the creation of a legal interest (for example an easement not created by deed); and
(d) restrictive covenants.

HMLR cannot register the benefit of equitable interests. However, the burden of the interest can be protected by the entry of a notice and/or restriction (as appropriate) in the register of an affected registered title.[2]

---

1 LPA 1925, s 1(3).
2 See 119 Notices and 153 Restrictions.

64 ESTATE, RIGHT OR INTEREST

When a vendor has doubts about his title to a piece of land, he may convey or transfer it for such 'estate, right or interest (if any)' as he may have in it. For example, he may believe either that he has lost, or is losing, his title to the land by adverse possession; or conversely that he has recently acquired, or is in the process of acquiring, title to the land by adverse possession. A conveyance containing such wording would not be a good root of title to such land; a good root must show nothing to cast doubt on the title of the disposing party.

Where the land conveyed or transferred for 'estate right or interest' is unregistered, any application for first registration of title to it should be supported by sufficient evidence to show title to that land. This is normally by way of statutory declaration or statement of truth; for example, a statement of truth in form ST1 in LRR 2003, Sch 4. Even though the title is open to objection, it may still be registered with absolute freehold, absolute leasehold, or good leasehold title (as the case may be) if HMLR is of the opinion that the defect will not cause the holding under the title to be disturbed.[1]

However, if a third party is in possession of the land and the applicant for first registration cannot account for that possession (for example by providing details of a subsisting lease or licence granted by the applicant or his predecessor in title), HMLR may not be prepared to grant any class of title in respect of that land and may exclude it from the registered title.

A vendor may convey or transfer his 'estate right or interest' in land where he is in adverse possession of the land but has been so for less than the requisite period. Where an applicant for first registration has not been in adverse possession for the requisite period under the LA 1980, no class of title can be granted. Similarly, where a person has not been in adverse possession for the requisite period specified in LRA 2002, Sch 6, no application to be registered as proprietor of a registered estate in land can be made under that Schedule.[2]

---

1 LRA 2002, ss 9(3) and 10(4). See 32 Classes of Title.

2 See 6 Adverse Possession.

65 EUROPEAN ECONOMIC INTEREST GROUPINGS

A European Economic Interest Grouping (EEIG) is formed of two or more legal bodies or natural persons, which have their central administrations or carry on their principal activities in different member states of the European Union. An EEIG must have at least two members from different EU states and can be formed by companies, firms or other legal entities and, in certain circumstances, individuals. It must have a registered office within the European Union. On 31 December 2020 any existing UK-registered EEIG automatically converted to a United Kingdom Economic Interest Grouping (UKEIG).[1] However, it remains possible for an EEIG to have an establishment in the United Kingdom provided it registers that establishment at Companies House.[2]

Only the manager (or, where there are two or more, each of the managers) may represent the EEIG in respect of dealings with third parties.[3] Accordingly, execution of a deed by an EEIG should be on the following lines:

> Signed as a deed by [*name of manager*] the [sole] or [joint] manager(s) of [*name of EEIG*] in the presence of …

An application to register an EEIG as the proprietor of a registered estate or of a registered charge should be supported by the usual documentation, accompanied by:

(a) the result of a recent search at Companies House against the EEIG together with all forms and documents submitted by them and showing the EEIG has a UK establishment; and
(b) evidence of appointment of the manager (if this is not clear from the other documents lodged).

Given the nature of an EEIG and the restrictions on its powers contained in Council Regulation (EEC) No 2137/85 and the European Economic Interest Grouping Regulations 1989 (SI 1989/638) (EEIG Regulations 1989), it may apply for a restriction on the following lines, if required, using form RX1:

> No disposition of the [registered estate] *or* [registered charge dated [*date*]] by the proprietor of [the registered estate] *or* [that registered charge] is to be completed by registration without a certificate signed by the conveyancer to [*name of EEIG*] that the manager or managers or its representative who has or have executed the deed, has or have been duly appointed and has or have the power to bind the proprietor; that the proprietor is not in receivership or administrative receivership and has not been wound up or dissolved and generally that the provisions of Council Regulation

(EEC) No 2137/85 and the European Economic Interest Grouping Regulations 1989 (SI 1989/638) have been complied with.

Where the EEIG does not have an indefinite duration, it may also apply for a restriction on the following lines, if required, using form RX1:[4]

> No disposition by the proprietor of the [registered estate] *or* [registered charge dated [*date*]] completed on or after [*date when duration of EEIG ceases*] is to be completed by registration unless its conveyancer has certified that the duration of the proprietor has been extended and that it remained a body corporate on the date of such disposition.

All deeds completed by an EEIG must indicate legibly:

(a) the name of the grouping preceded or followed either by the words 'European Economic Interest Grouping' or by the initials 'EEIG', unless those words or initials already occur in the name;
(b) the location of the registry in which the grouping is registered, together with the grouping's entry at that registry; and
(c) the grouping's official address.[5]

IA 1986, Pt III applies to establishments of EEIGs in the United Kingdom as if they were companies registered under the Companies Act 2006.[6] A receiver or manager or administrative receiver may be appointed, but not an administrator.

1 European Economic Interest Grouping (Amendment) (EU Exit) Regulations 2018 (SI 2018/1299). For further details about United Kingdom Economic Interest Groupings, see 180 United Kingdom Economic Interest Groupings.
2 Council Regulation (EEC) No 2137/85, art 10(1) as amended by European Economic Interest Grouping (Amendment) (EU Exit) Regulations 2018 (SI 2018/1299), reg 43.
3 Council Regulation (EEC) No 2137/85, art 20.
4 See 153.1 Application for entry of restriction.
5 Council Regulation (EEC) No 2137/85, art 25.
6 European Economic Interest Grouping Regulations 1989 (SI 1989/638) (EEIG Regulations 1989), reg 19(1).

66 EXCLUSIVE USE

Historically, particularly in the Midlands and the North of England, it has sometimes been the practice to include in a conveyance or lease of a dwelling house the exclusive use of or exclusive right to use other adjacent premises such as a lavatory or coal shed. Modern conveyances or leases also occasionally include reference to exclusive use, particularly in relation to the use of certain parts of a purpose-built development such as a bin store or car parking space.

The legal nature and effect of a grant of 'exclusive use' remains largely undefined by either statute or case law. Consequently, it can be difficult, when considering how to treat such a grant for land registration purposes, to determine whether the grant takes effect as a transfer or demise, or merely as an easement.

In *Reilly v Booth*,[1] a vendor granted exclusive use of a gateway. In a passage later cited with approval by the House of Lords in *Metropolitan Railway Company v Fowler*,[2] Lopes LJ said:

> The exclusive or unrestricted use of a piece of land, I take it, beyond all question passes the property or ownership in that land, and there is no easement known to law which gives exclusive and unrestricted use of a piece of land. It is not an easement in such a case, it is property that passes.

If, when applying for registration, the applicant specifically applies for the grant of the exclusive use to be registered as an estate in land, HMLR will consider it on that basis. However, for the grant to be treated as a transfer or demise of the land in question, the following conditions must be satisfied:

(a) the grantor must intend the grantee to have exclusive use of the land. If the grantor retains the ability to exercise a degree of control, so that the grantee cannot exclude all others from the land, the grant cannot operate as a transfer of the land. However, the grant may still operate as a transfer or demise if the grantor retains an interest in the boundaries or structures only that delimit the area (such as the ceilings, walls and floors), or the grantor's retained property has a right of support, or the grant imposes covenants to protect the grantor's retained property; and
(b) the area the subject of the grant must be well-defined. This will clearly be the case where the description includes details of the area's length, width and height or where the purpose of the grant (for example exclusive use of a storage room) in itself defines the area.

If the exclusive use *is* treated as a transfer or demise of the legal estate, HMLR will include it within the property description in the property register of the grantee's registered title. Where necessary, HMLR will make a reference to it on the title plan to supplement this. In the grantor's registered title, the land will be either excluded from the registered title (in the case of a transfer) or included in the notice of the burden of the lease (in the case of a demise).

The land will be limited to the area over which exclusive use has been granted; it will not therefore include the airspace over it or the soil beneath it, as the purpose of such a grant (rather than the transfer or demise of the entirety of the land outright) is presumably to except everything lying above or below it.

In other cases, HMLR will treat the grant of exclusive use as an easement but, because of its exclusive nature, it will make specific entries on both the grantee's and grantor's titles in relation to it. HMLR will not include the land over which it is granted within the red edging on the title plan of the grantee's registered title (other than where the land overlaps with the footprint of the red edging). Nor will it be included within the property description in the property register. Instead, HMLR will make a separate entry in the grantee's registered title in respect of the benefit of the grant of exclusive use. The entry will be along the lines of:

> A [*details of deed containing the grant of exclusive use*] dated [*date*] made between [*parties*] grants the exclusive use of the [*describe land, for example basement store room*] shown [*plans reference*] on the title plan.

If necessary to supplement the description of the relevant land in the register entry, HMLR will make a reference to it on the title plan. HMLR will make a separate entry even if the deed containing the grant also grants other easements.

The land subject to the grant of exclusive use will continue to be included within the grantor's registered title and HMLR will add a specific notice of the burden of the grant in the grantor's title, even if the deed containing the grant also grants other easements. The entry will be along the lines of:

> The land in this title is subject to the exclusive use of the [*describe land, for example basement store room*] shown [*plans reference*] on the title plan referred to in a [*details of deed containing the grant of exclusive use*] dated [*date*] made between [*parties*].

---

1 (1890) 44 Ch D 12 (CA) at 26.

2 [1893] AC 416 (HL) at 428.

67 FEES

Land Registration Fee Orders prescribe the fees payable for HMLR's services. The current Order is the Land Registration Fee Order 2024 (SI 2024/931) (the Fee Order).

The HMLR website contains a fee calculator for all types of application.[1]

An applicant must normally pay any fee on delivery of the application.[2] The permitted means of payment depends upon how the application was delivered and are set out in the following table:

Method of delivery	*Permitted payment methods*
Electronic means or by email and a notice given under LRR 2003, Sch 2 requires payment by direct debit	Direct debit
Other electronic means	Credit or debit card
Personal delivery or made orally in accordance with a notice given under LRR 2003, Sch 2	Cash Cheque or postal order crossed and made payable to HM Land Registry Credit or debit card Direct debit
Telephone in accordance with a notice given under LRR 2003, Sch 2	Credit or debit card
Otherwise	Direct debit Cheque or postal order crossed and made payable to HM Land Registry

When two or more instruments relating to the same land are delivered for registration as part of the same application, a separate fee is payable in respect of each; but when a sale and a sub-sale are effected by one instrument of transfer only one fee, assessed on the price paid by the purchaser or the sub-purchaser, whichever is the greater, is payable.[3] There are special provisions for 'large scale' applications involving large numbers of 'land units', as defined in the Fee Order.[4]

1 www.gov.uk/guidance/hm-land-registry-registration-services-fees.
2 Land Registration Fee Order 2024 (SI 2024/931) (the Fee Order), art 13(2).
3 Fee Order, art 3(4) and (5).
4 Fee Order, art 6.

68 FIRST REGISTRATION

The LRA 2002 provides for first registration of title to certain unregistered legal estates. Title to an estate in land may be capable of either voluntary or compulsory first registration.[1] Title to a rentcharge, a franchise or a profit à prendre in gross may be capable of voluntary first registration, but is not currently subject to compulsory first registration; nor is land consisting of mines and minerals held apart from the surface.[2]

68.1 Legal estates capable of first registration

An applicant may apply for first registration of an unregistered legal estate which is either:

(a) an estate in land;
(b) a rentcharge;
(c) a franchise; or
(d) a profit à prendre in gross.[3]

It is no longer possible to apply for first registration of title to an unregistered manor.

If the application relates to a leasehold estate in land, the lease must be either:

(a) for a discontinuous period; or
(b) for a term of which more than 7 years are unexpired.

In calculating the duration of the lease for this purpose, a person holding in the same right both a lease in possession and a lease to take effect in possession on, or within a month of, the end of the lease in possession, may, to the extent they relate to the same land, treat them as one continuous term.[4]

The applicant may apply to be registered as proprietor of the legal estate on first registration if:

(a) the estate is vested in him; or
(b) he is entitled to require the estate to be vested in him.[5]

For example, a person entitled solely and absolutely under a trust of land may apply.[6] A person who has contracted to buy an unregistered legal estate, however, cannot apply to be registered as proprietor before completion of the contract.[7] A person with a leasehold estate vested in him as mortgagee may not apply for first registration of that leasehold estate while there is a subsisting right of redemption.[8]

It is not possible to apply for first registration of a leasehold estate under:

(a) a relevant social housing tenancy;[9] or
(b) a PPP lease.[10]

68.2 Compulsory first registration

A person must apply for first registration of any freehold estate in land, or leasehold estate in land with more than 7 years left to run, on the occurrence of any of the following:[11]

(a) a transfer, conveyance or assignment for valuable or other consideration;[12]
(b) a transfer, conveyance or assignment by way of gift;[13]
(c) a transfer, conveyance or assignment in pursuance of an order of any court;
(d) an assent (including a vesting assent);
(e) a transfer, conveyance or assignment giving effect to a partition of land subject to a trust of land;
(f) a deed that appoints (or by virtue of Charities Act 2011, s 334 has effect as if it appointed) a new trustee or is made in consequence of the appointment of a new trustee;
(g) a vesting order under Trustee Act 1925, s 44 that is consequential on the appointment of a new trustee;
(h) a transfer, conveyance or assignment where Housing Act 1985 (HA 1985), s 171A applies (disposal by a landlord leading to a person's ceasing to be a secure tenant; the preserved right to buy applies);
(i) a first legal mortgage protected by the deposit of the title deeds (other than a mortgage of a lease with no more than 7 years to run at the date of the mortgage); and
(j) a grant by His Majesty out of demesne land of an estate in fee simple absolute in possession, other than a grant to himself.

A person must apply for first registration on the grant of any of the following leases out of an unregistered freehold estate in land or out of an unregistered leasehold estate in land where the lease has more than 7 years left to run at the date of the grant:[14]

(a) a lease for more than 7 years from the date of the grant for valuable or other consideration;[15]
(b) a lease for more than 7 years from the date of the grant by way of gift;
(c) a lease for more than 7 years from the date of the grant in pursuance of an order of any court;
(d) a lease for any length of term, which takes effect in possession more than 3 months from the date of the grant;[16]
(e) a lease for any length of term in pursuance of HA 1985, Pt 5 (the right to buy);
(f) a lease where the HA 1985, s 171A applies (disposal by a landlord leading to a person's ceasing to be a secure tenant; the preserved right to buy applies); and
(g) a lease by His Majesty out of demesne land for more than 7 years.

It is *not* compulsory to apply for first registration in respect of any of the following:

(a) an assignment of a mortgage term;
(b) an assignment or surrender of a lease to the owner of the immediate reversion where the term is to merge in that reversion;

(c) a mortgage by demise which is not a first legal mortgage protected by the deposit of the title deeds;
(d) any transaction relating to a rentcharge;
(e) any transaction relating to a franchise;
(f) any transaction relating to a profit à prendre in gross;
(g) a transfer or grant creating a trust where the settlor retains the whole of the beneficial interest;
(h) a transfer or grant uniting the bare legal title and the beneficial interest in property held under a trust under which the settlor retained the whole of the beneficial interest;
(i) any transaction relating solely to mines and minerals held apart from the surface;
(j) a transfer or grant of a lease that is a relevant social housing tenancy;[17]
(k) a transfer by operation of law;[18] and
(l) a general vesting declaration under the Compulsory Purchase (Vesting Declarations) Act 1981.

68.3 Duty to apply for first registration

Where compulsory first registration applies, the estate owner, or his successor in title, must apply for first registration within 2 months of the event triggering the duty to apply.[19] Where the event triggering compulsory first registration is a mortgage, it is the mortgagor, not the mortgagee, who must apply.[20] However, the mortgagee may apply for first registration in the name of the mortgagor, whether or not the mortgagor consents.[21] Where the mortgage is not a first legal mortgage protected by the deposit of the title deeds, the mortgagee may not apply for first registration without the consent of the mortgagor.

Any interested party may apply to HMLR for an order extending the period of 2 months in which the application for first registration must be made. Such application may be made by way of letter setting out the reasons why the order should be made. No fee is payable. If HMLR is satisfied there is good reason for doing so, it may by order provide that the period for registration ends on such later date as it may specify in the order.[22]

Where it is compulsory to apply for first registration but an application has not been made within 2 months, or by any later date stated in an order of HMLR, the transfer, grant or creation of a legal estate becomes void as regards the transfer, grant or creation of that legal estate.[23] In the case of a transfer, the title to the legal estate reverts to the transferor who holds it on a bare trust for the transferee. In the case of a lease or first mortgage, the grant or creation has effect as a contract made for valuable consideration to grant or create the legal estate concerned.[24]

If HMLR makes an order extending the period for registration where LRA 2002, s 7(1) has already applied, that application of s 7(1) is treated as not having occurred.[25] The possibility of reverter arising under s 7(1) is disregarded for the purposes of determining whether a fee simple is a fee simple absolute.

If the legal estate is retransferred, re-granted or recreated because of a failure to comply with the requirement for first registration, the transferee, grantee or mortgagor is liable to the other party for all the proper costs of and incidental to the retransfer, re-grant or recreation of the legal estate. That person is also liable to indemnify the other party in respect of any other liability reasonably incurred by him because of the failure to comply with the requirement of registration.[26]

68.4 Application for first registration

An applicant should deliver to HMLR:

(a) an application in form FR1;
(b) sufficient details, by plan or otherwise, so that the land can be clearly identified on the OS map;[27]
(c) in the case of a leasehold estate, the lease, if in the control of the applicant (and a certified copy, if the applicant wishes for the original to be returned);
(d) all deeds and documents relating to the title that are in the control of the applicant, including relevant Land Charges searches (with any entries accounted for and, where applicable, certified by a conveyancer as not affecting the estate);
(e) a list in duplicate in form DL of all the documents delivered;
(f) form DI giving the information as to overriding interests required by LRR 2003, r 28 including any documentary evidence of the interests;[28]
(g) the appropriate confirmation or evidence as to identity;[29]
(h) the appropriate LTT or SDLT certificate(s) or other evidence;[30] and
(i) the fee payable.[31]

If the applicant knows of any rights, interests or claims affecting the estate other than those disclosed in the title deeds or form DI, these should be disclosed in the form FR1. This would include, for example, any rights in the course of being acquired over the estate by adverse possession, or a disputed third-party claim relating to the estate.

For the position where the application is for first registration of an estate in mines and minerals held apart from the surface, see 115 Mines and Minerals.

Unless all the land above and below the surface is included in the application for first registration, the applicant must supply a plan of the surface on, under or over which the land to be registered lies, and sufficient information to define the vertical and horizontal extents of the land.[32] This requirement does not apply where only mines and minerals are excluded from the application.

Where the applicant for first registration cannot produce a full documentary title, the application must be supported by evidence to satisfy HMLR that the applicant is entitled, or required, to apply for first registration and, where appropriate, to account for the absence of documentary evidence of title.[33] This means that the evidence must show that the applicant has the legal estate vested in him or that he is entitled to require the legal estate to be vested in him. In practice, the evidence is usually in the form of a statutory declaration or statement of truth, exhibiting any appropriate supporting documents. A statement of truth may be in form ST3 in LRR 2003, Sch 1.[34]

Where the applicant for first registration comprises more than one person, panel 9 of form FR1 should be completed to confirm the basis of the trusts upon which the property will be held. This enables HMLR to decide whether the entry of a restriction in Form A will be necessary.[35] The wording of Form A is set out in Appendix IV.

HMLR will assume that the applicant requests the return of all documents relating to the title except any statutory declaration, statement of truth, subsisting lease, subsisting charge, LTT or SDLT certificate(s), or the latest document of title (for example the conveyance to the applicant). Those documents will be returned if the applicant lodges a certified copy with the application for first registration; he does not need to lodge certified copies of the other documents accompanying the application.

68.5 Examination of title

In examining the title shown by the documents accompanying an application for first registration, HMLR may have regard to:

(a) any examination by a conveyancer before the application; and
(b) the nature of the property.[36]

HMLR may:

(a) make searches and enquiries and give notices to other persons;
(b) direct the applicant to make searches and enquiries; and
(c) advertise the application.[37]

HMLR may register the applicant with absolute title if HMLR is of the opinion that the applicant's title to the estate is such as a willing buyer could properly be advised by a competent professional adviser to accept and (in the case of a leasehold estate) if HMLR approves the landlord's title to grant the lease. HMLR may disregard the fact that the title appears to it to be open to objection if it is of the opinion that the defect will not cause the holding under the title to be disturbed.[38]

For the classes of title which HMLR may grant following the examination of title and the effect of first registration with a particular class of title, see 32 Classes of Title.

HMLR may enter the benefit of an appurtenant right in the register on first registration if, on examining the title, HMLR is satisfied that the right subsists as a legal estate and benefits the registered estate.[39]

Where the existence of an appurtenant right is not apparent on the face of the title deeds, the applicant may apply in writing using form FR1 providing details of the right and evidence of its existence;[40] this evidence may be in the form of a statement of truth in form ST4 in LRR 2003, Sch 1, if appropriate.[41] The applicant should list this application in panel 5 of form FR1. If HMLR is satisfied that the right subsists as a legal estate and benefits the registered estate, it may enter it in the register. If HMLR is not so satisfied, it may enter details of the right claimed in the property register with such qualification as it considers appropriate; such an entry does not guarantee the validity of the claimed right.[42]

On first registration HMLR, whenever practicable, enters in the proprietorship register the price paid or value declared. That entry will remain until there is a change of proprietor or some other change in the register of title which HMLR considers would render the entry misleading.[43]

HMLR must enter a notice in the register of the burden of any interest which appears from its examination of title to affect the registered title.[44] This does not apply to:

(a) interests that, under LRA 2002, s 33 or s 90(4), cannot be protected by notice;[45]
(b) public rights;
(c) local land charges; or
(d) an interest which appears to HMLR to be of a trivial or obvious character, or the entry of a notice which would be likely to cause confusion or inconvenience.[46]

Where the applicant has provided information to HMLR in form DI about a disclosable overriding interest that affects the estate to which the application relates, HMLR may enter a notice in the register in respect of that interest.[47]

If it appears to HMLR on first registration that an agreement prevents the acquisition of rights of light or air for the benefit of the registered estate, it may make an entry in the property register of that estate.[48]

In defined circumstances, before completing an application for first registration with absolute title of a leasehold title, HMLR must serve notice of the application on the proprietor of the registered reversionary estate. Those circumstances are where:

(a) the lease was granted out of an unregistered legal estate, or the reversion was registered but the grant of the lease was not required to be completed by registration;
(b) at the time of the application the immediate reversion to the lease is registered;
(c) the lease is not noted in the register of that reversionary title; and
(d) it is not apparent from the application that the proprietor of that reversionary title consents to the registration.

On completing registration of the leasehold estate, HMLR must enter notice of the lease in the register of that reversionary title.[49]

Where a first legal mortgage is the event that triggers compulsory first registration, HMLR must enter the mortgagee as the proprietor of that charge if it is satisfied of that person's entitlement.[50] As regards any other legal mortgage which is either a charge on the legal estate that is being registered or a charge on such a charge, HMLR must enter the mortgagee as the proprietor of that charge if it is satisfied of that person's entitlement.[51]

If, while a person is required to apply for first registration of a legal estate, there is a dealing with that estate, LRA 2002 applies to that dealing as if the dealing had taken place after the date of first registration. Where the dealing is delivered for registration with the application for first registration, it has effect from the time of making that application.[52]

---

1 LRA 2002, ss 3(1) and 4(2).
2 LRA 2002, s 4(9).
3 LRA 2002, s 3(1).
4 LRA 2002, s 3(7).
5 LRA 2002, s 3(2).

6 *Saunders v Vaultier* (1841) 41 ER 482. Although, because of the difficulty in proving such claims, HMLR may refuse to register or award only a qualified title (see 32 Classes of Title).

7 LRA 2002, s 3(6).

8 LRA 2002, s 3(5).

9 LRA 2002, s 3(4A). LRA 2002, s 132(1) contains the definition of a 'relevant social tenancy'.

10 LRA 2002, s 90(1). A PPP lease is one within the meaning given by Greater London Authority Act 1999, s 218, which makes provision about leases created for PPPs relating to transport in London.

11 LRA 2002, ss 4(1) and 80.

12 If the estate transferred has a negative value, it is regarded as transferred for valuable or other consideration (LRA 2002, s 4(6)).

13 This includes gifts for the purposes of constituting a trust under which the settlor does not retain the whole of the beneficial interest, or uniting the bare legal title and the beneficial interest in property held under a trust under which the settlor did not, on constitution, retain the whole beneficial interest (LRA 2002, s 4(7)).

14 LRA 2002, ss 4 and 80.

15 If the estate granted has a negative value, it is regarded as granted for valuable or other consideration (LRA 2002, s 4(6)).

16 In the case of a sub-lease it is compulsory to register only if the lease out of which it is granted has, at the date of that grant, more than 7 years to run.

17 As defined in LRA 2002, s 132(1).

18 For example, the vesting of a deceased's estate in his personal representative(s).

19 LRA 2002, s 6.

20 LRA 2002, s 6(2).

21 LRR 2003, r 21.

22 LRA 2002, s 6(5).

23 LRA 2002, s 7(1)

24 LRA 2002, s 7(2).

25 LRA 2002, s 7(3)).

26 LRA 2002, s 8.

27 If the application is to register a register a rentcharge, franchise or profit à prendre in gross, the land to be identified is the land affected by that estate.

28 See 128.4 Duty to disclose overriding interests.

29 See 84 Identity Evidence.

30 For land in Wales, see 94 Land Transaction Tax or for land in England, see 168 Stamp Duty Land Tax.

31 See 67 Fees.

32 LRR 2003, r 26.

33 LRR 2003, r 27.

34 See 110 Lost or Destroyed Title Deeds.

35 See 92 Joint Proprietors.

36 LRR 2003, r 29.

37 LRR 2003, r 30.

38 LRA 2002, ss 9(2) and (3) and 10(2) and (4).

39 LRR 2003, r 33(1)(a).
40 LRR 2003, r 33(1)(b).
41 LRR 2003, r 33(3).
42 LRR 2003, r 33(2).
43 LRR 2003, r 8(2) and (3).
44 LRR 2003, r 35(1).
45 See 119 Notices.
46 LRR 2003, r 35(2).
47 LRR 2003, r 28(4).
48 LRR 2003, r 36.
49 LRR 2003, r 37.
50 LRR 2003, r 22.
51 LRR 2003, r 34.
52 LRR 2003, r 38.

69 FLOATING CHARGES

Companies use debentures to secure money raised by way of loan. A debenture may create a legal charge or an equitable charge; if equitable, it may be in the form of a fixed equitable charge or a floating charge.[1] A floating charge cannot be substantively registered but may be capable of protection by an entry in the register.

If a company has created a debenture containing a floating charge on its assets, it must disclose the existence of the charge when the company makes an application for the first registration of its title to an estate affected by the debenture. The applicant should supply a certified copy of the debenture with the application if it wishes HMLR to return the original. Where, on first registration of land held by a company, it appears to HMLR from its examination of the title that it is subject to a floating charge, it will enter a notice of it in the charges register.[2] If the debenture creating the floating charge contains a proviso which prohibits the creation of any other charges ranking in priority to or *pari passu* with the floating charge, HMLR will include a note of that proviso in the notice of the floating charge. The entry of a notice in respect of a floating charge in the charges register does not remove the need for it to be registered under the Companies Act 2011.

Where a company that has created a debenture acquires a registered estate or a registered charge, or where a company that is already the proprietor of a registered estate or a registered charge creates a debenture, HMLR will not make any entry in the register to protect any floating charge created by the debenture (whether registered at Companies House or not) without a specific application.

When a company creates a floating charge relating to registered land, the chargee cannot apply for an official search with priority using form OS1 or form OS2.

A chargee may protect a floating charge relating to registered land by an application for entry of an agreed notice or a unilateral notice.

69.1 Agreed notice

In addition to the usual documents required,[3] an applicant for entry of an agreed notice should deliver to HMLR the debenture creating the floating charge or a certified copy of it.

Where the consent of the registered proprietor is not available but, for example, the original debenture has been executed by him, this is likely to be sufficient to satisfy HMLR of the validity of the applicant's claim for the purposes of LRA 2002, s 34(3)(c).

The agreed notice in the register will give details of the interest protected.

If the chargee subsequently discharges the floating charge, a party should apply to cancel the agreed notice using form CN1[4] accompanied by an appropriate evidence of the discharge. This may consist of either:

(a) if the discharge was registered at Companies House before 1 October 2009, a copy of a declaration of satisfaction in Companies House form 403A stamped as 'registered';
(b) if the discharge was registered at Companies House between 1 October 2009 and 5 April 2013, a copy of a declaration of satisfaction in Companies House form MG02;
(c) if the discharge was registered at Companies House from 6 April 2013, a copy of a declaration of satisfaction in Companies House form MR04;
(d) a letter from Companies House confirming that the charge has been satisfied; or
(e) a letter from the chargee addressed to HMLR confirming that the charge has been satisfied and including (where appropriate) confirmation that there has been no assignment of the benefit of the charge. If there has been an assignment, the applicant must provide the normal conveyancing evidence of devolution of title.

Where a purchaser from the chargor company is seeking to have the notice of the floating charge cancelled, he should deliver application form CN1 to HMLR at the same time as his application to register the transfer. That application should be supported by a letter signed by the company's secretary or conveyancer to the effect that no event has occurred which would crystallise the charge. HMLR will normally accept this as sufficient evidence for the cancellation of the notice. HMLR will usually also accept a certificate to like effect from the chargee or its conveyancer. Where a lease by the chargor company is being registered with absolute leasehold title, the consent of the chargee under the floating charge will be required, otherwise HMLR may make a protective entry in the register.[5] This applies whether the floating charge is protected by an agreed notice or a unilateral notice.

69.2 Unilateral notice

An applicant may prefer to apply for entry of unilateral notice where he does not wish the terms of the charge to be open to public inspection and copying. The applicant should deliver to HMLR the usual documents required.[6]

The statement in panel 11 or conveyancer's certificate in panel 12 of form UN1 should be completed on the following lines to show the interest of the applicant:

> chargee having the benefit of a floating charge created by a [*specify the document creating the floating charge*] dated [*date*] made between [*registered proprietor*] and [*beneficiary of the unilateral notice*].

The unilateral notice in the register will give brief details of the interest protected and identify the beneficiary of that notice.

If the floating charge is subsequently discharged, the beneficiary should apply to cancel the unilateral notice using form UN2.[7] If the beneficiary fails to do so, the registered proprietor of the land may apply for cancellation of the unilateral notice using form UN4.[8] Evidence of discharge would not need to accompany either of these applications.

69.3 Crystallisation of floating charge

If a floating charge crystallises, the chargee should apply for an additional notice of the variation of the existing interest. This will show that the charge has become a fixed charge.[9] A chargee may apply for entry of an agreed notice or a unilateral notice, as above. Where the application is for entry of an agreed notice, evidence of the crystallisation should accompany the application. It will not normally be appropriate to apply to cancel or remove any existing notice, as the date of entry of that notice will be relevant for priority purposes.[10]

---

1 See 37 Companies and 49 Debentures.
2 LRR 2003, r 35.
3 See 119.1 Agreed notice.
4 See 119.2 Cancellation of a notice other than a unilateral notice or a home rights notice.
5 32.2 Titles to leasehold estates.
6 See 119.3 Unilateral notice.
7 See 119.5 Removal of a unilateral notice.
8 See 119.6 Cancellation of a unilateral notice.
9 LRR 2003, r 84(4).
10 See 138 Priorities.

70 FLYING FREEHOLDS

Sometimes the owner of a freehold property may own some or all of his property at one level or stratum, but not at all levels or strata. This can give rise to a so-called 'flying freehold'. A common example occurs where a room above a passageway is owned as part of a property, but the passageway itself is owned by the adjoining property.

When applying for first registration, unless all the land above and below the surface is included in the application for first registration, the applicant must provide a plan of the surface on, under or over which the land to be registered lies, and sufficient information to define the vertical or horizontal extents of the land.[1] This does not apply where it is only mines and minerals that are excluded from the application.[2]

Where the application for first registration shows that the land being registered is affected by a flying freehold, HMLR will make an appropriate entry in the property register. An example of such an entry is:

> NOTE: As to the part tinted blue on the title plan only the rooms over the passageway which form part of 15 Friar Street are included in the title.

Where a title was registered under LRA 1925, the Land Registration Rules 1925 provided that the registration of a person as proprietor of land vested in him all appurtenances appertaining or reputed to appertain to the land or any part of it, or, at the time of registration, demised, occupied, or enjoyed with the land, or reputed or known as part or parcel of or appurtenant to the land or any part of it.[3] The 1925 Rules also provided that this included the appropriate rights and interests which, had there been a conveyance of the land, would have passed under LPA 1925, s 62.

LRA 2002, ss 11(3) and 12(3) now provide that the registered freehold or leasehold estate is vested in the proprietor together with all interests subsisting for the benefit of the estate. In addition, LRA 2002, s 60 provides that where the boundary of a registered estate is a general boundary, that general boundary does not determine the exact line of the boundary. The result of these provisions is that if, for example, there is a room projecting over an adjoining owner's land or a cellar projecting under that land, this is usually included in the occupying owner's registered title even though it falls outside the red edging on the title plan, no details of the flying freehold having been supplied to HMLR at the time of registration.

Where a flying freehold has not been reflected by an entry in the property register, an application may be made for an alteration to the register by the making of such an entry on the title or titles affected. The applicant should deliver to HMLR:

(a) an application in form AP1;
(b) a statement of the alteration being applied for;
(c) all relevant evidence held by the applicant which is relevant to the application to alter the register; and
(d) the fee payable (if applicable).[4]

HMLR may make such enquiries as it thinks fit, which may include a survey where necessary, and must give notice of the proposed alteration to any person who would be affected by it, unless it is satisfied that such notice is unnecessary.[5]

1 LRR 2003, r 26(1).
2 LRR 2003, r 26(2).
3 Land Registration Rules 1925, r 251.
4 See 67 Fees.
5 LRR 2003, r 128. For further details, see 12.2 Alteration not pursuant to a court order.

71 FOREIGN LAW

Generally, the law relating to land is the law of the state in which the land is situated, i.e. the *lex situs*. In relation to registered estates under the LRA 2002, 'foreign law' is that of any country outside England and Wales. Accordingly, this includes the law of Scotland, Northern Ireland, the Channel Islands and the Isle of Man.

Issues of foreign law may, for example, sometimes arise in relation to a foreign power of attorney, divorce or bankruptcy. Any such issue will be considered by HMLR on an individual basis. For example, in the case of a foreign power of attorney, HMLR will consider whether the power is valid for land registration purposes and authorises the execution of the disposition in question.

72 FORESHORE

The foreshore is the shore and bed of the sea and of any tidal water, below the line of the medium high tide between the spring and neap tides.[1] In addition to the sea, tidal waters occur in river estuaries, harbours and any other water feature that adjoins the sea. There is a presumption that the Crown owns the foreshore in demesne, although in practice extensive tracts of the foreshore are in fact owned by other parties such as port authorities, local authorities or even private individuals.

Given the above presumption, where it appears to HMLR that any of the land in an application for first registration comprises foreshore, it must serve notice of the application on the Crown Estate Commissioners.[2] It must also serve notice on the Chancellor of the Duchy of Lancaster in the case of land in the county palatine of Lancaster and on the Port of London Authority in the case of land within its jurisdiction. In the case of land in the counties of Devon and Cornwall and the Isles of Scilly, HMLR must also serve notice on such person as the Duke of Cornwall, or the possessor for the time being of the Duchy of Cornwall, appoints. Where the land is within the jurisdiction of the Port of London Authority, HMLR must also serve notice of the application on such person as the Duke of Cornwall, or the possessor for the time being of the Duchy of Cornwall, appoints.

The notice must allow a period ending at 12 noon on the 20th working day after the date of issue of the notice in which to object to the application.[3] A working day is any day from Monday to Friday (inclusive) which is not Christmas Day, Good Friday or any other day either specified or declared by proclamation under Banking and Financial Dealings Act 1971, s 1 or appointed by the Secretary of State or certified by HMLR as being an 'interrupted day' due to delay or failure of a communication service or to some other event or circumstance causing substantial interruption in the normal operation of HMLR.

HMLR need not serve such a notice where, if it was served, it would be served on the applicant for first registration.[4]

Where the registered title comprises only foreshore, or comprises land and a separate parcel of foreshore, the description of the registered estate in the property register will describe the foreshore as such. However, HMLR will not refer to it separately where the registered estate comprises a single parcel of land which includes foreshore.

The effect of accretion and diluvion also applies to foreshore, so that the position of foreshore is moveable due to deposition and erosion. Sudden or violent changes, for example through the effects of a storm or the building of sea walls, do not affect the owner's rights. HMLR will therefore make an entry in the property register to reflect the effect of accretion and diluvion. On first registration, HMLR will either:

(a) enter a note in the property register for the property about the effect of accretion and diluvion, or
(b) if its investigation reveals an agreement about the operation of accretion and diluvion, enter a note of that agreement,

in the property register for the property.

Where there is an agreement about the operation of accretion and diluvion, HMLR will also add a note to confirm that it is registered for the purposes of LRA 2002, s 61(2). That is because that section provides such an agreement will only have effect if registered.

Where land is already registered and parties reach an agreement about the operation of accretion and diluvion, a party must apply to register it.[5] Such an application should be in form AP1 quoting the affected title numbers and must be made by, or be accompanied by the consent of, the proprietor of the registered estate and of any registered charge, unless they are party to the agreement.[6]

Where registered land consists of foreshore belonging to the King in right of the Crown or the Duchy of Lancaster or to the Duchy of Cornwall, the period of adverse possession required before an application may be made under LRA 2002, Sch 6, para 1(1) is 60 years rather than 10 years.[7] For these purposes land is treated as foreshore if it has been foreshore at any time in the 10 years before the application by the squatter for registration.[8] A similar period applies in respect of Crown foreshore which is unregistered.[9] The normal limitation periods apply to foreshore which is not Crown land. For foreshore which is Crown land, see also 51 Demesne Land.

Registration of title to foreshore does not affect existing public rights over foreshore. Such public rights are typically fishing and navigation,[10] although there may be other rights in a particular locality. Public rights are interests which override both first registration and registered dispositions.[11] Consequently, such interests are protected notwithstanding that there is no entry of them in the register.[12]

Public rights are not disclosable overriding interests under LRR 2003, r 28 or r 57. See also 2 Accretion and Diluvion.

1 LRA 2002, Sch 6, para 13(3).
2 LRR 2003, r 31.
3 LRR 2003, r 31(2).
4 LRR 2003, r 31(3).
5 LRA 2002, s 61(2).
6 LRR 2003, r 123.
7 LRA 2002, Sch 6, para 13(1).
8 LRA 2002, Sch 6, para 13(2).
9 LA 1980, s 15(7) and Sch 1, para 11(1).
10 *Blundell v Catterall* [1821] 5 B & Ald 268.
11 LRA 2002, Sch 1, para 5 and Sch 3, para 5.
12 LRA 2002, ss 11, 12, 29 and 30.

73 FORMS

A registrable disposition of a registered estate or registered charge has effect only if it complies with the requirements in the LRR 2003 as to form and content.[1] LRR 2003, Sch 1 contains several prescribed forms of application and disposition (Sch 1 forms) and Sch 3 contains a small number of miscellaneous forms which must be used in all matters to which they refer (Sch 3 forms), but which can be adapted with HMLR's consent. LRR 2003, Sch 9 contains approved forms of execution of Sch 1 and Sch 3 forms, which can be adapted with HMLR's consent. HMLR also publishes Welsh language versions of these scheduled forms. Specific forms are referred to under the relevant headings elsewhere in this book. See Appendix II for a list of forms. See Appendix V for the Sch 3 forms. See Appendix VI for the Sch 9 forms.

Most types of application and disposition have a prescribed form. LRR 2003, r 206(1) requires that the prescribed form must be used. Thus LRR 2003, r 58 states that a transfer must be in form TP1, TP2, TR1, TR2, TR5, AS1 or AS3, as appropriate. Also, r 59 prescribes the forms of transfer which must be used to effect a transfer by way of exchange and deals with the need for a receipt for equality money and suitable additional wording in the transfer. LRR 2003, r 60 covers transfers of leasehold land where the rent is being apportioned or the land is being exonerated.

A document affecting a registered title must refer to the title number.[2] HMLR may permit a person to make an application relying on a document that is not in the relevant Sch 1 or Sch 3 form if that person cannot obtain and lodge the relevant scheduled form or it is only possible to do so at unreasonable expense, if HMLR is satisfied that neither the rights of any person nor the keeping of the register are likely to be materially prejudiced by allowing the alternative document to be relied upon.[3]

Any application or document in one of the Sch 1 forms must:

(a) be printed on durable A4 size paper;
(b) be reproduced as set out in Sch 1 as to its wording, layout, ruling, font and point size (except for forms ST1, ST2, ST3 and ST4 where the special forms of execution provided in r 215A(4) and (5) may be used instead);
(c) contain all the information required in an easily legible form; and
(d) if it consists of more than one sheet of paper, or refers to an attached plan or a continuation sheet, be securely fastened together.

An 'additional provisions' panel may be used, where provided within a Sch 1 form. If (other than in form DL) the necessary information will not fit in the panel provided, the panel must be continued on a continuation sheet in form CS.[4]

Where a form is produced electronically:

(a) the depth of a panel may be increased or reduced to fit the material to be comprised in it, and a panel may be divided at a page break;
(b) the text outside of the panels (other than the name and description of the form at the top of the page, and any text after the final panel) may be omitted;
(c) inapplicable certificates and statements may be omitted;
(d) the plural may be used instead of the singular and the singular instead of the plural;
(e) panels which would contain only the panel number and the panel heading may be omitted, but such omission must not affect the numbering of subsequent panels;
(f) 'X' boxes may be omitted where all inapplicable statements and certificates have been omitted;
(g) the sub-headings in an additional provisions panel may be added to, amended, repositioned or omitted;
(h) 'Seller' may be substituted for 'Transferor' and 'Buyer' for 'Transferee' in a transfer on sale;
(i) the vertical lines which define the left and right boundaries of the panel may be omitted.[5]

If no form is prescribed, the document must be in such form as HMLR may direct or allow.

An applicant may seek HMLR's approval of a draft document:

(a) when it is desired to adapt a Sch 3 form for a particular matter;[6]
(b) when it is a document for which no form is prescribed;[7] or
(c) when it is desired to make an application for which there is a prescribed Sch 1 or Sch 3 form, but the applicant wishes to rely on an alternative document instead.[8]

The applicant should send the draft (with plan if any) and a copy to HMLR. No fee is currently payable. HMLR will limit any approval to matters of form; the person lodging the document for registration will be responsible for ensuring that it carries out the intention of the parties and for all other matters of substance, due execution, etc.

When requesting consent to use an alternative document in place of a prescribed form, the applicant must provide evidence to HMLR to show why:

(a) it is not possible to obtain and lodge the relevant prescribed form (duly executed, if appropriate); or
(b) it is only possible to do so at unreasonable expense.[9]

Before acceding to such a request, HMLR must be satisfied that neither the rights of any person nor the keeping of the register are likely to be materially prejudiced.[10] HMLR may make the acceptance of a non-scheduled document conditional on the provision of other documents or evidence in support of the application.[11]

Where several associated dispositions relating to a particular registered title are delivered for registration together, the applicant may number the application forms consecutively (for example when there are five applications: 1/5, 2/5, 3/5, 4/5 and 5/5), so that HMLR staff will readily identify that they should be dealt with together and in the order indicated. The appropriate number should be endorsed prominently at the top of the first page of each form.

---

1 LRA 2002, s 25(1).
2 LRR 2003, r 212(3).
3 LRR 2003, r 209.
4 LRR 2003, r 210.
5 LRR 2003, r 211.
6 LRR 2003, r 206(2).
7 LRR 2003, r 212.
8 LRR 2003, r 209.
9 LRR 2003, r 209(3).
10 LRR 2003, r 209(4).
11 LRR 2003, r 209(5).

74 FRANCHISES

A franchise is 'an incorporeal hereditament which has been authoritatively defined as a royal privilege or branch of the royal prerogative subsisting in the hands of a subject, by grant from the King'.[1] A franchise is normally created by a grant from the Crown in the form of a charter or letters patent, although it may also be claimed by prescription. A franchise does not carry with it ownership of the physical land to which it relates and is distinct from the freehold or leasehold estates in that land.

The most common franchise is the right to hold a market or fair. A right of market confers on the owner a monopoly right, in the form of the exclusive right to hold markets within a certain radius. A fair is a market held at rarer intervals.

A franchise can be confiscated by the Crown or abolished by Act of Parliament; for example, Wild Creatures and Forest Laws Act 1971, s 1(1) abolished franchises of forest, free chase, park or free warren. Franchises were not capable of registration under the LRA 1925 but may now be the subject of voluntary registration.[2] However, it is not compulsory to apply for first registration of the title to a franchise.

The LRR 2003 differentiate between an 'affecting franchise' and a 'relating franchise'.[3] An affecting franchise is one which relates to a defined area of land and is an adverse right affecting, or capable of affecting, the title to an estate or charge. A relating franchise is one which is not an affecting franchise.

HMLR's view is that most franchises are relating franchises. As such they will not constitute interests which override, because they do not affect an estate or charge. Thus in the case of a market franchise, it is considered that this will be a relating franchise because even if it relates to a definable area, it does not appear to give the franchisee the right to enter the land without the landowner's consent and so does not confer property rights adversely affecting the title to any estate or charge. Relating franchises cannot, therefore, be the subject of an application for entry of a notice in the register.

In the case of an affecting franchise, it is possible to register a caution against first registration both of that franchise and of any estate in land that it affects. Although it is possible to register a caution against first registration of a relating franchise (rather than against the land to which it relates), such a caution will not provide protection in relation to an application for first registration of the land to which it relates, as it does not 'affect' that land for the purposes of LRA 2002, s 15(1)(b).

Until 12 October 2013, the benefit of an affecting franchise was an unregistered interest which overrode first registration and registered dispositions.[4] There was a duty to disclose the burden of an affecting franchise under LRR 2003, r 28 or r 57. On first registration of title, HMLR will enter a notice in the register as to the burden of an affecting franchise, if it appears from its examination of the title to affect the land.

After the period of 10 years beginning on 13 October 2003, the automatic protection of an affecting franchise as an overriding interest ended.[5] The person having the benefit of the affecting franchise (if its priority has not already been previously defeated and it continues to subsist) should therefore protect it in the register. If he does not do so, the priority of the affecting franchise may be defeated on a subsequent first registration of unregistered burdened land or on a subsequent registration of a registrable disposition of registered burdened land for valuable consideration,[6] as the case may be. If the burdened land is unregistered he should apply for a caution against first registration. If the burdened land is registered he should apply for the entry of a notice in the register.

74.1 Caution against first registration

An applicant should deliver to HMLR the usual documents required.[7] The applicant should not exhibit any documents to the application; the statement should be self-contained. The statement of truth in panel 10 of form CT1 should be completed on the following lines to show the interest of the applicant:

> owner of the following franchise affecting the land: [*set out details of the franchise, including details of the grant under which it arose*].

The interest stated in form CT1 will appear in the caution register, together with a description of the legal estate to which the caution relates. For the effect of a caution against first registration, see 25 Cautions Against First Registration.

74.2 Agreed notice

An affecting (but not a relating) franchise may be protected by entry of an agreed notice. In addition to the usual documents required,[8] an applicant should deliver to HMLR the deed, order or instrument giving rise to the interest claimed or a certified copy of it, or (if there is no such deed, order or instrument) other details of the interest claimed to satisfy HMLR as to the nature of the applicant's claim.

Documentary evidence of the creation or existence of the franchise will normally be in the form of a certified copy (together with a certified translation if the copy document is in Latin) of the Charter or Letters Patent, together with evidence to demonstrate that the franchise is now vested in the applicant and remains actively exercised. Where the franchise is claimed by prescription, the applicant must provide evidence by way of statutory declaration or statement of truth of at least 20 years' prescriptive use.

The agreed notice in the register will give details of the interest protected.

Where the registered proprietor does not consent to the entry in the register of an agreed notice and the applicant cannot provide evidence to satisfy HMLR of the validity of his claim, he may still apply for entry of a unilateral notice.

74.3 Unilateral notice

An affecting (but not a relating) franchise may be protected by entry of a unilateral notice. An applicant should deliver to HMLR the usual documents required.[9]

The statement in panel 11 or conveyancer's certificate in panel 12 of form UN1 should be completed on the following lines to show the interest of the applicant:

> owner of the following franchise affecting the land: [*set out details of the franchise, including details of the grant under which it arose*].

The unilateral notice in the register will give brief details of the interest protected and identify the beneficiary of that notice.

74.4 First registration of a franchise

Both a relating franchise and an affecting franchise may be the subject of an application for first registration of title. However, to be capable of registration, a franchise must constitute a legal estate and be either:

(a) perpetual; or
(b) for a term of years absolute with more than 7 years unexpired.

The applicant should make clear whether he is applying for registration of a relating franchise or an affecting franchise.

In addition to the usual documents required,[10] an applicant should deliver to HMLR:

(a) (in the case of an affecting franchise) sufficient details, by plan or otherwise, so that the area of land to which the franchise relates can be clearly identified on the OS map;
(b) (in the case of a relating franchise) details of the current administrative area (i.e. the county or unitary authority) in which the franchise operates;
(c) the original (together with a certified translation if the document is in Latin) of the Charter or Letters Patent, or a certified copy; and
(d) (in the case of a franchise claimed by prescription) evidence by way of statutory declaration or statement of truth (which may be in form ST4 in LRR 2003, Sch 1) of at least 20 years' prescriptive use.

Where the applicant for first registration cannot produce a full documentary title, they must provide evidence to account for this. This will usually be in the form of a statutory declaration or statement of truth, exhibiting any appropriate supporting documents. A statement of truth may be in form ST3 in LRR 2003, Sch 1.[11]

Where two or more people apply to be registered as proprietors of a franchise and a sole proprietor or the survivor of joint proprietors will not be able to give a valid receipt for capital money, they must apply for entry of a restriction in Form A.[12] The wording of Form A is set out in Appendix IV.

HMLR will normally serve notice of an application for registration of a franchise upon the Crown. The applicant should lodge any relevant correspondence with the Crown as part of the application. In the case of an affecting franchise, HMLR will also serve notice on all the registered proprietors of estates in land, charges and relevant franchises within the defined area of the franchise and (where appropriate) on any known unregistered owners, chargees and relevant franchise-holders.

On first registration of an affecting franchise, HMLR will create a title plan based on the OS map and refer to it in the description of the registered estate in the property register. HMLR will also index the area affected on the index map. It will then be revealed on the result of an official search of the index map in respect of the land affected.

On first registration of a relating franchise, HMLR does not create any title plan. HMLR indexes relating franchises in the index of relating franchises and manors. This is an index of verbal descriptions of:

(a) registered franchises which are relating franchises;
(b) pending applications for first registration of relating franchises;
(c) registered manors;

(d) cautions against first registration where the subject of the caution is a relating franchise; and
(e) pending applications for such cautions.

The index contains the relevant title numbers, arranged by administrative area. HMLR does not reveal registered relating franchises on an official search of the index map, but does reveal them on the result of an official search of the index of relating franchises and manors made under LRR 2003, r 146. An application for an official search of the index of relating franchises and manors is made in form SIF.[13]

For first registrations generally, see 68 First Registration. For the classes of title which may be granted following the examination of title and the effect of first registration with a particular class of title, see 32 Classes of Title.

Registration of a franchise does not prejudice a right of the Crown to forfeit the franchise, and the priority of that right is automatically protected for the purposes of LRA 2002, s 29.[14]

74.5 Dispositions of registered franchises

The transfer or grant of a lease of a registered franchise is a registrable disposition which must be completed by registration. It will not operate at law until the registration requirements have been met.[15] This applies regardless of the length of the term of any such lease.

In the case of a transfer, the transferee should apply for registration in the normal way.[16]

Where there is a grant out of a lease of a registered franchise, the form of application depends upon the length of the term of the lease. If the lease is for a term of more than 7 years from the date of the grant, the application is completed by the entry in the register of:

(a) the grantee (or his successor in title) as proprietor of the lease; and
(b) a notice in respect of the lease.[17]

If the lease is for a term not exceeding 7 years from the date of the grant, the application is completed only by the entry of a notice in respect of the lease.[18] An application for entry of a notice of a lease which is for a term not exceeding 7 years from the date of the grant may be made in form AP1 or form AN1.[19]

A lease of a franchise is not required to be in the form of a prescribed clauses lease. An applicant should deliver to HMLR the usual documents required.[20]

---

1 *Spook Erection Ltd v Secretary of State for the Environment* [1989] QB 300 at 305 per Nourse LJ.
2 LRA 2002, s 3.
3 LRR 2003, r 217.
4 LRA 2002, ss 11, 12, 29 and 30, Sch 1, para 13 and Sch 3, para 13.
5 LRA 2002, s 117(1).
6 LRA 2002, ss 11, 12, 29 and 30.
7 See 25 Cautions Against First Registration.
8 See 119.1 Agreed notice.
9 See 119.3 Unilateral notice.
10 See 68 First Registration.
11 See 110 Lost or Destroyed Title Deeds.
12 LRR 2003, r 94(2A). See 92 Joint Proprietors.
13 See 124.2 Search of the index of relating franchises and manors.
14 LRR 2003, r 196B.
15 LRA 2002, s 27(1) and (2)(c).
16 See 176.1 Registration of transfer.
17 LRA 2002, Sch 2, para 4.
18 LRA 2002, Sch 2, para 5.
19 LRR 2003, r 90.
20 See 98.7 Registration of leases which are registrable dispositions.

75 FRAUD OR FORGERY

Property fraud can potentially occur in relation to registered land as well as unregistered land. However, separate principles apply in relation to registered estates. In particular, in contrast to the position in unregistered land, the entry of a person in the register as the proprietor of a registered legal estate vests the legal estate in him even where it would not otherwise have vested in him.[1] Accordingly if, for example, a person is registered as proprietor as the result of a forged or fraudulent transfer, the legal estate is still vested in him. This is the case whether the transfer is void or merely voidable. This principle reflects the importance of the fact of registration, but this does not mean that a person who has been the victim of fraud or forgery has no recourse.

75.1 Alteration and rectification

Although the legal estate has so vested, this does not prevent an application being made for alteration of the register under LRA 2002, Sch 4.[2] An alteration of the register will constitute 'rectification' if it:

(a) involves the correction of a mistake; and
(b) prejudicially affects the title of a registered proprietor.[3]

Rectification is therefore a specific form of alteration. The LRA 2002 imposes certain limitations on rectification of a registered estate in land against a 'proprietor in possession'. Land is in the possession of a proprietor if it is physically in his possession, or in that of a person who is entitled (other than as an adverse possessor under LRA 2002, Sch 6) to be registered as the proprietor of the registered estate.[4] In the following cases land which is (or is treated as being) in the possession of the second-mentioned person is to be treated for these purposes as in the possession of the first-mentioned person:

(a) landlord and tenant;
(b) mortgagor and mortgagee;
(c) licensor and licensee; and
(d) trustee and beneficiary.

Where an alteration which would constitute rectification affects the title of the proprietor of a registered estate in land, no order may be made by the court or HMLR without his consent in relation to land in his possession, unless:

(a) he has by fraud or lack of proper care caused or substantially contributed to the mistake; or
(b) it would be unjust for any other reason for the alteration not to be made.

For example, if A and B were the registered proprietors of land and A forged B's signature on a transfer into his sole name, on registration of the transfer the legal estate would vest in A alone. Because of his fraud, an order for alteration to the register to show A and B as registered proprietors would normally be made, even if A had remained in possession. However, if HMLR registered a transfer to an innocent purchaser from A before the forgery came to light, an order for rectification would not usually be made to affect that proprietor if he was in possession of the land. In that situation, B may be entitled to indemnity from HMLR for the loss he has suffered.

In *Dhillon v Barclays Bank PLC*,[5] the court refused to rectify against a lender despite a forgery. The court said to do so would be unjust because it would leave the claimant in a better position than she would have been had there been no fraud.

75.2 Indemnity

The distinction between rectification and alteration in general is also important in relation to entitlement to indemnity under LRA 2002, Sch 8. Where HMLR rectifies the register because of fraud or forgery, the question arises whether a person who has suffered loss by reason of the rectification is entitled to be indemnified by HMLR. For these purposes, the proprietor of a registered estate or charge claiming in good faith under a forged disposition is, where the register is rectified, to be regarded as having suffered loss by reason of such rectification as if the disposition had not been forged.[6]

Conversely, where the register is not rectified notwithstanding fraud or forgery, for example because of the protection conferred upon a proprietor in possession of land referred to above, a person who has suffered loss by reason of the fraud or forgery may be entitled to be indemnified by HMLR.[7]

HMLR is not liable to pay any indemnity for any loss suffered wholly or partly because of:

(a) the claimant's own fraud; or
(b) the claimant's lack of proper care.

Where any loss is suffered by a claimant partly because of his own lack of proper care, any indemnity payable to him will be reduced to such extent as is fair having regard to his share in the responsibility for the loss. For these purposes, any fraud or lack of proper care on the part of a person from whom the claimant derives title (otherwise than under a disposition for valuable consideration which is registered or protected by an entry in the register) is to be treated as if it were fraud or lack of care on the part of the claimant.[8] For further details, see 86 Indemnity.

75.3 Restriction

Where the registered proprietor of a title or charge believes there is the possibility of an attempt to register a forged or fraudulent disposition, he may apply to enter a restriction in Form LL. The wording of Form LL is set out in Appendix IV. This requires a conveyancer's certificate to be lodged with an application, certifying that he is satisfied that the person who executed the document submitted for registration as disponor is the same person as the proprietor.

Where it is considered that there is a higher risk of forgery or fraud, application a person may apply under LRA 2002, s 42(1)(a) for entry of a non-standard restriction in the following form:

> No disposition of the registered estate by the registered proprietor is to be completed by registration.

This form of restriction effectively 'freezes' the register, so that no disposition by the proprietor can be registered until the restriction is cancelled or disapplied. However, such a restriction would not prevent a disposition by a registered chargee in exercise of its power of sale.

The registered proprietor should deliver to HMLR the usual documents required.[9]

Panel 9 of form RX1 should set out the required restriction(s). A restriction in a standard Form LL in LRR 2003, Sch 4 does not require the approval of HMLR to the terms of the restriction under LRA 2002, s 43(3).

The statement in panel 12 or conveyancer's certificate in panel 13 of form RX1 should give the reasons for the application.

If the applicant is a private individual and does not live at the property, he may apply for entry of a restriction in Form LL using form RQ. No fee is currently payable if this form is used.

Instead of applying for a non-standard restriction in form RX1, a company may apply in form RQ(Co) for entry of a specific non-standard counter-fraud restriction in titles of which it is the registered proprietor. HMLR will currently enter the restriction in up to three titles without a fee. The wording of the restriction requires a conveyancer to certify that he is satisfied the company transferring or mortgaging the property is the same company as the owner. The conveyancer must also certify that he has taken reasonable steps to establish that anyone who executed the deed on behalf of the company held the stated office at the time of execution.

It is also important that a registered proprietor ensures that his address for service in the register is kept up to date, to ensure that notices and other correspondence from HMLR are delivered to him. He should also consider registering for Property Alert.[10]

---

1 LRA 2002, s 58.
2 See 12 Alteration of the Register and 148 Rectification.
3 LRA 2002, Sch 4, para 1.
4 LRA 2002, s 131.
5 [2019] EWHC 475 (Ch).
6 LRA 2002, Sch 8, para 1(2)(b).
7 LRA 2002, Sch 8, para 1(1)(b).
8 LRA 2002, Sch 8, para 5.
9 See 153.1 Application for entry of restriction.
10 See 142 Property Alert.

76 FREEZING ORDERS, RESTRAINT ORDERS AND INTERIM RECEIVING ORDERS

Where a person has applied to the court for a freezing order affecting a registered estate or charge, he has a sufficient interest to apply for entry of a restriction in Form CC or Form DD, as appropriate.[1] The wording of Forms CC and DD is set out in Appendix IV. Where a person has the benefit of a freezing order or an undertaking given in place of a freezing order affecting a registered estate or charge, he has a sufficient interest to apply for entry of a restriction in Form AA or Form BB, as appropriate.[2] The wording of Forms AA and BB is set out in Appendix IV.

This applies equally where the International Criminal Court applies for entry of a restriction in Forms AA, BB, CC or DD in respect of a freezing order, or an application for a freezing order, under International Criminal Court Act 2001, Sch 6.[3] The LRA 2002 applies in relation to freezing orders under the International Criminal Court Act 2001, as it applies in relation to orders affecting land made by the court for the purpose of enforcing judgments or recognisances, except that no notice may be entered in the register of title in respect of such orders.[4]

Generally, an application for a freezing order is not a pending land action. This is because it is an application to restrain the registered proprietor from exercising his powers of disposition, rather than to a proprietary claim.[5] However, certain statutes expressly provide that certain actions are to be treated, for the purposes of the LRA 2002, as pending land actions. These include:

(a) an application for a restraint order under Proceeds of Crime Act 2002, s 41 or Terrorism Act 2000, Sch 4, para 5(1) or (2);
(b) an application for a freezing order under the International Criminal Court Act 2001; and
(c) an application for an interim receiving order under Proceeds of Crime Act 2002, s 246.

In these cases, the application to the court may be protected as a pending land action, by application for entry of an agreed notice or a unilateral notice; this may be in addition to protection by the entry of an appropriate restriction. These statutory exceptions only relate to the application to the court; any order made by the court will not usually constitute a pending land action capable of protection by entry of a notice, but it may be capable of being protected by entry of a restriction.

A person who has applied for a restraint order under Terrorism Act 2000, Sch 4, para 5(1) or (2) or Proceeds of Crime Act 2002, s 41 affecting a registered estate or charge may apply for entry of a restriction in Form GG or Form HH, as appropriate.[6] The wording of Forms GG and HH is set out in Appendix IV. A person who has obtained such a restraint order may apply for entry of a restriction in Form EE or Form FF, as appropriate.[7]

A person who has applied for an interim receiving order under Proceeds of Crime Act 2002, s 246 affecting a registered estate or charge may apply for entry of a restriction in Form GG or Form HH, as appropriate.[8] A person who has obtained such an interim receiving order may apply for entry of a restriction in Form EE or Form FF, as appropriate.[9]

If the court considers it necessary or desirable to do so for the purposes of protecting a right or claim in relation to a registered estate or charge, it may make an order requiring HMLR to enter a restriction in the register.[10] The court may include in such an order a direction that an entry made in pursuance of the order is to have overriding priority; and may make the exercise of its power to make such a direction subject to such terms and conditions as it thinks fit. A restriction having overriding priority shall be in such form as HMLR determines to ensure the priority of the restriction ordered by the court is apparent from the register, and if entered during the priority period of a prior official search, HMLR must give notice of the entry to the person who applied for the search unless satisfied such notice is unnecessary.[11]

The applicant for entry of a restriction cannot apply for an official search with priority using form OS1 or form OS2.

HMLR must give notice of an application for a restriction to the proprietor of the registered estate or charge concerned, if it has not been made by or with his consent or a person entitled to be registered as such proprietor.[12] However, HMLR need not give notice where the application reflects a limitation under an order of the court, or an undertaking given in place of such an order.[13]

Under the LRA 1925, freezing orders were usually protected by inhibitions. The LRA 2002 applies to any inhibitions entered under the 1925 Act as it applies to restrictions under the 2002 Act.[14]

76.1 Agreed notice

Where the applicant wishes to apply for an agreed notice to protect a pending land action he should, in addition to the usual documents required,[15] deliver to HMLR a certified copy of the application to the court. This should satisfy HMLR of the validity of the applicant's claim in accordance with LRA 2002, s 34(3)(c).

The agreed notice in the register will give details of the interest protected.

76.2 Unilateral notice

Where the applicant wishes to apply for a unilateral notice to protect a pending land action he should deliver to HMLR the usual documents required.[16]

The statement in panel 11 or conveyancer's certificate in panel 12 of form UN1 should be completed on the following lines to show the interest of the applicant:

> applicant in an application for a [*restraint*] *or* [*freezing*] *or* [*interim receiving*] order in the [*name of court*] [*set out full court reference and parties*] to be made under [*state statutory provision*].

The unilateral notice in the register will give brief details of the interest protected and identify the beneficiary of that notice.

76.3 Restriction

In addition to the usual documents required,[17] the applicant for entry of a restriction should deliver to HMLR a certified copy of the court order, or of the application to the court, as the case may be.

As the consent of the registered proprietor is unlikely to be forthcoming, the statement in panel 12 or the conveyancer's certificate in panel 13 of form RX1 as to the nature of the applicant's interest should be completed on the following lines:

> The interest is that specified in rule 93 [(h) of the Land Registration Rules 2003 (SI 2003/1417), the applicant being a person with the benefit of a freezing order or an undertaking given in place of a freezing order *(as appropriate)*] *or* [(i) of the Land Registration Rules 2003 (SI 2003/1417), the applicant being a person who has applied for a freezing order] *or* [(r) of the Land Registration Rules 2003 (SI 2003/1417), the application being in respect of a freezing order or application for a freezing order *(as appropriate)* under Schedule 6 to the International Criminal Court Act 2001].

Panel 9 of form RX1 should set out the wording of the appropriate restriction.

A restriction in standard Forms AA, BB, CC, DD, EE, FF, GG or HH in LRR 2003, Sch 4 does not require the approval of HMLR to the wording of the restriction under LRA 2002, s 43(3).

---

1 LRR 2003, r 93(i).
2 LRR 2003, r 93(h).
3 LRR 2003, r 93(r).
4 International Criminal Court Act 2001, Sch 6, para 7.
5 See 132 Pending Land Actions.
6 LRR 2003, r 93(m).
7 LRR 2003, r 93(l).
8 LRR 2003, r 93(v).
9 LRR 2003, r 93(u).
10 LRA 2002, s 46.
11 LRA 2002, s 46(4) and LRR 2003, r 100.
12 LRA 2002, s 45.
13 LRA 2002, s 45(3)(c).
14 LRA 2002, Sch 12, para 2(2).
15 See 119.1 Agreed notice.
16 See 119.3 Unilateral notice.
17 See 153.1 Application for entry of restriction.

77 FRIENDLY SOCIETIES

Friendly societies were originally started by groups of individuals who joined together to make mutual provision for welfare issues that could affect individual members, such as sickness, disability or retirement, at a time when there were no general welfare provisions provided by the state. Although state welfare benefits and private insurance schemes are now available, friendly societies often offer other discretionary benefits to members in financial or other difficulties, in addition to providing tax-free savings policies, and therefore still exist and attract members. Various legislation was introduced to control and regulate the activities of friendly societies, culminating in the Friendly Societies Act 1974 and the Friendly Societies Act 1992.

The Friendly Societies Act 1992 provided a new framework for friendly societies, by allowing them to incorporate, conferring a wider range of powers on incorporated societies, and providing for more supervision to protect members. The 1992 Act came into force on 1 February 1993 and since that date no new friendly societies may be registered under the Friendly Societies Act 1974.

Friendly societies which are registered under the Friendly Societies Act 1992 are incorporated, while those still registered under the Friendly Societies Act 1974 are unincorporated. A friendly society which is not registered under either of those Acts will be an unincorporated association. If a friendly society was in existence on 1 February 1993, it can choose to become incorporated under the Friendly Societies Act 1992. If a friendly society is a charity, it is an exempt charity.[1]

77.1 Friendly societies registered under the Friendly Societies Act 1974

A friendly society registered under the 1974 Act may acquire land if this is permitted by its rules. The transfer should be to all the trustees. There is no limit to the number of trustees of a friendly society who can be registered as proprietors. The names of the trustees in the proprietorship register may be followed by an appropriate description such as: 'the trustees of the [*name*] Friendly Society'. If a trustee company has been appointed as trustee of a friendly society, the trustee company will be registered as proprietor.

The business address of the society should be given as an address for service.

If the survivor of the trustees will not be able to give a valid receipt for capital money, a restriction in Form A is required in the register. The wording of Form A is set out in Appendix IV.

A disposition by a friendly society should be executed by the current trustees of the society. If these are not also the existing registered proprietors, and the signatures have not been witnessed by the society's secretary, the society's solicitor or secretary should certify that they are the present trustees. A person dealing with the trustees is not required to enquire as to their authority to dispose of or deal with land.[2]

Where an unincorporated friendly society which is a registered proprietor has become incorporated under the Friendly Societies Act 1992, the trustees cease to hold office and the property formerly held by them on trust for the society automatically vests in the incorporated society.[3] The friendly society should therefore apply to bring the register up to date. It should deliver to HMLR:

(a) an application in form AP1;
(b) the original or a certified copy of the certificate of incorporation; and
(c) the fee payable.[4]

A branch of a friendly society registered under the Friendly Societies 1974 can acquire land only if its rules permit it to do so. Land, or a charge, acquired by a branch of a friendly society registered under the 1974 Act (whether or not the branch itself is so registered) vests in the trustees of the branch. Where a friendly society registered under the 1974 Act incorporates under the Friendly Societies

Act 1992, the property of its branches vests in the incorporated society unless a scheme to the contrary is made under s 6(5) of the 1992 Act.

77.2 Friendly societies registered under the Friendly Societies Act 1992

All friendly societies registered under the Friendly Societies Act 1992 are incorporated societies and have power to acquire, hold, charge and dispose of land. The last word of the name of an incorporated friendly society is 'Limited' or 'Cyfyngedig'. In the case of an incorporated friendly society which is a collecting society the last three words of the name are 'Collecting Society Limited' or 'Cymdeithas Casglu Cyfyngedig'.

Where HMLR registers a friendly society registered under the Friendly Societies Act 1992 as proprietor of registered land or of a registered charge, it will not usually enter a restriction in the register because of the protection afforded to a purchaser in good faith of property from a friendly society.[5]

An incorporated friendly society may execute a deed by either:

(a) affixing its common seal to a document that is expressed to be a deed in the presence of, and attested by, two persons who are stated to be either two members of the committee of management of the society or one such member and the secretary; or

(b) the document being signed by two persons who are stated to be either two members of the committee of management of the society or one such member and the secretary, and expressed (in whatever form of words) to be executed by the society as a deed.

In favour of a purchaser in good faith for valuable consideration, a document executed in accordance with (b) above is deemed to have been duly executed by the society.[6]

If the society executes a deed using a different method, the applicant for registration must lodge a certificate by either a conveyancer, or the secretary or a member of the committee of management of the society. The certificate must confirm that the deed has been duly executed in the manner authorised by the instrument constituting the society or regulating its affairs.

---

1 See 30 Charities.

2 Friendly Societies Act 1974, s 53(1).

3 Friendly Societies Act 1992, s 6(2).

4 See 67 Fees.
5 Friendly Societies Act 1992, s 9(4) and (5).
6 Friendly Societies Act 1992, Sch 6, para 2.

78 GIFTS

To pass a legal estate, a gift of land must be made by a deed. When the title to the land is unregistered, the gift may trigger compulsory first registration of title if it constitutes the transfer of a qualifying estate.[1] When the title to the land is registered, a transfer by way of gift must be in the appropriate prescribed form[2] and will constitute a registrable disposition which is required to be completed by registration.

78.1 Unregistered land

When the title to land is unregistered, the donee must apply for first registration if the gift 'triggers' compulsory first registration. The events triggering compulsory first registration under LRA 2002, s 4 include the transfer by way of gift (whether by conveyance, assignment, transfer or otherwise) of:

(a) a freehold estate in land; or
(b) of an existing leasehold estate in land with more than 7 years to run at the time of the transfer.

Also, the grant of a new leasehold estate in land out of a qualifying estate for a term of years absolute which is for a term of more than 7 years from the date of the grant, and which is by way of gift.

For these purposes, a 'gift' includes a transfer or grant for the purposes of constituting a trust under which the settlor does not retain the whole of the beneficial interest, or uniting the bare legal title and the beneficial interest in property held under a trust under which the settlor did not, on constitution, retain the whole beneficial interest. 'Land' for these purposes does not include mines and minerals held apart from the surface.[3] Therefore, the requirement to apply for first registration does not apply to a gift in respect of such mines and minerals.

The donee, as the person taking under the gift, must apply for first registration within 2 months of the gift. Where necessary, he may apply to HMLR for an order that the period for registration ends on a later date. That later date will be specified in the order, if made. HMLR will make such an order if it is satisfied that there is good reason for doing so.[4]

If the donee does not comply with the requirement of registration, the transfer or lease becomes void as regards the transfer or grant of a legal estate.[5] Consequently:

(a) in the case of a transfer by way of gift, the legal estate reverts to the donor who holds it on a bare trust for the donee; and
(b) in the case of the grant of a lease, the grant takes effect as a contract for valuable consideration to grant the lease.[6]

Where the registrar makes an order extending the period for registration, this will retrospectively undo the above.

If there must be a further deed because of the failure to apply for first registration following the original deed of gift, the donee will be liable for the proper costs of the donor in respect of the new deed.[7]

A donee applying for first registration should deliver to HMLR the usual documents required.[8]

78.2 Registered land

A transfer by way of gift of registered land must be made in the appropriate prescribed form. This will be either:

(a) form TR1 (for the whole of the land in a registered title);
(b) form TR4 (for a registered charge or a portfolio of charges);
(c) form TR5 (for a portfolio of titles as to whole or part); or
(d) form TP1 (for part of the land in a registered title).

Until the transfer of the registered estate or registered charge is completed by registration, it does not operate at law.[9]

The donee (not being a 'purchaser') is not able to apply for an official search with priority using form OS1 or form OS2.

A donee applying to register a transfer of registered land should deliver to HMLR the usual documents required.[10]

The priority of any interest affecting the registered estate is not affected by a gift of registered land (not being a disposition for valuable consideration), whether or not the interest or the gift is registered.[11]

Where a donee is seeking indemnity from HMLR under LRA 2002, Sch 8 (following rectification of the register, for example), any fraud or lack of proper care by the donor is treated as fraud or lack of proper care by the donee and may, therefore, preclude or reduce the payment of indemnity.[12]

For the position where an order of the court under IA 1986, ss 339, 340, 343 or 423 requires the register to be altered following the bankruptcy of the donor, see 19 Bankruptcy.

---

1 See 68.2 Compulsory first registration.
2 LRR 2003, r 58.
3 LRA 2002, s 4(9).
4 LRA 2002, s 6(5).
5 LRA 2002, s 7(1).
6 LRA 2002, s 7(2).
7 LRA 2002, s 8.
8 See 68.4 Application for first registration.
9 LRA 2002, s 27(1).
10 See 176.1 Registration of transfer.
11 LRA 2002, s 28.
12 LRA 2002, Sch 8, para 5. See 86 Indemnity.

79 HISTORICAL INFORMATION

The register of title only provides current details of the title at a particular point in time – it does not show how the title has changed historically. In most conveyancing transactions it is not necessary to consider historical editions of the registered title. However, these may be relevant when, for example, investigating whether certain registered titles were at some point in common ownership, to extinguish easements or restrictive covenants by unity of seisin. Another example is when investigating whether a former owner is liable on implied covenants for title, the benefit of which runs with the registered estate under Law of Property (Miscellaneous Provisions) Act 1994, s 7.

It is possible to apply for historical information about a registered title (including the title plan) where this is held by HMLR in electronic form.[1] This includes information that was but is no longer in the register. HMLR is not under an obligation to hold previous editions of a registered title in electronic form and register history information *may* be available for dates after 4 May 1993 and title plan information *may* be available for dates after 13 October 2003. Limited information is held about title plans before this date. The application should be made in form HC1 and should specify the date of the edition in question and indicate whether it is the last edition on that date, or all editions on that date, which are required. HMLR may reject an application which does not specify such a date. A fee is payable.[2]

Where HMLR is keeping in electronic form an edition of the registered title as it existed at the date specified in the application, it must issue a copy of it. If HMLR has kept only part of the edition requested in electronic form, HMLR must issue a copy of that part.

If the required information is not held in electronic form, HMLR may hold paper copies of earlier editions of the register or title plan. HMLR may be able to provide copies of these in response to an application under the Freedom of Information Act 2000.[3] Such an application should provide as much information as possible about the enquiry and the reason why the information is required. This will enable HMLR to determine if it can provide the information required.

1 LRA 2002, s 69 and LRR 2003, r 144.

2 See 67 Fees.

3 See 122.4 Freedom of Information Act 2000.

80 HM LAND REGISTRY

HMLR administers land registration. HMLR carries out its work principally under the authority of the LRA 2002 and the LRR 2003, and in accordance with HMLR's own practice and procedures.

HMLR, which was established in 1862, is a government agency whose main purpose is to register title to land and other registrable estates in England and Wales and to record dispositions, such as sales and mortgages, with registered titles. It also provides information in relation to registered titles and related data. It has a head office and local offices, details of which are set out in Appendix I.

81 HOME RIGHTS

'Home rights' means the rights of occupation of the home conferred upon a spouse or civil partner by FLA 1996, s 30. 'Home' means the dwelling house constituting the matrimonial or civil partnership home to which the home rights attach.

Home rights under the FLA 1996 constitute a charge on the home[1] which, if the title to the home is registered, should be protected by the entry of an agreed notice.[2] Such a notice is referred to in the LRR 2003 as a 'home rights notice'.[3] In the context of this topic:

(a) 'the spouse or civil partner' means the person whose home rights are protected or in need of protection; and
(b) 'the owning spouse or civil partner' means the other spouse or civil partner, who is the owner of the home.

A home rights charge arises on whichever is the latest of:

(a) the date when the owning spouse or civil partner acquires the home;
(b) the date of the marriage or civil partnership; and
(c) 1 January 1968 (being the date of commencement of the Matrimonial Homes Act 1967).[4]

Where the owning spouse or civil partner:

(a) is not the registered proprietor (or sole registered proprietor) of the home, but
(b) is entitled to occupy the home by virtue of a beneficial interest under a trust,

the spouse or civil partner may still be entitled to home rights which are capable of protection against the trustees' registered title. However, this will only be the case where the property is held on trust for:

(a) the owning spouse or civil partner only; or
(b) the owning spouse or civil partner and the spouse or civil partner only.[5]

Home rights will only continue so long as the marriage or civil partnership subsists, unless the court directs otherwise during the subsistence of the marriage or civil partnership by means of an order under FLA 1996, s 33(5).[6] If the court makes such an order and those home rights have not already been protected in the register, the spouse or civil partner should apply for a home rights notice. If the court makes such an order, and the home rights have already been protected in the register, the spouse or civil partner should apply for renewal of the registration.

A spouse's or civil partner's home rights may end in the following ways:

(a) by the death of either spouse or civil partner,[7] but subject to the power of the court to make an order under FLA 1996, s 33(5);
(b) by the ending of the marriage or civil partnership otherwise than by death,[8] but subject to the power of the court to make an order under FLA 1996, s 33(5);
(c) by an order of the court;[9] or
(d) by the spouse or civil partner voluntarily releasing the home rights in writing.[10]

For the effect of bankruptcy on home rights, see 19.16 Bankruptcy and home rights.

No protection under the FLA 1996 is necessary when the home is held jointly, both legally and beneficially, by both the spouses or civil partners. The protection of a home rights notice is only available in respect of one home at any one time. Before 14 February 1983, matrimonial home rights could also be protected by the entry of a caution against dealings.[11] The registration of a Class F land charge is relevant only to unregistered land and will confer no protection in relation to registered land.

The right of a spouse or civil partner to occupy the home conferred by the FLA 1996 is not capable of falling within LRA 2002, Sch 1, para 2 or Sch 3, para 2, which deal with the overriding status of interests of persons in actual occupation.[12] Even if the spouse or civil partner is occupying the home, such a right will not therefore constitute an interest which overrides first registration or registered dispositions and will need to be protected by entry of a home rights notice.

81.1 Home rights notice

A person applying to enter a home rights notice should deliver to HMLR an application in form HR1. No fee is currently payable. As home rights may subsist in respect only of one property at a time, the applicant must reveal any previous registration in form HR1 and HMLR will cancel such notices.[13] Where the application is made after the court has made an order under FLA 1996, s 33(5), the applicant must lodge an office copy of that order with form HR1. Alternatively, a conveyancer may certify in panel 10 of form HR1 that he holds such an office copy. HMLR will serve notice of the application to the registered proprietor.

81.2 Renewal of home rights notice

Where:

(a) the court has made an order under FLA 1996, s 33(5), directing that the home rights shall not be ended by the termination of the marriage or civil partnership, whether by death or otherwise, and
(b) those rights have already been protected in the register by means of a home rights notice or (before 14 February 1983) by a caution against dealings,

the spouse or civil partner should apply to protect the renewal in the register.

A person applying to renew the registration of a home rights notice should deliver to HMLR:

(a) an application in form HR2;
(b) an office copy of the court order made under FLA 1996, s 33(5). Alternatively, a conveyancer may certify in panel 8 of form HR2 that he holds such an office copy.

No fee is currently payable.

The renewal will be effected by the entry of a home rights notice referring to the order. It will not affect the priority of the original home rights charge.[14] HMLR will serve notice of the application for renewal upon the registered proprietor.

81.3 Cancellation of home rights notice

An application to cancel a home rights notice must be made in form HR4, accompanied by the evidence required by FLA 1996, Sch 4, para 4. That evidence will normally consist of:

(a) the death certificate or other sufficient evidence of death of either spouse or civil partner (but see also (e) below); or
(b) an office copy of a decree absolute of divorce, dissolution or nullity (but see also (e) below). If a decree of divorce by an overseas court is lodged, additional evidence as to residence, domicile or nationality, may be required and, if the decree is not in English, a notarially certified translation should be provided; or
(c) an office copy of an order of the court terminating the home rights; or
(d) a written release of the home rights by the spouse or civil partner; and
(e) where the supporting evidence is evidence of the spouse's or civil partner's death or a copy of a decree absolute produced in accordance with (a) or (b) above and the court has made an order under FLA 1996, s 33(5) and that order is referred to on the register, satisfactory evidence that the order has ceased to have effect.

No fee is currently payable.

81.4 Cancellation of home rights caution

Where home rights have been protected by a caution against dealings, application for removal of the caution may be made in one of the following ways:

(a) by application for cancellation in form CCD by the registered proprietor or a person who, but for the caution, would be entitled to be registered as proprietor;

(b) by withdrawal of the caution in form WCT signed by the spouse or civil partner (or by their personal representative where appropriate) or by his conveyancer; or
(c) by letter, accompanied by the appropriate evidence confirming one of the events described in (a), (b) or (c) in 81.3 Cancellation of home rights notice. If the court has made an order under FLA 1996, s 33(5) which is referred to in the register, the applicant must also supply satisfactory evidence that this order has ceased to have effect.

No fee is currently payable. As to cautions against dealings generally, see 24 Cautions Against Dealings.

81.5 Home rights search by a mortgagee

A mortgagee of a dwelling house who brings an action to enforce his security must serve notice of the action on a spouse or civil partner whose rights of occupation are protected at the relevant time by a notice or caution in the register and who was not a party to the relevant action.[15] A mortgagee of registered land that consists of or includes all or part of a dwelling house may apply in form HR3 or by telephone or electronically for an official certificate of the result of a search.[16] This will reveal if there is a home rights notice or a matrimonial home rights caution registered, or a pending application for entry of a home rights notice on the day list. The search will confer priority for a period of 15 days.[17] A fee is payable.[18]

---

1 Family Law Act 1996 (FLA 1996), s 31.
2 LRR 2003, r 80(a).
3 LRR 2003, r 217.
4 FLA 1996, s 31(3).
5 FLA 1996, s 31(4) and (5).
6 FLA 1996, s 31(8).
7 FLA 1996, s 31(8)(a).
8 FLA 1996, s 31(8)(b).
9 FLA 1996, Sch 4, para 4(1)(c).
10 FLA 1996, Sch 4, para 5(1).
11 See 24 Cautions Against Dealings.
12 FLA 1996, s 31(10).
13 FLA 1996, Sch 4, para 2.
14 FLA 1996, Sch 4, para 4(5).
15 FLA 1996, s 56.
16 LRR 2003, r 158.
17 FLA 1996, s 56(5).
18 See 67 Fees.

82 HOUSING ACTION TRUSTS

Housing action trusts are established by the Secretary of State or, in Wales, the Welsh Ministers in relation to a designated area which may be added to and which does not need to be contiguous.[1] Broadly, the aims of a housing action trust are to renovate an area of run-down housing and its general environment. In pursuance of this objective, the trust, which is a body corporate, has power to acquire, hold, manage, reclaim and dispose of land and other property and to carry on any business or undertaking and generally do anything necessary or expedient for the purposes of that objective. A housing action trust may acquire land in the following ways:

(a) by order of the Secretary of State or the Welsh Ministers ordering a transfer of housing accommodation from an LHA, a county council, a waste disposal authority, a joint body established under Local Government Act 1985, Pt IV or a residuary body established under Pt VII of that Act;
(b) by statutory vesting by an order of the Secretary of State or Welsh Ministers and, where appropriate, a minister of land which is owned by a public body or a statutory undertaker; or
(c) by agreement, or, provided the Secretary of State or Welsh Ministers consent, compulsorily.

While a housing action trust can dispose of land with the consent of the Secretary of State or Welsh Ministers, it may not dispose of a house which is for the time being subject to:

(a) a secure tenancy,
(b) an introductory tenancy,
(c) a tenancy which is a secure contract, or
(d) a tenancy which is an introductory secure contract,

except to a:

(a) non-profit registered provider of social housing;
(b) registered social landlord; or
(c) an LHA or other local authority. However, this does not prevent a disposal of a house under the right to buy provisions in HA 1985, Pt 5.[2]

82.1 Restrictions

Given the limitations on disposals by housing action trusts, when registering such a trust as the proprietor of a registered estate, an applicant should also apply for entry of a restriction on the following lines:

No disposition by the proprietor of the registered estate (other than a charge) is to be completed by registration without the consent of the [Secretary of State] *or* [National Assembly for Wales] unless either:

(i) it is a disposition of a house or flat under Part 5 of the Housing Act 1985 (Right to Buy); or
(ii) it is a disposition to one or more individuals and contains a certificate that it consists of a single house or flat; or
(iii) it contains a certificate that no part of the land consists of a house or a flat.

An application to register a disposition by a housing action trust should include the necessary evidence to meet the requirements of this restriction.

82.2 Disposal of land

A housing action trust has power, subject to any directions by, and with the consent of, the Secretary of State or Welsh Ministers, to dispose of any land that it owns. However, this is subject to limitation in relation to a house or flat which is the subject of a secure tenancy unless it is sold under the right to buy.[3] All disposals of land require the consent of the Secretary of State or Welsh Ministers which may be given generally or specifically. A disposal of land which includes a house or flat made without such consent is void unless the disposal is to an individual or to two or more individuals, and the disposal does not extend to any other house.[4] Where the land does not consist of a house or flat, then a purchaser is not concerned to enquire whether or not consent has been given and the disposal is not invalid.[5]

In the case of a disposal of a house or flat subject to a secure tenancy or an introductory tenancy to a registered social landlord, the registered social landlord cannot make any subsequent disposal (other than an exempt disposal[6]) without the consent of the Secretary of State or Welsh Ministers. The transfer effecting the disposal must state that the requirement applies to any such disposal.[7] Where the land has been mortgaged, this requirement for consent also applies to a disposal in exercise of the power of sale.

Where a transfer contains the statement required by Housing Act 1988 (HA 1988), s 81(1), HMLR must enter a restriction in Form X.[8] The wording of Form X is set out in Appendix IV.

---

1 Housing Act 1988 (HA 1988), Pt III, ss 60 to 92 and Sch 11.
2 HA 1988, s 79(2).
3 HA 1988, s 79.
4 HA 1988, s 80(1).

5 HA 1988, s 80(2).
6 As defined in HA 1988, s 81(8).
7 HA 1988, s 81(1).
8 HA 1988, s 81(10) and LRR 2003, r 95(2)(d).

83 HOUSING ASSOCIATIONS

The law relating to housing associations is largely contained in the Housing Associations Act 1985 in respect of unregistered housing associations and in the HA 1996 in respect of registered housing associations. In England, but not in Wales, the regulation of social housing was further amended by:

(a) the Housing and Regeneration Act 2008;
(b) the Localism Act 2011; and
(c) the Housing and Planning Act 2016.

Housing associations are affected by different regulatory regimes depending upon whether they are English or Welsh.

Housing Associations Act 1985, s 1 defines a housing association as a society, body of trustees or company:

(a) which is established for the purpose of, or amongst whose objects or powers are included those of, providing, constructing, improving or managing, or facilitating or encouraging the construction or improvement of, housing accommodation; and
(b) which does not trade for profit or whose constitution or rules prohibit the issue of capital with interest or dividend exceeding such rate as may be prescribed by the Treasury, whether with or without differentiation as between share and loan capital.

Many housing associations are charities and some of them are registered societies.[1] Registered housing associations will be private registered providers (in England) and registered social landlords (in Wales). Some housing associations were either never registered, or were registered but subsequently became deregistered. Different regulatory regimes will apply to a housing association, depending upon whether or not it is registered.

83.1 Registered housing associations

For housing associations which are private registered providers or registered social landlords, see 149 Registered Social Landlords and Private Registered Providers.

83.2 Registration of unregistered housing association as proprietor of land

Where an unregistered housing association acquires land, it may be grant-aided land. Grant-aided land is land:

(a) in respect of which a payment by way of annual grant or subsidy under the statutory provisions referred to in Housing Associations Act 1985, Sch 1, para 2 falls or fell to be made in respect of a period ending after 24 January 1974; or
(b) on which is, or has been, secured a loan made under the statutory provisions referred to in Sch 1, para 3, in respect of which a repayment (by way of principal or interest or both) falls or fell to be made after 24 January 1974.[2]

A disposition of grant-aided land by an unregistered housing association requires the consent of the Regulator of Social Housing, if the land is in England, or of the Welsh Ministers, if the land is in Wales.[3]

If:

(a) an applicant for registration as proprietor of a registered estate or registered charge is, or holds on trust for, an unregistered social landlord within the meaning of the Housing Associations Act 1985, and
(b) the application relates to grant-aided land as defined in Sch 1 to that Act,

the application must include a certificate to that effect.[4] This is in addition to any requirements arising from the fact that the applicant is a charity, a registered society or a company.[5] Where HMLR receives such a certificate relating to land in England, it will enter a restriction in the following wording in the proprietorship register for the property:

> No disposition by the proprietor of the land is to be registered and none shall take effect unless made with the consent of the Regulator of Social Housing when such consent if required under the provisions of section 9 of the Housing Associations Act 1985.

In the case of grant-aided land in Wales the restriction is in the following wording:

> No disposition by the proprietor of the registered estate is to be registered and none shall take effect unless made with the consent of the Welsh Ministers when such consent is required under the provisions of section 9 of the Housing Associations Act 1985.

If a registered estate in land is held on trust for an unregistered housing association and HMLR is entering two or more trustees as proprietors, HMLR will enter a restriction in Form A in the register. The wording of Form A is set out in Appendix IV. If an unregistered housing association is a charity, HMLR will add a charity restriction where appropriate.

83.3 Dispositions by unregistered housing associations

Applications to register dispositions by unregistered housing associations should meet the requirements of any restriction in the register. Where a restriction refers to the consent of the Regulator of Social Housing, or the Welsh Ministers, under Housing Associations Act 1985, s 9, an applicant need not lodge evidence of that consent where the disposal is an exempt disposal or other form of disposal where such consent is not required.

If an unregistered housing association is a charity, the disposition should include an appropriate charity statement, where necessary.[6]

---

1 See 30 Charities and 150 Registered Societies.
2 Housing Associations Act 1985, Sch 1 para 1.
3 Housing Associations Act 1985, s 9(1A).
4 LRR 2003, r 183A(2).
5 See 30.1 Dispositions in favour of charities, 150 Registered Societies and/or 37 Companies.
6 See 30.2 Dispositions by charities.

84 IDENTITY EVIDENCE

To reduce the risk of registration fraud, HMLR requires confirmation or evidence of identity to be provided for parties to certain dispositions and transactions which are the subject of an application for registration. HMLR's requirements will depend upon whether an application is lodged by a conveyancer or by a lay-person.[1]

HMLR will require evidence of identity for the following types of application:

(a) registration of a transfer of a registered estate or registered charge;
(b) registration of the appointment or retirement of a trustee;
(c) registration of an assent or transfer of registered land or charge by a personal representative;
(d) registration of a lease of a registered estate;
(e) closure of a registered leasehold title on surrender of the registered lease;
(f) compulsory first registration of freehold or leasehold land;

(g) voluntary first registration of freehold or leasehold land where the title documents have been lost or destroyed;
(h) registration of a legal charge of a registered estate or sub-charge of a registered charge or registration of such on first registration of the land;
(i) discharge or release of a registered charge in paper form (form DS1 or form DS3);
(j) registration of a deed of substituted security;
(k) alteration of the register following an individual's change of name by deed poll, statutory declaration or statement of truth; and
(l) alteration of the register to change an address for service where the application is by a non-conveyancer.

Although HMLR will not routinely require confirmation of identity in other situations, it may request this if it considers it necessary or desirable.[2] The evidence will be required in respect of the transferor and transferee, landlord and tenant, or mortgage lender, as the case may be. Evidence will also be required for an attorney of any of those parties.

Certain exceptions may apply:

(a) *The 'low-value' exception*, which applies where the true value of the land which is the subject of the disposal, discharge or release is £6,000 or less. In these cases, the conveyancer may instead lodge a certificate by someone qualified to give property valuations, such as a surveyor, confirming the value of the land.
(b) *The 'insolvency official, etc' exception*, which applies in respect of a person acting:

    (i) in the capacity of a trustee in bankruptcy, liquidator, supervisor, administrator or administrative receiver appointed under the IA 1986;
    (ii) as a receiver under the LPA 1925;
    (iii) as a deputy appointed under the Mental Health Act 2005; or
    (iv) as a guardian appointed under the Guardianship (Missing Persons) Act 2017.

    In each case, they must still lodge evidence of their appointment.
(c) *The 'not practicable' exception*, which applies where it is not practicable to provide evidence of identity. For example, where a tenant has 'disappeared' and application is made to close the leasehold title following its surrender by operation of law. The conveyancer should enclose a covering letter with the application explaining why it is not practicable to provide evidence of identity. Mere 'inconvenience' is not sufficient. If it is claimed it is not practicable to provide evidence of identity because a party has lost capacity,

the applicant should provide appropriate evidence of this such as a letter or report from a medical doctor.

(d) *The 'Land Registry facility letter' exception*, which applies where HMLR has issued a facility letter in respect of the identity of a private individual or corporate body dealing regularly with HMLR. A copy of the facility letter may be enclosed with any application in place of evidence of identity.

(e) *The 'retained evidence of identity' exception*, which applies where HMLR has approved draft forms of transfers and leases of part for specific developments.[3] Evidence of identity for any attorney acting for the transferor or landlord does not have to be lodged with each individual transfer or lease for registration where that evidence has been lodged with the draft for approval and has been retained by HMLR.

(f) *The 'Legal charge up to £10,000 to a local authority in respect of a service charge loan' exception*, which applies where an application is made to register a legal charge to a local authority, the value of the charge as stated on the charge deed or application form is up to £10,000, and the charge is in respect of a service charge loan and this is clearly stated in the charge deed or on the application form.

For most applications, a conveyancer should provide confirmation of identity by a conveyancer by completing the relevant panel(s) in forms AP1, FR1 or DS2 as the case may be. This will be in relation to the conveyancer's own client (the applicant) and the other party or parties involved. For any unrepresented party, the conveyancer must either confirm that sufficient steps have been taken to verify that party's identity or provide evidence of identity for that party using form ID1 or form ID3 (for a private individual) or form ID2 (for a corporate body). Where a conveyancer has completed identity checks via video call, they should also complete and lodge form ID5. A conveyancer should take care in completing the relevant panel(s) in the application forms; by doing so, he may be assuming a duty of care to the other parties.[4] In the case of an application for change of name by an individual which is not combined with any other application, a conveyancer may either confirm that sufficient steps have been taken to verify that party's identity or provide evidence of identity for that party using form ID1 or form ID3.[5]

Where a lay-person has lodged an application, he cannot provide confirmation of identity. Instead, he will need to provide evidence of identity for himself and for any other unrepresented party using form(s) ID1, ID2 or ID3, as appropriate.

Completed forms ID1, ID2, ID3 and ID5 are not open to public inspection or copying and normally a person may not apply for an official copy of them.[6]

To encourage the development and update of digital identity verification solutions, HMLR has provided a 'Safe Harbour' for conveyancers using certain digital systems. This provides that if a conveyancer verifies a person's identity using a digital system which meets HMLR's specifications, HMLR will not pursue rights of recourse against the conveyancer on the grounds that identity checks were inadequate if it transpires the person is a fraudster.[7]

Further guidance as to HMLR's requirements is contained in HMLR's *Practice Guide 67: evidence of identity*. This is available to view and download at the HMLR website.[8]

---

1 For the definition of 'conveyancer', see 41 Conveyancers.
2 LRR 2003, r 17.
3 See 52 Developing Estates.
4 *Ashraf v Lester Dominic Solicitors* [2023] EWCA Civ 4.
5 See 28 Change of Name.
6 LRR 2003, rr 133 and 135. See 122 Official Copies and Inspection.
7 HMLR's *Practice guide 81: encouraging the use of digital technology in identity verification*. This is available to view and download at the HMLR website: www.gov.uk/government/collections/land-registration-practice-guides.
8 www.gov.uk/government/collections/land-registration-practice-guides.

85 IMPLIED COVENANTS

A registrable disposition may be expressed to be made either with full title guarantee or with limited title guarantee or, in the case of an instrument in the Welsh language, gyda gwarant teitl llawn or gyda gwarant teitl cyfyngedig.[1] The effect of using these expressions is to imply covenants by the person making the disposition, as set out in Law of Property (Miscellaneous Provisions) Act 1994, Pt I.

A disposition 'with full title guarantee' or 'gyda gwarant teitl llawn' implies the following covenants:

(a) that the person making the disposition has the right (with the concurrence of any other person conveying the property) to dispose of the property as he purports to;
(b) that the person making the disposition will at his own cost do all that he reasonably can to give the person to whom he disposes of the property the title he purports to give;
(c) that the person making the disposition is disposing of the property free from all charges and incumbrances (whether monetary or not) and all other rights

exercisable by third parties, other than any charges, incumbrances or rights which that person does not and could not reasonably be expected to know about;

(d) (where the disposition is of leasehold land) that the lease is subsisting at the time of the disposition and there is no subsisting breach of a condition or tenant's obligation, and nothing which at that time would render the lease liable to forfeiture;

(e) (where the disposition is a mortgage of property subject to a rentcharge) that the mortgagor will fully and promptly observe and perform all the obligations under the instrument creating the rentcharge that are for the time being enforceable with respect to the property by the owner of the rentcharge in his capacity as such; and

(f) (where the disposition is a mortgage of leasehold land) that the mortgagor will fully and promptly observe and perform all the obligations under the lease subject to the mortgage that are for the time being imposed on him in his capacity as tenant under the lease.

A disposition 'with limited title guarantee' or 'gyda gwarant teitl cyfyngedig' implies the covenants set out at (a), (b), (d), (e) and (f) above, and the following covenant:

(g) that the person making the disposition has not since the last disposition for value:

  (i) charged or incumbered the property by means of any charge or incumbrance which subsists at the time when the disposition is made, or granted third-party rights in relation to the property which so subsist, or

  (ii) suffered the property to be so charged or incumbered or subjected to any such rights,

  and that he is not aware that anyone else has done so since the last disposition for value.

The implied covenantor in a registrable disposition made with either full or limited title guarantee is not liable under the implied covenants referred to in (a), (c), (d) or (g) above in respect of any particular matter to which the disposition is expressly made subject or which, at the time of the disposition, was entered in the register in relation to the interest in question.[2] Nor for anything that at the time of the disposition is within the actual knowledge, or which is a necessary consequence of facts that are within the actual knowledge, of the purchaser (for which purpose LPA 1925, s 198 is to be disregarded, so that registration in the Land Charges Department will not be deemed to constitute actual notice of an interest).[3]

The parties to an instrument may limit or extend the covenants which would otherwise be implied by Law of Property (Miscellaneous Provisions) Act 1994, Pt I by a provision of that instrument.[4]

One of the covenants referred to above is that contained in Law of Property (Miscellaneous Provisions) Act 1994 s 4(1)(b). This implies, in a disposition of leasehold land made with full title guarantee or limited title guarantee, a covenant that there is no subsisting breach of a condition or tenant's obligation, and nothing which at that time would render the lease liable to forfeiture. If the disposition is the grant of an underlease, the reference in the implied covenant to 'lease' is to the lease out of which the underlease is granted. Where a document effecting a registrable disposition contains a provision which limits or extends a covenant implied under Law of Property (Miscellaneous Provisions) Act 1994, s 4(1)(b), that document must do so by express reference to that section of that Act.[5] The LRR 2003 do not prescribe the form of statement, but may, for example, be in one of the following forms:

> The covenant set out in section 4(1)(b) of the Law of Property (Miscellaneous Provisions) Act 1994 shall [not] extend to [*insert relevant details*].

or:

> The [transferor] or [lessor] shall not be liable under any of the covenants set out in section 4(1)(b) of the Law of Property (Miscellaneous Provisions) Act 1994.

Where a registrable disposition of leasehold land limits or extends the implied covenant under Law of Property (Miscellaneous Provisions) Act 1994, s 4(1)(b), HMLR has discretion to refer to this in the register.[6] The form of entry will be along the following lines:

> The covenant implied under s 4(1)(b) of the Law of Property (Miscellaneous Provisions) Act 1994 in the disposition to the proprietor is modified.

HMLR will not make any other reference to any covenant implied by:

(a) Law of Property (Miscellaneous Provisions) Act 1994, Pt I in the register in any other circumstances; or
(b) LPA 1925, s 76 as applied by Law of Property (Miscellaneous Provisions) Act 1994, s 11(1).[7]

Right to buy transfers and leases must be made with full title guarantee, which should not be modified.[8]

The benefit of the implied covenants runs with the purchaser's estate or interest, so that a successor in title can enforce them.[9] However, the liability under the implied covenants does not attach to land retained by the vendor and so does not pass to his successors in title.

85.1 Transfers of pre-1996 leases

Landlord and Tenant (Covenants) Act 1995, s 1(3) defines a 'new tenancy' as a lease granted on or after 1 January 1996 otherwise than in pursuance of an agreement entered into, an option granted or a court order made before that date. An 'old tenancy' will therefore be a tenancy granted before 1 January 1996 or in pursuance of an agreement entered into, an option granted or a court order made before that date. Unless the contrary intention is expressed, the following covenants are implied in a transfer of a registered leasehold estate which is an 'old tenancy' rather than a 'new tenancy' for the purposes of Landlord and Tenant (Covenants) Act 1995, s 1:[10]

(a) (in the case of a transfer of the whole of the land comprised in the registered lease) the transferee covenants with the transferor that during the residue of the term granted by the registered lease the transferee and the persons deriving title under him will:

    (i) pay the rent reserved by the lease;
    (ii) comply with the covenants and conditions contained in the lease; and
    (iii) keep the transferor and the persons deriving title under him indemnified against all actions, expenses and claims on account of any failure to comply with clauses (i) and (ii);

(b) (in the case of a transfer of part of the land comprised in the registered lease) the transferee covenants with the transferor that during the residue of the term granted by the registered lease the transferee and the persons deriving title under him will:

    (i) where the rent reserved by the lease is apportioned, pay the rent apportioned to the part transferred;
    (ii) comply with the covenants and conditions contained in the lease so far as affecting the part transferred; and
    (iii) keep the transferor and the persons deriving title under him indemnified against all actions, expenses and claims on account of any failure to comply with clauses (i) and (ii);

(c) (in the case of a transfer of part of the land comprised in the registered lease where the transferor continues to hold land under that lease) the transferor covenants with the transferee that during the residue of the term granted by the registered lease the transferor and the persons deriving title under him will:

(i) where the rent reserved by the lease is apportioned, pay the rent apportioned to the part retained;
(ii) comply with the covenants and conditions contained in the lease so far as affecting the part retained; and
(iii) keep the transferee and the persons deriving title under him indemnified against all actions, expenses and claims on account of any failure to comply with clauses (i) and (ii).

Where a transfer of such a registered leasehold estate modifies or negatives any of the covenants implied under paragraphs (a) and (b) above, HMLR must make an entry in the register that the covenants have been so modified or negatived.[11]

As original tenant liability was abolished for new tenancies, the covenants implied into a transfer of an old tenancy will not, therefore, be implied into the transfer of a new tenancy. However, transfers of new tenancies will be subject to the implied covenants for title set out in the Law of Property (Miscellaneous Provisions) Act 1994 referred to above.

85.2 Transfer of a registered estate subject to a rentcharge

In addition to the covenants implied under Law of Property (Miscellaneous Provisions) Act 1994, Pt I, where a registered estate is transferred subject to a rentcharge, the covenants referred to in LPA 1925, s 77 and Sch 2 (as modified by LRR 2003, r 69) are also implied.

In a transfer for valuable consideration of the whole of the land affected by a rentcharge, there is implied a covenant by the transferee with the transferor that the transferee or the persons deriving title under him will at all times, from the date of the transfer or other date therein stated:

(a) duly pay the rentcharge and observe and perform all the covenants, agreements and conditions contained in the deed or other document creating the rentcharge, and thenceforth on the part of the owner of the land to be observed and performed; and
(b) save harmless and keep indemnified the transferor and his estate and effects from and against all proceedings, costs, claims and expenses on account of any omission to pay the rentcharge or any part thereof, or any breach of the said covenants, agreements and conditions.

Where a rentcharge has been apportioned in respect of any land, with the consent of the owner of the rentcharge, these covenants are implied in the transfer in the like manner as if the apportioned rentcharge were the rentcharge referred to and the document creating the rentcharge related solely to that land.

In a transfer for valuable consideration of part of the land affected by a rentcharge, subject to a part of that rentcharge which has been or is by that transfer apportioned (but in either case without the consent of the owner of the rentcharge) in respect of the land transferred, there is implied a covenant by the transferee with the transferor that the transferee or the persons deriving title under him will at all times, from the date of the transfer or other date therein stated:

(a) pay the apportioned rent and observe and perform all the covenants (other than the covenant to pay the entire rent) and conditions contained in the deed or other document creating the rentcharge, so far as the same relate to the land conveyed; and
(b) save harmless and keep indemnified the transferor and his respective estate and effects from and against all proceedings, costs, claims and expenses on account of any omission to pay the said apportioned rent, or any breach of any of the said covenants and conditions, so far as the same relate as aforesaid.

On a transfer of a registered estate subject to a rentcharge, any covenant implied by LPA 1925, s 77(1)(A) or (B) may be modified or negatived by adding suitable words to the transfer.[12]

The implied covenants referred to above do not apply to a rentcharge falling within Rentcharges Act 1977, s 2(3)(a) (i.e. family charges), in relation to which different covenants are implied.[13]

---

1 LRR 2003, r 67(1).
2 Law of Property (Miscellaneous Provisions) Act 1994, s 6(1) and (4).
3 Law of Property (Miscellaneous Provisions) Act 1994, s 6(2) and (3).
4 Law of Property (Miscellaneous Provisions) Act 1994, s 8(1).
5 LRR 2003, r 68.
6 LRR 2003, r 67(6).
7 LRR 2003, r 67(5).
8 Housing Act 1985 (HA 1985), Pt I, Sch 6, para 4A.
9 Law of Property (Miscellaneous Provisions) Act 1994, s 7.
10 LRA 2002, Sch 12, para 20.
11 LRR 2003, r 66.
12 LRR 2003, r 69(4).
13 Rentcharges Act 1977, s 11.

86 INDEMNITY

The LRA 2002 contains provisions relating to the payment of indemnity (i.e. statutory compensation) by HMLR under the 'state guarantee of title' in appropriate cases.[1] A person is entitled to be indemnified by HMLR if he suffers loss by reason of:

(a) rectification of the register;
(b) a mistake the correction of which would involve rectification of the register;
(c) a mistake in an official search;
(d) a mistake in an official copy;
(e) a mistake in a document kept by HMLR which is not an original and is referred to in the register;
(f) the loss or destruction of a document lodged at HMLR for inspection or safe custody;
(g) a mistake in the cautions register; or
(h) failure by HMLR to perform its duty under LRA 2002, s 50 to give notice of the creation of a statutory charge.

'Rectification' for these purposes means an alteration of the register which:

(a) involves the correction of a mistake; and
(b) prejudicially affects the title of a registered proprietor.

References to a mistake in something include anything mistakenly omitted from it as well as anything mistakenly included in it.[2]

A person who suffers loss by reason of the upgrade of a title under LRA 2002, s 62 is treated for the purposes of an indemnity claim as having suffered loss by reason of rectification of the register.[3]

Where the register is rectified following a forgery, the proprietor of a registered estate or charge claiming in good faith under the forged disposition is treated for the purposes of an indemnity claim as having suffered loss by reason of such rectification as if the disposition had not been forged.[4]

HMLR is not liable to pay indemnity:

(a) on account of any mines or minerals or the existence of any right to work or get mines or minerals, unless it is noted in the register that the registered title includes the mines and minerals;[5]
(b) on account of any loss suffered by a claimant wholly or partly as a result of his own fraud;[6] or

(c) on account of any loss suffered by the claimant wholly as a result of his own lack of proper care.[7]

Where a claimant suffers loss partly as a result of his own lack of proper care, any indemnity payable to him is reduced to such extent as is fair having regard to his share in the responsibility for the loss.[8]

When deciding whether there has been any fraud or lack of care on the part of the claimant, any fraud or lack of care on the part of a person from whom he derives title is treated as if it were the claimant's fraud or lack of care. However, this does not apply where the claimant derives title from such a person under a disposition for valuable consideration which is registered or protected by an entry in the register.[9]

Where the indemnity is payable in respect of an estate, interest or charge, the value of such estate, interest or charge is regarded, in a case where there is rectification, as not exceeding its value immediately before the rectification (but as if there were to be no rectification). Where correcting a mistake would involve rectification of the register but there is to be no rectification, the value of such estate, interest or charge is regarded as its value at the time when the mistake which caused the loss was made.[10]

For the position where indemnity is being sought in respect of costs, see 44 Costs.

Where a claimant cannot reach an agreement with HMLR about an indemnity claim, he may apply to the High Court or a county court for the determination of any question about:

(a) whether he is entitled to such indemnity; or
(b) the amount of the indemnity.

The requirement that the registrar consents to the incurring of costs or expenses does not apply to the costs of such an application to the court or of any legal proceedings arising out of such an application.[11]

86.1 Interest on indemnity

HMLR must pay interest on the amount of any indemnity paid at the applicable rate.[12] Where there has been rectification, interest is payable for the period from the date of rectification to the date of payment. Where there has not been rectification, interest is payable for the period from the date the loss is suffered by reason of the relevant mistake, loss, destruction or failure to the date of payment. No interest is payable for any period or periods where HMLR or the court is satisfied that the claimant has not taken reasonable steps to pursue with due diligence the claim for indemnity or, where relevant, the application for rectification.

In calculating the exact period in respect of which interest is payable, the date of payment is included but the date of the rectification, or the date the loss is suffered, is excluded.

The applicable rate of interest will be calculated as follows:

(a) Where the relevant period starts on or after 10 November 2008, at 1 per cent above the applicable Bank of England base rate or rates.
(b) Where the relevant period starts before that date:

   (i) for the part of the period before 10 November 2008, at the applicable rate or rates set for court judgment debts; and
   (ii) for the part of the period on or after 10 November 2008, at 1 per cent above the applicable Bank of England base rate or rates.

For the purposes of LRR 2003, r 195, 'Bank of England base rate' means:

(a) the rate announced from time to time by the Monetary Policy Committee of the Bank of England as the official dealing rate, being the rate at which the Bank is willing to enter into transactions for providing short-term liquidity in the money markets; or
(b) where an order under Bank of England Act 1998, s 19 is in force, any equivalent rate determined by the Treasury under that section.

86.2 Limitation

For the purposes of the LA 1980, a liability to pay an indemnity under LRA 2002, Sch 8 is a simple contract debt and the cause of action arises at the time when the claimant knows, or but for his own default might have known, of the existence of his claim.[13]

86.3 Rights of recovery

When HMLR pays an indemnity, including interest on an indemnity,[14] HMLR is entitled to recover the amount paid from any person who caused or substantially contributed to the loss by his fraud.[15] HMLR is also, for the purpose of recovering that amount, entitled to enforce the following rights of action:

(a) any right of action (of whatever nature and however arising) which the claimant would have been entitled to enforce had the indemnity not been paid; and

(b) where the register has been rectified, any right of action (of whatever nature and however arising) which the person in whose favour the register has been rectified would have been entitled to enforce had it not been rectified.[16]

This is without prejudice to any other rights HMLR may have.[17] For example, HMLR may be able to recover indemnity by enforcing an implied covenant for title given by the person who purported to transfer the estate to the claimant. There are also specific provisions under the Housing Acts that provide for a right of recourse against a local authority, if indemnity is paid where land has been registered in reliance on the accuracy of a certificate of title and there was an error in that certificate. Similar rights arise in cases where reliance has been placed on a certificate given by a housing action trust.

---

1 LRA 2002, s 103 and Sch 8.
2 LRA 2002, Sch 8, para 11(1).
3 See 181 Upgrade of Class of Title.
4 LRA 2002, Sch 8, para 1(2)(b). See also *Swift 1st Ltd v Chief Land Registrar* [2015] EWCA Civ 330.
5 LRA 2002, Sch 8, para 2.
6 LRA 2002, Sch 8, para 5(1)(a).
7 LRA 2002, Sch 8, para 5(1)(b).
8 LRA 2002, Sch 8, para 5(2).
9 LRA 2002, Sch 8, para 5(3).
10 LRA 2002, Sch 8, para 6.
11 LRA 2002, Sch 8, para 7.
12 LRR 2003, r 195.
13 LRA 2002, Sch 8, para 8.
14 LRA 2002, Sch 8, para 10(3).
15 LRA 2002, Sch 8, para 10(1)(a).
16 LRA 2002, Sch 8, para 10(2).
17 LRA 2002, Sch 8, para 10(1).

87 INDEMNITY COVENANTS

Where the proprietor of a registered estate has given an indemnity covenant, HMLR may make an entry in respect of it in the proprietorship register.[1] This applies whether the indemnity covenant is given in respect of a restrictive covenant or other matter that affects the registered estate or in respect of a positive covenant that relates to that estate.

If the existence of the indemnity covenant is apparent from the register in some other way, HMLR need not make an entry. This might arise where the indemnity covenant is included amongst restrictive covenants and is set out with them in the charges register. Where HMLR does make an entry, it must, where practicable, refer to the deed or document that contains the indemnity covenant.

There is no need to make a specific application for an entry in respect of an indemnity covenant when this is included in a deed or document lodged as part of an application in respect of a registrable disposition. HMLR will make the entry if it considers it appropriate.

Where HMLR has made an entry in respect of an indemnity covenant, it must remove it from the register if it appears to HMLR that the covenant does not bind the current proprietor of the registered estate.[2]

---

1 LRR 2003, r 65.

2 LRR 2003, r 65(3).

88 INDIVIDUAL VOLUNTARY ARRANGEMENTS

An IVA with creditors (as an alternative to bankruptcy) consists of either a composition in satisfaction of debts or a scheme of arrangement of affairs. In either case it must be approved by a meeting of creditors and is implemented by a licensed insolvency practitioner as the 'supervisor' of the IVA.[1] The effect of an IVA, if any, on the debtor's property depends on its terms. All the debtor's property will be included in the arrangement, unless specifically excluded.[2]

If the debtor is the sole proprietor of a registered estate or registered charge which he holds for his own benefit and the IVA creates an equitable charge, a contract for sale, option, or right of pre-emption in favour of the supervisor affecting that registered estate or registered charge, an application may be made for entry of an agreed notice or unilateral notice, in respect of the interest created.

If the debtor has a beneficial interest under a trust of land of a registered estate and the IVA creates an equitable charge, a contract for sale, option, or right of pre-emption in favour of the supervisor affecting that interest, or if the effect of the IVA is to create a trust and it affects a registered estate, the interest created cannot be protected by an agreed notice or unilateral notice.[3] However, it may be possible to protect this by an application for entry of a restriction. The appropriate form of restriction will depend upon the circumstances.

If the debtor is a sole registered proprietor who was holding the registered estate on trust for his own benefit before the IVA and is holding the property on trust for the creditors under the voluntary arrangement, an application may be made for entry of a restriction in Form A or Form II. The wording of Forms A and II is set out in Appendix IV.

If the IVA contains a provision that the debtor will not transfer, charge or otherwise deal with the property without the consent of the supervisor then, in addition to a restriction in Form A, application may also be made for a restriction in Forms L, N or NN. In the case of a registered charge, application may be made for a restriction in Forms S, T or OO. The wording of Forms L, N, NN, S, T and OO is set out in Appendix IV.

Where the registered estate is held by joint registered proprietors (one of whom may be the debtor) on trust for the debtor and others before the IVA, and the IVA contains a charge or assignment of the debtor's beneficial interest, or creates a trust in favour of the supervisor, an application may be made for the entry of a restriction in Form A, if such a restriction has not already been entered in the register. The supervisor may also apply for a restriction in Form II if the IVA contains an assignment of a debtor's beneficial interest, or if the debtor holds his beneficial share on a bare trust for the supervisor.

If the interest is held on trust by the debtor for the creditors or charged to the supervisor, no form of restriction other than a restriction in Form A (in relation to a registered estate, if not already entered in the register) can be applied for, as the interest of the supervisor or creditors will be derivative and will not therefore constitute a right or claim in relation to a registered estate or charge for the purposes of LRA 2002, s 42(1)(c).

No other form of restriction may be applied for without the consent of the registered proprietor(s).

A restriction does not confer any priority. However, it prevents an entry being made in the register relating to any disposition, or a disposition of a specified kind, unless the terms of the restriction have (where applicable) been complied with.

88.1 Agreed notice

In addition to the usual documents required,[4] an applicant should deliver to HMLR a certified copy of the IVA.

Where the consent of the registered proprietor is not available, the certified copy of the IVA is likely to be sufficient to satisfy HMLR of the validity of the applicant's claim for the purposes of LRA 2002, s 34(3)(c).

The agreed notice in the register will give details of the interest protected.

88.2 Unilateral notice

An applicant should deliver to HMLR the usual documents required.[5]

The statement in panel 12 or conveyancer's certificate in panel 13 of form UN1 should be completed to show details of the IVA, including:

(a) the date of the agreement;
(b) the debtor's name; and
(c) details of the provisions in the IVA claimed to give the supervisor an interest in the registered estate or charge.

The unilateral notice in the register will give brief details of the interest protected and identify the beneficiary of that notice.

88.3 Restriction

Where the supervisor is applying for a restriction, he should, in addition to the usual documents required,[6] deliver to HMLR (if the application is made by a person who claims that he has a sufficient interest in the making of the entry) a certified copy of the IVA.

The statement in panel 12 or conveyancer's certificate in panel 13 of form RX1 must be completed, setting out details of the IVA, including the provisions in the IVA claimed to give the supervisor an interest in the registered estate or charge.

Panel 9 of form RX1 should set out the wording of the appropriate restriction(s). A restriction in a standard form contained in LRR 2003, Sch 4 does not require the approval of HMLR to the terms of the restriction under LRA 2002, s 43(3).

A restriction in Form II does not of itself prevent a disposition, provided its terms are complied with. This is because the interest of the beneficiary will be overreached where the requirements of Form A have been met.[7]

A possible form of restriction based on the wording of Form L is:

> No [disposition *or specify type of disposition*] of the registered estate by the proprietor of the registered estate [or by the proprietor of any registered charge, not being a charge registered before the entry of this restriction] is to be registered without a certificate signed by [*name of supervisor*] of [*address*] [or [their conveyancer *or specify appropriate details*]] that the provisions of [*specify clause, paragraph or other particulars*] of the Individual Voluntary Agreement dated [*date*] made by [*party/ies*] have been complied with [or that they do not apply to the disposition].

A possible form of restriction based on the wording of Form N is:

> No [disposition *or specify type of disposition*] of the registered estate by the proprietor of the registered estate [or by the proprietor of any registered charge, not being a charge registered before the entry of this restriction] is to be registered without a written consent signed by [*name of supervisor*] of [*address*] [or [their conveyancer *or specify appropriate details*]].

A possible form of restriction based on the wording of Form NN is:

> No [disposition *or specify type of disposition*] of the registered estate [(other than a charge)] by the proprietor of the registered estate [or by the proprietor of any registered charge, not being a charge registered before the entry of this restriction] is to be registered without a written consent signed by [*name*] of [*address*] [or [their conveyancer *or specify appropriate details*]], or a certificate signed by [*name*] of [*address*] [or [their conveyancer *or specify appropriate details*]] that the provisions of [*specify clause, paragraph or other particulars*] of the Individual Voluntary Arrangement dated [*date*] made by [*party/ies*] have been complied with [or that they do not apply to the disposition].

The equivalent restrictions to those in Forms L, N and NN relating to a registered estate will, in the case of a registered charge, be Forms S, T and OO, respectively.

HMLR must give notice of such an application to the proprietor of the registered estate or charge concerned if it has not been made by or with his consent or a person entitled to be registered as such proprietor.[8]

---

1 IA 1986, Pt VIII.

2 IR 2016, r 8.3.

3 LRA 2002, s 33(a).

4 See 119.1 Agreed notice.

5 See 119.3 Unilateral notice.

6 See 153.1 Application for entry of restriction.

7 LPA 1925, ss 2 and 27.

8 LRA 2002, s 45.

89 INHERITANCE TAX

In some circumstances a registered estate may be subject to a liability for inheritance tax (IHT) (formerly known as capital transfer tax) in respect of deaths occurring after 12 March 1975. This tax replaced death duties (in practice, only estate duty) which applied in respect of deaths occurring on or before that date. The entry and/or removal of entries relating to IHT or death duties may therefore be relevant.[1]

89.1 Liability for death duties

Where the proprietor of a registered estate died before 13 March 1975 and it appeared that the registered estate was subject to a charge for death duties, HMLR would make the following entry (known as a notice in Form 60) in the register:

> Until the registration of a disposition in favour of a purchaser for money or money's worth, the land is liable to such death duties as may be payable or arise by reason of the death of [*name*] of [*address*] who died on [*date*].

HMLR will automatically cancel this entry upon the registration of a transfer of the registered estate on sale or other disposition for value. However, application to cancel this entry may be made at any time by lodging form CN1 completed by the Commissioners of HM Revenue and Customs (HMRC) (the Commissioners). No fee is currently payable.

89.2 Liability for capital transfer tax/inheritance tax

When IHT is due to the Commissioners, a statutory charge in their favour is imposed on the registered estate that is the subject of the gift. HMLR will not automatically make any entry in respect of this, but HMRC can, if it so wishes, apply in form AN1 to protect this charge by entering in the register an agreed notice[2] in the following form:

> Notice of an Inland Revenue charge (Reference number –) in respect of such tax as may arise.

A special rule of priority applies in relation to a charge under Inheritance Tax Act 1984, s 237 on the disposal of an estate or charge subject to such a charge. The priority of the statutory charge is to be determined in accordance with Inheritance Tax Act 1984, ss 237(6) and 238 rather than LRA 2002, ss 28 to 30. This imports a requirement of good faith and provides a purchaser in good faith for money or money's worth takes free from the charge in the absence of registration.

A disposition of the registered estate therefore takes subject to a subsisting Inland Revenue charge unless:

(a) the disposition is in favour of a purchaser within the meaning of the Inheritance Tax Act 1984; and
(b) the charge is not, at the time of registration of the disposition, protected by a notice in the register.

Such a notice will not be cancelled by HMLR, even when registering a transfer on sale, without receipt of form CN1 completed by the Commissioners. If the Commissioners have certified in the form CN1 that the application for cancellation is only to take effect upon the registration of a disposition to a purchaser, then HMLR will cancel the entry only when the form CN1 is accompanied by a proper application to register the transfer, or other specified disposition, in favour of the purchaser.

89.3 First registration

On an application for first registration not based on a disposition for value and where a gift has been made within 8 years of the date of the application, where no charge is disclosed and no Class D(i) land charge is registered, HMLR will not consider whether any liability to capital transfer tax or IHT has arisen.

If it appears from the application that the property being registered may be subject to a charge for IHT, HMLR will inform the applicant that it intends to make the following entry in the register:

> Notice of the possibility of an Inland Revenue charge in respect of such inheritance tax as may arise as a result of the death of [*name*] who died on [*date*].

However, if the applicant confirms in writing details of the surrounding circumstances of the case and that either no IHT was ever payable, or that it has been paid in full, HMLR will not make the entry. Alternatively, the applicant may supply a certificate of discharge from the Commissioners, or a letter from the Commissioners addressed to HMLR confirming the same.

89.4 Nil-rate band discretionary trusts

A nil-rate band discretionary trust is sometimes used in estate planning to reduce liability to IHT on the death of a surviving joint proprietor. However, their use is less common following the passing of the Finance Act 2008. The trustees have discretion as to the application of the trust income and how the trust assets will ultimately be distributed among a class of beneficiaries. Commonly, a property comprising the family home is an asset used in relation to such a trust. If the trust is created before the first death of a joint proprietor and the property is not already held under a tenancy in common, the proprietors sever their joint tenancy.[3]

If the trust is created after the first death, the surviving proprietor and his family may complete a deed of family arrangement to vary the disposition of the property comprised in the deceased's estate (for example under a right of survivorship) by effecting a post-death 'severance'. Provided this is done within 2 years after the first death, it has effect for tax purposes as though it had been made by the deceased proprietor.[4] However, such a 'severance' has no effect in general property law, so that the surviving beneficial joint tenant acquires the deceased's equitable share by survivorship in the normal way. An application to enter a Form A restriction based on such a 'severance' will not therefore be appropriate. The wording of Form A is set out in Appendix IV. The property may, however, become the subject of a trust because of other steps taken.

Typically, the value of the deceased proprietor's equitable share in the property will form part of the assets to be put into the nil-rate band discretionary trust. The value of this share cannot be realised without selling the property, and if the surviving proprietor wishes to carry on residing there, the deceased's personal representatives may instead charge the share to the trustees of the trust to satisfy the bequest. The personal representatives may then make an assent of the share, subject to the charge, to the beneficiary. Such an assent cannot be registered as it does not relate to the legal estate. The equitable charge of the equitable share cannot be registered or protected by notice.[5] Following such a charge and an assent, an application to cancel any existing Form A restriction would not be appropriate, given the charge created on the equitable share.

On the death of the deceased joint proprietor, an application should be made to remove his name from the register.[6] In most cases, the relevant form of application to reflect the existence of the nil-rate band discretionary trust will be for entry of any appropriate restriction(s). For example, a restriction in Form A (if one does not already appear in the register) and in Form B, if the trust contains limitations on the trustees' powers.[7] The wording of Form B is set out in Appendix IV.

1 See also 133 Personal Representatives.
2 LRR 2003, rr 80(b) and 81.
3 See 163 Severance of a Beneficial Joint Tenancy.
4 Inheritance Tax Act 1984, s 142.
5 LRA 2002, s 33.
6 See 92.2 Death of a joint proprietor.
7 See 178 Trusts of Land.

90 INHIBITIONS

An inhibition is an entry which was made in the register under LRA 1925, s 57 preventing the registration or entry of any dealing with registered land or with a registered charge. Inhibitions were usually entered to reflect an obligation not to deal with a registered estate or charge arising out of court proceedings, most often pursuant to:

(a) a freezing injunction;
(b) an undertaking given in lieu of such an injunction; or
(c) a restraint order.[1]

In rare cases, HMLR entered inhibitions for other reasons – for example, where a land certificate had been stolen or where there was other reason to believe that there was a risk of an application being made following an incident of fraud or forgery.

No new inhibitions can be entered in the register since 13 October 2003. By virtue of transitional provisions, any pre-existing inhibitions remain in the register, but the LRA 2002 applies to any such inhibitions as it applies to restrictions entered under that Act.[2] Special rules apply to bankruptcy inhibitions.[3] As to an inhibition entered in the register under LRA 1925, s 99 where the incumbent of a benefice was the registered proprietor, see 31.2 Incumbent of a benefice.

90.1 Effect of an inhibition

An inhibition will normally prevent the registration of a disposition. However, it cannot prevent the entry of a unilateral notice. Whether it prevents the entry of an agreed notice will depend upon the wording of the individual inhibition in the register. An inhibition that no disposition is to be 'registered' (without further wording) will not prevent the entry of an agreed notice. However, an inhibition that no disposition is to be 'registered or noted' will prevent the entry of an agreed notice in respect of a disposition, although it will not, for example, prevent the entry of such a notice in respect of a charging order as it is not a 'disposition'. An inhibition entered against a registered estate will not prevent the registration of a disposition by the proprietor of a registered charge in exercise of its power of sale, where the charge was registered before the entry of the inhibition.

90.2 Cancellation of an inhibition

An application to cancel an inhibition must be made in form RX3 and be accompanied by evidence to satisfy HMLR that the inhibition is no longer required.[4] Where HMLR entered the inhibition pursuant to an order of the court, normally it will be cancelled only pursuant to an order for its cancellation obtained from the court. If HMLR entered the inhibition pursuant to an order of the court under the Criminal Justice Act 1988, the Drug Trafficking Act 1994 or the Terrorism Act 2000, the written release by any prosecutor (as defined in those Acts) suffices in place of a court order.

An application in form RX4 to withdraw an inhibition will not normally be appropriate, given the circumstances in which inhibitions were usually entered in the register.

90.3 Modification or disapplication of an inhibition

HMLR may make an order modifying or disapplying an inhibition in relation to a specified disposition or class of dispositions.[5] An application for such an order must be made in form RX2.[6] The application must state whether it is to modify or disapply the inhibition, give details of the order sought (including details of the disposition or the kind of dispositions in question), explain why the applicant has a sufficient interest in the inhibition, and state why the applicant considers that HMLR should make the order.

HMLR must make a note of the terms of any order made by HMLR under LRA 2002, s 41(2) in the register.

---

1 See 76 Freezing Orders, Restraint Orders and Interim Receiving Orders.

2 LRA 2002, Sch 12, para 2(2).

3 See 19.3 Bankruptcy entries under the Land Registration Act 1925.

4 See 153.8 Cancellation of a restriction.

5 LRA 2002, s 41(2).

6 See 153.7 Application for an order that a restriction be disapplied or modified.

91 INTERNAL WATERS

The LRA 2002 extends to England and Wales only.[1] It applies to land covered by internal waters of the United Kingdom which are within England and Wales.[2] 'England' means, subject to any alteration of the boundaries under Local Government Act 1972, Pt IV, the area consisting of the counties established by s 1 of that Act, Greater London and the Isles of Scilly, while 'Wales' means the combined area of the counties which were created by Local Government Act 1972, s 20 as originally enacted, but subject to any alteration made under s 73 of that Act (consequential alteration of boundary following alteration of watercourse).[3] 'Internal waters' means waters to the landward side of the baseline used for defining the territorial limits of the United Kingdom and fixed in accordance with the Convention on the Territorial Sea and the Contiguous Zone of 1958. This baseline is normally, but not always, the low-water mark.

A coastal county or other administrative area normally extends up to the low-water mark on its seaward side.[4] In the case of estuaries, the county boundary is at the seaward limit of the estuary shown by the OS. The Channel Tunnel (as far as the frontier) is incorporated into England by Channel Tunnel Act 1987, s 10(1).

It is possible for the Lord Chancellor to extend by order the application of the LRA 2002 to other land covered by internal waters of the United Kingdom which is adjacent to England and Wales.[5] No such order has currently been made. Until such an order is made, land which falls within internal waters but outside the county boundaries of England and Wales is not registrable.

---

1 LRA 2002, s 136(3).
2 LRA 2002, s 130(a).
3 Interpretation Act 1978, s 5 and Sch 1.
4 *R v Keyn* (1876) 2 Ex D 63.
5 LRA 2002, s 130(b).

92 JOINT PROPRIETORS

Where joint proprietors are registered as proprietors of registered land, they hold the legal estate as joint tenants on a trust of land, whether or not they also hold the equitable interest as joint tenants.[1] The register records the ownership of the legal estate not the beneficial interests, and HMLR is not affected by notice of such a trust.[2] No more than four joint proprietors can be entered in the proprietorship register at any one time, unless the land is vested in trustees for charitable, ecclesiastical, or public purposes.[3]

The legal estate can never be severed and can only be held by two or more persons as beneficial joint tenants.[4] If one joint owner dies, the legal estate will pass by 'survivorship' and vest automatically in the surviving joint owner(s), regardless of the devolution of the equitable interest.

However, the equitable interest may, where there are two or more beneficiaries, be held as between themselves as beneficial joint tenants or tenants in common.

In the case of a beneficial joint tenancy, the whole equitable interest is held equally and the right of 'survivorship' applies so that, if one joint tenant dies, his interest passes automatically to the survivor(s). In the case of a beneficial tenancy in common, the equitable interest may be held in either equal or unequal undivided shares and the right of 'survivorship' does not apply, so that, if one tenant in common dies, his share passes under the terms of his will or intestacy. A tenant in common may also assign or dispose of his share during his lifetime.

Since 1926, a purchaser of land[5] need only be concerned with the legal estate, the devolution of which on death is clear, and does not need to investigate or be concerned with the equitable interest provided that, where necessary, 'overreaching' is effected.

Overreaching occurs where there is a:

(a) transfer,
(b) lease, or
(c) charge,

of land,[6] which is subject to a trust of land, and capital money arises. It is the mechanism under which the capital money is paid to at least two trustees (or to a sole personal representative acting as such) or to a trust corporation, so that the equitable interests of the beneficiaries under the trust are transferred to the capital monies (such as the proceeds of sale), leaving the purchaser to take free of those interests.[7]

If there is only a sole trustee of land held on a trust of land, that trustee (unless a trust corporation or a sole personal representative acting as such) will therefore need to appoint a co-trustee to act jointly with him in respect of a sale or charge of the land, so that there is a valid receipt for the capital money by not less than two trustees and overreaching is effected.

Only certain equitable interests can be overreached, being those which relate to an equitable interest under a trust of land rather than to the legal estate. For example, an equitable share in land, or an equitable charge on an equitable share in land, such as a charging order on the beneficial share of one of joint owners of land. Other equitable interests which relate to the legal estate cannot be overreached; for example, a restrictive covenant, equitable easement or equitable charge affecting the legal estate. Legal estates and interests, such as a leasehold estate in land or a legal easement, cannot be overreached.

A person dealing with a registered proprietor can assume that he has unlimited power to dispose of the registered estate or registered charge concerned, free from any limitation affecting the validity of the disposition, unless there is a restriction or other entry in the register limiting his powers, or a limitation imposed by or under the LRA 2002.[8] In the context of a trust of land, this means that, if two or more persons are registered as joint proprietors, a purchaser can safely acquire the legal estate from them, or from the survivor of them, unless there is a restriction or other entry to the contrary in the register.

92.1 Entry of Form A restriction

If HMLR enters two or more registered proprietors of a registered estate in land, it must enter a Form A restriction in the register where the survivor of them will not be able to give a valid receipt for capital money. The wording of Form A is set out in Appendix IV. The prescribed forms of transfer or assent of registered land[9] and clause LR14 of a prescribed clauses lease all contain a panel headed 'Declaration of trust' containing the following alternative declarations where the transferee is more than one person:

(a) The transferees are to hold the property on trust for themselves as joint tenants.
(b) The transferees are to hold the property on trust for themselves as tenants in common in equal shares.
(c) The transferees are to hold the property on trust [*to be completed as necessary*].

The appropriate option should be selected, depending upon whether the transferees are to hold the registered estate on trust for themselves as joint tenants beneficially, or as tenants in common in equal shares, or upon some other trust. Completion of the declaration in the transfer and execution of the transfer by the transferees is important, so that the transferees make an appropriate declaration as to the trusts upon which the registered estate will be held by them. This was emphasised by the House of Lords in *Stack v Dowden* [2007] UKHL 17 and by the Supreme Court in *Jones v Kernott* [2011] UKSC 53. A declaration of trust in a separate document may be executed if desired. The 'trust information' panel in application forms FR1 and ADV1 also include provision for similar confirmation to be given about the trusts upon which the property is to be held. As an alternative to completing the relevant panel in a prescribed form, a declaration in form JO may be lodged instead. The completed and signed form JO must be lodged with the relevant application for registration to which it relates.

Unless the transferees declare (or it is otherwise apparent from the application) that they are holding the property on trust for themselves as beneficial joint tenants, HMLR will enter a restriction in Form A, the wording of which is set out in Appendix IV.

The purpose of the Form A restriction is to reflect the existence of a trust of land and ensure that overreaching is effected on a disposition for value of the land.[10] The restriction will not 'catch' a disposition where no capital money arises, for example on the appointment of a new trustee.

In the case of other types of registered estate, as opposed to an estate in land, LRR 2003, r 94(2A) provides that where two or more persons apply to be registered as proprietors of an estate which is a:

(a) rentcharge,
(b) profit à prendre in gross,
(c) franchise, or
(d) manor,

they must also apply for entry of a restriction in Form A if a sole (surviving) proprietor will not be able to give a valid receipt for capital money.

HMLR will not enter a restriction in Form A in respect of a registered charge, because although a charge can be held on trust, the survivor of the registered chargees is always able to give a valid receipt for the money secured by it. This reflects LRA 2002, s 56 which provides that where a registered charge has two or more proprietors, a valid receipt for the money secured by it may be given by:

(a) the registered proprietors;
(b) the survivors or survivor of the registered proprietors; or
(c) the personal representative of the last survivor of the registered proprietors.

92.2 Death of a joint proprietor

Where a joint proprietor of a registered estate or a registered charge dies, an application may be made for alteration of the register by the removal of the deceased joint proprietor. The application may conveniently be made in application form AP1 or form DJP, although this is not essential. The application must be accompanied by evidence of the death.[11] Such an application can also be lodged electronically by a conveyancer, who must certify that he has seen the appropriate evidence of the death.

HMLR will delete the name of the deceased joint proprietor, leaving the names of the survivor(s) in the register. The only exception is where there is a 'partnership' restriction in Form Q (or similar) requiring the consent of the deceased proprietor's personal representative to any disposition. The wording of Form Q is set out in Appendix IV. Where such a restriction appears, HMLR will leave the name of the deceased in the register, but enter a note of his death.

92.3 Cancellation of Form A restriction

HMLR will not automatically cancel a Form A restriction on the death of a joint proprietor. If the trust of land continues to subsist and a sole survivor of joint proprietors remains as proprietor of land with a restriction in Form A in the register, a new trustee can be appointed and registered as proprietor jointly with him. This appointment will not be 'caught' by the restriction, which will remain in the register to reflect the fact the registered estate is still subject to a trust of land.

If, however, the sole surviving joint proprietor has become legally and beneficially entitled to the whole of the estate, he may apply for the cancellation of the restriction. The application should be made in form RX3[12] and supported by evidence of the equitable title showing that the surviving proprietor can give a valid receipt for capital money arising on a disposition of the estate. Usually, HMLR will accept a statutory declaration or statement of truth by the survivor (which may be in form ST5 in LRR 2003, Sch 1), or a certificate by a conveyancer with personal knowledge of the facts, which shows how he has become the sole beneficial owner by:

(a) explaining what has happened to the beneficial interest protected by the restriction;
(b) if it has devolved to the surviving proprietor, explaining how it has so devolved;
(c) confirming, if such be the case, that no one other than the surviving proprietor now has a beneficial interest in the property; and
(d) confirming, if such be the case, that no beneficial interest in the property has been encumbered (other than by a charge that is also of the legal estate).

The declaration, statement or certificate should be accompanied by any available documentary evidence, such as an assent relating to an undivided share. No fee is currently payable for the cancellation of the restriction.

If all the registered proprietors have died, the personal representatives of the last surviving proprietor can make a similar application adjusting the terms of the statutory declaration, statement of truth or certificate according to the individual circumstances.

An application for cancellation of the restriction may also be made, where appropriate, in other circumstances. For example, where a registered estate has been transferred into the sole name of one of the former joint proprietors and he has become legally and beneficially entitled to the whole of the estate or where the trusts upon which the joint proprietors hold the property have been replaced or amended, so that they now hold the registered estate upon trust for themselves as beneficial joint tenants rather than as tenants in common. Alternatively, an applicant may lodge a court order requiring the registrar to cancel the restriction.

In certain circumstances, HMLR may automatically cancel a restriction in Form A following completion of a disposition by registration. Thus HMLR will cancel a restriction in Form A on registration of a transfer on sale by two or more trustees or a trust corporation (except where the transfer is to one or more of the existing proprietors) under LRR 2003, r 99. A restriction in Form A cannot normally be withdrawn.[13]

92.4 Related matters

In addition to the matters discussed above in respect of joint proprietors, reference should be made, as appropriate, to:

(a) 39 Constructive and Resulting Trusts;
(b) 153 Restrictions;
(c) 163 Severance of a Beneficial Joint Tenancy; and
(d) 178 Trusts of Land.

---

1 LPA 1925, ss 34 and 36.
2 LRA 2002, s 78.
3 Trustee Act 1925, s 34.
4 LPA 1925, ss 1(6) and 34.
5 As defined in LPA 1925, s 205(1)(xxi) and which for this purpose includes a mortgagee.
6 *Baker v Craggs* [2018] EWCA Civ 1126 made it clear that other types of disposition, such as the grant of an easement, cannot overreach an earlier equitable interest.
7 LPA 1925, ss 2 and 27.
8 LRA 2002, s 26.
9 Forms AS1, AS3, TR1, TR2, TR5, TP1 and TP2.
10 LRA 2002, s 42(1)(b).
11 LRR 2003, r 164.
12 See 153.8 Cancellation of a restriction.
13 LRR 2003, r 98(3).

93 LAND REGISTRY ACT 1862

The Land Registry Act 1862 was the first statute under which the title to land could be registered. Application for registration was voluntary and the requirements for registration of title were stringent. The 1862 Act did not require subsequent dispositions of registered land to be registered and it was not essential for a land certificate to be issued. The Land Registry Act 1862 is now repealed.[1] Even before that repeal, Land Transfer Act 1875, s 125 and subsequently LRA 1925, s 137(1) provided that no application for the registration of an estate under the 1862 Act was to be entertained.

The Land Registry Act 1862 was largely replaced by the Land Transfer Act 1875 which (as subsequently amended by the Land Transfer Act 1897 to make provision for compulsory registration of title) introduced the land registration system which largely operated until 2003. The LRA 1925 was an important part of the great property reform legislation of 1925 which also included the LPA 1925. The LRA 2002 replaced the earlier legislation and came into force on 13 October 2003.

Any land which is registered under the Land Registry Act 1862 is now treated as being unregistered land and may be registered under the LRA 2002 by an application for first registration in the usual way.[2] If a land certificate issued under the 1862 Act is available, it should be lodged with the application for first registration.

If a person requires a copy of any information included in a record of title made under the Land Registry Act 1862, these are available on the HMLR website.[3]

1 LRA 2002, s 122.
2 See 67 First Registration.
3 https://digitalarchives.landregistry.gov.uk/.

94 LAND TRANSACTION TAX

LTT is a tax payable on the acquisition of a chargeable interest in land in Wales. It replaced SDLT for land in Wales from 1 April 2018 and was introduced by the Land Transaction Tax and Anti-avoidance of Devolved Taxes (Wales) Act 2017. The Welsh Revenue Authority (WRA) administers LTT.

For the purposes of LTT, 'acquisition' includes the creation, surrender and certain variations of a chargeable interest.[1] 'Chargeable interest' is either:

(a) an estate, interest, right or power in or over land in Wales; or
(b) the benefit of an obligation, restriction or condition affecting the value of any such estate, interest, right or power, other than an exempt interest.[2]

This is subject to the exceptions set out in Land Transaction Tax and Anti-avoidance of Devolved Taxes (Wales) Act 2017, s 5.

The rate of tax is a percentage of the 'chargeable consideration' for the transaction, which for LTT purposes comprises anything given for the transaction in money or money's worth. It therefore includes not only monetary consideration but also other forms of consideration such as the release or assumption of a debt; the provision of works and services; or the transfer of other property. Certain reliefs may be available in appropriate cases; such reliefs must be applied for.

Currently, different rates apply to residential property and to non-residential and mixed-use property. A supplemental charge applies on the purchase of an 'additional residential property' such as a buy-to-let property or a holiday home.

Where land falls partly in England and partly in Wales, its acquisition is treated as two separate land transactions. The applicant must apportion the consideration paid for the land on a just and reasonable basis.[3] Where appropriate, the applicant should notify both HMRC (in respect of SDLT) and the WRA (in respect of LTT).

Most land transactions are 'notifiable', which means the WRA must be informed about the transaction, even in cases where it is of a type which will not attract LTT. Conveyancers must notify the WRA using the online filing facility provided. Non-conveyancers must contact the WRA for a paper form. Companies and trusts purchasing residential property must also pay a higher rate of tax.

If a professional notifies the WRA online, they will be redirected to a site where they can download a WRA certificate. If the notification is in paper, the WRA will issue the WRA certificate once it has processed the return. Land Transaction Tax (Administration) Wales Regulations 2018 (SI 2018/2), reg 4 prescribes the contents of the WRA certificate.

An applicant must include a copy of any WRA certificate with any application to HMLR. HMLR cannot register or enter an agreed notice of the transaction without any necessary WRA certificate.[4]

Further details concerning LTT are available on the WRA website.[5]

---

1 Land Transaction Tax and Anti-avoidance of Devolved Taxes (Wales) Act 2017, s 6.

2 Land Transaction Tax and Anti-avoidance of Devolved Taxes (Wales) Act 2017, s 4(1).

3 Land Transaction Tax and Anti-avoidance of Devolved Taxes (Wales) Act 2017, s 9.

4 Land Transaction Tax and Anti-avoidance of Devolved Taxes (Wales) Act 2017, s 65(1).

5 www.gov.wales/land-transaction-tax.

95 LAND TRANSPARENCY

Levelling-up and Regeneration Act 2023 (LURA 2023), Part 11 contains powers to make regulations requiring the provision of information to:

(a) HMLR, or
(b) another person exercising public functions on behalf of the Crown,

for specified purposes.[1] The specified purposes are:

(a) the beneficial ownership purpose;
(b) the contractual control purpose; and
(c) the national security purpose.

Currently no such regulations are in force.

95.1 The beneficial ownership purpose

Information is within the scope of the beneficial ownership purpose if it appears to the Secretary of State that it would be useful for the purposes of:

(a) identifying persons who are beneficial owners of land in England or Wales; or
(b) understanding the relationship of those persons with the land that they beneficially own.[2]

95.2 The contractual control purpose

Information is within the scope of the contractual control purpose if it appears to the Secretary of State that it would be useful for the purposes of understanding rights:

(a) arising under a contract;[3]
(b) relating to the development or disposal of land in England or Wales; and
(c) which are held for the purposes of a business, charity or similar endeavour or the exercise of functions of a public nature.[4]

95.3 The national security purpose

Information is within the scope of the contractual control purpose if it appears to the Secretary of State that:

(a) it relates to land which the Secretary of State believes could constitute a threat to national security by reason of its location or anything situated or done on it;
(b) the information would be useful for the purposes of:

(i) identifying persons who:

(1) own relevant interests in the land;
(2) have relevant rights concerning the land; or
(3) have the ability, or are in a position that may involve the ability, to control or influence (directly or indirectly) the owner of a relevant interest in the land, or a person with a relevant right concerning the land, in the exercise of that ownership or right;

(ii) understanding the relationship of those persons with the land; and

(c) it appears to the Secretary of State that requiring the provision of the information under LURA 2023, s 219 would be justified in the interests of national security.[5]

For these purposes:

(a) 'Relevant interest in land' means an estate, interest, right or power in or over land in the United Kingdom, except an advowson, franchise or manor; and
(b) 'Relevant right concerning land' means a right or power, arising under a contract or otherwise, that is not a relevant interest in land but concerns the ownership, control or use of land in the United Kingdom.[6]

95.4 The information which must be provided

Regulations will specify the information which must be provided. Such information may include transactional information about instruments, contracts and other arrangements:

(a) creating, altering, extinguishing, evidencing, or transferring relevant interests in land; or
(b) conferring, amending, assigning, terminating or otherwise modifying relevant rights concerning land.[7]

'Relevant interests in land' and 'relevant right concerning land' have the meanings given above. 'Transactional information' means:

(a) details of the parties to a transaction;
(b) details of persons on whose behalf or for whose benefit the parties to a transaction are or were acting;
(c) details of the terms of a transaction;
(d) details of persons providing professional services in relation to a transaction;
(e) details of the source of any money paid or other consideration given in connection with a transaction; and
(f) copies of documents giving effect to or evidencing a transaction.

95.5 Providing the information

Regulations must specify:

(a) the person on whom the requirement to provide information falls;
(b) the occurrence or circumstances that gives or give rise to the requirement;
(c) the time limit for complying with the requirement; and
(d) the person to whom the required information is to be provided.[8]

Where the requirement to give information falls within the national security purpose, the occurrence which gives rise to the requirement must be the giving of notice to the person on whom the requirement falls. This may also be a trigger for the other purposes. In either case, regulations will provide further details about the giving of notice. This may include provisions deeming the giving of notice.[9]

Regulations may also:

(a) specify how the information is to be provided (including a requirement that it be provided by electronic means specified in the regulations);
(b) provide for, or make provision about, the application of the regulations to persons outside, or information held outside, the United Kingdom; and
(c) relate to things done or arising before the coming into force of LURA 2023, s 219.[10]

95.6 Enforcement

Once regulations are in effect:

(a) failure to provide the required information without reasonable excuse, and
(b) deliberately or recklessly providing misleading information,

will be criminal offences.[11] In addition, regulations may prevent HMLR from registering a transaction or entering or amending a notice and/or restriction to protect the relevant interest.[12]

---

1 LURA 2023, s 219.
2 LURA 2023, s 220.
3 Which for these purposes includes a deed and does not require consideration.
4 LURA 2023, s 221.
5 LURA 2023, s 222.
6 LURA 2023, s 227.
7 LURA 2023, s 223(1).
8 LURA 2023, s 219(4).
9 LURA 2023, s 219(5) and (6).
10 Which came into force on 26 October 2023.
11 LURA 2023, s 225.
12 LURA 2023, s 226.

96 LARGE SCALE APPLICATIONS

A large-scale application is one comprising a common deed or deeds affecting registered and/or unregistered land in areas covered by one or more HMLR office(s) and which either affects more than:

(a) 50 wholly registered titles; or
(b) any combination of registered titles and unregistered properties exceeding 50 in total.

When an applicant proposes to make a 'large-scale application', he should first contact the LSST to discuss the matter. The LSST will provide guidance about the preparation and lodging of the application and will also arrange for a nominated HMLR office to deal with the application or to act as a controller for a group of HMLR offices nominated to assist with the application. The LSST will coordinate the processing of the application and provide the applicant with written details of the required steps to take, the timetable of lodgement and the method of calculating the fees.

In some instances, the LSST can provide advice on the contents of transaction documents, such as form TR4 or form TR5, to minimise the likelihood of requisitions.

Once the application has been lodged at an HMLR office, that office will assume the operational responsibility, and the application becomes subject to the normal registration procedures.

97 LEASEHOLD ENFRANCHISEMENT

The Leasehold Reform Act 1967 confers upon qualifying tenants of a house held under a long tenancy at a low rent the right to acquire the freehold or an extended lease. 'House' does not include flats in a horizontally divided building and 'premises' includes any garage, outhouse, garden, yard and appurtenances let with the house.[1] 'Long tenancy' means any tenancy originally granted for a term exceeding 21 years whether or not it is determinable by notice or re-entry.[2] There are further conditions and exceptions that apply in particular circumstances.

Such a right may also be exercised by the personal representatives of a tenant who held the right at his death, so long as the tenancy is vested in them.[3] The personal representatives may not give notice of their desire to have the freehold or an extended lease later than 2 years after the grant of probate or letters of administration. For:

(a) extended leases under the Leasehold Reform Act 1967 or under the LRHUDA 1993, see 98.12 Acquisition of an extended lease under the Leasehold Reform Act 1967 and 98.13 Acquisition of a lease under the Leasehold Reform, Housing and Urban Development Act 1993; and
(b) collective enfranchisement under the LRHUDA 1993, see 34 Collective Enfranchisement.

Enfranchisement under the Leasehold Reform Act 1967 may be possible in circumstances where:

(a) the details of the lease and of the landlord are not fully known; and
(b) enlargement of the lease under LPA 1925, s 153 is precluded.[4]

97.1 Notice under Leasehold Reform Act 1967

Any right of a tenant or his personal representatives arising from a notice served on the landlord under the Leasehold Reform Act 1967 is not capable of being an interest within LRA 2002, Sch 1 or Sch 3 which overrides first registration and registered dispositions.[5] However, it may be the subject of a notice as if it were an estate contract and, where the landlord's reversionary title is registered, application may be made for the entry of an agreed notice or a unilateral notice.

97.1.1 Agreed notice

In addition to the usual documents required,[6] an applicant should deliver to HMLR a certified copy of the notice under the Leasehold Reform Act 1967.

Where the consent of the registered proprietor is not available, the notice under the 1967 Act is likely to be sufficient to satisfy HMLR as to the validity of the applicant's claim in accordance with LRA 2002, s 34(3)(c).

The agreed notice in the register will give details of the interest protected.

97.1.2 Unilateral notice

An applicant should deliver to HMLR the usual documents required.[7]

The statement in panel 11 or conveyancer's certificate in panel 12 of form UN1 should be completed on the following lines to show the interest of the applicant:

> intending purchaser, notice of enfranchisement under the Leasehold Reform Act 1967 having been given on [*date*] to [*name and address of landlord*].

Where the applicant has taken an assignment from the tenant of the benefit of the rights under notice in accordance with Leasehold Reform Act 1967, s 5(2), form UN1 should be completed on the following lines to show the interest of the applicant:

> assignee of rights under the Leasehold Reform Act 1967 by virtue of an assignment dated [*date*] made between [*former tenant*] and [*applicant*], the rights having arisen on [*date*] by the service of notice of enfranchisement on [*name and address of landlord*].

The unilateral notice in the register will give brief details of the interest protected and identify the beneficiary of that notice.

Any subsequent assignment of rights under the Leasehold Reform Act 1967 should not be included in a transfer of a registered leasehold estate but should instead be effected by a separate instrument 'off the register'. No entry of such an assignment will be made in the register, but if the rights are already protected in the register by a unilateral notice, the assignee should apply in form UN3 to be registered as the new beneficiary of the notice.[8]

97.2 Registration of transfer of the freehold

The application for the registration of the transfer of the freehold reversion should be made in the usual way.[9] The application should show, either by a statement in the transfer or on the application form, that the transfer is made under the Leasehold Reform Act 1967.

Any necessary request for merger should be included in the application. Where a deed of substituted security transferring a legal charge on a merged lease to the freehold estate is lodged, the charge will normally be registered against the tenant's freehold title. If the charge is only to be noted, form AN1 (for entry of an agreed notice) or form UN1 (for entry of a unilateral notice) should be lodged.[10]

Certain special considerations also apply, as discussed below.

97.3 Discharge of registered charges on the freehold title

The landlord's chargee may have expressly discharged the charge or released the land from it in the usual way. If not, and the tenant claims that he has paid to the chargee enough money to discharge the house from the charge, the tenant must lodge a verified copy of the chargee's (appropriately worded) receipt. Alternatively, if sufficient money to discharge or release the house from the charge has been paid into court by the tenant under Leasehold Reform Act 1967, s 13, there must be lodged a certified copy of the witness statement the tenant will have made for that purpose, and a certified copy of the court's official receipt.

If there has been an express discharge or release, or if, on the receipt of the appropriate evidence of payment to the chargee or into court HMLR is satisfied that the tenant may be registered as the freehold proprietor free from the charge, no entry of it will appear in the register of the tenant's freehold title. In appropriate cases, HMLR may serve notice upon the chargee explaining the nature of the transaction and inviting him to consent. If in response to the notice the chargee provides arguable grounds for objection, the application cannot proceed until the objection is disposed of either by agreement or in accordance with LRA 2002, s 73.[11]

In the case of a floating charge created by a landlord, HMLR will accept a certificate by the solicitor, secretary or other responsible officer of the landlord company or of the debenture holder that the charge had not crystallised at the date of the conveyance or transfer on enfranchisement for the registration of the tenant's freehold title free from the charge.

97.4 Rentcharges

The transfer or conveyance will normally take effect subject to any pre-existing rentcharges affecting the title.[12] However, where the rentcharge is more than the amount payable as rent under the lease, the tenant can require the landlord to discharge the house and premises from the rentcharge to the extent of the excess.[13] The appropriate evidence of discharge should be lodged. Where difficulties arise in paying the redemption price, provision is made for payment into court under Leasehold Reform Act 1967, s 11(4),[14] in which case evidence of such payment should be lodged in the form of a certified copy of the tenant's or landlord's witness statement and a verified copy of the court's receipt.

97.5 Rights and burdens under Leasehold Reform Act 1967, s 10

Leasehold Reform Act 1967, s 10(2) provides that the benefit and burden of certain rights that affect the leasehold interest shall automatically continue on enfranchisement, but without prejudice to any rights that may be expressly granted or reserved. The rights passing under s 10(2) take effect so far as the landlord is capable of granting them and consist of:

(a) rights of support;
(b) rights of access of light and air; and
(c) rights to the passage, use or maintenance of the usual common services, such as water, drainage, electricity, etc.

If HMLR is aware that a conveyance or transfer has been made under the Leasehold Reform Act 1967, it will make appropriate entries in the register of the benefit and burden of rights passing under s 10(2). If the conveyance or transfer expressly excludes or restricts any of the benefiting rights, HMLR will reflect this in the entry. If the conveyance or transfer includes new easements or restrictive covenants under s 10(3) or (4), HMLR will make entries in the register in respect of these.

Where the reversionary title over which the easement is granted is registered in the name of the landlord but under a different title number to that of the house, the applicant should also apply against that burdened title, or that where the servient title is unregistered, he should provide satisfactory evidence of title with his application.

In some instances, rights originally granted or reserved affecting the leasehold interest will, by virtue of Leasehold Reform Act 1967, s 10, now affect the freehold estate. If reference to the deed which granted or reserved those rights is required to be made in the register, this should be expressly requested and the original deed, or a certified copy or examined abstract of it, should be lodged.

97.6 Estate Management Scheme under the Leasehold Reform Act 1967

In certain circumstances on enfranchisement, Leasehold Reform Act 1967, s 19 provides for the landlord to retain management powers for the general benefit of the neighbourhood. This requires a scheme authorised by the Minister of Housing and Local Government (or the Secretary of State in Wales and Monmouthshire) and approved by the High Court. To be effective, such a scheme must be registered as a local land charge. Given the nature of the scheme, entry of a notice would not normally be appropriate. An exception to this would be where a scheme imposes a statutory charge, in which case this may be the subject of a notice in the register, although such a charge would have to be registered before it could be realised.[15] Rights under local land charges, unless and until registered or protected in the register of title, take effect as overriding interests under LRA 2002, Schs 1 and 3.[16]

---

1 Leasehold Reform Act 1967, s 2(1) to (3).
2 Leasehold Reform Act 1967, s 3.
3 Leasehold Reform Act 1967, s 6A.
4 See 60 Enlargement of Long Leases.
5 Leasehold Reform Act 1967, s 5(5).
6 See 119.1 Agreed notice.
7 See 119.3 Unilateral notice.
8 See 119.4 Registration of new or additional beneficiary of a unilateral notice.
9 See 68 First Registration or 176 Transfers, as appropriate.
10 See 119.1 Agreed notice and 119.3 Unilateral notice.
11 See 54 Disputes.
12 Leasehold Reform Act 1967, s 8(4)(b).
13 Leasehold Reform Act 1967, s 11(2).
14 Once LFRA 2024, s 41 comes into effect this will provide for payment to the appropriate tribunal.
15 LRA 2002, s 55.
16 See 109 Local Land Charges.

98 LEASES

Certain leases of unregistered estates are capable of being the subject of an application for first registration, which may be either a voluntary application or a compulsory application as a result of a 'trigger' for first registration having occurred. In the case of registered estates, certain leases are registrable dispositions which are required to be completed by registration if they are to take effect at law. Some leases may not be capable of substantive registration, but may be the subject of a notice in the register. Other leases may not be capable of either substantive registration or protection by the entry of a notice in the register.

98.1 Leases granted out of unregistered estates

A lease granted out of unregistered land need not contain the prescribed clauses,[1] but the parties may voluntarily choose to use them, if desired. If the parties do choose to use the prescribed clauses they may apply for entry of a standard restriction in clause LR13 rather than by using form RX1.[2] Such a lease may be subject to compulsory first registration upon its grant or assignment or may be the subject of a voluntary application for first registration.[3]

HMLR will enter a notice of the burden of an unregistered lease if it is disclosed on an application for first registration of the landlord's reversionary title, provided it is capable of being noted.[4]

If the landlord's title is registered and no notice of the lease appears in the register, HMLR must, when completing an application for first registration of the lease, enter a notice of the lease in the landlord's title.[5]

Where a lease granted out of unregistered land is not subject to compulsory first registration, the burden of it will be an interest which overrides first registration and registered dispositions.[6] If the landlord's title is later registered and HMLR do not enter a notice of the lease, the tenant may apply for entry of a notice in the landlord's title, provided the lease is granted for a term of more than 3 years.[7] A PPP lease cannot be noted.[8]

98.2 Leases which are registrable dispositions

A proprietor of a registered estate has full power to grant a lease (or, if it is a leasehold estate, an underlease for any term of years absolute of less duration than his own registered estate), subject to any entry in the register to the contrary.[9] A person's right to exercise owner's powers are, in favour of a tenant, taken to be free from any limitation affecting the validity of the lease, subject to any entry to the contrary in the register or any limitation imposed by or under the LRA 2002.[10] For example, a landlord may have to comply with a restriction their landlord title, or obtain a registered chargee's consent. Where an existing lease is registered with less than absolute class of leasehold title, see 32.2 Titles to leasehold estates.

Where the registered estate is an estate in land, the following grants of terms of years absolute must be completed by registration:[11]

(a) for a term of more than 7 years from the date of the grant;
(b) to take effect in possession after the end of the period of 3 months beginning with the date of the grant;
(c) under which the right to possession is discontinuous;
(d) in pursuance of the right to buy under HA 1985, Pt V; or
(e) in circumstances where the HA 1985, s 171A applies (leases of the reversion of land to a private sector landlord where the tenant has a right to buy).

Where the registered estate is a franchise or manor, the grant of any lease must be completed by registration.[12]

LRA 2002, Sch 2 sets out the registration requirements. Where there is a grant out of an estate in land of a term of years absolute which is required to be completed by registration, the grantee, or his successor in title, must be entered in the register as the proprietor of the lease and a notice in respect of the lease must be entered in the register of the reversionary title. In the case of a grant out of a registered franchise or manor of a lease for a term of more than 7 years from the date of the grant, the grantee, or his successor in title, must be entered in the register as the proprietor of the lease and a notice in respect of the lease must be entered in the register of the reversionary title. In the case of a grant out of a registered franchise or manor of a lease for a term not exceeding 7 years from the date of the grant, a notice in respect of the lease must be entered in the register of the reversionary title.

Most registrable dispositions consisting of a lease of a registered estate in land must be in the form of a prescribed clauses lease.[13] Where a lease of a registered estate is not required to be in the form of a prescribed clauses lease, it may be in any form provided that it refers to the landlord's title number[14] and, if it is a lease of part of the registered estate, it must normally include a plan enabling HMLR to identify the demised premises on the title plan of the landlord's title, unless it is already identified on that title plan.[15] The route of any easements and other rights must similarly be clearly identified.

98.3 Leases of land not exceeding 7 years

A leasehold estate in land granted for a term not exceeding 7 years from the date of the grant cannot usually be registered or, if for 3 years or less, noted in the register. It is an interest which overrides first registration and registered dispositions.[16] However, the following leases not exceeding 7 years are registrable dispositions and do not take effect as overriding interests:

(a) a grant of a term of years absolute to take effect in possession after the end of the period of 3 months beginning with the date of the grant;
(b) a grant of a term of years absolute under which the right to possession is discontinuous;
(c) a grant of a term of years absolute in pursuance of the right to buy under HA 1985, Pt V; or
(d) a grant of a term of years absolute in circumstances where HA 1985, s 171A applies (leases of the reversion of land to a private sector landlord where the tenant has a right to buy).

For the position where a lease not exceeding 7 years is an overriding interest and the lease contains:

(a) an option to renew or to purchase the reversion, see 125 Options; or
(b) a right of pre-emption, see 159 Rights of Pre-emption.

A notice may be entered in respect of a lease exceeding 3 years even when that lease is not required to be registered.

98.3.1 Agreed notice

In addition to the usual documents required,[17] an applicant for an agreed notice should deliver to HMLR the lease or a certified copy of it.

Where the consent of the registered proprietor is not available but the lease is signed by him, this is likely to be sufficient to satisfy HMLR of the validity of the applicant's claim for the purposes of LRA 2002, s 34(3)(c).

The agreed notice in the register will give details of the interest protected.

98.3.2 Unilateral notice

An applicant for a unilateral notice should deliver to HMLR the usual documents required.[18]

The statement in panel 11 or conveyancer's certificate in panel 12 of form UN1 should be completed on the following lines to show the interest of the applicant:

> person having the benefit of a lease dated [*date*] made between [*names*].

Where the lease was granted by a person who is not the current proprietor, the wording must establish the link between the current registered proprietor and the person who is to be shown as the beneficiary of the notice.

The unilateral notice in the register will give brief details of the interest protected and identify the beneficiary of that notice.

98.4 Leases which are incapable of substantive registration

There are certain leasehold interests created out of registered land which are incapable of substantive registration. These are:

(a) a lease granted for a term of 7 years or less, except for those mentioned in 98.3 Leases of land not exceeding 7 years;
(b) a lease for which a rent or premium is payable where the term commences more than 21 years from the date of the lease and the lease is void by virtue of LPA 1925, s 149(3);
(c) leases with no certain start date, so that the lease is not for a term of years certain;
(d) leases where the landlord and tenant are the same person and therefore of no effect;[19] and
(e) PPP leases.[20]

98.5 Noting of leases

On substantive registration of a lease, HMLR will enter a notice of the lease in the landlord's registered title. Where a lease granted out of a registered estate in land is not capable of substantive registration, the burden of it will be an interest which overrides registered dispositions, under LRA 2002, Sch 3, para 1. An application may nevertheless be made for entry of a notice in the landlord's registered title provided the lease is granted for a term of more than 3 years.[21] A PPP lease cannot be noted.[22]

98.6 Prescribed clauses leases

Since 19 June 2006 use of a prescribed clauses lease has (with certain limited exceptions) been compulsory for any lease granted out of a registered estate in land which is a registrable disposition under LRA 2002, s 27(2)(b).[23]

A prescribed clauses lease is a lease granted out of a registered estate in land on or after 19 June 2006 which is a registrable disposition required to be completed by registration under LRA 2002, s 27(2)(b) and which is not granted in a form *expressly* required:

(a) by an agreement entered into before 19 June 2006;
(b) by an order of the court;
(c) by or under an enactment; or
(d) by a necessary consent or licence for the grant of a lease given before 19 June 2006.[24]

If an applicant believes one of the above exceptions applies to a lease dated on or after 19 June 2016 which falls within LRA 2002, s 27(2)(b), he must lodge with his application for registration of that lease a certificate by a conveyancer to that effect or other evidence to satisfy HMLR of his claim.[25] However, this is not necessary where it appears to HMLR the lease is not a prescribed clauses lease.[26]

A lease by virtue of a variation of a lease which is a deemed surrender and re-grant is not a prescribed clauses lease; this exemption does not apply where a deed *expressly* provides for the surrender of an existing lease and the grant of a new lease in substitution.

A prescribed clauses lease must begin with the required wording (referred to below) or that wording must appear immediately after any front sheet. 'Front sheet' means a front cover sheet, or a contents or index sheet at the beginning of the lease, or a front cover sheet and contents or index sheet where the contents or index sheet is immediately after the front cover sheet.

'Required wording' means the wording in clauses LR1 to LR14 of LRR 2003, Sch 1A completed in accordance with the instructions in that schedule as appropriate for the particular lease. These clauses are set out in Appendix III. If a prescribed clauses lease is an electronic document to which LRA 2002, s 91 applies, the required wording will be such as is required by the relevant notice given under LRR 2003, r 54C; that wording must be to like effect to that given in paper form.

The prescribed clauses are therefore a standard set of clauses that must appear at the beginning of all such leases, containing relevant details which will assist in the registration of the lease. It is important that these clauses are correctly completed, as HMLR will prepare the register entries to complete registration of the lease from the information provided in the clauses. Also, if a clause is not completed this may result in any entry not being made.[27] The remainder of the lease can be in whatever form the parties require.

98.7 Registration of leases which are registrable dispositions

A person applying to register a lease granted out of a registered estate should deliver to HMLR:

(a) an application in form AP1;
(b) the lease or a certified copy of it;
(c) any consents or certificates required in respect of mortgages, charges or restrictions in the landlord's title;
(d) form DI giving the information as to overriding interests required by LRR 2003, r 57, including any documentary evidence of the interests;[28]
(e) the appropriate confirmation or evidence of identity;[29]
(f) the appropriate SDLT and/or LTT certificate(s) or other evidence;[30] and
(g) the fee payable.[31]

On registration of the lease, HMLR will:

(a) allot it its own title number; and
(b) enter a notice of the registered lease in the landlord's registered title without any need for a separate application or further fee.

LRR 2003, r 72A specifies certain entries which HMLR must make on registration of a lease granted out of a registered estate in land on or after 19 June 2006 which is required to be registered under LRA 2002, s 27(2)(b). Rule 72A also specifies situations where HMLR is required to make no entry. This applies to both prescribed clauses leases and other registrable leases.

On completion of such a lease by registration HMLR must (where appropriate) make entries in the relevant individual register in respect of interests contained in the lease which are of the nature referred to in clauses LR9 (rights of acquisition, etc), LR10 (restrictive covenants by the landlord in respect of other land), LR11 (easements granted or reserved) and LR12 (estate rentcharge).[32] The requirement to make an entry in respect of an interest referred to in clause LR12 is satisfied by entry, where appropriate, of notice of the interest created.

Where the lease is a prescribed clauses lease and contains a prohibition or restriction on disposing of the lease of the nature referred to in clause LR8 or it contains interests of the nature referred to in clauses LR9, LR10, LR11 and LR12, but the prohibition or restriction or the interests are not specified or referred to in those clauses, or the lease does not contain the required wording in respect of them, then HMLR need take no action in respect of them unless a separate application is made.[33] LRR 2003, r 6(2), which requires HMLR to make an entry on registration in respect of a prohibition or restriction on disposing of a lease, is amended accordingly. However, this does not apply where it appears to HMLR that the lease is not a prescribed clauses lease.[34]

HMLR need not make entries in respect of interests of the nature referred to in clauses LR9, LR10 or LR11 or a standard form of restriction set out in clause LR13 where:

(a) in the case of a prescribed clauses lease, the title numbers of the individual registers have not been given in clause LR2.2, or
(b) in any other case, the title numbers of the individual registers required by clause LR2.2 have not been given in panel 2 of the form AP1 lodged for the purpose of completing the lease by registration,

unless a separate application is made in respect of the interests or restriction.[35]

Where a separate application is made in form AP1 in respect of either a prohibition or restriction on disposal of the lease or the grant or reservation of an easement, the form AP1 must specify the particular clause, schedule or paragraph of a schedule, where the prohibition or restriction or easement is contained in the lease.[36]

An application for entry of a restriction may be made, where appropriate, contemporaneously with the application for registration of the lease. For example, a restriction in Form PP where a certificate signed by the landlord will be required before any disposition may be registered.[37] The wording of Form PP is set out in Appendix IV. LRR 2003, r 92 relaxes the requirement for a form RX1 to be lodged, where application for the entry of a standard restriction is made in clause LR13 of a 'relevant lease' which is defined as:

(a) a prescribed clauses lease; or
(b) any other lease which complies with the requirements as to form and content of a prescribed clauses lease and which either is required to be completed by registration under LRA 2002, s 27(2)(b) or is the subject of an application for first registration of the title to it.

On completion of the lease by registration, HMLR must enter a notice or other appropriate entry in respect of any interest which, at the time of registration, is the subject of a notice in the landlord's registered title and which HMLR considers may affect the registered lease.[38]

Where a lease contains a right of re-entry and the lease is a registrable disposition which is completed by registration, that is also sufficient to complete the grant of the right of re-entry[39] by registration, without any specific entry being made in relation to it in the register.[40]

98.8 Long leases of houses

Once in force, LFRA 2024 will ban:

(a) long residential leases of a house other than permitted leases; and
(b) assignments of leases granted on or after LFRA 2024, s 1 comes into effect where:

    (i) at the time of the assignment, the lease comprises a long residential leases of a house; but
    (ii) at the time of the grant it was not a long residential leases of a house.[41]

LFRA 2024, s 2 defines a long residential lease of a house and s 7 defines what comprises a permitted lease.

A long residential lease of a house granted or assignment made in breach of the above ban is not invalid; HMLR may still register it (subject to the restriction discussed below). However, the tenant (or a mortgagee in certain circumstances) has a right to acquire:

(a) the freehold of the land comprised in the lease, and
(b) any superior leasehold estate(s) in that land,

for no consideration.[42] LFRA 2024, ss 14 to 16 contain further details of that right and contain enabling provisions for the Secretary of State to make regulations further governing the exercise of the right.

Once LFRA 2024, s 1 comes into effect, if a lease has a long term and was granted after the relevant commencement date if it is:

(a) not a long residential lease of a house, or
(b) a permitted lease,

it must contain a statement to that effect.[43] Such a statement must be in such form as may be prescribed by Land Registration Rules made under the LRA 2002. Accordingly, it is anticipated there will be amendments to the prescribed clauses to facilitate this.

If HMLR approves an application to register a lease affected by the above requirement but which does not include the relevant statement, it must include a restriction in the register for the lease to the effect that no registerable disposition, other than the grant of a legal charge, is to be completed by registration.[44]

HMLR may remove the restriction if the registered lease is varied to include the required statement.

If a lease affected by a restriction as described above is varied in such a way as to take effect as a surrender and regrant of the lease,[45] HMLR must carry forward the restriction to the register for the new lease.[46] HMLR may remove the restriction from the register if satisfied the new lease is either not a long residential lease of a house or is a permitted lease.[47]

98.9 Leases for life or determinable on death, marriage or civil partnership

A lease may be expressed to:

(a) be for a life or lives;
(b) come to an end on the death of any person; or
(c) come to an end on the marriage or formation of civil partnership of the tenant.

Such a lease may fall within LPA 1925, s 149(6) if it terminates *automatically* on the specified event (i.e. on death, marriage or civil partnership) and is granted at a rent or in consideration of a premium. A lease falling within s 149(6) takes effect as a lease for 90 years determinable after the death, marriage or civil partnership, as the case may be, by giving at least one month's notice. Such a lease should be in the form of a prescribed clauses lease, where necessary.[48]

A lease which terminates *automatically* on the specified event but does not fall within s 149(6) generally constitutes only an equitable interest, which is incapable of substantive registration, although it may be the subject of a notice in the landlord's title (if registered). However, it is possible that a lease by way of a gift of a term of years subject to automatic determination on the marriage or civil partnership of the tenant may take effect at law,[49] in which case the lease should be in the form of a prescribed clauses lease, where necessary.[50]

A lease for a specified term determinable by the *service of notice* following death or marriage or civil partnership will not fall within s 149(6).[51] Accordingly, it does not take effect as a lease for 90 years and instead takes effect for the term referred to in the lease, subject to the provision for determination. Such a lease should be in the form of a prescribed clauses lease, where necessary.[52]

98.10 Variation of a lease

An applicant for registration of a deed of variation of a registered lease (other than one which takes effect as a surrender and re-grant[53]) should deliver to HMLR:

(a) an application in form AP1;
(b) the deed of variation or a certified copy of it;
(c) any consents or certificates required in respect of mortgages, charges or restrictions in the lessor's title;
(d) any consent to the variation from any chargee of the tenant's title;
(e) where the landlord's title is unregistered, evidence of that title;
(f) any other necessary evidence to show that the variation takes effect at law and;
(g) the fee payable.[54]

Where the variation has been made by an order pursuant to Landlord and Tenant Act 1987, s 35, that order should be lodged in place of the deed of variation.

If satisfied that the variation has effect at law, HMLR will make an entry relating to the deed in the property register of the tenant's title, together with a notice in the landlord's title (if registered).

If a chargee's consent is not lodged when required, the following note will be added to the register entry of the relevant title(s):

> NOTE: The proprietor of the registered charge dated [*date*] [of the landlord's/tenant's title number …] was not a party to the deed nor was evidence of its consent to the deed produced to the registrar.

An application may be made for entry of either an agreed notice using form AN1 or a unilateral notice using form UN1 in respect of a deed of variation, even when the lease is substantively registered, if sufficient evidence cannot be provided to satisfy HMLR that the variation takes effect at law under LRR 2003, r 129.[55]

If notice of an unregistered lease is entered in a landlord's title, an application may be made to enter a notice in respect of a variation of the lease. Such an application can be for entry of an agreed notice using form AN1, if the deed of variation can be provided and the lease is already protected by an agreed notice. Alternatively, application may be made in form UN1 for entry of a unilateral notice; for example, if the lease is already protected by way of unilateral notice or if the lease or/and the deed of variation cannot be provided.[56]

If the deed of variation contains easements which constitute a registrable disposition under LRA 2002, s 27, these will not operate at law until completed by registration.

The position regarding deeds of variation is similar in relation to a deed of rectification, where a lease is rectified to give effect to the original intention of the parties. For example, by the addition of covenants which were omitted from the lease by mistake.

Any party to a long lease of a flat may apply to a tribunal for an order varying the lease on the grounds that the lease fails to make satisfactory provision with respect to repair, maintenance, the provision of services, insurance, the recovery of expenses or the computation of service charges.[57] The tribunal may then make an appropriate order that will be binding on the parties to the lease and any other persons concerned.[58] Where an application is to be made for entry of a notice in respect of any variation of a lease effected by or under Landlord and Tenant Act 1987, s 38 (including any variation as modified by an order under s 39(4)), it must be for an agreed notice using application form AN1.[59]

98.10.1 Deeds of variation varying the term

If a tenant takes a new lease of the same property before the existing lease has expired, the original lease is treated as surrendered immediately before the new lease. As the term of a lease cannot be altered by means of a deed of variation, HMLR will treat any deed purporting to vary the term of a registered lease as being a new lease which will, therefore, have the effect of surrendering the original lease. The proper application in such a case will be for closure of the title to the original lease and registration of the new lease (if as varied, it is a registrable disposition). The deed of variation, in such a case, does not have to be in the form of a prescribed clauses lease.

For:

(a) surrenders of leases, see 98.18 Determination of registered leases;
(b) the position where the existing lease is not registered but is noted on the landlord's registered title, see 98.19 Cancellation of a noted lease;
(c) details of applications to register a new lease where it is granted out of unregistered land, see 68 First Registration; and
(d) details of applications to register a new lease where it is out of registered land, see 98.7 Registration of leases which are registrable dispositions.

As an alternative to use of a deed of variation, the landlord may grant an extension of a lease.[60]

98.10.2 Deeds of variation varying the extent

A deed of variation which *reduces* the extent of the premises demised by a lease will be treated as a surrender of the part in question.

As the extent of the premises demised by a lease cannot be *extended* by means of a deed of variation, HMLR will treat any deed purporting to increase the extent of the demised premises in a registered lease as being a new lease which will, therefore, have the effect of surrendering the original lease. The proper application in such a case will be for closure of the title to the original lease and registration of the new lease (if as varied, it is a registrable disposition). The deed of variation, in such a case, does not have to be in the form of a prescribed clauses lease. As an alternative to use of a deed of variation, the landlord may grant a supplemental lease or surrender the existing lease and replace it with a new lease of the combined extent. If so, the parties should use a prescribed clauses lease where necessary and apply to register the lease and any surrender.

For:

(a) surrenders of leases, see 98.18 Determination of registered leases;
(b) the position where the existing lease is not registered but is noted on the landlord's registered title, see 98.19 Cancellation of a noted lease;
(c) details of applications to register a new lease where it is granted out of unregistered land, see 68 First Registration; and
(d) details of applications to register a new lease where it is out of registered land, see 98.7 Registration of leases which are registrable dispositions.

98.11 Noting a declaration under the Leasehold Reform (Ground Rent) Act 2022

The Leasehold Reform (Ground Rent) Act 2022 limits the ground rent payable on many new long residential leases granted after 30 June 2022 to one peppercorn per year.

A lease containing terms in breach of the prohibition is not void. However, the reservation of a prohibited rent will be of no effect. Further, landlords and tenants may apply to either:

(a) the First-tier Tribunal (in England), or
(b) a leasehold valuation tribunal (in Wales),

for a declaration as to the effect of Leasehold Reform (Ground Rent) Act 2022, s 7 on their lease.[61] If satisfied the lease is regulated by the Act and contains the reservation of a prohibited rent, the appropriate tribunal must make a declaration of the effect of s 7.[62]

If the appropriate tribunal makes such an order, it may order the landlord to register the declaration at HMLR and pay the relevant fee for that application. Alternatively, the tenant may apply to HMLR to register the declaration.[63]

Any application to register such a declaration should be in form AP1 quoting the title numbers for the lease and reversion accompanied by:

(a) a certified copy of the tribunal's declaration; and
(b) the relevant fee.[64]

On completion of the application, HMLR will make an entry along the following lines in the tenant's title:

> By a declaration made on [*date*] the [*details of tribunal*] Tribunal declared the effect of section 7 of the Leasehold Reform (Ground Rent) Act 2022 on the terms of the registered lease.
>
> NOTE: Copy Declaration filed.

HMLR will also add notes along the following lines to the relevant entry in the schedule of leases in the landlord's title(s):

> NOTE 1: By a declaration made on [*date*] the [*details of tribunal*] Tribunal declared the effect of section 7 of the Leasehold Reform (Ground Rent) Act 2022 on the terms of the registered lease.
>
> NOTE 2: Copy Declaration filed under title number [*title number*].

98.12 Acquisition of an extended lease under the Leasehold Reform Act 1967

The Leasehold Reform Act 1967 confers on a tenant of a house held under a long tenancy at a low rent the right to acquire either the freehold on enfranchisement[65] or an extended lease of the house and premises expiring 50 years after the date on which the existing term is due to expire.[66] 'House' does not include flats in a horizontally divided building and 'premises' includes any garage, outhouse, garden, yard and appurtenances let with the house.[67] 'Long tenancy' means any tenancy originally granted for a term exceeding 21 years whether or not it is determinable by notice or re-entry.[68] There are further conditions and exceptions that apply in particular circumstances. Where the tenant holds under a sub-lease, there are complicated provisions in Sch 1 to the 1967 Act to determine which landlord is to act as reversioner on behalf of all the landlords where there are sub-leases.

Any right of a tenant or his personal representatives arising from a notice served on the landlord under the Leasehold Reform Act 1967 is not capable of being an interest within LRA 2002, Sch 1 or Sch 3 which overrides first registration or registered dispositions.[69] However, it may be the subject of a notice as if it were an estate contract and where the landlord's reversionary title is registered, application may be made for the entry of an agreed notice or a unilateral notice.

98.12.1 Agreed notice

In addition to the usual documents required,[70] an applicant should deliver to HMLR a certified copy of the notice under the Leasehold Reform Act 1967.

Where the consent of the registered proprietor is not available, this is likely to be sufficient to satisfy HMLR as to the validity of the applicant's claim for the purposes of LRA 2002, s 34(3)(c).

The agreed notice in the register will give details of the interest protected.

98.12.2 Unilateral notice

An applicant should deliver to HMLR the usual documents required.[71]

The statement in panel 11 or conveyancer's certificate in panel 12 of form UN1 should be completed on the following lines to show the interest of the applicant:

> tenant having on [*date*] given notice under the Leasehold Reform Act 1967 to [*name and address of the landlord*] in respect of the grant of an extended lease.

The unilateral notice in the register will give brief details of the interest protected and identify the beneficiary of that notice.

Where the applicant has taken an assignment from the tenant of the benefit of the rights under notice in accordance with Leasehold Reform Act 1967, s 5(2), no entry of such an assignment will be made in the register. However, if the rights are already protected in the register by a unilateral notice, the assignee should apply in form UN3 to be registered as the new beneficiary of the notice. Panel 11 of form UN3 should be completed on the following lines to show the entitlement of the applicant:

> assignee of rights under the Leasehold Reform Act 1967 by virtue of an assignment dated [*date*] made between [*name of former tenant*] and the applicant, the rights having arisen on [*date*] by the service of notice on [*name and address of the landlord*] in respect of the grant of an extended lease.

98.12.3 Registration of extended lease

The application for registration of the extended lease should be made in the usual way.[72] The application should show, either by a statement in the lease or on the application form, that the lease is made under the Leasehold Reform Act 1967.

The consent of the landlord's mortgagee (and any other person interested in the mortgage) should be lodged where the existing lease:

(a) was granted on or after 1 January 1968;
(b) was made after the date of the landlord's mortgage; and
(c) would not have been binding on the persons interested in the mortgage (i.e. it was outside any power to let the property retained by the landlord in the charge and the mortgagee did not consent to it).

Where any necessary consent is not lodged, HMLR will make a protective entry in the property register of the new title in the following wording:

> The title to the lease is, during the subsistence of the charge dated [*date*] in favour of [*lender*] affecting the landlord's title (and, to the extent permitted by law, any charge replacing or varying this charge or any further charge in respect of all or part of the sum secured by this charge), subject to any rights that may have arisen by reason of the absence of chargee's consent, unless the lease is authorised by section 99 of the Law of Property Act 1925.

When the applicant's title to his existing lease is unregistered but charged, satisfactory evidence of this should accompany an application for first registration of the extended lease, so that appropriate entries can be made in the register of title to the extended lease of any rights of a mortgagee of the existing lease.

If the extended lease incorporates the terms of an unregistered existing lease, the applicant should lodge a certified copy or examined abstract of it.

If an interest is protected in the register of a registered existing lease but does not affect the new extended lease, the applicant should apply as appropriate for the withdrawal or cancellation of the existing entry in respect of it. If the interest affects the extended lease, an application to protect it by means of a suitable entry in the register of the new title should accompany the application to register the extended lease.

Where the extended lease is being granted under the Leasehold Reform Act 1967, a mortgage secured on the existing lease does not transfer automatically to the extended lease and should, therefore, be either:

(a) discharged and replaced; or
(b) transferred to the extended lease by using a deed of substituted security.

Where the existing lease is registered, any chargees of the applicant's existing lease should be contacted before completion of the extended lease and the necessary arrangements made. If the mortgage is discharged then the appropriate form of discharge should be lodged with the application for registration. If a deed of substituted security is used, the deed should be lodged. Any new mortgage (with a certified copy, if the applicant wishes the original to be returned) should be lodged with the application for registration.

Where the existing lease is unregistered, if the mortgage is discharged then the discharged mortgage or other evidence of discharge should be lodged with the application for registration. If a deed of substituted security is used, the mortgage and the deed should be lodged. Any new mortgage (with a certified copy, if the applicant wishes the original to be returned) should be lodged with the application for registration.

If the mortgagee's co-operation cannot be secured, HMLR will endeavour to serve notice on him, and any other person appearing to be interested in the mortgage, giving relevant details of the applicant and the nature of the application. If there is no response to the notice, the application will be completed and a protective entry will be made to the effect that the extended lease is subject to such rights as may be subsisting in favour of the persons interested in a charge of the existing lease. The entry will not be a registration of the charge, but will take effect as a notice which will protect the priority of the charge in the register.

If, in response to the notice, the mortgagee lodges the original mortgage, either it will be registered or a notice will be entered in respect of it, as appropriate.

Where the existing lease is registered, the applicant should also apply to close that registered title and cancel the notice of that lease in the landlord's registered title.[73]

For the position where the existing lease is not registered but is noted in the landlord's registered title, see 98.19 Cancellation of a noted lease.

98.13 Acquisition of a lease under the Leasehold Reform, Housing and Urban Development Act 1993

The LRHUDA 1993, s 39 confers upon a qualifying tenant of a flat an individual right to acquire from the landlord a new lease in substitution for an existing lease. Such right may also be exercised by the personal representatives of a tenant who held the right at his death, so long as the tenancy is vested in them.[74] If the immediate landlord does not have sufficient interest to grant such a lease, the new lease must be granted by the nearest landlord whose lease is sufficient.[75] For the right to collective enfranchisement conferred upon qualifying tenants by the LRHUDA 1993, see 34 Collective Enfranchisement.

The new lease is at a peppercorn rent for a term expiring 90 years after the term date of the existing lease.[76] A premium, calculated under LRHUDA 1993, Sch 13, is payable.[77]

98.13.1 Notice to acquire new lease

The notice served by a qualifying tenant under LRHUDA 1993, s 42 claiming to exercise the right to acquire a new lease of the flat is not capable of being an interest which overrides first registration or registered dispositions.[78] However, it may be the subject of a notice as if it were an estate contract and, where the landlord's reversionary title is registered, the tenant may apply to enter an agreed notice or a unilateral notice.

98.13.1.1 Agreed notice

In addition to the usual documents required,[79] an applicant should deliver to HMLR a certified copy of the notice under LRHUDA 1993, s 42.

Where the consent of the registered proprietor is not available, this is likely to be sufficient to satisfy HMLR as to the validity of the applicant's claim for the purposes of LRA 2002, s 34(3)(c).

The agreed notice in the register will give details of the interest protected.

98.13.1.2 Unilateral notice

An applicant should deliver to HMLR the usual documents required.[80]

The statement in panel 11 or conveyancer's certificate in panel 12 of form UN1 should be completed on the following lines to show the interest of the applicant:

> qualifying tenant having given notice under section 42 of the Leasehold Reform, Housing and Urban Development Act 1993 on [*date*] to [*name and address of the landlord*] [and to [*name and address of any third party in the tenant's existing lease*]].

The unilateral notice in the register will give brief details of the interest protected and identify the beneficiary of that notice.

Where the applicant has taken an assignment from the tenant of the benefit of the rights under notice in accordance with LRHUDA 1993, s 42, no entry of such an assignment will be made in the register. However, if the rights are already protected in the register by a unilateral notice, the assignee should apply in form UN3 to be registered as the new beneficiary of the notice. Panel 11 of form UN3 should be completed on the following lines to show the entitlement of the applicant:

> assignee of rights under the Leasehold Reform, Housing and Urban Development Act 1993 by virtue of an assignment dated [*date*] made between [*name of former tenant*] and the applicant, the rights having arisen on [*date*] by the service of notice on [*name and address of the landlord*] in respect of the grant of a new lease.

98.13.2 Application for vesting order

If the qualifying tenant wishes to make a claim to exercise the right to acquire a new lease of his flat but the landlord cannot be found or his identity cannot be ascertained, the court may make a vesting order.[81] Such an order provides for the surrender of the tenant's lease of his flat and for the granting to him of a new lease of it on such terms as may be determined by the appropriate tribunal to be appropriate, with a view to the lease being granted to him as if he had given notice under LRHUDA 1993, s 42. An application for such a vesting order is treated as a pending land action[82] and cannot therefore be an interest which overrides first registration or registered dispositions.[83] Such an application may, however, be protected by entry of an agreed notice or a unilateral notice, and a restriction.

98.13.2.1 Agreed notice

In addition to the usual documents required,[84] an applicant should deliver to HMLR the application to the court for the vesting order or a certified copy of it. This should satisfy HMLR of the validity of the applicant's claim in accordance with LRA 2002, s 34(3)(c).

The agreed notice in the register will give details of the interest protected.

98.13.2.2 Unilateral notice

An applicant should for a unilateral notice deliver to HMLR the usual documents required.[85]

The statement in panel 11 or conveyancer's certificate in panel 12 of form UN1 should be completed on the following lines to show the interest of the applicant:

> qualifying tenants in an application under section 50(1) of the Leasehold Reform, Housing and Urban Development Act 1993 in the [*name* County Court] *or* [*name* Division of the High Court of Justice] [*state full court reference and parties*].

The unilateral notice in the register will give brief details of the interest protected and identify the beneficiaries of that notice.

98.13.2.3 Restriction

The applicant for a vesting order under LRHUDA 1993, s 50(1) is to be regarded as having a sufficient interest in relation to a registered estate or charge if he is applying for a restriction in Form N.[86] The wording of Form N is set out in Appendix IV. HMLR must give notice of the application for a restriction to the proprietor of the registered estate or charge concerned, if it has not been made by or with the consent of such proprietor or a person entitled to be registered as such proprietor.[87]

A restriction does not confer any priority. However, it prevents an entry being made in the register relating to any disposition, or a disposition of a specified kind, unless the terms of the restriction have (where applicable) been complied with.

In addition to the usual documents required,[88] the applicant should deliver to HMLR the application to the court for the vesting order or a certified copy of it.

As the application for a restriction is unlikely to be made by or with the consent of the registered proprietor, the statement in panel 12 or conveyancer's certificate in panel 13 of form RX1 must be completed, confirming that the applicants' interest is that specified in LRR 2003, r 93(q) and setting out details of the application to the court.

Panel 9 of form RX1 should set out the appropriate restriction. A possible form of restriction based on the wording of Form N is:

> No [disposition *or specify type of disposition*] of the registered estate by the proprietor of the registered estate [or by the proprietor of any registered charge, not being a charge registered before the entry of this restriction] is to be registered

> without a written consent signed by [*name*] of [*address*] [or [their conveyancer *or specify appropriate details*]].

A restriction in standard Form N in LRR 2003, Sch 4 does not require the approval of HMLR to the wording of the restriction under LRA 2002, s 43(3).

98.13.3 Vesting order

Where the court makes a vesting order under LRHUDA 1993, s 50(1), the LRA 2002 applies in relation to that order as it applies in relation to an order affecting land which is made by the court for the purpose of enforcing a judgment or recognisance.[89] Such a vesting order cannot be an interest which overrides first registration or registered dispositions,[90] but it may be protected by entry of an agreed notice or a unilateral notice, and a restriction.

98.13.3.1 Agreed notice

In addition to the usual documents required,[91] an applicant should deliver to HMLR the vesting order or a certified copy of it. This should satisfy HMLR of the validity of the applicants' claim in accordance with LRA 2002, s 34(3)(c).

The agreed notice in the register will give details of the interest protected.

98.13.3.2 Unilateral notice

An applicant should deliver to HMLR the usual documents required.[92]

The statement in panel 11 or conveyancer's certificate in panel 12 of form UN1 should be completed on the following lines to show the interest of the applicant:

> qualifying tenant having the benefit of an order under section 50(1) of the Leasehold Reform, Housing and Urban Development Act 1993 made by the [*name* County Court] *or* [*name* Division of the High Court of Justice] [*state full court reference and parties*].

The unilateral notice in the register will give brief details of the interest protected and identify the beneficiaries of that notice.

98.13.3.3 Restriction

A person who has obtained a vesting order under the LRHUDA 1993, s 50(1) is to be regarded as having a sufficient interest in relation to a registered estate or charge for the purposes of LRA 2002, s 42(1)(c) if he is applying for a restriction in Form L or Form N.[93] The wording of each is set out in Appendix IV. HMLR must give notice of the application for a restriction to the proprietor of the registered estate or charge concerned, if it has not been made by or with the consent of such proprietor or a person entitled to be registered as such proprietor.[94]

A restriction does not confer any priority. However, it prevents an entry being made in the register relating to any disposition, or a disposition of a specified kind, unless the terms of the restriction have (where applicable) been complied with.

In addition to the usual documents required,[95] the applicant should deliver to HMLR the vesting order or a certified copy of it.

As the application for a restriction is unlikely to be made by or with the consent of the registered proprietor, the statement in panel 12 or conveyancer's certificate in panel 13 of form RX1 must be completed, confirming that the applicant's interest is that specified in LRR 2003, r 93(p) and setting out details of the vesting order made by the court.

Panel 9 of form RX1 should set out the appropriate restriction. A possible form of restriction based on the wording of Form L is:

> No [disposition *or specify type of disposition*] of the registered estate by the proprietor of the registered estate [or by the proprietor of any registered charge, not being a charge registered before the entry of this restriction] is to be registered without a certificate signed by [*name*] of [*address*] [or [their conveyancer *or specify appropriate details*]] that the provisions of [*specify clause, paragraph or other particulars*] of [*specify details*] have been complied with [or that they do not apply to the disposition].

A possible form of restriction based on the wording of Form N is:

> No [disposition *or specify type of disposition*] of the registered estate by the proprietor of the registered estate [or by the proprietor of any registered charge, not being a charge registered before the entry of this restriction] is to be registered without a written consent signed by [*name*] of [*address*] [or [their conveyancer *or specify appropriate details*]].

A restriction in standard Form L or Form N in LRR 2003, Sch 4 does not require the approval of HMLR to the wording of the restriction under LRA 2002, s 43(3).

98.13.4 Grant of new lease

The new lease, which takes effect in substitution for the existing lease, is to be on the same terms as the existing lease but with such modifications as may be required or appropriate. A lease granted under the LRHUDA 1993 must contain a statement in the following form:[96]

> This lease is granted under section 56 of the Leasehold Reform, Housing and Urban Development Act 1993.

Where the lease is a prescribed clauses lease, this statement must be referred to in prescribed clause LR5.1.

Once the new lease has been granted to the tenant it must be registered. The application for registration should be made in the usual way.[97]

Unless the existing lease falls within the limited exception in LHRUDA 1993, s 58(2), the new lease is binding on the persons interested in any mortgage on the landlord's title, even where the grant of such a lease is otherwise unauthorised.[98] Consequently, it is usually unnecessary to include consents of mortgagees with the application to register the new lease. However, the consent of the landlord's mortgagee (and any other person interested in the mortgage) should be lodged where the existing lease:

(a) was granted on or after 1 November 1993;
(b) was made after the date of the landlord's mortgage; and
(c) would not have been binding on the persons interested in the mortgage (i.e. it was outside the mortgagor's leasing powers and the mortgagee did not concur in it).

Where any necessary consent is not lodged, HMLR will make a protective entry in the property register of the new title in the following wording:.

> The title to the lease is, during the subsistence of the charge dated [*date*] in favour of [*chargee*] affecting the landlord's title (and, to the extent permitted by law, any charge replacing or varying this charge or any further charge in respect of all or part of the sum secured by this charge), subject to any rights that may have arisen by reason of the absence of chargee's consent, unless the lease is authorised by section 99 of the Law of Property Act 1925.

If the existing lease is subject to a mortgage or charge immediately before surrender, on the grant of a new lease the mortgage or charge will attach to the new lease.[99] The application for registration should therefore include an application in respect of the registration of an existing mortgage or charge against the title of the new lease.

If the charge is to be protected by entry of a notice only, application should be made either for entry of an agreed notice, using form AN1 or for entry of a unilateral notice, using form UN1 as appropriate.[100] HMLR will serve notice on a chargee before closing the existing leasehold title, if registered. Any other entries in the register of the existing leasehold title, if registered, must be considered and the appropriate steps taken.

If the tenant's existing lease is unregistered and is subject to a mortgage entitling the mortgagee to possession of the documents of title relating to the existing lease, then, within one month of the registration of the new lease, it must be delivered to that mortgagee by the tenant.[101] Failure to do this has the same effect as the breach of an obligation under the existing mortgage.[102]

98.14 Easements in leases

Where a lease is lodged for registration, HMLR will, where appropriate, make an entry in the register in respect of easements granted and/or reserved by the lease. Where necessary, the entry will include any note qualifying or excluding an easement. The benefit of an equitable easement cannot be registered in the registered leasehold title, but the burden of it can be the subject of a notice in any registered burdened title.

98.14.1 Easements granted

In the case of a prescribed clauses lease, HMLR need only consider any easements granted that are referred to in clause LR11.1.[103] If the lease is not a prescribed clauses lease, HMLR will consider any easements granted in the lease and make the appropriate entry in the register.

Where the easement is granted over other land within the landlord's registered title out of which the lease is granted, a notice of the easements will appear in the register by virtue of the standard entry made in the landlord's title on registration of the lease:

> The parts of the land affected thereby are subject to the leases set out in the schedule of leases hereto. The leases grant and reserve easements as therein mentioned.

If the easement is granted over land within other registered titles, the title numbers must be stated in clause LR2.2 (in the case of a prescribed clauses lease) or panel 2 of form AP1 (in the case of other leases), otherwise HMLR need make no entry in those other titles.[104] In that event, unless a separate application is made against each registered title comprising the burdened land, the easements will not have been completed by registration for the purposes of LRA 2002, s 27 and

HMLR will not be able to register the benefit of the easement in the registered leasehold title as it will not have taken effect at law.

If the easement is granted over unregistered burdened land, any legal easement will bind any subsequent purchaser and the burden of it will take effect as an interest which overrides on first registration.[105] Satisfactory evidence of the grantor's unregistered title will need to be lodged before HMLR can register the benefit of the easement in the registered leasehold title.

If HMLR is satisfied the easements in the registered lease comprise legal easements and the landlord had power to grant them, it will enter the benefit in the property register of the new leasehold title. An example of such an entry may be:

> The land has the benefit of any legal easements granted by clause LR11.1 of the registered lease dated [*date*] referred to above.

98.14.2 Easements reserved

In the case of a prescribed clauses lease, HMLR need only consider any easements reserved (or granted for the benefit of land owned by a third party) in the lease which are referred to in clause LR11.2, unless separate application is made.[106]

If a prescribed clause lease contains both beneficial and subjective easements, HMLR will typically make an entry in the following wording instead of that referred to in 97.14.1 Easements granted:

> The title includes any legal easements referred to in clause LR11.1 of the registered lease but is subject to any rights that are granted or reserved by the lease and affect the registered land.

If the lease contains no beneficial easements (or these are not being registered because clause LR11.1 of a prescribed clauses lease has not been completed correctly), HMLR will make an entry in the charges register of the leasehold title in respect of the easements reserved by the lease. An example would be:

> The land is subject to any rights that are reserved by clause LR11.2 of the registered lease dated [*date*] and affect the registered land.

If the lease is not a prescribed clauses lease, HMLR will consider any easements reserved (or granted for the benefit of land owned by a third party) in the lease and make the appropriate entries in the register.

If the easement is reserved for the benefit of land in other registered titles, the title numbers must be stated in clause LR2.2 (in the case of a prescribed clauses lease) or panel 2 of form AP1 (in the case of other leases), otherwise HMLR need make no entry in those other titles unless separate application is made.[107]

Where the benefiting land is unregistered, the benefit of the easement will subsist for the benefit of that land. On first registration of the benefiting estate, the estate will vest in the proprietor together with the benefit of the easement.[108]

98.14.3 Easements in unregistered leases

Easements may be granted or reserved in 'unregistered leases', being leases:

(a) the grant of which is not a registrable disposition;
(b) the grant or assignment of which does not trigger compulsory first registration; and
(c) that are not the subject of voluntary first registration.

98.14.3.1 Easements granted

Where the burdened land is registered, the grant of such easements is a registrable disposition which must be completed by registration, even if the lease itself will not be substantively registered or the subject of a notice in the register of the landlord's title. An application should therefore be made in form AP1 or form AN1 to register the burden of the easements.[109]

Where the lease itself *is* capable of being noted, details of it may be provided in a form DI accompanying the application, and HMLR will normally then enter a notice in the register in respect of the lease at the same time.

If the easement is granted over unregistered burdened land, there is no register entry to be made; any legal easement will bind any subsequent purchaser and the burden of it will take effect as an overriding interest on first registration of the burdened estate.[110] However, the benefiting owner may also wish to consider applying for a caution against first registration against the burdened land.[111]

98.14.3.2 Easements reserved

As the burdened leasehold land is unregistered, the reservation is not a registrable disposition. Any legal easement will bind any subsequent purchaser and the burden of it will take effect as an overriding interest on first registration of the burdened estate.[112]

Application can, however, be made in form AP1 for the benefit of a legal easement to be registered in the register of any registered benefiting title.[113]

The benefiting owner may also wish to consider applying for a caution against first registration against the burdened land.[114]

98.14.4 Equitable easements in leases

An easement may be equitable rather than legal. For example, if the lease is merely in writing but not by deed, any easement granted or reserved within it can only be equitable. The effect of this is that:

(a) Where the burdened land is registered, the grant or reservation of such an easement is not a registrable disposition which is required to be completed by registration, although it should be noted in the register for the burdened land to protect its priority against future dispositions for valuable consideration.[115]
(b) The benefit of such an easement cannot be registered in the register of any registered benefiting title.
(c) Where an easement is granted or reserved and the burdened land is unregistered, that easement will need to be protected by way of a Class D(iii) land charge and the benefiting owner may also wish to consider applying for a caution against first registration against the burdened land.[116]

98.15 Restrictive covenants in leases

On registration of a person as proprietor of a leasehold estate, that estate is vested in him together with all interests subsisting for the benefit of the estate, but subject to implied and express covenants, obligations and liabilities incident to that estate.[117] It is not possible to enter a notice in the register in respect of the burden of restrictive covenants made between a landlord and tenant, so far as relating to the demised premises.[118] However, where a restrictive covenant between a landlord and tenant does not relate to the demised premises, it can be the subject of a notice in the register.

98.15.1 Covenants given by the landlord relating to other land

In the case of a prescribed clauses lease, no separate application is necessary to note restrictive covenants given by the landlord in respect of land other than the property provided:

(a) the relevant title number(s) appear in clause LR 2.1 and/or LR 2.2; and
(b) the parties have completed clause LR10 appropriately.

If such information is not included in the lease, HMLR need take no action in respect of the covenants unless separate application is made.[119]

If the lease is not a prescribed clauses lease, HMLR will consider any covenants given by the landlord in the lease and make the appropriate entries in the register. If the landlord gives covenants relating to land other than the title from which the lease is granted, that title number must be included in form AP1. Otherwise, HMLR need make no entry in those other titles unless separate application is made.[120]

98.15.2 Tenant covenants

If the tenant gives covenants affecting land other than that included in the demise, an application should be made for a notice to be entered in the affected title. The application may be for an agreed notice or a unilateral notice.

98.15.2.1 Agreed notice

In addition to the usual documents required,[121] an applicant should deliver to HMLR the document containing the restrictive covenant or a certified copy of it.

Where the consent of the registered proprietor is not available but, for example, the original document is signed by him, this is likely to be sufficient to satisfy HMLR as to the validity of the applicant's claim for the purposes of LRA 2002, s 34(3)(c).

The agreed notice in the register will give details of the interest protected.

98.15.3 Unilateral notice

An applicant should deliver to HMLR the usual documents required.[122]

The statement in panel 11 or conveyancer's certificate in panel 12 of form UN1 should be completed on the following lines to show the interest of the applicant:

> person having the benefit of a restrictive covenant contained in a [*lease*] *or* [*deed*] dated [*date*] and made between [*parties*] which, although made between a landlord and tenant, does not relate to the demised premises.

The unilateral notice in the register will give brief details of the interest protected and identify the beneficiaries of that notice.

98.16 Apportionment of rent

A transfer of a registered leasehold estate in land containing a legal apportionment of, or exoneration from, the rent reserved by the lease must include the statement prescribed by LRR 2003, r 60(1). Where the landlord does not consent to the apportionment, it will take effect in equity only. The statement must be in the additional provisions panel of the transfer and may contain any necessary alterations and additions. The statement is:

> Liability for the payment of [*if applicable* the previously apportioned rent of (amount) being part of] the rent reserved by the registered lease is apportioned between the Transferor and the Transferee as follows:
>
> – [*amount*] shall be payable out of the Property and the balance shall be payable out of the land remaining in title number [*title number of retained land*], or
> – the whole of that rent shall be payable out of the Property and none of it shall be payable out of the land remaining in title number [*title number of retained land*], or
> – the whole of that rent shall be payable out of the land remaining in title number [*title number of retained land*] and none of it shall be payable out of the Property.

Where in a transfer of part of a registered leasehold estate which is held under an old tenancy, that part is, without the consent of the landlord, expressed to be exonerated from, or charged with, the entire rent, the covenants in LRA 2002, Sch 12, para 20(3) or (4), if implied, are modified.[123] An 'old tenancy' is a tenancy which is not a new tenancy for the purposes of Landlord and Tenant (Covenants) Act 1995, s 1.[124]

The covenants in para 20(3) as modified are:

> The transferee covenants with the transferor that during the residue of the term granted by the registered lease the transferee and the persons deriving title under him will:
>
> (a) pay the entire rent,
> (b) comply with the covenants and conditions contained in the lease so far as affecting the part transferred but extended to a covenant to pay the entire rent, and
> (c) keep the transferor and the person deriving title under him indemnified against all actions, expenses and claims on account of any failure to comply with paragraphs (a) and (b).

The covenants in para 20(4) as modified are:

The transferor covenants with the transferee that during the residue of the term granted by the registered lease the transferor and the persons deriving title under him will:

(a) pay the entire rent,
(b) comply with the covenants and conditions contained in the lease so far as affecting the part retained but extended to a covenant to pay the entire rent, and
(c) keep the transferee and the persons deriving title under him indemnified against all actions, expenses and claims on account of any failure to comply with paragraphs (a) and (b).

Where a transfer of such a registered leasehold estate modifies or negatives any of the covenants implied under LRA 2002, Sch 12, para 20(3), HMLR must make an entry in the register that the covenants have been so modified or negatived.[125]

Where the rent has been apportioned by some other method,[126] the parties may apply to reflect this in the registers for the affected titles. Any such application should be in form AP1 accompanied by:

(a) either:

  (i) a certified copy of the deed or order effecting the apportionment; or
  (ii) where the apportionment is pursuant to Landlord and Tenant (Covenants) Act 1995, s 10 either:

    (1) a statutory declaration confirming the service of notice in accordance with s 10(1) attaching a copy of the notice and confirming that no objection was received in response;
    (2) a certified copy of the court order declaring the apportionment is binding on the appropriate person; or
    (3) a certified copy of the consent received from the appropriate person in response to the relevant notice; and

(b) the relevant fee.[127]

98.17 Extensions of leases (other than under the Leasehold Reform Act 1967 or the Leasehold Reform, Housing and Urban Development Act 1993)

Aside from the grant of an extended lease under the provisions of the Leasehold Reform Act 1967 or the LRHUDA 1993 discussed above, or the variation of an existing lease which takes effect as a deemed surrender and re-grant,[128] an existing lease may be extended by the grant of a new lease, either to take immediate effect or to commence on a future date.

98.17.1 Where the new lease takes immediate effect

In this case, the tenant is deemed to have surrendered his existing lease immediately before the new lease commences. This applies irrespective of the intention of the parties, because the new lease is inconsistent with the existing lease and therefore the tenant is estopped from denying that the existing lease has come to an end.[129]

The surrender of the existing lease must be effected in the register and the new lease registered in its place.

Before completing the new lease, the tenant should contact any chargee of the existing lease to ascertain his requirements. The chargee may prefer either to release his existing charge and take a fresh charge over the new leasehold estate, or to use a deed of substituted security.

However, if the new lease is made *expressly subject* to the existing lease, HMLR will accept that surrender of the existing lease does not occur, as the new lease (as a lease of the landlord's reversionary interest) is not inconsistent with the existing lease. In this event, the existing leasehold title, if registered, will not be closed. When registering such a new lease, HMLR will have regard to the possibility that any chargee of the existing lease has an interest in the new lease. Accordingly, when making an application to register such a new lease, it is also necessary to lodge any charges affecting the old lease or list them in panel 10 of form FR1 or panel 10 of form AP1. Where appropriate, an entry on the following lines will be made in the charges register of the registered title of the new lease:

> The land is subject to such rights as may be subsisting in favour of the persons interested in a charge dated [*date*] made between [*parties*] of the lease dated [*date*] referred to in the Schedule of leases hereto.

98.17.2 Where the new lease commences on a future date

The new lease may, when granted at a rent or for a premium, commence at any time up to 21 years from the date of the grant.[130] Therefore, if the existing lease has less than 21 years to run, the new lease may be granted to commence on its expiry. However, if the existing lease has more than 21 years to run, it will have to be shortened, either by a separate deed of variation, or by suitable wording in the new lease, so that the existing lease determines just before the commencement of the new lease. Otherwise, the grant of the new lease will take effect as an immediate surrender of the existing lease[131]

For surrenders of leases, see 98.18 Determination of registered leases. For the position where the existing lease is not registered but is noted on the landlord's registered title, see 98.19 Cancellation of a noted lease. For details of applications to register a new lease where it is granted out of unregistered land, see 68 First Registration. For details of applications to register a new lease where it is out of registered land, see 98.7 Registration of leases which are registrable dispositions.

98.18 Determination of registered leases

There are various ways in which a leasehold estate in land may come to an end. The evidence required in support of an application following the determination of a lease depends on the manner in which the leasehold estate has determined and upon whether the leasehold estate and/or the landlord's reversionary estate are registered.

98.18.1 Form of application

In addition to any documents that may be specified in the individual paragraphs set out below relating to the particular method by which the lease has been determined, an applicant for closure of a registered leasehold title should deliver to HMLR:

(a) an application in form AP1 to close the registered leasehold title on determination and (where applicable) to cancel the notice of that lease on the registered reversionary title;
(b) the original lease and/or counterpart lease, if in the applicant's possession;
(c) (if the reversionary estate is unregistered) an examined abstract or epitome of the landlord's unregistered title;
(d) (in the case of an application to close a registered leasehold title on surrender) the appropriate confirmation or evidence as to identity;[132] and
(e) the fee payable.[133]

HMLR will, where appropriate, serve notice of the application on any person appearing to be affected by it.

If the determined lease is unregistered but is the subject of a notice in a registered reversionary title, application may be made for cancellation or removal of that notice.[134]

98.18.2 Incumbrances affecting the determined lease

Any incumbrances affecting the leasehold estate being determined will need to be considered and any necessary action taken in respect of them, as follows:

(a) If a lease is determined by notice, effluxion of time, forfeiture or frustration, all incumbrances will normally end automatically with the determination of the lease. This is subject to the exception, in the case of determination by effluxion of time, to inferior leases which have been extended by either the Landlord and Tenant Act 1954 or the Local Government and Housing Act 1989 and which may therefore affect the reversionary estate (see (c) below).

(b) If a lease is being determined by merger, surrender or disclaimer, all incumbrances affecting the leasehold estate which is being determined must be dealt with as appropriate. Thus registered or noted charges, restrictions and cautions should be either discharged, withdrawn or cancelled, and the appropriate documentation lodged to effect this. Where an incumbrance consists of a registered charge, it may be possible to deal with the matter by way of a deed of substituted security, and an application made to register it against a registered reversionary title, where appropriate. Other incumbrances such as subjective easements and restrictive covenants will normally be carried forward to any registered reversionary title, unless they are already substantially repeated on that title.

(c) Where a lease has been determined by notice, forfeiture or frustration, any inferior leases (such as any underleases derived from that lease) will also determine. Where a lease has been determined by disclaimer, see 19.18 Disclaimer by trustee in bankruptcy or 108.4 Disclaimer by a liquidator. In other cases, any inferior leases will continue to subsist and may affect the reversionary estate, in which case they will be noted against any registered reversionary title unless evidence is produced that the inferior lease has also determined and, if the inferior lease is registered, an application is made to close that registered title.

(d) Where a leasehold estate is registered with a possessory leasehold class of title, it will not be possible to determine that registered leasehold title unless the applicant also lodges form UT1, or the title is otherwise capable of being upgraded to absolute leasehold title.[135] This reflects the fact that such a lease may be subject to other unregistered interests which might prevent determination.

98.18.3 Merger

Merger occurs where a leasehold estate and the reversionary estate come into the same ownership and are held in the same capacity, so that the lease is absorbed by the reversionary estate and thus determined. There must be an intention to merge the estates, so that even where a leasehold estate and its immediate reversionary title have become vested in the same person in the same capacity, it is a matter of intention whether or not the leasehold estate is to be determined on merger. The applicant should therefore always make it clear within the application that merger is intended.

Where a restriction in Form A appears in a registered leasehold title and/or in a registered reversionary title, it will not be possible to determine the registered leasehold title by merger unless the applicant can lodge satisfactory evidence that he holds both estates upon the same trusts. The wording of Form A is set out in Appendix IV. Similarly, if the leasehold estate or the reversionary estate is unregistered and there is an indication of a trust, the applicant must lodge satisfactory evidence that he holds both estates upon the same trusts.

As regards any benefiting easements affecting the leasehold estate, it needs to be considered whether the reversionary estate has the benefit of an equivalent easement where necessary and if not, whether the two estates should continue to be held separately and the lease not determined. In *Wall v Collins* [2007] EWCA Civ 444, the Court of Appeal held that an easement must be appurtenant to a dominant tenement, but not necessarily to a particular interest in that dominant tenement. In consequence, when a lease is extinguished on merger, the tenant may not automatically lose any benefiting easements granted for the benefit of the leasehold estate and those easements may continue to exist and to be exercisable by the occupier of the dominant tenement for the period for which they were granted. HMLR will not automatically enter the benefit of such easements in the registered title to the reversionary estate (if registered). However, an application may be made to register the benefit of such easements in the registered title to the reversionary estate, either at the time of merger or subsequently.[136]

98.18.4 Surrender by deed

When a tenant surrenders his lease to his immediate landlord, who accepts the surrender, the lease is absorbed by the reversionary estate and thus determined. A deed effecting a surrender of a leasehold estate must contain wording which clearly shows that the tenant is surrendering the lease. The application must be accompanied by the original deed of surrender and, as it will normally be a land transaction, the appropriate SDLT and/or LTT evidence.[137] If the landlord has not executed the deed and is not the applicant, the applicant must also provide evidence of the landlord's consent to the surrender. Where a restriction in Form A appears in the registered leasehold title, the surrender is a 'disposition' for the purposes of that restriction. If capital money arises and the surrender is by a sole registered proprietor who is not a trust corporation, the disposition will be caught by the terms of the restriction and the registered leasehold title cannot be closed.

98.18.5 Surrender by operation of law

Instead of surrender by deed, a surrender of a lease may be effected by operation of law, that is, as a result of the actions of both of the parties. For example, where the tenant gives up possession of the premises to the landlord, who then grants a new lease of the premises to a third party with the tenant's consent. It can also occur where the landlord grants a new lease of the same premises to the existing tenant. The application must be accompanied by satisfactory evidence of the acts which imply surrender.[138] This will normally consist of a statutory declaration or statement of truth made by a suitable person with full knowledge of the facts, together with any other available evidence relating to the surrender, such as a receipt for money paid for the surrender. If the tenant was occupying the property and has given vacant possession to the landlord, the statutory declaration or statement of truth must describe when and how the premises were vacated and the keys returned to the landlord. If a sub-tenant was occupying the property, the statutory declaration or statement of truth must contain evidence that the landlord is receiving the rent directly from that sub-tenant.

A statutory declaration or statement of truth will not be required where either:

(a) the landlord grants a new lease of the same premises to the existing tenant; or
(b) the leasehold estate and the reversionary estate are both registered and the application is made by or with the consent of the registered proprietors of both titles, provided the determined leasehold estate is registered with an absolute leasehold or a good leasehold class of title.

A surrender by operation of law is a land transaction for SDLT and/or LTT purposes. The appropriate SDLT and/or LTT evidence should therefore be lodged.[139]

Where a restriction in Form A appears in the registered leasehold title, the surrender is a 'disposition' for the purposes of that restriction. If capital money arises and the surrender is by a sole registered proprietor who is not a trust corporation, the disposition will be caught by the terms of the restriction and the registered leasehold title cannot be closed.

98.18.6 Disclaimer

When a person becomes bankrupt or a company becomes insolvent, either a trustee in bankruptcy or a liquidator respectively may, by giving the prescribed notice, disclaim certain onerous property, including leases. This has the effect of determining the lease. For disclaimer by a trustee in bankruptcy, see 19.18 Disclaimer by trustee in bankruptcy. For disclaimer by a liquidator, see 108.4 Disclaimer by a liquidator.

98.18.7 Effluxion of time

A lease for a fixed term will automatically determine when the fixed term expires, unless it is prolonged by virtue of the provisions of either the Landlord and Tenant Act 1954 or the Local Government and Housing Act 1989. The application must therefore be accompanied by confirmation that neither of those Acts affect the lease or that it has determined in accordance with their provisions. If the tenant has an option to renew the lease, satisfactory evidence that the option has not been, and cannot now be, exercised must also be lodged.

Where the lease is or appears to be of telecommunications equipment, it may continue under Electronic Communications Code, para 30.[140] Consequently, on an application to close a lease of such equipment relying on effluxion of time, HMLR will require confirmation that:

(a) the lease is within the Landlord and Tenant Act 1954 (and, if so, evidence that it has determined in accordance with that Act); or
(b) the lease is not within the Landlord and Tenant Act 1954 and either that:

    (i) the provisions of the Electronic Communications Code do not apply to it; or
    (ii) the lease has been determined in accordance with the provisions of the Electronic Communications Code. If such determination is by notice, the applicant must provide a certified copy of the notice.

98.18.8 Forfeiture

A lease containing a proviso for re-entry or 'forfeiture clause' may enable a landlord to forfeit the lease by taking court proceedings or by peaceable re-entry, because the tenant either has not paid the rent, has become insolvent or has breached some other covenant(s) in the lease. An interested person may apply to the court for relief from forfeiture. However, this is not in itself a valid ground for objection to an application based upon determination on forfeiture.

If the forfeiture is based on a *court order*, the application must be accompanied by a certified copy of an unconditional order for possession.

If the forfeiture is based on *peaceable re-entry*, the application must be accompanied by evidence in the form of a statutory declaration or statement of truth by a suitable person with full knowledge of the facts, proving the facts which, it is claimed, amount to a lawful re-entry on a specified date.

If the forfeiture is for *non-payment of rent*, the statutory declaration or statement of truth must establish whether a formal demand was required and, if so, whether it was made. Confirmation of the amount of rent arrears and that this was sufficient to trigger the proviso for re-entry must also be provided.

If the forfeiture is for *breach of covenant other than non-payment of rent*, the statutory declaration or statement of truth must establish:

(a) that the landlord served the requisite notice under LPA 1925, s 146(1) on the tenant on a stated date. If the leasehold estate is not registered, satisfactory evidence that the person served was the tenant must be lodged;
(b) in the case of a breach of a repairing covenant, that the service of the notice was known to the tenant, or to a sub-tenant where the tenant has only a nominal reversion, or to the person who last paid the rent due under the lease, either on his own behalf or as agent for the tenant or sub-tenant, and that a time reasonably sufficient to enable the repairs to be executed had subsequently elapsed;[141]
(c) in the case of a breach of a repairing covenant contained in a lease of which 3 years or more remained unexpired at the date of the notice served under LPA 1925, s 146, that the notice contained the required statement that the tenant was entitled to serve a counter-notice claiming the benefit of the Leasehold Property (Repairs) Act 1938 and did not do so; and
(d) that the tenant failed to comply with the notice served under LPA 1925, s 146.

If the demised premises are let as a dwelling, the only lawful method of enforcing a right of re-entry while anyone is lawfully residing there is by obtaining a court order.[142] For these purposes 'let as a dwelling' means premises which are let wholly or partly as a dwelling.[143] Therefore, if the demised premises include a dwelling, the statutory declaration or statement of truth must establish either that no one was residing in the premises or any part of them, or if someone was, that he was not lawfully residing there.

If the lease is a residential lease, the statutory declaration or statement of truth must establish that the following provisions either do not apply or have been complied with:

(a) HA 1996, s 81 which limits the landlord's right to forfeit a residential lease where there are arrears of service charges which are disputed by the tenant;
(b) Commonhold and Leasehold Reform Act 2002, s 166 which provides that a tenant under a long lease of a dwelling is not liable to make a payment of rent under the lease unless the landlord has given the tenant a notice relating to the payment and the date on which he is liable to make the payment is specified in the notice;

(c) Commonhold and Leasehold Reform Act 2002, s 167 which provides that a landlord under a long lease of a dwelling may not forfeit the lease for failure by the tenant to pay rent, service charge or administration charges unless the amount exceeds a prescribed sum (currently £350), or has been unpaid for a period in excess of a prescribed period (currently 3 years);
(d) Commonhold and Leasehold Reform Act 2002, s 168 which provides that a landlord under a long lease of a dwelling may not serve a notice under LPA 1925, s 146 for breach of covenant by the tenant unless the tenant has admitted the breach, or a period of 14 days has elapsed after a leasehold valuation tribunal or court has determined that the breach has occurred.

If the lease is a residential lease granted after 30 June 2022 and forfeiture is on the basis of non-payment of rent or administration charges relating to rent, the statutory declaration or statement of truth must establish that the rent and/or administration charge does not exceed that permitted by the Leasehold Reform (Ground Rent) Act 2022 and Commonhold and Leasehold Reform Act 2002, Sch 11, para 2A.

For the period from 26 March 2020 until:

(a) 30 September 2021 for residential tenancies, and
(b) 25 March 2022 for commercial tenancies,

landlords' ability to forfeit for non-payment of rent was suspended.[144] HMLR cannot complete any application to close a registered lease which appears to be in breach of this prohibition.

An assured tenancy (including an assured shorthold tenancy) is a tenancy of a home created after 15 January 1989 which meets the conditions of HA 1988, s 1. HA 1988, Sch 1 contains several exceptions which prevent a tenancy becoming an assured tenancy. A landlord can determine an assured tenancy only by obtaining a court order for possession under HA 1988, s 7 or, in the case of a fixed-term tenancy, by notice under a 'break clause'; it cannot be determined by forfeiture. Because the tenancy is not determined by forfeiture, it is not possible to claim relief against forfeiture. An assured tenancy will determine when the court order is executed.[145] Any incumbrances against the leasehold interest will determine when the lease itself determines. An application to determine a lease based on an order for possession made under HA 1988, s 7 should be accompanied by:

(a) a certified copy of the court order; and
(b) the sheriff's return, or a statutory declaration or statement of truth confirming that the order has been executed.

98.18.9 Notice

A lease for a fixed term may contain an option, usually called a 'break clause', allowing either one or both parties to the lease to determine the lease before the expiry of the fixed term. The option is usually only exercisable by written notice. The application must be accompanied by evidence of the determination of the lease by notice in accordance with the terms of the lease, such as a copy of the receipted notice, or a statutory declaration or statement of truth by the applicant, or a certificate by the applicant's conveyancer confirming the relevant facts.

98.18.10 Frustration

A lease may be determined under the doctrine of frustration, i.e. the occurrence of an unforeseen event that makes performance of the lease impracticable. Such cases will be rare and any application will be considered on its individual facts. This situation should be distinguished from the determination of a lease by notice on the occurrence of an event (such as the damage of the premises by fire to be beyond repair) referred to in a 'frustration clause' in the lease.

98.18.11 Enlargement

A tenant who holds the residue of a long lease of land may, under certain conditions, 'enlarge' it into a freehold. This is usually achieved by either the execution of a deed poll, or endorsement on one of the unregistered title deeds relating to an unregistered lease. On enlargement, the land remains subject to the same trusts and covenants that affected the original lease.[146]

98.19 Cancellation of a noted lease

Where a registered lease is determined, HMLR will cancel the notice of that lease in the landlord's registered title at the same time. Where an unregistered lease is determined and a notice of the lease appears in the landlord's registered title, an application should be made for that notice to be cancelled. An applicant should deliver to HMLR:

(a) an application in form CN1 (completing panels 9 and 10 as appropriate);
(b) documentary evidence to prove that the unregistered leasehold estate has determined;
(c) the original lease and/or counterpart lease, or an account for its absence;
(d) satisfactory evidence of title to the determining leasehold estate, consisting of either documents similar to those required on first registration or

(where the applicant is the landlord) the counterpart lease and copies of any assignments;

(e) a Land Charges search against the name of the tenant (with any entries accounted for and, where applicable, certified by a conveyancer as not affecting the estate);

(f) a list in duplicate in form DL of all the documents delivered; and

(g) the fee payable.[147]

If the lease is noted by way of a unilateral notice, an application must be made either to remove the unilateral notice using form UN2 or to cancel it using form UN4.[148]

98.20 Right to determine a registered lease

Where it appears to HMLR that a right to determine a registered estate is exercisable, it may enter the fact in the property register of the affected title.[149] Where a right to determine a registered leasehold estate has arisen, an applicant may apply for such an entry to be made by delivering to HMLR:

(a) an application in form AP1;

(b) evidence to satisfy HMLR that the applicant has the right to determine the registered leasehold estate and that the right is exercisable;[150] and

(c) the fee payable.[151]

Before making an entry, HMLR must give notice of the application to the proprietor of the registered estate to which the application relates and the proprietor of any registered charge on that estate.[152]

When such an entry has been made, an application to cancel it must be supported by evidence to satisfy HMLR that the right to determine the leasehold estate is not exercisable.[153] The application for cancellation may be made by:

(a) the person entitled to determine the registered estate;

(b) the proprietor of the registered estate to which the entry relates;

(c) a person entitled to be registered as proprietor of that estate; or

(d) any other person whom HMLR is satisfied has an interest in the removal of the entry.

---

1 See 98.6 Prescribed clauses leases.

2 LRR 2003, r 92.

3 See 68 First Registration for leases granted out of unregistered estates and 32.2 Titles to leasehold estates for the various classes of leasehold title.

4 LRR 2003, r 35.
5 LRR 2003, r 37.
6 LRA 2002, Sch 1, para 1 and Sch 3, para 1.
7 LRA 2002, ss 33(b) and 34.
8 LRA 2002, s 90.
9 LRA 2002, s 23(1).
10 LRA 2002, s 26.
11 LRA 2002, s 27(2).
12 See 74.5 Dispositions of registered franchises and 112.3 Lease of a registered manor.
13 See 98.6 Prescribed clauses leases.
14 LRR 2003, r 212.
15 LRR 2003, r 13.
16 LRA 2002, Sch 1, para 1 and Sch 3, para 1.
17 See 119.1 Agreed notice.
18 See 119.3 Unilateral notice.
19 See *Rye v Rye* [1962] AC 496.
20 LRA 2002, s 90.
21 LRA 2002, ss 33(b) and 34. See 119 Notices.
22 LRA 2002, s 90.
23 LRR 2003, r 58A(1).
24 LRR 2003, r 58A(4).
25 LRR 2003, r 58A(2).
26 An example might be where a copy of a court order specifying the form of the lease accompanies the application or where the recitals to the lease make clear it was granted in the form expressly required by an order of the court.
27 See 98.7 Registration of leases which are registrable dispositions.
28 See 128.4 Duty to disclose overriding interests.
29 See 84 Identity Evidence.
30 See 168 Stamp Duty Land Tax and/or 94 Land Transaction Tax.
31 See 67 Fees.
32 LRR 2003, r 72A(2).
33 LRR 2003, r 72A(3).
34 LRR 2003, r 58A(3). An example might be where a copy of a court order specifying the form of the lease accompanies the application or where the recitals to the lease make clear it was granted in the form expressly required by an order of the court.
35 LRR 2003, r 72A(4).
36 LRR 2003, r 72A(5).
37 See Appendix IV.
38 LRR 2003, r 72B.
39 Which is a registrable disposition under LRA 2002, s 27(2)(e).
40 LRR 2003, r 77.
41 LFRA 2024, s 1(1)–(2).
42 LFRA 2024, s 13(2).
43 LFRA 2024, s 11.
44 LFRA 2024, s 12(3).

45 See 98.10.1 Deeds of variation varying the term and 98.10.2 Deeds of variation varying the extent.
46 LFRA 2024, s 12(6).
47 LFRA 2024, s 12(7).
48 See 98.6 Prescribed clauses leases.
49 See LPA 1925, s 205(1)(xxvii).
50 See 98.6 Prescribed clauses leases.
51 See *Bass Holdings Ltd v Lewis* [1986] 2 EGLR 40.
52 See 98.6 Prescribed clauses leases.
53 See 98.10.1 Deeds of variation varying the term and 98.10.2 Deeds of variation varying the extent.
54 See 67 Fees.
55 See 119.1 Agreed notice or 119.3 Unilateral notice.
56 See 119.1 Agreed notice or 119.3 Unilateral notice.
57 Landlord and Tenant Act 1987, s 35.
58 Landlord and Tenant Act 1987, ss 38 and 39.
59 LRR 2003, r 80(d).
60 See 98.17 Extensions of leases (other than under the Leasehold Reform Act 1967 or the Leasehold Reform, Housing and Urban Development Act 1993).
61 Leasehold Reform (Ground Rent) Act 2022, s 15(1).
62 Leasehold Reform (Ground Rent) Act 2022, s 15(2).
63 Leasehold Reform (Ground Rent) Act 2022, s 15(5).
64 See 67 Fees.
65 See 34 Collective Enfranchisement.
66 Leasehold Reform Act 1967, s 1. Once in force, LFRA 2024, s 33 will entitle tenants to an extended lease expiring 990 years after the date on which the existing term is due to expire.
67 Leasehold Reform Act 1967, s 2(1) to (3).
68 Leasehold Reform Act 1967, s 3.
69 Leasehold Reform Act 1967, s 5(5).
70 See 119.1 Agreed notice.
71 See 119.3 Unilateral notice.
72 See 68 First Registration or 98.2 Leases which are registrable dispositions.
73 See 98.18 Determination of registered leases.
74 LRHUDA 1993, s 39(3A).
75 LRHUDA 1993, s 40.
76 LRHUDA 1993, s 56. Once in force, LFRA 2024, s 33(2) will extend this to 990 years after the term date of the existing lease.
77 Once in force, LFRA 2024, s 37 will determine the price payable.
78 LRHUDA 1993, s 97(1).
79 See 119.1 Agreed notice.
80 See 119.3 Unilateral notice.
81 LRHUDA 1993, s 50(1). Once in force, LFRA 2024, s 43(2) will transfer this power to the appropriate tribunal
82 LRHUDA 1993, s 97(2)(b).
83 LRA 2002, s 87(1) and (3).

84 See 119.1 Agreed notice.
85 See 119.3 Unilateral notice.
86 LRR 2003, r 93(q).
87 LRA 2002 s 45.
88 See 153.1 Application for entry of restriction.
89 LRHUDA 1993, s 97(2)(a).
90 LRA 2002, s 87(1) and (3).
91 See 119.1 Agreed notice.
92 See 119.3 Unilateral notice.
93 LRR 2003, r 93(p).
94 LRA 2002, s 45.
95 See 153.1 Application for entry of restriction.
96 LRR 2003, r 196(2).
97 See 68 First Registration and 98.2 Leases which are registrable dispositions, as the case may be.
98 LRHUDA 1993, s 58(1).
99 LRHUDA 1993, s 58(4).
100 See 119.1 Agreed notice and 119.3 Unilateral notice.
101 LRHUDA 1993, s 58(5).
102 LRHUDA 1993, s 58(6).
103 LRR 2003, r 72A(3).
104 LRR 2003, r 72A(4).
105 LRA 2002, Sch 1, para 3.
106 LRR 2003, r 72A(3).
107 LRR 2003, r 72A(4).
108 LRA 2002, ss 11(3) and 12(3).
109 LRR 2003, r 90.
110 LRA 2002, Sch 1, para 3.
111 See 25 Cautions Against First Registration.
112 LRA 2002, Sch 1, para 3.
113 LRR 2003, r 73A(1)(a).
114 See 25 Cautions Against First Registration.
115 See 138.2.1 Registrable dispositions of registered estates for valuable consideration and 119 Notices.
116 See 25 Cautions Against First Registration.
117 LRA 2002, s 12(4)(a).
118 LRA 2002, s 33(c).
119 LRR 2003, r 72A(3) and (4).
120 LRR 2003, r 72A(4).
121 See 119.1 Agreed notice.
122 See 119.3 Unilateral notice.
123 LRR 2003, r 60(2) and (3).
124 See also 85.1 Transfers of pre-1996 leases.
125 LRR 2003, r 66.
126 For example by a separate deed or ministerial order or using the procedure set out in Landlord and Tenant (Covenants) Act 1995, s 10.

127 See 67 Fees.
128 See 98.10 Variation of a lease.
129 *Allen v Rochdale BC* [2000] Ch 221.
130 LPA 1925, s 149(3).
131 *Re Ives Case* (1597) 5 Co Rep 11.
132 See 84 Identity Evidence.
133 See 67 Fees.
134 See 98.19 Cancellation of a noted lease.
135 See 181.2 Upgrading possessory or qualified leasehold to good leasehold.
136 See 101 Legal Easements.
137 See 168 Stamp Duty Land Tax and/or 94 Land Transaction Tax.
138 LRR 2003, r 161(1).
139 See 168 Stamp Duty Land Tax and/or 94 Land Transaction Tax.
140 Contained in Communications Act 2003, Sch 3A.
141 See Landlord and Tenant Act 1927, s 18(2).
142 Protection from Eviction Act 1977, s 2.
143 *Pirabakaran v Patel* [2006] EWCA Civ 685.
144 Coronavirus Act 2020, ss 81 and 82.
145 HA 1988, s 5(1A).
146 See 60 Enlargement of Long Leases.
147 See 67 Fees.
148 See 119.5 Removal of a unilateral notice or 119.6 Cancellation of a unilateral notice.
149 LRA 2002, s 64 and LRR 2003, r 125(1).
150 LRR 2003, r 125(2).
151 See 67 Fees.
152 LRR 2003, r 125(4).
153 LRR 2003, r 125(6).

99 LEGAL AID

Where legal aid services are made available to an individual, the aid provided constitutes a first charge on any property recovered or preserved by the individual in proceedings, or in any compromise, settlement or dispute in connection with which the services were provided, whether the property is recovered or preserved for the individual or another person. The system for legal aid is administered by the Legal Aid Agency on behalf of the Lord Chancellor. Previously, it was administered by the Legal Services Commission under the Access to Justice Act 1999 and, before that, by the Legal Aid Board under the Legal Aid Act 1988. Originally, it was administered by The Law Society.

A charge in favour of the Lord Chancellor may be:

(a) a statutory charge arising under Legal Aid, Sentencing and Punishment of Offenders Act 2012, s 25(1);[1]

(b) a contractual charge, which normally arises when the individual moves to a new property;[2]
(c) a voluntary charge, entered into voluntarily by the individual as security for monies owed;[3] or
(d) a sub-charge of an existing charge in favour of the individual.[4]

---

1 Previously, Legal Aid Act 1988, s 16(6) or Access to Justice Act 1999, s 10(7). See 170 Statutory Charges.
2 See 100 Legal Charges.
3 See 100 Legal Charges.
4 See 100.12 Sub-charges.

100 LEGAL CHARGES

A registered proprietor of a registered estate has power to create a charge expressed to be by way of legal mortgage and to charge the estate at law with the payment of money. It is no longer possible to charge a registered estate by a mortgage by demise or sub-demise.[1] A legal charge of a registered estate may be made in form CH1,[2] although its use is not compulsory. The grant of a legal charge must be completed by registration if it is to operate at law; until then it takes effect in equity only.[3] Registration of a charge is effected when the chargee or his successor in title is entered in the register as the proprietor of the charge.[4] On completion of registration, the charge has effect, if it would not otherwise do so, as a charge by deed by way of legal mortgage.[5]

For the position where a charge drawn as a legal charge cannot be registered, see 61 Equitable Charges. An example of when this might occur is where a consent is required under a restriction but that consent is not forthcoming.

100.1 Charges of registered land

An applicant to register a legal charge should deliver to HMLR:

(a) an application in form AP1;
(b) the charge (and a certified copy, if the applicant wishes for the original to be returned);
(c) where applicable, application for entry of a restriction (see below);
(d) form DI giving the information as to overriding interests required by LRR 2003, r 57, including any documentary evidence of the interests;[6]
(e) the appropriate confirmation or evidence of identity;[7] and
(f) the fee payable.[8]

Where an application is made to register a charge created by a company or an LLP, the applicant must produce to HMLR a certificate that the charge has been registered under Companies Act 2006 LRR 2003, r 111(1).[9] In addition, special evidence may be required in relation to particular kinds of chargors and chargees, such as charities.[10] If HMLR needs to see an incorporated document to complete the registration, it will request a copy.

On a charge of part of a registered estate, HMLR must:

(a) make an entry in the chargor's title as to the removal of the estate comprised in that charge (where the charged part is registered under a separate title from the uncharged part), or make a new edition of that title; and
(b) where appropriate, make entries in the relevant individual registers in respect of any rights, restrictive covenants, provisions or other matters created by the charge which are capable of being so entered. However, HMLR need make no such entries where the relevant title numbers have not been given in panel 2 of form AP1, unless separate application is made in respect of them.[11]

Charges of part of a registered estate sometimes contain the grant and/or reservation of rights in the nature of easements over the part of the land that has not been charged. Such rights are not easements as they do not have all the necessary characteristics of easements; in particular the benefiting land and burdened land remain in the same ownership. In consequence, they do not constitute registrable dispositions under LRA 2002, s 27 and cannot be registered as appurtenant to a registered title. They may take effect as quasi-easements and as such, if the chargee were to subsequently exercise his power of sale, they could become easements either under the rule in *Wheeldon v Burrows* (1879) LR 12 Ch D 31 or by virtue of LPA 1925, s 62. When registering such a charge of part, HMLR will not therefore make any entry as to the benefit of such rights. It will, however, make an entry in the title affected by the charge, referring to the fact that the charge contains provisions relating to the rights in question. In the alternative, specific application may be made using form UN1 for entry of a notice in the affected title as to the burden of such rights.[12]

If the chargee requires the entry of a restriction preventing registration of a disposition by the registered proprietor of the registered estate without the consent of the chargee, the application must be made in form RX1.[13] Alternatively, if a standard form of restriction is sought, the application may be contained in:

(a) panel 8 of form CH1;
(b) an electronic document to which LRA 2002, s 91 applies where the form of the document (including the application for the restriction) has first been approved by HMLR; or
(c) in an approved charge.

An 'approved charge' for these purposes is one the form of which (including the application for the restriction) has first been approved by HMLR.[14] A possible form of restriction based on Form P is:

> No [disposition *or specify type of disposition*] of the registered estate [(other than a charge)] by the proprietor of the registered estate [or by the proprietor of any registered charge, not being a charge registered before the entry of this restriction] is to be registered without a written consent signed by the proprietor for the time being of the charge dated [*date*] in favour of [*chargee*] referred to in the charges register [or [their conveyancer *or specify appropriate details*]].

The wording of Form P is set out in Appendix IV.

A restriction in a standard form contained in LRR 2003, Sch 4 does not require the approval of HMLR to the terms of the restriction under LRA 2002, s 43(3).

100.2 Digital charges

Since April 2018, it has been possible to register digital charges. Such charges must comply with the relevant notice issued by HMLR under LRR 2003, r 54C.[15]

Presently, the service is only available where:

(a) the transaction is a remortgage where there is an existing registered charge that will be discharged as part of the same transaction; and
(b) the charge is intended to take effect as a first charge, not a second or subsequent charge.

The digital deed is signed electronically using a service provided by HMLR. There is no need for a witness. Once the parties have signed the deed, their conveyancer must make it effective. This will result in the date being entered in the deed. They must then apply to HMLR to register it through HMLR's Business Gateway.[16]

HMLR will consider the application in the normal way.

100.3 Charges subsisting at the time of first registration

In the case of an unregistered estate in land, the creation of a protected first legal mortgage may be a 'trigger' for first registration.[17] Where a charge or mortgage subsists at the time of first registration, it must be disclosed in the application for first registration. The charge will be registered under LRR 2003, r 22 (in the case of a protected first legal mortgage) or r 34 (in the case of a subsequent legal charge).

Where a charge or mortgage has been created contemporaneously with the purchase of land which has triggered compulsory first registration, this will need to be completed by registration as a 'dealing' taking place before completion of the first registration.[18] In such a case, the charge should be lodged for registration with the application for first registration of the estate and it will be registered on completion of the first registration; the registration of the charge has effect from the time of the making of the application for first registration.[19]

If a charge accompanies an application for first registration in form FR1, no separate application or fee for its registration will be necessary.

100.4 Approved forms of charge

HMLR has a facility to approve standard forms of charge (not being in form CH1) and major lenders are encouraged to apply for such approval. An approved form of charge is given a unique 'MD reference', which assists in the processing of an application to register the charge. Re-approval is necessary if changes are made to the approved form. Application is made in form ACD and no fee is currently payable.

100.5 Further advances

The proprietor of a registered charge may make further advances on the security of the charge ranking in priority to a subsequent charge if he has not received from the subsequent chargee notice of the creation of the subsequent charge.[20] Such notice is treated as having been received at the time when, in accordance with LRR 2003, r 107, it ought to have been received. Rule 107 sets out details of various methods of the giving of the notice and of the time when the notice ought to have been received when given by one of those methods.

The proprietor of a registered charge may also make further advances on the security of the charge ranking in priority to a subsequent charge if the advance is made pursuant to an obligation and, at the time of the creation of the subsequent charge, the obligation was entered in the register.[21] Where the proprietor of a registered charge, or a person applying to be so registered, is under an obligation to make further advances on the security of that charge, he may apply for the obligation to be entered in the register. The application must be in form CH2 unless it is contained in:

(a) panel 8 of form CH1;
(b) an electronic legal charge; or
(c) a charge the form of which has been approved by HMLR.[22]

The proprietor of a registered charge may also make further advances on the security of the charge ranking in priority to a subsequent charge if the parties to the prior charge have agreed a maximum amount for which the charge is security and, at the time of the creation of the subsequent charge, the agreement was entered in the register.[23] Where the parties have agreed such a maximum amount, the proprietor of a registered charge, or a person applying to be registered as proprietor, may apply for such agreement to be entered in the register. The application must be made in form CH3.

Other than as set out above, tacking in relation to a charge over registered land is possible only with the agreement of the subsequent chargee.[24]

100.6 Collateral charges

A collateral charge is one that runs parallel to another charge (i.e. the primary security) secured on other property. It usually arises where a lender is only prepared to advance additional money to the borrower if additional security is provided. It does not in itself secure any new money but merely extends the lender's security to include the property subject to the collateral charge. The lender will protect his interest in the additional security by registering a collateral charge on it.[25]

100.7 Priorities

Subject to any entry in the register to the contrary, registered charges on the same registered estate, or on the same registered charge, are taken to rank as between themselves in the order shown in the register.[26]

Where a deed or other document alters the priority between registered charges, an application should be made for an entry in the register to reflect that altered priority. Such a deed is often referred to as a 'deed of postponement'. The application must be made by or with the consent of the proprietor, or a person entitled to be registered as the proprietor, of any registered charge whose priority is adversely affected by the alteration.[27] However, such consent is not required from a person who has executed the deed or document which alters the priority.

The applicant should deliver to HMLR:

(a) an application in form AP1;
(b) the deed or document altering the priority of the registered charges or a certified copy of it;
(c) any consent required (or a conveyancer's certificate confirming that he holds any necessary consents); and
(d) the fee payable.[28]

In relation to deeds of postponement in respect of a registered charge and a noted charge, HMLR may, on application, make an entry in the register referring to an agreement which it is claimed relates to priorities between a registered charge and a charge which is the subject of a notice in the register.[29]

100.8 Consolidation

A chargee who has a right of consolidation in relation to a registered charge may apply for an entry in respect of that right to be made in the register in which the charge is registered.[30] The chargee should deliver to HMLR:

(a) an application in form AP1 (or form FR1, if part of an application for first registration);
(b) form CC;
(c) certified copies of any unregistered charges that are consolidated; and
(d) the fee payable.[31]

100.9 Deeds of variation

An application to register a deed or other document varying the terms of a registered charge must be made by, or with the consent of, the proprietor of the registered charge and the proprietor of the estate charged. It must be accompanied by the consent of the proprietor, or a person entitled to be registered as proprietor, of any registered charge of equal or inferior priority (and the proprietor of any sub-charge derived directly or indirectly from such a charge) that is prejudicially affected by the variation.[32] However, such consent is not required from any person who has executed the deed of variation or whose consent is not required under the terms of his charge (or sub-charge).

The applicant should deliver to HMLR:

(a) an application in form AP1;
(b) the deed of variation of the registered charge or a certified copy of it;
(c) any consent required (or a conveyancer's certificate confirming that he holds any necessary consents); and
(d) the fee payable.[33]

A note of the variation is made in the register if HMLR is satisfied that the proprietor of any other registered charge of equal or inferior priority to that of the varied charge who is prejudicially affected by the variation is bound by it. If HMLR is not so satisfied, it may make an entry to the effect that a deed which is expressed to vary the terms of the registered charge has been entered into.

100.10 Remedies of a registered chargee

A registered chargee will have several methods of enforcing his security. Unless there are entries in the register to the contrary, the proprietor of a registered charge is taken to have the powers of disposition conferred by law on the owner of a legal mortgage.[34] This has effect only for the purpose of preventing the title of a disponee being questioned and does not affect the lawfulness of a disposition.[35]

No period of limitation under LA 1980, s 16 shall run against any person in relation to a registered estate in land or rentcharge.[36] Accordingly, even where a mortgagee is in possession, the mortgagor does not lose his right to redeem.

A mortgagee must serve notice on a spouse or civil partner, who is not a party to the action and who has the benefit of a home rights notice or a matrimonial homes right caution, of an action for enforcement of the mortgagee's security.[37] The mortgagee may apply in form MH3 for an official search certificate of the result of search for this purpose, which will reveal whether a home rights notice or matrimonial home rights caution is entered in the register, and whether there is a pending application for the entry of a home rights notice.[38]

The most common method of enforcing the security of a registered chargee is the exercise of the chargee's power of sale. A chargee may also apply for an order for foreclosure. A legal mortgagee also has a statutory power to appoint a receiver under LPA 1925, s 101.[39]

100.10.1 Power of sale

A transfer of a registered estate by the proprietor of a registered charge under the power of sale must be in form TR2 (for a transfer of whole) or form TP2 (for a transfer of part).[40] The transfer must be completed by registration if it is to operate at law.[41]

A sale by the chargee is subject to any matters which appear in the register and have priority over the charge under which the power of sale is being exercised. It overreaches any caution registered in the proprietorship register, other than a matrimonial home rights caution registered before the charge and not subsequently postponed to the charge. Interests in existence at the time of registration of the charge which took effect as interests which override first registration or registered dispositions under LRA 2002, Sch 1 or Sch 3 are not overreached by a transfer under the power of sale.

A transfer by a chargee in exercise of his power of sale is subject to any charges which have priority over the chargee's charge (for which a discharge will therefore be required if it is to be removed from the register), but otherwise the purchaser will take free of any other legal or equitable charges, which will be cancelled automatically upon registration of the transfer.

Where the chargee has a surplus arising from the sale after discharging prior charges, the expenses of the sale and his own charge, he holds it on trust to pay it to the person entitled to the mortgaged property.[42] For these purposes, a person is taken to have notice of anything in the register immediately before the disposition on sale.[43] As a result, the chargee should inspect the register to ascertain whether there is any subsequent chargee to whom he should pay the balance of the proceeds of sale.

If there is an entry affecting the charge under which the power of sale is exercised to the effect that it may be subject to Companies Act 2006, s 859H (or any similar preceding legislation),[44] HMLR may enter a note in the proprietorship register on registration of the transferee to the effect that the registration of the proprietor pursuant to that transfer is or may be subject to any estate, right and interest or any liquidator, administrator or creditor of the chargor.

100.10.2 Foreclosure

Foreclosure is a judicial procedure by which a chargee acquires the land freed from the chargor's interest in it. Where a person has obtained an order for foreclosure absolute, he should deliver to HMLR:

(a) an application in form AP1;
(b) the foreclosure order absolute or an office copy of it or a certified copy of it (or a conveyancer's certificate confirming that he holds such order or office copy); and
(c) the fee payable.[45]

On completion of the application, the registration of the charge in respect of which the order was made, and any entry in respect of an interest over which that charge has priority, will be cancelled. The applicant is entered as proprietor of the registered estate.[46]

100.11 Discharge of registered charge

A discharge of a registered charge, in documentary form, should be in form DS1 and a release of part of the registered estate from a registered charge should be in form DS3. Forms DS1 and DS3 must be executed as deeds or authenticated in such other manner as HMLR may approve. HMLR may also accept and act upon any other proof of satisfaction of a charge that it may regard as sufficient.[47]

Where a charge is registered in the name of two or more proprietors, a valid receipt for the money secured by it may be given by:

(a) the registered proprietors;
(b) the survivors or survivor of the registered proprietors; or
(c) the personal representative of the last survivor of the registered proprietors.

A person applying to register the discharge or release of a registered charge should deliver to HMLR:

(a) an application in form AP1 or form DS2 (for use with form DS1 only);
(b) a discharge in form DS1 or form DS3;
(c) where necessary, the appropriate confirmation or evidence as to identity;[48] and
(d) any evidence necessary to show that the correct person has executed form DS1 or form DS3.

No fee is currently payable.

Discharges of part of a registered charge sometimes contain the grant and/or reservation of rights in the nature of easements over the part of the land that has not been charged. Such rights are not easements. Similar comments apply to those in relation to such rights contained in charges of part of a registered estate.[49]

LRR 2003, r 115 provides for discharges and releases of registered charges in electronic form. The release of part of a registered charge in electronic form is not currently permitted. The electronic discharge (ED) method is used by several major lending institutions. An ED cancels the charge entries automatically and, in most cases, immediately. No DS1 and no formal paper application to discharge the charge is therefore required and the process is completely automated. The ED method has been supplemented by the introduction of the e-DS1, which is an electronic form of discharge submitted through HMLR portal. The e-DS1 acts as both the evidence of discharge and the application to cancel the charge from the register. Currently, the e-DS1 service is designed for corporate chargees and their agents only.

Generally, HMLR will cancel any restriction that specifically relates to the charge automatically when the charge is discharged. However, if a restriction in favour of the chargee does not specifically refer to the charge being discharged, a separate withdrawal of that restriction in form RX4 must be lodged, otherwise the restriction will remain in the register.

In relation to the discharge of registered charges, a policy of 'early completion' was introduced by HMLR on 3 August 2009 with the purpose of ensuring that individual applications for registration are, where possible, completed rather than being delayed as a result of failure to provide evidence of satisfaction of an existing registered charge. The policy applies to all situations where an application for a discharge of the whole has been made with another application, but evidence of satisfaction of the charge has not been provided. For example, it applies in the common scenario where an application is made in form AP1 for the registration of a discharge of an existing charge, a transfer and a new charge. Three distinct applications are being made. Without evidence of satisfaction of the existing charge, HMLR will reject the application for discharge but complete the other applications where possible. The entries relating to the existing charge will be left in the register until evidence of satisfaction is provided.

If there is a restriction registered in favour of the existing chargee which provides that no disposition and/or that no charge of the registered estate shall be registered without the consent of that chargee, HMLR will requisition for evidence of discharge or evidence that the terms of the restriction have been met. If the requisition is not dealt with HMLR will, in the case of a restriction against the registration of any disposition, cancel not only the application for discharge but also the application to register the transfer and charge. In the case of a restriction against the registration of a charge only, HMLR will complete the registration of the transfer, cancelling the other applications and leaving the entries relating to the existing charge in the register. A 'stand-alone' application made only for discharge of a registered charge is substantially defective if evidence of satisfaction is not lodged with the application and will therefore be rejected.

100.12 Sub-charges

A proprietor of a registered charge has power to charge at law with the payment of money indebtedness secured by the registered charge. A sub-charge of a registered charge may not be created in any other way.[50] The grant of a sub-charge of a registered charge must be completed by registration, with the sub-chargee or his successor in title being entered in the register as proprietor of the sub-charge.[51]

The registered proprietor of a sub-charge has the same powers as the sub-chargor in relation to the property subject to the principal charge or any intermediate charge.[52]

An applicant to register a sub-charge should deliver to HMLR:

(a) an application in form AP1;
(b) the sub-charge or a certified copy of it; and
(c) the fee payable.[53]

100.13 Transfer of charge

The transfer of a registered charge must be in form TR4 or form AS2, as appropriate.[54] The transfer must be completed by registration with the transferee, or his successor in title, being entered in the register as proprietor of the charge.[55]

An applicant to register a transfer of a registered charge should deliver to HMLR the usual documents required.[56]

100.14 Related topics

For:

(a) equitable charges, see 61 Equitable Charges;
(b) charges created by debenture, see 49 Debentures; and
(c) statutory charges, see 170 Statutory Charges.

---

1 LRA 2002, s 23.
2 LRR 2003, r 103.
3 LRA 2002, s 27.
4 LRA 2002, Sch 2, para 8.
5 LRA 2002, s 51.
6 See 128.4 Duty to disclose overriding interests.
7 See 84 Identity Evidence.
8 See 67 Fees.
9 See 37 Companies and 105.2 Registration of charge created by a UK limited liability partnership.
10 See 30.4 Mortgages by non-exempt charities.
11 LRR 2003, r 72.
12 See 119.3 Unilateral notice.
13 See 153.1 Application for entry of restriction.
14 LRR 2003, r 92.

15 Currently Notice 1 (under rule 54C of the Land Registration Rules 2003): HM Land Registry Network Services – arrangements for the creation and registration of digital mortgages (effective 21 January 2019), www.gov.uk/government/publications/land-registration-act-2002-schedule-2/notice-1-hm-land-registry-network-services-creation-and-registration-of-digital-mortgages.

16 See 56 Electronic Services.

17 See 68 First Registration.

18 LRR 2003, r 38.

19 LRR 2003, r 38(2)

20 LRA 2002, s 49(1).

21 LRA 2002, s 49(3).

22 LRR 2003, r 108.

23 LRA 2002, s 49(4).

24 LRA 2002, s 49(6).

25 See 100.1 Charges of registered land.

26 LRA 2002, s 48(1) and LRR 2003, r 101.

27 LRR 2003, r 102.

28 See 67 Fees.

29 LRR 2003, r 116A.

30 LRR 2003, r 110.

31 See 67 Fees.

32 LRR 2003, r 113.

33 See 67 Fees.

34 LRA 2002, s 52(1).

35 LRA 2002, s 52(2).

36 LRA 2002, s 96(2).

37 FLA 1996, s 56.

38 See 81.5 Home rights search by a mortgagee.

39 See 146 Receivers Appointed under the Law of Property Act 1925.

40 LRR 2003, r 58.

41 See 176 Transfers.

42 LPA 1925, s 105.

43 LRA 2002, s 54.

44 See 37.5 Registration of a charge created by a UK company.

45 See 67 Fees.

46 LRR 2003, r 112.

47 LRR 2003, r 114.

48 See 84 Identity Evidence.

49 See 100.1 Charges of registered land.

50 LRA 2002, s 23(2)(b) and (3).

51 LRA 2002, s 27(3)(b) and Sch 2, para 11.

52 LRA 2002, s 53.

53 See 67 Fees.

54 LRR 2003, r 116.

55 LRA 2002, s 27(3)(a) and Sch 2, para 10.

56 See 176.1 Registration of transfer.

101 LEGAL EASEMENTS

An easement is a right which one piece of land has over another piece of land. For an easement to subsist at law, there are four essential characteristics which must be present:[1]

(a) there must be a benefiting tenement and a burdened tenement, as an easement cannot exist in gross;
(b) the easement must benefit the benefiting land by making it a better and more convenient property, rather than it being a purely personal right;
(c) the benefiting land and burdened land must not be both owned *and* occupied by the same person. A landowner cannot have an easement over his own land – rights exercised by him over part of his land will take effect only as quasi-easements. This does not, however, prevent an easement arising in favour of a tenant over other land of his landlord, as the landlord does not own *and* occupy both tenements; and
(d) the easement must be capable of forming the subject matter of a grant. No right can exist as an easement unless it could have been validly granted by deed. This principle in turn has four elements:

    (i) the right must be within the general nature of rights capable of being granted as easements;[2]
    (ii) the right must be sufficiently definite;
    (iii) there must be a capable grantor; and
    (iv) there must be a capable grantee.

Most easements are expressly granted or reserved, in either a deed of grant, a transfer or a lease, but they can also arise through implication or through long use. Implied easements are easements arising by implication:

(a) under the LPA 1925, s 62;
(b) under the rule in *Wheeldon v Burrows*;[3]
(c) by virtue of necessity; or
(d) by virtue of being 'intended easements', i.e. easements which were intended to be granted or reserved, but which for some reason were not expressly set out in the conveyance or other deed.

Prescriptive easements are legal easements which arise by virtue of user as of right (i.e. without permission, force, or secrecy) over a long period of time, rather than having arisen by way of a formal grant or by implication.

A legal easement must subsist for an interest equivalent to an estate in fee simple absolute in possession or a term of years absolute.[4]

101.1 Legal easements on first registration

101.1.1 Beneficial easements

On first registration of title, the estate is vested in the registered proprietor together with all interests subsisting for the benefit of the estate.[5] This includes the benefit of any subsisting legal easements, whether or not these are the subject of an entry in the register. If, at the time of first registration, HMLR is satisfied that a right subsists as a legal estate and benefits the registered estate, it may enter the benefit of that appurtenant right in the register.[6] This will be as the result of HMLR's examination of the title or its consideration of a written application providing details of the right and evidence of its existence. Where the easement arose by prescription or is an implied easement, the evidence will usually be in the form of a statutory declaration or statement of truth.[7] If HMLR is not satisfied that the right subsists as a legal interest benefiting the registered estate, it may enter details of the right claimed in the property register with such qualification as it considers appropriate.[8] The applicant must therefore lodge evidence that the grantor had power to grant the right, otherwise HMLR may either omit the right or enter a qualification note to an entry in the register relating to the right.

Where the burdened estate is registered, the consent of any chargee of the burdened estate whose charge has priority over the grant of the easement and who has not joined in the grant, should be lodged. If the chargee has not consented to the grant, the easement is liable to be overridden if the chargee exercises his power of sale. If the consent cannot be lodged, the application may be completed but with a note along the following lines being added to the register entry for the benefiting title:

> NOTE: The consent of the proprietor of the charge dated [*date*] in favour of [*name*] affecting title(s) [*title number(s)*] was not produced on registration and the rights [granted by *or* granted in clause(s) [*number*]] of the deed may be overridden in the event of the exercise of the power of sale.

The note can be cancelled without fee if an application is subsequently made in form AP1 enclosing the consent. Any restriction (including a restriction in favour of a chargee) in the register of the burdened title must be complied with as necessary. If there is a caution against dealings or a notice of (intended) deposit in the register of the burdened title and the consent to the registration of the easement does not accompany the application, HMLR may serve notice upon the cautioner or depositee.

Where the burdened estate is unregistered, evidence of the grantor's title to it, commencing with a good root more than 15 years old at the date of the application, must accompany the application. The consent of any legal mortgagee of the burdened estate to the grant of the easement should also be lodged, unless he has joined in the grant. If this consent is not lodged, the application may be completed but with a note being added to the register entry for the benefiting title in the form referred to above.

If the easement was granted over an unregistered estate that has since been registered, it may be necessary for a notice as to the burden of the easement to be entered in the register of the burdened title at the same time as the benefit is entered in the register of the benefiting title. This will be done by HMLR as part of the first registration, normally after service of notice on the proprietor of the burdened title.

101.1.2 Subjective easements

On first registration, the estate is vested in the registered proprietor subject to any easements which are an interest which overrides first registration under LRA 2002, Sch 1, or are the subject of an entry in the register in relation to the estate, and/or, in the case of a leasehold title, which are incident to the leasehold estate.[9] HMLR must enter a notice in the register of the burden of any easement which appears from its examination of the title to affect the registered estate, except any which appear to it to be of a trivial or obvious character, or the entry of a notice in respect of which would be likely to cause confusion or inconvenience.[10] Even where no entry is made as to a subjective legal easement on first registration, it is an interest falling within LRA 2002, Sch 1, para 3, which therefore overrides first registration.

A person applying for first registration must provide information to HMLR in form DI about any legal easements which are within his actual knowledge and affect the estate to which the application relates, including any documentary evidence of the interests.[11] HMLR may enter a notice in the register in respect of any such legal easement.[12]

101.2 Legal easements arising after first registration

The express grant or reservation of a legal easement over registered land (other than a grant as a result of the operation of LPA 1925, s 62) must be completed by registration if it is to operate at law.[13] Registration is completed by the entry of a notice of the easement in the register of the burdened title and, if the title to the benefiting estate is registered, by an entry in the property register of that title.[14] Until completed by registration, such an easement is only equitable.

The benefit of a legal easement can be entered in the register only as appurtenant to a registered estate; it cannot be registered independently.[15]

Where the benefiting and/or burdened estate is registered, an application to complete the grant by registration *must* be made in form AP1 to meet the registration requirements. This is the case even if only the benefiting estate is registered.[16] An application for entry of an agreed or unilateral notice against the burdened title will *not* meet the registration requirements. In that event, a subsequent application may be made in form AP1 to complete the easement by registration so that it does take effect at law. Until then, it takes effect in equity only and the benefit cannot be registered in the property register of the benefiting estate.

If the estate benefiting from the grant is unregistered but the burdened estate is registered, an application to complete the grant by registration *must* be made in form AP1 or AN1 to meet the registration requirements.[17] An application for entry of a unilateral notice will *not* meet the registration requirements. In that event, a subsequent application may be made in form AP1 or form AN1 to complete the easement by registration so that it does take effect at law. Until then, it takes effect in equity only.

Where the easement is contained in a transfer or charge of part of a registered title, only an application to register the transfer or charge is necessary; no separate application in respect of the easements is required. HMLR will make the necessary entries as a matter of course when registering the transfer, provided the relevant title numbers are provided in panel 2 of the form AP1 or separate application is made.[18]

An applicant for registration of an easement contained in a deed of grant should deliver to HMLR:

(a) an application in form AP1;
(b) the deed of grant or a certified copy of it;
(c) any consents or certificates required in respect of mortgages, charges or restrictions relating to the burdened title;
(d) (if the right is granted over an unregistered estate) an abstract or epitome showing the grantor's title to the burdened estate;
(e) the appropriate confirmation or evidence of identity;[19]
(f) the appropriate SDLT and/or LTT certificate(s) or other evidence;[20] and
(g) the fee payable.[21]

The title numbers of all the registered titles involved must be specified in panel 2 of form AP1, otherwise HMLR is not obliged to make any entry unless separate application is made.[22] The easement will be completed by registration, with entries being made in the register of the burdened estate and (if registered) the benefiting estate.[23]

Where the grant or reservation of an easement is not a registrable disposition, it will be effective at law when made. However, an application may be made for the benefit of the easement to be registered as appurtenant to the benefiting estate, if registered.[24] The application must be made in form AP1, accompanied by an abstract or epitome showing the grantor's title to the unregistered burdened estate and any consents or certificates required in respect of mortgages, charges or restrictions relating to the burdened estate. Where HMLR is not satisfied that the right claimed subsists as a legal estate appurtenant to the applicant's registered estate, it may enter details of the right claimed in the property register with such qualification as it considers appropriate.

Where the benefiting estate is unregistered, application may be made for the entry of a notice in respect of an easement affecting a registered title. Where it appears to HMLR that a registered estate is subject to a legal easement, it may enter a notice in the register in respect of that easement.[25] In that case, HMLR must give notice to the registered proprietor and to any person who appears to it to be entitled to the interest protected by the notice or whom HMLR otherwise considers appropriate.[26] However, if the registered proprietor applies for the entry of the notice, or consents to an application for such an entry, HMLR is not obliged to give notice to him.[27] HMLR is also not obliged to give notice to any person who has applied for, or consented to, the entry of the notice, nor is it so obliged if that person's name and address for service are not set out in the registered title in question.[28]

101.3 Prescriptive easements

Prescription is the acquisition of a right through long use or enjoyment (user) so that the law presumes that the right was lawfully granted. There are three methods of acquiring an easement by prescription:

(a) at common law;
(b) by lost modern grant; and
(c) under the Prescription Act 1832.

Whichever method is relied on, the user must have been exercised:

(a) for at least 20 years;
(b) as of right, i.e. without force, without secrecy and without permission;
(c) by or on behalf of a freehold owner against another freehold owner, so that where the burdened land is occupied by a tenant, the user must normally have started before the tenancy began; and
(d) continuously, with no long, unexplained periods of non-user. Where the claim is made under the Prescription Act 1832, a break is not treated as an

'interruption' in user for the purposes of that Act until acquiesced in for one year.

In addition, the right claimed must be one that could have been lawfully granted. This point was considered by the House of Lords in *Bakewell Management Ltd v Brandwood*.[29] Consequently, if the right could not have been lawfully granted by deed (for example a right to pollute a river contrary to a statutory prohibition), then it cannot be acquired by prescription.

LPA 1925, s 193(4) makes it a criminal offence to drive a vehicle over a common. Road Traffic Act 1988, s 34 makes it a criminal offence to drive a motor vehicle over land that is not a road and that is a restricted byway or over which a public footpath or bridleway runs. However, both offences are only committed if driving over the land is 'without lawful authority'. Since a right to drive over the land concerned *could* in most cases have been lawfully granted, it can in those cases be acquired by prescription.

A prescriptive easement over a registered estate does not have to be completed by registration to take effect at law and it will subsist for the benefit of any registered or unregistered estate to which it is appurtenant, notwithstanding that it is not the subject of an entry in the register. However, its validity will only be guaranteed for registration purposes if it is registered as appurtenant to a registered estate.

An application for registration of the benefit of a prescriptive easement may be made in either form FR1 at the time of an application for first registration of the benefiting estate;[30] or form AP1 at any time subsequently.[31] If the burdened land is registered, the title number must be given in the application form. Where the application is only to note the burden of an easement in the register of a registered burdened estate (for example where the benefiting estate is unregistered), the application should be made in form AN1 for entry of an agreed notice or form UN1 for entry of a unilateral notice, as appropriate.[32]

The application must be accompanied by satisfactory supporting evidence, normally in the form of a statement of truth (which may be in form ST4 in LRR 2003, Sch 1) or statutory declaration by the applicant and any predecessors in title setting out the relevant details of the user of the easement claimed, for the requisite period of 20 years or more (and a certified copy of each, if the applicant wishes for the original to be returned). If the title to the applicant's estate is unregistered, he should lodge evidence of his title. Similarly, the applicant should lodge evidence of title in respect of the burdened estate if that is unregistered. If an inspection of the land is necessary, an additional fee to cover the cost of this will also be payable.

If HMLR completes the application, the register entries will depend upon whether both the benefiting estate and burdened estate are registered or only one of them is registered. Also, where the burdened estate is unregistered, whether satisfactory evidence of title to it has been lodged.

Where both the benefiting estate and the burdened estate are registered, HMLR will give notice of the application to the registered proprietor and any registered chargee of the burdened title. If HMLR does not receive any objection, it will register the benefit of the easement as appurtenant to the benefiting title and enter a notice of the burden in the burdened title.

Where the benefiting estate is registered but the burdened estate is unregistered, if the applicant lodges evidence of title to the burdened estate and the address of the freehold owner, HMLR will give notice of the application to the freehold owner and any other person who may have an interest in the burdened estate. If HMLR does not receive any objection, it will register the benefit of the easement as appurtenant to the benefiting estate. However, if (as may often be the case) the applicant is not able to lodge evidence of title to the burdened estate and the address of the freehold owner, HMLR is likely to make only a note in the register to the effect that the applicant claims the benefit of the easement.[33] This entry will be in the following form:

> The registered proprietor claims that the land has the benefit of a right [*terms of right as claimed by claimant*]. The right claimed is not included in this registration. The claim is supported by [*dates and details of statement(s) of truth or statutory declaration(s) and who has made them*].

Where the burdened estate is registered but the benefiting estate is unregistered, HMLR will give notice of the application to the registered proprietor and any registered chargee of the burdened estate. If HMLR does not receive any objection, it will enter a notice of the burden in the burdened estate in the appropriate form, depending upon whether the application is for an agreed notice or a unilateral notice.

Where the benefit of a prescriptive easement is entered in the register of a registered benefiting estate, the entry will indicate that the right was acquired through long user and will refer to the statement(s) of truth or statutory declaration(s) lodged in support of the application, which will be open to inspection and copying.

If HMLR receives a valid objection in response to a notice of an application which cannot be disposed of by agreement, the matter will have to be dealt with in accordance with LRA 2002, s 73.[34]

101.4 Unregistered legal easements which override registered dispositions

Although all legal easements override first registration, the position is not the same for registered dispositions. A legal easement (not being one registered under the CRA 1965) overrides a registered disposition only if:

(a) at the time of the disposition it is within the actual knowledge of the person to whom the disposition is made; or
(b) at the time of the disposition it would have been obvious on a reasonably careful inspection of the land over which the easement is exercisable; or
(c) the person entitled to the easement proves that it has been exercised in the period of one year ending with the day of the disposition.[35]

However, any easement which was an overriding interest immediately before 13 October 2003, but which would satisfy the above if created on or after 13 October 2003, continues to be an overriding interest.[36] For a period of 3 years beginning on 13 October 2003, any unregistered legal easement overrode a registered disposition.[37] An unregistered easement over registered land arising on or after 13 October 2003 is a legal easement only if it is an implied or prescriptive easement; the grant of an easement which constitutes a registrable disposition will be equitable unless completed by registration.[38]

A person applying to register a registrable disposition of a registered estate must provide information to HMLR in form DI about any legal easements falling within LRA 2002, Sch 3, para 3 which are within his actual knowledge and affect the estate to which the application relates.[39] The applicant must produce to HMLR any documentary evidence of the existence of any such legal easements as is under his control. HMLR may enter a notice in the register in respect of any such legal easements.[40]

101.5 Extinguishment of easements

When an easement is referred to in the register of title and has been extinguished, an appropriate application may be made for the relevant entry or entries to be removed. Extinguishment may arise where, for example, there has been a deed of release, or through unity of ownership of both the benefiting and burdened estates, or through abandonment. The application should be accompanied by evidence to satisfy HMLR that the easement has been extinguished.

Where the benefit of the easement has been registered in a registered benefiting title, the application should be made in form AP1; otherwise (where only the burden has been noted in the register of a registered burdened title) the application should be in form CN1 (for cancellation of an agreed notice), form UN2 (for removal of a unilateral notice) or form UN4 (for cancellation of a unilateral notice) as appropriate.[41]

101.6 Related topics

For:

(a) equitable easements, see 62 Equitable Easements;
(b) profits à prendre, see 139 Profits à Prendre;
(c) easements in leases, see 98.14 Easements in leases;
(d) rights to light and air, see 158 Rights of Light and Air.

---

1 *Re Ellenborough Park* [1956] Ch 131.
2 For a discussion on this, see *Regency Villas Title Ltd and Others v Diamond Resorts (Europe) Ltd and Another* [2018] UKSC 57.
3 (1879) LR 12 Ch D 31.
4 LPA 1925, s 1(2)(a).
5 LRA 2002, ss 11(3) and 12(3).
6 LRR 2003, r 33(1).
7 See 101.3 Prescriptive easements.
8 LRR 2003, r 33(2).
9 LRA 2002, ss 11(4)(a) and 12(4)(a) and (b).
10 LRR 2003, r 35.
11 See 128.4 Duty to disclose overriding interests.
12 LRR 2003, r 28(4).
13 LRA 2002, s 27(2)(d) and (7).
14 LRA 2002, Sch 2, para 7.
15 LRA 2002, s 59(1).
16 LRR 2003, r 13.
17 LRR 2003, r 90.
18 LRR 2003, r 72(4) and (5).
19 See 84 Identity Evidence.
20 See 168 Stamp Duty Land Tax and/or 94 Land Transaction Tax.
21 See 67 Fees.
22 LRR 2003, r 72C(3).
23 LRR 2003, r 72C(2).
24 LRR 2003, r 73A(1)(a).
25 LRA 2002, s 37.
26 LRR 2003, r 89(1).
27 LRR 2003, r 89(2).
28 LRR 2003, r 89(3).
29 [2004] UKHL 14.

30 LRR 2003, r 33.
31 LRR 2003, r 73A.
32 See 119.1 Agreed notice or 119.3 Unilateral notice, as appropriate.
33 LRR 2003, r 73A(5).
34 See 54 Disputes.
35 LRA 2002, Sch 3, para 3.
36 LRA 2002, Sch 12, para 9.
37 LRA 2002, Sch 12, para 10.
38 LRA 2002, s 27(2)(d) and (7).
39 See 128.4 Duty to disclose overriding interests.
40 LRR 2003, r 57.
41 See 119.2 Cancellation of a notice other than a unilateral notice or a home rights notice, 119.5 Removal of a unilateral notice or 119.6 Cancellation of a unilateral notice, as appropriate.

102 LEGAL ESTATES

There can only be two legal estates in land:[1]

(a) an estate in fee simple absolute in possession (the freehold estate); and
(b) a term of years absolute (the leasehold estate).

HMLR may register these two legal estates with their own individual title if they fall within the categories of registrable estates prescribed by the LRA 2002.[2]

1 LPA 1925, s 1(1).
2 See 68.1 Legal estates capable of first registration.

103 LEGAL INTERESTS

There are five types of legal interest in land:[1]

(a) easements, rights or privileges;
(b) rentcharges;
(c) charges by way of legal mortgage;
(d) certain charges not created by an instrument (for example a statutory charge);
(e) rights of entry (for example under the terms of a lease or rentcharge).

These interests are only legal interests if they take effect at law. So, for example, an easement granted by deed may take effect at law and be a legal interest, but if granted in writing (but not by deed) it will take effect only in equity and be an equitable interest. Where it is a registrable disposition, the grant of the easement would need to be completed by registration to take effect at law; until then, it operates in equity only.[2]

Of these legal interests, only rentcharges, profits in gross and franchises can be registered with their own individual title.[3]

The remaining interests, being easements, profits appurtenant (i.e. a profit that exists for the benefit of a piece of land) and charges by way of legal mortgage, can be registered by way of entry in an existing registered title.[4]

---

1 LPA 1925, s 1(2).
2 LRA 2002, s 27.
3 See 68.1 Legal estates capable of first registration.
4 See 101 Legal Easements and 100 Legal Charges and Profits à Prendre.

104 LICENCES

Bare licences and contractual licences are not, without more, interests in land binding on a purchaser, even if he has notice.[1] For the position where, on the facts of a particular case, a constructive trust or an equity by estoppel has arisen, see 39 Constructive and Resulting Trusts and 143 Proprietary Estoppel.

Whether a licence coupled with an interest (i.e. a licence collateral to a proprietary interest) is an interest which overrides first registration and also overrides registered dispositions depends on the status of that interest. For example, where a person has a licence to enter on land in the exercise of a legal profit à prendre, the legal profit is capable of being an interest which overrides[2] and the licence has the same status. If the profit is only equitable, then neither it nor the licence has overriding status and should be protected by entry of a notice,[3] where the burdened estate is registered. The entry of a notice in respect of the profit in practice protects the licence as well, since this is irrevocable while the interest subsists. If the burdened estate is unregistered, application for registration of a caution against first registration should be made.[4] For the protection of a profit à prendre generally, see 139 Profits à Prendre.

The benefit of a licence is not in itself capable of being registered, as it is not a legal estate which can be registered as appurtenant to a registered estate.

For the purposes of the LRA 2002, land in the possession of a licensee is treated as being in the possession of the licensor.[5] This applies, for example, when establishing that the proprietor is in possession for the purposes of upgrading a possessory title under LRA 2002, s 62(5), or when establishing whether the proprietor is in possession for the purposes of LRA 2002, Sch 4, paras 3(2) or 6(2) where rectification of the register is sought.

1 *Ashburn Anstalt v W J Arnold and Co* [1989] Ch 1.
2 Under LRA 2002, Sch 1, para 3 or Sch 3, para 3.
3 See 119.1 Agreed notice or 119.3 Unilateral notice.
4 See 25 Cautions Against First Registration.
5 LRA 2002, s 131.

105 LIMITED LIABILITY PARTNERSHIPS

A limited liability partnership (LLP) incorporated in England and Wales or in Scotland under the Limited Liability Partnerships Act 2000 has full powers to deal with land. It is a body corporate with a legal personality separate from that of its members and is registered at Companies House. The name of an LLP must end with one of the following expressions or abbreviations: limited liability partnership, llp or LLP or (being the Welsh equivalents) partneriaeth atebolrwydd cyfyngedig, pac, or PAC. The Limited Liability Partnerships Act (Northern Ireland) 2002 applied to LLPs incorporated in Northern Ireland, which are registered at Companies House in Belfast. However, as a result of the Companies Act 2006, the Limited Liability Partnerships Act 2000 now also applies to LLPs incorporated in Northern Ireland. A UK LLP is one incorporated in the United Kingdom under the Limited Liability Partnerships Act 2000 or the Limited Liability Partnerships Act (Northern Ireland) 2002.

An LLP should not be confused with a partnership or a limited partnership.[1]

105.1 Registration of a UK limited liability partnership as proprietor

Where a UK LLP applies to be registered as proprietor of a registered estate or a registered charge, the application must state the LLP's registered number. In practice the registered number is usually stated in a prescribed form of disposition or application, such as panel 5 of a transfer in form TR1 or in panel 6 of application form FR1. The registered number commences 'OC' for LLPs registered in England and Wales, 'SO' for LLPs registered in Scotland, or 'NILLP' for LLPs registered in Northern Ireland. The LLP itself, not its individual members, will be registered as proprietor. The registered number is included in the entry of the LLP as proprietor in the proprietorship register or charges register.[2]

105.2 Registration of charge created by a UK limited liability partnership

In the case of a UK LLP, registration of the charge at Companies House within 21 days of its creation should precede an application for registration to HMLR. Registration of a charge of registered land at Companies House alone is not sufficient – it should also be completed by registration to take effect at law.[3] Conversely, registration of a charge in a debenture at HMLR does not remove the need for it to be registered under the Companies Act 2006.

Although LRA 2002, s 121 allows the Lord Chancellor to make rules about the transmission, by HMLR to the Registrar of Companies, of applications for registration of charges under the Companies Act 2006, no such rules have yet been made. The application to Companies House must therefore be made separately. Since 6 April 2013, such application may be made electronically, in which case the certificate of registration will be issued electronically. It is still possible to apply in paper form and the certificate of registration will be issued in paper form; the charge itself will no longer be stamped with the Companies House stamp.

When making an application for registration of a charge created by a UK LLP, the applicant must produce to HMLR the certificate issued under Companies Act 2006, s 859I that the charge has been registered at Companies House under s 859A,[4] together with a Companies House official copy of the charge or a certificate or confirmation in writing by the lender or a conveyancer that the charge lodged for registration is identical to the copy charge filed at Companies House and is the charge to which the certificate of registration relates.

If the certificate is not produced, HMLR must enter a note in the register stating that no evidence of registration of the charge in accordance with Companies Act 2006, s 859A has been lodged. Similar provisions applied before 6 April 2013 in relation to Companies Act 2006, s 860 or s 878 and, before 1 October 2009, in relation to Companies Act 1985, s 395 or s 410, with any necessary note in the register referring to the relevant section. The note reflects the fact that where the charge is not registered with Companies House within the prescribed period, the charge is void against the liquidator or administrator of the LLP and any creditor of the LLP.

An LLP, like a limited company, may create a debenture.[5]

105.3 Execution of deeds by limited liability partnerships

Like a limited company, an LLP can execute a deed under seal or under the provisions of Companies Act 2006, s 44. In transfers of registered land and other deeds whose form is prescribed, the attestation clause in Form F(i) or F(ii) of LRR 2003, Sch 9 must be used when an LLP executes a deed. If, instead, an LLP uses a seal, HMLR can accept this provided the attestation clause is in similar form to Form C in LRR 2003, Sch 9, but with two members witnessing the affixing of the seal.

105.4 Conversion of a partnership or corporate body to a limited liability partnership

Under the Limited Liability Partnerships Act 2000, existing partnerships and companies may choose to convert to LLP status. Any two or more persons associated for carrying on business can become an LLP. An LLP is formed when those persons incorporate as an LLP by registration at Companies House. This is a similar process to company incorporation.

When an existing corporate body or partnership becomes an LLP, property of the former corporate body or partnership which is to be held by the LLP will need to be transferred to the newly formed LLP. If the property comprises a registered estate or charge, it should be transferred in the normal way to the LLP. If the estate is unregistered and the transfer triggers compulsory first registration, the appropriate application should be made. If the transfer does not trigger compulsory first registration, a voluntary application may still be made.[6]

105.5 Dissolution of a limited liability partnership

Under the Limited Liability Partnerships (Application of Companies Act 2006) Regulations 2009 (SI 2009/1804), Companies Act 2006, s 1012 is modified to apply to a UK LLP. On dissolution, therefore, all the property and rights of a UK LLP (other than property held on trust for another) are deemed to be bona vacantia and will belong to the Crown or to the Duchy of Lancaster or the Duke of Cornwall, as the case may be.[7] Where a corporation which is the proprietor of a registered estate or registered charge has been dissolved, HMLR may enter a note of that fact in the proprietorship register or charges register, as appropriate.[8]

105.6 Registration of an overseas limited liability partnership as proprietor

For details of the evidence needed to register an overseas LLP as proprietor, see 37.2 Registering entities which are not a UK company as proprietor.

---

1 See 130 Partnerships and 107 Limited Partnerships.
2 LRR 2003, r 8(1)(b).
3 LRA 2002, s 27(2)(f).
4 LRR 2003, r 111.
5 See 49 Debentures.
6 See 68 First Registration.
7 Companies Act 2006, s 1012 as from 1 October 2006; previously Companies Act 1985, s 654.
8 LRR 2003, r 185.

106 LIMITED OWNER'S CHARGE

A limited owner's charge arises where a tenant for life or statutory owner of settled land discharges IHT or any other liabilities to which special priority is given by statute. The charge may be overreached by a disposition under SLA 1925, s 72(3) or LPA 1925, s 2(2) and (3). As to settled land generally, see 162 Settlements.

No notice may be entered in the register in respect of a limited owner's charge.[1] The relevant form of protection for a limited owner's charge is the entry of a restriction in Forms G, H or I, as appropriate, to ensure capital money arising under the settlement is paid to at least two trustees or a trust corporation. If there is no such restriction entered in the proprietorship register, the person having the benefit of the limited owner's charge is entitled to apply for entry of the appropriate restriction.[2]

HMLR must give notice of an application for a restriction to the proprietor of the registered estate or charge concerned if it has not been made by or with his consent or a person entitled to be registered as such proprietor.[3]

A restriction does not confer any priority. However, it prevents an entry being made in the register relating to any disposition, or a disposition of a specified kind, unless the terms of the restriction have (where applicable) been complied with.

If applying for entry of a restriction in Forms G, H or I, the person having the benefit of a limited owner's charge should deliver to HMLR the usual documents required.[4]

If the application is made by a person who claims that he has a sufficient interest in the making of the entry, the statement in panel 12 or a conveyancer's certificate in panel 13 of form RX1 must be completed, setting out details of the limited owner's charge and confirming that 'the applicant's interest is an interest in settled land as specified in Schedule 7 paragraph 3(2) of the Land Registration Rules 2003 (SI 2003/1417)'. Any supporting documents should be listed in panel 5 of form RX1 or in a separate form DL.

Panel 9 of form RX1 should set out the wording of the restriction in Forms G, H or I, as appropriate. The wording of Forms G, H and I is set out in Appendix IV.

Form G is applicable where the tenant for life is the registered proprietor of the settled land and there are trustees of the settlement.

Form H is applicable where the statutory owners are the trustees of the settlement and registered proprietors of the settled land.

Form I is applicable where the tenant for life is the registered proprietor of the settled land and there are no trustees of the settlement.

A restriction in Forms G, H or I in LRR 2003, Sch 4 does not require the approval of HMLR under LRA 2002, s 43(3).

---

1 LRA 2002, s 33(a).
2 LRR 2003, Sch 7, para 3(2).
3 LRA 2002, s 45.
4 See 153.1 Application for entry of restriction.

107 LIMITED PARTNERSHIPS

A partnership is the relationship which subsists between persons carrying on a business in common with a view to profit.[1] A limited partnership is a special type of partnership set up under the Limited Partnership Act 1907. It enables a person, who has contributed financially to the partnership but is not involved with the management of it, to become a 'sleeping' partner with only a limited liability to creditors of the partnership. In a limited partnership, there must be at least one partner whose liability is not limited in this way. A limited partnership therefore consists of one or more 'general' partners, who are liable for all debts and obligations of the firm, and one or more 'limited' partners, who contribute a sum or sums of money as capital, or property valued at a stated amount. Limited partners are not liable for the debts and obligations of the partnership beyond the amount contributed.[2]

Companies House maintains an index and a register of limited partnerships. When a limited partnership is formed, it must be registered with Companies House, otherwise it will be regarded as a general partnership and both the general and the limited partners will be equally responsible for any debts and obligations of the partnership. A limited partnership registered at Companies House has a registration number with the prefix 'LP'.

A limited partnership created under the Limited Partnership Act 1907 is not a separate legal entity. It does not have the corporate status of an LLP incorporated under the Limited Liability Partnerships Act 2000.[3] Different principles apply to a limited partnership in Scotland, and to overseas limited partnerships.

The Limited Partnership Act 1907 was amended by the Legislative Reform (Private Fund Limited Partnerships) Order 2017 (SI 2017/514) to introduce a new form of limited partnership: the private fund limited partnership. This is for use by private investment funds (i.e. funds that may not be promoted to retail consumers, for example private equity and venture capital funds) that are structured as a limited partnership, and is intended to reduce the administrative and financial burdens previously affecting private funds that use a limited partnership structure. The designation as a private fund limited partnership on original registration of the limited partnership, or the change from an existing limited partnership to a private fund limited partnership, has effect from the date shown in the certificate of registration (or designation) issued by Companies House.[4]

107.1 Registration and entry of restriction(s)

A transfer or charge to a limited partnership must be to the individual partners or general partner(s), not to the partnership name. If there are more than four partners or general partners, the transfer should be to four of them to hold the legal estate on trust for the partnership. No reference to the partnership is made in the register, nor is its registration number as a limited partnership set out in the register. However, the proprietors may specifically apply to have the limited partnership's name entered in the proprietorship register. This will appear in the following format:

> [*Name*] of [*address*] as General Partner of [*name of limited partnership*].

In the case of a registered estate in land, as the beneficial interests are held under a tenancy in common, HMLR will enter a restriction in Form A in the proprietorship register.[5] The wording of Form A is set out in Appendix IV. In the case of other registered estates, the proprietors should make an application for entry of such a restriction.[6]

The partners may also, if they wish, apply for entry of a restriction in Form Q. The wording of Form Q is set out in Appendix IV.

If the partnership deed contains specific provisions requiring any consent to be obtained to a disposition, application should be made for entry of a restriction in Form B.[7] The wording of Form B is set out in Appendix IV.

An application for entry of a restriction should normally be made in form RX1. However, form RX1 does not need to be used if the application is for a standard form restriction and is contained in either the 'additional provisions' panel of a prescribed form of transfer or assent, or in clause LR13 of a prescribed clauses lease (or any other lease containing clauses LR1 to LR14 of LRR 2003, Sch 1A).[8] A restriction in a standard form contained in LRR 2003, Sch 4 does not require the approval of HMLR to the terms of the restriction under LRA 2002, s 43(3).

---

1 Partnership Act 1890, s 1
2 Limited Partnership Act 1907, s 4(2).
3 See 105 Limited Liability Partnerships.
4 Limited Partnership Act 1907, s 8C.
5 LRA 2002, s 44(1).
6 LRR 2003, r 94(2A).
7 TLATA, s 8(2) and LRR 2003, r 94(4).
8 LRR 2003, r 92(7).

108 LIQUIDATORS

Where a company which is the registered proprietor of a registered estate or registered charge is in liquidation, its liquidator may apply for an entry to be made in the register as to his appointment. HMLR will not make such an entry automatically. A specific application is required. The application must be supported by evidence of the liquidator's appointment.[1] Alternatively, a liquidator may provide evidence of his appointment to a purchaser or other disponee, which should be lodged with the application for registration of the transfer or other disposition.

108.1 Entry of notice of liquidator's appointment

The liquidator should deliver to HMLR:

(a) an application in form AP1;
(b) evidence of appointment;[2] and
(c) the fee payable.[3]

When notice of the appointment is entered in the register, the liquidator may also make an application for entry of any appropriate restriction(s) required.

108.2 Evidence of appointment

The evidence required varies depending on the type of liquidation. The same evidence is required whether for entry of a notice of the liquidator's appointment or for the registration of a transfer or other disposition by him.

108.2.1 Creditors' voluntary winding up

The following documents are required:

(a) a certified copy of the resolution passed at the company's meeting that the company be wound up and appointing a liquidator; and
(b) one of the following:

    (i) for appointments made before 8 December 2017:

        (1) a certified copy of the notice of the liquidator's appointment in Companies House form 600; or
        (2) a certified copy of the resolution passed at the creditor's meeting appointing the liquidator under IA 1986, s 100(1); or

    (ii) for appointments made on or after 8 December 2017:

        (1) a certified copy of the liquidator's appointment in Companies House form 600CH;
        (2) a certificate by the liquidator appointed at the company's meeting (or his conveyancer) that the meeting of the creditors was duly held in accordance with IA 1986, s 98(1) at which either the appointment of the liquidator by the company's meeting was confirmed or no resolution nominating a liquidator was passed;[4]
        (3) a copy of the creditors' decision notice (certified as a true copy by the liquidator or their conveyancer); or
        (4) a certificate by the liquidator or their conveyancer that the liquidator's appointment was confirmed by a creditors' qualifying decision procedure or deemed consent procedure.

108.2.2 Members' voluntary winding up

The following documents are required:

(a) either:

  (i) a certificate by the secretary of the company (or his conveyancer) or by the liquidator (or his conveyancer) that a statutory declaration of solvency complying with the requirements of IA 1986, s 89 has been filed with Companies House; or
  (ii) Companies House form LIQ1; and

(b) one of:

  (i) a certified copy of the resolution passed by the general meeting of the company appointing the liquidators (under IA 1986, s 91(1));
  (ii) a copy of the notice of the liquidator's appointment in Companies House form 600 where the appointment was made before 8 December 2017; or
  (iii) a copy of the notice of the liquidator's appointment in Companies House form 600CH where the appointment was made on or after 8 December 2017.

108.2.3 Winding up by the court

The following documents are required:

(a) a certified copy of the winding-up order; and
(b) either:

  (i) a certified copy of the order of the court appointing the liquidator; or
  (ii) a certified copy of the appointment of the liquidator by the Secretary of State; or
  (iii) a certified copy of the resolution passed at the contributories' meeting appointing the liquidator, and a certificate by the liquidator appointed at the contributories' meeting (or his conveyancer) that the contributories' meeting either confirmed the appointment of the liquidator or did not pass a resolution nominating a liquidator;[5] or
  (iv) a certified copy of the resolution passed at the creditors' meeting appointing the liquidator (under IA 1986, s 139(2))[6] where the appointment was made before 8 December 2017; or

(v) a copy of the notice of the liquidator's appointment in Companies House form 600CH where the appointment was made on or after 8 December 2017.

108.3 Dispositions by a liquidator

If a transfer or other disposition of a registered estate or registered charge by or in favour of a company in liquidation is lodged for registration (and notice of the appointment has not previously been entered, in the case of a disposition by the company), evidence of the liquidator's appointment as set out above will be required. This will also apply in relation to an application for first registration. A disposition by a company in liquidation should be executed by the liquidator by either:

(a) affixing the company seal and signing the document to attest that the seal has been affixed in his presence; or
(b) by signing the document as a deed in the name and on behalf of the company.

108.4 Disclaimer by a liquidator

A liquidator may disclaim any onerous property comprised in the insolvent estate and is entitled to do so even if he has taken possession of the property or attempted to sell it.[7] In the case of land, it is normally a leasehold estate which is disclaimed, although disclaimer of a registered freehold estate is also possible. The notice operates to determine the rights, interests and liabilities of the company in respect of the property. It does not, however, otherwise affect the rights or liabilities of any other person. The disclaimer of a lease is not effective unless a copy of it has been served on any sub-tenant or mortgagee claiming under the company and either no application for a vesting order is made to the court within a period of 14 days from the day on which the last copy notice was served, or the court has directed that the disclaimer is to take effect.[8]

Any person claiming an interest in the disclaimed property may apply to the court for a vesting order vesting the property in him or in a trustee on his behalf.[9] A person who is under a liability in respect of a disclaimed property, which liability will not be discharged by the disclaimer, may also apply for a vesting order.

If no vesting order is made, a lease which has been disclaimed vests in the landlord and so will determine. If no vesting order is made, a freehold which has been disclaimed vests in the Crown or the relevant Royal Duchy by escheat.

The liquidator must send to HMLR a copy of the notice of disclaimer of a registered estate or of a registered charge as soon as reasonably practicable after it has been authenticated (i.e. signed) and dated by the liquidator.[10] No formal application in form AP1 is necessary at this stage and no fee is payable. HMLR will make the following note in the register:

> A notice dated [*date*] by the liquidator of [*name of company*] stated that the [registered estate in this title] *or* [registered charge dated [*date*] referred to above] was being disclaimed under section 178 of the Insolvency Act 1986.

A liquidator who has disclaimed a registered lease may apply for formal notice of the disclaimer to be entered in the register with or without an application to close the title under LRR 2003, r 79. Where the disclaimed lease is unregistered but has been noted against a registered title, application may be made to cancel notice of the unregistered lease in the landlord's title.

108.4.1 Registered disclaimed lease

Where a liquidator has disclaimed a registered lease, an applicant should deliver to HMLR:

(a) an application in form AP1;
(b) a copy of the notice of disclaimer, unless the note referred to above already appears in the register;
(c) evidence of the appointment of the liquidator;[11]
(d) the original lease, or a satisfactory explanation of why it cannot be lodged; and
(e) the fee payable.[12]

HMLR will serve notice of the application on the registered proprietor of the freehold or other superior leasehold title in which the disclaimed lease is noted, on any chargee or sub-tenant and on any other party whose interest would be affected by closure of the title.

If there is no evidence of any registered or noted charge, sub-lease or other third-party rights affecting the disclaimed leasehold title, or satisfactory evidence is supplied that every such interest has also come to an end, HMLR will close the leasehold title and cancel any notice of the lease in the landlord's registered title.

However, as determination of a lease by disclaimer does not affect the rights and liabilities acquired before the disclaimer by persons other than the tenant, HMLR will not close the registered leasehold title if there is a registered or noted charge in the disclaimed leasehold title, unless the application includes an application either to discharge the registered charge or to cancel the entry of the noted charge; or evidence that the chargee's application for a vesting order has been dismissed (so that the chargee is excluded from all interest in the property); or evidence of forfeiture of the lease.

If the registered leasehold title cannot be closed (or the application is only for a formal notice of the disclaimer to be entered in the register), HMLR will make the following entries in the property register of the disclaimed leasehold title:

> This lease was disclaimed by the liquidator of the registered proprietor on [*date*] pursuant to section 178 of the Insolvency Act 1986.

A restriction will at the same time be entered in the proprietorship register, to the effect that no disposition of the registered estate is to be completed by registration.

HMLR will also add the following note to the notice of the disclaimed lease in the landlord's title:

> This lease was disclaimed by the liquidator of the registered proprietor on [*date*]. The registered leasehold title has not been closed because there is a subsisting [registered] *or* [noted] charge in favour of [*name*] dated [*date*].

The leasehold title for a disclaimed lease may be closed if there is no registered or noted charge but there is a registered sub-lease or other third-party rights noted in title, in which case appropriate entries referring to the disclaimer will be made in the landlord's title and any registered sub-leasehold title.

108.4.2 Unregistered disclaimed lease

Where the disclaimed lease has not been registered but has been noted against a registered title, an applicant should deliver to HMLR:

(a) an application in form CN1, panel 9 being completed by entering details of the lease and placing an 'X' against 'disclaimer';
(b) the original lease or a satisfactory explanation of why it cannot be lodged;
(c) the deeds and documents relating to the leasehold title;
(d) a copy of the notice of disclaimer, unless the note referred to above already appears in the register;
(e) evidence of the appointment of the liquidator;[13] and
(f) the fee payable.[14]

Where there is no evidence of any charge, sub-lease or of other third party-rights affecting the disclaimed noted lease, then the notice of the lease in the landlord's title may be cancelled.

Where there is evidence of a continuing charge, sub-lease or other third-party rights affecting the disclaimed noted lease, the notice of the lease cannot be cancelled, but appropriate entries referring to the disclaimer will be made in the landlord's title and any registered sub-leasehold title.

108.4.3 Vesting order relating to registered disclaimed lease

Where the property has been disclaimed and an order has been made by the court vesting the property in some other person, an applicant should deliver to HMLR:

(a) an application in form AP1;
(b) an office copy of the court order;[15] and
(c) the fee payable.[16]

108.4.4 Disclaimer of registered freehold estate

In the unusual situation where a registered freehold estate has been disclaimed, application may be made for formal notice of the disclaimer to be entered in the register of the freehold title.[17] The requirements are similar to those where application is made to close a registered leasehold title following disclaimer.[18] HMLR will not close the registered title unless and until it registers either a grant from the Crown of a new freehold estate or a transfer from one of the Royal Duchies.[19] In the interim, it will make the following entry in the property register:

> The registered estate in this title has determined on disclaimer by the liquidator of the registered proprietor on [*date*] pursuant to section 178 of the Insolvency Act 1985.

HMLR will also enter a restriction to prevent any further dealings with the estate.

If the escheated freehold title is subject to a registered lease or other inferior interest, the following entry will be made in the property register for that title:

> The [*landlord's (or as the case may be)*] registered estate has determined on disclaimer by the liquidator on [*date*] pursuant to section 178 of the Insolvency Act 1986 but the entries relating to the estate continue in the register.

HMLR may qualify the above entries where there is some doubt as to whether escheat has in fact taken place.[20]

108.5 Dissolution

On dissolution, all the property and rights of a company (other than property held on trust for another) are deemed to be bona vacantia and will belong to the

Crown or to the Duchy of Lancaster or the Duke of Cornwall, as the case may be.[21] Where a company which is the proprietor of a registered estate or registered charge has been dissolved, HMLR may enter a note of that fact in the proprietorship register or charges register, as appropriate.[22]

108.6 Liquidation of foreign companies

In the case of an overseas liquidation, the liquidation of a foreign company in its country of incorporation is recognised by English law. An application to register a disposition made by or on behalf of such a company must be made in form AP1, accompanied by appropriate evidence of the liquidation and of its effect. This may include:

(a) certified copies of the court orders or other documents relied upon including the appointment of the foreign liquidator; and
(b) the written opinion of a lawyer qualified to practise company law in the country of incorporation as to the nature and effect of the proceedings on the company and as to the powers of the liquidator or other person representing the company, including the power to execute documents on behalf of the company.

An applicant must supply certified translations of any documents not in English or Welsh.

In the case of a liquidation in the United Kingdom, a foreign company that has been carrying on business in the United Kingdom may be wound up as an unregistered company under the IA 1986 even though it may already have been dissolved or otherwise ceased to exist under the law of its country of incorporation. The winding up will be by order of the court and the relevant evidence specified in 108.2.3 Winding-up by the court would need to be lodged.

As explained in 37.4 Dispositions by non-UK companies, a specified insolvency practitioner may lodge a certificate in form OE1 in specified circumstances. However, at the time of writing, the secondary legislation setting out who comprises a specified insolvency practitioner and what the specified circumstances are has not been passed.

---

1 LRR 2003, r 184.

2 See 108.2 Evidence of appointment.

3 See 67 Fees.

4 If the general meeting of the company and the creditors' meeting nominate different liquidators, the person nominated by the creditors will act unless an order is made by

the court on an application made within 7 days of the creditors' nomination (IA 1986, ss 100(2) and (3)).

5 If the creditors' and the contributories' meetings nominate different liquidators, the person nominated by the creditors will act unless an order is made by the court on an application made within 7 days of the creditors' nomination (IA 1986, ss 139(3) and (4)).

6 A copy of the liquidator's appointment in Companies House form 600 is acceptable.

7 IA 1986, s 178.

8 IA 1986, s 179.

9 IA 1986, s 181.

10 IR 2016, r 91.2(3)(b).

11 See 108.2 Evidence of appointment.

12 See 67 Fees.

13 See 108.2 Evidence of appointment.

14 See 67 Fees.

15 LRR 2003, r 161(2).

16 See 67 Fees.

17 LRR 2003, rr 79 and 173.

18 See 108.4.1 Registered disclaimed lease.

19 See 21 Bona Vacantia and Escheat.

20 LRR 2003, r 173(2).

21 Companies Act 2006, s 1012 as from 1 October 2006; previously Companies Act 1985, s 654.

22 LRR 2003, r 185. See 21 Bona Vacantia and Escheat.

109 LOCAL LAND CHARGES

109.1 Introduction

Local Land Charges Act 1975, ss 1 and 2 define what comprises a local land charge. Broadly, they are charges, restrictions or obligations affecting land which are enforceable by certain public authorities and are binding on successive owners of the land affected. Common types of local land charges include:

(a) conditions imposed in a planning permission;
(b) listed buildings;
(c) conservation areas;
(d) tree preservation orders;
(e) planning and enforcement notices; and
(f) light obstruction notices.

Previously, registers of local land charges were maintained by the local authority for the area in which the affected property was situated. However, Infrastructure

Act 2015, s 34 and Sch 5 make provision for HMLR to become the sole registering authority and holder of a local land charges register and index, which may be kept in electronic form. The intention is that, ultimately, there will be a single local land charges register and index for the whole of England and Wales, and that it will be held in electronic form.

109.2 Migration of the local land charges register to HMLR

Infrastructure Act 2015 provides that HMLR may take over responsibility for the individual registers, held by each local authority, on a 'staged' basis, by means of the service of a notice by HMLR upon a local authority.[1] The notice will specify the date upon which HMLR is to assume responsibility.

At the time of writing, HMLR has assumed responsibility for some, but not all, local authority areas. The HMLR Local Land Charges Programme website[2] contains a list of the local authority areas which have migrated to HMLR and the date of such migration.

Once HMLR takes on responsibility for the local land charges register for an area:

(a) the changes to the Land Charges Act 1975 made by the Infrastructure Act 2015 will come into effect for that area; and
(b) the Local Land Charges Rules 2018 (SI 2018/273) will replace the Local Land Charges Rules 1977 (SI 1977/985) for that area.

HMLR's *Practice guide 79: Local Land Charges* contains full details of:

(a) registration of local land charges;
(b) searches of the local land charges register;
(c) obtaining copy documents; and
(d) rights to compensation for mistakes in the register.

This is available to view and download at the HMLR website.[3]

109.3 Local land charges and the register of title

A local land charge is an unregistered interest which overrides both first registration and registered dispositions.[4] This includes a local land charge the status of which as an overriding interest under the LRA 1925 was preserved by Local Land Charges Act 1975, s 19(3).[5] The duty to disclose information about interests which override on an application for first registration or on an application to register a registrable disposition does not apply to information about local land charges.[6]

Although a local land charge is an interest which overrides, it may be protected by entry of a notice or restriction. If it is protected by a notice, it ceases to be an interest which overrides, and does not revert to being an overriding interest if the notice is subsequently cancelled.[7] In practice, a local land charge is usually registered in the local land charges registers but is not entered in the register of title at HMLR.

109.4 Monetary charges

Some local land charges create monetary charges. These are charges on a property imposed under various statutes, such as Public Health Act 1936, s 291, to recover costs incurred by a local authority. For example, the costs of cleansing and clearing land, or repairing or demolishing buildings, structures and services, which are a hazard to health or safety. Such a charge is a statutory charge and, although not created by a deed executed by the owner, takes effect as a charge by way of legal mortgage when registered as a local land charge, but without prejudice to its priority.[8]

A charge over registered land which is a local land charge may be protected by entry of a notice, but may be realised only if the charge is registered.[9] An application to register the title to such a charge must be supported by evidence of the charge.[10] As there will be no formal deed of charge, such evidence may be the declaration in writing creating the charge, where that is required by legislation, or a sealed resolution of the local authority which recites the facts giving rise to the charge and resolves that application is made for its registration.

When applying for substantive registration of a monetary local land charge, the applicant authority should deliver to HMLR:

(a) an application in form AP1;
(b) documentary evidence of the charge or a certified copy of it; and
(c) the fee payable.[11]

If the statutory charge has effect to postpone a charge which is already entered in the register or is the basis for an entry in the register, the applicant authority must also deliver form SC with the application.[12] The usual basis for claiming priority over an existing charge is that a statutory provision expressly provides that the charge is a charge on the premises and on all estates and interests in it (and is thus a charge on a prior registered charge); or that the charge secures the cost of works which have resulted in an improvement to the property, which has benefited not only the proprietor of the registered estate, but also others who have an interest in it.

Where the applicant satisfies HMLR that the statutory charge has the priority specified in form SC, HMLR must make an entry in the charges register showing that priority.[13] If the applicant does not satisfy HMLR that the statutory charge has that priority, but HMLR considers that the applicant has an arguable case, HMLR may make an entry in the charges register that the applicant claims that priority.[14] In either case, HMLR must give notice to the registered proprietor of any existing registered charge and any person who appears to HMLR to be entitled to a charge protected by a notice.[15] In the case of a charge protected by a notice, HMLR is obliged to serve notice only if the chargee's name and address for service appear in the register of the title in question.[16] A person who suffers loss by reason of a failure by HMLR to give such notice may be entitled to indemnity.[17]

Where an entry as to claimed priority has been made, an application may be made for the entry to be removed, or to be replaced with an entry that the statutory charge in question does have the priority specified in the form SC.[18] The applicant must provide evidence to satisfy HMLR that it should take the action sought by the applicant.[19] HMLR must serve notice of the application upon the proprietors of registered charges affected by the application.[20]

---

1 Infrastructure Act 2015, Sch 5, para 40.

2 www.gov.uk/government/publications/hm-land-registry-local-land-charges-programme/local-land-charges-programme.

3 www.gov.uk/government/collections/land-registration-practice-guides.

4 LRA 2002, Sch 1, para 6 and Sch 3, para 6.

5 LRA 2002, Sch 12, para 13.

6 LRR 2003, rr 28(2)(d) and 57(2)(c). See also 128.4 Duty to disclose overriding interests.

7 LRA 2002, ss 29(3) and 30(3).

8 Local Land Charges Act 1975, s 7.

9 LRA 2002, s 55.

10 LRR 2003, r 104.

11 See 67 Fees.

12 LRA 2002, s 50 and LRR 2003, r 105(1).

13 LRR 2003, r 105(2).

14 LRR 2003, r 105(3).

15 LRR 2003, r 106(1).

16 LRR 2003, r 106(2).

17 See 86 Indemnity.

18 LRR 2003, r 105(5).

19 LRR 2003, r 105(7).

20 LRR 2003, r 105(8).

110 LOST OR DESTROYED TITLE DEEDS

Where the unregistered title deeds have been lost or destroyed, an applicant for first registration must provide evidence to satisfy HMLR that he is:

(a) entitled to apply voluntarily for first registration under LRA 2002, s 3(2) because the unregistered legal estate sought to be registered is vested in him or he is entitled to require the estate to be vested in him; or (as the case may be)
(b) required to apply for compulsory first registration under LRA 2002, s 6(1) on the occurrence of a 'trigger' for compulsory registration listed in s 4.

The supporting evidence must also account for the absence of the deeds.[1] The evidence may consist of, or include, a statutory declaration or statement of truth (which may be in form ST3 in LRR 2003, Sch 1) setting out the facts and exhibiting any appropriate supporting documents.[2] The evidence required in each individual case will depend on the particular facts, but it will need to cover the following:

(a) the circumstances of the loss or destruction;
(b) the reconstruction of the title;
(c) possession of the estate; and
(d) evidence of identity of the applicant, where necessary.

110.1 Application for first registration

In addition to the usual documents required,[3] an applicant should deliver to HMLR evidence as to the applicant's title by way of statutory declaration(s) or statement(s) of truth (which may be in form ST3) and a certified copy of each if the applicant wishes for the original to be returned.

The applicant may be called upon to pay an additional fee to meet the cost of a survey or special enquiries.[4]

110.2 Circumstances of the loss or destruction

The evidence lodged must cover:

(a) where and by whom the deeds were held immediately before their loss or destruction;
(b) why the person in possession had custody of the deeds; for example, whether they were held for safekeeping or as security for a loan;

(c) the full circumstances of their loss or destruction;
(d) the efforts made to recover the deeds;
(e) whether or not at the time of the loss or destruction the applicant had created any mortgage, charge or lien on the property or deposited the deeds with any person, firm or body as security for money;
(f) whether the applicant is in occupation of the estate or in receipt of the rents and profits from it; and
(g) that the applicant is entitled to apply for first registration as the legal estate is vested in him or he is entitled to require it to be vested in him.

If the deeds were lost or destroyed whilst in the custody of (or being sent in the post from) a conveyancer, building society, bank or other well-known institution, the above information should normally be supplied by a member of that firm or organisation.

110.3 Reconstruction of the title

The best available secondary evidence of how title has devolved to the applicant must be produced. The nature and quality of this will vary depending on the circumstances of the individual case. Copies or drafts of lost deeds may often be obtained from solicitors or other conveyancers who acted at the time of a previous sale or purchase of the property. If the property is mortgaged, evidence of the mortgage should be included. If there is no mortgage on the property, the declaration should specifically confirm that at the time of the loss or destruction the owner had not created any mortgage, charge or lien on the land and had not deposited the deeds by way of security for money.

Where the property is leasehold, copies of the deeds may be available from the landlord, who should also be able to confirm who has paid the rent. The landlord may also have details about licences to assign, where this is a requirement of the lease.

Where the land falls within the areas covered by any of the former deeds registries for Middlesex or Yorkshire, copies of deeds or of memorials of deeds may be available from the appropriate archive service. Memorials did not, though, normally show whether the land was subject to restrictive covenants.

110.4 Possession of the estate

The applicant should also provide satisfactory evidence that since the date of acquisition he has been in actual occupation of the whole of the estate or in receipt of its rents and profits (particulars of which, supported by copies of leases, rent books or receipts, should be given) without any adverse claim. Any other relevant facts should be provided. The registrar may, if it considers it necessary, arrange for OS to inspect the land.

Evidence of possession is relevant not only in helping to satisfy HMLR that the applicant is entitled to apply for registration, but because a possessory title (which is the most commonly granted class of title in these circumstances) can only be granted where HMLR is satisfied that the applicant is in actual possession of the land or in receipt of the rents and profits from it.[5]

110.5 Evidence of identity

In some cases, HMLR may require evidence of identity. This can assist in demonstrating that the applicant does hold the legal estate and in combating property fraud. HMLR does not usually require such evidence when the application is lodged by:

(a) a conveyancer who is applying for registration because the title deeds were lost or destroyed whilst in his custody; or
(b) a major mortgage lender, where the deeds were being held as security for the lender's mortgage and were lost whilst in its custody; or
(c) a duly authorised official of a local authority, government department or nationally well-known body, where the deeds relating to its land, or land on which it holds a mortgage, were lost whilst in its custody; or
(d) a receiver or liquidator of a company, where evidence of the appointment is supplied, together with a certified copy of the mortgage or charge where the applicant is a receiver appointed under such a deed.

Where the applicant is required to provide evidence of identity, see 83 Identity Evidence.

110.6 Class of title

Where HMLR is satisfied as to the applicant's title and the circumstances of the loss or destruction, it may grant a registered title. Although each application is considered on its merits, normally HMLR will not grant absolute title (nor good leasehold title, in the case of a leasehold estate) where the loss or destruction of the deeds cannot be adequately explained. Instead, HMLR will usually grant a possessory title. An applicant may be registered with possessory title if HMLR is of the opinion that the applicant is in actual possession of the land, or in receipt of the rents and profits of the land, by virtue of the estate, and that there is no other class of title with which he may be registered.[6] If the applicant remains in possession of the registered estate for the requisite period, or if the title deeds are subsequently found, application may be made to upgrade the class of title.[7]

HMLR may enter a protective entry in the register if it considers there is a risk that the land may be subject to undisclosed restrictive covenants, easements or rentcharges. HMLR will make an entry in respect of the benefit of legal easements in the register only if the applicant has shown satisfactory evidence of title to HMLR.[8]

---

1 LRR 2003, r 27(1)(b).
2 LRR 2003, r 27(2).
3 See 68 First Registration.
4 Fee Order, r 11.
5 LRA 2002, ss 9(5) and 10(6).
6 LRA 2002, ss 9(5) and 10(6).
7 See 181 Upgrade of Class of Title.
8 LRR 2003, r 33.

111 MALADMINISTRATION

As a public body, HMLR should carry out its functions in accordance with the Principles of Good Administration published by the PHSO.[1] Failure to do so may amount to maladministration.

Examples of possible maladministration by HMLR include:

(a) failure to follow procedures laid out in the LRA 2002 or LRR 2003;
(b) departing from published practice without good reason;
(c) excessive delay;
(d) providing incorrect advice; and
(e) being, or being perceived to be, biased in favour of one party.

The most common form of alleged maladministration is excessive delay. The existence of a backlog of applications and consequent delay in processing an application is not by itself maladministration. To qualify as maladministration, the complaint must show his case has taken significantly longer than comparable applications or that HMLR has otherwise not acted in accordance with its guidance. Examples include (but are not limited to):

(a) where HMLR has failed to process an expedited application within the relevant timeframe;

(b) where HMLR has rejected an application outside the published timeframe for rejection and the rejection point could potentially have been dealt with by requisition; and
(c) where HMLR has delayed considering a response to a requisition for an unreasonable period.

111.1 Remedies for maladministration

The principal remedies for maladministration by HMLR are:

(a) an apology;
(b) compensation for any resultant financial loss; and/or
(c) where appropriate, a consolatory payment.

These are in line with guidance given by the PHSO on the appropriate remedies for maladministration.[2]

111.1.1 Compensation

If HMLR's maladministration has resulted in an applicant incurring additional costs (for example because he has incurred further legal costs determining what has occurred or re-lodging an incorrectly cancelled application), HMLR will usually reimburse such costs provided they are reasonable.

A claimant must provide evidence that:

(a) he has suffered the loss claimed;[3] and
(b) the loss complained of was caused by the relevant maladministration.

HMLR will want to be satisfied both that it was reasonable for the claimant to incur such costs and that the costs themselves are reasonable. In some instances, HMLR may ask for further evidence of the reasonableness of the sums sought. Usually, this will be a breakdown of:

(a) the additional steps taken as a result of the maladministration;
(b) the purpose of each step;
(c) the cost of each step; and
(d) how that cost has been calculated.

In assessing how much to reimburse, HMLR may take account of any contributory negligence or other factors.

111.1.2 Consolatory payments

The purpose of a consolatory payment is to underpin an apology given by HMLR and to provide a tangible recognition of HMLR's regret for the inconvenience or distress that it has caused. It is not intended to put a value on someone's time or to address a claimed financial loss.

In deciding:

(a) whether to make such a payment, and
(b) if so, the amount of such a payment,

HMLR will have regard to the PHSO's severity of injustice scale.[4]

---

1 www.ombudsman.org.uk/about-us/our-principles/principles-good-administration.
2 www.ombudsman.org.uk/organisations-we-investigate/putting-things-right.
3 For example, copies of relevant invoices.
4 www.ombudsman.org.uk/organisations-we-investigate/putting-things-right/financial-remedy.

112 MANORS

Manors are of ancient origin dating from pre-Norman times, with the extent of each manor normally being determined by the original grant from the Crown or superior lord. A manor was self-contained with its own customs and rights within its defined area. A manor can comprise three separate elements which may affect registered land:

(a) The title of lord of the manor, which confers the right upon the person holding the title to refer to himself as lord of that manor; for example, 'Lord of the manor of [*name of manor*]'.
(b) Manorial land, comprising the freehold or leasehold land within the defined area of the manor.
(c) Manorial rights, comprising rights which were part of the manorial title and which were usually retained by the lord on any disposal of part of the manorial land; for example, the right to hunt, shoot or fish.

The lordship title cannot be sub-divided, but the manorial land and the manorial rights can be, so that these three elements may remain combined or they may have become separated. When dealing with a manor, it is therefore important to consider, and where necessary distinguish between, each of these elements.

112.1 Lordship of a manor

The lordship of a manor is an incorporeal hereditament. It is no longer possible to register the title to a lordship of a manor.[1] Manors which were registered under the LRA 1925 remain in the register, but the proprietor of a registered manor may apply for the title to the manor to be removed from the register.[2]

The registered title to a manor has no title plan and HMLR does not hold any definitive record of the extent of the original manor. Registrations of manors are listed in the index of franchises and manors, which can be searched in respect of any particular administrative area using form SIF.[3] The result of such a search does not, however, reveal any caution against first registration of a manor which may have been in existence on 13 October 2003. To ascertain whether there is such a caution, a search of the index map using form SIM is required.[4] No caution against first registration in respect of a manor may be lodged under the LRA 2002.

112.2 Transfer of a registered manor

A transfer of a registered manor is a registrable disposition which must be completed by registration if it is to operate at law.[5]

112.3 Lease of a registered manor

Where there is a grant of a lease out of a registered manor, an application must be made to register the lease.[6] Any lease, however short, out of a registered manor must be registered. If this is not desired, consideration should be given to deregistering the manor.[7]

If the lease is for a term of more than 7 years from the date of the grant, the application is completed by the entry in the register of the grantee (or his successor in title) as proprietor of the lease; and a notice in respect of the lease.[8]

If the lease is for a term not exceeding 7 years from the date of the grant, the application is completed only by the entry of a notice in respect of the lease.[9] An application for entry of a notice of a lease which is for a term not exceeding 7 years from the date of the grant may be made in form AP1 or form AN1.[10]

An applicant should deliver to HMLR the usual documents required.

For registration of leases generally, see 98 Leases.

112.4 Deregistration of a registered lordship of a manor

An applicant for the title to a lordship of a manor to be removed from the register should deliver to HMLR an application in form AP1, showing the nature of application as 'deregistration of manor'.

No fee is currently payable for the removal of a registered lordship of a manor from the register. Upon deregistration the lordship continues to subsist, but not as a registered estate.

112.5 Manorial land

Manorial land is the land that was originally part of the landholdings of the lordship of the manor and which has not been separated from the lordship title. Manorial land can be extensive if the manor remains largely intact, or if the manor has been broken up, it can consist of a collection of small pieces of land remaining in the manor and scattered across a large area, including manorial waste, such as some highway verges. Manorial land is subject to the same requirements as to compulsory first registration, and the completion of registrable dispositions by registration, as any other corporeal land.[11]

Registrations of manorial land are recorded in the index map, which can be searched using form SIM.[12]

112.6 Manorial rights

A lord of the manor may exercise certain rights usually known as 'manorial rights' or 'manorial incidents'. Such rights could no longer be created after 1925. Manorial rights are not defined in the LRA 2002, but were defined in the LRA 1925 as having the same meaning as in Law of Property Act 1922, Pt V. They include:

(a) any right of the lord or tenant in or to any mines, minerals, limestone, lime, clay, stone, gravel, pits, or quarries, and any associated rights of search, winning, working and carrying away;
(b) the rights, franchises, royalties, or privileges of the lord in respect of any fairs, markets, rights of chase or warren, piscaries, or other rights of hunting, shooting, fishing, fowling, or otherwise taking game, fish or fowl; and
(c) any liability subsisting on 1 January 1926 for the construction, maintenance, cleansing, or repair of any dykes, ditches, canals, sea or river walls, piles, bridges, levels, ways and other works required for the protection or general benefit of any land within a manor or for abating nuisances therein.

Manorial rights arise in relation to land which was formerly copyhold, being rights which were reserved to the lord of the manor on enfranchisement.[13]

Where on first registration the title deduced reveals that the land is subject to manorial rights, HMLR will enter a notice to that effect in the property register.

Any unregistered manorial rights were interests which overrode both first registration or a registered disposition.[14] Such interests were therefore protected notwithstanding that there was no entry in the register in respect of them.[15]

Such rights ceased to have overriding status at the end of 10 years from 13 October 2003. The person having the benefit of a manorial right (if its priority has not already been previously defeated and it continues to subsist) should therefore protect it in the register. If he does not do so, the priority of the right is liable to be defeated in favour of a subsequent registrable disposition for valuable consideration which is completed by registration.[16] If the burdened land is unregistered, he should apply for a caution against first registration. If the burdened land is registered, he should apply for the entry of a notice if one does not already appear in the register.

As to an application for a caution against first registration, or an application for entry of a notice in the register, to protect manorial rights, see 42 Copyhold.

---

1 LRA 2002, s 3.
2 LRA 2002, s 119.
3 LRR 2003, r 146.
4 See 124.1 Search of the index map.
5 LRA 2002, s 27. See 176 Transfers.
6 LRA 2002, s 27(2)(c).
7 See 112.4 Deregistration of a registered lordship of a manor.
8 LRA 2002, Sch 2, para 4.
9 LRA 2002, Sch 2, para 5.
10 LRR 2003, r 90.
11 See 68 First Registration and Transfers.
12 LRR 2003, r 145. See 124.1 Search of the index map.
13 See 42 Copyhold.
14 LRA 2002, Sch 1, para 11 and Sch 3, para 11.
15 LRA 2002, ss 11, 12, 29 and 30.
16 LRA 2002, s 29.

113 MENTAL INCAPACITY

Where a person is suffering from a lack of mental capacity, either permanently or temporarily, someone must be appointed to manage his property on his behalf. A mentally incapacitated person is not barred from holding registered land, and any registered land held by him when he became incapacitated remains vested in him. However, he will lack capacity to effect a valid disposition of that registered land. Any valid enduring power or lasting power of attorney given by a person is not revoked by his subsequent mental incapacity and the attorney can therefore act on his behalf.[1] However, in the absence of such a power of attorney, special provision may need to be made by the court in relation to the management of the incapacitated person's property and affairs.

Mental incapacity in relation to property is dealt with under the Mental Capacity Act 2005. Where a person is suffering from mental incapacity, the court may by order make decisions on behalf of that person or may appoint a 'deputy' to make decisions on his behalf. A deputy will have such powers as the court confers upon him in relation to the personal welfare and the property and affairs of the incapacitated person, including powers in relation to real property.[2] A deputy will therefore normally have power to buy and sell property on behalf of the incapacitated person.

The appointment of a receiver under the Mental Health Act 1983 remains effective notwithstanding the repeal of that Act by the Mental Capacity Act 2005. However, the 2005 Act applies as if the receiver were a deputy appointed by the court for the incapacitated person, but with the functions that he had as a receiver. Orders made under the 1983 Act did not always empower the receiver to buy or sell property on behalf of the incapacitated person; where this is the case, a further order of the court authorising the disposition will be required.

113.1 Address(es) for service

If the incapacitated person is:

(a) the registered proprietor of land or a registered charge,
(b) the beneficiary of a unilateral notice,
(c) the cautioner under a caution against first registration,
(d) the person named in a restriction which requires his consent or certificate or the service of notice upon him, or
(e) a person entitled to be notified of an application for adverse possession under LRR 2003, r 194,

and the order gives the deputy power to take decisions regarding the incapacitated person's property, the deputy should consider whether he has access to the address(es) for service in the register. If not, he should apply to either add or substitute an address to which he does have access. Any such application should be accompanied by a certified copy of the deputyship order. See also 3 Address for Service.

113.2 Registered land

113.2.1 Disposals of registered land

Where the incapacitated person is the sole proprietor of registered land, any transfer or other registrable disposition by him should:

(a) be expressed to be made by the proprietor who has lost capacity acting by the deputy; and
(b) be signed by the deputy in the name of the incapacitated individual and his own name and duly witnessed.

An application to register such a disposition must be accompanied by the order appointing the deputy or a certified copy of it. Where a deputy is a receiver appointed under the Mental Health Act 1983, a certified copy of the order appointing him must be provided, together with (where necessary) a certified copy of the order authorising the sale or other disposition.

The deputy must take decisions in the best interests of the person who has lost capacity. The deputy may be in breach of his fiduciary duties to the patient if he disposes of the patient's property to himself or a connected person at less than full market value. Indeed, such a transaction may be void. This is because the provisions regarding gifts of the patient's property in most orders mirrors that in Mental Capacity Act 2005, s 12, and *Chandler v Lombardi*[3] confirmed that a gift in breach of such provisions was void. Where the deputy applies to register any disposition of the patient's property in favour of himself or a connected person, he should include either:

(a) evidence that the transaction is at full market value (such as a valuer's report); or
(b) an order of the Court of Protection under Mental Capacity Act 2005, s 16 authorising the disposition.

113.2.2 Acquisitions of land

Notwithstanding his mental incapacity, property may be acquired on behalf of an incapacitated person. Where unregistered land is acquired for an incapacitated person and this triggers compulsory first registration of title, the deputy should apply for first registration in the name of the incapacitated person. Similarly, where registered land is acquired for an incapacitated person, the deputy should apply for registration in the name of the incapacitated person. He must lodge with the application a certified copy of the order appointing him to act as deputy and also a certified copy of the order authorising the acquisition, which may be a separate order or form part of the powers conferred within the order appointing the deputy. Where a deputy is a receiver appointed under the Mental Health Act 1983, a certified copy of the order appointing him must be provided, together with (where necessary) a copy of the order authorising the acquisition.

Before 1 October 2007, the receiver of an incapacitated person could apply to be registered as proprietor of that person's property. If the receiver did, HMLR would normally enter a restriction against the title of the receiver, preventing the registration of any disposition unless the disposition was made pursuant to an order of the court under the Mental Health Act 1983. Since 1 October 2007, the deputy of an incapacitated person may not apply to be registered as proprietor unless specifically authorised by the Court of Protection.

113.2.3 Restrictions reflecting mental incapacity

HMLR will not enter a restriction reflecting a proprietor's mental incapacity unless the deputy expressly applies for this. A deputy is entitled to apply for entry of a restriction in Form RR.[4] The wording of Form RR is set out in Appendix IV.

Any application for cancellation of such a restriction should be made using form RX3, accompanied by an appropriate order or direction of the Court of Protection. No fee is currently payable for the cancellation of a restriction.[5]

113.3 Registered land held on trust

It may be that a mentally incapacitated person holds registered land on trust. A deputy cannot be given power to act on behalf of a patient in respect of trust property.[6] Where a patient is a trustee, a deputy should not therefore make the disposition on behalf of the patient in conjunction with the other trustee(s). Instead, when a trustee is unfit to act, or incapable of acting, in respect of the trusts conferred upon him, a new trustee should be appointed in his place. This power would lie first with any person whom the trust instrument nominated to do so. If there is no one to make the appointment, or no one who is willing and able to do so, then the continuing trustees may appoint a new trustee in his place.[7] If a trustee who is incapable is also entitled to some beneficial interest in the trust property, only the person nominated by the trust instrument may appoint a new trustee in his place, unless the Court of Protection has given leave to the continuing trustees to make the appointment.[8] If both or all the trustees are mentally incapacitated, an order of the court under Trustee Act 1925, s 41 will be required.

If a trustee who is incapable does not have an entitlement to some beneficial interest in the trust property and there is no one who is entitled or willing to appoint a trustee in his place, the beneficiaries may give a deputy of the incapacitated trustee a written direction to appoint the person named in the direction to be the trustee in place of the incapable person.[9] The beneficiaries may only give this direction if they are of full age and capacity, and are together absolutely entitled to the trust property. They may also give a similar direction to a person authorised for this purpose by the Court of Protection, or to the donee of an enduring power or lasting power of attorney with authority to act on behalf of the incapacitated trustee where the power has been registered under the Mental Capacity Act 2005.

An incapable trustee should generally be removed and a new one appointed before the trustees deal with the legal estate. However, even without taking those steps, the trustees may deal with the legal estate if the donee of an enduring power or lasting power of attorney is entitled to act in the dealing on the incapable trustee's behalf.[10] While this power subsists, it would not be necessary to discharge the incapable trustee or appoint a new trustee.

An attorney for an incapacitated trustee or incapacitated trustees under an enduring power or lasting power of attorney which has been registered under the Mental Capacity Act 2005 may have power to make an appointment of an additional trustee on behalf of the trustee or trustees.[11] This power would not appear to enable such an attorney to appoint himself as such a trustee.

An appointment of a new trustee must be completed by registration.[12]

A trustee of a registered estate or registered charge that requires the consent of the Court of Protection to any disposition is entitled to apply for entry of a restriction in Form SS.[13] The wording of Form SS is set out in Appendix IV.

113.4 Severance of beneficial joint tenancy of registered land

A deputy may apply for the entry of a restriction in Form A following the severance of a beneficial joint tenancy where the incapacitated person is one of the beneficial owners. The wording of Form A is set out in Appendix IV. The application must be supported, where necessary, by evidence to satisfy HMLR that the deputy has power to make the application. An order made under the Mental Capacity Act 2005 giving the deputy general authority includes (unless otherwise qualified in the order) the power to sever the joint tenancy of a patient. If the deputy is a receiver appointed under the Mental Health Act 1983, his power to sever the joint tenancy will depend on the terms of the order. If the order does not specifically authorise the receiver to sever the joint tenancy, the written authority of the court to do this will be required. If the deputy has the power to sever the joint tenancy, any application should be made in the patient's name and the usual evidence of severance will be required.[14]

113.5 Adverse possession of registered land

No one who has been in adverse possession of a registered estate may apply to be registered as proprietor of that estate during any period in which the existing registered proprietor is unable because of mental disability to make decisions about issues of the kind to which such an application would give rise, or unable to communicate such decisions because of mental disability or physical impairment.[15] Where it appears to HMLR that this applies, it may include a note to that effect in the register.[16] For these purposes, 'mental disability' means a disability or disorder of the mind or brain, whether permanent or temporary, which results in an impairment or disturbance of mental functioning.[17] Where it is desired that HMLR should make such a note in the register, application should be made using application form AP1, supported by appropriate evidence of the mental disability or physical impairment. For adverse possession of registered land generally, see 6 Adverse Possession.

---

1 See 136 Powers of Attorney.
2 Mental Capacity Act 2005, ss 16 and 18.
3 [2022] EWHC 22 (Ch).
4 LRR 2003, r 93(aa).
5 See 153.8 Cancellation of a restriction.
6 Mental Capacity Act 2005, s 20(3).
7 Trustee Act 1925, s 36(1).
8 Trustee Act 1925, s 36(9).
9 TLATA, s 20(2).
10 LPA 1925, s 22(3).
11 Trustee Act 1925, s 36(6)(b), (6A), (6B), (6C) and (6D).
12 LRA 2002, s 27.
13 LRR 2003, r 93(bb).
14 See 163 Severance of a Beneficial Joint Tenancy.
15 LRA 2002, Sch 6, para 8(2).
16 LRA 2002, Sch 6, para 8(4).
17 LRA 2002, Sch 6, para 8(3).

114 MERE EQUITIES

A mere equity is an equitable right which falls short of being an equitable interest. The courts have not laid down what distinguishes an equitable interest from a mere equity but the latter appears usually to involve a claim to discretionary relief in equity which relates to property. Examples are the right to rectify a deed for mutual mistake, a right to set aside a transfer for fraud or undue influence, and a right to seek relief from forfeiture of a lease after peaceable re-entry.

In relation to registered land, a mere equity has effect from the time the equity arises as an interest capable of binding successors in title, subject to the rules about the effect of dispositions on priority.[1] For the rules about the effect of dispositions on priority, see 138 Priorities.

The purchaser of a later equitable interest in the registered title does not therefore take free from the mere equity, even though he has no notice of it. This is different from the position with unregistered land, where the purchaser would take free in this case.[2]

This applies to mere equities which arose both before and after the section came into force on 13 October 2003.

To protect the priority of a mere equity affecting registered land against a registrable disposition made for valuable consideration, application may be made for entry of a notice in the register. Given the inchoate nature of a mere equity, in the absence of the consent of the registered proprietor it will normally be appropriate to make an application for entry of a unilateral notice rather than an agreed notice, due to the difficulty of being able to satisfy HMLR of the validity of the applicant's claim under LRA 2002, s 34(3)(c). For example, in the case of a claimed right to have a deed rectified for mutual mistake.

An applicant for entry of a unilateral notice should deliver to HMLR the usual documents required.[3]

The statement in panel 11 or conveyancer's certificate in panel 12 of form UN1 should be completed on the following lines to show the interest of the applicant:

> person having the right [*insert details of the mere equity, for example to have a transfer dated [date] made between (parties) rectified for mutual mistake*].

The unilateral notice in the register will give brief details of the interest protected and identify the beneficiary of that notice.

---

1 LRA 2002, s 116.

2 *Phillips v Phillips* (1861) 4 De GF & J 208.

3 See 119.3 Unilateral notice.

115 MINES AND MINERALS

Mines and minerals are 'land' for the purposes of the LRA 2002.[1] They are rebuttably presumed to be included in the registered title of a registered estate in the surface land. This is in accordance with the common law position regarding mines and minerals where the surface land is unregistered. However, no indemnity is payable in respect of mines and minerals unless there is a specific note in the register that title to them is included.[2] Such a note can be entered following a specific application either on first registration or subsequently and will only be made where evidence of title to the mines and minerals sufficient to satisfy HMLR that those mines and minerals are included in the registered estate is lodged.[3]

Where HMLR cannot make a note in the register that the title to the registered estate includes mines and minerals, but the description of the registered estate refers to mines and minerals, HMLR may make an entry along the following lines:[4]

> NOTE: The description of the registered estate is an entry made under rule 5(a) of the Land Registration Rules 2003 (SI 2003/1417) and is not a note to which paragraph 2 of Schedule 8 to the Land Registration Act 2002 refers that the registered estate includes the mines or minerals. The mines and minerals under the land are only included in the registration to the extent that they were so included before the Transfer dated [*date*] made between [*parties*].

LRR 2003, r 5(a) provides that the property register must contain a description of the registered estate. Such an entry may be used, for example, where a transfer of part of a registered estate is expressed to include the mines and minerals, but the register of the transferor's title does not include a note for the purposes of LRA 2002, Sch 8, para 2. HMLR will therefore wish to ensure that any reference to mines and minerals in the description in the transferee's property register is not a note for the purposes of Sch 8, para 2.

Under the general law, as part of the Crown's prerogative, all mines of gold and silver belong to the Crown other than, exceptionally, where they have been granted to a subject. Petroleum in its natural state is also vested in the Crown. Most interests in coal are vested in the Mining Remediation Authority.[5] The Mining Remediation Authority may also have title to other mines and minerals in coal-mining areas. A registered estate will not therefore include any of these interests.

115.1 First registration of mines and minerals

Although a voluntary application may be made, it is never compulsory to apply for first registration of mines and minerals held apart from the surface.[6] Where the mines and minerals constitute the surface of land, the normal rules regarding compulsory first registration apply.

Where an application for first registration of mines and minerals is made, investigation of title often needs to go beyond the normal 15-year root. Evidence, typically by way of statutory declaration(s) or statement(s) of truth, as to the working of the mines and minerals will assist in showing a good title. If the land was formerly copyhold, evidence to show the effect of enfranchisement on the mines and minerals should be lodged. Mines and minerals were often retained by the lord on enfranchisement. In many areas, mines and minerals were reserved to the Crown on the original grant of the land; where appropriate, a disclaimer of ownership by the Crown might be lodged. If the land was subject to inclosure, the Inclosure Act and Award should be considered, since these often deal with the ownership of mines and minerals.

In addition to the usual documents required,[7] an applicant for first registration of mines and minerals should deliver to HMLR:

(a) a plan of the surface under which the mines and minerals lie;
(b) any other sufficient details, by plan or otherwise, so that the mines and minerals can be clearly identified; and
(c) full details of rights incidental to the working of the mines and minerals.[8]

Due to the difficulties in establishing a good title to mines and minerals, HMLR will in many cases only be in a position to grant a qualified, rather than an absolute, class of title. The qualification will be on the following lines:

> The inclusion of all or any of the mines and minerals and powers of working and getting them in this title does not affect or prejudice the enforcement of any estate right or interest therein existing before [*date of first registration*].

In the case of an application for first registration of a lease of mines and minerals, where the landlord's title to the mines and minerals cannot be satisfactorily established, HMLR will grant a good leasehold class of title rather than title absolute.[9]

Where HMLR is satisfied, on first registration of an estate comprising or including the land beneath the surface, that the mines and minerals are included in or excluded from the applicant's title, it must make an appropriate note in the register.[10]

115.2 Registered surface land

If a registered estate includes mines or minerals but there is no note in the register to that effect, the registered proprietor of that estate may apply for a note to be entered that the registered estate includes the mines or minerals or specified mines or minerals.[11] The applicant should deliver to HMLR:

(a) an application in form AP1;
(b) evidence (in similar form to that outlined above in respect of first registration) to satisfy HMLR that the mines or minerals were vested in the applicant for first registration of the registered estate at the time of first registration and were so vested in the same capacity as the remainder of the estate in land then sought to be vested; and
(c) the fee payable.[12]

Where HMLR is satisfied that those mines and minerals are included in the registered estate, it must enter the appropriate note in the register. The form of the note will be:

> NOTE: For the purposes of paragraph 2 of Schedule 8 to the Land Registration Act 2002 [*details of mines and minerals*] are included in this title.

115.3 Transfer of mines and minerals out of a registered title

Where a transfer of mines and minerals is granted out of a registered title to mines and minerals, or to surface land, which contains a note regarding the inclusion of those mines and minerals, the new title will be registered with the same class of title as the existing class of title. Where there is no such note, the new title will be registered with the same class of title as the existing class of title but with the following entry being made in the register under LRR 2003, r 70:

> NOTE: The description of the registered estate is an entry made under rule 5(a) of the Land Registration Rules 2003 (SI 2003/1417) and is not a note to which paragraph 2 of Schedule 8 to the Land Registration Act 2002 refers that the registered estate includes the mines or minerals under the land. The mines and minerals under the land are only included in the registration to the extent that they were included in title number [*title number of the transferor's title*].

Such a transfer will be a registrable disposition which must be completed by registration if it is to operate at law.[13]

Where a registered title contains a note that expressly includes mines and minerals or is silent about the inclusion or exclusion of mines and minerals, any transfer of or out of that title that excepts the mines and minerals will have the effect of severing the mines and minerals from the surface land. In such circumstances, if the transfer is of the whole of the registered title, HMLR will create a new title for the mines and minerals retained by the transferor. If the transfer is of part of the registered title, the mines and minerals will be retained by the transferor in the existing registered title.

115.4 Lease of mines and minerals out of registered surface land

Where a lease of mines and minerals is a registrable disposition and is granted out of an absolute registered title where there is a note in the title regarding the inclusion of those mines and minerals within the landlord's registered title, HMLR can grant an absolute leasehold title. Where there is no such note and the landlord is registered with an absolute title, then an absolute leasehold title can still be granted but with the following entry being made after the description of the registered estate:[14]

> NOTE: The description of the registered estate is an entry made under rule 5(a) of the Land Registration Rules 2003 (SI 2003/1417) and is not a note to which paragraph 2 of Schedule 8 to the Land Registration Act 2002 refers that the registered estate includes the mines or minerals under the land. The mines and minerals under the land are only included in the registration to the extent that they were included in [*title number of the landlord's title*].

The purpose of this note is discussed above. In those cases where the landlord is registered with a qualified or possessory title, HMLR will register a good leasehold title. As to leases generally, see 98 Leases.

115.5 Profits à prendre

A right to enter on to land and extract minerals may in some instances constitute a profit à prendre, rather than a freehold or leasehold estate in land, depending upon the nature and terms of the grant or reservation. Thus, rights in respect of mines and minerals reserved to the lord of the manor on enfranchisement under Copyhold Act 1852, s 48, Copyhold Act 1894, s 23 or Law of Property Act 1922, Sch 12, para 5 do not constitute a freehold estate in land, but may constitute a profit in gross.[15]

115.6 Overriding interests

The burden of certain rights and interests relating to mines and minerals may take effect as an interest which overrides both first registration and registered dispositions notwithstanding that there is no entry in the register in respect of them. LRA 2002, Schs 1 and 3 specify such rights and interests which have overriding status. These are:

(a) Interests in any coal or coal mine, the rights attached to any such interest and the rights of any person under Coal Industry Act 1994, ss 38, 49 or 51.[16] No notice may be entered in the register in respect of any such rights.[17]
(b) In the case of land which was registered before 1898, unregistered rights to mines and minerals and incidental rights created before 1898 override both first registration and registered dispositions.[18]
(c) In the case of land which was registered between 1898 and 1925 inclusive, unregistered rights to mines and minerals and incidental rights created before the date of registration of the title override both first registration and registered dispositions.[19]

As to manorial rights relating to mines and minerals, see 42 Copyhold and 112 Manors.

115.7 Indemnity

No indemnity under LRA 2002, Sch 8 is payable on account of any mines or minerals or the existence of any right to work or get mines or minerals, unless it is noted in the register that the title of the registered estate concerned includes the mines and minerals.[20] Although mines and minerals are rebuttably presumed to be included in a registered title if there is no entry excluding them in the register, this does not of itself give any entitlement to indemnity if, for example, it subsequently transpires that the title does not in fact include them. There must be a specific note in the register that they are included in the title. As to indemnity generally, see 86 Indemnity.

---

1 LRA 2002, s 132(1)(c).
2 LRA 2002, Sch 8, para 2.
3 LRR 2003, r 71.
4 LRR 2003, r 70.
5 See 33 Coal.
6 LRA 2002, ss 3 and 4(9).
7 See 68.4 Application for first registration.
8 LRR 2003, r 25.
9 See 32.2 Titles to leasehold estates.

10 LRR 2003, r 32.
11 LRR 2003, r 71.
12 See 67 Fees.
13 LRA 2002, s 27.
14 LRR 2003, r 70.
15 See 42 Copyhold and 139 Profits à Prendre.
16 LRA 2002, Sch 1, para 7 and Sch 3, para 7.
17 LRA 2002, s 33(e). See 33 Coal.
18 LRA 2002, Sch 1, para 8 and Sch 3, para 8.
19 LRA 2002, Sch 1, para 9 and Sch 3, para 9.
20 LRA 2002, Sch 8, para 2.

116 MINORS

A minor is a person who has not attained the age of majority. A person attains the age of majority at the first moment of the 18th anniversary of his birth.[1] A minor cannot hold a legal estate in land.[2] He may hold an equitable interest only. Nevertheless, situations do arise where, through inadvertence, a legal estate or legal charge is purported to be vested in a minor.

116.1 Transfer of land to a minor

After 1996 a purported transfer to one or more minors is not effective to pass the legal estate but operates as a declaration that the land is held in trust for the minor or minors (or if it purports to transfer it to the minors in trust for any persons, for those persons).[3] Such a transfer is not, therefore, capable of registration, but an application should be made in form RX1 for entry of a restriction in Form A, if this does not already appear in the register. The wording of Form A is set out in Appendix IV.

Since no evidence of the age of an applicant is required to be produced to HMLR, a conveyancer may discover that a person is under the age of 18 only after he has been registered as proprietor. This will represent a mistake in the register and an application for alteration of the register should be made to reinstate the previous proprietor and enter a Form A restriction if this does not already appear in the register.

An applicant for alteration of the register should deliver to HMLR:

(a) an application in form AP1;
(b) a statement by the conveyancer briefly summarising the facts and stating the alteration sought;

(c) evidence of minority (for example a birth certificate) or a certified copy of it;
(d) an application in form RX1 for entry of the appropriate restriction mentioned above;[4] and
(e) the fee payable.[5]

116.2 Transfer of land to a minor jointly with an adult

After 1996 a purported transfer to one or more minors and an adult or adults operates to vest the land in the adult or adults in trust for the minor or minors and the adult or adults (or if it purports to convey it to them in trust for any persons, for those persons).[6] Such a transfer is capable of registration, but only the adult or adults will be registered as proprietors and an application should be made in form RX1 for entry of a restriction in Form A, if this does not already appear in the register.

Since no evidence of the age of an applicant is required to be produced to HMLR, a conveyancer may discover that a person is under the age of 18 only after he has been registered as one of the proprietors. This will represent a mistake in the register and an application for alteration of the register should be made to remove the minor as proprietor and enter a Form A restriction, if this does not already appear in the register.

An applicant for alteration of the register should deliver to HMLR:

(a) an application in form AP1;
(b) a statement by the conveyancer briefly summarising the facts and stating the alteration sought;
(c) evidence of minority (for example a birth certificate);
(d) an application in form RX1 for entry of the appropriate restriction mentioned above;[7] and
(e) the fee payable.[8]

116.3 Charge in favour of a minor or to a minor jointly with an adult

After 1996 any purported grant or transfer of a charge to one or more minors (or to one or more minors and one or more adults) operates in the same way as a purported transfer of land.[9] Where the grant of a charge is to a minor, it cannot be registered, nor, since it is an interest under a trust of land, can a notice be entered in the register, but a Form A restriction should be entered. Where the grant of a charge or transfer of a charge is to a minor and an adult, the charge may be registered showing the adult as proprietor of the charge.

Where a minor has been registered as proprietor inadvertently, an application for alteration of the register should be made on the same lines as explained above in respect of a transfer of land.

---

1 Family Law Reform Act 1969, s 9.
2 LPA 1925, s 1(6).
3 TLATA, s 2(6) and Sch 1, para 1(1).
4 See 153.1 Application for entry of restriction.
5 See 67 Fees.
6 TLATA, s 2(6) and Sch 1, para 1(2).
7 See 153.1 Application for entry of restriction.
8 See 67 Fees.
9 TLATA, s 23(2) and Sch 1, para 1.

117 MISSING PERSONS

When a person goes missing, he is presumed alive until the contrary is declared. During his absence, it may be necessary to deal with his property. The Guardianship (Missing Persons) Act 2017 provides a statutory framework which allows the High Court to appoint one or more guardians to deal with the missing person's property during his absence. The Act covers who may apply for a guardianship order, the powers and duties of a guardian, how guardians are to be supervised and how guardianship orders can be varied and revoked. The Ministry of Justice has also published a code of practice providing further details.[1] A guardian must have regard to the code of practice.[2]

Once appointed, a guardian will be the agent of the missing person in relation to the property specified in the order.[3] The guardian's powers are defined by the Guardianship (Missing Persons) Act 2017 and the terms of the guardianship order.

Subject to the general duties contained in the Guardianship (Missing Persons) Act 2017 and the terms of the guardianship order a guardian may (*inter alia*):

(a) sell, let or mortgage the missing person's property;
(b) execute deeds and other documents on the missing person's behalf;
(c) resign trusteeships held by the missing person; and
(d) make gifts of the missing person's property.[4]

A guardian cannot:

(a) purchase property on behalf of the missing person; or
(b) deal with property held by the missing person (whether alone or jointly) on trust for another person.[5]

In exercising his powers, the guardian must act in the best interests of the missing person[6] and he cannot profit personally from the appointment unless authorised to do so by the terms of his appointment.[7]

117.1 Recording the appointment of a guardian

If a missing person is the registered proprietor of an estate in land registered at HMLR or a charge registered against such an estate, once appointed, the guardian should apply to HMLR to record his appointment.

The guardian should deliver to HMLR:

(a) an application in form AP1;
(b) a certified copy of the guardianship order appointing the guardian named in the application;
(c) if the order requires a security bond to be put in place, either:

    (i) a conveyancer's certificate that such security is in place; or
    (ii) a copy of a security certificate issued by the bond provider;

(d) if the order is more than 12 months old, a statutory declaration confirming that it has not been revoked;
(e) the fee payable.[8]

On completion of the application, HMLR will make an entry in the register along the following lines:

> By an order of the High Court made on [*date*] (reference [*court reference*]), [*name of guardian*] of [*address*] was appointed as guardian for [*name of missing person*] pursuant to the Guardianship (Missing Persons) Act 2017.

The entry or entries can be subsequently cancelled upon an application in form AP1 supported by a copy of a revocation order made by the High Court.

117.2 Restriction

The guardian should also apply to enter a restriction to reflect his appointment.

Where the missing person is the sole registered proprietor of the estate or charge and the guardianship order allows the guardian to dispose of the missing person's property, the guardian may apply in form RX1 for entry of a restriction in Form N. The wording of Form N is set out in Appendix IV.

Otherwise, the guardian may apply for a non-standard restriction to reflect his appointment. A suggested form of wording is:

> RESTRICTION: No disposition of the registered estate executed in the name and on behalf of [*name of missing person*] is to be completed by registration unless either (a) made by [*name of guardian*] of [*address of guardian*] appointed and authorised by an order of the High Court dated [*date of guardianship order*], (reference [*court reference*]), pursuant to the Guardianship (Missing Persons) Act 2017, or by a subsequent order, or (b) accompanied by a certificate by a conveyancer confirming that any such appointment (including any variation thereof) has come to an end.

In either case, the application should be made in form RX1 accompanied by a certified copy of the guardianship order and, if the order requires a security bond, evidence that this is in place. A fee will be payable.[9]

HMLR will automatically cancel any restriction referring to the guardianship order on registration of a transfer of whole of the relevant estate or charge provided the disposition is by the guardian or accompanied by the relevant certificate.

A guardian may apply to withdraw any restriction in which they are named using form RX4.[10]

An applicant may apply to cancel a restriction entered to protect a guardian's interest. As well as the usual evidence required,[11] the applicant should deliver to HMLR:

(a) evidence that the missing person or guardian has died;
(b) evidence that the guardianship order has time expired; or
(c) if the guardianship order has been revoked, a certified copy of the revocation order.

The missing person cannot apply to cancel the restriction without evidence to show the guardianship order has been revoked.

117.3 Dispositions

117.3.1 Sales, leases and charges to a third party

Unless prohibited by the guardianship order, a sale, lease or charge to a third party by a guardian is permissible.

Where co-owners have gone missing and the same person has been appointed as guardian for each of them, that guardian cannot give a valid receipt for capital monies and overreaching will not occur.

When applying to register a disposition, as well as the usual evidence required,[12] the applicant should deliver to HMLR:

(a) a certified copy of the guardianship order appointing the guardian named in the application;
(b) if the order requires a security bond to be put in place, either:

    (i) a conveyancer's certificate that such security is in place; or
    (ii) a copy of a security certificate issued by the bond provider; and

(c) if the order is more than 12 months old, a statutory declaration confirming that it has not been revoked.

117.3.2 Transfers and leases to third parties not for value

A guardian must always act in the best interests of the missing person. Consequently, a transfer of the missing person's property should normally be for its full market value.

A transfer not for value might possibly be a gift. If so, it would have to be expressly authorised by the order appointing the guardian or by a variation of that order (and HMLR would require a copy of such an order in addition to the evidence mentioned in 116.3.1 Sales, leases and charges to a third party).[13]

117.3.3 Dispositions to the guardian

A guardian is an agent of the missing person. Accordingly, the guardian cannot profit personally from his appointment unless authorised to do so by the order appointing him.

Provided he has authority to make the relevant disposal, a guardian is not prohibited from acquiring the property or relevant interest in it.[14] However, the guardian's duty to act in the best interests of the missing person mean he must pay full market value for the relevant interest. Further, in addition to the evidence mentioned in 117.3.1 Sales, leases and charges to a third party, the guardian would need to provide evidence that the acquisition was at full market value (such as a valuation report from a surveyor to that effect) with any application to register the disposition.

117.4 Resigning trusteeships

A guardian cannot exercise a power vested in the missing person as a trustee in relation to another person's property.[15] However, he may resign any trusteeships held by the missing person.[16] This will free any remaining trustees to deal with the trust property (although where there is a restriction in Form A in the register and the resignation means there is only one remaining trustee, that trustee cannot effect overreaching and it will remain necessary to appoint a replacement trustee).

When registering a resignation by a guardian on behalf of a missing person, in addition to any other evidence required, the applicant should provide HMLR with the documents listed in 117.3.1 Sales, leases and charges to a third party.

For further information on trusts generally, see 178 Trusts of Land.

117.5 Execution of deeds

There is no prescribed form of execution by a guardian. HMLR recommends guardians execute deeds using the following wording:

> Signed as a deed by [*name of missing person*] acting by [*name of guardian*] pursuant to an Order of the Court dated [*date of guardianship order*] in the presence of:
>
> Signature: [*Guardian to sign in the name of the missing individual and their own name for example, Joseph Bloggs by his guardian Ann Other*]
> Signature of witness:
>
> Name (IN BLOCK CAPITALS):
> Address:

---

1 https://assets.publishing.service.gov.uk/government/uploads/system/uploads/attachment_data/file/822418/missing-people-code-of-practice.pdf.

2 Guardianship (Missing Persons) Act 2017, s 22(2).

3 Guardianship (Missing Persons) Act 2017, s 8(2).
4 Guardianship (Missing Persons) Act 2017, s 6(4).
5 Guardianship (Missing Persons) Act 2017, s 6(5)(b).
6 Guardianship (Missing Persons) Act 2017, s 8(1).
7 Guardianship (Missing Persons) Act 2017, s 9(2).
8 See 67 Fees.
9 See 67 Fees.
10 See 153.9 Withdrawal of a restriction.
11 See 153.8 Cancellation of a restriction.
12 See 97 Leases, 99.1 Charges of registered land or 176.1 Registration of transfer.
13 Guardianship (Missing Persons) Act 2017, s 6(7).
14 Although the Code of practice suggests getting express authorisation from the court (Guardianship (Missing Persons) Act 2017 – Code of Practice, para 5.40).
15 Guardianship (Missing Persons) Act 2017, s 6(5)(b).
16 Guardianship (Missing Persons) Act 2017, s 6(4)(f).

118 MORTGAGE CAUTIONS

Under the LRA 1925, it was possible to protect a mortgage by a caution known as a mortgage caution. Its effect was to prevent the registration of any dealing with the registered title until notice had been served on the cautioner. The mortgage caution was used only rarely and no new mortgage caution (or sub-mortgage caution) has been capable of registration since 30 August 1977.

A proprietor of a sub-charge could (before 30 August 1977) protect that sub-charge by a sub-charge caution. Substantive registration of the sub-charge is not possible until the principal charge is itself substantively registered.

Land Registration Act 2002 (Transitional Provisions) Order 2003 (SI 2003/1953) (LRA (TP) Order 2003), art 16 preserves the position of mortgage cautions and sub-mortgage cautions under the LRA 2002, so that they continue to have the same effect under the LRA 2002 as they did under the 1925 Act.

It is possible to substantively register the charge protected by the mortgage caution.[1] The application must (where title to the protected mortgage is vested in someone other than the cautioner) include the documents proving devolution of title to the applicant. On registration, the following note will be added to the entry of the charge:

> This charge was formerly protected by a mortgage caution and has priority, under Article 16(5) of the Land Registration Act 2002 (Transitional Provisions) Order 2003 (SI 2003/1953), with effect from [*date*], the date on which the caution was entered.

If there are any existing charges in the register dated after the date of the caution, a corresponding note will be added to the existing charge entry.

It is not possible to apply to cancel a mortgage caution, but application may be made in form WCT to remove it, accompanied by satisfactory evidence of the discharge of the mortgage. No fee is currently payable.

If an application for registration is lodged where a mortgage caution appears in the register and no withdrawal of the caution is lodged, HMLR will serve notice of the application on the mortgage cautioner. This notice will confirm that the mortgage caution cannot be removed, even where the cautioner fails to respond to the notice, as an application cannot have the effect of a warning-off of a mortgage caution.

---

1 See 100 Legal Charges.

119 NOTICES

A notice is an entry in the register in respect of the burden of an interest affecting a registered estate or a registered charge. The entry of a notice does not necessarily mean that the interest is valid but does protect the priority of the interest, if valid, for the purposes of LRA 2002, ss 29 and 30.[1] For details of this priority protection, see 138 Priorities. Matters typically protected by a notice are contracts for sale and agreements for lease, adverse easements, leases, rentcharges, restrictive covenants, and home rights. Also orders of a court affecting the registered estate.

No notice may be entered in the register in respect of any of the following interests:[2]

(a) an interest under a trust of land;
(b) an interest under a settlement under the SLA 1925;
(c) a leasehold estate in land which is granted for a term of 3 years or less from the date of the grant and which is not required to be registered;
(d) an interest under a relevant social housing tenancy;[3]
(e) a restrictive covenant made between a landlord and tenant, so far as relating to the demised premises;
(f) an interest which is capable of being registered under the CRA 1965;
(g) an interest in any coal or coal mine, the rights attached to any such interest and the rights of any person under Coal Industry Act 1994, ss 38, 49 or 51; and
(h) leases created for PPPs relating to transport in London.[4]

In many cases HMLR will enter a notice as a matter of course, without the need for a separate application, as part of the registration process. Such as notice is referred to as a 'registrar's notice' and takes effect as an agreed notice. For example, HMLR may enter a notice as a result of its examination of title on first registration,[5] or where it finds that the title is affected by an unregistered interest which overrides first registration and which is capable of being noted.[6] In the latter example, HMLR must give notice to the registered proprietor and to any person who appears to HMLR to be entitled to the interest protected by the notice or whom it otherwise considers appropriate.[7] HMLR need not give notice to a registered proprietor who applies for the entry of the notice or consents to the application for the notice. Nor need HMLR give notice to any other person if that person has applied for, or consented to, the notice, or whose name and address for service do not appear in the register of the title in question.[8]

Where a registrable disposition requires completion of registration by the entry of a notice, HMLR must enter such a notice in the register.[9] This includes, for example, the entry of a notice of a lease in the landlord's title on the registration of a lease, or the entry of a notice in the grantor's title on the express grant of a legal easement.

Aside from the circumstances when HMLR enters a notice, as described above, HMLR may also enter a notice upon specific application. A person claiming to be entitled to the benefit of an interest affecting a registered estate or registered charge may apply for the entry of either an agreed notice or a unilateral notice.[10] The right to apply for the entry of a notice must not be exercised without reasonable cause. This duty to act reasonably is owed to any person who suffers damage in consequence of its breach.[11] A person in breach of such duty is therefore liable in damages to a person who suffers loss in consequence.

119.1 Agreed notice

HMLR may approve the entry of an agreed notice only if:

(a) the applicant is the registered proprietor of the estate or charge in question;
(b) the applicant is a person entitled to be registered as proprietor of the estate or charge in question;
(c) the registered proprietor of the estate or charge in question, or the person entitled to be registered as such, consents to the entry of the notice; or
(d) HMLR is satisfied of the validity of the applicant's claim.[12]

An applicant for an agreed notice should deliver to HMLR:

(a) an application in form AN1;
(b) a plan of the affected land (where the interest claimed affects only part of the land in the registered title);
(c) the deed, order or instrument giving rise to the interest claimed, or (if there is no such deed, order or instrument) other details of the interest claimed to satisfy HMLR of the nature of the applicant's claim;
(d) (if the application is made with the consent of, rather than by, the registered proprietor or person entitled to be so registered) the relevant consent, which may be given in panel 11 of form AN1, or (if the application is not made with such consent) evidence to satisfy HMLR of the validity of the applicant's claim in accordance with LRA 2002, s 34(3)(c);
(e) (if the application is made by or with the consent of a person entitled to be registered as proprietor) evidence to satisfy HMLR of that person's entitlement to be registered as proprietor;
(f) where applicable, the appropriate SDLT or LTT certificate(s) or other evidence;[13] and
(g) the fee payable.[14]

Before HMLR can enter an agreed notice in respect of an interest comprising a land transaction, it must ensure that the appropriate SDLT and/or LTT certificate(s) accompanies the application where this is required.[15]

Where the application is for entry of a home rights notice or its renewal, the appropriate application form is form HR1 or form HR2.[16]

An agreed notice must be entered in the charges register of the title affected. The agreed notice will give details of the interest protected and, in the case of a notice of a variation of an interest protected by a notice, details of the variation.[17]

119.2 Cancellation of a notice other than a unilateral notice or a home rights notice

An applicant for the cancellation of a notice other than a unilateral notice or a home rights notice should deliver to HMLR:

(a) an application in form CN1;
(b) (if the application relates to part only of the land to which the agreed notice relates) a plan or other sufficient details to allow the extent in question to be clearly identified on the OS map.
(c) evidence to satisfy HMLR that the interest has determined. Where appropriate, this should include evidence of devolution to prove determination

of the interest and/or the right of the applicant to apply for the notice to be cancelled; and

(d) the fee payable.[18]

Where HMLR is satisfied that the interest protected by the notice has come to an end, it must cancel the notice or make an entry in the register that the interest in question has come to an end. If the interest in question has come to an end in part only, an appropriate entry must be made in the register to reflect this.[19]

119.3 Unilateral notice

HMLR may enter a unilateral notice without the consent of the registered proprietor and without having to be satisfied of the validity of the applicant's claim. Also, the applicant may prefer to apply for entry of a unilateral notice where he does not wish the terms of the deed, order or document giving rise to the interest claimed to be open to public inspection and copying.[20]

An applicant cannot apply for entry of a unilateral notice for the following interests:

(a) a home rights notice;
(b) an IHT notice;
(c) a notice in respect of an order under the Access to Neighbouring Land Act 1992 (ANLA 1992);
(d) a notice of any variation of a lease effected by or under an order under Landlord and Tenant Act 1987, s 38, including any variation as modified by an order under s 39(4);
(e) a notice in respect of a public right; or
(f) a notice in respect of a customary right.

Instead, the applicant must apply for entry of an agreed notice to protect such an interest.[21]

Where HMLR enters a unilateral notice, it must give notice of the entry to the registered proprietor of the registered estate or registered charge affected.[22]

An applicant for a unilateral notice should deliver to HMLR:

(a) an application in form UN1;
(b) a plan of the affected land (where the interest claimed affects only part of the land in the registered title);
(c) where applicable, the appropriate SDLT or LTT certificate(s) or other evidence;[23] and
(d) the fee payable.[24]

The statement in panel 11 or conveyancer's certificate in panel 12 of form UN1 should be completed as appropriate, with the relevant details of the applicant's interest.

Before HMLR can enter a unilateral notice in respect of an interest comprising a land transaction, it must ensure that the appropriate SDLT and/or LTT certificate(s) accompanies the application where this is required.[25]

A unilateral notice must be entered in the charges register of the title affected.[26] The first part of a unilateral notice in the register identifies that it is a unilateral notice and gives brief details of the interest protected. The second part identifies the beneficiary of the notice.[27]

119.4 Registration of new or additional beneficiary of a unilateral notice

A person entitled to the benefit of an interest protected by a unilateral notice may apply to be entered in the register in place of, or in addition to, the existing registered beneficiary.[28] An applicant to be registered as beneficiary of an existing unilateral notice should deliver to HMLR:

(a) an application in form UN3;
(b) evidence to satisfy HMLR of the applicant's title to the interest protected by the unilateral notice (for example a transfer of the interest to the applicant);
(c) where applicable, the consent of the existing registered beneficiary if he has not signed the form UN3; and
(d) the fee payable.[29]

Before entering the applicant in the register, HMLR must serve notice on the registered beneficiary of the unilateral notice[30] unless:

(a) the registered beneficiary signs the form UN3 or otherwise consents to the application; or
(b) if the applicant is the registered beneficiary's personal representative and evidence of his appointment accompanies the application.[31]

If HMLR completes the application, it will enter details of the applicant in place of the existing registered beneficiary or jointly with that registered beneficiary as the case may be.

119.5 Removal of a unilateral notice

The registered beneficiary of a unilateral notice may apply in form UN2 for the removal of the notice from the register.[32] No fee is currently payable. The application may also be made by the personal representative or trustee in bankruptcy of the registered beneficiary, in which case evidence of his appointment must accompany the application. If HMLR is satisfied that the application is in order, it must remove the unilateral notice.

119.6 Cancellation of a unilateral notice

The registered proprietor, or a person entitled to be registered as proprietor, of the registered estate or registered charge to which the unilateral notice relates, may apply at any time for the cancellation of that notice.[33]

The application must be made in form UN4. No fee is currently payable. Where the application is by a person entitled to be registered as proprietor, it must be accompanied by evidence to satisfy HMLR of his entitlement, or his conveyancer must complete the certificate in panel 9 of form UN4 to certify that he is satisfied that the applicant is entitled to be registered as proprietor.[34] If the application relates to part only of the land to which the unilateral notice relates, a plan or other sufficient details to allow the extent in question to be clearly identified on the OS map must be lodged.

HMLR must give the registered beneficiary notice of the application and inform him that if he does not exercise his right to object within the relevant period, HMLR must cancel the unilateral notice.[35] The relevant period is the period ending at 12 noon on the 15th working day after the date of issue of the notice or such longer period as HMLR may allow following a request by the beneficiary.[36] The beneficiary must set out in such a request why a longer period should be allowed and must make the request before the expiry of the period ending at 12 noon on the 15th working day after the date of issue of the notice.[37] HMLR may, if it considers it appropriate, seek the views of the person who applied for cancellation. If, after considering such views and all other relevant matters, HMLR is satisfied that a longer period should be allowed, it may allow such period as it thinks appropriate, whether or not the period is the same as any period requested by the beneficiary.[38] The longer period may never exceed a period ending at 12 noon on the 30th working day after the issue of the notice.[39] A working day is any day from Monday to Friday (inclusive) which is not Christmas Day, Good Friday or any other day either specified or declared by proclamation under Banking and Financial Dealings Act 1971, s 1 or appointed by the Secretary of State or certified by HMLR as being an 'interrupted day' due to delay or failure of a communication service or to some other event or circumstance causing substantial interruption in the normal operation of HMLR.[40]

Only the person shown in the register as the beneficiary of the unilateral notice or a person entitled to be registered as the beneficiary of the unilateral notice may object to an application for cancellation of that notice.[41] Where there are two or more persons who are shown in the register as beneficiary of the unilateral notice or who are entitled to be registered as beneficiary, each such person is a beneficiary of the unilateral notice and therefore has a right to object to its cancellation.

If the registered beneficiary or person entitled to be registered as beneficiary does not exercise his right to object to the cancellation of the unilateral notice within the relevant period, HMLR must cancel the unilateral notice.[42]

Where the registered beneficiary or person entitled to be registered as beneficiary does wish to object to the cancellation of the unilateral notice, he must deliver an objection to HMLR. That objection must comply with LRR 2003, r 19.[43] If it receives such an objection before the relevant deadline, HMLR will proceed as set out in 54 Disputes.

In addition to statutory procedure for cancellation of a unilateral notice, the court has an inherent jurisdiction to modify or remove unilateral notices.[44] For the procedure to reflect any such order on the register, see 12.1 Alteration pursuant to a court order.

---

1 LRA 2002, s 32.
2 LRA 2002, ss 33 and 90(4).
3 As defined in LRA 2002, s 132(1).
4 As defined in Greater London Authority Act 1999, s 218 (PPP leases).
5 LRR 2003, r 35.
6 LRA 2002, s 37(1).
7 LRA 2002, s 37(2) and LRR 2003, r 89(1).
8 LRR 2003, r 89(2).
9 LRA 2002, s 38.
10 LRA 2002, s 34.
11 LRA 2002, s 77.
12 LRA 2002, s 34(3).
13 See 168 Stamp Duty Land Tax and/or 94 Land Transaction Tax.
14 See 67 Fees.
15 Finance Act 2003, s 79(1) and Land Transaction Tax and Anti-avoidance of Devolved Taxes (Wales) Act 2017, s 65(1).
16 See 81.1 Home rights notice and 81.2 Renewal of home rights notice.
17 LRA 2002, s 84.

18 See 67 Fees.
19 LRR 2003, s 87.
20 See 122 Official Copies and Inspection.
21 LRR 2003, r 80.
22 LRA 2003, s 35(1).
23 See 168 Stamp Duty Land Tax and/or 94 Land Transaction Tax.
24 See 67 Fees.
25 Finance Act 2003, s 79(1) and Land Transaction Tax and Anti-avoidance of Devolved Taxes (Wales) Act 2017, s 65(1).
26 LRR 2003, r 84(1).
27 LRA 2002, s 35(2).
28 LRR 2003, r 88(1).
29 See 67 Fees.
30 LRR 2003, r 88(4).
31 LRR 2003, r 88(5).
32 LRA 2002, s 35(3) and LRR 2003, r 85.
33 LRA 2002, s 36(1).
34 LRR 2003, r 86(2).
35 LRA 2002, s 36(2).
36 LRR 2003, r 86(3).
37 LRR 2003, r 86(4) and (6).
38 LRR 2003, r 86(5).
39 LRR 2003, r 86(3).
40 LRR 2003, r 217(1).
41 LRR 2003, r 86(7).
42 LRA 2002, s 36(3).
43 See 54.1 Objections.
44 *Nugent v Nugent* [2013] EWHC 4095 (Ch).

120 NOTICES OF DEPOSIT

Instead of registering a mortgage with HMLR and holding a charge certificate, a lender used to be able to hold a borrower's land or charge certificate as security for the loan. Before 3 April 1995, the lender could apply for an entry to be made in the register giving notice that the certificate had been deposited with him. A notice of deposit, or notice of intended deposit, was entered in the register in respect of a lien created under LRA 1925, s 66. It has not been possible to make such an entry since the coming into force of the Land Registration Rules 1995 (SI 1995/140) on 3 April 1995. In the light of the decision in *United Bank of Kuwait v Sahib*,[1] it appears that it was not possible to create an equitable charge by deposit of a land certificate or charge certificate after the coming into force of the Law of Property (Miscellaneous Provisions) Act 1989, s 2 on 27 September 1989.

Where a notice of deposit, or a notice of intended deposit, of a land certificate or of a charge certificate has been entered in the register before 3 April 1995, it operates as a caution against dealings under LRA 1925, s 54.[2] The transitional provisions contained in LRR 2003, rr 218 to 223 therefore apply. This is so even if HMLR has destroyed the land certificate or charge certificate in accordance with the power contained in LRA (TP) Order 2003, art 24(3) and (4).

Any entry of a notice of deposit or notice of intended deposit still subsisting in the register therefore continues to take effect as a caution against dealings.[3] A notice of deposit, or notice of intended deposit, can be 'warned off' in the same way as a caution against dealings; a consent to cancellation may be given by the depositee or his personal representative or by his conveyancer.

When an entry of a notice of deposit or notice of intended deposit still subsists in the register and there is to be a transfer of part of the registered estate, or when a lease or rentcharge is to be granted out of the registered estate, a depositee usually provides a letter of consent which can then be sent to HMLR with the application to register the transfer or grant. When necessary, the consent must refer to a plan enabling the estate to which it relates to be identified on the title plan. A depositee's consent to a disposition may be by way of a letter or it may be endorsed by way of reply on a notice sent by HMLR to the depositee. Consent may be given by the depositee or his personal representative or by his conveyancer. A transfer of whole should be accompanied by a withdrawal of the notice of (intended) deposit.

HMLR will accept the following evidence as discharge for the purposes of cancelling an entry of a notice of deposit or notice of intended deposit:

(a) an application in form 86 to the Land Registration Rules 1925, provided it is dated before 13 October 2003;
(b) the duplicate part of the original application forms 85A, 85B or 85C for entry of the notice (under the Land Registration Rules 1925), provided it is dated before 13 October 2003;
(c) a withdrawal in form WCT by the chargee in whose favour the notice was made; or
(d) an application in form CCD by the proprietor of the registered estate or registered charge to which the notice relates, provided it is shown that the notice does not protect a valid interest, or that the interest has come to an end.

No fee is currently payable.

---

1 [1997] Ch 107.

2 Land Registration Rules 1925, r 239(1) and LRA 2002, Sch 12, para 3.

3 See 24 Cautions Against Dealings.

121 OCCUPATION CONTRACTS UNDER THE RENTING HOMES (WALES) ACT 2016

The Renting Homes (Wales) Act 2016 (RH(W)A 2016) enhances the rights of tenants or licensees of residential properties in Wales. In particular, the RH(W)A 2016 grants tenants/licensees greater security with changes to notice periods, restrictions on possession notices and proceedings and simplified standard rental contracts.

Where it applies, the RH(W)A 2016 creates an occupation contract between the landlord/licensor and the tenant/licensee. The explanatory note to the act states:

> In effect, the occupation contract, with all of its rights and obligations, will sit on top of the tenancy or licence with a view to helping the parties to the tenancy or licence to have clarity as to what their rights and obligations are, and what the other party's rights and obligations are, regardless of the legal basis for the occupation.[1]

The landlord/licensor must give the tenant/licensee a written statement setting out prescribed information within 14 days of the occupation date.[2]

There are two different forms of occupation contract:

(a) a secure contract; and
(b) a standard contract.[3]

Subject to exceptions set out in the RH(W)A 2016, generally an occupation contract made with a private landlord will be a standard contract and one made with a community landlord[4] will be a secure contract.[5] A standard occupation contract may be for a fixed or periodic term. Where it is for a fixed term, it may be capable of substantive registration or noting. A secure contract will always be a periodic tenancy (and so incapable of substantive registration or noting) but allows for repossession by the landlord/licensor in more limited circumstances than a standard contract.

To be an occupation contract for the purposes of the RH(W)A 2016, the lease or licence must:

(a) be made between a landlord and at least one individual;
(b) confer on the individual (or, if there is more than one individual, on one or more of them) the right to occupy a dwelling as a home; and
(c) require payment of a rent or other consideration.[6]

Certain leases or licences can never be occupation contracts, these include tenancies or licences with a fixed term of over 21 years. For further details of what can be an occupation contract, see RH(W)A 2016, s 7.

Where an existing lease or licence met the requirements of RH(W)A 2016, s 7 on 1 December 2022, subject to limited exceptions, it will have been converted into an occupation contract.[7]

121.1 Registration of an Occupation Contract

If an occupation contract is for a term of more than 7 years, it may be capable of substantive registration at HMLR.

A person applying to register an occupation contract should provide HMLR with:

(a) an application in form AP1;
(b) the occupation contract or a certified copy of it;
(c) any consents or certificates required in respect of mortgages, charges or restrictions in the landlord's title;
(d) form DI giving the information as to overriding interests required by LRR 2003, r 57, including any documentary evidence of the interests;[8]
(e) the appropriate confirmation or evidence of identity;[9]
(f) any appropriate LTT certificate(s) or other evidence;[10] and
(g) the fee payable.[11]

HMLR will consider the occupation contract to ensure it meets the requirements of RH(W)A 2016. On completion of registration, HMLR will enter a note in the property register for the title stating that the occupation contract was granted under the RH(W)A 2016 and a restriction in the following wording:

> RESTRICTION: No disposition is to be completed by registration unless authorised by an order of the court or unless a conveyancer certifies that the provisions of the Renting Homes (Wales) Act 2016 have been complied with.

HMLR will also note the occupation contract in the landlord's title.

121.2 Noting an Occupation Contract

If an occupation contract is for a fixed term of more than 3 but less than 7 years, the tenant may apply to note it on their landlord's title by way of an agreed or unilateral notice.

121.2.1 Agreed notice

If applying to register an agreed notice, in addition to the usual documents required,[12] an applicant should deliver to HMLR:

(a) the occupation contract or a certified copy of it; and
(b) any consents or certificates required in respect of mortgages, charges or restrictions in the landlord's title.

The agreed notice in the register will give details of the interest protected.

121.2.2 Unilateral notice

An applicant for entry of a unilateral notice should deliver to HMLR the usual documents required.[13]

The statement in panel 11 or conveyancer's certificate in panel 12 of form UN1 should be completed on the following lines to show the interest of the applicant:

> tenant of an occupation contract dated [*date*] and made between [*parties*] pursuant to the Renting Homes (Wales) Act 2016.

The unilateral notice in the register will give brief details of the interest protected and identify the beneficiary of that notice.

121.3 Dealings with an occupation contract

Most dealings with an occupation contract are prohibited unless permitted by an express term of the occupation contract or the dealing is in accordance with a family property order.[14] Further, the RH(W)A 2016 does permit:

(a) inclusion of an optional clause permitting additional people to be added as contract holders;[15] and
(b) inclusion of an optional clause permitting removal of a joint contract holder.[16]

RH(W)A 2016, ss 69 and 72 provide a transfer of an occupation contract must be signed by all parties to it but need not be by deed. However, the RH(W)A 2016 does not disapply LRR 2003, r 58 or r 206(3). Consequently, if such a dealing is permitted, any transfer of the occupation contract should be in the relevant Sch 1 form. Further, as LRR 2009, Sch 9 makes no reference to a transfer (other than an assent) being executed otherwise than by deed, it may be safest to have any transfer of an occupation contract signed as deed using the appropriate prescribed form of execution.

Where the occupation contract is substantively registered, the parties should apply to update the register in the normal way.[17]

Where the occupation contract is protected by an agreed notice, there is no need to alter the register to reflect any transfer of the noted occupation contract.

Where the occupation contract is protected by a unilateral notice, the new tenant should apply to update the unilateral notice. In addition to the usual documents required,[18] an applicant should deliver to HMLR:

(a) the transfer or a certified copy of it;
(b) the certificate required to comply with the restriction in the occupation contract title;
(c) any necessary consent from the landlord; and
(d) any appropriate LTT certificate(s) or other evidence.[19]

121.4 Survivorship and succession

Most occupation contracts have succession rights allowing up to two successions. However, this may be overridden by the terms of the occupation contract. Where a tenancy converted to an occupation contract on 1 December 2022, a right of succession applies only if immediately before 1 December 2022 the tenancy was:

(a) a secure tenancy under HA 1985, s 89;
(b) an introductory tenancy under HA 1996, s 133 or s 143; or
(c) an assured tenancy which vested in the contract holder under HA 1988, s 17 or Rent Act 1977, Sch 1, Part 3.[20]

If, on the death of a contract holder, there is no qualifying successor nor any transfer under a family property order, the contract will terminate.[21] For further details, see 121.5 Determination.

121.4.1 Sole contract holder

Where a sole contract holder dies either:

(a) their qualified successor[22] succeeds to the contract,[23] or
(b) the occupation contract may be transferred in the course of administration of their estate,[24]

depending on the terms of the occupation contract.

In either case, the parties should update the register.

121.4.1.1 Substantively registered occupation contract

Where the occupation contract is substantively registered, an applicant should deliver to HMLR:

(a) an application in form AP1;
(b) a certified copy of the death certificate or grant of representation for the registered proprietor of the title;
(c) in the case of an application by a qualifying successor, a certificate from a conveyancer confirming:

    (i) the occupation contract is one to which RH(W)A 2016, s 73 applies; and
    (ii) either:

        (1) the applicant is the only qualified successor for the purposes of RH(W)A 2016, s 73; or
        (2) the applicant is the person identified in accordance with RH(W)A 2016, s 78 to succeed the deceased contract holder;

(d) in the case of an application following a transfer in the course of administration of an estate:

    (i) an assent in form AS1; and
    (ii) a certificate from a conveyancer that the occupation contract is one to which RH(W)A 2016, s 139 applies; and

(e) the relevant fee.[25]

In the case of an assent by the deceased proprietor's personal representative, HMLR will always need to see an original or certified copy of the grant of representation.[26]

121.4.1.2 Noted occupation contract

Where the occupation contract is the subject of an agreed notice, no further action is necessary.

Where the occupation contract is protected by a unilateral notice, the new tenant should apply to update the unilateral notice. In addition to the usual documents required,[27] an applicant should deliver to HMLR:

(a) a certified copy of the death certificate or grant of representation for the registered proprietor of the title;
(b) in the case of an application by a qualifying successor, a certificate from a conveyancer confirming:

    (i) the occupation contract is one to which RH(W)A 2016, s 73 applies; and
    (ii) either:

        (1) the applicant is the only qualified successor for the purposes of RH(W)A 2016, s 73; or
        (2) the applicant is the person identified in accordance with RH(W)A 2016, s 78 to succeed the deceased contract holder; and

(c) in the case of an application following a transfer in the course of administration of an estate:

    (i) an assent; and
    (ii) a certificate from a conveyancer that the occupation contract is one to which RH(W)A 2016, s 139 applies.

In the case of an assent by the deceased proprietor's personal representative, HMLR will always need to see an original or certified copy of the grant of representation.[28]

121.4.2 Joint contract holders

Where there are joint contract holders and one of them dies, their share will either:

(a) pass to the remaining contract holders,[29] or
(b) their share in the occupation contract may be transferred in the course of administration of their estate,[30]

depending on the terms of the occupation contract.

In either case, the remaining tenants should apply to update the register in the normal way.[31]

Any disposition of the deceased contract holder's share by their personal representative must be of their beneficial interest in the occupation contract, not the legal estate. Consequently, it is not capable of registration.[32] However, where the occupation contract is substantively registered, it may entitle the beneficiary to apply for entry of a Form A restriction in the register.[33] The wording of Form A is set out in Appendix IV.

121.5 Determination

An occupation contract can only be terminated in accordance with:

(a) the fundamental provisions incorporated into the contract under the RH(W)A 2016;
(b) the terms of another enactment;
(c) the law on frustration; or
(d) the law on recission.[34]

Where there is more than one tenant, they must generally all act together to end the contract.

A landlord may not forfeit an occupation contract or serve notice to quit.[35] Generally, a landlord must obtain a possession order to recover possession of the property. However, RH(W)A 2016, ss 152 to 155 contain provisions where the landlord can terminate without a court order.

Where an occupation contract has come to an end the parties should apply to update the register.

121.5.1 Closing a registered title

Where the occupation contract is substantially registered, the parties should apply to close the register. An applicant should deliver to HMLR:

(a) an application in form AP1;
(b) evidence that the occupation contract has come to an end;
(c) any appropriate LTT certificate(s) or other evidence;[36] and
(d) the fee payable.[37]

HMLR will automatically remove the notice of the occupation contract from the landlord's title on completion of the application, there is no need for a further application.

121.5.2 Removing a notice of an occupation contract

Where the occupation contract is protected by an agreed notice, in addition to the usual documents required,[38] an applicant should deliver to HMLR:

(a) documents of title to the determining occupation contract showing evidence of title to the occupation contract; and
(b) evidence that the occupation contract has come to an end;
(c) any appropriate LTT certificate(s) or other evidence;[39] and
(d) any fee payable.[40]

Where the occupation contract is protected by a unilateral notice, either:

(a) the beneficiary may apply to withdraw it;[41] or
(b) the registered proprietor(s) may apply to cancel it.[42]

---

1 Renting Homes (Wales) Act 2016 (RH(W)A 2016), Explanatory note, para 7.
2 RH(W)A 2016, s 31. For the prescribed information, see RH(W)A 2016, s 32. RH(W)A 2016, s 245 defines the occupation date.
3 RH(W)A 2016, s 8(1).
4 As defined in RH(W)A 2016, s 9.
5 For exceptions to these general rules, see RH(W)A 2016, ss 11, 12 and 17.
6 RH(W)A 2016, s 7.
7 RH(W)A 2016, s 240.
8 See 128.4 Duty to disclose overriding interests.
9 See 84 Identity Evidence.
10 See 94 Land Transaction Tax.
11 See 67 Fees.
12 See 119.1 Agreed notice.
13 See 119.3 Unilateral notice.
14 RH(W)A 2016, s 57.
15 RH(W)A 2016, s 49.
16 RH(W)A 2016, s 130.
17 See 176.1 Registration of transfer.
18 See 119.4 Registration of new or additional beneficiary of a unilateral notice.
19 See 94 Land Transaction Tax.
20 RH(W)A 2016, Sch 12, para 20.
21 RH(W)A 2016, s 155.
22 As determined by RH(W)A 2016, s 74.
23 RH(W)A 2016, s 73. Where there is more than one potential successor, RH(W)A 2016, s 78 determines who shall succeed.
24 RH(W)A 2016, s 139.
25 See 67 Fees.
26 For further details of the evidence required, see 133 Personal Representatives.
27 See 119.4 Registration of new or additional beneficiary of a unilateral notice.
28 For further details of the evidence required, see 133 Personal Representatives.
29 RH(W)A 2016, s 52.
30 RH(W)A 2016, s 142.
31 See 92.2 Death of a joint proprietor or 119.4 Registration of new or additional beneficiary of a unilateral notice.

32 Although the parties may update the register or any unilateral notice to reflect the death. See 92.2 Death of a joint proprietor or 119.4 Registration of new or additional beneficiary of a unilateral notice.
33 See 178.2 Entry of restrictions.
34 RH(W)A 2016, s 148.
35 RH(W)A 2016, s 232.
36 See 94 Land Transaction Tax.
37 See 67 Fees.
38 See 119.1 Agreed notice.
39 See 94 Land Transaction Tax.
40 See 67 Fees.
41 See 119.5 Removal of a unilateral notice.
42 See 119.6 Cancellation of a unilateral notice.

122 OFFICIAL COPIES AND INSPECTION

Any person may, subject to formalities and fee, inspect and make copies of:

(a) the register of any individual registered title (including any title plan);
(b) any document kept by HMLR which is referred to in the register;
(c) any other document kept by HMLR which relates to an application to it; and
(d) the caution register of an individual caution against first registration (including any caution plan).[1]

However, the general right to inspect and make copies is subject to certain limitations imposed by LRR 2003, rr 133 and 135 which provide that the following 'excepted documents' are excepted from the general right:

(a) exempt information documents;
(b) an edited information document which has been replaced by another edited information document under LRR 2003, r 136(6) or r 138(4);
(c) form EX1A (reasons for exemption in support of an application to designate a document as an exempt information document);
(d) form CIT and any form which has been attached to form CIT (application in connection with investigation or enforcement proceedings), together with any documents or copy documents prepared by HMLR in connection with the application;
(e) any document relating to an application for a network access agreement under LRA 2002, Sch 5, para 1(4);
(f) an 'identity document' (any document within LRA 2002, s 66(1)(c) provided to, or prepared or obtained by, the Registry as evidence of identity of any person (such as an applicant)); and

(g) an 'investigation of crime document', being any document within LRA 2002, s 66(1)(c) (other than an identity document) which relates to the prevention or detection of crime – *unless* it is a document:

  (i) lodged as part of or in support of either an application to the Registry or an objection to an application; or
  (ii) prepared by, or at the request of, the Registry as part of the process of considering an application or objection but which is not prepared principally in connection with the prevention or detection of crime.

In addition, correspondence and documents relating to claims for indemnity under LRA 2002, Sch 8 are also excepted from the general right. Also, the general right to inspect does not extend to the index of proprietors' names. However, these exceptions are in turn subject to special provision under LRR 2003, r 140, in relation to applications made in form CIT in connection with court proceedings, insolvency and tax liability.

122.1 Personal inspection

A person may apply in form PIC to make a personal inspection of the register and the documents referred to in LRA 2002, s 66(1) or (during the currency of a relevant notice given under LRR 2003, Sch 2) any part of them, subject to the exceptions referred to above. A separate form PIC is required for each title to be inspected. Fees are payable for inspection, depending upon the subject matter. If the title number is not known, an additional fee may be payable. An applicant must make an appointment to inspect at least 5 working days before his proposed attendance. Appointments are available between 9 am and 4 pm Mondays to Fridays excluding public holidays.[2]

122.2 Official copies

An application may be made using form OC1 for:

(a) an official copy of an individual register or (during the currency of a relevant notice given under LRR 2003, Sch 2) any part of it;
(b) an official copy of any title plan of an individual register;
(c) an official copy of an individual caution register and caution plan; and
(d) a certificate of inspection of any title plan.

A separate application must be made for each registered title or caution against first registration.[3] A fee is payable.[4]

A certificate of inspection of a title plan will be issued by HMLR in form CI and reveals whether the land in question is in the relevant title and whether it is affected by any colour or other reference shown on the title plan. The accuracy of the certificate will be guaranteed, but it will not confer on the applicant priority for the registration of any disposition.

An application may be made using form OC2 for an official copy of any document referred to in the register of title and kept by HMLR, and any other document relating to an application that is kept by HMLR or (during the currency of a relevant notice given under LRR 2003, Sch 2) any part of such documents. Form EX2 is used for requests for official copies of exempt information documents.[5]

Official copies of registers and title plans are always timed and dated to show that they represent a true record at that specific time. Where there are pending substantive applications, the date and time will be backdated to immediately before receipt of the earliest pending application. An official search can also be made, to provide details of the pending application(s) if required. Official copies of documents are not dated because, once registered or otherwise referred to in the register, documents are not normally altered.

An official copy of the register, or of any document kept by HMLR which is referred to in the register or which relates to an application, is admissible in evidence to the same extent as the original.[6] If there is a mistake in the official copy, a person who relies on that copy is not liable for loss suffered by another person by reason of the mistake[7]. A person is entitled to be indemnified by HMLR if he suffers loss by reason of a mistake in an official copy.[8]

Official copies are often of documents kept by HMLR which are not originals. As between the parties to a disposition relating to a registered title, the copy document kept by HMLR is to be taken to be correct and to contain all the material parts of the original document. No party to such disposition is to be affected by any provision of the original document not contained in the copy kept by HMLR, nor can any party require production of the original document.[9]

122.3 Exempt information documents

A person may apply for HMLR to designate a document an 'exempt information document' if he claims that the document contains prejudicial information.[10] The document must be one referred to in the register of title, or one that relates to an application to HMLR, the original or a copy of which is kept by HMLR. Such application may accompany the application that will lead to the document being kept by HMLR. 'Prejudicial information' in this context means:

(a) information that relates to an individual who is the applicant and, if disclosed to other persons (whether to the public generally or specific persons) would, or would be likely to, cause substantial unwarranted damage or substantial unwarranted distress to the applicant or another; or
(b) information that if disclosed to other persons (whether to the public generally or specific persons) would, or would be likely to, prejudice the commercial interests of the applicant.[11]

The application to designate a document an exempt information document must be made in forms EX1 and EX1A. A fee is payable.[12] Form EX1A states the reasons for exemption. It should be borne in mind that form EX1A is excepted from the general right of inspection and copying, but form EX1 is not, nor are any accompanying letters. In addition to the document in question, the applicant must deliver to HMLR a copy which excludes the prejudicial information (with the words 'excluded information' inserted instead wherever information has been excluded within the document) and which is certified as being a true copy of the document from which the prejudicial information has been excluded except that it excludes the prejudicial information and includes the above wording instead.

Provided HMLR is satisfied that the applicant's claim is not groundless, it must designate the document an exempt information document and may make an appropriate entry in the register of any affected registered title. If, however, it considers that so designating it could prejudice the keeping of the register, it may cancel the application. Where a document is designated an exempt information document, the edited copy is known as the 'edited information document' and it is this which is supplied in response to a request for an official copy using form OC2. The benefit of the designation of an exempt information document cannot be transferred to another person; for example, on a transfer of the registered estate to which it relates.

Where a document has been designated an exempt information document, it is possible to make another application so that further information is excluded from the edited information document and a new edited information document is prepared.[13]

It is possible for a person to apply for an official copy of an exempt information document using form EX2 and stating why he considers that an official copy of the edited information document is not sufficient for his purposes.[14] A fee is payable.[15] The applicant also must state in form EX2 why he considers that none of the information omitted from the edited information document is prejudicial information. Alternatively, if he accepts that some or all of the information is prejudicial information, he must give details and state why he considers that the public interest in providing an official copy of the exempt information document outweighs the public interest in not doing so.

HMLR must give notice of any such application to the person who applied for the document to be designated an exempt information document, unless it is satisfied that such notice is unnecessary or impracticable.[16]

HMLR will supply an official copy of the exempt information document if it decides that none of the information excluded from the edited information document is prejudicial information. HMLR will also do so if it decides that, although some or all of the information excluded is prejudicial information, the public interest in providing an official copy of the exempt information document to the applicant outweighs the public interest in not doing so.[17] Application for an official copy of an exempt information document may also be made under LRR 2003, r 140 using form CIT, in connection with court proceedings, insolvency or tax liability.

A person who applied for a document to be designated an exempt information document may apply in form EX3 to have the designation removed.[18] No fee is currently payable. HMLR must remove the designation and any entry in the register which relates to that designation, if it is satisfied that the application is in order. Where a document has been made an exempt document as a result of more than one application by different persons, HMLR must replace the existing edited information document with one that reflects only the current exemptions.

122.4 Freedom of Information Act 2000

The Freedom of Information Act 2000 generally allows inspection of all documents held by HMLR as a 'public authority'. Any person has the right to ask a public authority for information and, if that authority holds it, to have that information disclosed to them unless there are justifiable reasons why this should not be done. Under the right of access provisions of the Freedom of Information Act:

(a) a request must be in writing (which includes email or fax) and must include a name and address to which a response can be sent;
(b) the request does not have to mention the Freedom of Information Act 2000;
(c) the request can be made to any part of the public authority;
(d) the authority must reply within 20 working days;
(e) the authority has a duty to provide assistance to the applicant; and
(f) the authority may charge a fee for providing the information.

A request to HMLR for information covered by the Freedom of Information Act 2000 may only be refused in the following circumstances:

(a) where HMLR reasonably requires further information to identify and locate the information requested but the applicant has failed to supply it; or
(b) where the request is 'vexatious' or repeated, for example where HMLR has previously complied with an identical or similar request from the same applicant and a reasonable time has not elapsed between compliance with the previous request and the making of the current request;[19] or
(c) where HMLR estimates that the cost of complying with the request would exceed the 'appropriate limit' (currently £600);[20] or
(d) where an exemption applies, and applying the 'public interest test' (if applicable) leads to the decision that it is not in the public interest to disclose the information (see below).

Exemptions from the obligation to disclose information can be absolute or non-absolute. If an absolute exemption applies, the information requested need not be disclosed and, in many cases, HMLR is not obliged to comply with the duty to confirm or deny whether it holds the requested information. Absolute exemption applies to requests for information reasonably accessible by other means.[21] This means that the Freedom of Information Act 2000 does not apply, for example, to requests for official copies of registers and title plans, and documents relating to applications or to requests for historical copies of registers, as these are available under the general right under LRA 2002, s 66(1). Applications in that regard should therefore be made in the appropriate form, such as form OC1 or form OC2, as the case may be.

Information covered by HMLR's Publication Scheme is also absolutely exempt. The Freedom of Information Act 2000 requires HMLR to adopt and maintain a publication scheme setting out classes of information which it intends to make available to the public as a matter of course, the manner in which the information is to be made available and whether the information will be provided free or for a charge.[22] The HMLR Publication Scheme is available on its website.[23] Other examples of information covered by absolute exemption are information supplied by or relating to court records.

In the case of non-absolute exemptions, the Freedom of Information Act 2000 requires HMLR to consider whether or not the exemption applies and, if it does, then to consider the 'public interest test' before withholding or disclosing information.[24] Examples of information covered by the non-absolute exemptions are personal information about third parties and information that constitutes a trade secret or the disclosure of which would, or would be likely to, prejudice the commercial interests of any person. Under the public interest test there is likely to be a public interest in disclosing information where it:

(a) facilitates accountability and transparency in the spending of public money; or
(b) allows individuals to understand decisions affecting their lives and, in some cases, assists individuals in challenging those decisions; or
(c) brings to light information affecting public safety.

The LRA 2002 and the LRR 2003 were drafted to take account of the provisions of the Freedom of Information Act 2000, so it appears unlikely that inspection of exempt information would be allowed under that Act where it would not be allowed under the LRR 2003. However, it remains a possibility, which should be borne in mind when drafting documents relating to registered land.

In relation to a request under the Freedom of Information Act 2000 for personal inspection and copying, or for a copy of a document, or for historical information (as opposed to an application under the LRR 2003), the request should be made in accordance with the requirements set out above, for consideration by HMLR. There is no requirement to provide reasons for the request, but it may assist in cases where the public interest test needs to be applied.

In relation to a request for an official copy of an exempt information document under the Freedom of Information Act 2000 (as opposed to an application under the LRR 2003 in form EX2), the request should be made in accordance with the requirements set out above, for consideration by HMLR. Again, there is no requirement to provide reasons for the request, but it may assist HMLR in deciding whether the full copy of the document can be provided.

Under the Freedom of Information Act 2000, HMLR may need to determine whether the excluded information is 'personal data' for the purposes of the Data Protection Act 2018.[25] If it is, the information may be exempt from the general right of access under the Freedom of Information Act 2000.[26] If it does not fall within that absolute exception, HMLR must apply the public interest test in deciding whether a full copy of the document can be provided.[27] HMLR will normally serve notice of the request upon any third party who may be affected by the decision and he will have the opportunity to make representations, which HMLR will take into account in making its decision.

A fee may be payable for a request under the Freedom of Information Act 2000. If the information cannot be provided within 20 working days, HMLR will inform the applicant in advance and provide an estimated time for dealing with the request. If HMLR decides to refuse a request for information, it will inform the applicant of this and the reasons for the decision.

122.5 Environmental Information Regulations 2004

The Environmental Information Regulations 2004 (SI 2004/3391) give members of the public the right to access environmental information held by public authorities.[28] It is possible that some of the information held by HMLR comprises environmental information (particularly some of the information relating to local land charges[29]).

A request may be made by letter, email, telephone or in person.

The Environmental Information Regulations 2004 (SI 2004/3391) contain several exceptions to the general right. HMLR need not release the relevant information if:

(a) an exception applies; and
(b) in all the circumstances of the case, the public interest in maintaining the exception outweighs the public interest in disclosing the information.[30]

If no exceptions apply and HMLR does hold environmental information, it must release it to the requestor as soon as possible and no later than 20 working days after the date of receipt of the request.[31]

The Information Commissioner's Office website contains further details about the Environmental Information Regulations 2004 (SI 2004/3391).[32]

122.6 The United Kingdom General Data Protection Regulation and the Data Protection Act 2018

The United Kingdom General Data Protection Regulation (UK GDPR) and the Data Protection Act 2018 set out data subjects' rights to require:

(a) confirmation as to whether or not personal data concerning him are being processed; and
(b) where that is the case, access to the personal data and the additional information set out in UK GDPR, Art 15(1).[33]

The UK GDPR comprises those parts of the EU GDPR[34] as were retained in UK domestic law following Brexit.[35]

At the time of writing, Parliament is considering whether the above right should be limited to such confirmation, personal data and other information as the controller is able to provide based on a reasonable and proportionate search for the personal data and other information.[36]

The above rights affect HMLR, but do not apply to most of the data that it holds because information that is already publicly available is exempt; for example, under the general right to inspect and make copies under LRA 2002, s 66(1).[37] An application relating to such information should be made in the appropriate prescribed form, such as form OC1 or form OC2, as the case may be.

A 'data subject' may make a request for personal data that is not already publicly available. There is no prescribed format for the request and it need not be in writing.

If HMLR accedes to the request, it must:

(a) provide the relevant information to the data subject in a concise, transparent, intelligible and easily accessible form, using clear and plain language;
(b) provide the relevant information in writing or by other means. Where the data subject so requests, HMLR may provide the information orally provided the data subject has proven his identity; and
(c) provide the relevant information without undue delay and in any event within one month of receipt of the request. That period may be extended by 2 further months where necessary, taking into account the complexity and number of the requests. HMLR must inform the data subject of any such extension within one month of receipt of the request, together with the reasons for the delay.

HMLR must provide the information and copy documents free of charge. HMLR may charge a reasonable fee based on administrative costs for any further copies requested. Where the data subject makes the request by electronic means, and unless otherwise requested by the data subject, HMLR must provide the information in a commonly used electronic form.

If HMLR does not accede to the subject access request, it must:

(a) inform the data subject of the refusal without delay and at the latest within one month of receipt of the request;
(b) give reasons for the refusal; and
(c) provide information on the possibility of lodging a complaint with the Information Commissioner and seeking a judicial remedy.[38]

HMLR must deal with the request within 40 days. The response will provide details of the personal data held about the applicant, the purposes for which it is being used, and those to whom the data may be disclosed. If the data requested contains details about other living persons, HMLR may need to obtain their consent to divulge the data or it may edit the data to exclude those details. In this case, the 40-day period may be extended.

---

1 LRA 2002, s 66.

2 Notice 6: Applications made orally at an HM Land Registry office (effective 21 November 2022), given under LRR 2003, Sch 2 (www.gov.uk/government/publications/land-registration-act-2002-schedule-2/notice-6-applications-made-orally-at-an-hm-land-registry-office-customer-information-centre).

3 LRR 2003, r 134.

4 See 67 Fees.

5 See 122.3 Exempt information documents.

6 LRA 2002, s 67(1).

7 LRA 2002, s 67(2).

8 LRA 2002, Sch 8, para 1(1)(d). See 86 Indemnity.

9 LRA 2002, s 120.

10 LRR 2003, r 136.

11 LRR 2003, r 131.

12 See 67 Fees.

13 LRR 2003, r 136(6).

14 LRR 2003, r 137.

15 See 67 Fees.

16 LRR 2003, r 137(3).

17 LRR 2003, r 137(4).

18 LRR 2003, r 138.

19 Freedom of Information Act 2000, s 14.

20 Freedom of Information and Data Protection (Appropriate Limit and Fees) Regulations 2004 (SI 2004/3244), reg 3(2).

21 Freedom of Information Act 2000, s 21.

22 Freedom of Information Act 2000, s 19.

23 www.gov.uk/government/organisations/land-registry/about/publication-scheme.

24 Freedom of Information Act 2000, s 2(1)(b) and (2)(b).

25 See 122.6 The United Kingdom General Data Protection Regulation and Data Protection Act 2018.

26 Freedom of Information Act 2000, s 2(3)(f) and (fa).

27 Freedom of Information Act 2000, s 2.

28 Environmental Information Regulations 2004 (SI 2004/3391), reg 5. 'Environmental information' is defined in reg 2.

29 See 109 Local Land Charges.

30 Environmental Information Regulations 2004 (SI 2004/3391), reg 12.

31 Environmental Information Regulations 2004 (SI 2004/3391), reg 5(2).

32 https://ico.org.uk/for-organisations/eir-and-access-to-information/guide-to-the-environmental-information-regulations/.

33 United Kingdom General Data Protection Regulation (UK GDPR), Art 15(1).

34 Regulation (EU) 2016/679.

35 In particular, by virtue of European Union (Withdrawal) Act 2018, s 3 and Data Protection, Privacy and Electronic Communications (Amendments etc) (EU Exit) Regulations 2019 (SI 2019/419), Sch 1 and as further amended by the Data Protection Act 2018.

36 Data (Use and Access Bill) 2024–25, s 78(1).

37 UK GDPR, Sch 2, para 5(1).

38 UK GDPR, Art 12.

123 OFFICIAL SEARCHES

To obtain up-to-date information about all subsisting entries in the register of a title (including any which may have been made since the applicant obtained an official copy of the register) and details of any pending applications in respect of a registered title, it is necessary to apply for an official search of the register. The LRA 2002 provides for a system of official searches of the register, which is operated in accordance with the LRR 2003. An application may be made for an official search with priority or an official search without priority. A fee is payable.[1]

123.1 Official search with priority

An official search with priority may be made only by a purchaser of the title in question. The search may be in respect of the individual register of a registered title or of a pending application for first registration.[2] A 'purchaser' for this purpose is a person who has entered into, or intends to enter into, a registrable disposition of a registered estate or registered charge for valuable consideration as disponee. 'Valuable consideration' does not include marriage consideration or a nominal consideration in money.[3]

The purpose of such a search is to enable a purchaser to obtain an official certificate of the entries in the register of the disponor's title immediately before completion and to ensure that (if he applies to register the disposition within the priority period conferred by the search) he will be unaffected by any entry made between the date of this certificate and the registration of his protectable disposition.

123.1.1 Lodging of official search

The application should be made in form OS1 for a search of the whole of the estate in a registered title or application for first registration, and in form OS2 for a search of part. No plan need accompany form OS2 if the part affected is a numbered plot on an estate plan approved by HMLR relating to a developing estate, provided that the plot number(s) and the date of HMLR's approval are stated on form OS2. Where there is no approved estate plan, form OS2 must be accompanied by a plan in duplicate; this plan should be a copy of the plan intended to be used in the protectable disposition.

123.1.2 The 'search from' date

Application for an official search with priority must be from a date (the 'search from' date) which is the date shown on an official copy of the register of the individual registered title as the date on which the entries shown on that official copy were subsisting. A time is also printed on the official copy but this need not be quoted on an application for an official search.

123.1.3 Official certificate of search

The result of a search is contained in an official search certificate issued by HMLR. It reveals details of any adverse entries made in the individual register on or after the day specified in the application as the 'search from' date. Details of any entries made in the register and subsequently cancelled during the period searched may not be given. It also reveals any pending application or pending official search with priority affecting the registered title entered on the day list. The date and time at which the priority period commences and expires are stated.

Additionally, in the case of a search in respect of an estate which is the subject of a pending application for first registration, the official search certificate will also enable the purchaser to satisfy himself that the estate searched is the subject of a pending first registration application and will state by whom the application was made and on what date the application was received. It will not contain details of any entries that may be made in the register of title arising from the deeds or other evidence of title produced with the application for first registration. The same priority protection is conferred as that in relation to an official search of an existing registered title, but no guarantee is given that any registered title will be granted or, if granted, that it will be of the class of title sought.

Accuracy of an official search certificate is guaranteed and indemnity may be payable by HMLR as a result of any mistake in an official search.[4]

If the extent of the property to which the search relates is not wholly comprised within the registered title, the official search certificate will be limited to the extent which falls within the title. The details of the limitation and the reason for it will normally be included with the official search certificate, but the applicant should not seek to rely on this as a means of 'confirming' the registered proprietor's title and should instead rely on a proper investigation of that title.

123.1.4 Priority period of official search

The priority period provided by the official search is the period beginning at the time when the application for the official search is entered on the day list and ending at midnight marking the end of the 30th working day thereafter. A working day is any day from Monday to Friday (inclusive) which is not Christmas Day, Good Friday or any other day either specified or declared by proclamation under Banking and Financial Dealings Act 1971, s 1 or appointed by the Secretary of State or certified by HMLR as being an 'interrupted day' due to delay or failure of a communication service or to some other event or circumstance causing substantial interruption in the normal operation of HMLR.[5]

For the position where two or more official search certificates with priority relating to the same registrable estate or charge or to the same registered land have been issued, see 138.4 Priority of applications.

The priority period resulting from an official search in respect of a registrable disposition is also conferred on any prior registrable disposition affecting the same registered land on which that application is dependent.[6] For example, in the common situation where a person is purchasing registered land and is entering into a legal charge at the same time, a search by the intending chargee confers the same priority period on the intending transferee. The same applies where the search relates to a pending first registration. Where an application is lodged, or deemed to be lodged, at the same time as the priority period of a search expires, the application is taken as being made within that priority period.[7]

123.1.5 Effect of priority

An official search certificate with priority confers priority upon an application to register the protected disposition, over applications relating to other registrable dispositions and other matters which were not entered on the day list before that search and are not themselves protected by an earlier official search with priority.

An application protected by an official search with priority will have priority over an application protected by another official search with priority, in respect of the same registered estate or charge, where the first search is deemed to have been delivered before the second one.

If the completion of the protected disposition is delayed to an extent likely to preclude the delivery of the application for registration within the priority period, a second application for an official search may be made, whether the priority period under the first official search certificate is still subsisting or has expired. However, the second official search certificate will *not* operate to 'extend' the priority afforded by the first. It will only provide a separate priority period, which will not provide priority over any application lodged before its priority period commences.

Any entry made in the register during the priority period conferred by an official search will be postponed to a subsequent application to register the protectable disposition to which the priority period relates, unless the earlier entry was itself protected by an official search with a priority period ranking ahead of the one relating to the subsequent application.[8] For this reason, where an official search with priority has not yet expired and has priority over an application on the day list, HMLR will not normally complete that application until the priority period of the search has expired.[9]

123.1.6 Withdrawal of official search with priority

A person who has made an application for an official search with priority may withdraw that official search.[10] On withdrawal, the priority period ceases to have effect. Where an entry has already been made in the register in respect of a disposition protected by the search, the search cannot be withdrawn.

123.2 Official search without priority

Any person may apply for an official search without priority using form OS3.[11] This form of official search is available to a person who is not a 'purchaser';[12] for example, a mortgagee who intends to protect his mortgage in the register by entry of a notice. Such a search can only be made in respect of a registered title; it cannot be used to search against a pending first registration. The position with regard to plans for a search of part is the same as that for official searches in form OS2.[13]

Similar information is supplied with the result of an official search without priority as with the result of an official search with priority, but no priority period is given. The accuracy of the certificate is guaranteed but it will not confer on the applicant priority for the registration of any disposition.

123.3 Official search by a mortgagee in form HR3

The proprietor of a registered charge or a mortgagee of registered land may search the register to enable him to comply with the provisions of FLA 1996, s 56(3).[14]

---

1 See 67 Fees.

2 LRR 2003, r 147.

3 LRA 2002, s 132(1).

4 LRA 2002, Sch 8, para 1(1)(c). See 86 Indemnity.
5 LRR 2003, r 217(1).
6 LRR 2003, r 151.
7 LRR 2003, r 154.
8 LRA 2002, s 72(2) and (3).
9 LRA 2002, s 72(5).
10 LRR 2003, r 150.
11 LRR 2003, r 155.
12 See 123.1 Official search with priority.
13 See 123.1.1 Lodging of official search.
14 See 81.5 Home rights search by a mortgagee.

124 OFFICIAL SEARCHES OF THE INDICES

Under LRA 2002, s 68 and LRR rr 10 and 11, HMLR must keep certain indices. These are an index map, an index of verbal descriptions of relating franchises and manors and an index of proprietors' names. Both the index map and the index of verbal descriptions of relating franchises and manors are open to inspection and any person may apply for an official search of the indices. The index of proprietors' names is not open to general inspection, but the LRR 2003 provides for certain limited rights to make an official search of that index.

124.1 Search of the index map

The index map is a large-scale map from which it is possible to ascertain, in relation to a parcel of land, whether there is:

(a) a pending application for first registration (other than in respect of title to a relating franchise);
(b) a pending application for a caution against first registration (other than where the subject of the caution is a relating franchise);
(c) a registered estate in land;
(d) a registered rentcharge;
(e) a registered profit à prendre in gross;
(f) a registered affecting franchise; or
(g) a caution against first registration (other than where the subject of the caution is a relating franchise).

If there is such a registered estate or caution, the index map provides the title number.

An affecting franchise is a franchise which relates to a defined area of land and is an adverse right affecting, or capable of affecting, the title to an estate or charge. A relating franchise is a franchise which is not an affecting franchise.[1]

An application for an official search of the index map is made using form SIM. The application must clearly describe the land to which it relates. The description should include the postal number or description, the road name, the locality, the town, the local authority serving the property, the postcode and/or OS map reference (if known) and any known title number. If the search is in respect of a particular flat in a block of flats, this should be made clear in the description. A plan may not be necessary if the land can be identified by postal description. If, however, HMLR so requires, an applicant must provide a copy of an extract from the OS map on the largest scale published showing the land to which the application relates.[2] A fee is payable.[3]

The result of an official search of the index map will include the date and time of the official search certificate; a description of the land searched; details of any of the matters referred to in (a) to (g) above which affect the land; and, if there is a registered estate or caution, the title number.

It should be remembered that the index map is only an index and that any plan attached to the result of an official search is merely illustrative and does not define the extent of the land in a title. If more specific information is required about a title revealed by the result of a search of the index map, the applicant should obtain official copies of the register and title plan of that title.[4]

124.2 Search of the index of relating franchises and manors

The index of relating franchises and manors is an index of verbal descriptions of:

(a) pending applications for first registrations of title to relating franchises;
(b) pending applications for cautions against first registration where the subject of the caution is a relating franchise;
(c) registered franchises which are relating franchises;
(d) registered manors; and
(e) cautions against first registration where the subject of the caution is a relating franchise.

If there are any such registered estates and cautions, the index provides the title numbers arranged by administrative area.

An application for an official search of the index of relating franchises and manors is made using form SIF. A fee is payable.[5]

In form SIF the applicant must specify whether he is searching in respect of manors or relating franchises or both, and must also specify the administrative areas (i.e. the relevant counties and/or unitary authorities) in respect of which he is searching.

The result of an official search of the index of relating franchises and manors will include the date and time of the official search certificate; a description of the administrative area(s) searched; details of any of the matters referred to in (a) to (e) above which affect the administrative area(s); and, if there is a registered estate or caution, the title number.

It should be remembered that the index of relating franchises and manors is only an index and that if more specific information is required about a title revealed by the result of a search of the index, the applicant should obtain official copies of the register and title plan of that title.[6]

124.3 Search of the index of proprietors' names

The index of proprietors' names shows for each individual register the name of the proprietor of the registered estate and the proprietor of any registered charge together with the title number.[7] Until every register is kept electronically, the index need not contain the name of any corporate or joint proprietor of an estate or of a charge registered as proprietor before 1 May 1972. The index of proprietors' names is not open to general inspection. However, in addition to the special right to a search made in form CIT (application in connection with court proceedings, insolvency and tax liability), any person may apply for a search to be made in the index in respect of either his own name, the name of a corporation aggregate, or the name of some other person in whose property he can satisfy HMLR that he is interested generally. For example, he may be interested as personal representative or trustee in bankruptcy.

An application for a search in the index of proprietors' names is made using form PN1. Only one name can be searched on each form; where there is a former name or alternative name, a separate form PN1 should be used for each. Every address which may have been used as an address for service in the register should be stated. A fee is payable.[8]

The reply to the application will state whether or not the person named in the search appears in the index and, if he does, the reply will also give the relevant title number(s). The reply does not constitute an official search for the purposes of the LRA 2002.

---

1 See 74 Franchises.
2 LRR 2003, r 145(3).
3 See 67 Fees.
4 See 122.2 Official copies.
5 See 67 Fees.
6 See 122.2 Official copies.
7 LRR 2003, r 11.
8 See 67 Fees.

125 OPTIONS

An option to purchase, or to renew a lease of, registered land may be protected by the entry in the register of an agreed notice or a unilateral notice, and possibly (depending on the terms of the option agreement) a restriction. A notice does not necessarily mean that the option is valid but does protect the priority of the option on any registered disposition.[1] A restriction does not confer any priority. However, it prevents an entry being made in the register relating to any disposition, or a disposition of a specified kind, unless the terms of the restriction have (where applicable) been complied with. The protection given to the option may also extend to the subsequent estate contract when the option is exercised.[2]

An option is not itself an interest which overrides either first registration or registered dispositions. A beneficiary should protect its priority by entry of a notice in the register. However, even where an option relating to registered land is not protected by a notice, it may still override a later registered disposition for valuable consideration if, at the time of that later disposition, the person having the benefit of the option is in actual occupation of the land to which the option relates. If he is in actual occupation of only part of the land to which the option relates, he has an overriding interest only in respect of the part he is occupying.[3]

The interest of the person in actual possession does not override a registered disposition if enquiry was made of him before the disposition and he failed to disclose the option when he could reasonably have been expected to do so. Nor does the option override a registered disposition if it belongs to a person whose occupation would not have been obvious on a reasonably careful inspection of the land at the time of the disposition, and if the person to whom the disposition is made does not have actual knowledge of the option at the time of the disposition.[4]

Where the option is contained in a lease that is an unregistered interest falling within LRA 2002, Sch 3, para 1 which overrides registered dispositions, the option may be protected by an entry in the register even where no entry may be made as to the lease itself.[5] This applies even if the interest to be granted under the option is another lease which will be an interest which overrides registered dispositions.

The option should be granted and signed by the proprietor of the registered estate, or a satisfactory chain of title shown between the person granting the option and the registered proprietor. For example, if the registered proprietor has contracted to sell a registered title to A, and A then grants to B an option to purchase the land in the title, B's option can be protected by a notice, whether or not A's contract is also protected by a notice.

An option granted before 6 April 2010 may become void for remoteness if it breaches the rule against perpetuities.[6] An option granted after that date is no longer subject to the rule against perpetuities.[7]

Before HMLR can enter an agreed notice or unilateral notice in respect of an interest comprising a land transaction, it must ensure that the appropriate SDLT and/or LTT certificate(s) accompanies the application where this is required.[8]

125.1 Agreed notice

In addition to the usual documents required,[9] an applicant should deliver to HMLR the original document granting the option or a certified copy of it.

Where the option is granted by a person with the benefit of a contract for sale, the contract or a certified copy of it should be included with the application. This is not necessary if there is already an agreed notice in respect of the contract in the register.

Where the consent of the registered proprietor is not available but, for example, the document granting the option is signed by him, this is likely to be sufficient to satisfy HMLR of the validity of the applicant's claim for the purposes of LRA 2002, s 34(3)(c).

The agreed notice in the register will give details of the interest protected.

The applicant may prefer to apply for entry of a unilateral notice where he does not wish the terms of the option to be open to public inspection and copying.

125.2 Unilateral notice

An applicant should deliver to HMLR the usual documents required.[10]

The statement in panel 11 or conveyancer's certificate in panel 12 of form UN1 should be completed on the following lines to show the interest of the applicant:

> person having the benefit of an option [to purchase] or [to take or renew a lease] contained in a [*description of document*] dated [*date*] made between [*names*].

Where the option is granted by a person with the benefit of a contract for sale, the contract should also be referred to. The wording must establish the link between the registered proprietor and the person who is to be shown as the beneficiary of the notice.

The unilateral notice in the register will give brief details of the interest protected and identify the beneficiary of that notice.

125.3 Restriction

HMLR may not enter any restriction for the purpose of protecting the priority of an interest which is, or could be, the subject of a notice.[11] However, this does not prevent the entry of a restriction in addition to the notice of the option, where appropriate. Although the notice will protect the priority of the option, a restriction may be used to ensure that any conditions in relation to another disposition by the registered proprietor are complied with. The consent of the registered proprietor to the entry of the restriction is required, unless the document granting the option contains a provision which limits the registered proprietor's powers to enter into any further disposition. HMLR must give notice of the application for a restriction to the proprietor of the registered estate or charge concerned, if it has not been made by or with the consent of such proprietor or a person entitled to be registered as such proprietor.[12]

An applicant should deliver to HMLR the usual documents required.[13]

If the application is made by a person who claims that he has a sufficient interest in the making of the entry, a statement in panel 12 of form RX1 signed by the applicant or a certificate by his conveyancer in panel 13 of form RX1 must be provided, setting out details of the option and of the provision in the document granting the option limiting the registered proprietor's powers to enter into a disposition.

Panel 9 of form RX1 should set out the required restriction(s). A restriction in a standard form contained in LRR 2003, Sch 4 does not require the approval of HMLR to the terms of the restriction under LRA 2002, s 43(3). A possible form of restriction based on Form L is:

> No disposition of the registered estate by the proprietor of the registered estate is to be registered without a written certificate signed by [*purchaser*] of [*address*] or their conveyancer that the provisions of [*clause, paragraph or other particulars*] of [*details of document granting the option*] have been complied with or that they do not apply to the disposition.

The wording of Form L is set out in Appendix IV.

Form RX1 does not need to be used if the application is for a standard form restriction and is contained in either the 'additional provisions' panel of a prescribed form of transfer or assent, or in clause LR13 of a prescribed clauses lease (or any other lease containing clauses LR1 to LR14 of LRR 2003, Sch 1A).[14]

125.4 Options contained in registrable dispositions

Although an option may be granted by way of a separate transaction, it can also form part of the terms of a registrable disposition such as a transfer or a lease. In the case of a transfer of part of a registered title, HMLR must (where appropriate) make entries in the relevant registered title in respect of any rights, provisions or other matters created by the transfer which are capable of being so entered. However, HMLR need make no such entries where the relevant title numbers have not been given in panel 2 of form AP1, unless separate application is made in respect of them.[15] Similar provisions apply in the case of a transfer of the whole of a registered title, or other registrable disposition.[16]

In the case of a lease granted out of a registered estate in land which is required to be registered under LRA 2002, s 27(2)(b), LRR 2003, r 72A specifies certain entries which HMLR must make on registration of the lease. This applies to both prescribed clauses leases and other leases. On completion of such a lease by registration, HMLR must (where appropriate) make entries in the relevant registered title in respect of interests contained in the lease which are of the nature referred to in clause LR9 (rights of acquisition, etc). However, where the lease is a prescribed clauses lease and the rights are not specified or referred to in clause LR9, HMLR need take no action in respect of them unless a separate application is made. Equally, HMLR need not make any entries where, in the case of a prescribed clauses lease, the title numbers of the relevant registered titles have not been given in clause LR2.2; or in any other case, the title numbers of the relevant registered titles required by clause LR2.2 have not been given in panel 2 of form AP1 lodged for the purpose of completing the lease by registration, unless a separate application is made.

---

1 LRA 2002, ss 29, 30 and 32.
2 *Armstrong & Holmes Ltd v Holmes* [1994] 1 All ER 826.
3 LRA 2002, ss 29 and 30 and Sch 3, para 2.
4 LRA 2002, Sch 3, para 2.
5 I.e. because the lease is for a term not exceeding 3 years and is not otherwise registrable.
6 Perpetuities and Accumulations Act 1964, ss 9 and 10.
7 Perpetuities and Accumulations Act 2009, s 1.
8 Finance Act 2003, s 79(1) and Land Transaction Tax and Anti-avoidance of Devolved Taxes (Wales) Act 2017, s 65(1).
9 See 119.1 Agreed notice.
10 See 119.3 Unilateral notice.
11 LRA 2002, s 42(2).
12 LRA 2002, s 45.
13 See 153.1 Application for entry of restriction.
14 LRR 2003, r 92(7).
15 LRR 2003, r 72.
16 LRR 2003, r 72C.

126 OVERAGE

See 10 Agreement to pay further consideration.

127 OVERREACHING

Overreaching occurs where there is a disposition of land, which is subject to a trust of land, and capital money arises; for example, on a sale of the property. It is the mechanism under which the capital money is paid to not less than two trustees (or to a sole personal representative acting as such) or to a trust corporation, so that the equitable interests of the beneficiaries under the trust are transferred to the capital monies (such as the proceeds of sale), leaving the purchaser to take free of those interests.[1] Only a:

(a) transfer,
(b) lease, or
(c) legal charge

can have overreaching effect. A disposition of another sort, such as the grant of an easement, cannot overreach an earlier equitable interest.[2] Further, it appears the requirements to pay capital monies to two trustees or a trust corporation applies only where capital monies arise; where a disposition is for no capital monies but the transferee, tenant or chargee remains a purchaser (as defined in LPA 1925, s 205(1)), payment to a single trustee may effect overreaching.[3]

Knight v Fernley[4] indicates it is apparently possible to overreach an unregistered transfer (even where the unregistered transferee is in actual occupation of the land in question at the time of the later transfer such that his interest would otherwise comprise an overriding interest[5]).

In relation to registered estates which are subject to a trust of land, the entry of a restriction in Form A in the register reflects the existence of the trust and ensures that overreaching is effected on a disposition for value of the land.[6] The wording of Form A is set out in Appendix IV.

Overreaching is discussed in more detail in the relevant sections of this book. See, in particular, 92 Joint Proprietors, 133 Personal Representatives and 178 Trusts of Land.

---

1 LPA 1925, ss 2 and 27.
2 *Baker v Craggs* [2018] EWCA Civ 1126.
3 *State Bank of India v Sood* [1997] Ch 276.
4 [2021] EWHC 1343 (Ch).
5 See 128.2.2 Interests of persons in actual occupation.
6 LRA 2002, s 42(1)(b) and LRR 2003, r 94.

128 OVERRIDING INTERESTS

Overriding interests (referred to in the LRA 2002 as 'interests which override') are unregistered interests which will override first registration or registered dispositions, as the case may be, notwithstanding that no entry in respect of them is made in the register. However, an interest will not be binding on a successor if it has been overreached even if it would otherwise override.[1]

Unlike the LRA 1925, the LRA 2002 draws a distinction between unregistered interests which override first registration[2] and unregistered dispositions which override registered dispositions.[3] Although many of the interests are the same in both schedules, there are certain important differences.

128.1 Unregistered interests which override first registration

On first registration, the registered estate is vested in the proprietor subject to any of the following interests which affect the estate at that time and which are not the subject of an entry in the register of that estate.[4]

128.1.1 Leasehold estates in land

A lease of land granted for a term not exceeding 7 years from the date of the grant overrides first registration, unless such lease is one required to be registered under LRA 2002, s 4(1)(d), (e) or (f). A grant out of an unregistered freehold estate, or leasehold estate with more than 7 years to run, which is to take effect in possession after the end of the period of 3 months beginning with the date of the grant, must be registered under LRA 2002, s 4(1)(d). A grant of a lease out of an unregistered legal estate in land pursuant to HA 1985, Pt 5 (the right to buy) must be registered under LRA 2002, s 4(1)(e). A grant of a lease out of an unregistered legal estate in land in circumstances where HA 1985, s 171A applies (disposal by landlord which leads to a person's no longer being a secure tenant; the preserved right to buy) must be registered under LRA 2002, s 4(1)(f).

128.1.2 Interests of persons in actual occupation

An interest belonging to a person in actual occupation, so far as relating to land of which he is in actual occupation, except for an interest under a settlement under the SLA 1925, overrides first registration. Such an overriding interest extends only to land in the registered title which is actually occupied by the person having the interest. It is the interest, not the occupation, which takes effect as an overriding interest. The interest protected is not therefore confined to a right of occupation; for example, an option to purchase in favour of the person in actual occupation may be an overriding interest. However, the protection of the interest extends only to that land of which the person is in actual occupation; if a person only occupies part of the land to which an interest relates, the interest only has overriding status for that part. It should be noted that, unlike the position under the LRA 1925, the receipt of rents and profits is not sufficient for these purposes. Further, the interest must be proprietary in nature, a personal right will not be protected by actual occupation.[5] In *Orchard v Dhillon*,[6] the court concluded the right to rescind a contract under Financial Services and Markets Act 2000, s 26 was a mere equity capable of protection by actual occupation.

128.1.3 Easements and profits à prendre

A legal easement or profit à prendre overrides first registration. This will not be the case in relation to an equitable easement.

128.1.4 Customary rights

A customary right overrides first registration. Customary rights are rights enjoyed by members of a local community or a defined class of such community members. They are usually ancient in origin.

128.1.5 Public rights

A public right overrides first registration. Public rights are rights which are exercisable by any member of the public, such as a public right of way over a highway.[7] The vesting of the fee simple of a highway in the highway authority may be a public right for this purpose.[8]

128.1.6 Local land charges

A local land charge overrides first registration.[9]

128.1.7 Mines and minerals

Certain interests relating to mines and minerals override first registration.[10]

128.1.8 Franchise

A franchise was formerly an interest which overrode first registration. However, a franchise ceased to be an overriding interest at the end of 10 years from 13 October 2003.[11]

128.1.9 Manorial rights

A manorial right was formerly an interest which overrode first registration. However, a manorial right ceased to be an overriding interest at the end of 10 years from 13 October 2003.[12]

128.1.10 Crown rents

A right to rent which was reserved to the Crown on the granting of any freehold estate (whether or not the right is still vested in the Crown) was formerly an interest which overrode first registration. A Crown rent includes, but may not be limited to, the rent payable to the Crown for freehold land in a manor of ancient demesne, or the rent reserved to the Crown under the grant of a freehold estate, whether or not that estate was situated in a manor of ancient demesne. In practice such Crown rents occur most commonly on conveyances of foreshore by the Board of Trade.

Such Crown rents ceased to be overriding interests at the end of 10 years from 13 October 2003.[13] The person having the benefit of the interest (if its priority has not already been previously defeated and it continues to subsist) should therefore protect it. In the case of unregistered burdened land, he should apply for a caution against first registration. If he does not do so, the priority of the interest is liable to be defeated on a subsequent first registration of unregistered burdened land.[14]

A person applying for a caution against first registration should deliver to HMLR the usual documents required.[15]

Either the cautioner (or at least one of them, if there is more than one cautioner), or someone authorised by the cautioner, or the cautioner's conveyancer must make the statement of truth in panel 10 of form CT1. No documents should be exhibited, as the statement should be self-contained. The statement of truth should be completed on the following lines to show the interest of the applicant:

> the person entitled to the benefit of a Crown rent of [*specify details*] charged on [*insert description*] arising by reason of [*summarise the basis on which the interest arises, including evidence of devolution to the applicant where necessary*] and which continues to be payable by [*specify relevant details*].

The interest stated in the form CT1 will appear in the caution register, together with a description of the legal estate to which the caution relates. For the effect of the caution against first registration, see 25 Cautions Against First Registration.

128.1.11 Non-statutory rights in respect of an embankment or sea or river wall

The benefit of a non-statutory right in respect of an embankment or sea or river wall overrides first registration.[16]

128.1.12 Rights to payment in lieu of tithe

A right to payment in lieu of tithe was formerly an interest which overrode first registration. In practice these rights are only likely to be corn rents where the liability to pay arises by an Act other than a Tithe Act and is in commutation of tithes.

Such rights ceased to be overriding interests at the end of 10 years from 13 October 2003.[17] The person having the benefit of the interest (if its priority has not already been previously defeated and it continues to subsist) should therefore protect it. In the case of unregistered burdened land, he should apply for a caution against first registration. If he does not do so, the priority of the interest is liable to be defeated on a subsequent first registration of unregistered burdened land.[18]

A person applying for a caution against first registration should deliver to HMLR the usual documents required.[19]

Either the cautioner (or at least one of them, if there is more than one cautioner), or someone authorised by the cautioner, or the cautioner's conveyancer must make the statement of truth in panel 10 of form CT1. No documents should be exhibited, as the statement should be self-contained. The statement of truth should be completed on the following lines to show the interest of the applicant:

> the person entitled to a right to payment in lieu of tithe [*specify details*] payable out of or charged on [*insert description*] arising under [*insert details of relevant statutory provision and include details of devolution to the applicant where necessary*] and which continues to be payable by [*specify relevant details*].

The interest stated in the form CT1 will appear in the caution register, together with a description of the legal estate to which the caution relates. For the effect of the caution against first registration, see 25.1 Effect of a caution against first registration.

128.1.13 Rights in respect of the repair of a church chancel

A right in respect of the repair of a church chancel was formerly an interest which overrode first registration. However, such rights ceased to be an overriding interest at the end of 10 years from 13 October 2003.[20]

128.1.14 Public-private partnership leases relating to transport in London

A PPP lease overrides first registration.[21]

128.1.15 Rights acquired under the LA 1980

For the period of 3 years beginning on 13 October 2003, a right acquired under the LA 1980 before 13 October 2003 overrode first registration.[22] This applied even if the squatter was no longer in actual occupation. The 3-year period expired on 12 October 2006.

128.2 Unregistered interests which override registered dispositions

A registrable disposition for valuable consideration of a registered estate or registered charge is subject to any interest falling within LRA 2002, Sch 3 which affects the estate at the time of the disposition and which is not the subject of an entry in the register of that estate.[23] Any interest which has been the subject of a notice in the register at any time on or after 13 October 2003 is not treated as falling within LRA 2002 Sch 3 for these purposes.[24]

The unregistered interests which override registered dispositions are mainly the same as those described above as overriding first registration. The differences are as follows.

128.2.1 Leasehold estates in land

A lease the grant of which constitutes a registrable disposition does not override another registrable disposition. However, leases granted before 13 October 2003 for a term of less than 21 years retain the overriding status they enjoyed by virtue of the LRA 1925, s 70(1)(k).[25]

128.2.2 Interests of persons in actual occupation

In addition to the exception of interests under settlements referred to in 128.1.2 Interests of persons in actual occupation, the following interests of a person in actual occupation are not included in LRA 2002, Sch 3:

(a) an interest of a person of whom enquiry was made before the disposition and who failed to disclose the right when he could reasonably have been expected to do so;
(b) an interest which belongs to a person whose occupation would not have been obvious on a reasonably careful inspection of the land at the time of the disposition and of which the person to whom the disposition is made does not have actual knowledge at that time; and

(c) a leasehold estate in land granted to take effect in possession after the end of the period of 3 months beginning with the date of the grant and which has not taken effect in possession at the time of the disposition.

Under the LRA 1925, s 70(1)(g) an interest could be an overriding interest by virtue of a person's receipt of rents and profits. Such an interest subsisting on 13 October 2003 will continue to override registered dispositions provided the receipt of rents and profits continues.[26] Such an interest does not override if enquiry was made of the person having the benefit of it before the disposition and that person failed to disclose the right when he could reasonably have been expected to do so.

128.2.3 Easements and profits à prendre

Although all legal easements and profits à prendre override first registration, the position is not the same for registered dispositions. Under LRA 2002, Sch 3, para 3, a legal easement or profit à prendre overrides a registered disposition only if:

(a) at the time of the disposition it is within the actual knowledge of the person to whom the disposition is made; or
(b) at the time of the disposition it would have been obvious on a reasonably careful inspection of the land over which the easement or profit is exercisable; or
(c) the person entitled to the easement or profit proves that it has been exercised in the period of one year ending with the day of the disposition; or
(d) in the case of a profit à prendre, it is registered under the CRA 1965.

However, any easement or profit à prendre which was an overriding interest immediately before 13 October 2003, but which would not fall within LRA 2002, Sch 3, para 3 if created on or after 13 October 2003, continues to be an overriding interest.[27] This includes equitable easements that were openly exercised and enjoyed as appurtenant to the dominant tenement which took effect as overriding interests on the registered servient title under the Land Registration Rules 1925, r 258.

For a period of 3 years beginning on 13 October 2003, the exceptions referred to in (a) to (d) above did not apply, so that any unregistered legal easement or profit à prendre overrode a registered disposition.[28] The 3-year period expired on 12 October 2006. Any unregistered easement or profit à prendre over registered land arising on or after 13 October 2003 will be a legal easement or profit only if it is an implied or prescriptive easement or profit.

128.2.4 Local land charges

Certain local land charges which had overriding status by virtue of LRA 1925, s 70(1)(i) will retain that status indefinitely.[29]

128.2.5 Crown rents

Crown rents ceased to be overriding interests at the end of 10 years from 13 October 2003.[30] The person having the benefit of the interest (if its priority has not already been previously defeated and it continues to subsist) should therefore protect it in the register. If he does not do so, the priority of the interest is liable to be defeated on a subsequent registration of a registrable disposition of registered burdened land for valuable consideration.[31] In the case of registered burdened land, he should apply for the entry in the register of an agreed notice or a unilateral notice.

In addition to the usual documents required,[32] a person applying for an agreed notice should deliver to HMLR the deed, order or instrument giving rise to the interest claimed or a certified copy of it, or (if there is no such deed, order or instrument) other details of the interest claimed to satisfy HMLR of the nature of the applicant's claim.

Documentary evidence of the Crown rent will normally consist of a certified copy of the grant under which the Crown rent arises and, where the applicant is not the Crown, evidence of the devolution of the Crown rent to the applicant and confirmation that the Crown rent is still payable.

The agreed notice in the register will give details of the interest protected.

Where the registered proprietor does not consent to the entry in the register of an agreed notice and evidence to satisfy HMLR of the validity of the applicant's claim cannot be lodged, an application for entry of a unilateral notice may still be made.

A person applying for a unilateral notice should deliver to HMLR the usual documents required.[33]

The statement in panel 11 or conveyancer's certificate in panel 12 of form UN1 should be completed on the following lines to show the interest of the applicant:

> owner of the following Crown rent affecting the land: [*set out details of the Crown rent including details of the grant under which it arose and, where the applicant is not the Crown, details of the devolution of the Crown rent to the applicant and confirmation that the Crown rent is still payable*].

The unilateral notice in the register will give brief details of the interest protected and identify who are the beneficiaries of that notice.

128.2.6 Rights to payment in lieu of tithe

A right to payment in lieu of tithe ceased to be an overriding interest at the end of 10 years from 13 October 2003.[34] The person having the benefit of the right (if its priority has not already been previously defeated and it continues to subsist) should therefore protect it in the register. If he does not do so, the priority of the right is liable to be defeated on a subsequent registration of a registrable disposition of registered burdened land for valuable consideration.[35] In the case of registered burdened land he should apply for the entry in the register of an agreed notice or a unilateral notice.

In addition to the usual documents required,[36] a person applying for an agreed notice should deliver to HMLR the deed, order or instrument giving rise to the interest claimed or a certified copy of it, or (if there is no such deed, order or instrument) other details of the interest claimed to satisfy HMLR of the nature of the applicant's claim.

Documentary evidence of the right to payment in lieu of tithe will normally consist of confirmation of the statutory provision on which the payment is based, evidence of the devolution to the applicant of the benefit of the right to the payment and confirmation that the payment is still payable.

The agreed notice in the register will give details of the interest protected.

Where the registered proprietor does not consent to the entry in the register of an agreed notice and evidence to satisfy HMLR of the validity of the applicant's claim cannot be lodged, an application for entry of a unilateral notice may still be made.

A person applying for a unilateral notice should deliver to HMLR the usual documents required.[37]

The statement in panel 11 or conveyancer's certificate in panel 12 of form UN1 should be completed on the following lines to show the interest of the applicant:

> owner of the following right to payment in lieu of tithe affecting the land: [*set out details of the corn rent or other payment, including details of the statutory provision on which the payment is based, details of devolution to the applicant where necessary and confirmation that the corn rent is still payable*].

The unilateral notice in the register will give brief details of the interest protected and identify who are the beneficiaries of that notice.

128.2.7 Rights acquired under the LA 1980

For the period of 3 years beginning with 13 October 2003, the right to apply to be registered as proprietor of a registered estate under LRA 2002, Sch 12, para 18 was included in LRA 2002, Sch 3.[38] LRA 2002, Sch 12, para 18(1) provides that where a registered estate in land is held in trust for a person by virtue of LRA 1925, s 75(1) immediately before 13 October 2003, he is entitled to be registered as the proprietor of the estate. The position under LRA 1925, s 75(1) was that where a registered proprietor's title had been extinguished by adverse possession, it was open to the squatter to apply for the closure of the registered proprietor's title which was deemed, in the meantime, to be held on trust for the squatter by the registered proprietor.[39]

128.3 Interests which cannot take effect as overriding interests

Certain types of interest can never be overriding interests. These are:

(a) an interest under a settlement under the SLA 1925.[40] However, an interest under a trust of land can have overriding status if it otherwise qualifies;
(b) a pending land action, a writ or order affecting land issued or made by a court for the purpose of enforcing a judgment or recognisance, an order appointing a receiver or sequestrator, or a deed of arrangement;[41]
(c) a spouse's or civil partner's right of occupation under the FLA 1996 as amended by the Civil Partnership Act 2004;[42]
(d) in the case of registered dispositions only, a lease granted to take effect in possession more than 3 months ahead, and which has not taken effect in possession at the time of the disposition. This reflects the requirement to register such a lease;[43]
(e) rights of tenants arising from a desire notice under the Leasehold Reform Act 1967;[44]
(f) in the case of dispositions only, exercise of the Preserved Right to Buy;[45]
(g) rights under an access order made under the ANLA 1992;[46]
(h) rights of tenants under the LRHUDA 1993;[47] and
(i) rights arising from a request to a landlord for the grant of an overriding lease under the Landlord and Tenant (Covenants) Act 1995.[48]

128.4 Duty to disclose overriding interests

A person applying for first registration must provide information to HMLR in form DI about any of the overriding interests set out in LRA 2002, Sch 1 that affect the estate to which the application relates and are within the actual knowledge of the applicant, but are not apparent from the deeds and documents accompanying the application.[49] An applicant is not required to provide information about local land charges, or public rights, or a leasehold estate in land which falls within LRA 2002, Sch 1, para 1 but, at the time of the application, has one year or less to run.[50] Form FR1 requires the applicant to confirm whether disclosable overriding interests affect the estate and, if so, to enclose form DI with the application.

A person applying to register a disposition of a registered estate must provide information to HMLR in form DI about any of the overriding interests set out in LRA 2002, Sch 3 that affect the estate to which the application relates and are within the actual knowledge of the applicant.[51] An applicant is not required to provide information about local land charges, or public rights, or a leasehold estate in land which falls within LRA 2002, Sch 3, para 1 but, at the time of the application, has one year or less to run.[52] The applicant must produce to HMLR any documentary evidence of the disclosed interest that is under his control.[53] Form AP1 requires the applicant to confirm whether the application relates to a registrable disposition and disclosable overriding interests affect the estate, and if so to enclose form DI with the application.

An applicant is not required, however, to provide information about interests that, under LRA 2002, s 33 or s 90(4), cannot be protected by a notice.[54]

HMLR may enter a notice in the register in respect of any overriding interest disclosed.[55] Upon entry of such a notice, the interest ceases to be an overriding interest.[56]

---

1 *City of London Building Society v Flegg* [1987] UKHL 6. See 130 Overreaching.
2 As set out in LRA 2002, Sch 1 and s 90.
3 As set out in LRA 2002, Sch 3 and s 90.
4 LRA 2002, ss 11 and 12.
5 *Scott v Southern Pacific Mortgages Ltd and Others* [2014] UKSC 52.
6 [2025] EWHC 834 (Ch).
7 *Overseas Investment Services Ltd v Simcobuild Construction Ltd* (1995) 70 P & CR 322.
8 *Secretary of State for the Environment, Transport and the Regions v Baylis (Gloucester) Ltd* (2000) 80 P & CR 324.
9 See 109 Local Land Charges.
10 See 33 Coal and 115.6 Overriding interests.

11 LRA 2002, s 117(1). See 74 Franchises.
12 LRA 2002, s 117(1). See 112.6 Manorial rights.
13 LRA 2002, s 117(1).
14 LRA 2002, ss 11 and 12.
15 See 25 Cautions Against First Registration.
16 See 58 Embankments or Sea or River Walls.
17 LRA 2002, s 117(1).
18 LRA 2002, ss 11 and 12.
19 See 25 Cautions Against First Registration.
20 Land Registration Act 2002 (Transitional Provisions) (No 2) Order 2003 (SI 2003/2431). See 26 Chancel Repair.
21 See 145 Public-Private Partnership Leases Relating to Transport in London.
22 LRA 2002, Sch 12, para 7.
23 LRA 2002, ss 29 and 30.
24 LRA 2002, ss 29(3) and 30(3).
25 LRA 2002, Sch 12, para 12.
26 LRA 2002, Sch 12, para 8.
27 LRA 2002, Sch 12, para 9.
28 LRA 2002, Sch 12, para 10.
29 LRA 2002, Sch 12, para 13. See 109 Local Land Charges.
30 LRA 2002, s 117(1).
31 LRA 2002, ss 29 and 30.
32 See 119.1 Agreed notice.
33 See 119.3 Unilateral notice.
34 LRA 2002, s 117(1).
35 LRA 2002, ss 29 and 30.
36 See 119.1 Agreed notice.
37 See 119.3 Unilateral notice.
38 LRA 2002, Sch 12, para 11.
39 See 6.8 Transitional provisions.
40 LRA 2002, Sch 1, para 2 and Sch 3, para 2(a).
41 LRA 2002, s 87(3).
42 FLA 1996, s 31(10).
43 LRA 2002, Sch 3, para 2(d).
44 Leasehold Reform Act 1967, s 5(5).
45 HA 1985, Sch 9A, para 6(1).
46 ANLA 1992, s 5(5).
47 LRHUDA 1993, s 97(1).
48 Landlord and Tenant (Covenants) Act 1995, s 20(6).
49 LRR 2003, r 28(1).
50 LRR 2003, r 28(2).
51 LRR 2003, r 57(1).
52 LRR 2003, r 58(2).
53 LRR 2003, r 57(4).
54 LRR 2003, rr 28(2)(a) and 57(2)(a). These are listed in 119 Notices.
55 LRR 2003, rr 28(4) and 57(5).
56 LRA 2002, ss 29(3) and 30(3).

129 OVERSEAS INSOLVENCY PROCEEDINGS

Aside from the special provisions applying before Brexit for proceedings in member states of the European Union[1] and those governing the separate parts of the United Kingdom,[2] the general principle is that the courts of England and Wales will recognise that the courts of a foreign country have jurisdiction over a debtor if:

(a) he was domiciled in that country at the time of presentation of the petition for insolvency; and
(b) he submitted to the court by presenting the petition himself or by entering an appearance in the proceedings.

A foreign bankruptcy order, even if recognised by the courts in England and Wales, will not have the effect of automatically vesting the debtor's assets in the foreign trustee in bankruptcy. Such a vesting may, however, be effected under an order of a court in England and Wales. In 2006, special provisions were introduced in relation to cross-border insolvency, as discussed below.

129.1 Insolvency proceedings commenced in a member state of the European Union (excluding Denmark) before Brexit

Where insolvency proceedings were opened in a member of the European Union (other than Denmark) before Brexit, special provisions applied which allowed a relevant person to apply for a note of a judgment opening insolvency proceedings in the register. Such provisions are now only available where the proceedings were commenced before the end of the relevant transitional period.[3]

129.2 Cross-Border Insolvency Regulations 2006

The Cross-Border Insolvency Regulations 2006 (SI 2006/1030) give effect to the United Nations Commission on International Trade Law Model Law on Cross-Border Insolvency (the Model Law), which is intended to cover cases where, for example, a debtor has assets in more than one state. The Model Law provides for a court in England and Wales to determine whether a foreign proceeding is to be recognised and if so, whether as a 'main' or 'non-main' proceeding (depending on whether the foreign proceeding is taking place in the country where the debtor's main centre of operations is located). An order for recognition automatically triggers a suspension of the debtor's right to transfer, encumber or otherwise dispose of his assets, as if a bankruptcy order had been made against him.

However, no bankruptcy order is made and no trustee in bankruptcy is appointed. This automatic suspension can be modified or terminated by an order of the court.

The Model Law also provides, in the alternative, for a court to grant either interim relief (during the period between the filing of the application for recognition and its determination) or discretionary relief upon recognition of the foreign proceeding to the foreign insolvency representative for the benefit of any recognised foreign proceeding. This includes relief to suspend the debtor's right to dispose of or encumber his assets.

Where an order is made by the court, the Cross-Border Insolvency Regulations 2006 (SI 2006/1030) provide for the foreign representative to make the appropriate application to the registrar to give effect to the terms of the order. The form of application and the type of entry which can be made will depend upon whether the debtor is a sole registered proprietor or a joint registered proprietor.

Where the debtor is the registered proprietor of a registered estate which he holds for his own sole benefit, the application will be for entry of a restriction.[4] This will be in a non-standard form, to the effect that no disposition of the registered estate by the registered proprietor of that estate is to be completed by registration within the meaning of LRA 2002, s 27 except under a further order of the court. In any other case, the application will be for such entry as shall be necessary to reflect the effect of the court order.

The application should be made in form RX1 accompanied by a certified copy of the court order. A fee will be payable.[5]

It is possible that the court may direct HMLR to enter a restriction using its powers under LRA 2002, s 46. In such a case, the appropriate form of application will be in form AP1 accompanied by a certified copy of the court order. A fee will be payable.[6]

The same principles will apply where the debtor is the sole registered proprietor of a registered charge, except that the restriction will relate to dispositions of the registered charge rather than of the registered estate.

Where the debtor is a joint proprietor of a registered estate and holds a beneficial interest in the property under a trust of land, by analogy with the position in bankruptcy, only the beneficial interest of the debtor would be affected by a court order suspending his right to transfer, encumber or dispose of his assets.

In such circumstances, the foreign representative would normally have sufficient interest to apply for entry of a standard restriction in Form II, but not the non-standard restriction referred to above. The wording of Form II is set out in

Appendix IV. A restriction in Form J[7] would be inappropriate as there is no actual bankruptcy or appointment of a trustee in bankruptcy under the IA 1986. The wording of Form J is set out in Appendix IV. However, where the court has directed HMLR to enter a particular form of restriction under LRA 2002, s 46, the restriction will be entered notwithstanding that the debtor is not the sole proprietor.

---

1 See 129.1 Insolvency proceedings commenced in a member state of the European Union (excluding Denmark) before Brexit.
2 See 19.19 Insolvency proceedings commenced in another part of the United Kingdom.
3 Insolvency (Amendment) (EU Exit) Regulations 2019 (SI 2019/146), r 4(2).
4 See 153.1 Application for entry of restriction.
5 See 67 Fees.
6 See 67 Fees.
7 See 19.8 Bankruptcy of a joint proprietor.

130 PARTNERSHIPS

A partnership is the relationship which subsists between persons carrying on a business in common with a view to profit.[1] A partnership is not a corporate body.[2]

130.1 Registration

A transfer or charge to a partnership must be to the names of the individual partners, not to the partnership name. If there are more than four partners, the transfer should be to four of them to hold the legal estate on trust for the partnership. No reference to the partnership is made in the register. In the case of a registered estate in land, as the beneficial interests are held under a tenancy in common, HMLR will enter a restriction in Form A in the proprietorship register in accordance with its obligation under LRA 2002, s 44(1). The wording of Form A is set out in Appendix IV. In the case of other registered estates, the proprietors should make an application for entry of such a restriction.[3]

The partners may also, if they wish, apply for entry of a restriction in Form Q. The wording of Form Q is set out in Appendix IV.

If the partnership deed contains specific provisions requiring any consent to be obtained to a disposition, application should be made for entry of a restriction in Form B.[4] The wording of Form B is set out in Appendix IV.

An application for a restriction should be made in form RX1. However, this form does not need to be used if the application is for a standard form restriction and is contained in either the 'additional provisions' panel of a prescribed form of transfer or assent, or in clause LR13 of a prescribed clauses lease (or any other lease containing clauses LR1 to LR14 of LRR 2003, Sch 1A).[5]

Although no reference to the partnership is made in the register, the proprietors may specifically apply to have any trading name entered in the proprietorship register. This will appear after the last address for service in the entry of the proprietors, in the form 'trading as [*trading name*]'.

---

1 Partnership Act 1890, s 1.

2 For LLPs incorporated under the Limited Liability Partnerships Act 2000, see 105 Limited Liability Partnerships, and for limited partnerships, see 107 Limited Partnerships.

3 LRR 2003, r 94(2A).

4 TLATA, s 8(2) and LRR 2003, r 94(4).

5 LRR 2003, r 92(7). See 153.1 Application for entry of restriction.

131 PARTY WALL ETC ACT 1996

The purpose of the Party Wall etc Act 1996 is to regulate the manner in which works to party walls and other works adjacent to boundaries are carried out. In general, the Party Wall etc Act 1996 does not affect ownership of land and hence no notice or other entry may be made in the register in respect of any of the following arising under that Act:

(a) a party structure notice;
(b) a party wall award; or
(c) a notice under s 1(2) in respect of a proposed new wall.

However, Party Wall etc Act 1996, s 14 provides that the expenses of building a party wall or party fence wall or carrying out works under that Act may be apportioned between the building owner and the adjoining owner (as defined in that Act). Until the adjoining owner has paid the appropriate share of the expenses to the building owner, the part of the party wall on the adjoining owner's land vests in the building owner.

If the adjoining owner's title is registered, the building owner can apply to protect his ownership rights by the entry of an agreed notice or a unilateral notice in the register.[1] The notice should be confined to the land affected and the position of the wall must be described sufficiently to enable a verbal description or a reference on the title plan to be given for so much of the wall as falls within the adjoining owner's title.

A party wall agreement may be made under the provisions of the Party Wall etc Act 1996 or under the general law; its effect for land registration purposes will depend upon its provisions.

A party wall agreement which provides that ownership of a wall or fence is split longitudinally between two neighbouring registered titles represents a 'provision as to boundary structures' and an application may be made in form AP1 for the register to be altered to include an entry in respect of the agreement in the relevant title(s). A fee is payable.[2]

A party wall agreement may also contain the mutual grant of easements. If granted over a registered estate, these may constitute a registrable disposition required to be completed by registration[3] and the appropriate application should be made in respect of them.[4]

---

1 See 119.1 Agreed notice and 119.3 Unilateral notice.
2 See 67 Fees.
3 LRA 2002, s 27(2)(d).
4 See 101.2 Legal easements arising after first registration.

132 PENDING LAND ACTIONS

A pending land action is defined as 'any action or proceeding pending in court relating to land or any interest in or charge on land'.[1] For this purpose, 'land' does not include a beneficial interest in land under a trust. A pending land action would include, for example, an application for a declaration of the existence of an easement, or for forfeiture of a lease. However, an action for a pure money judgment, or for damages for breach of a restrictive covenant, would not constitute a pending land action. An action relating solely to a beneficial interest under a trust is not a pending land action, because an undivided share is excluded from the definition of 'land' for this purpose. However, it is arguable that an action which relates to the issue of whether the land is subject to a trust of land and/or to the appointment of a new or additional trustee may constitute a pending land action.[2]

For the position where a pending land action relates to an application for a property adjustment order in matrimonial proceedings, see 141 Property Adjustment Orders. For a pending land action relating to an application for an access to neighbouring land order, see 1.1 Notice of a pending land action. For a pending land action relating to an application for a charging order, see 29.1 Notice in respect of a pending land action. For a pending land action relating to an application under the LRHUDA 1993, see 34 Collective Enfranchisement and 98 Leases.

A pending land action is treated as an interest affecting an estate or charge for the purposes of the LRA 2002.[3] It cannot, however, be an interest belonging to a person in actual occupation falling within LRA 2002, Sch 1, para 2 or Sch 3, para 2 which will override first registration or registered dispositions.[4]

A pending land action may be protected by the entry in the register of an agreed notice or a unilateral notice, and possibly a restriction. The application may be made by the person taking the action or proceedings, or his assignee or chargee.[5] A notice will protect the priority of the pending land action as against a subsequent registered disposition for valuable consideration.[6] A restriction does not confer any priority. However, it prevents an entry being made in the register relating to any disposition, or a disposition of a specified kind, unless the terms of the restriction have (where applicable) been complied with. The entry in the register in respect of a pending land action will only protect the action itself; if the court action is successful, a separate application should therefore be made to protect any order made by the court as appropriate. If the court action is unsuccessful, application should be made for removal from the register of an entry relating to the pending land action.

132.1 Agreed notice

In addition to the usual documents required,[7] an applicant should deliver to HMLR the sealed claim form and notice of issue. This should satisfy HMLR of the validity of the applicant's claim in accordance with LRA 2002, s 34(3)(c).

The agreed notice in the register will give details of the interest protected.

132.2 Unilateral notice

Where the applicant wishes to apply for a unilateral notice, he should deliver to HMLR the usual documents required.[8]

The statement in panel 11 or conveyancer's certificate in panel 12 of form UN1 should be completed on the following lines to show the interest of the applicant:

> applicant in an action in the [*name* Division of the High Court] *or* [*name* County Court] [*set out full court reference and parties*] for [*state nature of the action*].

The unilateral notice in the register will give brief details of the interest protected and identify the beneficiary of that notice.

132.3 Restriction

HMLR may not enter any restriction made for the purpose of protecting the priority of an interest which is, or could be, the subject of a notice.[9] However, this does not prevent a restriction being entered in addition to a notice of the pending land action where appropriate. In most cases the existence of a pending land action will not make a disposition by the registered proprietor unlawful or invalid and the existence of the action itself will not be sufficient for the entry of a restriction; only in cases where the action gives rise to some limitation on the proprietor's powers of disposition would an application for a restriction be appropriate.

In addition to the usual documents required,[10] an applicant should deliver to HMLR the sealed claim form and notice of issue.

As the application for a restriction is unlikely to be made by or with the consent of the registered proprietor, the statement in panel 12 or conveyancer's certificate in panel 13 of form RX1 must be completed, setting out details of the application to the court.

Panel 9 of form RX1 should set out the required restriction(s). The form of restriction sought depends on the nature of the pending land action. A restriction in a standard form contained in LRR 2003, Sch 4 does not require the approval of HMLR to the terms of the restriction under LRA 2002, s 43(3). A possible form of restriction based on Form N is:

> No [disposition *or specify type of disposition*] of the registered estate by the proprietor of the registered estate [or by the proprietor of any registered charge, not being a charge registered before the entry of this restriction] is to be registered without a written consent signed by [*name*] of [*address*] [or [their conveyancer *or specify appropriate details*]].

The wording of Form N is set out in Appendix IV.

HMLR must give notice of the application for a restriction to the proprietor of the registered estate concerned, if it has not been made by or with his consent or a person entitled to be registered as such proprietor.[11]

---

1 Land Charges Act 1972, s 17(1).
2 See *Godfrey v Torpey and Others* [2006] EWHC 1423 (Ch).
3 LRA 2002, s 87(1).
4 LRA 2002, s 87(3).
5 LRR 2003, r 172.
6 LRA 2002, ss 29, 30 and 32.

7 See 119.1 Agreed notice.
8 See 119.3 Unilateral notice.
9 LRA 2002, s 42(2).
10 See 153.1 Application for entry of restriction.
11 LRA 2002, s 45.

133 PERSONAL REPRESENTATIVES

Where a sole or sole surviving proprietor dies, the legal estate in registered land will vest in his executor or administrator by operation of law.[1] This vesting is not a disposition which is required to be completed by registration to take effect at law.[2] In the case of joint proprietors, the legal estate cannot be severed and can only be held on a legal joint tenancy.[3] The principle of 'survivorship' therefore applies, so that if one joint proprietor dies, the legal estate will automatically vest in the survivor(s) by operation of law regardless of devolution of the equitable interest. For the death of a sole proprietor or joint proprietor, see 48.1 Death of a sole proprietor, and 92.2 Death of a joint proprietor.

133.1 Registration of personal representative

On the death of a sole proprietor, or of the survivor of joint proprietors, of a registered estate or registered charge, the personal representative of such proprietor may apply to become registered as proprietor of that estate or charge. Although the personal representative is not obliged to become registered before exercising his powers of disposition, a disadvantage of not doing so is that the register remains out of date longer than it would if he was registered as soon as the grant of representation was made. Whilst the register is out of date, any notice sent by HMLR and addressed to the deceased proprietor may not be received by the personal representative.

The personal representative should deliver to HMLR:

(a) an application in form AP1;
(b) evidence of the appointment of the personal representative in the form of either:

 (i) the original or a certified copy or office copy of the grant of probate or letters of administration to the estate of the deceased proprietor and, where Administration of Estates Act 1925, s 7 applies, the original grant of probate showing the chain of representation, to prove that the applicant is his personal representative; or

(ii) the original or a certified copy or office copy of the letters of administration showing the applicant as personal representative of the deceased proprietor;
(iii) a court order appointing the applicant as the deceased's personal representative, or a certified copy or office copy of it; or
(iv) (where a conveyancer is acting for the applicant) a certificate given by the conveyancer that he holds the original or an office copy of such grant of probate, letters of administration or court order;[4]

(c) the appropriate confirmation or evidence of identity;[5] and
(d) the fee payable.[6]

Where a personal representative is seeking to become registered jointly with another personal representative who is already registered as proprietor,[7] HMLR will serve notice on that existing proprietor.[8]

Where a personal representative is seeking to become registered in place of another personal representative who is already registered as proprietor, the application must also be accompanied by evidence to show that the appointment of the personal representative whom the applicant is replacing has been terminated.[9]

Where the register states that the deceased was the administrator of the estate of a deceased proprietor, a grant of letters of administration *de bonis non* to the estate of that deceased proprietor must be obtained, and the administrator *de bonis non* can then apply to be registered as proprietor. Similarly, when the register states that the deceased was the executor of a deceased proprietor, but the executor has died intestate, his administrator is not entitled to be registered in the deceased executor's place; a grant of letters of administration *de bonis non* to the estate of the original testator is necessary, and the administrator *de bonis non* can then apply to be registered as proprietor. These exceptions apply because the 'chain of representation' does not apply in these circumstances.

A chain of representation arises where the executor of a deceased proprietor himself dies without having completed the administration of the estate. If the executor has left a will appointing an executor, then on proving that will, that latter executor also automatically becomes executor of the deceased proprietor's estate as well. The chain of representation only applies to executors not administrators and if the chain of successive executorships is broken then a grant *de bonis non* to the deceased proprietor's estate would then be required. If an applicant relies upon a chain of representation, evidence of any additional grant of probate showing the chain will also need to be lodged, as well as the grant to the deceased proprietor's estate.

Where the personal representative is registered as proprietor, the following is added after the personal representative's name:

> [executor *or* executrix] *or* [administrator *or* administratrix] of [*name*] deceased.

Where the land was settled before the death of the sole or last surviving joint proprietor and not by his will and the settlement continues after his death, an application to register the special personal representatives in whom the registered land vests under the Administration of Estates Act 1925 must be accompanied by the grant limited to the settled land.[10] In that case the following is added after the personal representative's name:

> [special executor *or* executrix] *or* [administrator *or* administratrix] of [*name*] deceased.

133.2 Entry of restrictions

A person dealing with a registered proprietor can assume that he has unlimited power to dispose of the registered estate or registered charge concerned, free from any limitation affecting the validity of the disposition, unless there is a restriction or other entry in the register limiting his powers, or a limitation imposed by or under the LRA 2002.[11]

In the case of a personal representative, it is the duty of the executor or administrator to apply for any necessary restriction(s), although a person who has an interest in the due administration of the estate may also apply. A restriction does not confer any priority. However, it prevents an entry being made in the register relating to any disposition, or a disposition of a specified kind, unless the terms of the restriction have (where applicable) been complied with.

LPA 1925, s 27(2) does not affect the right of a sole personal representative *acting as such* to give a valid receipt for capital money. Therefore, HMLR will not automatically enter a restriction in Form A when registering a personal representative as proprietor of a registered estate. The wording of Form A is set out in Appendix IV. However, any existing such restriction will remain in the register because, in that case, the personal representative will be succeeding the deceased as trustee of the trust. For the same reason, HMLR will enter a restriction in Form A on first registration when registering the personal representative of a deceased proprietor who was a sole trustee or (except where he was the survivor of beneficial joint tenants) the last surviving trustee.

Where the personal representative holds the registered estate on a trust of land created by the deceased's will, or on a trust of land arising under the laws of intestacy which is subsequently varied, and his powers have been limited by

TLATA 1996, s 8, he must apply for entry of a restriction in Form C.[12] The wording of Form C is set out in Appendix IV. Where there are two or more personal representatives of a deceased proprietor, an application by one or more of them satisfies the obligation to apply for entry of the restriction. If an application is not made, any person who has an interest in the due administration of the estate may apply for entry of a restriction in Form C.[13] The applicant should deliver to HMLR the usual documents required.[14]

Where the applicant is a person who has an interest in the due administration of the deceased's estate, the statement in panel 12 or conveyancer's certificate in panel 13 of form RX1 should be completed on the following lines:

> The interest is that specified in rule 93(d) of the Land Registration Rules 2003 (SI 2003/1417), the applicant being a person interested in the due administration of the estate of [*name*] deceased.

Panel 9 of form RX1 should set out the restriction in Form C.

A restriction in Form C in LRR 2003, Sch 4 does not require the approval of HMLR to the wording of the restriction under LRA 2002, s 43(3).

HMLR must give notice of the application for a restriction to the proprietor of the registered estate concerned if it has not been made by or with his consent or a person entitled to be registered as such proprietor.[15]

Where a trust of land imposes limitations on the powers of the trustees under TLATA 1996, s 8, for example a requirement to obtain a consent before sale, and the legal estate is vested in the personal representatives of a sole or last surviving trustee, the personal representatives must apply for entry of a restriction in Form B.[16] The wording of Form B is set out in Appendix IV. This does not apply if the land is held on charitable, ecclesiastical or public trusts.[17] Where there are two or more persons registered as proprietor of the estate, an application by one or more of them satisfies the obligation to apply for entry of the restriction.[18] If such an application is not made, any person who has an interest under the trust of land where the powers of the trustees are limited under TLATA 1996, s 8 may apply for the entry of a restriction in Form B.[19] The applicant should deliver to HMLR the usual documents required.[20]

Where the applicant is a person who has an interest under a trust of land, the statement in panel 12 or conveyancer's certificate in panel 13 of form RX1 should be completed on the following lines:

> The interest is that specified in rule 93(c) of the Land Registration Rules 2003 (SI 2003/1417), the applicant being a person who has an interest in the registered

estate held under a trust of land where the powers of the trustees are limited by section 8 of the Trusts of Land and Appointment of Trustees Act 1996.

Panel 9 of form RX1 should set out the restriction in Form B.

A restriction in Form B in LRR 2003, Sch 4 does not require the approval of HMLR to the wording of the restriction under LRA 2002, s 43(3).

HMLR must give notice of the application for a restriction to the proprietor of the registered estate concerned if it has not been made by or with his consent or a person entitled to be registered as such proprietor.[21]

133.3 Dispositions by personal representatives

The personal representative may deal with the registered estate in accordance with his powers in that capacity, subject to any entry to the contrary in the register, whether or not he has been registered as proprietor in place of the deceased. For assents by personal representatives, see 17 Assents. Other than assents, there are no prescribed forms of transfer by a personal representative. Accordingly, on a transfer other than an assent, the personal representative must use the form of transfer generally prescribed for such a transfer.[22] This is the case irrespective of whether the personal representative has been registered as proprietor or not.

HMLR is not under a duty to investigate the reasons a transfer of registered land by a personal representative of a deceased sole proprietor or last surviving joint proprietor is made. Nor is it required to consider the contents of the will. Provided the terms of any restriction in the register are complied with, HMLR must assume, whether or not it knows of the terms of the will, that the personal representative is acting correctly and within his powers.[23]

In addition to the usual documents required,[24] a person applying to register a transfer by a personal representative should deliver to HMLR evidence of the appointment of the personal representative (if not already registered as proprietor) similar to that required by LRR 2003, r 163(2) as specified in 133.1 Registration of personal representative.[25]

If a restriction in Form A appears in the register when the transfer is registered, it will be cancelled by HMLR if the transfer is by two or more personal representatives or a trust corporation, as the equitable interests under the trust of land will have been overreached.[26] However, if the transfer is by a sole personal representative (not being a trust corporation) of a sole surviving proprietor, the application will be caught by the restriction as if it were an application to register a transfer on sale by the deceased. Therefore, unless HMLR is satisfied that the equitable interests have been overreached, it will be necessary either to appoint a new co-trustee to act jointly with the personal representative and give a joint receipt for the purchase money, or for evidence of the equitable title to be lodged to satisfy HMLR that the trust of land has come to an end. The reason for this is because although a sole personal representative *acting as such* can give a valid receipt for the purposes of overreaching, that will not apply where (as is the case in this situation) the personal representative is acting in a capacity of trustee under a trust of land.

Any other restrictions appearing in the register will also need to be complied with or cancelled or withdrawn, as appropriate. Thus, where a restriction in Form C appears in the register, the appropriate certificate, statutory declaration or statement of truth will need to be provided; on registration of the transfer the restriction will then be automatically cancelled.

133.4 First registration

Where a legal estate is currently unregistered, the vesting of that estate in the personal representative by operation of law will not 'trigger' compulsory first registration.[27] However, an assent or transfer of that estate may be a 'trigger' for compulsory first registration. If so, the beneficiary or transferee should apply for registration of the estate.[28] Also, the personal representative may apply for voluntary first registration if desired, in which case the requisite evidence of his appointment[29] must accompany the application.

133.5 Inheritance tax, capital transfer tax and death duties

In some circumstances a registered estate may be subject to a liability for IHT (formerly known as capital transfer tax) in respect of deaths occurring after 12 March 1975. The entry and/or removal of entries relating to IHT or death duties may therefore be relevant.[30]

---

1 Administration of Estates Act 1925, s 1(1).

2 LRA 2002, s 27(5).

3 LPA 1925, ss 1(6), 34 and 36.

4 LRR 2003, r 163(2).

5 See 84 Identity Evidence.

6 See 67 Fees.

7 This sometimes occurs where a will appoints several executors but one or more of them do not wish to prove the grant. Power in the initial grant will be granted to the proving executors with power reserved to the remaining executor(s). If the remaining executors later wish to participate in the administration of the estate, they may apply for the grant of double probate.

8 LRR 2003, r 163(5).
9 LRR 2003, r 163(3).
10 LRR 2003, Sch 7, para 11.
11 LRA 2002, s 26.
12 LRR 2003, r 94(3).
13 LRR 2003, r 93(d).
14 See 153.1 Application for entry of restriction.
15 LRA 2002, s 45.
16 LRR 2003, r 94(4) and (7).
17 LRR 2003, r 94(6).
18 LRR 2003, r 94(9).
19 LRR 2003, r 93(c).
20 See 153.1 Application for entry of restriction.
21 LRA 2002, s 45.
22 See 176 Transfers.
23 LRR 2003, r 162(2).
24 See 176.1 Registration of transfer.
25 LRR 2003, r 162(1).
26 LPA 1925, ss 2 and 27.
27 LRA 2002, s 4(3).
28 See 68 First Registration.
29 See 133.1 Registration of personal representative.
30 See 89 Inheritance Tax.

134 PLANS

HMLR title plans are produced using the OS's large scale digital map data. Although this data is supplied in a single consistent format, it is surveyed and digitised at different scales. It is not possible to achieve perfect accuracy in drawing features on a plan. The degree of variation between the actual position on the ground and that recorded on the map is known as the specified accuracy tolerance. This means that measurements scaled between features shown on OS mapping may not exactly match the actual distance measured between the same features on the ground. Different levels of accuracy apply dependent on the scale of the map and the original survey method used to create it. As a general guide, the width of a line on a 1:1250 OS map roughly represents 0.3 metres on the ground. The width of a line on a 1/2500 OS map roughly represents 0.6 metres on the ground. The OS publishes expected confidence levels in the accuracy of its maps in terms of relative and absolute accuracy.

Relative accuracy compares the scaled distance between features measured from the map data with distances measured between the same features on the ground. For example, if at a scale of 1:1250 the distances between well-defined points of detail 60 metres apart were measured on the ground, there would be an expectation that 95 per cent would be represented on the OS map by scaled distances of between 59.1 metres and 60.9 metres. Similarly, if at a scale of 1:2500 the measured distances between points of detail were 100 metres apart there would be an expectation that 95 per cent would be represented on the OS map by scaled distances of between 98.1 metres and 101.9 metres. Further information and examples appear on the OS website.[1]

Absolute accuracy is the measure which indicates how closely the coordinates of a point in OS map data agree with the 'true' National Grid coordinates of the same point on the ground. As the true position can never be known exactly, the statistic is quoted relative to the best-known position determined by precise survey methods.

Where an OS map has been enlarged from its original scale, the degree of accuracy remains the same as the original map specification. For example, a plan surveyed at 1:2500 and enlarged to 1:1250 will still be subject to the survey specifications of 1:2500 mapping. The copying, reducing or enlarging of a plan is likely to distort its accuracy.

The OS map shows permanent physical features, normally at ground surface level, together with a variety of descriptive information and symbols. Generally, the OS map shows features more than 30 cm high such as walls, fences, hedges or building outlines by firm black lines. Features less than 30 cm high, such as kerbs or where two different surfaces meet, are shown by dotted black lines. Dotted black lines can also represent features that overhang, such as the outline of a building above ground surface level or where a roadway passes underneath.

The only features the OS map shows within private gardens are permanent buildings more than 12 m^2 in area, and roads and tracks over 100 m long.

The scale of the OS map also dictates how physical features are shown on a title plan. Where, for example, a hedge and a wall run close together on the ground, it may be that they are shown on the plan by a single firm black line because the gap between the two features cannot be shown at the scale in question. Even where only one physical feature is represented by a firm black line on the OS map, it may be a wide hedge or a narrow fence. Again, a small projection in a boundary might be shown on a plan surveyed at 1:1250 scale where a plan surveyed at 1:2500 scale would show a straight line. Even if the latter plan is enlarged to 1:1250 scale, it will still not show the projection.

In *Alan Wibberley Building Ltd v Insley*,[2] Lord Hope of Craighead said:

> The use of maps or plans such as those published by the OS is now widespread and has obvious advantages. OS maps are prepared to a high standard of accuracy and are frequently and appropriately used to fix boundaries by reference, for example, to OS field numbers. But like all maps they are subject to limitations. The most obvious are those imposed by scale. No map can reproduce to anything like the same scale of detail every feature which is found on the ground. Furthermore the OS does not fix private boundaries. The purpose of the survey is topographical, not taxative. Even the most detailed OS map may not show every feature on the ground which can be used to identify the extent of the owner's land. In the present case the OS map shows the hedge, but it does not show the ditch. So there is no reason in principle in this case for preferring the line on the map to other evidence which may be relevant to identify the boundary.

Plans for use in transfers of part or other deeds relating to an application to HMLR should be prepared bearing in mind the following guidelines. The plan should:

(a) be drawn accurately to a stated scale;
(b) show its scale;
(c) preferably be at 1:1250 or 1:500 scale for urban properties or 1:2500 for rural properties;
(d) be based on a scale of metric measurement;
(e) not be reduced in scale or distorted by copying;
(f) show its orientation (for example by a north point);
(g) show sufficient detail to be identified on the OS map;
(h) clarify its general location by showing roads, road junctions or other landmarks;
(i) not be marked or referred to as for identification purposes only;
(j) not contain a disclaimer under the Property Misdescriptions Act 1991;
(k) show the whole of the property including any garage, parking space, bin store or garden ground;
(l) show buildings and other features in their correct or intended positions;
(m) show access drives or pathways if they form part of the property boundaries;
(n) show clearly the land in question, for example by edging, colouring or hatching;
(o) have edgings of a thickness that does not obscure any other detail;
(p) show undefined boundaries accurately and, where necessary, by reference to measurements;
(q) show measurements that correspond as far as possible to scaled measurements;
(r) show measurements in metric units, to two decimal places;
(s) show where the property falls in relation to the external footprint of the building and/or in relation to surrounding detail on the OS map;
(t) identify different floor levels (where appropriate);
(u) show the extent at each floor level, if necessary by using separate plans;

(v) for subsoil or airspace, show the levels between which the land falls or relates the land to OS datum (mean sea level);
(w) show intricate boundaries with a larger scale or inset plan;
(x) show separate parts by suitable plan markings (house, garage, parking space, bin store, etc);
(y) agree with the verbal description contained in the deed; and
(z) correctly shows all markings referred to in the deed.

For title plans and boundaries, see 22 Boundaries.

---

1 www.ordnancesurvey.co.uk.
2 [1999] UKHL 15.

135 POSITIVE COVENANTS

Where the proprietor, or any previous proprietor, of a registered estate has given a positive covenant relating to that estate, HMLR may make an entry in respect of it in the proprietorship register.[1]

If the existence of the positive covenant is apparent from the register in some other way, HMLR need not make a separate entry. This might be the case where the positive covenant is included:

(a) in a deed which is referred to elsewhere in the register and is stated to have a copy filed at HMLR; or
(b) among restrictive covenants and set out with them in the charges register.

Where HMLR does make an entry, it must, where practicable, refer to the deed that contains the positive covenant.[2]

There is no need to make a specific application for an entry relating to a positive covenant when this is included in a deed lodged as part of an application in respect of a registrable disposition, such as a transfer. HMLR will make an entry as part of that application, if it considers it appropriate.

Where HMLR has made an entry relating to a positive covenant, it must remove it from the register if it appears to HMLR that the covenant does not bind the current proprietor of the registered estate.[3]

The burden of positive covenants does not run with freehold land.[4] Positive covenants may be made enforceable against successors in title of the covenantor by creating an estate rentcharge for a nominal amount.[5]

Positive covenants are sometimes protected by ensuring that a subsequent purchaser enters into a new deed of covenant with the person having the benefit of the original covenant. This arrangement may itself involve a positive covenant requiring that this be done and, in the case of registered land, may be supported by an application for a restriction.

135.1 Restriction

The consent of the registered proprietor to the entry of the restriction is required, unless the deed containing the positive covenant contains a provision which limits the registered proprietor's powers to enter into any further disposition.

In addition to the usual documents required,[6] an applicant for a restriction should deliver to HMLR (if the application is made by a person who claims that he has a sufficient interest in the making of the entry) a certified copy of the deed containing the positive covenant.

The statement in panel 12 of form RX1 signed by the applicant or a certificate by his conveyancer in panel 13 of form RX1 must be completed, setting out details of the deed and of the provision in the deed limiting the registered proprietor's powers to enter into a disposition.

Panel 9 of form RX1 should set out the restriction required. A restriction in a standard form contained in LRR 2003, Sch 4 does not require the approval of HMLR to the terms of the restriction under LRA 2002, s 43(3). A possible form of restriction based on Form L is:

> No disposition of the registered estate by the proprietor of the registered estate is to be registered without a written certificate signed by [*purchaser*] of [*address*] or their conveyancer that the provisions of [*clause, paragraph or other particulars*] of [*details of contract for sale*] have been complied with or that they do not apply to the disposition.

The wording of Form L is set out in Appendix IV.

Alternatively, where the certificate of the registered proprietor of a specified title number is to be required, a similar restriction based upon Form M may be appropriate. The wording of Form M is set out in Appendix IV. If the consent of the person having the benefit of the positive covenant is to be required, then a restriction in Form N may be appropriate. The wording of Form N is set out in Appendix IV. A restriction in Form O may be appropriate where the consent of the registered proprietor of a specified title number, or the provision of a certificate as an alternative to such consent, is to be required.[7] The wording of Form O is set out in Appendix IV.

Form RX1 does not need to be used if the application is for a standard form restriction and is contained in either the 'additional provisions' panel of a prescribed form of transfer or assent, or in clause LR13 of a prescribed clauses lease (or any other lease containing clauses LR1 to LR14 of LRR 2003, Sch 1A).[8]

HMLR must give notice of the application for a restriction to the proprietor of the registered estate or charge concerned, if it has not been made by or with the consent of such proprietor or a person entitled to be registered as such proprietor.[9]

135.2 Positive covenants imposed by statute

Although normally the burden of a positive covenant does not run with the land, certain statutes make provision for a positive covenant entered into pursuant to that statute enforceable as though it was a restrictive covenant. Such statutes include:

(a) Local Government (Miscellaneous Provisions) Act 1982, s 33;
(b) Mission and Pastoral Measure 2011 (2011/3), s 75;
(c) Wildlife and Countryside Act 1981, s 39; and
(d) Water Industry Act 1991, s 156(6).

HMLR will treat such covenants in the same way as restrictive covenants, but will omit the word 'restrictive' from the register entry.

---

1 LRR 2003, r 64(1).
2 LRR 2006, r 64(2).
3 LRR 2003, r 64(3).
4 *Rhone v Stephens* [1994] 2 All ER 65 (HL).
5 For the protection of estate rentcharges, see 151 Rentcharges.
6 See 153.1 Application for entry of restriction.
7 See Appendix IV for the wording of these restrictions.
8 LRR 2003, r 92(7).
9 LRA 2002, s 45.

136 POWERS OF ATTORNEY

A power of attorney is a deed by which one person (the donor) gives another person (the attorney) power to act on his behalf. It may be granted either for general purposes or for a specific purpose. If it is granted for a specific purpose, it should be ensured that it contains clear authority to enter into the disposition, as powers of attorney are interpreted strictly. It is not possible to note the appointment of an attorney by a registered proprietor in the register.

Any deed lodged for registration that has been executed under a power of attorney must be accompanied by one of the following:[1]

(a) the original power; or
(b) a certified copy of the power in accordance with Powers of Attorney Act 1971 (PAA 1971), s 3; or
(c) a document which under:

    (i) Evidence and Powers of Attorney Act 1940, s 4; or
    (ii) Mental Capacity Act 2005, Sch 1, para 16 or Sch 4, para 16,

    is sufficient evidence of the power; or
(d) a certificate by a conveyancer in Form 1 of LRR 2003, Sch 3. The wording of Form 1 is set out in Appendix V.

If an order or direction under Mental Capacity Act 2005, s 22 or s 23 or Sch 4, para 16 has been made in relation to a power or the donor of the power or the attorney appointed under it, the order or direction must be produced to HMLR.

HMLR will scan and destroy the evidence lodged. Therefore, if the applicant wishes to keep the original, he should lodge a certified copy with the application.[2] The different types of power of attorney are as follows.

136.1 General powers under Powers of Attorney Act 1971, s 10

The PAA 1971 provides a short form of general power of attorney that can be used by a sole beneficial owner of land. Such a power must follow the form set out in Sch 1 to that Act or be in a form to the like effect and expressed to be made under that Act. The donor must execute the power as a deed. It confers upon the attorney authority to do anything that the donor can lawfully do by an attorney. However, powers in that form dated before 1 March 2000 are not appropriate for dealing with land of which the donor is a joint proprietor. Those dated after 29 February 2000 may only be used by a joint proprietor if certain conditions are satisfied under Trustee Delegation Act 1999, s 1.[3] The donor may revoke such a power at any time and the death, bankruptcy or mental incapacity of the donor will automatically revoke it.

136.2 Other general and specific powers

As an alternative to the form set out in the PAA 1971, the donor of a power of attorney may use any form of wording, giving the attorney either general authority to act or limited powers. For example, in connection with a particular transaction or in relation only to a specified property. The donor must execute the power as a deed. Such a power may be used on behalf of a donor who is a joint proprietor only if certain conditions are satisfied under Trustee Delegation Act 1999, s 1. Unless it is a security power, the donor may revoke such a power and the death, bankruptcy or mental incapacity of the donor will automatically revoke it.

136.3 Security powers

A security power is a power of attorney that is expressed to be irrevocable and is given to secure a proprietary interest of the attorney or the performance of an obligation owed to the attorney. While the attorney retains the interest or until the obligation is discharged, the donor can revoke the power only with the attorney's consent, and the death, bankruptcy or mental incapacity of the donor does not revoke it.

136.4 Enduring powers of attorney

The Enduring Powers of Attorney Act 1985 was repealed by the Mental Capacity Act 2005 and in consequence no new enduring powers can be created after 30 September 2007. Enduring powers created before 1 October 2007 will continue to have effect, but are now subject to the provisions of Mental Capacity Act 2005, Sch 4.[4] An enduring power must be in one of the prescribed forms according to the date of execution of the power.

Enduring powers dated after 29 February 2000 may be used by a donor who is a joint proprietor if certain conditions are satisfied under Trustee Delegation Act 1999, s 1.[5] There were transitional provisions for enduring powers dated before 1 March 2000 under which such powers could be used by a donor who was a joint proprietor until 1 March 2001. From 1 March 2001 an enduring power dated before that date can only be used by a donor who is a joint proprietor if:

(a) the donor has a beneficial interest in the property and there is no indication in the power that the donor did not intend the attorney to exercise trustee functions; or
(b) the power is registered with the Court of Protection following an application to the court before 1 March 2001; or
(c) an application made to the court before 1 March 2001 for registration of the power has not been finally refused.

Enduring powers of attorney continue to be effective even after the donor has lost capacity, provided the power has been registered with the Court of Protection or the Public Guardian, as appropriate. Otherwise, the attorney cannot use it to act on behalf of the donor if the donor lacks capacity.

If two or more attorneys are appointed jointly, they must all execute a deed on behalf of the donor. If they are appointed jointly and severally, only one need execute it.

If an enduring power of attorney has been registered at the Court of Protection or with the Office of the Public Guardian and any order or direction has been made by the court under Mental Capacity Act 2005, Sch 4, para 16 with respect to the power or to the donor or to the attorney, the order or direction, or an official copy or certified copy of it, must be lodged with the application for registration of a deed executed under the power.[6]

136.5 Lasting powers of attorney

Lasting powers of attorney were introduced by the Mental Capacity Act 2005 and replaced enduring powers as the primary way for a donor to choose an attorney (or 'decision maker) to act in the event of loss of mental capacity. In addition to a 'property and financial affairs' lasting power, a donor is able to appoint an attorney to make decisions about his own welfare using a 'health and welfare' lasting power for a time when he lacks capacity to make such decisions himself.

Lasting Powers of Attorney, Enduring Powers of Attorney and Public Guardian Regulations 2007 (SI 2007/1253), Sch 1, Pt 1 prescribes the form which must be used for a 'property and financial affairs' lasting power of attorney and it must be executed in accordance with reg 9. A lasting power may only be used once it has been registered with the Office of the Public Guardian.

If two or more attorneys are appointed jointly, they must all execute a deed on behalf of the donor. If they are appointed jointly and severally, only one need execute it.

If a lasting power of attorney has been registered with the Office of the Public Guardian and any order or direction has been made by the court under Mental Capacity Act 2005, s 22 or s 23 with respect to the power or to the donor or attorney, the order or direction, or an official or certified copy of it, must be lodged with the application for registration of a deed executed under the power.[7]

136.6 Powers of attorney by joint proprietors and other trustees

Trustees holding property upon trust (which includes joint owners who are holding on trust for themselves as beneficial joint tenants or tenants in common) can only delegate their duties and powers when they have authority to do so. However, several statutory provisions now allow for delegation.

It should be borne in mind that where overreaching is necessary, the attorney must act with at least one other person, unless the donor is a trust corporation, to ensure there is a valid receipt by at least two trustees in accordance with LPA 1925, ss 2 and 27. If a transfer is lodged in such circumstances which has been executed by only one person, both as proprietor and as attorney for the other proprietor or as attorney for all the proprietors, HMLR will return it for execution by the donor(s). If the transfer is not re-executed HMLR will retain any restriction in Form A in the register to reflect the fact that overreaching has not been effected and that there may therefore be beneficial interests that continue to subsist. The wording of Form A is set out in Appendix IV.

136.6.1 Trustee Act 1925, s 25

Under this section, a trustee can delegate the exercise of his powers for a maximum of 12 months from the start of the delegation or, if there is no provision for when the delegation starts, for 12 months from the execution of the power by the trustee. The power must be in the form set out in Trustee Act 1925, s 25(6) or in a form to the like effect and expressed to be made under s 25.

136.6.2 Trustee Delegation Act 1999, s 1

This section allows a power of attorney to be used in relation to trust property after 1 March 2000 if:

(a) there is no indication in the power that the donor does not intend the attorney to exercise trustee functions; and
(b) at the time the power of attorney is used, the donor has a beneficial interest in the property. This delegation is not limited in duration. This applies to general powers, certain enduring powers and lasting powers.[8]

A signed statement by the attorney made within 3 months of the date of the disposition will be conclusive evidence of the donor having had a beneficial interest at that time. The statement can be included within the transfer or other disposition or it may be made separately provided it is dated within 3 months of the date of the disposition.

If such a statement cannot be produced, HMLR will consider other evidence, such as a statutory declaration or statement of truth, confirming that the donor had a beneficial interest at the relevant time. In the absence of satisfactory evidence of the donor's beneficial interest, the disposition will need to be executed by the donor of the power.

136.6.3 Trusts of Land and Appointment of Trustees Act 1996, s 9

All the trustees of a trust of land may jointly delegate their functions to a beneficiary or beneficiaries of full age and beneficially entitled to an interest in possession. The delegation may be for any period or indefinite.

However, these 'beneficiary' attorneys are not treated as trustees for the purposes of receiving capital money, so that the trustees themselves will need to join in any disposition under which capital money arises in order to effect overreaching.[9] Consequently, this type of power will only be appropriate when no capital money is passing; for example, on the grant of a lease without payment of a premium.

Statutory protection is given to a third party who in good faith deals with an attorney to whom trustee powers were delegated as a beneficiary, but who in fact was not a beneficiary to whom the trustee functions could be delegated. The attorney is presumed to have been a person to whom the trustee functions could be delegated unless the third party had knowledge that they were not such a person.[10] In consequence, where a beneficiary has executed a deed under a power of attorney, HMLR may require a statutory declaration or statement of truth from the disponee to confirm that he acted in good faith and had no knowledge at the time of completion of the disposition that the attorney was not a person to whom the functions of the trustees in relation to the land could be delegated. Alternatively, the disponee's conveyancer can provide a certificate to the effect that at the time of completion his client had no such knowledge.[11]

136.7 Gifts and dispositions at undervalue by an attorney

An attorney owes a fiduciary duty to the donor. In general therefore, an attorney cannot use the power to confer a benefit on himself or others to the detriment of the donor. Where an application for registration of such a disposition is lodged, HMLR's approach will depend upon the type of power used.

In the case of a general power, HMLR will regard the disposition as within the authority of the attorney even though, potentially, it could be set aside as being in breach of fiduciary duty. This is because the disposition is voidable rather than void, but HMLR will usually serve notice upon the donor as a precaution.

In the case of an enduring power or lasting power, there are considerable limitations upon gifts being made. A disposition in breach of these limitations will be void.[12] HMLR will therefore reject applications to register such dispositions unless the disposition is re-executed in person by the donor or satisfactory evidence of authority to make the gift is lodged. For example, if an enduring power is registered and the disposition has been approved by the court under Mental Capacity Act 2005, Sch 4, para 16.

Where it is claimed, in relation to a disposition by an attorney under an enduring or lasting power granted by a joint proprietor, that there is no element of gift because the donor had no beneficial interest in the property, this may cause a consequential problem in relation to powers granted by a joint proprietor.[13]

136.8 Powers more than 12 months old – evidence of non-revocation

A purchaser from a person who has dealt with an attorney is entitled to assume that the power of attorney has not been revoked if the transaction in question took place within 12 months of the date when the power came into question.[14] Although under LRR 2003, r 62, HMLR may require evidence of non-revocation if the power of attorney is more than 12 months old, such evidence will not normally be required. On the rare occasions when HMLR does require such evidence, this must be in Form 2 in LRR 2003, Sch 3, being either a statutory declaration or statement of truth made by the person dealing with the attorney or a certificate by that person's conveyancer.[15] The wording of Form 2 is set out in Appendix V. As powers of attorney under Trustee Act 1925, s 25 can only operate for 12 months, evidence of non-revocation is unnecessary for such powers.

136.9 Execution of deeds by an attorney

There is no prescribed attestation clause, but HMLR's *Practice guide 8: execution of deeds* contains forms of execution which are acceptable for land registration purposes. This is available to view and download at the HMLR website.[16]

136.10 Powers of attorney given to receivers in debentures

See 49 Debentures.

---

1 LRR 2003, r 61.

2 LRR 2003, r 203.

3 See 136.6.2 Trustee Delegation Act 1999, s 1.

4 See 136.7 Gifts and dispositions at undervalue by an attorney.
5 See 136.6.2 Trustee Delegation Act 1999, s 1.
6 LRR 2003, r 61(2).
7 LRR 2003, r 61(2).
8 See 136.1 General powers under Powers of Attorney Act 1971, s 10, 136.4 Enduring powers of attorney and 136.5 Lasting powers of attorney.
9 TLATA 1996, s 9(7).
10 TLATA 1996, s 9(2).
11 LRR 2003, r 63 and Forms 2 and 3 in Sch 3 (see Appendix V).
12 *Chandler v Lombardi* [2022] EWHC 22 (Ch).
13 See 136.6.2 Trustee Delegation Act 1999, s 1
14 Powers of Attorney Act 1971, s 5(4).
15 See Appendix V.
16 www.gov.uk/government/collections/land-registration-practice-guides.

137 PRE-SUBMISSION ENQUIRY SERVICE

The pre-submission enquiry service gives those dealing with complex commercial transactions initial guidance when submitting such transactions to HMLR for registration. It provides:

(a) support if a customer is left with questions after reading an HMLR practice guide;
(b) general lodgement or registration guidance before submitting such an application; and
(c) general guidance on whether plans or documents are likely to meet registration requirements.

An applicant wishing to use the application management service must apply using form PSS1. No fee is payable.

The HMLR website[1] provides further details of the service, including details of what HMLR considers comprises a complex commercial transaction.

1 www.gov.uk/guidance/submit-complex-commercial-or-infrastructure-development-enquiries-and-transactions-to-hm-land-registry.

138 PRIORITIES

The LRA 2002 contains specific provision for rules of priority in relation to registered land.

138.1 Basic rule of priority

The basic rule is that the priority of an interest affecting a registered estate or charge is not affected by a disposition of the estate or charge.[1] It makes no difference for this purpose whether the interest or disposition is registered. In effect, therefore, the basic rule is that the first in time by reference to date of creation prevails. This basic rule is, however, subject to considerable modification in the common event of a disposition for valuable consideration of a registered estate or a registered charge (as to which, the special rule of priority discussed below applies), and also in the less common event of an Inland Revenue charge. For the relative priority of registered charges as between themselves, see 100.7 Priorities.

138.2 Special rule of priority

The LRA 2002 provides for the application of a special rule of priority in relation to a registrable disposition of a registered estate or of a registered charge which is completed by registration.[2]

138.2.1 Registrable dispositions of registered estates for valuable consideration

A 'registrable disposition' means a disposition, such as a transfer or charge, which is required to be completed by registration under LRA 2002, s 27. 'Valuable consideration' does not include marriage consideration or a nominal consideration in money.[3] Completion by registration of a registrable disposition for valuable consideration of a registered estate has the effect of postponing to the interest under the disposition any interest affecting the estate immediately before the disposition whose priority is not protected at the time of registration.[4] The priority of an interest is 'protected' for these purposes if it:

(a) is a registered charge or the subject of a notice in the register;
(b) is an interest falling within LRA 2002, Sch 3 which overrides registered dispositions; or
(c) appears from the register to be excepted from the effect of registration.[5]

Additionally, in the case of a disposition of a leasehold estate, the priority of an interest is also protected if the burden of the interest is incident to the estate;[6] for example, covenants by a tenant contained in the registered lease.

For interests falling within LRA 2002, Sch 3 which override registered dispositions, see 128.2 Unregistered interests which override registered dispositions. Any interest which has been the subject of a notice in the register at any time on or after 13 October 2003 is not treated as an overriding interest for these purposes.[7]

Where the grant of a leasehold estate in land out of a registered estate does not involve a registrable disposition, LRA 2002, s 29 has effect as if the grant involved such a disposition and the disposition were registered at the time of the grant.[8] This would apply to the grant of a lease for a term of 7 years or less provided it was not one falling in LRA s 27(b)(ii) to (v) (inclusive).

The following example illustrates the working of the rules of priority in LRA 2002, ss 28 and 29:

- A is registered proprietor of a freehold estate in land.
- On 6 January 2025, A enters into a restrictive covenant with B affecting the whole of the estate in A's title. B does not apply for a notice to be registered in A's title.
- On 5 February 2025, A grants C an estate contract affecting the whole of the estate and a notice of the estate contract is entered in the register on 10 February 2025.
- On 5 March 2025, A transfers part of the land in the title by way of gift to D and D is registered as proprietor of the new title so created on 10 March 2025.
- On 4 April 2025, A transfers the remainder of the land in the original title on sale to E and E is registered as proprietor on 9 April 2025.

Considering the relative priorities on 12 April 2025: B's interest has priority to C's interest under the basic rule in s 28, because they are both equitable interests and B's interest was created first in time. D's registered estate is subject to the interests of both B and C under the basic rule in s 28, because although the transfer to D was a registrable disposition, it was not made for valuable consideration and the special rule in s 29 does not therefore apply to it. E's registered estate is subject only to the interest of C, which was protected by notice at the relevant time, as the transfer to E was a registrable disposition for valuable consideration and it was completed by registration.

138.2.2 Registrable dispositions of registered charges for valuable consideration

A 'registrable disposition' means a disposition, such as a transfer or charge, which is required to be completed by registration under LRA 2002, s 27. 'Valuable consideration' does not include marriage consideration or a nominal consideration in money.[9] Completion by registration of a registrable disposition for valuable consideration of a registered charge has the effect of postponing to the interest under the disposition any interest affecting the charge immediately before the disposition whose priority is not protected at the time of registration.[10] The priority of an interest is 'protected' for these purposes if it:

(a) is a registered charge or the subject of a notice in the register;
(b) is an interest falling within LRA 2002, Sch 3 which overrides registered dispositions; or
(c) appears from the register to be excepted from the effect of registration.[11]

Additionally, in the case of a disposition of a charge which relates to a leasehold estate, the priority of an interest is also protected if the burden of the interest is incident to the estate.[12]

For interests falling within LRA 2002, Sch 3 which override registered dispositions, see 128.2 Unregistered interests which override registered dispositions. Any interest which has been the subject of a notice in the register at any time on or after 13 October 2003 is not treated as an overriding interest for these purposes.[13]

138.3 Inland Revenue charges

Inheritance Act 1984, ss 237(6) and 238 determine the effect of a disposition of a registered estate or registered charge on a charge under Inheritance Tax Act 1984, s 237. For further details, see 89 Inheritance Tax.

138.4 Priority of applications

The operation of the special rule of priority is subject to the operation of the rules applicable to the priority of applications, including the rules relating to the priority period conferred by an official search with priority. An application for an entry is 'protected' if it is:

(a) one to which a priority period relates; and
(b) it is made before the end of that period.[14]

Where an application for an entry in the register is protected, any entry made in the register during the priority period relating to the application is postponed to any entry made in pursuance of it.[15] However, this does not apply if the earlier entry was itself made in pursuance of a protected application and its priority period ranks ahead of the later application.[16] If it appears to HMLR that the above might apply to an entry,[17] it may defer dealing with the application for such entry.[18]

Where a court makes an order under LRA 2002, s 46(3) that an entry is to have overriding priority,[19] this prevails over an application for another entry.[20]

A purchaser may obtain a priority period for his application by applying for an official search with priority using form OS1 or form OS2, as appropriate.[21] The priority period is the period beginning at the time when the application for the official search is entered on the day list and ending at midnight marking the end of the 30th working day thereafter.[22] A working day is any day from Monday to Friday (inclusive) which is not Christmas Day, Good Friday or any other day either specified or declared by proclamation under Banking and Financial Dealings Act 1971, s 1 or appointed by the Secretary of State, or certified by HMLR as being an 'interrupted day' due to delay or failure of a communication service or to some other event or circumstance causing substantial interruption in the normal operation of HMLR.[23]

Where two or more official search certificates with priority relating to the same registrable estate or charge or to the same registered land have been issued and are in operation, the certificates take effect, in respect to the priority conferred, in the order the applications for search were entered on the day list, unless the applicants agree otherwise.[24] Where one transaction is dependent upon another, HMLR must assume, unless the contrary appears, that the applicants have agreed that their applications for search have priority to give effect to the sequence of the documents effecting the transactions.[25]

Where two or more applications relating to the same registered title are made at the same time by the same applicant, they rank in such order as he may specify.[26] Where the applications are not made by the same applicant, they rank in such order as the applicants specify that they have agreed.[27] If the applicants have not specified the agreed order of priority, HMLR notifies them and requests them to agree within a specified time.[28] Should the applicants not agree within this period, HMLR proposes the order of priority and serves notice of its proposal on the applicants.[29] If any applicant objects to this proposal, there is in consequence a dispute between the applicants.[30] Where one transaction is dependent upon another, HMLR must assume, unless the contrary appears, that the applicants have specified that the applications are to have priority to give effect to the sequence of the documents effecting the transactions.[31]

---

1 LRA 2002, s 28.
2 LRA 2002, ss 29 and 30.
3 LRA 2002, s 132(1).
4 LRA 2002, s 29(1).
5 LRA 2002, s 29(2)(a).
6 LRA 2002, s 29(2)(b).
7 LRA 2002, s 29(3).
8 LRA 2002, s 29(4).
9 LRA 2002, s 132(1).
10 LRA 2002, s 30.
11 LRA 2002, s 30(2)(a).
12 LRA 2002, s 30(2)(b).
13 LRA 2002, s 30(3).
14 LRA 2002, s 72(1).
15 LRA 2002, s 72(2).
16 LRA 2002, s 72(3).
17 Usually, where there is an outstanding official search with priority but HMLR has not yet received the protected application.
18 LRA 2002, s 72(5).
19 For further details, see 153.3 Court order for entry of restriction.
20 LRA 2002, s 72(4).
21 LRR 2003, r 147(3). See 123.1 Official search with priority.
22 LRR 2003, r 131.
23 LRR 2003, r 217(1).
24 LRR 2003, r 153(1).
25 LRR 2003, r 153(2).
26 LRR 2003, r 55(2).
27 LRR 2003, r 55(3).
28 LRR 2003, r 55(4).
29 LRR 2003, r 55(5).
30 For details of how this may be resolved, see 54 Disputes.
31 LRR 2003, r 55(7).

139 PROFITS À PRENDRE

A profit à prendre is a right to take something from another person's land, such as the right to take fish, game or peat. A legal profit must subsist for an interest equivalent to an estate in fee simple absolute in possession or a term of years absolute.[1] Under the LRA 1925, the benefit of a profit à prendre appurtenant (i.e. one attached to land) could be registered as appurtenant to a registered estate in land, but the benefit of a profit in gross (i.e. one not attached to any land) could not be registered. However, the LRA 2002 provides for profits à prendre in gross to be capable of substantive registration in their own right.[2] It is not, however, compulsory to apply for first registration of the title to a profit à prendre in gross. It is not possible to register a profit which is appurtenant to land separately from that land.[3]

A 'right of common' is a form of profit à prendre and some rights of common will be profits à prendre in gross. However, not all profits à prendre in gross will be rights of common. This distinction is important, because rights of common over land capable of being registered under the CRA 1965 and CA 2006 cannot be registered under the LRA 2002.[4] Nor can the burden of such rights be the subject of a notice in the register of land subject to them.[5]

139.1 Legal profits à prendre on first registration

139.1.1 Beneficial profits à prendre

On first registration of title, the estate is vested in the registered proprietor together with all interests subsisting for the benefit of the estate.[6] This includes the benefit of any subsisting appurtenant legal profits, whether or not these are the subject of an entry in the register. If, at the time of first registration, HMLR is satisfied that a right subsists as a legal estate and benefits the registered estate, it may enter the benefit of that appurtenant right in the register.[7] This will be as a result of HMLR's examination of the title or its consideration of a written application providing details of the right and evidence of its existence. Where the profit has arisen by implication or prescription, the evidence will usually be in the form of a statutory declaration or statement of truth.[8] If HMLR is not satisfied that the right subsists as a legal interest benefiting the registered estate, it may enter details of the right claimed in the property register with such qualification as it considers appropriate.[9]

The applicant must therefore lodge evidence that the grantor had power to grant the profit, otherwise HMLR may either omit the right or enter a qualification note to an entry in the register relating to the appurtenant profit.

Where the burdened estate is registered, the applicant should supply the consent of any chargee of that estate, whose charge has priority over the grant of the profit and who has not joined in the grant. If the chargee has not consented to the grant, the profit is liable to be overridden if the chargee exercises his power of sale. If the consent cannot be lodged, the application may be completed but with a note along the following lines being added to the register entry for the benefiting title:

> NOTE: The consent of the proprietor of the charge dated [*date*] in favour of [*name*] affecting title(s) [*title number(s)*] was not produced on registration and the rights [*referred to above or as the case may be*] may be overridden in the event of the exercise of the power of sale.

The note can be cancelled without fee if an application is subsequently made in form AP1 enclosing the consent. Any restriction (including a restriction in favour of a chargee) in the register of the burdened title must be complied with so far as necessary. If there is a caution against dealings or a notice of (intended) deposit in the register of the burdened title and the consent to the registration of the profit does not accompany the application, HMLR may serve notice upon the cautioner or depositee.

Where the burdened estate is unregistered, evidence of the grantor's title to it, commencing with a good root more than 15 years old at the date of the application, must accompany the application. The consent of any legal mortgagee of the burdened estate to the grant of the profit should also be lodged, unless he has joined in the grant. If this consent is not lodged, the application may be completed but with a note being added to the register entry for the benefiting title in the form referred to above. In addition, if the grantor's title is leasehold, full evidence of title to any superior leasehold titles (whether of the land or profit) relating to the burdened land should be lodged.

If the profit was granted over an unregistered estate that has since been registered, it may be necessary for a notice of the burden of the profit to be entered in the register of the burdened title at the same time as the benefit is entered in the register of the benefiting title. This will be done by HMLR as part of the first registration, normally after service of notice on the proprietor of the burdened title.

139.1.2 Subjective profits à prendre

On first registration, the estate is vested in the registered proprietor subject to any profit which is an interest which overrides first registration under LRA 2002, Sch 1, or is the subject of an entry in the register in relation to the estate, and/or, in the case of a leasehold title, which is incident to the leasehold estate.[10] HMLR must enter a notice in the register of the burden of any profit which appears from its examination of the title to affect the registered estate, except any which appears to it to be of a trivial or obvious character, or the entry of a notice in respect of which would be likely to cause confusion or inconvenience.[11] No notice may be entered in the register in respect of a profit which is a right of common capable of being registered under the CRA 1965 or CA 2006.[12] Even where no entry is made of a subjective legal profit on first registration, it is an interest falling within LRA 2002, Sch 1, para 3 which therefore overrides first registration.

A person applying for first registration must provide information to HMLR in form DI about any legal profits which are within his actual knowledge and affect the estate to which the application relates, other than any which are capable of being registered under the CRA 1965 or CA 2006.[13] HMLR may enter a notice in the register in respect of any such legal profit.[14]

139.2 Legal profits à prendre arising after first registration

The express grant or reservation of a legal profit (other than one capable of being registered under the CRA 1965[15] or CA 2006[16] and other than a grant as a result of the operation of LPA 1925, s 62[17]) over registered land must be completed by registration if it is to operate at law.[18] The profit may be created in either a deed of grant, a transfer or a lease. Registration in the case of an appurtenant legal profit is completed by the entry of a notice of the profit in the register of the burdened estate and, if the benefiting estate is registered, an entry in the property register of that estate.[19] Until completed by registration, such a profit is only equitable. In the case of a legal profit in gross, the grantee must be registered as proprietor of the profit and a notice in respect of the profit must be entered in the register.[20]

If the grant of a profit over a registered burdened estate is a registrable disposition, an application to complete the grant by registration *must* be made in form AP1 or form AN1 to meet the registration requirements.[21] This is the case even if only the burdened estate is registered. Therefore, an application for entry of a unilateral notice in form UN1 will *not* meet the registration requirements. In that event, a subsequent application may be made in form AP1 or AN1 to complete the profit by registration so that it does take effect at law. Until then, it takes effect in equity only and, if it is an appurtenant profit, the benefit cannot be registered in the register of the benefiting estate (if registered).

Where the profit is contained in a transfer or charge of part of a registered estate, only an application to register the transfer or charge is necessary; no separate application in respect of the profit is required. HMLR will make the necessary entries as a matter of course when registering the transfer, provided the relevant title numbers are provided in panel 2 of form AP1 or separate application is made.[22] On registration of the transfer or charge, entries are made in the new title created and the retained or uncharged title, in respect of any appurtenant legal profits granted or reserved in the transfer or charge. An entry in respect of a profit in gross is made in the burdened title and a new title created in respect of the profit. In the case of a charge of part of a registered estate, such entries are made only if HMLR decides that the charged part is to be comprised in a separate registered title from the uncharged part.

An applicant for registration of the benefit of an appurtenant legal profit contained in a deed of grant should deliver to HMLR:

(a) an application in form AP1;
(b) the deed of grant or a certified copy of it;
(c) any consents or certificates required in respect of mortgages, charges or restrictions relating to the burdened title;
(d) (if the right is granted over unregistered land) an abstract or epitome showing the grantor's title to the unregistered estate;
(e) a commons registration search showing the right is not a right of common unless:

    (i) the property is in the New Forest, Epping Forest, the Forest of Dean or any other land excepted from the CRA 1965 by ministerial order; or
    (ii) the right is held for a term of years or from year to year;

(f) the appropriate confirmation or evidence of identity;[23]
(g) the appropriate SDLT or LTT certificate(s) or other evidence;[24] and
(h) the fee payable.[25]

The title numbers of all the registered titles involved must be specified in panel 2 of form AP1, otherwise HMLR is not obliged to make any entry unless separate application is made.[26] The profit will be completed by registration, with entries being made in the register of the burdened estate and (if registered) the benefiting estate.[27]

Where the grant or reservation of a profit is not a registrable disposition, it will be effective at law when made. However, an application may be made for the benefit of the profit to be registered as appurtenant to a registered benefiting estate.[28] The application must be made in form AP1, accompanied by:

(a) an abstract or epitome showing the grantor's title to the unregistered burdened land;
(b) any consents or certificates required in respect of mortgages, charges or restrictions relating to the burdened land; and
(c) a commons registration search showing the right is not a right of common unless:

    (i) the property is in the New Forest, Epping Forest, the Forest of Dean or any other land excepted from the CRA 1965 by ministerial order; or
    (ii) the right is held for a term of years or from year to year.

Where HMLR is not satisfied that the right claimed subsists as a legal estate appurtenant to the applicant's registered estate, it may enter details of the right claimed in the property register with such qualification as it considers appropriate.[29]

Where the benefiting estate having the benefit of a profit appurtenant is unregistered, or an unregistered profit in gross exists, application may be made for the entry of a notice in respect of such a profit where it affects a registered estate. Where it appears to HMLR that a registered estate is subject to a legal profit à prendre, it may enter a notice in the register in respect of that profit.[30] In that case HMLR must give notice to the registered proprietor and to any person who appears to it to be entitled to the interest protected by the notice or whom HMLR otherwise considers appropriate.[31] However, if the registered proprietor applies for the entry of the notice, or consents to an application for such an entry, HMLR is not obliged to give notice to him.[32] HMLR is also not obliged to give notice to any person who has applied for, or consented to, the entry of the notice, nor is it so obliged if that person's name and address for service are not set out in the registered title in question.[33]

139.3 Prescriptive profits à prendre

Prescription is the acquisition of a right through long use or enjoyment (user) so that the law presumes that the right was lawfully granted. There are three methods of acquiring a profit by prescription: at common law; by lost modern grant; and under the Prescription Act 1832 (except that this Act does not apply to a profit in gross). Whichever method is relied on, the user must have been exercised:

(a) for at least 20 years (or at least 30 years if the claim to a profit appurtenant is made under the Prescription Act 1832[34]);
(b) as of right, that is, without force, without secrecy and without permission;
(c) by or on behalf of a freehold owner against another freehold owner, so that where the burdened land is occupied by a tenant, the user must normally have started before the tenancy began; and
(d) continuously, with no long, unexplained periods of non-user. Where the claim is made under the Prescription Act 1832, a break is not treated as an 'interruption' in user for the purposes of that Act until acquiesced in for one year.[35]

In addition, the right claimed must be one that could have been lawfully granted.[36] Consequently, if the right could not have been lawfully granted by deed, then it cannot be acquired by prescription.

A prescriptive profit over a registered estate that has arisen by prescription does not have to be completed by registration to take effect at law. It will subsist either in gross or (as the case may be) for the benefit of any registered or unregistered estate to which it is appurtenant, notwithstanding that it is not the subject of an entry in the register. However, its validity will only be guaranteed for registration purposes if it is registered as a profit in gross or (as the case may be) as appurtenant to a registered estate.

139.3.1 Registration of a prescriptive appurtenant profit à prendre

An application for registration of the benefit of a prescriptive profit appurtenant may be made in either:

(a) form FR1 at the time of an application for first registration of the benefiting estate;[37] or
(b) form AP1 at any time subsequently.[38]

If the burdened estate is registered, the title number must be given in the application form. Where the application is only to note the burden of a profit, the application should be made in form AN1 for entry of an agreed notice or form UN1 for entry of a unilateral notice,[39] as appropriate.

The application must be accompanied by satisfactory supporting evidence, normally in the form of a statement of truth (which may be in form ST4 in LRR 2003, Sch 1) or statutory declaration by the applicant and any predecessors in title setting out the relevant details of the user of the profit claimed, for the requisite period of 20 years[40] or more. If the title to the applicant's estate is unregistered, he should lodge evidence of his title. Similarly, the applicant should lodge evidence of title in respect of the burdened estate if that is unregistered. If an inspection of the land is necessary, an additional fee to cover the cost of this will also be payable.

If HMLR completes the application, the register entries will depend upon whether both the benefiting estate and burdened estate are registered or only one of them is registered. Also, where the burdened estate is unregistered, whether satisfactory evidence of title to it has been lodged.

Where both the benefiting estate and burdened estate are registered, HMLR will give notice of the application to the registered proprietor and any registered chargee of the burdened title. If no objection is received, HMLR will enter the benefit of the profit as appurtenant to the benefiting estate and enter a notice of the burden in the burdened estate.

Where the benefiting estate is registered but the burdened estate is unregistered, if the applicant lodges evidence of title to the burdened estate and the address of the freehold owner, HMLR will give notice of the application to the freehold owner and any other person who may have an interest in the burdened land. If no objection is received, the benefit of the profit will be registered as appurtenant to the benefiting estate. However, if (as may often be the case) the applicant is not able to lodge evidence of title to the burdened estate and the address of the freehold owner, HMLR is likely to make only a note in the register to the effect that the applicant claims the benefit of the profit.[41] This entry will be in the following form:

> The registered proprietor claims that the land has the benefit of a right [*terms of profit as claimed by claimant*]. The right claimed is not included in this registration. The claim is supported by [*dates and details of statement(s) of truth or statutory declaration(s) and who has made them*].

Where the burdened estate is registered but the benefiting estate is unregistered, HMLR will give notice of the application to the registered proprietor and any registered chargee of the burdened estate. If no objection is received, a notice of the burden will be entered in the burdened estate in the appropriate form, depending upon whether the application is for an agreed notice or a unilateral notice.

Where the benefit of a prescriptive profit appurtenant is entered in the register of a registered benefiting estate, the entry will indicate that the right was acquired through long user and will refer to the statement(s) of truth or statutory declaration(s) lodged in support of the application, which will be open to inspection and copying.

If a valid objection is received in response to a notice of an application and it cannot be disposed of by agreement, HMLR must deal with it in accordance with LRA 2002, s 73.[42] Similar procedures, adapted as necessary, apply where a profit has arisen by implied grant rather than by prescription.

139.3.2 Registration of a prescriptive profit à prendre in gross

An application for registration of the benefit of a prescriptive profit à prendre in gross may be made in form FR1.

The application must be accompanied by satisfactory supporting evidence, normally in the form of a statement of truth[43] or statutory declaration by the applicant and any predecessors in title setting out the relevant details of the user of the profit claimed, for the requisite period of 20 years or more. If the title to the burdened estate is unregistered, he should lodge evidence of title in respect of that estate. If the applicant cannot deduce title to the unregistered burdened estate, HMLR will not usually proceed with his application. Instead, HMLR may suggest he register a caution against first registration.[44] If an inspection of the land is necessary, an additional fee to cover the cost of this will also be payable.

The applicant must also provide a commons registration search showing the right is not a right of common unless the property is in the New Forest, Epping Forest, the Forest of Dean or any other land excepted from the CRA 1965 by ministerial order.

If there are any rights, interests or claims affecting the profit which are known to the applicant, other than those disclosed in the statement of truth or statutory declaration or form DI, these should be disclosed in form FR1. This would include, for example, a disputed third-party claim relating to the profit.

Assuming the application is in order, HMLR will give notice of it to the registered proprietor and any registered chargee of the burdened estate. If no objection is received, HMLR will register the prescriptive profit à prendre in gross. On registration of the profit, it is allotted its own title number. The register for the profit will indicate that the right was acquired through long user and will refer to the statement(s) of truth or statutory declaration(s) lodged in support of the application, which will be open to inspection and copying.[45] HMLR will also usually prepare a title plan showing the land affected by the profit.[46] HMLR enters notice of the registered profit in the register for the burdened estate's registered title without any need for a separate application or further fee.

Because it is not possible to possess a profit à prendre in gross, HMLR cannot award a possessory title.[47] Neither will the title be sufficiently clear from doubt to allow HMLR to award absolute title.[48] Consequently, HMLR will usually register a prescriptive profit à prendre in gross with qualified title.[49] An example of such a qualification which might be used in a fishing profit is:

> Title to the profit a prendre in gross of fishing rights produced on first registration commences with the [*statutory declaration/statement of truth*] dated [*date*] referred to in the Property Register. No prior title to either the river bed or the fishing rights was produced on first registration. There are accordingly excepted from the effect of registration all estates rights and interests of any person who may be entitled to or have an interest in the river or the land over which the river runs.

Where two or more persons apply to be registered as proprietors of a profit à prendre in gross and a sole proprietor or the survivor of joint proprietors will not be able to give a valid receipt for capital money, application must be made for entry of a restriction in Form A.[50] The wording of Form A is set out in Appendix IV. HMLR will not usually enter such a restriction without application because LRA 2002, s 44(1) applies only to estates in land, and a profit à prendre in gross is an interest in land.[51]

An easement over other land can exist as appurtenant to a profit à prendre in gross. On first registration, HMLR will consider the statement of truth or statutory declaration accompanying the application as it would any other claimed prescriptive easement[52] and may register them as appurtenant to the profit and note them on the burdened estate. Rights which are effectively part of the profit à prendre in gross, such as a right of access over land adjoining a river bank in order to exercise a right to fish, will form part of the description of the profit à prendre in gross in the register.

If a valid objection is received in response to a notice of an application and it cannot be disposed of by agreement, HMLR must deal with it in accordance with LRA 2002, s 73.[53]

139.4 Unregistered legal profits à prendre which override registered dispositions

Although all legal profits à prendre override first registration, the position is not the same for registered dispositions. A legal profit overrides a registered disposition only if:

(a) at the time of the disposition it is within the actual knowledge of the person to whom the disposition is made; or
(b) at the time of the disposition it would have been obvious on a reasonably careful inspection of the land over which the profit is exercisable; or
(c) the person entitled to the profit proves that it has been exercised in the period of one year ending with the day of the disposition; or
(d) it is registered under the CRA 1965.[54]

Any profit, however, which was an overriding interest immediately before 13 October 2003, but which would not fall within LRA 2002, Sch 3, para 3 if created on or after 13 October 2003, continues to be an overriding interest.[55] For a period of 3 years beginning on 13 October 2003 any unregistered legal profit overrode a registered disposition.[56] An unregistered profit over registered land arising on or after 13 October 2003 is a legal profit only if it is an implied or prescriptive profit; the grant of a profit which constitutes a registrable disposition will be equitable unless completed by registration.[57]

A person applying to register a registrable disposition of a registered estate must provide information to HMLR in form DI about any legal profits (other than those capable of being registered under the CRA 1965[58]) falling within LRA 2002, Sch 3, para 3 which are within his actual knowledge and affect the estate to which the application relates.[59] The applicant must produce to HMLR any documentary evidence of the existence of any such legal profits as is under his control.[60] HMLR may enter a notice in the register in respect of any such legal profit.[61]

139.5 First registration of profit à prendre in gross

In addition to the usual documents required,[62] an applicant should deliver to HMLR:

(a) sufficient details, by plan or otherwise, so that the area of land which is affected by the profit can be clearly identified on the OS map;
(b) in the case of a leasehold profit in gross, the lease, if in the control of the applicant (and a certified copy, if the applicant wishes for the original to be returned); and
(c) a commons registration search showing the right is not a right of common unless:

    (i) the property is in the New Forest, Epping Forest, the Forest of Dean or any other land excepted from the CRA 1965 by ministerial order; or
    (ii) the right is held for a term of years or from year to year;

If the grantor's title is leasehold, full evidence of title to any superior leasehold titles (whether of the land or profit) relating to the burdened land should be lodged.

If there are any rights, interests or claims affecting the profit which are known to the applicant, other than those disclosed in the title deeds or form DI, these should be disclosed in form FR1. This would include, for example, a disputed third-party claim relating to the profit. For first registration generally, see 68 First Registration.

Leases of profits à prendre in gross may only be the subject of first registration if at the date of the application more than 7 years of the term are unexpired.[63] The provision in LRA 2002, s 3(4), which enables discontinuous leases of any length to be the subject of first registration, relates only to an estate in land. If the term of a discontinuous lease is not sufficiently clear for the purposes of s 3(3), HMLR may decide to grant only a qualified class of title. Notice of a lease of an unregistered profit à prendre in gross may be entered in the register of an affected servient registered title even if less than 7 years of the term are unexpired.

The property register of a registered profit à prendre in gross must contain a description of the profit and, where practicable, sufficient particulars of any instrument which created it to enable it to be identified.[64] An easement over other land can exist as appurtenant to a profit à prendre in gross. On first registration, HMLR will examine the title to the profit à prendre in gross and register appurtenant easements to which good title can be shown. Rights which are effectively part of the profit à prendre in gross, such as a right of access over land adjoining a river bank in order to exercise a right to fish, will form part of the description of the profit à prendre in gross in the register.

Where the applicant for first registration is unable to produce a full documentary title, the application must be supported by evidence to account for this, usually in the form of a statutory declaration or statement of truth, exhibiting any appropriate supporting documents. A statement of truth may be in form ST3 in LRR 2003, Sch 1.[65]

Where two or more persons apply to be registered as proprietors of a profit à prendre and a sole proprietor or the survivor of joint proprietors will not be able to give a valid receipt for capital money, application must be made for entry of a restriction in Form A.[66] HMLR will not usually enter such a restriction without application because LRA 2002, s 44(1) applies only to estates in land, and a profit à prendre in gross is an interest in land.[67]

139.6 Registration of profit à prendre in gross created over registered land

The express grant of a profit à prendre in gross out of a registered estate (other than one capable of being registered under the CRA 1965) is a registrable disposition.[68] In the case of a deed of grant, an applicant should deliver to HMLR:

(a) an application in form AP1;
(b) the deed creating the profit or a certified copy of it;
(c) any consents or certificates required in respect of mortgages, charges or restrictions in the grantor's title;
(d) a commons registration search showing the right is not a right of common unless:

    (i) the property is in the New Forest, Epping Forest, the Forest of Dean or any other land excepted from the CRA 1965 by ministerial order; or
    (ii) the right is held for a term of years or from year to year;

(e) form DI giving the information about overriding interests required by LRR 2003, r 57, including any documentary evidence of the interests;[69]
(f) the appropriate confirmation or evidence of identity;[70]
(g) the appropriate SDLT or LTT certificate(s) or other evidence;[71] and
(h) the fee payable.[72]

On registration of the profit, it is allotted its own title number. Notice of the registered profit is entered on the grantor's registered title without any need for a separate application or further fee. Where two or more persons apply to be registered as proprietors of a profit à prendre and a sole proprietor or the survivor of joint proprietors will not be able to give a valid receipt for capital money, application must be made for entry of a restriction in Form A.[73] HMLR will not usually enter such a restriction without application because LRA 2002, s 44(1) applies only to estates in land, and a profit à prendre in gross is an interest in land.[74]

Where the disposition consists of the grant of a lease of a profit à prendre in gross out of a registered estate, this will be a registrable disposition, regardless of the length of the term.[75] However, where the term of the lease is 7 years or less, the registration requirements are simply that the profit is noted in the register for the burdened estate.[76] For the noting of a lease for a term of 7 years or less, see 98.3.1 Agreed notice and 98.3.2 Unilateral notice. For the registration of a lease for a term exceeding 7 years, see 98.7 Registration of leases which are registrable dispositions. In the case of a discontinuous lease, HMLR may decide to enter a qualifying note in the leasehold title, if the lease is being substantively registered with its own title and the term of the lease is not sufficiently clear for the purposes of the registration requirements in LRA 2002, Sch 2, para 6.

139.7 Dispositions of a registered profit à prendre in gross

The proprietor of a registered profit à prendre in gross may transfer or lease it subject to any rule of law, express provision in the grant of the profit, or entry in the register to the contrary.[77] A lease of a registered profit à prendre in gross is a registrable disposition, regardless of the length of the term.[78] The transfer or lease may be in respect of the whole of the registered profit, or part of it. In the latter case, the part may relate to either a geographical division of the area over which the profit subsists (for example by splitting off a right to fish in a specific part of the river over which the right subsists), or a division of the subject matter of right (for example by splitting off a right to fish for salmon from a general right to fish in a river).

139.8 Extinguishment of profits à prendre

When a profit is referred to in the register of title and has been extinguished, an appropriate application may be made for the relevant entry or entries to be removed. Extinguishment may occur by virtue of statute; release (express or implied); merger by unity of ownership and possession; exhaustion of the subject matter of the profit;[79] or disclaimer.[80] In that event, application may be made for removal of the relevant entry or entries and/or (in the case of a registered estate consisting of a profit à prendre in gross) closure of the registered title. The application must be accompanied by evidence to satisfy HMLR that the profit has been extinguished.

If a valid objection is received in response to a notice of the application served by HMLR which cannot be disposed of by agreement, the matter will have to be dealt with in accordance with LRA 2002, s 73.[81]

In the case of a registered profit à prendre in gross, or a profit appurtenant which has been registered in a registered benefiting title, the application should be made in form AP1. Otherwise (where only the burden has been noted in the register of a registered burdened estate), the application should be in form CN1 (for cancellation of an agreed notice),[82] form UN2 (for removal of a unilateral notice)[83] or form UN4 (for cancellation of a unilateral notice),[84] as appropriate.

139.9 Related matters

An equitable profit à prendre may exist. In such a case, reference may usefully be made to the principles applicable to equitable easements.[85] As to legal easements, see 101 Legal Easements.

---

1 LPA 1925, s 1(2)(a).
2 LRA 2002, s 2.
3 LRA 2002, s 59(1).
4 CRA 1965, s 1(1) and CA 2006, s 3(7).
5 LRA 2002, s 33(d).
6 LRA 2002, ss 11(3) and 12(3).
7 LRR 2003, r 33(1).
8 See 139.3 Prescriptive profits à prendre.
9 LRR 2003, r 33(2).
10 LRA 2002, ss 11(4)(a) and 12(4)(a) and (b).
11 LRR 2003, r 35.
12 LRA 2002, s 33(d).
13 See 128.4 Duty to disclose overriding interests.
14 LRR 2003, r 28.
15 CRA 1965, s 1(1).
16 CA 2006, s 3(7).
17 LRA 2002, s 27(7).
18 LRA 2002, s 27(1) and (2)(d).
19 LRA 2002, Sch 2, para 7.
20 LRA 2002, Sch 2, para 6. See 139.6 Registration of profit à prendre in gross created over registered land.
21 LRR 2003, r 90.
22 LRR 2003, r 72(4) and (5).
23 See 84 Identity Evidence.

24 See 168 Stamp Duty Land Tax and/or 94 Land Transaction Tax.
25 See 67 Fees.
26 LRR 2003, r 72C(3).
27 LRR 2003, r 72C(2).
28 LRR 2003, r 73A(1)(a).
29 LRR 2003, r 73A(5).
30 LRA 2002, s 37.
31 LRR 2003, r 89(1).
32 LRR 2003, r 89(2).
33 LRR 2003, r 89(3).
34 Prescription Act 1832, s 1.
35 Prescription Act 1832, s 4.
36 *Bakewell Management Ltd v Brandwood* [2004] UKHL 14.
37 LRR 2003, r 33.
38 LRR 2003, r 73A.
39 See 119.1 Agreed notice and 119.3 Unilateral notice.
40 Or 30 years where the claim is for an appurtenant profit and the applicant is relying on the Prescription Act 1832.
41 LRR 2003, r 73A(5).
42 See 54 Disputes.
43 Which may be in form ST4 in LRR 2003, Sch 1.
44 See 25 Cautions Against First Registration.
45 LRR 2003, r 7.
46 LRR 2003, r 5. However, LRR 2003, r 5(a) does not require a title plan for profit à prendre in gross titles and HMLR may not create a title plan if the area affected by the profit is too large and cannot be conveniently split onto A0 title plans.
47 LRA 2002, s 9(5).
48 LRA 2002, s 9(2).
49 LRA 2002, s 9(4).
50 LRR 2003, r 94(2A). See 92 Joint Proprietors.
51 LPA 1925, s 1(2).
52 See 101.3 Prescriptive easements.
53 See 54 Disputes.
54 LRA 2002, Sch 3, para 3.
55 LRA 2002, Sch 12, para 9.
56 LRA 2002, Sch 12, para 10.
57 LRA 2002, s 27(1) and (2)(d).
58 LRR 2003, r 57(2)(a).
59 LRR 2003, r 57(1). See 128.4 Duty to disclose overriding interests.
60 LRR 2003, r 57(4).
61 LRR 2003, r 57(5).
62 See 68.4 Application for first registration.
63 LRA 2002, s 3(3).
64 LRR 2003, rr 5 and 7.
65 See 110 Lost or Destroyed Title Deeds.
66 LRR 2003, r 94(2A). See 92 Joint Proprietors.

67 LPA 1925, s 1(2).
68 LRA 2002, s 27(2)(d).
69 See 128.4 Duty to disclose overriding interests.
70 See 84 Identity Evidence.
71 See 168 Stamp Duty Land Tax and/or 94 Land Transaction Tax.
72 See 67 Fees.
73 LRR 2003, r 94(2A). See 92 Joint Proprietors.
74 LPA 1925, s 1(2).
75 LRA 2002, s 27(2)(d).
76 LRA 2002, Sch 2, para 7.
77 LRA 2002, s 23.
78 LRA 2002, s 27(2)(d). See 139.6 Registration of profit à prendre in gross created over registered land for the registration of such leases.
79 This occurs where the subject matter of the profit no longer exists and cannot be regenerated. It does not apply where the exhaustion is because of the deliberate actions of the servient owner(s). For example, if cattle eat all the grass in a field, it will naturally regenerate and the profit will revive. However, if all the peat in a peat bog has been removed, the profit will be extinguished by exhaustion.
80 See 19.18 Disclaimer by trustee in bankruptcy, 21 Bona Vacantia and Escheat and 108.4 Disclaimer by a liquidator.
81 See 54 Disputes.
82 See 119.2 Cancellation of a notice other than a unilateral notice or a home rights notice.
83 See 119.5 Removal of a unilateral notice.
84 See 119.6 Cancellation of a unilateral notice.
85 See 62 Equitable Easements.

140 PROPER OFFICE

Unless lodged electronically or in accordance with a written arrangement about delivery made between HMLR and the applicant or his conveyancer, all applications and correspondence should be delivered to:

(a) the 'proper office', as designated by an order of the Secretary of State as the proper office for the receipt of applications;[1] or
(b) if no such order subsists, to HMLR under the provisions of any relevant direction by the registrar under LRA 2002, s 100(4) as to the address to be used for the delivery of applications.[2]

Currently, there is no order of the Secretary of State in force. Direction 1: Addresses for HM Land Registry for the receipt of applications and correspondence (effective 17 February 2025), given under LRA 2002, s 100(4), specifies the addresses to which an applicant must deliver paper applications.[3] Different addresses apply depending on whether the customer is a business or non-business customer.

The Royal Mail address for non-business customers is: HM Land Registry Citizen Centre, PO Box 7806, Bilston WV1 9QR. They may also hand deliver applications to HM Land Registry, Tŷ Cwm Tawe, Phoenix Way, Swansea Enterprise Park, Swansea SA7 9FQ.

Business users of land registration services who have a written arrangement as to delivery should send applications to their designated 'Customer Team' within an HMLR office. Other such business users should send their applications to the applicant's closest office.

The Royal Mail address for business customers is: HM Land Registry, [*insert customer team's office name, or if none, the name of the closest office*], PO Box 7803, Bilston WV1 9QN.

The DX address for business customers is: HM Land Registry, [*insert customer team's office name, or if none, the name of the closest office*], DX 427301, Bilston 3.

Business customers may also hand deliver applications to HM Land Registry, [*insert customer team's office name, or if none, the name of the closest office*], HMLR Mailroom, Restore Digital, EDM House, Village Way, Bilston WV14 0UJ.

For electronic applications, see 56 Electronic Services.

---

1 LRA 2002, s 100(3).

2 LRR 2003, r 15(3)(a).

3 www.gov.uk/government/publications/directions-under-the-land-registration-act-2002/direction-1-addresses-for-hm-land-registry-for-the-receipt-of-applications-and-correspondence.

141 PROPERTY ADJUSTMENT ORDERS

An application for a property adjustment order under Matrimonial Causes Act 1973, s 24, or under the equivalent provisions in Civil Partnership Act 2004, s 72 and Schs 5 and 7, which affects the legal estate in registered land is a pending land action.[1] As such, it is treated as an interest affecting an estate or charge for the purposes of the LRA 2002.[2] It cannot, however, be an interest belonging to a person in actual occupation falling within LRA 2002, Sch 1, para 2 or Sch 3, para 2 which overrides first registration or registered dispositions.[3] Such an application may be protected by entry in the register of an agreed notice or a unilateral notice.

An application for a property adjustment order which does not affect the legal estate in registered land is not a pending land action and cannot be protected by entry of a notice. For example, an application for an order only in respect of a beneficial interest held by the other spouse or civil partner under a trust of land, where the dispute is not about the existence of the trust, but about who is entitled to a beneficial interest under it. This is because the interest in dispute does not constitute 'land' for this purpose. By contrast, an application where the existence of the trust is in dispute (for example an application for a declaration that a sole proprietor holds on an implied trust), or an application for the appointment of a new or additional trustee, may affect the legal estate and is therefore arguably a pending land action which may be protected by entry of a notice.[4]

Where the spouses or civil partners already hold the property as beneficial joint tenants, consideration should be given to severing the equitable joint tenancy.[5]

Once the court has made a final order, there will no longer be a 'pending' action and the appropriate action will need to be taken in respect of the order itself. A property adjustment order affecting the legal estate may be protected by entry of an agreed notice or a unilateral notice, although in most cases it will be more appropriate to complete and register a disposition (such as a transfer or charge) giving effect to its terms.

The order of the court may provide for the immediate sale of the property and the distribution of the proceeds of sale. Such an order does not need to be the subject of an entry in the register.

Where the order provides that one party should enter into a charge in favour of the other, the protection of such charge depends on whether it is a registrable charge or an equitable charge.[6]

A property adjustment order that has the effect only of either creating a trust of land, or of declaring the beneficial interests under a trust of land, cannot be protected by entry of a notice.[7] Such an order may be protected by entry of a restriction, where appropriate, in which case the form of the restriction will depend upon the nature of the order. Where the order has the effect of creating a trust, or of severing an existing beneficial joint tenancy, application should be made for a restriction in Form A, if such a restriction has not already been entered in the register. The wording of Form A is set out in Appendix IV. A restriction does not confer any priority. However, it prevents an entry being made in the register relating to any disposition, or a disposition of a specified kind, unless the terms of the restriction have (where applicable) been complied with.

141.1 Agreed notice

In addition to the usual documents required,[8] an applicant should deliver to HMLR a certified copy of application for a property adjustment order or a certified copy of the property adjustment order made by the court, as the case may be. This should be sufficient to satisfy HMLR of the validity of the applicant's claim in accordance with LRA 2002, s 34(3)(c).

The agreed notice in the register will give details of the interest protected.

141.2 Unilateral notice

An applicant should deliver to HMLR the usual documents required.[9]

Where the application relates to an application for a property adjustment order, the statement in panel 11 or conveyancer's certificate in panel 12 of form UN1 should be completed on the following lines to show the interest of the applicant:

> applicant for a property adjustment order under the [Matrimonial Causes Act 1973] *or* [Civil Partnership Act 2004] in the [*name of court*] [*set out full court reference and parties*].

Where the application relates to a property adjustment order which has been made by the court, the statement in panel 11 or conveyancer's certificate in panel 12 of form UN1 should be completed on the following lines to show the interest of the applicant:

> person who has obtained a property adjustment order under the [Matrimonial Causes Act 1973] *or* [Civil Partnership Act 2004] dated [*date*] made in the [*name of court*] [*set out full court reference and parties*] which provides that [*set out the effect of the order*].

The unilateral notice in the register will give brief details of the interest protected and identify the beneficiary of that notice.

141.3 Restriction

In addition to the usual documents required,[10] an applicant should deliver to HMLR a certified copy of the property adjustment order made by the court.

As the application for a restriction is unlikely to be made by or with the consent of the registered proprietor, the statement in panel 12 or conveyancer's certificate in panel 13 of form RX1 must be completed, setting out details of the applicant's interest under the property adjustment order.

Panel 9 of form RX1 should set out the appropriate restriction(s).

If there is no restriction in Form A already in the register, a person having a beneficial interest under a trust of land has a sufficient interest to apply for entry of a restriction in Form A, to ensure that a survivor of the joint proprietors (unless a trust corporation) will not be able to give a valid receipt for capital money.[11]

The person having a beneficial interest under a trust of land also has a sufficient interest to apply for entry of a restriction in Form II to ensure that he receives notice of a disposition. The wording of Form II is set out in Appendix IV.

This restriction does not prevent a disposition, provided its terms are complied with. This is because the interest of the beneficiary will be overreached where the requirements of Form A have been met.[12]

A restriction in standard Form A or Form II in LRA 2002, Sch 4 does not require the approval of HMLR to the wording of the restriction under LRA 2002, s 43(3).

HMLR must give notice of an application for a restriction to the proprietor of the registered estate or charge concerned if it has not been made by or with his consent or a person entitled to be registered as such proprietor.[13]

---

1 See 132 Pending Land Actions.
2 LRA 2002, s 87(1).
3 LRA 2002, s 87(3).
4 See *Godfrey v Torpey and Others* [2006] EWHC 1423 (Ch).
5 See 163 Severance of a Beneficial Joint Tenancy.
6 See 100 Legal Charges and 61 Equitable Charges, as appropriate.
7 LRA 2002, s 33(a).
8 See 119.1 Agreed notice.
9 See 119.3 Unilateral notice.
10 See 153.1 Application for entry of restriction.
11 LRR 2003, r 93(a).
12 LPA 1925, ss 2 and 27.
13 LRA 2002, s 45.

142 PROPERTY ALERT

Property Alert is a free service offered by HMLR to combat registration fraud. It allows registered users to monitor up to 10 title numbers. The user needs either the postcode or the title number(s) of the property/properties he wishes to monitor. The user does not have to be the registered proprietor of the property/ properties he is monitoring.

Once registered, HMLR will email the user if it receives:

(a) an application, or
(b) an application for an official search,

against a monitored title. The email will give details of:

(a) the application received;
(b) the applicant;
(c) when HMLR received the application; and
(d) how to contact HMLR if the user believes the application may be fraudulent.

Those who do not have access to the internet can register by phone. Further details about Property Alert, including how to sign up are on the Property Alert website.[1]

1 https://propertyalert.landregistry.gov.uk/.

143 PROPRIETARY ESTOPPEL

Where the owner of land creates an expectation in another person that that person will receive some right or interest over the land and that person acts to his detriment as a result of that expectation, an equity may arise in favour of that person by estoppel. If the owner refuses to grant the right or interest in question, an application for relief may be made to the court. The court has discretion regarding the form of relief it grants.[1] In recent years, the courts have sometimes sought to limit the circumstances in which an estoppel may arise.[2]

There has been doubt about the nature of the interest after the proprietary estoppel has arisen but before the court has made its decision. LRA 2002, s 116 declares for the avoidance of doubt that, in relation to registered land, an equity by estoppel has effect from the time the equity arises as an interest capable of binding successors in title, subject to the rules about the effect of dispositions on priority. For the rules about the effect of dispositions on priority, see 138 Priorities.

LRA 2002, s 116 applies to estoppels created both before and after that section came into force on 13 October 2003.

Between the time the equity by estoppel arises and the time the court gives effect to it, the interest may be protected by entry of a notice. If the person claiming the equity is in actual possession of the land over which the equity is claimed, it may take effect as an interest falling within LRA 2002, Sch 1, para 2 or Sch 3, para 2 which overrides first registration and registered dispositions. If an application for entry of a notice is made, this will normally be for a unilateral notice, unless the facts claimed to give rise to the interest are unequivocal, in which case application may be made for an agreed notice.

143.1 Agreed notice

In addition to the usual documents required,[3] an applicant should deliver to HMLR details of the facts claimed to have given rise to the proprietary estoppel, including the name of the proprietor of the registered estate against whom the equity is claimed to have arisen, together with any documentary evidence available.

As the consent of the registered proprietor is unlikely to be forthcoming, the evidence lodged must be sufficient to satisfy HMLR of the validity of the applicant's claim in accordance with LRA 2002, s 34(3)(c).

The agreed notice in the register will give details of the interest protected.

143.2 Unilateral notice

An applicant should deliver to HMLR the usual documents required.[4]

The statement in panel 12 or conveyancer's certificate in panel 13 of form UN1 should be completed on the following lines to show the interest of the applicant:

> person having an equity arising by proprietary estoppel as a result of [*set out facts which give rise to the proprietary estoppel, including the name of the proprietor of the registered estate against whom the equity is claimed to have arisen*].

The unilateral notice in the register will give brief details of the interest protected and identify the beneficiary of that notice.

---

1 See, for example, *Crabb v Arun District Council* [1976] Ch 179, *Taylor Fashions v Liverpool Victoria Friendly Society* [1981] 1 All ER 897 and *Gillett v Holt* [2001] Ch 210.

2 See, for example, *Yeoman's Row Management Ltd v Cobbe* [2008] UKHL 55.

[3] See 119.1 Agreed notice.
[4] See 119.3 Unilateral notice.

144 PUBLIC AUTHORITY CERTIFICATES OF TITLE

HMLR has made arrangements with many local and other public authorities whereby when the authority sells unregistered land, it gives the purchaser a certificate of the title in an agreed form, instead of deducing title in the ordinary way. The certificate contains a statement of the incumbrances that affect the land. HMLR will accept this statement, and accordingly, when the purchaser applies for first registration of his title, he need not produce the normal conveyancing evidence of the authority's title. It also makes it unnecessary for a Land Charges search to be made by the purchaser against the name of the authority.

This procedure will be used, for example, on purchases of property under the right to buy scheme. Under HA 1985, s 154(2), a landlord must give a tenant who exercises his right to buy under that Act a certificate of title in a form approved by HMLR. Three such forms of certificate of title have been so approved: form PSD1 (where the landlord conveys a freehold dwelling house); form PSD2 (where the landlord owns the freehold and grants a lease of a house or grants a shared ownership lease of a house or flat); and form PSD3 (where the landlord does not own the freehold and grants an underlease of a house or flat).

Similarly, forms PSD13, PSD14 and PSD15 have been approved for use in preserved right to buy cases and form PSD16 has been approved for use in extended right to buy cases. Form PSD17 has been approved for use on the conveyance, lease or assignment of housing land or buildings, where the disposal is subject to a preserved right to buy or is a voluntary disposal with the consent of the Secretary of State, or is a disposal by a Housing Action Trust. Forms PSD11 (freehold dwelling) and PSD12 (leasehold dwelling) have been approved for use in relation to the compulsory registration of title to defective dwellings repurchased under HA 1985, Sch 20, para 17.

These forms of certificate of title are only for use in the specified cases and should not be used in any other circumstances. The certificate must be signed as provided and, in the case of a local authority, by the chief executive officer or by some other officer approved by HMLR. In reliance upon the certificate, the property will be registered subject to any incumbrances specified in the certificate, any contained in the deed inducing registration, and any created by the applicant. The authority is responsible for the accuracy of the certificate and must refund to HMLR any indemnity paid because the certificate was incorrect.

145 PUBLIC-PRIVATE PARTNERSHIP LEASES RELATING TO TRANSPORT IN LONDON

PPP leases for the purposes of the LRA 2002 are leases created for PPPs relating to transport in London within the meaning given by Greater London Authority Act 1999, s 218.[1] No application for voluntary registration of such a lease may be made, nor does the requirement of registration apply on the grant or transfer of a leasehold estate in land under a PPP lease.[2]

The grant of a term of years absolute under a PPP lease is not required to be completed by registration.[3] The express grant of an interest falling within LPA 1925, s 1(2) (for example a legal easement) is not required to be completed by registration where the interest is created for the benefit of a leasehold estate in land under a PPP lease.[4]

No notice may be entered in the register in respect of an interest under a PPP lease.[5]

A PPP lease is an unregistered interest which overrides first registration and registered dispositions, as though it were included within LRA 2002, Schs 1 and 3.[6] An applicant is not, however, required to provide any information about a PPP lease under the duty to disclose interests which override those imposed by LRR 2003, rr 28 and 57.[7]

1 LRA 2002, s 90(6).
2 LRA 2002, s 90(1) and (2).
3 LRA 2002, s 90(3)(a).
4 LRA 2002, s 90(3)(b).
5 LRA 2002, s 90(4).
6 LRA 2002, s 90(5).
7 See 128.4 Duty to disclose overriding interests.

146 RECEIVERS APPOINTED UNDER THE LAW OF PROPERTY ACT 1925

Receivers appointed either under the statutory powers of appointment conferred by LPA 1925, s 109, or under an express power contained in a mortgage or debenture, who do not meet the requirements for an administrative receiver, are commonly referred to as 'Law of Property Act' or 'LPA' receivers.

For:

(a) administrative receivers, see 4 Administrative receivers;
(b) for receivers appointed under the Mental Health Act 1983, see 113 Mental Incapacity;
(c) for receivers appointed by court order, see 147 Receivers Appointed by Order of the Court.

A receiver is more commonly appointed where the mortgagor is a company, but appointment is also possible where the mortgagor is an individual. Where more than one receiver is appointed, the instrument of appointment must make it clear whether they can act jointly and severally, or jointly only.

In the case of a mortgage or debenture created by deed, a statutory power arises when the mortgage money has become payable and the power of sale is exercisable.[1] This statutory power may be varied, extended or excluded by the mortgage or debenture, which may contain an express power to appoint.[2]

In the case of a company mortgagor, where an administrator has been appointed before the appointment of the receiver, the consent of the administrator (or the permission of the court) to the appointment of the receiver must be lodged with any application to register a disposition by the receiver, otherwise HMLR will serve notice on the administrator, giving him the opportunity to object, before the application can proceed further. The appointment of a receiver does not prevent an administrator being subsequently appointed, although the receiver is not automatically dismissed if this occurs. However, the receiver must vacate office if required to do so by the administrator.

An entry in respect of the mortgage or debenture under which the receiver is appointed should already appear in the register by virtue of it having been registered as a registered charge or protected by entry of a notice. As the property remains vested in the mortgagor, the receiver cannot be registered as proprietor nor can a note of the receiver's appointment be entered in the register. However, the receiver may apply for any necessary changes to the mortgagor's address for service in the register.

146.1 Address for service

The receiver should ensure that the mortgagor's address for service shown in the register is such as will allow notices to be received. If an additional address for service (up to three are permitted) or an amended address for service is required, the receiver should deliver to HMLR:

(a) an application in form AP1;
(b) a certified copy of the appointment of the receiver;
(c) evidence that the receiver has power to apply on behalf of the mortgagor; and
(d) a certified copy of the debenture or charge under which the receiver is appointed (if not already noted or registered and a copy filed with HMLR).

No fee is currently payable.

146.2 Sale by a receiver

A receiver has only limited statutory powers under LPA 1925, s 109. These are normally extended by the mortgage or debenture. The statutory powers must be extended if the receiver is to have power to dispose of the mortgagor's property.

An LPA 1925 receiver (LPA receiver) has no statutory power to execute on behalf of the company. The mortgage or debenture will normally include a power of attorney in favour of the receiver. Such a power is not a security power and will not survive liquidation if the mortgagor is a company. If the receiver executes as attorney under such a specific power, even if the power is under 12 months old, the application for registration of the disposition will need to be accompanied by a statutory declaration or statement of truth confirming that the applicant did not, at the time of the completion of the transaction, know of any revocation of the power or know of the occurrence of any event (such as the winding up of a company mortgagor or bankruptcy, death or mental incapacity of an individual mortgagor) which had the effect of revoking the power. A conveyancer's certificate to the like effect may be provided instead.

Usually, the mortgage or debenture will also give the receiver the right to sell or otherwise dispose of the mortgagor's property and this includes the power to execute in the name and on behalf of the mortgagor. If the receiver executes under such a power, evidence of non-revocation will not be required.

In the case of a company mortgagor, a deed can also, at the direction of the receiver, be sealed by the company using its common seal in the presence of the duly authorised officers of the company, or signed as a deed by a director and secretary or by two directors of the company (or by a single director if that signature is witnessed and attested).

A receiver is the agent of the mortgagor. On liquidation of a company mortgagor this agency comes to an end, but the receiver continues to have power to act for the purposes of holding and disposing of the company's property and may use the company's name for that purpose.[3]

In a winding up of a corporate mortgagor by the court, any disposition of the company's property after commencement of the winding-up is void unless sanctioned by an order of the court.[4] However, where a debenture has been created before the winding up, any subsequent disposition by the debenture holder or receiver under powers contained in the debenture does not require an order of the court.

The IA 1986 provides for transactions at an undervalue, preferences, extortionate credit transactions and the avoidance of certain floating charges[5] which may have the effect of invalidating the debenture wholly or in part. Therefore, when making an application for registration of a disposition by a receiver, the applicant must disclose any such challenge of which he is aware and if there is any suggestion that the liquidator may be seeking to have the debenture avoided under these provisions, HMLR may serve notice upon the liquidator, giving him the opportunity to object. If a valid objection is received which cannot be disposed of by agreement, the matter will have to be dealt with in accordance with LRA 2002, s 73.[6] Similar considerations are likely to apply where it appears that a trustee in bankruptcy may seek to avoid the mortgage under IA 1986, ss 339, 340, 343 or 423 (while having regard to the provisions of s 342(2) and (2A)).

If the debenture confers a power of attorney upon the receiver, this power is not a security power and it will be revoked by the winding up of the company. However, the right to sell, or otherwise dispose of, the company's property will include the right to execute in the name and on behalf of the company and such a right will continue after winding up commences.[7]

A receiver is the agent of the mortgagor not of the mortgagee or debenture holder and therefore has no power to discharge the mortgagor's property from any mortgage or charge (including the mortgage or debenture under which he was appointed), regardless of the date of creation of the mortgage or charge. Consequently, on a sale of a property by a receiver, the purchaser must, where appropriate, ensure that a release or discharge is obtained for all mortgages and charges, including the mortgage or debenture under which the receiver was appointed.

In addition to the usual documents required,[8] a transferee of a registered title from a receiver should deliver to HMLR:

(a) a certified copy of the receiver's appointment;
(b) a certified copy of the mortgage or debenture under which the receiver was appointed (unless this is already noted in the register and a copy is filed at HMLR);

(c) evidence that the power of appointment of a receiver under the mortgage has arisen (which may be in the form of a certificate by the mortgagee, or by a conveyancer on his behalf, that the power of appointment under the mortgage has arisen, unless this is evident from a full copy of the mortgage or debenture filed at HMLR);
(d) if the receiver executes as attorney, evidence of non-revocation where appropriate:
(e) a discharge or release in respect of any charges appearing in the title;
(f) details of any challenge to the validity of the debenture that is within the actual knowledge of the receiver or the applicant. Where the mortgagor is a company and the challenge is by a liquidator or administrator of the company, or the mortgagor is an individual and the challenge is by a trustee in bankruptcy, details of the name and address of the liquidator, administrator or trustee in bankruptcy should be provided; and
(g) the consent of any previously appointed administrator, or the permission of the court, to the appointment of the receiver where required.

Any existing restrictions in the register will need to be complied with. If a restriction in Form A appears in the register, consideration must be given both to whether the terms of the restriction have been complied with to enable the transfer to be registered and, if so, whether overreaching has been effected to enable the existing restriction to be cancelled from the register. The wording of Form A is set out in Appendix IV.

If there are joint mortgagors, a transfer executed by a single receiver on their behalf will comply with the restriction and can be registered, as it is not a disposition by a sole proprietor. This reflects the fact that the joint mortgagors (as trustees) have power to mortgage the land and can delegate to the receiver the power to sell and convey the mortgaged land. Delegation by more than one mortgagor to a single receiver will be effective for registration purposes, as it represents 'collective delegation' for the purposes of Trustee Act 2000, s 11, so that the joint mortgagors are acting through a single agent. However, execution by a single receiver would not appear to fulfil the requirements for overreaching to be effected under LPA 1925, ss 2(1)(ii) and 27.[9] As the transfer is not by the mortgagee, the overreaching provisions relating to a conveyance by a mortgagee contained in LPA 1925, s 2(1)(iii) will not apply. In consequence, upon registration of the transfer, the restriction will not be automatically cancelled by HMLR pursuant to LRR 2003, r 99, as it will not be in a position to be satisfied that the beneficial interests under the existing trust of land have necessarily been overreached. Although application may be made under LRR 2003, r 97 for the restriction to be cancelled, such an application would have to be supported by evidence to satisfy HMLR that the restriction is no longer required because the mortgagors were the only persons with a beneficial interest in the land and the land was not, or is no longer, subject to any beneficial interest in favour of a third party.

If there are joint mortgagors and the transfer is executed by two or more joint receivers on their behalf, this will both comply with the restriction in Form A and effect overreaching, so that the restriction will be cancelled on registration of the transfer.

If there is a sole mortgagor, a transfer executed by either a single receiver or joint receivers on his behalf cannot be registered as it is a disposition by a sole proprietor and so caught by the restriction in Form A; nor will it effect overreaching.

The position will be similar if the disposition is a lease granted out of the mortgaged registered title, except that if the lease is registered in circumstances where a restriction in Form A appears in the register of the mortgaged title and overreaching has not been effected, the restriction will not be carried forward to the register of the new leasehold title. The powers of the receiver would have to have been extended beyond the limited statutory powers in the LPA 1925, to enable such a lease to be granted.

---

1 LPA 1925, ss 101(1)(iii), 109 and 109.
2 LPA 1925, ss 101(4) and 109(3).
3 *Sowman v David Samuel Trust Ltd* [1978] 1 All ER 616.
4 IA 1986, s 127.
5 IA 1986, ss 238 to 241, 244 and 245.
6 See 54 Disputes.
7 *Barrows v Chief Land Registrar*, *The Times*, 20 October 1977.
8 See 176.1 Registration of transfer.
9 Trustee Delegation Act 1999, s 7.

147 RECEIVERS APPOINTED BY ORDER OF THE COURT

An order appointing a receiver is treated as an interest affecting an estate or charge for the purposes of the LRA 2002.[1] It cannot, however, constitute an interest belonging to a person in actual occupation falling within LRA 2002, Sch 1, para 2 or Sch 3, para 2 which overrides first registration and registered dispositions.[2] No notice of an order appointing a receiver may be entered in the register.[3] Such an order may, however, be protected by the entry of a restriction.

The receiver is to be regarded as a person having a sufficient interest in the entry of a restriction if he is applying for a restriction in Form L or Form N.[4] The wording of Forms L and M is set out in Appendix IV. A restriction does not confer any priority. However, it prevents an entry being made in the register relating to any disposition, or a disposition of a specified kind, unless the terms of the restriction have (where applicable) been complied with.

For:

(a) administrative receivers, see 4 Administrative receivers;
(b) LPA receivers, see 146 Receivers Appointed under the Law of Property Act 1925;
(c) receivers appointed under the Mental Health Act 1983, see 113 Mental Incapacity.

147.1 Restriction

In addition to the usual documents required,[5] the receiver should deliver to HMLR a certified copy of the order of the court appointing the receiver.

As the application for a restriction is unlikely to be made by or with the consent of the registered proprietor, the statement in panel 12 or conveyancer's certificate in panel 13 of form RX1 should be completed on the following lines:

> The interest is that specified in rule 93(s) of the Land Registration Rules 2003 (SI 2003/1417), the applicant being the receiver appointed by [*name*] Court on [*date*].

Panel 9 of form RX1 should set out the appropriate restriction.

A possible form of restriction based on the wording of Form L is:

> No [disposition *or specify type of disposition*] of the registered estate by the proprietor of the registered estate [or by the proprietor of any registered charge, not being a charge registered before the entry of this restriction] is to be registered without a certificate signed by [*name*] of [*address*] [or [their conveyancer *or specify appropriate details*]] that the provisions of [*specify clause, paragraph or other particulars*] of [*specify details*] have been complied with [or that they do not apply to the disposition].

A possible form of restriction based on the wording of Form N is:

> No [disposition *or specify type of disposition*] of the registered estate by the proprietor of the registered estate [or by the proprietor of any registered charge, not being a charge registered before the entry of this restriction] is to be registered without a written consent signed by [*name*] of [*address*] [or [their conveyancer *or specify appropriate details*]].

A restriction in standard Form L or Form N does not require the approval of HMLR to the wording of the restriction under LRA 2002, s 43(3).

HMLR must give notice of the application for a restriction to the proprietor of the registered estate concerned, if it has not been made by or with his consent or a person entitled to be registered as such proprietor.[6]

---

1 LRA 2002, s 87(1)(c).
2 LRA 2002, s 87(3).
3 LRA 2002, s 87(2).
4 LRR 2003, r 93(s).
5 See 153.1 Application for entry of restriction.
6 LRA 2002, s 45.

148 RECTIFICATION

For the purposes of the LRA 2002, 'rectification' is an alteration of the register which involves the correction of a mistake and which prejudicially affects the title of a registered proprietor[1]. Rectification is therefore a form of alteration, but not all alterations amount to rectification. For alterations which do not amount to rectification, see 12 Alteration of the Register. Where there is an issue of rectification, indemnity may be payable by HMLR to a person who suffers loss as a result.[2] A person may apply to the court for an order for rectification of the register.[3] They may also apply to HMLR for rectification of the register without a court order.[4] The power to rectify the register extends to changing for the future the priority of any interest affecting the registered estate or charge concerned.[5] The effect of rectification is therefore prospective and takes effect for the future only; it does not operate retrospectively from the time of the original mistake.

148.1 Rectification pursuant to an order of the court

Where rectification of a title to a registered estate in land by court order is sought and the proprietor of that estate is in possession of the land, the court can make such an order only if:

(a) the proprietor consents to it; or
(b) he has caused or substantially contributed to the mistake by fraud or lack of proper care; or
(c) it would be for any other reason unjust for the alteration not to be made.

A proprietor is in possession of the land if it is physically in his possession or in that of a person who is entitled to be registered as the proprietor.[6] Land in the possession of a tenant is treated as in the possession of the landlord, and similarly in the cases of mortgagee and mortgagor, licensee and licensor, and beneficiary and trustee.[7] A proprietor's title, for this purpose, includes his title to any registered estate which subsists for the benefit of his registered estate in the land; for example, a beneficial easement.

Dhillon v Barclays Bank PLC[8] contains an example where the court refused to rectify despite the registered proprietor being in possession.

Where rectification of a registered estate in land by court order is sought and the proprietor of that estate is not in possession of the land, the court must make such an order if it has power to do so, unless there are exceptional circumstances which justify its not doing so.[9]

A court order for alteration of the register must state the title number of the title affected and the alteration that is to be made. It must also direct HMLR to make the alteration.[10] Service on HMLR of such an order must be made by making an application for HMLR to give effect to the order, accompanied by the order.[11]

An applicant for an alteration of the register pursuant to an order of the court should deliver to HMLR:

(a) an application in form AP1;
(b) the court order for alteration of the register or a sealed copy of that court order; and
(c) the fee (if applicable).[12]

148.2 Rectification other than pursuant to an order of the court

Where application is made direct to HMLR for an alteration which amounts to rectification, the same principles as to the protection of a proprietor in possession of a registered estate in land apply. Equally, where the proprietor is not in possession and HMLR has power to make the alteration, it must approve the application, unless there are exceptional circumstances which justify not making the alteration.

An application for alteration, other than under a court order, must be supported by evidence to justify the alteration.[13] HMLR may make such enquiries as it thinks fit and must give notice of the proposed alteration to any person who would be affected by it, unless it is satisfied that such notice is unnecessary.[14] However, where there is a specific rule dealing with the alteration sought, HMLR must follow that rule in preference to these general provisions.

An applicant for an alteration of the register otherwise than pursuant to a court order should deliver to HMLR:

(a) an application in form AP1;
(b) a statement of the alteration being applied for;
(c) all relevant evidence held by the applicant which is relevant to the application to alter the register; and
(d) the fee (if applicable).[15]

Where the application leads to a valid objection which cannot be disposed of by agreement, any dispute will have to be dealt with in accordance with LRA 2002, s 73.[16]

---

1 LRA 2002, Sch 4, para 1.
2 See 86 Indemnity.
3 LRA 2002, Sch 4, para 2.
4 LRA 2002, Sch 4, para 5.
5 LRA 2002, Sch 4, para 8.
6 LRA 2002, s 131(1).
7 LRA 2002, s 131(2).
8 [2019] EWHC 475 (Ch). Discussed in 75.1 Alteration and rectification.
9 LRA 2002, Sch 4, para 3(3).
10 LRR 2003, r 127(1).
11 LRR 2003, r 127(2).
12 See 67 Fees.
13 LRR 2003, r 129.
14 LRR 2003, r 128.
15 See 67 Fees.
16 See 54 Disputes.

149 REGISTERED SOCIAL LANDLORDS AND PRIVATE REGISTERED PROVIDERS

In England, but not Wales, the regulation of social housing was amended by the Housing and Regeneration Act 2008, and again by the Localism Act 2011. In Wales, the Welsh Ministers have passed the Regulation of Registered Social Landlords (Wales) Act 2018. Registered providers of social housing are therefore affected by different regulatory regimes depending upon whether they are English or Welsh.

In England, the Regulator of Social Housing (previously the Homes England and before that the Homes and Communities Agency) maintains a register of providers of social housing, which may be public (for example local authorities) or private (for profit or not for profit). Such private providers were formerly known as registered social landlords but are now referred to as private registered providers.

In Wales, private providers continue to be referred to as registered social landlords where they are registered within the register maintained by the Welsh Ministers under HA 1996, s 1.

In either case, such a body may be a registered charity which is a housing association. Alternatively, it may be a registered society or a registered company which satisfies the conditions for registration.

For:

(a) housing associations which are unregistered social landlords, see 83 Housing Associations;
(b) registered societies, see 150 Registered Societies.

149.1 Registration of registered social landlords or private registered providers as proprietor

If an applicant for registration as proprietor of a registered estate or registered charge in England is, or holds on trust for, a private registered provider of social housing, or a registered social landlord within the meaning of the HA 1996, the application must include a certificate to that effect.[1] This is in addition to any requirements arising from the fact that the applicant is a charity, a registered society or a company, for which see 30 Charities, 150 Registered Societies or 37 Companies, respectively.

If a registered estate in land is held on trust for a private registered provider or a registered social landlord and two or more trustees are being entered as proprietors, a restriction in Form A will be entered by HMLR in the register. The wording of Form A is set out in Appendix IV. If an unregistered housing association is a charity, HMLR will enter a charity restriction, where appropriate.

149.2 Housing administration orders

In England, where a private registered provider is a corporate entity of the type specified in Housing and Planning Act 2016, s 95(1)(a), the court may make a housing administration order.[2] Such an order appoints one or more qualified insolvency practitioners as a housing administrator. He/they must manage the private registered proprietor's affairs, business and property with a view to achieving the objectives set out in Housing and Planning Act 2016, s 96.

Once appointed, the housing administrator(s) should apply to HMLR to reflect their appointment in the register. A housing administrator should deliver to HMLR:

(a) an application in form AP1;
(b) the court order appointing them or a sealed copy of that court order; and
(c) the fee (if applicable).[3]

On completion of the application, HMLR will make an entry in the proprietorship register along the following lines:

> By an order of the court made on [*date*] [*name(s) of housing administrator(s)*] of [*address*] were appointed housing administrators of [*name of private registered provider*].

149.3 Dispositions by registered social landlords or private registered providers

Historically, HMLR entered restrictions in the registers of estates owned by or held on trust for registered social landlords or private registered providers. These restrictions reflected the statutory limitations on the proprietor's ability to dispose of their property. Such restrictions can now be disregarded for dispositions taking place on or after:

(a) 6 April 2017 in England; or
(b) 15 August 2018 in Wales.

Applications to register dispositions by private registered providers or registered social landlords should meet the requirements of any other restriction in the register. If a private registered provider or registered social landlord is a charity, the appropriate charity statement should be included within the disposition, where necessary.[4]

Where a house is sold by a private registered provider or registered social landlord at a discount, the transfer will contain a covenant to repay a proportion of the discount if the purchaser disposes of the house within 5 years.[5] This takes effect as a charge[6] and HMLR will make an entry in respect of it in the charges register of the purchaser's title.

Where the disposal is of a house in a National Park, a national landscape or an area designated as a rural area, the transfer or conveyance may contain a covenant limiting the freedom of the purchaser to dispose of the property. In such case, HMLR will automatically enter a restriction in Form V or Form Y in the proprietorship register.[7] The wording of Forms V and Y is set out in Appendix IV.

Where the disposal consists of a lease, application could previously be made for entry of a restriction in Form KK in the register of the title to the lease. Form KK prohibited variations to the registered lease without the consent of the relevant body. All Form KK restrictions in England were cancelled on 1 October 2008. Since 15 August 2018 it has not been possible to apply for a new restriction in Form KK in Wales.[8] Where a Form KK remains in the register, it must be complied with. Alternatively, it may be cancelled. In addition to the usual documents required,[9] the applicant should deliver to HMLR either:

(a) written confirmation that the tenant has purchased 100% of the equity; or
(b) a certificate that the final staircasing purchase has been completed.

---

1 LRR 2003, r 183A(1), as amended by Regulation of Registered Social Landlords (Wales) Act 2018 (Consequential Amendments) Regulations 2018 (SI 2018/870), reg 4(b).
2 Housing and Planning Act 2016, s 100.
3 See 67 Fees.
4 See 30 Charities.
5 HA 1985, s 155 in England; Housing Act 1996 (HA 1996), s 11 in Wales.
6 HA 1985, s 156 in England; HA 1996, s 11B in Wales.
7 LRA 2002, s 44(2) and LRR 2003, r 95(2)(h).
8 Regulation of Registered Social Landlords (Wales) Act 2018 (Consequential Amendments) Regulations 2018 (SI 2018/870), reg 4(c)(ii).
9 See 153.8 Cancellation of a restriction.

150 REGISTERED SOCIETIES

Registered societies are registered under the Co-operative and Community Benefit Societies Act 2014 (CCBSA 2014). They replaced industrial and provident societies and all existing societies that were registered under the Industrial and Provident Societies Act 1965 became registered societies on 1 August 2014.

The purpose of the CCBSA 2014 was to consolidate the existing legislation relating to industrial and provident societies, co-operatives, community benefit societies, and other societies registered under the Industrial and Provident Societies Act 1965.

Registered societies registered after 1 August 2014 can be either co-operative societies or community benefit societies.

They are corporate bodies which, unless their rules state to the contrary, possess the power to purchase or take a lease of land in their own name. Once registered as proprietors of land they may sell, lease, exchange or mortgage it.

Many (but not all) housing associations are registered societies.

The FCA maintains the register of registered societies. Although registered societies are treated as companies for tax purposes and the Companies Act 2006 requires the name of a registered society to be registered in the Companies House index of company names, they are regulated by the FCA and must register any charges over their assets with the FCA, not at Companies House. Charges by registered societies are therefore not subject to the filing requirements for companies under Companies Act 2006, Pt 25, or to the requirement in LRR 2003, r 111.

A purchaser, assignee, mortgagee or tenant is not bound to enquire as to the authority for any such dealing with the land by the society.[1] As a result, a restriction does not need to be entered in the proprietorship register merely because the proprietor is a registered society.

On an application to register a registered society as proprietor, a copy of its registered rules, or a certificate by its conveyancer in Form 8 in LRR 2003, Sch 3, should be lodged.[2] The wording of Form 8 is set out in Appendix V. In practice, arrangements are often made by registered societies with the head office of HMLR so that the rules do not need to be lodged with every application. For the position where the society is also a charity, housing association or private registered provider or registered social landlord, see 30 Charities, 83 Housing Associations and 149 Registered Social Landlords and Private Registered Providers, respectively. See also 45 Credit Unions.

The registration number of a registered society will be entered in the proprietorship register immediately after the name of the society.

A registered society may execute deeds either under its common seal authenticated in accordance with the society's rules and expressed to be a deed; or by being signed by a member of the committee and its secretary or by two members of the committee and expressed (in whatever form of words) to be executed by the society.[3]

---

1 CCBSA 2014, s 46.

2 LRR 2003, r 183.

3 CCBSA 2014, s 53.

151 RENTCHARGES

A rentcharge is any sum of money charged on land payable annually or periodically, other than rent reserved by a lease or interest charged under a mortgage.[1] 'Land' for this purpose has the same meaning as in LPA 1925, s 205(1). Rentcharges are sometimes described in deeds as rent charges, chief rents, quit rents, fee farm rents or some similar term. A rentcharge is usually perpetual, but can be granted for a term of years so that it is terminable. The land affected by a rentcharge can be either freehold or leasehold; in the latter case, the rentcharge will always be terminable because the lease itself will eventually come to an end.

A rentcharge is usually created by way of a conveyance or transfer, where the vendor of the land reserves an annual rent, payable to him and his successors in title and charged upon the land sold. In modern times, most new rentcharges created are 'estate rentcharges', which are discussed below. A rentcharge is capable of being bought and sold or charged. A rentcharge may be capable of being substantively registered with its own title and the burden of it may be the subject of a notice in the register of registered land affected by it.

The Rentcharges Act 1977 made several important changes to the law relating to rentcharges. It provides for the extinguishment, apportionment and redemption of certain rentcharges and limits the scope for the creation of new rentcharges. Its main provisions came into operation on 22 August 1977. After 21 August 1977 the only new rentcharges which may be created (either at law or in equity) are those falling within Rentcharges Act 1977, s 2, including rentcharges arising out of an order of the court, and estate rentcharges. In practice, the only new rentcharges likely to be created are estate rentcharges. An estate rentcharge is defined by Rentcharges Act 1977, s 2(4) and (5) as being a rentcharge of either:

(a) a nominal amount for the purpose of making covenants to be performed by the owner of the land affected by the rentcharge enforceable by the rent owner against the owner for the time being of the land; or
(b) a reasonable amount to meet, or contribute towards, the cost of the performance by the rent owner of covenants for the provision of services, the carrying out of maintenance or repairs, the effecting of insurance or the making of any payment by him for the benefit of the land affected by the rentcharge or for the benefit of that and other land.

Rentcharges Act 1977, s 3 provides (subject to certain exceptions) for the extinguishment of rentcharges after a period of 60 years. Sections 4 to 10 deal with apportionment and redemption.

LFRA 2024, s 113 amended the law concerning enforcement of rentcharges falling outside Rentcharges Act 1977, s 2. It refers to such rentcharges as regulated rentcharges. In particular, the owner of a regulated rentcharge cannot take action to recover arrears due unless he serves a demand for payment complying with the statutory formalities set out in LPA 1925, s 120B. Further, the owner of a regulated rentcharge no longer has the statutory remedies in LPA 1925, s 121.

151.1 Rentcharges created out of unregistered land

In relation to an estate which is subject to a rentcharge, on first registration of title to that estate, the estate is vested in the registered proprietor subject to any rentcharges which are the subject of an entry in the register in relation to the estate.[2] HMLR must enter a notice in the register of the burden of any rentcharge which appears from its examination to affect the registered estate.[3]

In relation to the title to an unregistered rentcharge, it is not compulsory to register the title to a legal rentcharge created out of unregistered land, either on its creation or on a subsequent sale or transfer. However, it is possible to make a voluntary application to register a legal rentcharge which is either perpetual, or is held for a term of years of which more than 7 years are unexpired at the date of the application for first registration of the rentcharge.[4] The rentcharge must be based either on a deed dated before 22 August 1977; or on a deed dated on or after 22 August 1977 where its creation is not prohibited by Rentcharges Act 1977, s 2. The fact that a rentcharge is subject to extinguishment in accordance with the provisions of the Rentcharges Act 1977 does not of itself prevent it from being 'perpetual' or for a term of years 'absolute' for the purposes of registration. It was also possible to register a legal rentcharge under the LRA 1925. Rentcharges that subsist as equitable interests only, for example because of the mode of their creation or because they are informally apportioned parts of a legal or equitable rentcharge, cannot be registered but they may be protected in the register by means of a notice.[5]

In addition to the usual documents required,[6] an applicant for first registration of a legal rentcharge should deliver to HMLR:

(a) sufficient details, by plan or otherwise, so that the area of land which is affected by the rentcharge can be clearly identified on the OS map;
(b) the deed creating the rentcharge and those deeds proving devolution of title to the applicant.

If there are any rights, interests or claims affecting the rentcharge which are known to the applicant, other than those disclosed in the title deeds or form DI, these should be disclosed in the form FR1. This would include, for example, any rights in the course of being acquired over the rentcharge by adverse possession, or a disputed third-party claim relating to the rentcharge. For first registration generally, see 68 First Registration.

Where the applicant for first registration cannot produce a full documentary title, the application must be supported by evidence to account for this, usually in the form of a statutory declaration or statement of truth, exhibiting any appropriate supporting documents. A statement of truth may be in form ST3 in LRR 2003, Sch 1.[7]

Where two or more persons apply to be registered as proprietors of a rentcharge and a sole proprietor or the survivor of joint proprietors will not be able to give a valid receipt for capital money, application must be made for entry of a restriction in Form A.[8] The wording of Form A is set out in Appendix IV.

151.2 Registration of rentcharge created over registered land

The express grant or reservation of a legal rentcharge over registered land is a registrable disposition which must be completed by registration.[9] Until completed by registration, the rentcharge takes effect in equity only. The registration requirements are:

(a) In the case of a rentcharge granted in fee simple or for a term of more than 7 years, the grantee must be registered as proprietor of the rentcharge and a notice of the rentcharge must be entered in the register of the title out of which it was created.
(b) In the case of a rentcharge granted for a term of less than 7 years, a notice of the rentcharge must be entered in the register of the title out of which it was created.[10]

A legal rentcharge may be created as a disposition of registered land in one of two ways. It may be the subject of a deed of grant by the proprietor of the land; or it may be granted in a transfer or lease of registered land by the transferee or tenant to the transferor or landlord, charged upon the land transferred or demised. Typically, the latter will be the case where there is a transfer or lease of a plot on a developing estate, where an estate rentcharge is imposed on each plot. In both cases an application for the registration of the rentcharge should be made in form AP1.

In the case of a rentcharge granted for a term of less than 7 years, application for entry of a notice of the rentcharge in the grantor's title may be made in form AP1 or form AN1.[11]

In the case of a rentcharge granted in a transfer or lease, a single form AP1 can cover both registration of the land and registration of the rentcharge if desired. HMLR is not obliged to substantively register the rentcharge unless specific application is made in the form AP1.[12] The rentcharge cannot be registered until the transfer or lease itself has been completed by registration and therefore taken effect at law.

If a legal rentcharge is granted out of leasehold land registered with good leasehold title, and more than a qualified title to the rentcharge is desired, satisfactory evidence must be produced to show that the lease (and any superior lease) was validly granted.

Every deed creating a rentcharge out of registered land must contain a reference to the title number of that land[13] and particulars, by plan if necessary, to enable the land charged to be identified on the title plan of the grantor's title.[14]

If completed by registration, HMLR will register the rentcharge under its own individual title (where it is capable of substantive registration) and/or enter a notice of the burden in the register of title of the land charged.

If not completed by registration, the rentcharge will take effect in equity only, although the burden will still be capable of being protected by a notice in the register of the title to the land charged.[15]

A right of re-entry relating to a rentcharge created out of registered land on or after 13 October 2003 must itself be completed by registration if it is to take effect at law.[16] In the case of such a right created in a lease for a term of years absolute which is itself a registrable disposition, completion by registration of the lease will be sufficient to meet the registration requirements for the right of re-entry and no additional entry needs to be made in respect of it.[17]

An applicant for registration of a rentcharge granted by a deed of grant should deliver to HMLR:

(a) an application in form AP1;
(b) the deed creating the rentcharge (and a certified copy, if the applicant wishes for the original to be returned);
(c) any consents or certificates required in respect of mortgages, charges or restrictions in the grantor's title;
(d) form DI giving the information on overriding interests required by LRR 2003, r 57, including any documentary evidence of the interests;[18]
(e) the appropriate confirmation or evidence of identity;[19]
(f) the appropriate SDLT and/or LTT certificate(s) or other evidence;[20] and
(g) the fee payable.[21]

Where two or more persons apply to be registered as proprietors of a rentcharge and a sole proprietor or the survivor of joint proprietors will not be able to give a valid receipt for capital money, HMLR will not automatically enter a restriction in Form A and instead application must be made for entry of the restriction.[22]

151.3 Rentcharges granted by a UK company or UK limited liability partnership

Previously, such rentcharges were specifically exempted from the requirement for registration at Companies House. However, as a result of the Companies Act 2006 (Amendment of Part 25) Regulations 2013 (SI 2013/600), which came into force on 6 April 2013, it appears that this specific exemption may no longer apply. Where necessary therefore, when an application for substantive registration of such a rentcharge granted on or after 6 April 2013 is made to HMLR, evidence of registration at Companies House[23] should be lodged. If this is not done, HMLR may enter a note in the register of the rentcharge title, indicating that it is subject to the provisions of Companies Act 2006, s 859H, if and so far as that section applies to the rentcharge.

151.4 Rentcharges which cannot be registered

Rentcharges which subsist only as equitable interests cannot be registered, but the burden of such rentcharges should be protected in the register of the title to the land out of which they were created, where that land is registered.

When an equitable rentcharge is created out of a registered estate, a notice of the burden of the rentcharge should be entered in the register of the title to the estate charged. If an equitable rentcharge is created by the transferee in a transfer of a registered estate, a notice of the burden will be entered in the register of the transferee's title as a matter of course when the transfer is registered.[24]

If an equitable rentcharge is created by the tenant in a prescribed clauses lease and the requisite details are inserted in clause LR12, a notice of the burden will be entered in the register of the tenant's title as a matter of course when the lease is registered.[25] If created in a non-prescribed clauses lease, a notice of the burden will be entered in the register of the tenant's title as a matter of course when the lease is registered.[26]

In any other case of an equitable rentcharge created out of a registered estate, a separate application should be made to enter a notice of the rentcharge in the register of the title of the estate charged.

151.5 Entry of notice of rentcharge

When an estate is first registered, HMLR will enter a notice of the burden of any subsisting rentcharge, whether legal or equitable, charged on the estate and appearing in the title, in the charges register of the title to the estate charged, together with details of any apportionments and exonerations.

On the completion by registration of a legal rentcharge created out of a registered estate, HMLR will enter a notice of the burden of the rentcharge in the register of the title to the estate charged, in accordance with the registration requirements.[27]

If a rentcharge is a registrable disposition under LRA 2002, s 27 but is not completed by registration, it takes effect in equity only, but the burden of it will still be capable of being protected by entry of a notice in the register of the title to the estate charged. In the case of a rentcharge granted in a transfer or lease, HMLR will enter such a notice as a matter of course when registering the transfer or lease itself.[28]

On the creation, out of a registered estate, of a rentcharge which cannot be registered, a specific application for the entry of an agreed notice or a unilateral notice in respect of the rentcharge in the register of the title to the estate out of which the rentcharge issues will be necessary. The application should be made in form AN1 for entry of an agreed notice or form UN1 for entry of a unilateral notice, as appropriate.[29]

Often, rentcharges contain a contractual right of entry if the estate owner does not pay the relevant sum(s).[30] Before 13 October 2003, such rights were not required to be noted on the register. However, since then, they must be completed by registration if they are to take effect in law.[31] On first registration, or when completing by registration a legal rentcharge created out of a registered estate which contains such a right, HMLR will automatically enter a note of the contractual right of re-entry.[32]

151.6 Dispositions of registered rentcharges

A registered rentcharge can be transferred, leased or charged in the same way and subject to the same rules as a registered estate in land, so far as the nature of a rentcharge permits. The guidance appearing elsewhere in this book, whilst primarily relating to registered estates in land, also applies generally to registered rentcharges.[33] However, a rentcharge owner cannot create easements or restrictive covenants.

Any transfer of a rentcharge should provide for the express assignment of the benefit of the grantor's covenant to pay the rent, as such a covenant does not run at law with the rentcharge to enable the rentcharge owner to sue under it.

Dispositions of rentcharges have the same SDLT and/or LTT requirements as other dispositions of registered land, as a rentcharge is for this purpose 'land'.[34]

151.7 Transfer of registered estate subject to a rentcharge

LRR 2003, r 69 makes provision in relation to implied covenants in respect of such a transfer.[35]

151.8 Apportionment and redemption of rentcharges

Apportionment is the division of a rentcharge. A formally apportioned rentcharge can be dealt with separately in its own right.

Exoneration is the release of part of the land charged from any liability for payment.

An apportionment or an exoneration may each be formal or informal. There are two types of formal apportionment. The most common is by a ministerial order (or certificate of apportionment) given by the Secretary of State. The other is a deed made between all the relevant parties. To be formal (and to have full effect at law), all the owners of the land affected by the rentcharge and the rentcharge owner must join in the deed.

An informal apportionment or exoneration arises where not all the relevant parties join in the deed; this often occurs where there is a transfer or lease of part of the land in a registered title and the rentcharge owner is not a party to the apportionment or exoneration.

A registered title which relates to an estate in land or to a rentcharge may be affected by a ministerial order apportioning a rentcharge or by a ministerial certificate that a rentcharge has been redeemed. If it is not known whether the title to the land or rentcharge is registered, a search of the index map may be made in form SIM.[36]

An application should be made for effect to be given to the order or the certificate in the registered title(s) affected. Where an apportionment is made conditional on the redemption of the rentcharge, the application should not be made until after the redemption has taken place. The application should be made in form AP1, referring to 'Apportionment of rentcharge' or 'Redemption of rentcharge' as the case may be. It should be supported by an official copy of the order and/or an official copy of the certificate of redemption as appropriate. A fee is payable.[37] However, no fee is payable if the application is accompanied by an application upon which a scale fee is payable; for example, where the order or certificate has been obtained in anticipation of a sale of the registered land or rentcharge and the application for the registration of the order or certificate is lodged with the application for the registration of the transfer on sale of the land or rentcharge.

Where a rentcharge has been formally exonerated, this acts as an extinguishment of the rentcharge.

151.9 Extinguishment of rentcharges

Rentcharges Act 1977, s 3(1) provides that, subject to certain exceptions, every rentcharge shall (if it has not then ceased to have effect) be extinguished at the expiry of the period of 60 years beginning with the passing of that Act (22 July 1977), or the date on which the rentcharge first became payable, whichever is later. This section will not extinguish any rentcharge payable wholly or partly in lieu of tithes or of a kind referred to in Rentcharges Act 1977, s 2(3) (disregarding s 2(5), which relates to estate rentcharges). Variable rentcharges are also excluded from extinguishment under Rentcharges Act 1977, s 3(1), but where a variable rentcharge ceases to be variable s 3(1) will apply as if the date on which the rentcharge first became payable was the date on which it ceased to be variable.

Apart from extinguishment under the Rentcharges Act 1977, a rentcharge may also be determined or extinguished by a number of other means, including;

(a) merger;
(b) a deed of release whereby the rentcharge owner releases the rentcharge to the owner of the land charged;
(c) re-entry after an order of the court, where the rentcharge owner has obtained possession of the land charged by order of the court;
(d) a certificate of redemption given by the Secretary of State or the Welsh Ministers;[38]
(e) effluxion of time, in the case of a terminable rentcharge;
(f) adverse possession where, by virtue of non-payment of the rent, the rentcharge has become statute barred;[39]
(g) cessation of the estate in the land charged; for example, on forfeiture of a leasehold estate subject to a terminable rentcharge; and
(h) informal letter or receipt from the rentcharge owner.

An application following the extinguishment of a rentcharge, other than by ministerial certificate, should be made supported by appropriate evidence of extinguishment. The application should be made in form AP1 (where both the land and the rentcharge are registered, or only the rentcharge is registered). Otherwise, it should be made in form CN1 for cancellation of an agreed notice, or form UN4 for cancellation of a unilateral notice (where only the land charged is registered).[40] A fee is payable (unless the application is accompanied by an application upon which a scale fee is payable, when no fee is payable).[41]

151.10 Adverse possession of rentcharges

It is unclear whether it is currently possible to adversely possess a registered or unregistered rentcharge. This is because of changes made to LA 1980, s 38 by Tribunal Courts and Enforcement Act 2007, Sch 14. These amendments were intended to facilitate the abolition of rent distress but have amended LA 1980, s 38 in such a way that they appear to abolish the limitation regime for rentcharges, by removing rentcharges from the definition of 'land' for the purposes of LA 1980, s 15. Commentators believe this was not the intended consequence of the amendment. As a result of this uncertainty, HMLR will take a cautious approach when considering an application to close a rentcharge title or remove a notice of a rentcharge from the register.

Previously, a person may have been in adverse possession of a rentcharge if he failed to pay the rent due under the rentcharge, or if he paid the rent to a person who is not entitled to receive it. In the first case, the proprietor of the estate subject to the charge was in adverse possession of the rentcharge. In the second, the person who received the rent from him was in adverse possession of the rentcharge. The period of adverse possession ran from the date at which the proprietor of the charge received the last rent.[42]

Where a rentcharge:

(a) affects both an applicant's estates and other estates, and
(b) has not been formally apportioned,

the applicant must establish that no other person has paid the rent due. If any other person has paid the rent due, time will not start to run.[43] In such circumstances, HMLR may refuse to proceed or, where the rentcharge is protected by an agreed notice but not substantively registered, make an entry to the effect that the registered proprietor claims the rentcharge has come to an end.

151.10.1 Adverse possession of a registered rentcharge

The LRA 2002 and the LRR 2003 make provision for adverse possession of a registered rentcharge. LRR 2003, r 191 applies the provisions of LRA 2002, Sch 6 to rentcharges in the modified form set out in LRR 2003, Sch 8. This provides for a procedure similar to that in respect of adverse possession of registered land.[44] Accordingly, subject to the uncertainty mentioned above, a person may apply under LRA 2002, Sch 6, para 1 (as modified) to be registered as proprietor of the registered rentcharge if he has been in adverse possession of the registered rentcharge for a period of 10 years ending on the date of the application. The registered rentcharge need not have been registered throughout this period. A person may not make such an application if:

(a) he is a defendant in proceedings by the registered proprietor of the registered rentcharge for recovery of the rent or to enter into possession of the land out of which the registered rentcharge issues;
(b) judgment in favour of the registered proprietor of the registered rentcharge in respect of proceedings of the nature mentioned in (a) above has been given against him in the last 2 years; or
(c) the registered proprietor of the registered rentcharge of which that person was in adverse possession has entered into possession of the land out of which the registered rentcharge issues.

If HMLR elects to proceed with the application, it must give notice of it to the registered proprietor of the rentcharge. That notice will usually refer to the uncertainty caused by Tribunal Courts and Enforcement Act 2007, Sch 14.

If a person given notice of an application requires that it is dealt with under LRA 2002, Sch 6, para 5 (as modified), the applicant is entitled to be registered as the new proprietor only if either of the following conditions in para 5 (as modified) is met.

The first condition is that:

(a) it would be unconscionable because of an equity by estoppel for the registered proprietor to seek to assert his title to the registered rentcharge against the applicant; and
(b) the circumstances are such that the applicant ought to be registered as the proprietor.

The second condition is that the applicant is for some other reason entitled to be registered as the proprietor of the registered rentcharge. The third condition in Sch 6, para 5, which applies in relation to adverse possession of a registered estate in land, does not apply to adverse possession of a rentcharge and is therefore omitted from Sch 6 (as modified).

Where the applicant cannot bring himself within either condition his application is rejected. He may then make a further application to be registered as proprietor of the registered rentcharge under LRA 2002, Sch 6, para 6 (as modified) if he is in adverse possession of that rentcharge from the date of the application until the last day of the period of 2 years beginning with the date of its rejection.

There are restrictions on making applications, similar to those relating to applications based on adverse possession of land.[45]

Where a person is entitled to be registered as proprietor of a registered rentcharge under LRA 2002, Sch 6 (as modified) as a result of non-payment of the rentcharge, the registered rentcharge title is closed or (if the title also comprises other rentcharges) the registered rentcharge is cancelled; this reflects the fact that the rentcharge has effectively been merged with the applicant's existing estate. This does not apply if, were that person to be registered as proprietor of that rentcharge, he would be subject to a registered charge or registered lease or other interest protected in the register.[46] Where a person is entitled to be registered as proprietor of a registered rentcharge as a result of having received the payment of rent due under the rentcharge, HMLR will not remove the entry of the rentcharge from the register but will instead register the applicant as the new proprietor.

Where, as a result of an application under LRA 2002, Sch 6 (as modified), a person is registered as proprietor of a registered rentcharge or that registered title is closed or the registered rentcharge is cancelled (the title comprising also other rentcharges), no previous registered proprietor of the rentcharge may recover any rent due under the rentcharge from a person who has been in adverse possession of the rentcharge.[47] This applies whether the adverse possession arose as a result of non-payment of the rent or by receipt of the rent from the person liable to pay it.

151.10.1.1 Application under Land Registration Act 2002, Sch 6, para 1 (as modified) for registration by a person in adverse possession of registered rentcharge

An applicant making an application under LRA 2002, Sch 6, para 1 (as modified) should deliver to HMLR:

(a) an application in form ADV1;
(b) a statutory declaration or statement of truth made by the applicant not more than one month before the application, together with any necessary supporting

statutory declarations or statements of truth, to provide evidence of adverse possession of the rentcharge against which the application is made for a period of not less than 10 years ending on the date of application. A statement of truth may be made in form ST2 in LRR 2003, Sch 4, although its use is not compulsory;

(c) any additional evidence which the applicant considers necessary to support the claim;
(d) a list in duplicate in form DL of all the documents delivered;
(e) the appropriate confirmation or evidence of identity;[48] and
(f) the fee payable.[49]

The statutory declaration or statement of truth by the applicant must also contain:

(a) confirmation that LRA 2002, Sch 6, para 1(2) (as modified) does not apply. Paragraph 1(2) provides that a person may not make an application if he is a defendant in proceedings by the registered proprietor of the rentcharge for recovery of the rent or to enter into possession of the land out of which the rentcharge issues, or if judgment in such proceedings has been given against him in the last 2 years. It also provides that he may not make such an application if the registered proprietor of the rentcharge of which he was in adverse possession has entered into possession of the land out of which the rentcharge issues;
(b) confirmation that to the best of his knowledge the restriction on applications in LRA 2002, Sch 6, para 8 (as modified) does not apply;[50]
(c) confirmation that to the best of his knowledge the rentcharge is not, and has not been during any of the period of alleged adverse possession, subject to a trust (other than one where the interest of each of the beneficiaries is an interest in possession);
(d) confirmation that the proprietor of the registered rentcharge has not re-entered the land out of which the rentcharge issues; and
(e) if, should a person given notice of the application require that it be dealt with under LRA 2002, Sch 6, para 5 (as modified), it is intended to rely on one or both of the conditions set out in that paragraph, the facts supporting such reliance.

The applicant must also supply such additional evidence as HMLR may require after it has considered the application.[51]

The effect of registration under LRA 2002, Sch 6, para 1 (as modified), including that in relation to registered charges (and the provision for apportionment of charges, where appropriate), is similar to that in relation to a registered estate in land.[52]

151.10.1.2 Application under Land Registration Act 2002, Sch 6, para 6 (as modified) for registration by a person in adverse possession of registered rentcharge

Where an applicant has had an application under LRA 2002, Sch 6, para 1 (as modified) rejected, he may be able to make a further application under LRA 2002, Sch 6, para 6 (as modified) if he has been in adverse possession of the registered rentcharge for a further 2 years from the date of rejection. However, a person may not make an application under this paragraph if:

(a) he is a defendant in proceedings by the registered proprietor of the registered rentcharge for recovery of the rent or to enter into possession of the land out of which the registered rentcharge issues;
(b) judgment in favour of the registered proprietor of the registered rentcharge in respect of proceedings of the nature mentioned in sub-paragraph (a) has been given against him in the last 2 years; or
(c) the registered proprietor of the registered rentcharge of which that person was in adverse possession has entered into possession of the land out of which the registered rentcharge issues.

The special form of notice required by Sch 6, para 2 (as modified) and the right to require the application to be dealt with under Sch 6, para 5 (as modified) do not apply to such applications. Instead, under LRR 2003, r 17, HMLR will give 15 working days' notice of the application to the proprietor of the registered rentcharge and certain other persons.[53]

An applicant should deliver to HMLR:

(a) an application in form ADV1;
(b) a statutory declaration or statement of truth made by the applicant not more than one month before the application, together with any necessary supporting statutory declarations or statements of truth, to provide evidence of adverse possession of the rentcharge against which the application is made for a period of not less than 2 years beginning with the date of rejection of the original application and ending on the date of application. A statement of truth may be made in form ST2 in LRR 2003, Sch 4, although its use is not compulsory;
(c) any additional evidence which the applicant considers necessary to support the claim;
(d) a list in duplicate in form DL of all the documents delivered;
(e) the appropriate confirmation or evidence of identity;[54] and
(f) the fee payable.[55]

The statutory declaration or statement of truth by the applicant must also contain:

(a) full details of the previous rejected application;
(b) confirmation that to the best of his knowledge the restriction on applications in LRA 2002, Sch 6, para 8 (as modified) does not apply;[56]
(c) confirmation that to the best of his knowledge the rentcharge is not, and has not been during any of the period of alleged adverse possession, subject to a trust (other than one where the interest of each of the beneficiaries is an interest in possession);
(d) confirmation that the proprietor of the registered rentcharge has not re-entered the land out of which the rentcharge issues; and
(e) confirmation that LRA 2002, Sch 6, para 6(2) (as modified) does not apply. Paragraph 6(2) (as modified) provides that a person may not make an application if he is a defendant in proceedings by the registered proprietor of the rentcharge for recovery of the rent or to enter into possession of the land out of which the rentcharge issues, or if judgment in such proceedings has been given against him in the last 2 years. It also provides that he may not make such an application if the registered proprietor of the rentcharge of which he was in adverse possession has entered into possession of the land out of which the rentcharge issues.

The applicant must also supply such additional evidence as HMLR may require after it has considered the application.[57]

The effect of registration under LRA 2002, Sch 6, para 6 (as modified), including that in relation to registered charges (and the provision for apportionment of charges, where appropriate), is similar to that in relation to a registered estate in land.[58]

151.10.1.3 Transitional provisions

Under LRA 2002, Sch 12, para 18(5) and LRR 2003, r 224, if title to a rentcharge was acquired by adverse possession before 13 October 2003, and it was held in trust under LRA 1925, s 75(1) immediately before that date, the beneficiary of that trust may apply either to be registered as proprietor of the rentcharge, or for the registration of the rentcharge to be cancelled.[59] In such circumstances, the issues identified in relation to the Tribunal Courts and Enforcement Act 2007, Sch 14 do not arise because the applicant will have completed his adverse possession before Sch 14 came into effect.

151.10.2 Adverse possession of unregistered rentcharges

Adverse possession may arise in relation to a rentcharge the title to which is unregistered; in such a case reference may usefully be made to the principles applicable to adverse possession of an unregistered estate in land.[60] If the applicant completed the relevant period of adverse possession of the unregistered rentcharge before 6 April 2014, the issues identified in relation to Tribunal Courts and Enforcement Act 2007, Sch 14 do not arise.

If the unregistered rentcharge is the subject of an agreed notice in the register, the applicant should apply to cancel it using form CN1 accompanied by:

(a) a statutory declaration or statement of truth made by the applicant, together with any necessary supporting statutory declarations or statements of truth, to provide evidence of adverse possession of the rentcharge against which the application is made for a period of not less than 12 years. A statement of truth may be made in form ST2 in LRR 2003, Sch 4, although its use is not compulsory;
(b) any additional evidence which the applicant considers necessary to support the claim; and
(c) the fee payable.[61]

---

1 Rentcharges Act 1977, s 1.
2 LRA 2002, ss 11(4) and 12(4).
3 LRR 2003, r 35.
4 LRA 2002, s 3.
5 See 151.4 Rentcharges which cannot be registered.
6 See 68.4 Application for first registration.
7 See 110 Lost or Destroyed Title Deeds.
8 LRR 2003, r 94(2A). See 92 Joint Proprietors.
9 LRA 2002, s 27(2)(e).
10 LRA 2002, s 27 and Sch 2, Part 1, paras 6 and 7.
11 LRR 2003, r 90.
12 LRR 2003, rr 72(6) and 72C(4).
13 LRR 2003, r 212(3).
14 LRR 2003, r 213.
15 See 151.5 Entry of notice of rentcharge.
16 LRA 2002, s 27(2)(e).
17 LRR 2003, r 77.
18 See 128.4 Duty to disclose overriding interests.
19 See 84 Identity Evidence.
20 See 168 Stamp Duty Land Tax and/or 94 Land Transaction Tax.
21 See 67 Fees.
22 LRR 2003, r 94(2A). See 92 Joint Proprietors.

23 See 37.5 Registration of a charge created by a UK company and 105.2 Registration of charge created by a UK limited liability partnership.
24 LRR 2003, rr 72(4) and 72C(2).
25 LRR 2003, r 72A(2) and (3).
26 LRR 2003, r 72C(2).
27 See 151.2 Registration of rentcharge created over registered land.
28 LRR 2003, rr 72(4), 72A(2) and 72C(2).
29 See 119.1 Agreed notice and 119.3 Unilateral notice.
30 In addition to the statutory right conferred by LPA 1925, s 121(3).
31 LRA 2002, s 27(2)(e).
32 LRR 2003, rr 35, 72(4), 72A(2) and 72C(2).
33 See in particular 176 Transfers and 98 Leases.
34 See 168 Stamp Duty Land Tax and/or 94 Land Transaction Tax.
35 See 85.2 Transfer of a registered estate subject to a rentcharge.
36 See 124.1 Search of the index map.
37 See 67 Fees.
38 See 151.8 Apportionment and redemption of rentcharges.
39 See 151.10 Adverse possession of rentcharges.
40 See 119.2 Cancellation of a notice other than a unilateral notice or a home rights notice and 119.6 Cancellation of a unilateral notice.
41 See 67 Fees.
42 LA 1980, ss 15(1) and 38(8).
43 *Adnam v The Earl of Sandwich* (1877) 2 QBD 485 and *Woodcock v Titterton* (1864) 12 WR 865.
44 See 6 Adverse Possession.
45 See 6 Adverse Possession and LRR 2003, Sch 8.
46 LRR 2003, r 192.
47 LRR 2003, r 193.
48 See 84 Identity Evidence.
49 See 67 Fees.
50 See 6.3 Application under Land Registration Act 2002, Sch 6, para 1 for registration by person in adverse possession of registered land and LRR 2003, Sch 8.
51 LRR 2003, r 17.
52 See 6.3 Application under Land Registration Act 2002, Sch 6, para 1 for registration by person in adverse possession of registered land, 6.6 Registered charges and LRR 2003, Sch 8.
53 See 6.5 Application under Land Registration Act 2002, Sch 6, para 6 for registration by person in adverse possession of registered land.
54 See 84 Identity Evidence.
55 See 67 Fees.
56 See 6.3 Application under Land Registration Act 2002, Sch 6, para 1 for registration by person in adverse possession of registered land and LRR 2003, Sch 8.
57 LRR 2003, r 17.
58 See 6.5 Application under Land Registration Act 2002, Sch 6, para 6 for registration by person in adverse possession of registered land, 6.6 Registered charges and LRR 2003, Sch 8.

59 See 6.8 Transitional provisions.
60 See 6.9 Application for first registration.
61 See 67 Fees.

152 REQUISITION, REJECTION AND CANCELLATION POLICY

If an application appears to HMLR to be substantially defective, it may reject it on delivery or it may cancel it at any time thereafter.[1] If an application is not in order, HMLR may raise such requisitions as it considers necessary and specify a period (being not less than 20 working days) within which the applicant must comply with the requisitions. If the applicant fails to do so, HMLR may cancel the application or may extend the period when this appears to be reasonable in the circumstances.

If it considers it necessary or desirable, HMLR may refuse to complete or proceed with an application until further documents or evidence are supplied or notice is given.[2]

If it will not be possible to reply to requisitions in the time specified, an applicant should request an extension. The request should:

(a) state the reason for the delay;
(b) explain what is being done to resolve the problem; and
(c) indicate when it is expected that a full reply to the requisition can be supplied.

If an applicant makes such a request supported by a proper reason, HMLR may allow an extension, but if the applicant does not make any request, HMLR may cancel the application. HMLR's *Practice guide 49: Return and rejection of applications for registration* and *Practice guide 50: requisition and cancellation procedures* contain full details of its policy and practice on the rejection of defective applications and on requisitions and cancellation. These are available to view and download at the HMLR website.[3]

1 LRR 2003, r 16.
2 LRR 2003, r 17.
3 www.gov.uk/government/collections/land-registration-practice-guides.

153 RESTRICTIONS

A restriction is an entry in the register regulating the circumstances in which a disposition of a registered estate or charge may be the subject of an entry in the register. It therefore represents a limitation on the exercise of the 'owner's powers' contained in LRA 2002, s 23, for the purposes of ss 26 and 52 of that Act. It may prohibit the making of an entry in respect of any disposition, or of certain kinds of disposition, indefinitely or for a specified period or until the occurrence of a specified event. For example, a restriction may prohibit the registration of a disposition of a registered estate without the written consent of a named person.

Where a restriction is entered in the register, no entry may be made in respect of a disposition to which the restriction applies unless it is in accordance with the terms of the restriction or HMLR makes an order. HMLR may by order disapply or modify a restriction in respect of a particular disposition or class of dispositions.[1]

A restriction affecting a registered estate may also affect a charge that is subsequently registered, if its wording is sufficiently wide to catch dispositions by both a registered proprietor and a registered chargee; it will not, however, affect a charge which was registered before the entry of the restriction. A restriction affecting a registered charge will not catch dispositions by the proprietor of the registered estate and a separate restriction in that regard would be necessary. Nor will it affect a charge which was registered before the entry of the restriction.

HMLR may enter a restriction if it appears to it that it is necessary or desirable to do so for the purpose of:

(a) preventing invalidity or unlawfulness in relation to dispositions of a registered estate or charge;
(b) securing that interests which are capable of being overreached on a disposition of a registered estate or charge are overreached; or
(c) protecting a right or claim in relation to a registered estate or charge.[2]

Although HMLR enters most restrictions following an application, HMLR may enter such restriction without an application having been made. If it does so, it must give notice of the entry to the registered proprietor.[3] HMLR must enter a restriction in certain circumstances.[4] The court may make an order requiring HMLR to enter a restriction if it appears necessary or desirable to do so for the purposes of protecting a right or claim in relation to a registered estate or registered charge.[5]

HMLR may not enter any restriction for the purpose of protecting the priority of an interest which is, or could be, the subject of a notice.[6] However, this does not necessarily prevent the entry of a restriction in addition to a notice. Although the notice will protect the priority of the interest, a restriction may be used to ensure that any conditions in relation to another disposition by the registered proprietor are complied with. For example, a notice may be entered to protect the priority of a right of pre-emption and at the same time a restriction entered to ensure that there is no disposition of the land to a third party without the written consent of the person having the benefit of the right of pre-emption.

A right or claim may only be protected by a restriction if it relates to a registered estate or registered charge; that is, to the legal estate. This does not therefore include rights or claims that relate only to an equitable interest in an estate or charge under a trust of land.[7] In most cases, entry of a restriction in Form A will be appropriate, to ensure that overreaching takes place on a disposition that gives rise to capital monies. The wording of Form A is set out in Appendix IV. A specific exception to this is a charging order affecting a beneficial interest under a trust, which may nevertheless be protected by a restriction in Form K.[8] The wording of Form K is set out in Appendix IV.

An applicant must not exercise the right to apply for the entry of a restriction without reasonable cause.[9] This duty to act reasonably is owed to any person who suffers damage in consequence of its breach.[10]

153.1 Application for entry of restriction

A person may apply for the entry of a restriction if he is the registered proprietor or entitled to be so registered; or if he has the consent of the registered proprietor or the person entitled to be so registered; or if he otherwise has a sufficient interest in the making of the entry.[11] LRR 2003, r 93 lists various different classes of person who are automatically regarded as having sufficient interest in the making of an entry. These are dealt with in the appropriate sections of this book. This list is not exhaustive, but a person not falling within any of the categories listed will have to lodge evidence that he has a sufficient interest in the entry of the restriction.

An applicant for entry of a restriction should deliver to HMLR:

(a) an application in form RX1 (but see also below);
(b) (if the application is made with the consent of, rather than by, the registered proprietor or person entitled to be so registered) the relevant consent unless this is given in panel 11 of form RX1 or the applicant's conveyancer certifies in panel 8 of form RX1 that he holds such consent;

(c) (if the application is made by or with the consent of a person entitled to be registered as proprietor) evidence to satisfy HMLR of that person's entitlement to be registered as proprietor. This may take the form of a certificate by the applicant's conveyancer in panel 8 of form RX1 that he is satisfied that the applicant, or the person consenting to the application, is entitled to be registered as proprietor and that he holds the originals of the documents that contain evidence of that person's entitlement, or an application for registration of that person as proprietor is pending at HMLR;
(d) (if the application is made by a person who claims that he has a sufficient interest in the making of the entry) a statement in panel 12 of form RX1 signed by the applicant or a certificate by his conveyancer in panel 13 of form RX1, giving details of the nature of the applicant's interest in the entry of the required restriction (or, if the interest is one of those specified in LRR 2003, r 93, stating which of them) and details of how the applicant's interest arose. Any supporting documents should be listed in panel 5 of form RX1 or in a separate form DL; and
(e) the fee payable.[12]

Panel 9 of form RX1 should set out the required restriction(s). If a restriction requires notice to be given to a person, or requires a person's consent or certificate, or is a standard form restriction that refers to a named person and requires his address, that person's address for service must be stated. A restriction in one of the standard forms set out in LRR 2003, Sch 4 does not require the approval of HMLR to the wording of the restriction under LRA 2002, s 43(3). For non-standard restrictions, such approval will be required.[13]

If the restriction affects the registered estate, HMLR will enter it in the proprietorship register. If it affects a registered charge, HMLR will enter it in the charges register.

An application for a restriction need not be made in form RX1 provided it is for a *standard* form of restriction and the application is instead made in one of the following:

(a) the additional provisions panel of a prescribed form of transfer or assent in forms TP1, TP2, TR1, TR2, TR4, TR5, AS1, AS2 or AS3;
(b) panel 8 of form CH1, or in a charge which has first been approved by HMLR, or in an electronic document to which LRA 2002, s 91 applies where the form of the document (including the application for the restriction) has first been approved by HMLR;
(c) clause LR13 of a prescribed clauses lease (or any other lease containing clauses LR1 to LR14 of LRR 2003, Sch 1A and which is required to be

completed by registration under LRA 2002, s 27(2)(b) or is the subject of an application for first registration of title to it); or

(d) (in the case of application for a Form A restriction following the severance of a beneficial joint tenancy by agreement or notice) form SEV.[14]

HMLR must give notice of the application for entry of a restriction and of the right to object to the registered proprietor, unless:

(a) the application was made by him or with his consent;
(b) the application was made by or with the consent of a person entitled to be registered as proprietor;
(c) the application was required to be made by LRR 2003, r 94 (which lists various cases where an application must be made); or
(d) the restriction reflects a limitation under an order of the court or HMLR, or under an undertaking given in place of such an order.[15]

HMLR may not determine the application before the end of the specified period unless each person notified has indicated that he is not objecting or his objection has been disposed of.[16] The specified period is the period ending at 12 noon on the 15th working day after the date of issue of the notice or, if more than one such notice is issued, after the date of issue of the latest notice.[17] A working day is any day from Monday to Friday (inclusive) which is not Christmas Day, Good Friday or any other day either specified or declared by proclamation under Banking and Financial Dealings Act 1971, s 1 or appointed by the Secretary of State, or certified by HMLR as being an 'interrupted day' due to delay or failure of a communication service or to some other event or circumstance causing substantial interruption in the normal operation of HMLR.[18] For the position where the registered proprietor objects to the entry of the restriction, see 54 Disputes.

153.2 Forms of restriction

LRR 2003, Sch 4 sets out the standard forms of restriction. Some of the standard forms contain variables and LRR 2003, r 91A allows certain amendments to be made to the standard forms. Other than that, the amendment of a standard form will result in a restriction being non-standard. Use of the standard forms of restriction is recommended if at all possible.

If no standard form is suitable, application may be made to enter a non-standard form of restriction. Because the definition of registered in LRR 2003, r 91(3) applies only to standard forms of restriction, an applicant for a non-standard restriction should refer to applications being completed by registration in the text of the restriction. Where an application is made for a non-standard restriction, HMLR may approve the application only if it appears to it that:

(a) the terms of the restriction are reasonable; and
(b) applying the restriction would:

 (i) be straightforward; and
 (ii) not place an unreasonable burden on HMLR.[19]

It is therefore prudent to check with HMLR that an application for such restriction will be approved before the parties agree the terms of a non-standard restriction. For example, it is unlikely HMLR will accept an application for a restriction that expressly prevents the entry of a notice.

The standard forms of restriction are set out in full in Appendix IV.

153.3 Court order for entry of restriction

If it appears to the court that it is necessary or desirable to do so for the purpose of protecting a right or claim in relation to a registered estate or charge, it may make an order requiring HMLR to enter a restriction in the register.[20] This may be a standard or non-standard restriction, but such an order may not be made for the purpose of protecting the priority of an interest which is, or could be, the subject of a notice.[21] Although the order may be addressed directly to HMLR, a formal application for the restriction to be entered should be made, as HMLR may not otherwise be aware of the order. It is not necessary to use form RX1 to apply for the entry of the restriction; instead, the court order and form AP1 should be delivered to HMLR, together with the fee payable.[22]

The court may include in such an order a direction that the entry of the restriction made in pursuance of the order is to have overriding priority.[23] Where this is done, HMLR makes an entry in the register to ensure that the priority of the restriction ordered by the court is apparent. Since such a direction of the court overrides an existing priority protection given by an official search with priority, HMLR must give notice of the entry to the person who applied for the official search (or the conveyancer or agent who applied on his behalf), unless HMLR is satisfied that such notice is unnecessary.[24]

153.4 Obligatory restrictions

In addition to the making of a court order made under LRA 2002, s 46(1), there are certain other circumstances where HMLR must enter a restriction without an application being made.

Where two or more persons are registered as proprietors of a registered estate in land, HMLR must enter a restriction in Form A unless the survivor will be able to give a valid receipt for capital money.[25] This is to ensure that interests which are capable of being overreached on a disposition of a registered estate or charge are overreached.

Certain statutes require HMLR to enter a restriction. LRR 2003, r 95(2) sets out details of some of these statutory provisions and the appropriate restrictions. These restrictions are dealt with in the appropriate sections of this book.

HMLR must enter a bankruptcy restriction under LRA 2002, s 86(4).[26]

153.5 Compliance with a restriction

An application must, where necessary, comply with the terms of a restriction before it can be completed.[27] Where the restriction requires a consent or certificate, this may be in form RXC (although its use is not mandatory). LRR 2003, r 91B contains provisions relating to a certificate or consent by a corporation required under the terms of a restriction.

153.6 Updating a restriction

Sometimes it is necessary to alter the wording of a restriction to allow it to continue to work as intended when circumstances change. Examples, may include where:

(a) the person named in the restriction's address has changed;
(b) the title number referred to in the restriction has changed;
(c) there was an error in the deed or application form applying for the restriction; and
(d) the restriction requires the consent or certificate of a specified person as office holder (for example liquidator or trustee in bankruptcy) and that person has changed.

An applicant seeking to modify a restriction should deliver to HMLR:

(a) an application in form AP1;
(b) a covering letter giving details of the alteration sought;
(c) where the update is based on a change of an office holder,[28] evidence of that change;
(d) where a personal representative applies to be registered in place of a deceased beneficiary, evidence that the interest protected by the restriction

was vested in the deceased and has devolved in accordance with his will or intestacy;[29]

(e) where the restriction is in favour of a specified person with no personal interest,[30] evidence to show:

  (i) that individual's only interest was by virtue of the office he formerly held; and
  (ii) that interest has transferred to the new holder of that office;

(f) where there has been a transfer of the interest protected by the restriction, evidence of such transfer;
(g) where there was a mistake in the restriction originally applied for, evidence to justify an alteration under LRR 2003, r 130.[31] When discussing why it is not practicable to deal with the matter by other means, the applicant must explain why it is not practicable to deal with the mistake by way of an application to cancel or withdraw the restriction accompanied by an application to enter a restriction in the preferred wording;[32] and
(h) the fee payable, if any.[33]

153.7 Application for an order that a restriction be disapplied or modified

An applicant who appears to HMLR to have a sufficient interest in a restriction may apply for HMLR to make an order disapplying or modifying the restriction.[34] For example, a restriction might:

(a) require the consent of a person who can no longer be traced. In which case, an application to disapply the restriction may be appropriate; or
(b) prohibit all dispositions when it was clearly not intended to prevent charges by the registered proprietor. In which case, an application to modify the restriction may be appropriate.

An applicant should deliver to HMLR an application form RX2 setting out:

(a) whether the application is to disapply or modify the restriction and, if the latter, the details of the modification sought;
(b) why the applicant has a sufficient interest in the restriction to make the application;
(c) details of the disposition or the kind of disposition that will be affected by the order; and
(d) why the applicant considers that HMLR should make the order.[35]

A fee is payable.[36]

HMLR may make such enquiries and serve such notices as it thinks fit and it may require the applicant to supply further evidence.[37] If an order is made it must, if appropriate, be noted in the register.[38]

If HMLR:

(a) disapplies a restriction, it will remain on the register following registration of the relevant disposition;
(b) modifies a restriction, it will remain on the register in its modified form.

153.7.1 Disapplication of a restriction, further evidence

HMLR will not usually exercise the statutory discretion to disapply a restriction unless satisfied the applicant has used its best endeavours to comply with it. In addition to the items listed in 153.7 Application for an order that a restriction be disapplied or modified, an applicant for disapplication should include:

(a) a certified copy of any document referred to in the restriction (unless HMLR already holds a copy of the document);
(b) evidence of the steps taken to comply with the restriction;[39] and
(c) evidence of the steps taken by the applicant to procure the consent or certificate required by the restriction.[40]

153.7.2 Modification of a restriction, further evidence

Modification of a restriction should not be confused with an update to a restriction.[41] The power to modify a restriction is much more limited. For example, HMLR cannot modify a restriction to make it apply to a wider class of disposition.

HMLR will not usually exercise the statutory discretion to modify a restriction unless satisfied the change cannot be achieved by other means. In particular, HMLR will want to be sure the applicant cannot achieve the same result by applying to withdraw or cancel the existing restriction and replace it with a new restriction in the required form.[42] Accordingly, an applicant for modification of a restriction should include evidence to show why this is the case.

153.8 Cancellation of a restriction

Any person may apply to cancel a restriction that is no longer required. The application must be made in form RX3[43] and no fee is currently payable. The application must be accompanied by evidence to satisfy HMLR that the restriction is no longer required.[44] If HMLR is satisfied with the evidence it must cancel the restriction.[45] Where the restriction gives an address for service for any person who is not the applicant for cancellation, HMLR will send notice of the application to that person.[46]

When registering a disposition of a registered estate, HMLR must cancel a restriction entered for the purpose of protecting an interest, right or claim arising under a trust of land if it is satisfied that such estate is no longer subject to that trust of land.[47] Thus HMLR will, for example, automatically cancel a restriction in Form A where the beneficial interests under the trust of land have clearly been overreached on a transfer on sale.

HMLR may cancel a restriction without an application being made where it is satisfied that the entry is superfluous.[48] For example, HMLR will cancel a restriction requiring the consent of the proprietor of a registered charge when the charge is discharged, or a restriction may reflect a limitation on the powers of a previous proprietor, which does not apply to the current proprietor.

153.9 Withdrawal of a restriction

A person with the benefit of a restriction may apply for it to be removed from the register without regard to the question of whether it still serves any purpose.[49] The application must be made in form RX4 and no fee is currently payable. The application must be accompanied by the required consent,[50] which is either:

(a) where the restriction requires the consent of a specified person, the consent of that person;
(b) where the restriction requires a certificate to be given by a specified person, the consent of that person;
(c) where the restriction requires notice to be given to a specified person, the consent of that person;
(d) where the restriction requires the consent of a specified person, or alternatively a certificate to be given by a specified person, the consent of all such persons; or
(e) in any other case, the consent of all persons who appear to HMLR to have an interest in the restriction.[51]

A certificate may be given by the applicant's conveyancer that he holds any consents required.[52] This certificate may be given in panel 10 of form RX4.

In general, a 'voluntary' restriction (i.e. one applied for voluntarily rather than entered in pursuance of an obligation under the LRA 2002) cannot be removed from the register as a matter of course when a disposition is registered, even where the terms of the restriction have been complied with and the disposition is a transfer on sale, for example. Therefore, if it is intended that the restriction should not remain in the register following the registration of the disposition, an express withdrawal should normally be obtained.

No application may be made to withdraw a restriction that:

(a) is entered to prevent invalidity or unlawfulness in relation to dispositions and reflects some limitation on the registered proprietor's powers of disposition imposed by statute or the general law;
(b) is entered by someone who was under an obligation to apply under LRR 2003, r 94;
(c) HMLR is obliged to enter;
(d) reflects a limitation under an order of the court or of HMLR, or an undertaking given in lieu of such an order; or
(e) the court has ordered HMLR to enter under LRA 2002, s 46.[53]

153.10 Restrictions entered under the Land Registration Act 1925

The LRA 2002 applies to restrictions entered in the register before 13 October 2003 in the same way that it applies to restrictions entered on or after that date under the LRA 2002.[54] The effect of a restriction under the LRA 1925 is preserved. For example, a restriction preventing the noting of a disposition is not treated as preventing the entry of a unilateral notice, since the restriction would not have prevented the entry of a caution against dealings.

153.11 Inhibitions entered under the Land Registration Act 1925

Although it has not been possible to enter a new inhibition in the register since 13 October 2003, an inhibition entered before that date will continue to have effect and will be treated as a restriction for the purposes of the LRA 2002.[55] Inhibitions prohibit, wholly or partially, the exercise of a proprietor's powers of disposition. Inhibitions, other than bankruptcy inhibitions,[56] are very uncommon. An application to cancel an inhibition must be made to the court if the inhibition was originally entered pursuant to an order of the court; otherwise it must be made to HMLR. No fee is currently payable for cancellation.

---

1 LRA 2002, s 41.
2 LRA 2002, s 42(1).
3 LRA 2002, s 42(3).

4 See 153.4 Obligatory restrictions.
5 See 153.3 Court order for entry of restriction.
6 LRA 2002, s 42(2).
7 Which can generally be the subject of a restriction for the purposes of LRA 2002, s 42(1)(a) or (b).
8 See 29.4 Restriction where the charging order is over a beneficial interest.
9 LRA 2002, s 77(1).
10 LRA 2002, s 77(2).
11 LRA 2002, s 43(1).
12 See 67 Fees.
13 See 153.2 Forms of restriction.
14 LRR 2003, r 92(7).
15 LRA 2002, s 45(1) and (3).
16 LRA 2002, s 45(2).
17 LRR 2003, r 92(9).
18 LRR 2003, r 217(1).
19 LRA 2002, s 43(3).
20 LRA 2002, s 46(1).
21 LRR 2003, r 46(2).
22 See 67 Fees.
23 LRA 2002, s 46(3).
24 LRR 2003, r 100.
25 LRA 2002, s 44(1) and LRR 2003, r 95(2)(a).
26 See 19 Bankruptcy.
27 LRA 2002, s 41(1).
28 For example, on the appointment of an insolvency practitioner as trustee in bankruptcy in place of the Official Receiver.
29 Such as a statutory declaration or statement of truth to this effect annexing supporting evidence.
30 For example, a named charity trustee.
31 See 43 Correction of Mistakes in an Application or Accompanying Document.
32 See 153.8 Cancellation of a restriction, 153.9 Withdrawal of a restriction and 153.1 Application for entry of restriction.
33 See 67 Fees.
34 LRA 2002, s 41(3).
35 LRR 2003, r 96(2).
36 See 67 Fees.
37 LRR 2003, r 96(3) and (4).
38 LRR 2003, r 96(5).
39 For example, if the restriction protected a covenant by the registered proprietor to ensure any disponee complete a deed of covenant in favour of a specified person, HMLR would want to see the deed of covenant. Alternatively, if the applicant was applying to disapply a restriction in advance of a disposition, any order disapplying the restriction would likely be made conditional on the applicant for registration providing such a deed.

40 Usually this would comprise copies of any correspondence between the applicant for disapplication and the beneficiary of the restriction.
41 See 153.6 Updating a restriction.
42 See 153.8 Cancellation of a restriction, 153.9 Withdrawal of a restriction and 153.1 Application for entry of restriction.
43 LRR 2003, r 97(1).
44 LRR 2003, r 97(2).
45 LRR 2003, r 97(3).
46 If that person objects to the cancellation, HMLR will proceed as set out in 54 Disputes.
47 LRR 2003, r 99.
48 LRA 2002, Sch 4, para 5(d).
49 LRA 2002, s 47.
50 LRR 2003, r 98(1).
51 LRR 2003, r 98(2).
52 LRR 2003, r 98(4).
53 LRR 2003, r 98(3).
54 LRA 2002, Sch 12, para 2(2).
55 LRA 2002, Sch 12, para 2(2).
56 See 19.3 Bankruptcy entries under the Land Registration Act 1925.

154 RESTRICTIVE COVENANTS

The LRA 2002 is a register of legal estates and interests and does not therefore provide for the entry of the benefit of equitable rights in the register. Consequently, HMLR cannot make any entry in the register of the benefit of a restrictive covenant, as such a benefit is an equitable not a legal right. Entitlement to the benefit of a restrictive covenant must therefore subsist 'off the register'. The burden of a restrictive covenant usually needs to be protected by way of a notice in the register. For restrictive covenants between a landlord and tenant, however, see 98.15 Restrictive covenants in leases. The fact that an interest is the subject of a notice does not necessarily mean that the interest is valid, but does mean that the priority of the interest, if valid, is protected.[1]

154.1 Restrictive covenants on first registration

When the deeds and documents lodged on first registration show that the estate is subject to restrictive covenants, HMLR will enter notice of the covenants in the register.[2] This does not apply to covenants between a landlord and tenant affecting the demised premises in the lease.[3] The entry in the charges register will refer to the deed containing the covenants and provide details of the covenants (including any covenanting clause) either by setting out the covenants verbatim in the register or by referring to a filed document containing them. Sometimes neither the original deed nor a certified copy nor examined abstract will accompany the application. The action taken by HMLR will then depend on the circumstances:

(a) If an unverified copy or abstract of the covenants accompanies the application and HMLR considers the risk of it being inaccurate to be so small that it can properly be treated as though it were verified (for example if the evidence consists of an apparently accurate typewritten copy or a photocopy), it will be so treated and an entry made in the register as above.

(b) If an unverified copy or abstract of the covenants accompanies the application but cannot properly be treated as though it were verified and if a solicitor so requests, HMLR will make an entry (in accordance with an agreement made between The Law Society and HMLR) in the charges register along the following lines:

> A [*specify deed type*] of the land in this title [and other land] dated [*date*] made between [*parties*] contains restrictive covenants but no verified particulars of them were produced on first registration. The details set out [in the schedule of restrictive covenants hereto] of what purport to be the said covenants were provided by [*solicitor*] acting for a vendor in [*specify details*].

As this entry is qualified, no indemnity will be payable by HMLR if the details referred to are not complete or correct.

(c) If an unverified copy or abstract of the covenants accompanies the application, but cannot be treated as verified and is not the subject of a request by a solicitor as in (b) above, an entry will be made in the register referring to the deed containing the covenants and stating that it contains restrictive covenants but that:

> … neither the original deed nor a certified copy nor an examined abstract thereof was produced on first registration.

Such an entry will also be made when no particulars, verified or unverified, of the covenants or stipulations accompany the application.

Particulars of the words of covenant should be provided whenever possible, but when only particulars of restrictive stipulations without the words of covenant accompany an application, a modified form of entry indicating that the words of covenant were not available, will be used. The fact that a notice in the register does not necessarily mean that a restrictive covenant is valid means that the entry on first registration of a restrictive covenant which was void for non-registration as a land charge does not confer any fresh validity on such a covenant.[4]

154.2 Restrictive covenants and registered land

If a transfer of the whole or part, or other registrable disposition, of a registered estate under LRA 2002, s 27(2) imposes restrictive covenants, HMLR will automatically enter a notice of these covenants in the register of the burdened title upon registration of the transfer or other disposition.[5] However, if the transfer or other disposition imposes restrictive covenants on any other title, the relevant title number(s) must be given in panel 2 of the form AP1, otherwise HMLR is not obliged to make any entry in that title and a specific application for entry of a notice of the covenants on that title will be necessary.[6]

If restrictive covenants are imposed upon a registered estate other than in a transfer or other registrable disposition, for example by a deed of covenant, an application must be made for entry of a notice in the register of title to the burdened estate. It is important to identify the burdened estate clearly (by plan if necessary) and also to identify the estate intended to be benefited by the covenants. The application may be for entry of an agreed notice or a unilateral notice.

154.2.1 Agreed notice

In addition to the usual documents required,[7] an applicant should deliver to HMLR the deed of covenant or a certified copy of it.

Where the consent of the registered proprietor is not available but, for example, the deed of covenant is signed by him, this is likely to be sufficient to satisfy HMLR of the validity of the applicant's claim for the purposes of LRA 2002, s 34(3)(c).

The agreed notice in the register will give details of the interest protected.

154.2.2 Unilateral notice

An applicant should deliver to HMLR the usual documents required.[8]

The statement in panel 11 or conveyancer's certificate in panel 12 of form UN1 should be completed on the following lines to show the interest of the applicant:

> person having the benefit of restrictive covenants contained in a Deed dated [*date*] made between [*parties*] [as varied by a deed dated [*date*] made between [*parties*]].

The unilateral notice in the register will give brief details of the interest protected and identify the beneficiary of that notice.

154.3 Release, waiver or modification of restrictive covenants

An application for entry of a notice in respect of a deed of release or variation should be made in form AN1 for an agreed notice or form UN1 for a unilateral notice, if made by the person claiming the benefit of the covenants;[9] or in form AP1 if made by the registered proprietor of the burdened title. In the case of an agreed notice of a variation of an interest protected by a notice, the entry in the register must give details of the variation.[10]

An application for cancellation of an existing notice (other than a unilateral notice) in respect of restrictive covenants based upon a deed of release should be made in form CN1.[11] In practice it is often difficult, if not impossible, to prove that a deed purporting to release, waive, discharge or modify restrictive covenants is fully effective, because of the difficulty in identifying the extent of the estate having the benefit of the covenants and ensuring that all parties having an interest in the covenants have joined into the deed. It is therefore the practice of HMLR in most cases (unless the position is beyond doubt) to retain the original notice of the covenants in the register and enter a notice of such a deed in the register stating that it is 'expressed' to release or vary the covenants.[12]

Where it is claimed that restrictive covenants protected in the register by a notice (other than a unilateral notice) are void for non-registration as a land charge following first registration, application may be made in form CN1 to cancel the notice, accompanied by evidence to satisfy HMLR that the covenants are void.[13] It should be noted that:

(a) registration as a land charge is not necessary for matters contained in a deed dated after 27 July 1971 which attracts compulsory registration;[14]
(b) under HMLR 'D31 procedure' (abolished in March 1976), land charge registrations were cancelled on completion of first registration of title. The fact the land charge no longer appears may not therefore be conclusive that it was not registered at the relevant time;
(c) land charges in favour of local authorities are not void for want of registration as a land charge, if registered as local land charges before 1 August 1977;[15] and
(d) in relation to a disposition which is *not* to a purchaser, such as a deed of gift to a donee or an assent to a beneficiary, the disponee (not being a purchaser) will be bound by the covenant even if it has not been not registered as a land charge.

If the existing notice in respect of restrictive covenants is a unilateral notice, application may be made in form UN2 for removal or in form UN4 for cancellation of the notice.[16]

When the Upper Tribunal (Lands Chamber) – formerly the Lands Tribunal – has made an order under LPA 1925, s 84 for modification or discharge of restrictive covenants, application may be made for this to be reflected in the register. The action taken by HMLR will depend upon the terms of the order.

The Equalities Act 2010, s 142(1) provides that a contractual term is unenforceable if it constitutes, promotes or provides for treatment of a person which is of a description prohibited by that Act. In 2017, HMLR undertook an exercise to remove any obviously discriminatory covenants from the register. However, some discriminatory covenants will remain on the register. If HMLR comes across a discriminatory covenant, it will remove it from the register and inform the proprietor of the affected title. If HMLR has not spotted such a covenant, a person may write to HMLR to draw its attention to the covenant and request its removal.

154.4 Positive covenants imposed by statute

Although normally the burden of a positive covenant does not run with the land, certain statutes make provision for a positive covenant entered into pursuant to that statute enforceable as though it was a restrictive covenant. Such statutes include:

(a) Local Government (Miscellaneous Provisions) Act 1982, s 33;
(b) Mission and Pastoral Measure 2011 (2011/3), s 75;
(c) HA 1985, s 609;
(d) National Trust Act 1937, s 8;
(e) Wildlife and Countryside Act 1981, s 39; and
(f) Water Industry Act 1991, s 156.

HMLR will treat such covenants in the same way as restrictive covenants, but will omit the word 'restrictive' from the register entry.

---

1 LRA 2002, s 32(3).
2 LRR 2003, r 35(1).
3 LRA 2002, s 33(c).
4 LRA 2002, s 32(3).
5 LRR 2003, rr 72(4) and 72C(2).
6 LRR 2003, rr 72(5) and 72C(3)
7 See 119.1 Agreed notice.
8 See 119.3 Unilateral notice.
9 See 119.1 Agreed notice and 119.3 Unilateral notice.
10 LRR 2003, r 84(4).
11 See 119.2 Cancellation of a notice other than a unilateral notice or a home rights notice.

12 LRR 2003, r 87(4).
13 LRR 2003, r 87(1).
14 Land Charges Act 1972, s 14(3).
15 Land Charges Act 1972, s 1(3A).
16 See 119.5 Removal of a unilateral notice and 119.6 Cancellation of a unilateral notice.

155 RETENTION, DESTRUCTION AND RETURN OF DOCUMENTS

HMLR may destroy any document which it retains if it is satisfied that it has made and retained a sufficient copy of the document or further retention of the document is unnecessary.[1] HMLR may release any document retained by it upon such terms, if any, for its return as it considers appropriate.[2]

See also 16 Applications to HM Land Registry and 68 First Registration.

1 LRR 2003, r 203(2).
2 LRR 2003, r 205.

156 RIGHT TO BUY AND RIGHT TO ACQUIRE UNDER THE HOUSING ACTS

In England, many tenants of local authorities and certain other public sector landlords have the right to buy their houses or flats under the HA 1985. This right to buy was originally introduced by the Housing Act 1980 and is now dealt with in HA 1985, Pt V. Many other tenants of registered social landlords have the right to acquire their houses or flats under the HA 1996. The right to acquire operates in the same way as the right to buy, but only applies to qualifying tenants of registered social landlords who live in houses or flats provided with public money and which have remained in the social rented sector.

In the case of a freehold house, the freehold is transferred to the tenant when he exercises his right to buy and, in the case of a flat or leasehold house, a lease is granted to him,[1] usually for 125 years (depending upon the nature of the landlord's reversionary title).[2] The tenant is given a discount on the purchase price.

In Wales, subject to certain limited exceptions,[3] the right to buy was abolished with effect from 26 January 2019.[4]

156.1 Charges on landlord's title

Where the right to buy is exercised, no discharge or release is required in respect of any registered or noted charge, nor is the consent of any chargee under a restriction required.[5]

In the case of the exercise of the right to acquire from a registered social landlord, the tenant receives either:

(a) evidence of the release from the charge provided by the chargee; or
(b) a certificate from the landlord given under HA 1985, Sch 6, para 23(1) or (3).[6] Such a certificate is effective to release the house or flat from the charge.

156.2 Rentcharges

A transfer under the right to buy or right to acquire is made subject to any existing rentcharge. Where the property being transferred is, with other land, subject to the rentcharge, the transfer must contain a covenant by the landlord to indemnify the tenant and his successors in title in respect of any liability arising under the rentcharge.[7] A lease granted under the right to buy or right to acquire is not affected by any rentcharge on the landlord's interest.[8]

156.3 Statutory easements

Unless excluded or modified, a transfer or lease under the right to buy or right to acquire is deemed to include a grant and reservation of the easements contained in HA 1985, Sch 6, para 2 so far as the seller has power to grant such rights. These include rights of support, rights of light and air, and rights of drainage and other domestic services. HMLR will automatically make an entry in respect of these statutory easements in the register when registering the transfer. A transfer or lease may also include non-statutory easements, as well as restrictive and other covenants.

156.4 Discount charges

Where a tenant exercises the right to buy or right to acquire, he is entitled to a discount on the purchase price.[9] The tenant covenants in the transfer to repay the discount if there is a disposal within 5 years.[10] Certain disposals do not result in the repayment of discount.[11] The covenant takes effect as a charge[12] and HMLR will make an entry automatically on registration of the transfer.

156.5 Right of first refusal

Under the HA 1985, s 156A (as inserted by HA 2004, s 188) and the Housing (Right of First Refusal) (England) Regulations 2005 (SI 2005/1917), right to buy disposals by local authorities and right to acquire disposals by registered social landlords of land in England dated on or after 10 August 2005 may contain a covenant not to dispose of the land unless certain prescribed conditions, relating to a right of first refusal in favour of the landlord, are satisfied. The Housing (Right of First Refusal) (Wales) Regulations 2005 (SI 2005/2680) allowed such disposals of land in Wales dated on or after 28 September 2005 to contain a similar covenant. The covenant applies to disposals made within a period of 10 years beginning with the date of the conveyance or grant by the landlord. Certain disposals are exempted or do not constitute relevant disposals for this purpose.

HMLR must enter a restriction in the register reflecting the limitation imposed by any such covenant.[13] The restriction will be to the effect that no disposition within the relevant period is to be registered unless accompanied by a certificate from the relevant authority that the transfer or lease complies with the requirements of HA 1985, s 156A or is an exempt disposal or is otherwise not a relevant disposal.

156.6 Property to which Housing Act 1985, s 37 or s 157 applies

Where the sale to the tenant is of a house in a National Park, a national landscape or an area designated as a rural area, the transfer or conveyance may contain a covenant limiting the freedom of the purchaser to dispose of the property. In such case where the sale is under the right to buy, HMLR will automatically enter a restriction in Form V in the proprietorship register.[14] The wording of Form V is set out in Appendix IV.

Where the sale is a voluntary sale to which HA 1985, s 37 applies, HMLR will automatically enter a restriction in Form U in the proprietorship register.[15] The wording of Form U is set out in Appendix IV.

156.7 Preserved right to buy

Where public sector landlords dispose of their housing stock to social or private sector landlords, the tenant's right to buy may be preserved, even though the new landlord is not one which would otherwise be subject to the right to buy. Where this occurs, the transfer to the new landlord must contain:

(a) a statement that the transfer is, so far as it relates to dwelling houses occupied by secure tenants, a transfer to which HA 1985, s 171A applies; and
(b) a list of the dwelling houses transferred which are occupied by secure tenants.[16]

Such a statement may be along the following lines:

> Section 171A of the Housing Act 1985 applies to this deed so far as it relates to dwelling houses occupied by secure tenants. The [purchaser] *or* [lessee] applies for entry of the notice and restriction required by paragraph 4 of Schedule 9A to that Act.

A transfer of unregistered land, or a lease out of unregistered land, to which HA 1985, s 171A applies is subject to compulsory registration.[17]

On registration of a transfer containing a statement that HA 1985, s 171A applies, HMLR automatically enters:

(a) a notice of the rights of the qualifying tenants, and
(b) a restriction in Form W,

in the register.[18] The wording of Form W is set out in Appendix IV.

The rights of the tenant having the preserved right to buy are not interests within LRA 2002, Sch 3 which override registered dispositions and so the priority of such rights is liable to be postponed under LRA 2002, s 29 in favour of a registered disposition for valuable consideration unless protected by a notice in the register. Where the tenants are moved to another registered property, the landlord should apply for the notice and restriction to be entered in respect of that registered title, if there is no entry in that title.

Where the registered proprietor supplies a certificate that the registered title, or a specified part of it, is not subject to any rights of a qualifying person under the preserved right to buy, application may be made for the notice and restriction to be cancelled or modified,[19] as appropriate.

In certain circumstances, a transfer by a local authority or a housing action trust requires the consent of the Secretary of State or the Welsh Ministers. A transferee of housing stock following such consent may itself be subject to a requirement for similar consent on a subsequent transfer. A statement to this effect should be made in the transfer and a restriction in Form X is entered automatically in the proprietorship register. The wording of Form X is set out in Appendix IV

Exempt disposals as defined by the HA 1988, s 81(8) are:

(a) the disposal of a dwelling house to a person having the right to buy it under HA 1985, Pt V (whether the disposal is, in fact, made under that Part or otherwise);
(b) the disposal of a dwelling house to a person having the right to buy it under Housing and Regeneration Act 2008, s 180;
(c) a compulsory disposal within the meaning of HA 1985, Pt V;
(d) the disposal of an easement or rentcharge;
(e) the disposal of an interest by way of security for a loan;
(f) the grant of a secure tenancy or what would be a secure tenancy but for any of HA 1985, Sch 1, paras 2 to 12;
(g) the grant of an assured tenancy or an assured agricultural occupancy, within the meaning of HA 1988, Pt I, or what would be such a tenancy or occupancy but for any of Sch 1, paras 4 to 8 to that Act; and
(h) the transfer of an interest held on trust for any person where the disposal is made in connection with the appointment of a new trustee or in connection with the discharge of any trustee.

---

1 HA 1985, s 118(1).
2 HA 1985, s 139(1).
3 See Abolition of the Right to Buy and Associated Rights (Wales) Act 2018 (Consequential Amendments and Savings Provisions) Regulations (SI 2019/110), reg 5.
4 Abolition of the Right to Buy and Associated Rights (Wales) Act 2018, s 6.
5 HA 1985, Sch 6, paras 20 and 21.
6 Inserted by Housing (Right to Acquire) Regulations 1997, Sch 1, para 41(g).
7 HA 1985, Sch 6, para 21(3).
8 HA 1985, Sch 6, para 20.
9 HA 1985, ss 129 and 130.
10 HA 1985, s 155.
11 HA 1985, s 160.
12 HA 1985, s 156.
13 HA 1985, s 156A(12).
14 LRA 2002, s 44(2) and LRR 2003, r 95(2)(c).
15 LRA 2002, s 44(2) and LRR 2003, r 95(2)(b).
16 HA 1985, s 171G and Sch 9A, para 1.
17 LRA 2002, s 4(1)(b) and (f). See 68.2 Compulsory first registration.
18 HA 1985, s 171G and Sch 9A, para 4, LRA 2002, s 44(2) and LRR 2003, r 95(2)(f).
19 See 119 Notices.

157 RIGHT TO MANAGE COMPANIES

Commonhold and Leasehold Reform Act 2002, Pt 2 provides for the management functions of the landlord (and certain third parties) to be exercisable by a right to manage (RTM) company in place of the landlord. An RTM company is a special company limited by guarantee, the membership of which is restricted to qualifying tenants (generally a tenant under a long lease) and landlords (once the company has obtained the RTM).

157.1 Recording the right to manage on the register

The RTM is not an adverse right affecting the landlord's title. Consequently, HMLR will reject any application for an agreed or unilateral notice or caution against first registration relating to the RTM. However, LRR 2003, r 79A does allow for application to be made in form AP1 for an entry to be made in the proprietorship register of the landlord's title to record the acquisition of the RTM by an RTM company. Such an application must be accompanied by evidence to satisfy HMLR that:

(a) the applicant is an RTM company;
(b) the RTM is in relation to the premises comprised in the registered estate;
(c) the registered proprietor of the registered estate is the landlord under a lease of the whole or part of the registered estate; and
(d) the RTM the premises has been acquired, and remains exercisable, by the RTM company.

Such evidence may be provided by way of a conveyancer's certificate. If HMLR is so satisfied, it must make the appropriate entry in the proprietorship register. Such an entry may be along the following lines:

> [*Name and company registration number of RTM company*] of [*address*] has lodged evidence under rule 79A of the Land Registration Rules 2003 (SI 2003/1417) that it is a RTM company and has acquired the right to manage the land in this title pursuant to Chapter 1 of Part 2 of the Commonhold and Leasehold Reform Act 2002.

The entry does not guarantee that the RTM has been acquired or that, if acquired, it remains exercisable, but it does highlight to those proposing to deal with the landlord's title that there is an RTM company which claims to have acquired the RTM in respect of the premises concerned. A fee is payable.[1]

157.2 Consents and certificates given by a right to manage company

The management functions taken over by the RTM company may include the giving of consents or certificates required to comply with restrictions in the register. Consequently, provided:

(a) the restriction protects the landlord (or relevant party's) management function under the lease, and
(b) the RTM company complies with the relevant statutory formalities,[2]

the RTM company may be able to provide the necessary consent or certificate instead of the landlord (or other relevant party).

Where a person seeks to rely on a consent or certificate given by an RTM company instead of the landlord or other named beneficiary of a restriction, in addition, they must provide either:

(a) where there is an entry in the register of the type referred to in 157.1 Recording the RTM on the register, a certificate from the RTM company or its conveyancer confirming that:

    (i) the RTM company gave the notice required by Commonhold and Leasehold Reform Act 2002, s 98 in respect of the consent or certificate required under the terms of the restriction; and
    (ii) the requisite notice period has expired without any objection being made; or

(b) where there is no such entry in the register, a certificate from the RTM company or its conveyancer confirming:

    (i) the person named in the restriction is the landlord or other specified party (for example management company) under the relevant lease;
    (ii) the restriction protects the landlord or other party's management functions under the relevant lease;
    (iii) the company giving the consent:

        (1) is a RTM company; and
        (2) has acquired the RTM in respect of the landlord or other party's management functions under the relevant lease;

    (iv) the RTM company gave the notice required by Commonhold and Leasehold Reform Act 2002, s 98 in respect of the consent or certificate required under the terms of the restriction; and
    (v) the requisite notice period has expired without any objection being made.

HMLR may serve a notice on the beneficiary of the restriction before proceeding with the registration. If they dispute that the RTM Company has power to give the required consent or certificate or that it has complied with the relevant formalities before doing so, HMLR will proceed as set out in 54 Disputes. HMLR will not usually serve notice if the applicant includes the written consent of the person named in the restriction which confirms that the RTM company may give consents or certificates to the disposition concerned as required by the terms of the restriction because the landlord management functions vest in the RTM.

---

1 See 67 Fees.

2 Set out in Commonhold and Leasehold Reform Act 2002, s 98.

158 RIGHTS OF LIGHT AND AIR

The right to receive natural light through a defined aperture (such as a window or skylight) can be a form of easement.[1] However, there are special rules associated with such rights.

HMLR must often record:

(a) easements to receive light and air;
(b) restrictive covenants relating to light and air;[2] and/or
(c) provisions in deeds relating to light and air.

HMLR must also add, amend or remove entries where parties agree to vary or release the rights.[3]

158.1 Registration of rights of light and air

Where a deed expressly or impliedly grants or reserves rights of light and air, HMLR will treat the grant or reservation as it would the grant or reservation of any other easement.[4]

A right to light and air may also arise through long use:

(a) by common law prescription;
(b) under the doctrine of lost modern grant; or
(c) under the Prescription Act 1832.

Subject to the comments in 158.1.1 Light obstruction notices, common law prescription and the doctrine of lost modern grant operate for rights to light and air as they do for other easements.[5] However, most applicants applying to register prescriptive claims to light and air rely on the Prescription Act 1832

Prescription Act 1832, s 3 contains special provisions which apply to rights to light. These disapply some of the restrictions which otherwise apply to the acquisition of prescriptive easements under the Act. In particular:

(a) there is no requirement that use be as of right.[6] Provided an applicant can show 20 years' continuous use before their application, a right may arise under the Prescription Act 1832;
(b) any consent must be in writing to prevent a right to light accruing. An oral permission does not prevent a right from arising under the Prescription Act 1832;[7]
(c) it is not necessary that the enjoyment is by or against a freehold owner. Accordingly:

    (i) a tenant can acquire an easement over other land owned by his landlord; and
    (ii) it does not matter whether the burdened land was subject to a tenancy during the relevant 20-year period; and

(d) there is no need for a capable grantor to grant the right.

However, no right to light will arise under the Prescription Act 1832 where the benefiting and burdened land were in the possession of the same person for all or part of the relevant 20-year period.[8]

It is not possible to acquire rights to light under the Prescription Act 1832 over Crown land.[9]

158.1.1 Light obstruction notices

It is possible effectively to stop the period of prescription from running by obtaining a certificate from the Upper Tribunal and registering a light obstruction notice as a local land charge, pursuant to the Rights of Light Act 1959. Such a notice, once registered, acts as a notional obstruction to the access of light to the dominant building across the servient land and prevents time from running for the purposes of a prescriptive easement claim:

(a) until the registration is cancelled;
(b) for the period of one year beginning with the date of registration; or
(c) until the expiry date (in the case of a temporary certificate issued under Rights of Light Act 1959, s 2(3)(b)).

Accordingly, in addition to the usual documents required,[10] an applicant for:

(a) registration of a prescriptive right to light and air, or
(b) entry of an agreed notice of such a right where the proprietor of the burdened land does not consent to its entry,

should deliver to HMLR a local land charges search showing either:

(a) that no light obstruction notice affects the property, or
(b) where such a notice does affect the property:

    (i) the notice took effect after the prescriptive right arose (in the case of a claim under the doctrine of lost modern grant); or
    (ii) in the case of a claim under the Prescription Act 1832, that the notice was registered less than one year before the date of the application and more than 19 years and one day after the use started.

158.2 Provisions relating to rights of light and air

Often deeds contain provisions designed to prevent a property from acquiring future rights to light or air, for example, a statement that the access of light or air to the property has a transferor's permission. HMLR may make a note of this in the property register for the land affected.[11]

158.2.1 Provisions in leases

HMLR does not make any entry in the register of provisions contained in leases. This is because the lease is incorporated in and becomes part of the register.[12]

Where the landlord's title is subject to an entry in respect of such a provision, HMLR may replicate that entry in the register for the new lease.

158.2.2 Provisions on first registration

Where HMLR sees that a freehold property is subject to a provision relating to light or air on first registration, it usually either:

(a) sets out the provision in the register; or
(b) adds an entry to the register stating that the deed contains provisions and file a copy of the deed.

However, where the provision is intermixed with other restrictive covenants or rights granted or reserved which it is setting out in the register, HMLR will include the provision with them and not make any separate entry in the property register.

158.2.3 Provisions in dispositions and other dealings with registered land

Where there is a provision relating to rights to light and air in a deed (other than a lease) which is being registered, such as a transfer, the applicant does not need to make a separate application to enter the provision in the registers of the land affected provided all affected title numbers are included in the application.

Where the deed containing the provision is not being registered, an applicant can apply to enter the provision using form AP1 accompanied by:

(a) the original or a certified copy of the relevant deed; and
(b) the relevant fee.[13]

If the application is in order, HMLR will usually either:

(a) set out the provision in the register; or
(b) add an entry to the register stating that the deed contains restrictive covenants and file a copy of the deed.

However, where the provision is embedded with other restrictive covenants or rights granted or reserved which HMLR is setting out in the register, HMLR will include the provision with them and not make any separate entry in the property register.

158.2.4 The title benefiting from the provision

LRR 1925, r 197 previously allowed HMLR to make an entry on the register for the title which benefited from the provision. There is no equivalent in the LRR 2003. Accordingly, HMLR no longer makes such an entry.

Where HMLR encounters an entry made under the LRR 1925, it will not remove it. However, HMLR will not carry such an entry forward to any new title granted out of the benefiting title (for example on any transfer of part or lease).

158.3 Further information

HMLR's *Practice guide 62A: rights to light or air* contains full details of HMLR's policy and practice on rights to light and air. This is available to view and download at the HMLR website.[14]

1 See 62 Equitable Easements and 101 Legal Easements.
2 See 157 Restrictive Covenants.
3 See 101.5 Extinguishment of easements.
4 See 62 Equitable Easements and 101 Legal Easements.
5 See 101.3 Prescriptive easements.
6 *Collis v Home and Colonial Stores* [1904] AC 179.
7 *Plasterers Co v Parish Clerks Co* (1851) 6 Exch 630.
8 *Harbidge v Warwick* (1849) 3 Exch 552.
9 *Perry v Eames* [1891] 1 Ch 658.
10 See 101.3 Prescriptive easements and 119.1 Agreed notice.
11 LRR 2003, rr 36 and 76.
12 *R (HCP (Hendon) Ltd) v Chief Land Registrar* [2020] EWHC 1278 (Admin).
13 See 67 Fees.
14 www.gov.uk/government/collections/land-registration-practice-guides.

159 RIGHTS OF PRE-EMPTION

The grant of a right of pre-emption imposes an obligation upon the grantor as owner of the land not to sell it without first giving the grantee the right to purchase it. Following the decision in *Pritchard v Briggs*,[1] the status of a right of pre-emption as an interest in land has remained doubtful. However, in the case of rights of pre-emption created on or after 13 October 2003, a right of pre-emption in relation to registered land has effect from the time of creation as an interest capable of binding successors in title, subject to the rules about the effect of dispositions on priority.[2]

A right of pre-emption in respect of registered land may be protected by the entry in the register of an agreed notice or a unilateral notice, and possibly by a restriction.[3] A notice does not necessarily mean that the right of pre-emption is valid but does protect the priority of that right on any registered disposition.[4] A restriction does not confer any priority. However, it prevents an entry being made in the register relating to any disposition, or a disposition of a specified kind, unless the terms of the restriction have (where applicable) been complied with.

A right of pre-emption is not itself an interest which overrides either first registration or registered dispositions. A beneficiary should protect its priority by entry of a notice in the register.

However, even where a right of pre-emption relating to registered land is not protected by a notice, it may still override a later registered disposition for valuable consideration if, at the time of that later disposition, the person having the benefit of the right of pre-emption is in actual occupation of the land to which the right relates. If he is in actual occupation of only part of the land to which the right of pre-emption relates, he has an overriding interest only in respect of the part he is occupying.[5]

The interest of the person in actual possession does not override a registered disposition if enquiry was made of him before the disposition and he failed to disclose the right of pre-emption when he could reasonably have been expected to do so. Nor does the right of pre-emption override a registered disposition if it belongs to a person whose occupation would not have been obvious on a reasonably careful inspection of the land at the time of the disposition, and if the person to whom the disposition is made does not have actual knowledge of the right of pre-emption at the time of the disposition.[6]

Where the right of pre-emption is contained in a lease that is an unregistered interest falling within LRA 2002, Sch 3, para 1 which overrides registered dispositions, the right of pre-emption may be protected by an entry in the register even where no entry may be made of the lease itself (i.e. because the lease is for a term not exceeding 3 years and is not otherwise registrable).

The right of pre-emption should be granted and signed by the proprietor of the registered estate, or a satisfactory chain of title between the person granting the right of pre-emption and the registered proprietor shown. For example, if the registered proprietor has contracted to sell a registered title to A, and A then grants to B a right of pre-emption in respect of the land in the title, B's right of pre-emption can be protected by a notice, whether or not A's contract is also protected by a notice.

A right of pre-emption granted before 6 April 2010 may become void for remoteness if it breaches the rule against perpetuities.[7] A right of pre-emption granted after that date is no longer subject to the rule against perpetuities.[8]

159.1 Agreed notice

In addition to the usual documents required,[9] an applicant should deliver to HMLR the original document granting the right of pre-emption or a certified copy of it.

Where the right of pre-emption is granted by a person with the benefit of a contract for sale, the applicant should include the contract or a certified copy of it with the application. This is not necessary if there is already an agreed notice of the contract in the register.

Where the consent of the registered proprietor is not available but, for example, the document granting the right of pre-emption is signed by him, this is likely to be sufficient to satisfy HMLR of the validity of the applicant's claim for the purposes of LRA 2002, s 34(3)(c).

The agreed notice in the register will give details of the interest protected.

The applicant may prefer to apply for entry of a unilateral notice where he does not wish the terms of the pre-emption to be open to public inspection and copying.

159.2 Unilateral notice

An applicant should deliver to HMLR the usual documents required.[10]

The statement in panel 11 or conveyancer's certificate in panel 12 of form UN1 should be completed on the following lines to show the interest of the applicant:

> person having the benefit of a right of pre-emption contained in a [*description of document*] dated [*date*] made between [*names*].

Where the right of pre-emption is granted by a person with the benefit of a contract for sale, the applicant should also refer to that contract. The wording must establish the link between the registered proprietor and the person who is to be shown as the beneficiary of the notice.

The unilateral notice in the register will give brief details of the interest protected and identify the beneficiary of that notice.

159.3 Restriction

HMLR may not enter any restriction for the purpose of protecting the priority of an interest which is, or could be, the subject of a notice.[11] However, this does not prevent a restriction being entered in addition to the notice of the right of pre-emption. Although the notice will protect the priority of the right of pre-emption, a restriction may be used to ensure that any conditions in relation to another disposition by the registered proprietor are complied with. The consent of the registered proprietor to the entry of the restriction is required, unless the document granting the right of pre-emption contains a provision which limits the registered proprietor's powers to enter into any further disposition.

In addition to the usual documents required,[12] an applicant should deliver to HMLR (if the application is made by a person who claims that he has a sufficient interest in the making of the entry) a certified copy of the document granting the right of pre-emption. The statement in panel 12 or conveyancer's certificate in panel 13 of form RX1 must be completed, setting out details of the right of pre-emption and of any provision in the document granting the right of pre-emption which limits the registered proprietor's powers to enter into a disposition.

Panel 9 of form RX1 should set out the required restriction(s). A restriction in a standard form contained in LRR 2003, Sch 4 does not require the approval of HMLR to the terms of the restriction under LRA 2002, s 43(3). A possible form of restriction based on Form L is:

> No disposition of the registered estate by the proprietor of the registered estate is to be registered without a written certificate signed by [*purchaser*] of [*address*] or their conveyancer that the provisions of [*clause, paragraph or other particulars*] of [*details of document granting the right of pre-emption*] have been complied with or that they do not apply to the disposition.

The wording of Form L is set out in Appendix IV.

Form RX1 does not need to be used if the application is for a standard form restriction and is contained in either the 'additional provisions' panel of a prescribed form of transfer or assent, or in clause LR13 of a prescribed clauses lease (or any other lease containing clauses LR1 to LR14 of LRR 2003, Sch 1A).[13]

HMLR must give notice of the application for a restriction to the proprietor of the registered estate or charge concerned, if it has not been made by or with the consent of such proprietor or a person entitled to be registered as such proprietor.[14]

159.4 Rights of pre-emption contained in registrable dispositions

Although a right of pre-emption may be granted by way of a separate transaction, it can also form part of the terms of a registrable disposition such as a transfer or a lease. In the case of a transfer of part of a registered title, HMLR must (where appropriate) make entries in the relevant registered title in respect of any rights, provisions or other matters created by the transfer which are capable of being so entered.[15] However, HMLR need make no such entries where the relevant title numbers have not been given in panel 2 of the form AP1, unless separate application is made in respect of them.[16] Similar provisions apply in the case of a transfer of the whole of a registered title, or other registrable disposition.[17]

In the case of a lease granted out of a registered estate in land which is required to be registered under LRA 2002, s 27(2)(b), LRR 2003, r 72A specifies certain entries which HMLR must make on registration of the lease. This applies to both prescribed clauses leases and other leases. On completion of such a lease by registration, HMLR must (where appropriate) make entries in the relevant registered title in respect of interests contained in the lease which are of the nature referred to in clause LR9 (rights of acquisition, etc).[18] However, where the lease is a prescribed clauses lease and the rights are not specified or referred to in clause LR9, HMLR need take no action in respect of them unless a separate application is made.[19] Equally, HMLR need not make any entries where, in the case of a prescribed clauses lease, the title numbers of the relevant registered titles have not been given in clause LR2.2; or in any other case, the title numbers of the relevant registered titles required by clause LR2.2 have not been given in panel 2 of the form AP1 lodged for the purpose of completing the lease by registration, unless a separate application is made.[20]

---

1 [1980] Ch 338.
2 LRA 2002, s 115. For the rules about the effect of dispositions on priority, see 138 Priorities.
3 Depending on the terms of the agreement and whether it expressly or impliedly limits the registered proprietor's powers of disposition.
4 LRA 2002, ss 29, 30 and 32.
5 LRA 2002, ss 29 and 30 and Sch 3, para 2.
6 LRA 2002, Sch 3, para 2.
7 Perpetuities and Accumulations Act 1964, ss 9 and 10.
8 Perpetuities and Accumulations Act 2009, s 1.
9 See 119.1 Agreed notice.
10 See 119.3 Unilateral notice.
11 LRA 2002, s 42(2).
12 See 153.1 Application for entry of restriction.
13 LRR 2003, r 92(7).
14 LRA 2002, s 45.
15 LRR 2003, r 72(4).
16 LRR 2003, r 72(5).
17 LRR 2003, r 72C(2) and (3).
18 LRR 2003, r 72A(2).
19 LRR 2003, r 72A(3).
20 LRR 2003, r 72A(4).

160 RIGHTS OF REVERTER

In the 19th century, various statutes made provision to facilitate the donation of land for certain purposes, for example as a site for the erection of a school or a place of worship. To overcome difficulties which could arise from alienation of such land by way of gift, in particular in relation to land which was settled land, these statutes included provision for a right of reverter in favour of the grantor. The effect of such a right was that, if the land ceased to be used for the purpose for which it had been granted, title to it would revert to the grantor or his successors. A grant subject to such a right of reverter took effect as a determinable fee simple, but this did not prevent it from being a legal estate. The statutes in question (the relevant enactments) were the School Sites Acts of 1841, 1844, 1849, 1851 and 1852; the Literary and Scientific Institutions Act 1854; and the Places of Worship Sites Act 1873.

The Reverter of Sites Act 1987 came into force on 17 August 1987. It was intended to overcome some of the problems which could arise where an event triggering determination of the determinable fee simple and reverter of title (a reversion event) occurred. Section 1 provides that where any relevant enactment provides for reverter, that enactment shall have effect (and be deemed always to have had effect) so that instead of reverting automatically to the grantor, the land is to be held on trust after the reversion event.[1] The trustees are the persons who held it immediately before the reversion event and they hold it on a trust of land for the revertee. The trustees will be under a duty to convey the land to a revertee who is of full age and capacity,[2] but they do have a power of sale whilst the land is vested in them.[3] Accordingly, a sale by two or more trustees or a trust corporation will overreach the beneficial interest of the revertee.[4]

There are two exceptions to the imposition of such a trust:

(a) where the trustees have extinguished the right of a revertee before 17 August 1987.[5] This would be the case where, for example, the trustees had, before that date, been in possession of the land for more than 12 years after the reversion event. In such a case, the trustees will hold the land on trust, but there will be no beneficiary of the trust and the trustees' powers are limited to those that they could have exercised if the Reverter of Sites Act 1987 had not been passed, or to applying to either the Charity Commission or the Secretary of State for Education for a Charity Commission's Scheme or Education Act Scheme (as the case may be) in accordance with the provisions of the 1987 Act; and
(b) where the trustees have traced the beneficiaries, but either the beneficiaries do not want to claim the property or for some other reason it is felt desirable that actual or potential beneficiaries should have their rights extinguished

and a charitable purposes scheme created. In such a case, the trustees may apply under Reverter of Sites Act 1987, s 2 or s 5 to either the Charity Commission or the Secretary of State for Education for a Charity Commission's Scheme or Education Act Scheme (as the case may be) in accordance with the provisions of the 1987 Act.

160.1 Restriction

Where a registered estate becomes subject to a trust of land, other than on a registrable disposition, or where the estate is held on a trust of land and there is a change in the trusts, and a sole or last surviving trustee will not be able to give a valid receipt for capital money, the registered proprietor must apply for entry of a restriction in Form A.[6] The wording of Form A is set out in Appendix IV. If such an application is not made, a revertee entitled to the beneficial interest in the land has a sufficient interest to apply for entry of such a restriction, to ensure that a survivor of the joint proprietors (unless a trust corporation) will not be able to give a valid receipt for capital money.[7]

A restriction does not confer any priority. However, it prevents an entry being made in the register relating to any disposition, or a disposition of a specified kind, unless the terms of the restriction have (where applicable) been complied with.

An applicant should deliver to HMLR the usual documents required.[8]

No fee is currently payable where the application is in respect of a restriction in Form A only.

Where the applicant is a person who has an interest under a trust of land, the statement in panel 12 or conveyancer's certificate in panel 13 of form RX1 should be completed on the following lines:

> The interest is that specified in rule 93(a) of the Land Registration Rules 2003 (SI 2003/1417), the applicant being a person who has an interest in the registered estate held under a trust of land as a result of [*set out details of provision for reverter and of the reversion event*].

Panel 9 of form RX1 should set out Form A. A restriction in Form A in LRR 2003, Sch 4 does not require the approval of HMLR to the wording of the restriction under LRA 2002, s 43(3).

HMLR must give notice of the application for a restriction to the proprietor of the registered estate concerned if it has not been made by or with his consent or a person entitled to be registered as such proprietor.[9]

160.2 Transfer to revertee

If a revertee becomes beneficially entitled, he should take a transfer of the land from the trustees and apply for registration in the usual way.[10] The application should be accompanied by a letter confirming, if such be the case, that the land is not affected by anything done by the revertee before 17 August 1987, the validity of which is preserved by Reverter of Sites Act 1987, s 1(4).

---

1 Reverter of Sites Act 1987, s 1(1).
2 *Saunders v Vaultier* (1841) 41 ER 482.
3 Reverter of Sites Act 1987, s 1(2).
4 See 127 Overreaching.
5 Reverter of Sites Act 1987, s 1(4).
6 LRR 2003, r 94(1) and (2).
7 LRR 2003, r 93(a).
8 See 153.1 Application for entry of restriction.
9 LRA 2002, s 45.
10 See 176.1 Registration of transfer.

161 SEQUESTRATORS

Sequestrators appointed by the court under a writ of sequestration have a duty to enter on the property of the contemnor and take possession of all his estate. An order appointing a sequestrator is treated as an interest affecting an estate or charge for the purposes of the LRA 2002.[1] However, it cannot be an interest belonging to a person in actual occupation falling within LRA 2002, Sch 1, para 2 or Sch 3, para 2 which overrides first registration or registered dispositions.[2] Nor can HMLR enter a notice of an order appointing a sequestrator in the register.[3] Such an order may therefore be protected only by entry of a restriction in the register.

The sequestrator may be treated as a person having a sufficient interest if he is applying for entry of a restriction in Form L or Form N.[4] The wording of Forms L and N is set out in Appendix IV. A restriction does not confer any priority. However, it prevents an entry being made in the register relating to any disposition, or a disposition of a specified kind, unless the terms of the restriction have (where applicable) been complied with.

161.1 Restriction

In addition to the usual documents required,[5] the sequestrator should deliver to HMLR a certified copy of the court order appointing the sequestrator.

As the application for a restriction is unlikely to be made by or with the consent of the registered proprietor, the statement in panel 12 or conveyancer's certificate in panel 13 of form RX1 should be completed on the following lines:

> The interest is that specified in rule 93(s) of the Land Registration Rules 2003 (SI 2003/1417), the applicant being the sequestrator appointed by [*name*] Court on [*date*].

Panel 9 of form RX1 should set out the wording of the appropriate restriction. A restriction in a standard form contained in LRR 2003, Sch 4 does not require the approval of HMLR to the terms of the restriction under LRA 2002, s 43(3). A possible form of restriction based on the wording of Form L is:

> No [disposition *or specify type of disposition*] of the registered estate by the proprietor of the registered estate [or by the proprietor of any registered charge, not being a charge registered before the entry of this restriction] is to be registered without a certificate signed by [*name*] of [*address*] [or [their conveyancer *or specify appropriate details*]] that the provisions of [*specify clause, paragraph or other particulars*] of [*specify details*] have been complied with [or that they do not apply to the disposition].

A possible form of restriction based on the wording of Form N is:

> No [disposition *or specify type of disposition*] of the registered estate by the proprietor of the registered estate [or by the proprietor of any registered charge, not being a charge registered before the entry of this restriction] is to be registered without a written consent signed by [*name*] of [*address*] [or [their conveyancer *or specify appropriate details*]].

HMLR must give notice of such an application to the proprietor of the registered estate or charge concerned if it has not been made by or with his consent or a person entitled to be registered as such proprietor.[6]

---

1 LRA 2002, s 87(1)(c).
2 LRA 2002, s 87(3).
3 LRA 2002, s 87(2).
4 LRR 2003, r 93(s)
5 See 153.1 Application for entry of restriction.
6 LRA 2002, s 45.

162 SETTLEMENTS

Registered land which is settled land must be registered in the name of the tenant for life or the statutory owner or the special personal representatives in whom the legal estate would be vested if the land were unregistered.[1] The rights of beneficiaries, which are overreached by dispositions under the SLA 1925, do not appear in the register but are protected by the entry of appropriate restrictions in the register. An interest under a settlement under the SLA 1925 is not an unregistered interest which overrides first registration or registered dispositions even where the interest belongs to a person in actual occupation of the land.[2] HMLR cannot enter any notice in the register in respect of an interest under an SLA 1925 settlement.[3]

Since 1 January 1997 it has not been possible to create any new settlement under the SLA 1925.[4] As regards existing settlements, LRA 2002, s 89 provides that rules may make provision in relation to the application of the SLA 1925 to registered land and this is dealt with in LRR 2003, r 186 and Sch 7.

162.1 Settled land forms of restriction

Applications for first registration of settled land must be accompanied by an application for entry of a restriction in Form G, H or I as appropriate.[5] The wording of Forms G, H and I is set out in Appendix IV. There is a similar requirement where registered land is transferred into settlement or bought with capital money of the settlement.[6] In addition to those forms of restriction, the registered proprietor of settled land is under a duty to apply for such other restrictions as may be appropriate. In that case the application should be completed to show that the restrictions applied for are required for the protection of the beneficial interests and powers under the settlement.[7] LRR 2003, Sch 4 contains the following forms:

(a) Form G (Tenant for life as registered proprietor of settled land, where there are trustees of the settlement);
(b) Form H (Statutory owners as trustees of the settlement and registered proprietors of settled land); and
(c) Form I (Tenant for life as registered proprietor of settled land – no trustees of the settlement).

A house is not a mansion house if it is usually occupied as a farmhouse or where the site of the house and grounds does not exceed 25 acres.[8]

The restrictions may be modified on application or as HMLR sees fit, according to the circumstances. Where one of the prescribed restrictions should have been entered in the register and has not been, any person who has an interest in the settled land can apply for such restriction (modified if appropriate) to be entered. The persons interested under the settlement may apply for any additional restriction(s) necessitated by the provisions of the settlement.

Except in the instances referred to in LRR 2003, Sch 7, para 8 (proprietor ceasing in his lifetime to be the tenant for life) and para 14 (discharge of registered land from beneficial interests and powers under a settlement), the restrictions bind the proprietor in his lifetime but do not affect dispositions by his personal representatives.

162.2 Transfer of land into settlement

A transfer of registered land into settlement must include the following provisions, with any necessary alterations and additions:[9]

> The Transferor and the Transferee declare that—
>
> (a) the property is vested in the Transferee upon the trusts declared in a trust deed dated (*date*) and made between (*parties*),
> (b) the trustees of the settlement are (*names*),
> (c) the power of appointment of new trustees is vested in (*name*),
> (d) the following powers relating to land are expressly conferred by the trust deed in addition to those conferred by the Settled Land Act 1925: (*insert additional powers*).
>
> *or*, if the tenant for life is a minor and the transferees are the statutory owner—
>
> (a) the property is vested in the Transferee as statutory owner under a trust deed dated (*date*) and made between (*parties*),
> (b) the tenant for life is (*name*), a minor, who was born on (*date*),
> (c) the trustees of the settlement are (*names*),
> (d) during the minority of the tenant for life the power of appointment of new trustees is vested in the Transferee,
> (e) the following powers relating to land are expressly conferred by the trust deed in addition to those conferred by the Settled Land Act 1925: (*insert additional powers*).

An application must also be made for a restriction in Forms G, H or I, as appropriate.[10]

162.3 Registered land bought with capital money

Where registered land is acquired with capital money, the transfer must include the following provisions, with any necessary alterations and additions:[11]

The Transferee declares that—

(a) the consideration has been paid out of capital money,
(b) the property is vested in the Transferee upon the trusts declared in a trust deed dated (*date*) and made between (*parties*),
(c) the trustees of the settlement are (*names*),
(d) the power of appointment of new trustees is vested in (*name*),
(e) the following powers relating to land are expressly conferred by the trust deed in addition to those conferred by the Settled Land Act 1925: (*set out additional powers*).

An application must also be made for a restriction in Forms G, H or I, as appropriate.[12]

162.4 Registered land brought into settlement

Where registered land has been settled and the existing registered proprietor is the tenant for life under the settlement, the registered proprietor must make a declaration in Form 6 in LRR 2003, Sch 3 and apply for a restriction in Form G modified as appropriate.[13] The wording of Form 6 is set out in Appendix V. This arises only where the settlement is a variation of a settlement created before 1 January 1997, or derives from such a settlement, and falls within TLATA, s 2(2).

162.5 Proprietor ceasing in his lifetime to be tenant for life

Where a registered proprietor ceases in his lifetime to be a tenant for life and has not become absolutely entitled, he must transfer the land to his successor in title, or, if the successor is a minor, to the statutory owner.[14] On the registration of the successor in title or statutory owner, the trustees of the settlement, if the settlement is continuing, must apply for any necessary alteration in the restrictions in the register.[15]

162.6 Registration of special personal representatives

Where land was settled before the death of the sole or last surviving joint registered proprietor and not by his will, and the settlement continues after his death, the personal representatives in whom the registered land vests under the Administration of Estates Act 1925 may apply to be registered as proprietor in place of the deceased proprietor.[16] The application must be accompanied by the grant of probate or letters of administration of the deceased proprietor limited to the settled land.[17] The personal representatives must be registered in place of the deceased proprietor and the following added:[18]

> [special executor *or* executrix] *or* [administrator *or* administratrix] of [*name*], deceased.

162.7 Transfer on death of tenant for life

Where the settlement continues after the death of the registered proprietor who was tenant for life, the personal representatives will assent the land using form AS1 or form AS2 to the person entitled. In addition to the usual documents required,[19] an applicant should deliver to HMLR:

(a) (if the personal representatives are not already registered as proprietors) the grant of probate or letters of administration limited to, or including, settled land; and
(b) an application for entry of a restriction in Form G or Form H, as appropriate. This may be made in the additional provisions panel of form AS1 or form AS2 or in form RX1.[20]

The assent in form AS1 or form AS2 must contain the following provisions with any necessary alterations or additions:[21]

> The Personal Representatives and the Transferee declare that—
>
> (a) the property is vested in the Transferee upon the trusts declared in [a trust deed dated (*date*) and made between (*parties*) *or* the will of *(name of deceased)* proved on *(date)*],
> (b) the trustees of the settlement are (*names*),
> (c) the power of appointment of new trustees is vested in (*name*),
> (d) the following powers relating to land are expressly conferred by the [*trust deed*] *or* [*will*] in addition to those conferred by the Settled Land Act 1925: (*set out additional powers*).

Where the settlement ends on the death of the proprietor, an application by the personal representatives to register a transfer to the person entitled should be accompanied by the grant of probate or letters of administration (if the personal representatives are not already registered as proprietors) and form RX3 for cancellation of the restriction relating to the settlement.[22]

162.8 Registration of statutory owner during a minority otherwise than on death

If a minor becomes entitled in possession to registered land otherwise than on a death (or will be so entitled on attaining full age), the statutory owner during the minority is entitled to have the land transferred to him and to be registered as proprietor.[23] The transfer must be in form TR1 and must not refer to the settlement.[24] An application to register the transfer must be accompanied by an application for a restriction in Form H.[25]

162.9 Minority where settlement arises under a will or intestacy

During a minority, the personal representatives under a will or intestacy of a person who died before 1 January 1997 under which a settlement of registered land is created or arises, must be registered as proprietors and will have all the powers conferred by the SLA 1925 on a tenant for life and on the trustees of the settlement.[26]

When the minor becomes beneficially entitled to an estate in fee simple or a term of years absolute in registered land or would, if he were of full age, be or have the powers of a tenant for life, the personal representatives must (unless they are themselves the statutory owner) during the minority give effect in the register to the directions of the statutory owner.[27] The statutory owner must direct the personal representatives to apply for a restriction in Form H.[28]

HMLR is under no duty to call for any information regarding why an application is made, or the terms of the will or devolution under the intestacy, or the directions of the statutory owner. Instead, HMLR can assume that the personal representatives are acting according to the directions given and that the directions were given and were correct.[29]

A disponee dealing with the personal representatives who complies with the Form H restriction is not concerned to see or enquire whether any directions have been given by the statutory owner with regard to the disposition to him.[30]

162.10 Changes to settlement

As changes take place under a settlement of registered land, the registered proprietor or his personal representatives must execute the instruments necessary to give effect to the changes in the register and must apply for any necessary changes in the restrictions appearing in the register. An appropriate prescribed form in LRR 2003, Sch 1 should be used, modified where necessary according to the facts.

New trustees are appointed in the usual way.[31] However, where a restriction in Form G appears in the register, an application to update the restriction by substituting the new names is necessary. This should be made in form AP1 accompanied by evidence of the death or retirement and appointment of new trustees, as appropriate.[32]

162.11 End of settlement other than on death

Where the settlement comes to an end otherwise than on the death of the registered proprietor, the trustees of the settlement may enter into a deed of discharge in accordance with SLA 1925, s 17. An application to cancel the restriction relating to the settlement should be made in form RX3 accompanied by the deed of discharge.[33]

---

1 LRR 2003, Sch 7, paras 1 and 11.
2 LRA 2002, Sch 1, para 2 and Sch 3, para 2.
3 LRA 2002, s 33(a).
4 TLATA, s 2.
5 LRR 2003, Sch 7, para 2.
6 LRR 2003, Sch 7, para 6(2).
7 LRR 2003, Sch 7, para 7(2).
8 Settled Land Act 1925, s 65(2).
9 LRR 2003, Sch 7, para 4(1).
10 LRR 2003, Sch 7, para 4(2).
11 LRR 2003, Sch 7, para 6(1).
12 LRR 2003, Sch 7, para 6(2).
13 LRR 2003, Sch 7, para 5.
14 LRR 2003, Sch 7, para 8(a).
15 LRR 2003, Sch 7, para 8(b).
16 LRR 2003, Sch 7, para 11(1).
17 LRR 2003, Sch 7, para 11(2).
18 LRR 2003, Sch 7, para 11(3).
19 See 17 Assents.
20 LRR 2003, Sch 7, para 12(1)(a).
21 LRR 2003, Sch 7, para 12(1)(b).
22 LRR 2003, Sch 7, para 12(2).
23 LRR 2003, Sch 7, para 10(1).
24 LRR 2003, Sch 7, para 10(2).
25 LRR 2003, Sch 7, para 10(3).
26 LRR 2003, Sch 7, para 13(1)(a).
27 LRR 2003, Sch 7, para 13(1)(b).

[28] LRR 2003, Sch 7, para 13(1)(c).
[29] LRR 2003, Sch 7, para 13(3).
[30] LRR 2003, Sch 7, para 13(4).
[31] See 178.5 Vesting of registered land in new trustees.
[32] See 153.6 Updating a restriction.
[33] See 153.8 Cancellation of a restriction.

163 SEVERANCE OF A BENEFICIAL JOINT TENANCY

A registered proprietor may sever a beneficial joint tenancy. The severance may be effected by a deed of declaration entered into by the joint proprietors, but is more commonly effected by one of the joint proprietors serving notice on the other joint proprietor(s) under LPA 1925, s 36(2). Severance may also occur where, for example, one of the joint proprietors has been declared bankrupt or has charged his beneficial share to a third party. Where there has been severance, the proprietors of a registered estate must apply for entry of a restriction in Form A, since the estate is held on a trust of land and, as a result of a change in the trusts, the survivor of joint proprietors will not be able to give a valid receipt for capital money.[1] The wording of Form A is set out in Appendix IV.

163.1 Restriction in Form A

An applicant for entry of a restriction in Form A should deliver to HMLR an application in form RX1 or (where the severance has been effected by agreement or by the service of notice) in form SEV. No fee is payable where the application is in respect of a restriction in Form A only.

If applying in form RX1, panel 9 should set out the wording of Form A.

If the application has not been made by or with the consent of all the registered proprietors, the statement in panel 12 or conveyancer's certificate in panel 13 of form RX1 must be completed, setting out details of the severance. In the case of form SEV, the details in panel 8 should be completed as appropriate. In addition, whether form RX1 or form SEV is used, the application must be accompanied (where the severance was effected by notice) by either:

(a) the original or a certified copy of the notice of severance given by one proprietor to the other(s) together with a certificate by the applicant or his conveyancer confirming that notice has been served on the other proprietor(s); or

(b) the original or a certified copy of the notice of severance signed by the proprietor(s) on whom it has been served, or a certificate by the applicant's conveyancer confirming that he holds the original of such a notice.

Where severance has been effected by a document, such as a deed of declaration signed by all of the registered proprietors, the original or a certified copy of the document should be lodged, or a certificate by the applicant's conveyancer confirming that he holds the original or a certified copy of such a document. If the application has been made by or with the consent of all the registered proprietors, evidence of the severance need not be lodged.

Where the application has not been made by all the registered proprietors or with their consent, HMLR is not obliged to give notice of the application for a restriction to the other proprietor(s) of the registered estate or charge concerned under LRA 2002, s 45. This is because the application is one which the applicant is obliged to make under LRR 2003, r 94; HMLR will, however, notify the other proprietor(s) of completion of the application.

A restriction does not confer any priority. However, it prevents an entry being made in the register relating to any disposition, or a disposition of a specified kind, unless the terms of the restriction have (where applicable) been complied with. A restriction in Form A reflects, rather than effects, the severance. It ensures that a survivor of the joint proprietors (unless a trust corporation) will not be able to give a valid receipt for capital money and that the beneficial interests will be overreached on a sale under LPA 1925, ss 2 and 27.

For the position where the beneficial joint tenancy has been severed as a result of the bankruptcy of one of the joint proprietors, see 19.8 Bankruptcy of a joint proprietor. For the position where the beneficial joint tenancy has been severed as a result of a charging order being created over the beneficial share of one of the joint proprietors, see 29.4 Restriction where the charging order is over a beneficial interest. For joint proprietors generally, see 92 Joint Proprietors.

---

1 LRR 2003, r 94(1)(b).

164 SHARED OWNERSHIP LEASES

A shared ownership lease differs from a conventional lease in allowing a tenant to purchase a share in the equity of the property. This assists tenants who might otherwise be unable to afford to buy a property outright. The purchaser, as tenant, is granted a lease of the property at a premium which represents the value of the share purchased. The rent is calculated to take account of the value of the share in the property that has not been purchased. Provisions in the lease allow the tenant to purchase further shares in the property, a procedure called 'staircasing'. The rent is reduced when further shares are purchased. There may also be further provisions allowing the tenant the option to call for a transfer of the landlord's interest in the property or, in the case of a flat, to call for a conventional lease of the flat.

A shared ownership lease sometimes contains a discount charge. A notice of the discount charge is entered in the charges register.

HA 1988, s 5(5A) permits a landlord to include within a shared ownership lease a right of pre-emption in his favour, and to enforce that right.

A shared ownership lease granted out of a registered estate in land must normally be in the form of a prescribed clauses lease.[1]

164.1 Registration of the lease

An application for registration of a shared ownership lease is made in the same way as for a conventional lease. Where the lease is granted out of a registered estate, see 98.7 Registration of leases which are registrable dispositions.

On registration of the lease, HMLR:

(a) allots it its own title number; and
(b) enters a notice of the registered lease in the landlord's registered title.

Where the lease contains an option for the tenant to call for a transfer of the landlord's interest or to call for the grant of a lease in conventional form, HMLR will enter notice of the option in the landlord's title. HMLR will not make any entry of such option in the tenant's title.

Where the lease contains a provision requiring the tenant to offer a surrender to the landlord if the tenant wishes to assign before he has purchased all the equity in the property, HMLR will make a note of this obligation in the property register of the tenant's title. HMLR will also enter a note if the lease contains a right of pre-emption in favour of the landlord.

Where the lease is granted out of unregistered land, see 98.1 Leases granted out of unregistered estates.

Where the lease contains an option for the tenant to call for a transfer of the landlord's interest or to call for the grant of a lease in conventional form and the landlord's title is unregistered, HMLR will not make any entry of such option in the tenant's title. The tenant should register a Class C(iv) land charge in respect of the landlord's unregistered title.

Where the lease is granted by a registered social landlord, application could previously be made in Form RX1 or clause LR13 of a prescribed clauses lease (or a lease containing the prescribed clauses) for entry of a restriction in Form KK. On 1 October 2008, the Housing Corporation applied to cancel all Form KK restrictions affecting properties in England. Any remaining need not be complied with. Since 15 August 2018, it has not been possible to apply for a Form KK restriction for a property situated in Wales.[2] However, any remaining on Welsh titles must be complied with for a variation of the shared ownership lease dated before 15 August 2018. An applicant may apply to cancel such a restriction on purchasing 100 per cent of the equity. In addition to the usual documents required,[3] an applicant should deliver to HMLR:

(a) written confirmation that the tenant has purchased 100 per cent of the equity; or
(b) a certificate that the final staircasing purchase has been completed.

The tenant may assign the benefit of any options in the lease granted in his favour. This may be done when the tenant mortgages the leasehold estate. HMLR does not make any entry in the register of any such assignment.

164.2 Staircasing

The acquisition by the tenant of further shares in the property does not require any entry to be made in the register unless, at the same time, a deed is entered into varying the terms of the lease, usually by reducing the rent, or a discount charge arises on such acquisition.

Where there is a deed of variation of the lease, the tenant should deliver to HMLR:

(a) an application in form AP1;
(b) the deed of variation or a certified copy; and
(c) the fee payable.[4]

If satisfied that the variation has effect at law, HMLR will make an entry relating to the deed in the property register of the tenant's title, together with a notice in the landlord's title (if registered).

Where the further shares are acquired at a discount and the liability to repay the discount takes effect as a charge, specific application should be made to register the charge or enter a notice in respect of it, as appropriate.

---

1 See 98.6 Prescribed clauses leases.
2 Regulation of Registered Social Landlords (Wales) Act 2018 (Consequential Amendments) Regulations 2018 (SI 2018/870), reg 4.
3 See 153.8 Cancellation of a restriction.
4 See 67 Fees.

165 SOUVENIR LAND

During the 1970s and 1980s, schemes were set up for the sale of very small plots of land which had sentimental or commemorative value only and which were often promoted for conservation purposes. All such land was known as 'souvenir land'. At that time, the small size of the plots and the number of titles in a very small area posed considerable potential problems for HMLR. In consequence, the Land Registration (Souvenir Land) Rules 1972 (SI 1972/985) provided that HMLR could declare an area of land to be subject to a souvenir land scheme if that area consisted wholly or mainly of land which had been, or was proposed to be, disposed of in souvenir plots. A plot of souvenir land was defined by Land Registration and Land Charges Act 1971, s 4(5) as:

> any piece of land which being of inconsiderable size and little or no practical utility, is unlikely to be wanted in isolation except for the sake of pure ownership or for sentimental reasons or commemorative purposes.

The effect of that declaration was that disposals of individual plots within the designated area took effect as if the title were not registered. An entry on the following lines appeared in the property register of the affected title:

> The land [*edged and numbered (number) in blue on the filed plan*] is subject to a Souvenir Land scheme.
> NOTE: Declaration dated … filed.

Only a few registered titles were affected by such a declaration. A souvenir land declaration could also be made in respect of unregistered land. It is no longer possible to make a souvenir land declaration in relation to either registered or unregistered land and dispositions must now be registered, or (as the case may be) the subject of an application for first registration, in the normal way.

Where a souvenir land declaration has been entered in the register and any unregistered transaction with that land has been made, the proprietor must not dispose of that land otherwise than in a manner which gives effect to the interests of any third parties who have become entitled to apply to be registered as proprietor of any part of that land.[1]

The particulars of the declaration entered in the register take effect as a restriction and HMLR may amend the register to substitute for the declaration in the property register a restriction in the proprietorship register.[2] The wording of the restriction is:

> No disposition is to be registered without the consent of the person or persons (if any) entitled to apply to be registered as proprietor of the land disposed of, or any part of it, as the result of any unregistered transaction effected since [*the date of the declaration as noted in the register*].

165.1 Cancellation of entries relating to souvenir land

Where the registered proprietor can establish to the satisfaction of HMLR that there has been no unregistered transaction with the souvenir land after the declaration was made, so that no third party has become entitled to be registered as proprietor of it, he may apply using form AP1 for cancellation of the entry in the register relating to the souvenir land. The application may be made in respect of a particular part of the souvenir land only.

165.2 Application for registration by a third party

A third party may apply to be registered as proprietor of part of the souvenir land using application form AP1 if he is able to establish to the satisfaction of HMLR that one or more unregistered transactions were effected since the declaration was made and that, as a result of them and any other events that have taken place:

(a) the legal estate in the land is vested in him; or
(b) a legal estate granted out of the land is vested in him; or
(c) a legal estate such as is referred to in (a) or (b) above has been transferred to him, directly or indirectly, by the person in whom it has become vested.

HMLR will give notice of such application to the registered proprietor. The restriction referred to above must be complied with, where appropriate.

---

1 LRA (TP) Order 2003, art 11.

2 LRA (TP) Order 2003, art 11(4) and (5).

166 SPECIAL POWERS OF APPOINTMENT

A special power of appointment is a power under which the donee of the power, who may not be the registered proprietor, is able to appoint the property among a limited class of persons. Such a power of appointment takes effect in equity[1] and allows the donee of the power to transfer an equitable interest only.

A power of appointment cannot be protected by entry of a notice in the register.[2] However, the donee of a special power of appointment has a sufficient interest to apply for the entry of a restriction in relation to the registered land affected by the power.[3] A restriction does not confer any priority. However, it prevents an entry being made in the register relating to any disposition, or a disposition of a specified kind, unless the terms of the restriction have (where applicable) been complied with.

166.1 Restriction

An applicant should deliver to HMLR the usual documents required.[4]

Where the applicant is a person who is the donee of a special power of appointment, the statement in panel 12 or conveyancer's certificate in panel 13 of form RX1 should be completed on the following lines:

> the applicant's interest is that specified in rule 93(e) of the Land Registration Rules 2003 (SI 2003/1417), the applicant being the donee of a special power of appointment which affects the registered estate.

Panel 9 of form RX1 should set out the wording of the appropriate restriction. A restriction in a standard form contained in LRR 2003, Sch 4 does not require the approval of HMLR to the terms of the restriction under LRA 2002, s 43(3). A possible form of restriction based on Form N is:

> No [disposition *or specify type of disposition*] of the registered estate by the proprietor of the registered estate [or by the proprietor of any registered charge, not being a charge registered before the entry of this restriction] is to be registered without a written consent signed by [*name*] of [*address*] [or [their conveyancer *or specify appropriate details*]].

The wording of Form N is set out in Appendix IV.

HMLR must give notice of the application for a restriction to the proprietor of the registered estate concerned if it has not been made by or with his consent or a person entitled to be registered as such proprietor.[5]

1 LPA 1925, s 1(7).
2 LRA 2002, s 33.
3 LRR 2003, r 93(e).
4 See 153.1 Application for entry of restriction.
5 LRA 2002, s 45.

167 SPORTING RIGHTS

Sporting rights are those relating to shooting, fishing and hunting and may potentially be of considerable commercial value. Most sporting rights will take effect as profits à prendre, although fishing rights may relate to a corporeal fishery.

167.1 Profits à prendre, franchises and manorial rights

Sporting rights which are profits à prendre mainly exist in gross rather than as appurtenant to land. Profits à prendre in gross may be the subject of a voluntary application for first registration; an application for first registration is never compulsory. For the registration and protection of profits à prendre in gross and appurtenant profits, see 139 Profits à Prendre.

As a result of Law of Property Act 1922, Twelfth Schedule, there are preserved to the lord of the manor in relation to copyhold land enfranchised under that Act, the rights, franchises, royalties or privileges of the lord in respect of any rights of chase or warren, piscaries or other rights of hunting, shooting, fishing, fowling or otherwise taking game, fish or fowl. Copyhold Act 1852, s 48 and Copyhold Act 1894, s 23 excepted similar rights in respect of enfranchisement under those Acts. Any franchises of forest, free chase, park or free warren were abolished by Wild Creatures and Forest Laws Act 1971, s 1(1). For the registration and protection of franchises and manorial rights, see 74 Franchises and 112 Manors.

167.2 Corporeal fisheries

There is a presumption that the owner of a several fishery in a non-tidal river is the owner of the bed of the river.[1] This presumption prevails over the better-known presumption that the owner of the land abutting a non-tidal river owns the bed to the middle of the stream. Both presumptions are rebuttable on the particular facts of a case. A similar presumption arises, in the case of a several fishery in a tidal river, that ownership of the fishery includes the soil under the fishery. Such a fishery must have been created by a grant of the Crown before Magna Carta 1297.[2] After Magna Carta 1297 such a fishery would have to have been created by statute.

A corporeal fishery, being land, is subject to compulsory first registration in the usual way.[3]

---

1 *Hanbury v Jenkins* [1901] 2 Ch 401.

2 See for instance *Duke of Beaufort v John Aird and Co* (1904) 20 TLR 602 where the evidence commenced with an extract from the Domesday Book.

3 See 68.2 Compulsory first registration.

168 STAMP DUTY LAND TAX

SDLT is a tax payable on certain land transactions completed on or after 1 December 2003. It was introduced by the Finance Act 2003 and replaced stamp duty for most land transactions. 'Land transaction' means the acquisition of a chargeable interest in land located in the United Kingdom. Finance Act 2003, s 48(1) defines 'Chargeable interest' and includes freehold and leasehold estates in land, and rights over another's land. The definition includes both legal and beneficial interests. Consequently, a wide range of transactions are within the scope of SDLT. It is payable in respect of transactions rather than deeds. Therefore, a liability to SDLT can arise even in cases where no deed has been executed; for example, the surrender of a lease by operation of law.

The rate of tax is a percentage of the 'chargeable consideration' for the transaction, which for SDLT purposes comprises anything given for the transaction in money or money's worth. It therefore includes not only monetary consideration but also other forms of consideration such as the release or assumption of a debt; the provision of works and services; or the transfer of other property. Certain reliefs may be available in appropriate cases; such reliefs must be applied for.

Currently, different rates apply to residential property and to non-residential and mixed use property. A 'higher rate' of SDLT is currently chargeable on the purchase of an 'additional residential property' such as a buy-to-let property or a holiday home.

Most land transactions are 'notifiable', which means HMRC must be informed about the transaction, even in cases where it is of a type which will not attract SDLT. Notification is given by means of the submission of a return in form SDLT1. HMLR cannot register the transaction (or enter a notice in the register in respect of it) unless the application is accompanied by evidence that HMRC has been notified.[1] Such evidence will be either a Land Transaction Return certificate (form SDLT5), or a printed submission certificate as generated when a person applies electronically for an SDLT5 certificate.

Other transactions and interests which are exempt from SDLT or outside the scope of SDLT do not require notification to HMRC. A 'self certificate' in form SDLT60 was previously required for these, but this was abolished with effect from 12 March 2008. Finance Act 2003, s 48(2) describes exempt instruments. These include, for example, a legal or equitable charge, a discharge of a charge or a contract for sale. Certain transactions are exempt transactions (as opposed to exempt interests) and thus do not need to be notified to HMRC. Finance Act 2003, Sch 3 defines these. They include transactions in connection with divorce and assents. Certain other transactions, although not exempt transactions,[2] are also not notifiable. These include a transaction dated on or after 22 July 2004 but before 12 March 2008 that consists entirely of residential property where the total consideration for the transaction (together with any linked transaction) is less than £1,000. HMLR can register such transactions without SDLT evidence being lodged, but in cases where the position is not clear, an applicant should lodge a covering letter confirming the position with the application.

There are still a few transactions on which stamp duty (rather than SDLT) is payable. These will mainly be based on pre-11 July 2003 contracts. Where a document is lodged which is endorsed with stamp duty and, if appropriate, with a 'produced' stamp, HMLR will not raise any query and no covering letter is necessary. A transfer for value (not relating to a share) dated after 30 November 2003 on which stamp duty would still be payable but which is below the stamp duty threshold, should be lodged with a form L(A)451 and a covering letter of explanation. Where appropriate, a transfer may contain a certificate under the Stamp Duty (Exempt Instruments) Regulations 1987 (SI 1987/516) and should be lodged with a covering letter explaining why the certificate is appropriate.

On 1 April 2015, the Land and Buildings Transaction Tax replaced SDLT in Scotland. From April 2018, LTT replaced SDLT in Wales.[3] Where land falls partly in England and partly in Wales, its acquisition is treated as two separate land transactions. The applicant must apportion the consideration paid for the land on a just and reasonable basis.[4] Where appropriate, the applicant should notify both HMRC (in respect of SDLT) and the WRA (in respect of LTT).

Further details concerning SDLT are available on the HMRC website.[5]

---

1 Finance Act 2003, s 79.

2 As defined in Finance Act 2003, Sch 3.

3 See 94 Land Transaction Tax.
4 Land Transaction Tax and Anti-avoidance of Devolved Taxes (Wales) Act 2017, s 9.
5 www.hmrc.gov.uk/sdlt.

169 STATEMENTS OF TRUTH

The LRR 2003 make provision for use of a statement of truth as a means of providing evidence in support of an application to HMLR; for example, an application based upon adverse possession or a prescriptive easement. It provides an alternative to the use of a statutory declaration in most circumstances. Except where a prescribed application form incorporates a statement of truth,[1] an applicant may use a statutory declaration for supporting evidence, if preferred.

Certain standard forms of statement of truth, to cover common forms of application, are contained in LRR 2003, Sch 1, although their use is not compulsory:

(a) form ST1 – Statement of truth in support of an application for registration of land based upon adverse possession.
(b) form ST2 – Statement of truth in support of an application for registration of a rentcharge based upon adverse possession.
(c) form ST3 – Statement of truth in support of an application for registration of land based on lost or destroyed title deeds.
(d) form ST4 – Statement of truth in support of an application for registration and/or noting of a prescriptive easement.

Also available is form ST5 – Statement of truth in support of an application to cancel a Form A restriction.

For land registration purposes, a statement of truth is defined in LRR 2003, r 215A and must comply with the following requirements:

(a) it must be made by an individual in writing;
(b) it must contain a declaration of truth in the following form: 'I believe that the facts and matters contained in this statement are true';
(c) it must (except where he cannot read or sign it) be signed by the person who makes it;
(d) it need not be sworn or witnessed;
(e) if a conveyancer makes the statement of truth or signs it on someone's behalf, the conveyancer must sign in his own name and state his capacity.

If a statement of truth is made by a person who is unable to read, it must be signed in the presence of a conveyancer and contain a certificate made and signed by the conveyancer in the form set out in LRR 2003, r 215A(4)(b). If a statement of truth is made by a person who is unable to sign it, it must state the person's name, be signed by a conveyancer at his direction, and contain a certificate made and signed by the conveyancer in the form set out in r 215A(5)(c).

1 Such as forms ADV2 and CT1.

170 STATUTORY CHARGES

Statutory charges are charges created by or under a statute. Some statutory charges will be local land charges, such as a charge imposed under Public Health Act 1936, s 291, in favour of a local authority.[1] Other statutory charges, such as those in favour of the Lord Chancellor, in relation to legal aid, on property recovered or preserved[2] are not local land charges.

A statutory charge which is not a local land charge and which charges the legal estate must be completed by registration and does not operate at law until the registration requirements are met.[3] Such a statutory charge may be protected by entry of an agreed notice or unilateral notice in the register, but will take effect in equity only, until it is completed by registration.

170.1 Registration

An applicant to register a statutory charge should deliver to HMLR:

(a) an application in form AP1;
(b) a statement of charge[4] or a certified copy of it;
(c) (where the charge has priority over existing charges (see below) an application in form SC; and
(d) the fee payable.[5]

Some charges created by or under a statute have effect to postpone a charge which at the time of registration of the statutory charge is entered in the register or is the basis for an entry in the register. Where application form SC is lodged and HMLR is satisfied that the statutory charge has the priority specified in that form, HMLR must make an entry in the charges register showing that priority.[6] If the applicant does not satisfy HMLR that the statutory charge has that priority, but HMLR considers that the applicant has an arguable case, it may make an entry in the charges register that the applicant claims that priority.[7] In either case, HMLR must give notice of the statutory charge to the proprietor of any registered charge appearing in the affected title at the time of registration of the statutory charge. It must also give notice to any person who appears to be entitled to a charge protected by a notice in the register where that person's name and address appear in the register of the title in question.[8] A person who suffers loss by reason of a failure by HMLR to give such notice may be entitled to indemnity.[9]

Where an entry as to claimed priority has been made, a party may apply for the entry to be:

(a) removed; or
(b) replaced with an entry that the statutory charge in question does have the priority specified in the form SC.

The applicant must provide evidence to satisfy HMLR that it should take the action sought by the applicant. HMLR must serve notice of the application upon the proprietors of registered charges affected by the application.[10]

170.2 Restriction

Where a statutory charge takes effect as a charge over a beneficial interest in registered land, rather than as a charge on the legal estate, it cannot be registered or protected by entry of a notice. It may, however, be capable of protection by entry of a restriction. If the statutory charge has the effect of severing a beneficial joint tenancy, application may be made for entry of a restriction in Form A, if such a restriction does not already appear in the register. The wording of Form A is set out in Appendix IV. The purpose of this restriction is to ensure that a survivor of the joint proprietors (unless a trust corporation) will not be able to give a valid receipt for capital money and that the requirements for overreaching in LPA 1925, ss 2 and 27 are complied with.

Where a statutory charge has arisen in favour of the Lord Chancellor under Legal Aid Act 1988, s 16(6), Access to Justice Act 1999, s 10(7) or Legal Aid, Sentencing and Punishment of Offenders Act 2012, s 25(1) over a beneficial interest in registered land held under a trust of land, he has a sufficient interest to apply for entry of a restriction in Form JJ.[11] The wording of Form JJ is set out in Appendix IV.

Panel 9 of form RX1 should set out the required restriction(s). A restriction in a standard form contained in LRR 2003, Sch 4 does not require the approval of HMLR to the terms of the restriction under LRA 2002, s 43(3).

HMLR must give notice of the application for a restriction to the proprietor of the registered estate or charge concerned, if it has not been made by or with the consent of such proprietor or a person entitled to be registered as such proprietor.[12]

---

1 See 109.4 Monetary charges.

2 Legal Aid Act 1988, s 16(6), Access to Justice Act 1999, s 10(7) or Legal Aid, Sentencing and Punishment of Offenders Act 2012, s 25(1). See 99 Legal Aid.

3 LRA 2002, s 27.

4 For example, in the case of a charge under Legal Aid, Sentencing and Punishment of Offenders Act 2012, s 25(1), a statement given by a person stated to hold the rank of, or equivalent to, Civil Service Grade 7 or above.

5 See 67 Fees.

6 LRR 2003, r 105(2).

7 LRR 2003, r 105(3).

8 LRR 2003, rr 105(4) and 106.

9 LRA 2002, Sch 8 para 1(1)(h). See 86 Indemnity.

10 LRR 2003, r 105(5)–(8).

11 LRR 2003, r 94(w).

12 LRA 2002, s 45.

171 STATUTORY VESTING

There are several statutory provisions under which land may be transferred automatically and vest in a particular person or body by operation of law. In the case of unregistered land, a vesting by operation of law will not 'trigger' compulsory first registration,[1] but a voluntary application may be made. A transfer of unregistered land pursuant to a court order will, however, be a 'trigger' for compulsory first registration.[2]

In relation to a registered estate, the compulsory purchase or statutory vesting will need to be completed by registration to take effect at law, including situations where there is a vesting by operation of law.[3] In the case of a transfer by virtue of a court order, an application for registration should be made accompanied by the court order.[4]

---

1 LRA 2002, s 4(3).

2 LRA 2002, s 4(1)(a). See 68.2 Compulsory first registration.

3 LRA 2002, s 27(5).

4 LRR 2003, r 127(2) or r 161(2). See 176 Transfers.

172 SUBROGATION

Subrogation is a remedy not a cause of action. It is available in a wide variety of situations to reverse the defendant's unjust enrichment.[1]

Where a lender makes a loan and that money is used to pay off an existing registered charge on the property, that lender may be subrogated to the rights of the original chargee, even though the entry in respect of the registered charge has been removed from the register. This may even be the case where the lender contemplated making only an unsecured loan, if otherwise a third party would be unjustly enriched at the lender's expense.[2] A lender who obtains some security, but less than what he bargained for, is not necessarily precluded from claiming further security by subrogation.[3] Where a lender's legal charge over a property is defective, it may be entitled by subrogation to an unpaid vendor's lien over the property, on the basis that the owner has been unjustly enriched at the lender's expense.[4]

An example of where subrogation could arise might be when a lender makes a loan to be secured by a first charge and part of the money advanced is used to discharge an existing charge. The application to register the lender's charge is not made during the priority period of the official search relating to it and, before the application for registration is lodged, an application to register another charge is lodged by a third party. The third party's charge will therefore have priority over the lender's unprotected charge.[5] The lender may, however, be entitled to be subrogated to the original charge to the extent that its loan was used to redeem the original charge.

Where it is considered that a person has an interest in land as a result of subrogation, an application to protect that interest by entry of a notice may be made. In practice, the fact that documentation is usually not immediately available to satisfy HMLR of the validity of the applicant's claim means that application for a unilateral notice rather than for an agreed notice is more likely to be appropriate.

172.1 Unilateral notice

An applicant should deliver to HMLR the usual documents required.[6]

The statement in panel 11 or conveyancer's certificate in panel 12 of form UN1 should set out the nature of the interest claimed and how it has arisen by subrogation.

The unilateral notice in the register will give brief details of the interest protected and identify the beneficiary of that notice.

---

1 *Boscawen v Bajwa* [1995] 4 All ER 769 (CA).
2 *Banque Financière de la Cité v Parc (Battersea) Ltd* [1998] UKHL 7.
3 *Cheltenham & Gloucester PLC v Appleyard* [2004] EWCA Civ 291.
4 *Bank of Cyprus UK Ltd v Menelaou* [2015] UKSC 66.
5 LRA 2002, s 29.
6 See 119.3 Unilateral notice.

173 TIME SHARE

In a time share lease, the right to possession under the lease is discontinuous. A single property may be the subject of several discontinuous leases, under each of which the tenant is entitled to occupy the property for a specified period; typically, a specific week or specific weeks every year for a certain number of years.

Such a lease may be the subject of an application for first registration no matter how short a period of the term is unexpired.[1] First registration, on the grant of such a lease out of unregistered land or the transfer or first mortgage of such an unregistered lease, is compulsory only where the term at the time of the grant, transfer or mortgage has more than 7 years to run. A grant is also subject to compulsory registration where it is out of an unregistered freehold, or leasehold with more than 7 years to run, and it is to take effect in possession after the end of the period of 3 months beginning with the date of the grant.[2]

A time share lease takes effect as a lease for a single term equivalent to the aggregate of the individual periods during which the tenant is entitled to occupy the demised premises.[3] For example, the term of a lease for 2 specified weeks every year for 25 years is 50 weeks.

A grant of a term of years absolute out of a registered estate in land under which the right to possession is discontinuous is required to be completed by registration.[4] Where necessary, this should be in the form of a prescribed clauses lease.[5]

Before 13 October 2003, most leases granted for a term not exceeding 21 years were overriding interests under LRA 1925, s 70(1). A lease which was an overriding interest under the LRA 1925 immediately before 13 October 2003 continues to be an unregistered interest which overrides both first registration and registered dispositions.[6]

For applications for first registration of leases, see 68 First Registration, and for applications for registration of leases which are registrable dispositions, see 98.2 Leases which are registrable dispositions. A copy of any calendar used to define the weeks during which the tenant is entitled to occupy the land (where such a calendar does not form part of the lease) should accompany any application for registration.

No notice may be entered in the register in respect of a lease which is granted for a total term of 3 years or less from the date of the grant and is not required to be registered.[7]

---

1 LRA 2002, s 3(4).
2 LRA 2002, s 4.
3 *Cottage Holiday Associates Limited v Customs and Excise Commissioners* [1983] QB 735.
4 LRA 2002, s 27(2)(b)(iii).
5 See 98.6 Prescribed clauses leases.
6 LRA 2002, Sch 12, para 12.
7 LRA 2002, s 33(b).

174 TITLE INFORMATION DOCUMENT

Although it is not required by the LRR 2003, as a matter of practice HMLR issues a Title Information Document whenever an application is completed. The document consists of a frontsheet with an official copy of the register attached. It is envisaged that a conveyancer will pass this document on to his client.

175 TOWN OR VILLAGE GREENS

As a result of the CRA 1965, all town or village greens in England and Wales were required to be registered with the appropriate council specified in that Act during a period ending on 31 July 1970.[1] After that date no land capable of being registered under the CRA 1965 is deemed to be a town or village green unless so registered. 'Town or village green' is defined in the CRA 1965 as land which has been allotted by or under any Act for the exercise or recreation of the inhabitants of any locality; or on which the inhabitants of any locality have a customary right to indulge in lawful sports and pastimes; or on which the inhabitants of any locality have indulged in such sports and pastimes as of right for not less than 20 years.[2]

The purpose of the CRA 1965 was to establish a record of land in England and Wales which was either common land, a town green or a village green; the rights of common existing over such land; and the ownership of the land. The CA 2006 is not fully in force yet, but when it is, it will repeal the CRA 1965 and the regulations passed under its authority. As to common land, see 36 Commons. Common land does not include a town or village green. No person was to be registered as owner of any land the freehold estate to which was already registered at HMLR.

Once a town or village green is registered at HMLR, HMLR notifies the appropriate council accordingly. The council then deletes the registration of ownership and indicates that the land is registered at HMLR.[3]

The New Forest, Epping Forest and the Forest of Dean are exempted from the effect of the CRA 1965 and CA 2006.[4] The CRA 1965 also allowed the Minister to exempt land by order. For a list of areas in respect of which such an order was made, see 36 Commons.

Where a town or village green was registered under the CRA 1965 and the Commons Commissioner, following enquiry, was not satisfied that any person was the owner of the land, he could direct the registration authority to register as owner the parish council or other appropriate local authority as set out in CRA 1965, s 8. On registration under s 8, the land vested in that local authority. Any such direction should be revealed on a subsequent application for first registration of the land.

Where, after 2 January 1970, any land becomes a town or village green, an application for that land, and for the rights of common over it and claims of ownership to it, to be entered in the appropriate registers maintained under the CRA 1965 or CA 2006 should be made in accordance with the:

(a) Commons Registration (England) Regulations 2014 (SI 2014/3038) where the land is in one of the areas where the CA 2006 is in force;
(b) Commons (Registration of Town or Village Greens) (Interim Arrangements) (Wales) Regulations 2007 (SI 2007/2396) where the land is in Wales; or
(c) Commons Registration (New Land) Regulations 1969 (SI 1969/1843) otherwise.

For the position where there are any rights of common over such a town or village green, see 36 Commons.

The Common Land (Rectification of Registers) Act 1989 made provision for removal from the register of town or village greens, on application by the owner, of dwelling houses and land ancillary to dwelling houses. Any such application had to be made by 22 July 1992. A copy of any order made under that Act should be lodged with any application for first registration of the land in question.

The CA 2006 provides for application to be made by any person for registration of a town or village green where a significant number of the inhabitants of any locality, or of any neighbourhood within a locality, have indulged as of right in lawful sports and pastimes on the land for a period of at least 20 years; and they continue to do so at the time of the application.[5] The CA 2006 also provides for such an application to be made in certain circumstances where such use of the land by the inhabitants has previously ceased.[6]

The Planning (Wales) Act 2015 amends the CA 2006 in relation to town and village greens located in Wales.

Town and village greens do not consist only of open areas of grassland; they may also consist of a lake, woodland or even a beach. See, for example, *R (Newhaven Port and Properties Ltd) v East Sussex County Council and Another*.[7]

175.1 First registration of a town or village green

In addition to the usual documents required,[8] an applicant should deliver to HMLR a copy of the entries in the register of common land, town greens and village greens.

Where there is a discrepancy between the town or village green's ownership register and the deeds, this must be accounted for. Registration as owner under the CRA 1965 or CA 2006 is not conclusive proof of ownership; the applicant must provide HMLR with evidence of his title in the normal way. An exception to this is where the land has been vested in a local authority under s 8 as mentioned above.

175.2 Dispositions of a registered town or village green

A transfer, lease or other disposition of a registered town or village green must, where appropriate, be completed by registration in the normal way.

---

1 CRA 1965, s 1(2) and Commons Registration (Time Limits) Order 1966 (SI 1966/1470).

2 CRA 1965, s 22(1)(b).

3 CRA 1965, s 12 and Commons Registration (England) Regulations 2014 (SI 2014/3038), reg 47.

4 CRA 1965, s 11 and CA 2006, s 5.

5 CA 2006, s 15(2).

6 CA 2006, s 15(3) and (4).
7 [2013] EWCA Civ 276.
8 See 68.4 Application for first registration.

176 TRANSFERS

A transfer of a registered estate must be in forms TP1, TP2, TR1, TR2, TR5, AS1 or AS3, as appropriate, unless it is effected by an electronic document to which LRA 2002, s 91 applies.[1] Forms AS1 and AS3 are transfers by way of assent.[2]

Form TP1 is a transfer of part of the registered estate comprised within one or more registered titles and form TP2 is a similar transfer by the proprietor of a registered charge under power of sale. Form TR1 is a transfer of the whole of one or more registered titles and form TR2 is a similar transfer by the proprietor of a registered charge under the power of sale. Form TR5 is a transfer of a portfolio of titles, comprising the whole or part of the registered estate comprised within each of the titles in the portfolio.

A transfer of a registered charge must be in form TR4 or form AS2, as appropriate.[3] Form TR4 is a transfer of a charge or portfolio of charges.[4] Form AS2 is a transfer by way of assent.[5]

A transfer affecting two or more registered titles may, on the written request of the applicant, be registered as to some or only one of the registered titles.[6] The applicant may later apply to have the transfer registered as to any other of the registered titles affected by it.[7]

A transfer of part of the land in a registered title must have attached to it a plan signed by the transferor and clearly identifying the land transferred.[8] If the land transferred is clearly identified on the title plan, it may instead be described by reference to the title plan.[9]

Where any registered estate is transferred wholly or partly in consideration of a transfer of another estate, it must still be effected by a transfer in one of the prescribed forms, such as form TR1 or form TP1, as appropriate.[10] A receipt for any equality money must be given in the receipt panel and the following provision must be included in the additional provisions panel:[11]

> This transfer is in consideration of a transfer [*or conveyance, or as appropriate)*] of [*brief description of property exchanged*] dated today [*if applicable and of the sum stated above paid for equality of exchange*].

If a transfer is made by way of exchange, a separate transfer should be used for each part of the exchange, with the 'receipt' and 'additional provisions' panels in each transfer being completed as appropriate.

In the case of a sale and sub-sale, a single form of transfer may be used, with the registered proprietor being the transferor and the sub-purchaser being the transferee. Details of the sub-vendor should be included in the 'additional provisions' panel in the transfer, along with any other relevant details or provisions as appropriate. However, if there is to be a specific transfer by the sub-vendor to the sub-purchaser, two separate transfers should be used.

If a transfer subject to a charge is being effected, the 'consideration' and 'additional provisions' panels in the transfer should be completed with the relevant details or provisions as appropriate, including any release by the chargee (who should be made a party to the transfer) and any covenant(s) in respect of the charge.

Where a transfer is made in connection with the transfer of an equitable share in the registered estate, the assignment of the share and the transfer of the legal estate may be effected by separate instruments. However, a single form of transfer to effect the whole transaction may be used, with the 'consideration' and 'additional provisions' panels in the transfer being completed with the relevant details or provisions as appropriate. HMLR will not cancel any existing Form A restriction in the register unless an application is made in form RX3 for its cancellation, accompanied by evidence lodged to satisfy HMLR that it is no longer required.[12] The wording of Form A is set out in Appendix IV.

A transfer of a registered estate must be registered and does not operate at law until the transferor or his successor in title is entered in the register as the proprietor.[13] In the case of a transfer of part of a registered estate, the following entries are also made in the registered title of the retained land:

(a) an entry in the property register referring to the removal of the estate comprised in the transfer;[14] and
(b) (where appropriate) entries relating to any rights, restrictive covenants, provisions, and other matters created by the transfer which are capable of being so entered.[15] However, HMLR need make no such entries where the relevant title numbers have not been given in panel 2 of the form AP1, unless separate application is made in respect of them.[16]

Instead of making the entry referred to at (a) above, HMLR may make a new edition of the registered title out of which the transfer is made and, if it considers it desirable, it may allot a new title number to that title.[17]

Entries are also made in the new registered title and any other affected titles relating to any rights, restrictive covenants, provisions, and other matters created by the transfer which are capable of being so entered.[18] However, HMLR need make no such entries in any other affected titles where the relevant title numbers have not been given in panel 2 of the form AP1, unless separate application is made in respect of them.[19]

In the case of a transfer of the whole of a registered estate, entries are made in the registered title and any other affected titles relating to any rights, restrictive covenants, provisions and other matters created by the transfer which are capable of being so entered.[20] However, HMLR need make no such entries in any other affected titles where the relevant title numbers have not been given in panel 2 of the form AP1, unless separate application is made in respect of them.[21]

A transfer of a registered leasehold estate in land which contains a legal apportionment of or exoneration from the rent reserved by the lease must include the following statement, with any necessary alterations and additions:[22]

> Liability for the payment of [*if applicable* the previously apportioned rent of [*amount*] being part of] the rent reserved by the registered lease is apportioned between the Transferor and the Transferee as follows –
>
> > [*amount*] shall be payable out of the Property and the balance shall be payable out of the land remaining in title number [*title number of retained land*];
> > the whole of that rent shall be payable out of the Property and none of it shall be payable out of the land remaining in title number [*title number of retained land*];
> > *or*
> > the whole of that rent shall be payable out of the land remaining in title number [*title number of retained land*] and none of it shall be payable out of the Property.

A person applying to register a transfer of a registered estate must provide information to HMLR in form DI about any of the overriding interests (subject to certain exceptions set out in LRR 2003, r 57(2) and including local land charges or public rights) set out in LRA 2002, Sch 3 that affect the estate to which the application relates and are within the actual knowledge of the applicant.[23] For details, see 128.4 Duty to disclose overriding interests. The applicant must produce to HMLR any documentary evidence of the interest which is under his control.[24] HMLR may enter a notice in the register in respect of any such interest.[25]

176.1 Registration of transfer

An applicant to register a transfer should deliver to HMLR:

(a) an application in form AP1;
(b) a transfer in the appropriate prescribed form;

(c) form DI giving the information of overriding interests required by LRR 2003, r 57, including any documentary evidence of the interest;[26]
(d) the appropriate confirmation or evidence of identity;[27]
(e) the appropriate SDLT and/or LTT certificate(s) or other evidence;[28] and
(f) the fee payable.[29]

176.2 Related topics

For:

(a) transfers under power of sale, see 100.10.1 Power of sale;
(b) transfers relating to mines and minerals, see 115.3 Transfer of mines and minerals out of a registered title;
(c) transfers to two or more proprietors, see 92 Joint Proprietors;
(d) implied covenants in transfers, see 85 Implied Covenants;
(e) HMLR forms in general, see 73 Forms.

---

1 LRR 2003, r 58.
2 See 17 Assents.
3 LRR 2003, r 116.
4 See 100.13 Transfer of charge.
5 See 17 Assents.
6 LRR 2003, r 56(1).
7 LRR 2003, r 56(2).
8 LRR 2003, r 213(1) and (2).
9 LRR 2003, r 213(4).
10 LRR 2003, r 59(1).
11 LRR 2003, r 59(2).
12 See 92.3 Cancellation of Form A restriction.
13 LRA 2002, s 27 and Sch 2.
14 LRR 2003, r 72(1).
15 LRR 2003, r 72(4).
16 LRR 2003, r 72(5).
17 LRR 2003, r 72(2).
18 LRR 2003, r 72(4).
19 LRR 2003, r 72(5).
20 LRR 2003, r 72C(2).
21 LRR 2003, r 72C(3).
22 LRR 2003, r 60(1).
23 LRR 2003, r 57(1).
24 LRR 2003, r 57(4).
25 LRR 2003, r 54(5).
26 See 128.4 Duty to disclose overriding interests.

27 See 84 Identity Evidence.
28 See 168 Stamp Duty Land Tax and/or 94 Land Transaction Tax.
29 See 67 Fees.

177 TRIBUNAL

LRA 2002, s 108(1) provides for the Tribunal to determine:

(a) objections referred to it under LRA 2002, s 73(7);[1] and
(b) appeals under LRA 2002, Sch 5, para 4 relating to e-conveyancing network access agreements.[2]

Also, the Tribunal may make any order which the High Court could make for the rectification or setting aside of a document which:

(a) effects a qualifying disposition of a registered estate or charge;
(b) is a contract to make such a disposition; or
(c) effects a transfer of an interest which is the subject of a notice in the register.[3]

For this purpose a 'qualifying disposition' is:

(a) a registrable disposition required to be completed by registration under LRA 2002, s 27; or
(b) a disposition which created an interest which may be the subject of a notice in the register.[4]

An application for such rectification or setting aside should be made direct to the Tribunal and not to HMLR. A successful applicant may apply to HMLR to update the register if the Tribunal makes such an order.[5]

The Tribunal is staffed by specialist judges versed in the field of land registration and property law. It deals with matters in accordance with the Tribunal Rules.

1 See 54 Disputes.
2 See 56 Electronic Services.
3 LRA 2002, s 108(2).
4 LRA 2002, s 108(3).
5 See 12 Alteration of the Register.

178 TRUSTS OF LAND

A 'trust of land' is any trust of property which consists of or includes land, except for settled land (as defined in the SLA 1925) and land to which the Universities and Colleges Estates Act 1925 applies.[1] This includes any description of trust, whether express, implied, resulting or constructive. It therefore includes a bare trust or a trust for sale, but not a settlement under the SLA 1925. 'Land' for this purpose includes an undivided share in land.

Where a sole owner of land holds both the legal estate (in the case of registered land, the registered title) and the underlying equitable or beneficial interest, the legal estate and equitable interest are merged and there is no trust of land. The essential characteristic of a trust of land is that the legal estate to the land is separated from the equitable interest, with the legal estate being vested in the trustee(s) and the equitable interest being vested in the beneficiary or beneficiaries. A trust of land may:

(a) be expressly created in writing;[2]
(b) be a 'bare trust' arising where the trustee is merely the nominee for a beneficiary of full age;[3]
(c) arise by operation of law as an implied, resulting or constructive trust (for example where the proprietor has purchased the land using funds provided by a third party);[4] or
(d) arise by operation of law as a statutory trust (for example the statutory trust automatically imposed by LPA 1925, ss 34 and 36 where two or more persons own land jointly, so that they hold the legal estate on a trust of land even if they are holding the equitable interest on trust for themselves).[5]

A trust of land may therefore exist where the trustees are holding on trust:

(a) for themselves only;
(b) for themselves and a third party; or
(c) for a third party only.

The legal estate can never be severed and can only be held by two or more persons as beneficial joint tenants.[6] Upon the death of one of the trustees, the legal estate will pass by 'survivorship' and vest automatically in the surviving trustee(s) (or in the personal representative of a deceased sole or sole surviving trustee), regardless of the devolution of the equitable interest.[7]

Land which is held on a trust of land should be vested in the trustees. In relation to registered land, the register records the ownership of the legal estate, not the beneficial interests. HMLR is not affected with notice of a trust.[8]

It is not possible to enter a notice in the register to protect an interest under a trust of land.[9] The trustees should apply for the entry of appropriate restrictions to reflect any limitations on their powers of disposition contained in the trust deed.

178.1 Registration of trustees

There are no prescribed forms specifically for dispositions to trustees; the standard forms prescribed in LRR 2003, Sch 1 must be used where the title is already registered.[10] In the case of the grant of a lease out of a registered estate, this should where necessary be in the form of a prescribed clauses lease.[11]

As with unregistered land, the number of trustees of a private trust of registered land cannot exceed four; if more than four are named, only the first four named who are able and willing to act will be registered as proprietors.[12] This limitation does not apply to charitable trusts.[13]

The appropriate panel of the transfer, assent, prescribed clauses lease or (where the application is for first registration) of form FR1 should make clear the basis upon which the applicants are holding the land on trust. Alternatively, the applicants may use form JO. If this is not done, HMLR may have to enter a restriction in Form A by default in pursuance of its obligation under LRA 2002, s 44(1).[14] The wording of Form A is set out in Appendix IV.

178.2 Entry of restrictions

A person dealing with a registered proprietor can assume that he has unlimited power to dispose of the registered estate or registered charge concerned, free from any limitation affecting the validity of the disposition, unless there is a restriction or other entry in the register limiting his powers, or a limitation imposed by or under the LRA 2002.[15] In the context of a trust of land, this means that, if two or more people are registered as joint proprietors, a purchaser can safely acquire the legal estate from them, or from the survivor of them, unless there is a restriction or other entry to the contrary in the register.

A restriction does not confer any priority. However, it prevents an entry being made in the register relating to any disposition, or a disposition of a specified kind, unless the terms of the restriction have (where applicable) been complied with.

In the case of a private trust (i.e. one not for charitable, ecclesiastical or public purposes), it is the duty of the trustees to apply for any necessary restriction(s), although a beneficiary may also apply.[16] HMLR must enter a restriction without application in only one circumstance, though it may do so in certain other cases if it appears to be necessary or desirable.

If HMLR enters two or more registered proprietors of a registered estate in land, it must enter a Form A restriction where the survivor of them will not be able to give a valid receipt for capital money.[17] In the case of other registered estates, the proprietor(s) should make an application for entry of such a restriction.[18]

HMLR will not enter a restriction in Form A in respect of a registered charge, because although a charge can be held on trust, the survivor of the registered chargees is always able to give a valid receipt for the money secured by it.[19]

When a trust corporation applies to be registered as sole proprietor of an estate, which it holds on trust, it must apply for a Form A restriction. Although it will be able to give a valid receipt for capital money arising on a disposition, the restriction is needed in case the proprietor ceases to be a trust corporation at any time, or is replaced by another trustee.

LPA 1925, s 27(2) does not affect the right of a sole personal representative *acting as such* to give a valid receipt for capital money. Therefore, HMLR will not automatically enter a restriction in Form A when registering a personal representative as proprietor of a registered estate. However, any existing such restriction will remain in the register because, in that case, the personal representative will be succeeding the deceased as trustee of the trust. For the same reason, HMLR will enter a restriction in Form A on first registration when registering the personal representative of a deceased proprietor who was a sole trustee or (unless he was the survivor of beneficial joint tenants) the last surviving trustee.

Where a registered estate becomes subject to a trust of land, other than on a registrable disposition, or where the estate is held on a trust of land and there is a change in the trusts, and a sole or last surviving trustee will not be able to give a valid receipt for capital money, the registered proprietor must apply for entry of a restriction in Form A.[20] Where there are two or more people registered as proprietor of the estate, an application by one or more of them satisfies the obligation to apply for entry of the restriction.[21] If such an application is not made, any person who has an interest under the trust of land has a sufficient interest to apply for the restriction in Form A.[22] An applicant should deliver to HMLR the usual documents required.[23]

No fee is currently payable where the application is for a Form A restriction only.

Where the applicant is a person who has an interest under a trust of land, the statement in panel 12 or conveyancer's certificate in panel 13 of form RX1 should be completed on the following lines:

> The interest is that specified in rule 93(a) of the Land Registration Rules 2003 (SI 2003/1417), the applicant being a person who has an interest in the registered estate held under a trust of land as a result of [*set out relevant details*].

Panel 9 should set out the restriction in Form A. A restriction in Form A in LRR 2003, Sch 4 does not require the approval of HMLR to the wording of the restriction under LRA 2002, s 43(3).

HMLR must give notice of the application for a restriction to the proprietor of the registered estate concerned if it has not been made by or with his consent or a person entitled to be registered as such proprietor.[24]

Where the trust imposes limitations on the powers of the trustees under TLATA 1996, s 8 (for example the requirement to obtain a consent before effecting any sale), the registered proprietors must apply for entry of a restriction in Form B.[25] The wording of Form B is set out in Appendix IV. This does not apply if the land is held on charitable, ecclesiastical or public trusts,[26] but does apply where the legal estate is vested in the personal representatives of a sole or last surviving trustee.[27] Where there are two or more persons registered as proprietor of the estate, an application by one or more of them satisfies the obligation to apply for entry of the restriction.[28] If such an application is not made, any person who has an interest under the trust of land where the powers of the trustees are limited under TLATA 1996, s 8 has a sufficient interest to apply for entry of the restriction in Form B.[29] An applicant should deliver to HMLR the usual documents required.[30]

Where the applicant is a person who has an interest under a trust of land, the statement in panel 12 or conveyancer's certificate in panel 13 of form RX1 should be completed on the following lines:

> The interest is that specified in rule 93(c) of the Land Registration Rules 2003 (SI 2003/1417), the applicant being a person who has an interest in the registered estate held under a trust of land where the powers of the trustees are limited by section 8 of the Trusts of Land and Appointment of Trustees Act 1996.

Panel 9 should set out the restriction in Form B.

A restriction in Form B in LRR 2003, Sch 4 does not require the approval of HMLR to the wording of the restriction under LRA 2002, s 43(3).

HMLR must give notice of the application for a restriction to the proprietor of the registered estate concerned if it has not been made by or with his consent or a person entitled to be registered as such proprietor.[31]

Where personal representatives hold a registered estate on a trust of land created by the deceased's will, or on a trust of land arising under the laws of intestacy which is subsequently varied, and their powers have been limited by TLATA 1996, s 8, they must apply for entry of a restriction in Form C.[32] The wording of Form C is set out in Appendix IV. Where there are two or more personal representatives of a deceased proprietor, an application by one or more of them satisfies the obligation to apply for entry of the restriction.[33] If such an application is not made, any person who has an interest in the due administration of the estate has a sufficient interest to apply for entry of a restriction in Form C.[34] An applicant should deliver to HMLR the usual documents required.[35]

Where the applicant is a person who has an interest in the due administration of the deceased's estate, the statement in panel 12 or conveyancer's certificate in panel 13 of form RX1 should be completed on the following lines:

> The interest is that specified in rule 93(d) of the Land Registration Rules 2003 (SI 2003/1417), the applicant being a person interested in the due administration of the estate of [*name*] deceased.

Panel 9 of form RX1 should set out the restriction in Form C.

A restriction in Form C does not require the approval of HMLR to the wording of the restriction under LRA 2002, s 43(3).

HMLR must give notice of the application for a restriction to the proprietor of the registered estate concerned if it has not been made by or with his consent or a person entitled to be registered as such proprietor.[36]

TLATA 1996, s 6(6) provides that the powers of an absolute owner of land conferred by that section shall not be exercised in contravention of, or of any order made in pursuance of, any other enactment or any rule of law or equity. TLATA 1996, s 6(8) provides that where any enactment other than that section confers on trustees authority to act subject to any restriction, limitation or condition, trustees of land may not exercise the powers conferred by that section to do any act which they are prevented from doing under the other enactment by reason of the restriction, limitation or condition. Any person who has a sufficient interest in preventing a contravention of TLATA 1996, s 6(6) or (8) has a sufficient interest to apply for a restriction to prevent such a contravention.[37]

178.3 Dispositions by trustees

There are no prescribed forms specifically for dispositions to trustees; the standard forms prescribed in LRR 2003, Sch 1 must be used where the title is already registered.[38] In the case of the grant of a lease out of a registered estate, this should where necessary be in the form of a prescribed clauses lease.[39]

Any restriction(s) in the register will, where necessary, need to be complied with before HMLR can register a disposition by the trustees. In the case of a restriction in Form A, where capital money arises as a result of the disposition and a sole or sole surviving trustee (not being a trust corporation) cannot give a valid receipt, at least one new co-trustee will need to be appointed to join in the disposition. The appointment may be effected within the form of disposition, such as a transfer, or by separate deed. In the case of a restriction in Form B, the appropriate certificate, statutory declaration or statement of truth will need to be provided.

In certain circumstances, an existing restriction may be cancelled automatically following completion of a disposition by registration. For example, HMLR will cancel a restriction in Form A on registration of a transfer on sale by two or more trustees or a trust corporation (except where the transfer is to one or more of the existing proprietors) under LRR 2003, r 99. A restriction in Form B will be cancelled on registration of a transfer on sale by the trustees when the appropriate certificate, statutory declaration or statement of truth has been provided. In other cases, application may be made to cancel a restriction where appropriate. The application should be made in form RX3, accompanied by evidence to satisfy HMLR that the restriction is no longer required. If HMLR is so satisfied, it must cancel the restriction.[40]

178.4 Powers of attorney granted by trustees

There are several statutory provisions enabling trustees to delegate their functions, individually or collectively.[41] Under TLATA 1996, s 9, the trustees, acting jointly, can delegate their functions to a beneficiary or beneficiaries by means of a power of attorney. But the attorneys cannot give a valid receipt for capital money, even if they are two or more.[42] If capital money arises on a disposition, the trustees (or their individual attorneys appointed under Trustee Act 1925, s 25) will therefore have to execute the deed to give the receipt. However, an attorney under TLATA 1996, s 9 can execute a disposition under which no capital money arises.

178.5 Vesting of registered land in new trustees

It is important that the names and addresses for service of trustees in the register are kept up to date and that any change of trustees is reflected in the register. An appointment of a new trustee will not be effective to vest the registered title in the new and any continuing trustees until it has been completed by registration. There are several methods of effecting the appointment and discharge of trustees of land.

Where new trustees have been appointed in place of existing trustees, the simplest course is to proceed by way of a transfer in form TR1 from the registered proprietors to the new trustees. The additional provisions panel of the transfer should include a statement that the transfer is made for the purpose of giving effect to the appointment of new trustees. The legal estate passes to the new trustees only when they are registered as proprietors.[43]

Where a deed of appointment or retirement of trustees has an express or implied vesting declaration to which Trustee Act 1925, s 40 applies, an application may be made to register this disposition by operation of law without executing a transfer.[44] This might be appropriate, for example, where a person other than the existing registered proprietors has the power of appointing new trustees. The limitations on using this procedure in respect of charges and leases requiring a consent to alienation should be noted.[45] An applicant to register such a disposition should deliver to HMLR:

(a) an application in form AP1;
(b) the deed of appointment or retirement or a certified copy of it;
(c) a certificate from the conveyancer acting for the persons making the appointment or effecting the retirement that they are entitled to do so, or other evidence to satisfy HMLR that the persons making the appointment or effecting the retirement are entitled to do so;[46]
(d) form DI giving the information of overriding interests required by LRR 2003, r 57, including any documentary evidence of the interest;[47]
(e) the appropriate confirmation or evidence of identity;[48]
(f) the appropriate SDLT and/or LTT certificate(s) or other evidence;[49] and
(g) the fee payable.[50]

Under Trustee Act 1925, s 41, the court may by vesting order appoint a new trustee. Where it relates to a registered estate, such an order must be completed by registration.[51] Where the court has made a vesting order an applicant should deliver to HMLR:

(a) an application in form AP1;
(b) the vesting order[52] or a certified copy of it;
(c) form DI giving the information of overriding interests required by LRR 2003, r 57, including any documentary evidence of the interest;[53]
(d) the appropriate confirmation or evidence of identity;[54]
(e) the appropriate SDLT and/or LTT certificate(s) or other evidence;[55] and
(f) the fee payable.[56]

In certain cases where trustees may be appointed or discharged by resolution of a meeting of the trustees or other persons, for example under Trade Union and Labour Relations (Consolidation) Act 1992, ss 13 and 129, a vesting declaration is implied by statute in the memorandum or written record of the resolution. If the trust property is a registered estate or a registered charge, this declaration must be completed by registration.[57] The existing registered proprietors may execute a transfer to the new and any continuing trustees.[58] Alternatively, application may be made to register the implied vesting declaration itself, which should accompany the application.

Where an implied vesting declaration has arisen, an applicant should deliver to HMLR:

(a) an application in form AP1;
(b) a certified copy of the memorandum or resolution and evidence of the provision under which it operates to vest the estate in the trustees;[59]
(c) form DI giving the information of overriding interests required by LRR 2003, r 57, including any documentary evidence of the interest;[60]
(d) the appropriate confirmation or evidence of identity;[61]
(e) the appropriate SDLT and/or LTT certificate(s) or other evidence;[62] and
(f) the fee payable.[63]

In the case of unregistered land, the appointment of a new trustee may be a 'trigger' for compulsory first registration.[64]

When a trustee has died, an application to remove his name from the register, or an application to register a disposition by the remaining trustees, should be accompanied by evidence of the death.[65]

---

1 TLATA 1996, s 1.
2 LPA 1925, s 53(1)(b).
3 See 20 Bare Trusts.
4 See 39 Constructive and Resulting Trusts.
5 See 92 Joint Proprietors.
6 LPA 1925, ss 1(6) and 34.
7 See 92.2 Death of a joint proprietor.
8 LRA 2002, s 78.
9 LRA 2002, s 33(a).
10 See 17 Assents and 176 Transfers.
11 See 98.6 Prescribed clauses leases.
12 Trustee Act 1925, s 34(2).
13 See 30 Charities.
14 See 178.2 Entry of restrictions.
15 LRA 2002, s 26.

16 LRR 2003, rr 94(1) to (5) and 93(a) to (d).
17 LRA 2002, s 44(1).
18 LRR 2003, r 94(2A).
19 LRA 2002, s 56.
20 LRR 2003, r 94(1) and (2).
21 LRR 2003, r 93(9).
22 LRR 2003, r 93(a).
23 See 153.1 Application for entry of restriction.
24 LRA 2002, s 45.
25 LRR 2003, r 94(4).
26 LRR 2003, r 94(6).
27 LRR 2003, r 94(7).
28 LRR 2003, r 94(9).
29 LRR 2003, r 93(c).
30 See 153.1 Application for entry of restriction.
31 LRA 2002, s 45.
32 LRR 2003, r 94(3).
33 LRR 2003, r 94(9).
34 LRR 2003, r 93(d).
35 See 153.1 Application for entry of restriction.
36 LRA 2002, s 45.
37 LRR 2003, r 93(b).
38 See 17 Assents and 176 Transfers.
39 See 98.6 Prescribed clauses leases.
40 LRR 2003, r 97. See 153.8 Cancellation of a restriction.
41 See 136.6 Powers of attorney by joint proprietors and other trustees.
42 TLATA 1996, s 9(7).
43 LRA 2002, s 27. See 176 Transfers.
44 LRA 2002, s 27(5).
45 Trustee Act, s 40(4).
46 LRR 2003, r 161(3).
47 See 128.4 Duty to disclose overriding interests.
48 See 84 Identity Evidence.
49 See 168 Stamp Duty Land Tax and/or 94 Land Transaction Tax.
50 See 67 Fees.
51 LRA 2002, s 27(5).
52 LRR 2003, r 161(2).
53 See 128.4 Duty to disclose overriding interests.
54 See 84 Identity Evidence.
55 See 168 Stamp Duty Land Tax and/or 94 Land Transaction Tax.
56 See 67 Fees.
57 LRA 2002, s 27(5).
58 See 176 Transfers.
59 LRR 2003, r 161(1).
60 See 128.4 Duty to disclose overriding interests.
61 See 84 Identity Evidence.

62 See 168 Stamp Duty Land Tax and/or 94 Land Transaction Tax.
63 See 67 Fees.
64 See 68.2 Compulsory first registration.
65 LRR 2003, r 164.

179 UNINCORPORATED ASSOCIATIONS

An unincorporated association consists of a group of individuals who have come together to achieve some common purpose, such as clubs, societies (including unincorporated friendly societies) and trade unions. In general, there are three types of unincorporated association: partnerships formed for profit; not for profit associations which are not (or not exclusively) charitable; and associations formed for charitable purposes. Unlike corporate bodies, unincorporated associations do not have their own legal personality. Therefore they cannot be registered in their own right as the proprietor of registered land. Instead, where an unincorporated association holds land, the legal estate must be vested in trustees, or a trust corporation, in trust for the members of the association. For the position where an unincorporated association is a charity, see 30 Charities.

179.1 Registration of trustees

A transfer or charge to an unincorporated association must be to the names of the individual members, not to the association itself. If there are more than four members and the unincorporated association is not a charity, the transfer should be to four of them to hold the legal estate on trust for all the members of the association. The names of the trustees in the proprietorship register may be followed by an appropriate description such as: 'the trustees of [*name of unincorporated association*]'.

As a sole trustee or the survivor of two or more trustees (unless a trust corporation) will be unable to give a valid receipt for capital money, entry of a restriction in Form A will be required, and if necessary should be applied for. The wording of Form A is set out in Appendix IV. In the case of a registered estate in land, HMLR will, when entering joint proprietors, enter a restriction in Form A in the proprietorship register in accordance with its obligation under LRA 2002, s 44(1). In the case of other registered estates, the proprietor(s) should make an application for entry of such a restriction.[1]

If no other restriction is entered, the proprietors' powers of disposition are taken, in favour of any disponee, as being free from any limitation affecting the validity of a disposition.[2] Therefore, the trustees should consider applying for any further restriction which may be necessary, such as one to ensure compliance with club rules. For example, they may apply for a restriction in Form R. The wording of Form R is set out in Appendix IV.

If the rules of the association contain any limitation on the trustees' powers of disposition, they should apply for entry of a restriction in Form B.[3] The wording of Form B is set out in Appendix IV.

For further details, see 178.2 Entry of restrictions.

179.2 Dispositions by trustees

The trustees shown in the register as proprietors must execute any disposition by the trustees of an unincorporated association. If any of them have died, evidence of death must be lodged and the survivor(s) must execute the deed and comply with the terms of any restriction in the register.

179.3 Change of trustees

The normal rules on the appointment, retirement or removal of trustees apply to the trustees of an unincorporated association. For the position where the registered estate is to be vested in new trustees of an unincorporated association, see 178.5 Vesting of registered land in new trustees.

---

1 LRR 2003, r 94(2A).
2 LRA 2002, s 26.
3 TLATA, s 8(2) and LRR 2003, r 94(4).

180 UNITED KINGDOM ECONOMIC INTEREST GROUPINGS

On 31 December 2020 any existing UK-registered EEIG automatically converted to a UKEIG.[1] All UKEIGs were formerly an EEIG. It is not possible to register any new UKEIG.

A UKEIG is a corporate body.[2] It must have at least two members based in different countries, either:

(a) from two different EU member states; or
(b) one from an EU member state and one from the United Kingdom.[3]

A UKEIG's official address must be in the United Kingdom.

Following automatic conversion, Companies House will have amended the EEIG's suffix to UKEIG and issued a certificate of conversion to the UKEIG. If the entity remains registered as proprietor of an estate or legal charge in its former name, it may apply to update the register.[4] In addition to the usual documents required,[5] the applicant should deliver to HMLR a certified copy of the certificate of conversion.

Only the manager (or, where there are two or more, each of the managers) may represent the UKEIG in respect of dealings with third parties. Where the manager is not a natural person, it must designate one or more natural persons to represent it.[6] Accordingly, execution of a deed by a UKEIG should be on the following lines:

> Signed as a deed by [*name of manager*] the [sole] *or* [joint] [representative of the] manager(s) of [*name of UKEIG*] in the presence of …

An application to register a UKEIG as the proprietor of a registered estate or of a registered charge should be supported by the usual documentation, accompanied by:

(a) the result of a recent search at Companies House against the UKEIG together with all forms and documents submitted by it;
(b) evidence of appointment of the manager (if this is not clear from the other documents lodged); and
(c) the certificate of conversion to a UKEIG issued by Companies House.

Given the nature of a UKEIG and the restrictions on its powers contained in Council Regulation (EEC) No 2137/85 and the European Economic Interest Grouping Regulations 1989 (as amended by the European Economic Interest Grouping (Amendment) (EU Exit) Regulations 2018 (SI 2018/1299)), it may apply for a restriction on the following lines, if required, using form RX1:

> No disposition of the [registered estate] *or* [registered charge dated [*date*]] by the proprietor of [the registered estate] *or* [that registered charge] is to be completed by registration without a certificate signed by the conveyancer to [*name of UKEIG*] that the manager or managers or its representative who has or have executed the deed, has or have been duly appointed and has or have the power to bind the proprietor; that the proprietor is not in receivership or administrative receivership and has not been wound up or dissolved and generally that the provisions of Council Regulation (EEC) No 2137/85 and the European Economic Interest Grouping Regulations 1989 (SI 1989/638) (as amended by the European Economic Interest Grouping (Amendment) (EU Exit) Regulations 2018 (SI 2018/1299)) have been complied with.

Where the UKEIG does not have an indefinite duration, it may also apply for a restriction on the following lines, if required, using form RX1:[7]

> No disposition by the proprietor of the [registered estate] *or* [registered charge dated [*date*]] completed on or after [*date when duration of UKEIG ceases*] is to be completed by registration unless its conveyancer has certified that the duration of the proprietor has been extended and that it remained a body corporate on the date of such disposition.

All deeds completed by a UKEIG must indicate legibly:

(a) the name of the grouping preceded or followed either by the words 'UK Economic Interest Grouping' or by the initials 'UKEIG', unless those words or initials already occur in the name; and
(b) the grouping's official address.[8]

IA 1986, Pts III[9] and V[10] apply to UKEIGs as if they were companies registered under the Companies Act 2006. A receiver or manager or administrative receiver may be appointed, but not an administrator. The matters set out under 4 Administrative Receivers, 108 Liquidators and 146 Receivers Appointed under the Law of Property Act 1925, therefore apply. At the end of 3 months from the date of receipt by the companies registry of a notice of the conclusion of the liquidation of a UKEIG, the UKEIG is dissolved.[11]

---

1 European Economic Interest Grouping (Amendment) (EU Exit) Regulations 2018 (SI 2018/1299). For further details about EEIGs, see 65 European Economic Interest Groupings.

2 Council Regulation (EEC) No 2137/85, art 1 as amended by European Economic Interest Grouping (Amendment) (EU Exit) Regulations 2018 (SI 2018/1299), reg 33.

3 Council Regulation (EEC) No 2137/85, art 4(2) as amended by European Economic Interest Grouping (Amendment) (EU Exit) Regulations 2018 (SI 2018/1299), reg 37.

4 Although this is not strictly necessary due to Council Regulation (EEC) No 2137/85, art 1A(3) as amended by European Economic Interest Grouping (Amendment) (EU Exit) Regulations 2018 (SI 2018/1299), reg 34.

5 See 28.2 Change of name of corporate bodies.

6 European Economic Grouping Regulations 1989 (SI 1989/638), reg 5(1).

7 See 153.1 Application for entry of restriction.

8 Council Regulation (EEC) No 2137/85, art 25 as amended by European Economic Interest Grouping (Amendment) (EU Exit) Regulations 2018 (SI 2018/1299), reg 51.

9 EEIG Regulations 1989, reg 19(1).

10 EEIG Regulations 1989, reg 8(1).

11 EEIG Regulations 1989, reg 8(2).

181 UPGRADE OF CLASS OF TITLE

Where a registered estate has been awarded a class of title which is less than absolute, an application to upgrade it may be made under LRA 2002, s 62. For the classes of title which may be granted in relation to registered titles, see 32 Classes of Title. HMLR has power to upgrade the class of title where it is satisfied as to the title, applying the same standards as on an application for first registration.[1] This usually means that the defect that resulted in the grant of the particular class of title on first registration has been remedied. Before approving an application for upgrading, HMLR may require the production of further documents or evidence, or serve such notices, as it considers necessary or desirable.[2]

An application for upgrading of title must be made in form UT1.[3] The applicant must state the class of title to which he is applying for the title to be upgraded and also state in what capacity he is entitled to apply for upgrading of title. Confirmation must be given that no claim adverse to the title of the proprietor has been made by virtue of an estate, right or interest whose enforceability is preserved by virtue of the existing entry about the class of title.

HMLR may upgrade a possessory freehold title to absolute freehold if satisfied as to the title to the estate.[4] It may upgrade a possessory leasehold title to good leasehold if satisfied as to the title to the estate or to absolute leasehold if satisfied both as to the title to the estate and as to the superior title.[5] The applicant must lodge evidence of title to overcome the defect which caused the possessory class of title to be granted in the first place.[6] For example, where lost pre-registration title deeds subsequently come to light after first registration has taken place.

HMLR may also upgrade a possessory freehold title to absolute where (in the case of a freehold estate in land) the estate has been registered with possessory title for a period of at least 12 years.[7] It may upgrade a possessory leasehold title to good leasehold where (in the case of a leasehold estate in land) the estate has been registered with possessory title for a period of at least 12 years.[8] A proprietor is in possession if the land is physically in his possession, or in that of a person who is entitled to be registered as the proprietor of the registered estate. Land in the possession of a tenant is treated as being in the possession of the landlord. Land in the possession of a mortgagee is treated as being in the possession of the mortgagor. Land in the possession of a licensee is treated as being in the possession of the licensor. Land in the possession of a beneficiary is treated as being in the possession of the trustee.[9]

HMLR may upgrade a good leasehold title to absolute if it is satisfied as to the superior title.[10] The applicant must lodge evidence to establish that the landlord had power to grant the lease.[11]

HMLR may upgrade a qualified freehold title to absolute freehold if satisfied as to the title to the estate.[12] HMLR may upgrade a qualified leasehold title to good leasehold if satisfied as to the title to the estate or to absolute leasehold if satisfied both as to the title to the estate and as to the superior title.[13] The applicant must lodge documentary evidence to satisfy HMLR as to the title.

An application to upgrade the class of title of a registered estate may be made only by:

(a) the proprietor of that estate;
(b) a person entitled to be registered as proprietor;
(c) the proprietor of a registered charge affecting that estate; or
(d) a person interested in a registered estate which derives from that estate.[14]

None of the powers to upgrade the title in LRA 2002, s 62 is exercisable if there is outstanding any claim adverse to the title of the registered proprietor which is made by virtue of an estate, right or interest the enforceability of which is preserved by virtue of the existing entry about the class of title.[15] For the effect of a caution against conversion registered under the Land Registration Rules 1925, see 23 Cautions Against Conversion.

Where a registered freehold or leasehold estate is upgraded to absolute, the proprietor ceases to hold the estate subject to any estate, right or interest the enforceability of which was preserved by virtue of the previous entry about the class of title. This also applies where the title is upgraded to good leasehold, except that then the upgrading does not affect or prejudice the enforcement of any estate, right or interest affecting, or in derogation of, the title of the landlord to grant the lease.[16]

181.1 Upgrading possessory or qualified freehold to absolute

An applicant should deliver to HMLR:

(a) an application in form UT1;
(b) documentary evidence to satisfy HMLR as to the title[17] (this is not required where the title to a registered estate in freehold land has been registered as possessory for at least 12 years and panel 10 of form UT1 has been completed to show the proprietor is in possession);
(c) where the application is by a person entitled to be registered as the proprietor of the estate sought to be upgraded, evidence of that entitlement;[18]

(d) where the application is by a person interested in a registered estate which derives from the estate sought to be upgraded, evidence of the applicant's interest where this is not apparent from the register (panel 9 of form UT1 must also be completed with details of the interest claimed);[19] and
(e) the fee payable.[20]

181.2 Upgrading possessory or qualified leasehold to good leasehold

An applicant should deliver to HMLR:

(a) an application in form UT1;
(b) documentary evidence to satisfy HMLR as to the title[21] (this is not required where the title to a registered estate in leasehold land has been registered as possessory for at least 12 years and panel 10 of form UT1 has been completed to show the proprietor is in possession);
(c) where the application is by a person entitled to be registered as the proprietor of the estate sought to be upgraded, evidence of that entitlement;[22]
(d) where the application is by a person interested in a registered estate which derives from the estate sought to be upgraded, evidence of the applicant's interest where this is not apparent from the register (panel 9 of form UT1 must also be completed with details of the interest claimed);[23] and
(e) the fee payable.[24]

181.3 Upgrading good leasehold to absolute

An applicant should deliver to HMLR:

(a) an application in form UT1;
(b) documentary evidence to satisfy HMLR as to any superior title which is not registered;[25]
(c) where any superior title is registered with possessory, qualified or good leasehold title, documentary evidence to satisfy HMLR that that title qualifies for upgrading to absolute title;[26]
(d) evidence of any consent to the grant of the lease required from any chargee of any superior title and any superior landlord;[27]
(e) where the application is by a person entitled to be registered as the proprietor of the estate sought to be upgraded, evidence of that entitlement;[28]
(f) where the application is by a person interested in a registered estate which derives from the estate sought to be upgraded, evidence of the applicant's interest where this is not apparent from the register (panel 9 of form UT1 must also be completed with details of the interest claimed);[29] and
(g) the fee payable.[30]

No fee is currently payable where the application is accompanied by an application upon which a scale fee is payable. Since the effect of registration with an absolute title is to confer an absolute title to any easements granted in the lease, the title of the landlord to grant the easements should also be shown. Where HMLR is not satisfied on this point, it may make an entry in the register excluding the easement concerned from the registration.

181.4 Upgrading possessory or qualified leasehold to absolute

An applicant should deliver to HMLR:

(a) an application in form UT1;
(b) documentary evidence to satisfy HMLR as to the title to the estate sought to be upgraded (this is not required where the title to a registered estate in land has been registered as possessory for at least 12 years and panel 10 of form UT1 has been completed to show the proprietor is in possession);
(c) documentary evidence to satisfy HMLR as to any superior title which is not registered;
(d) where any superior title is registered with possessory, qualified or good leasehold title, documentary evidence to satisfy HMLR that that title qualifies for upgrading to absolute title;
(e) evidence of any consent to the grant of the lease required from any chargee of any superior title and any superior landlord;[31]
(f) where the application is by a person entitled to be registered as the proprietor of the estate sought to be upgraded, evidence of that entitlement;[32]
(g) where the application is by a person interested in a registered estate which derives from the estate sought to be upgraded, evidence of the applicant's interest where this is not apparent from the register (panel 9 of form UT1 must also be completed with details of the interest claimed);[33] and
(h) the fee payable.[34]

Since the effect of registration with an absolute title is to confer an absolute title to any easements granted in the lease, the title of the landlord to grant the easements should also be shown. Where HMLR is not satisfied on this point, it may make an entry in the register excluding the easement concerned from the registration.

---

1 LRA 2002, s 62(8).
2 LRR 2003, r 17.
3 LRR 2003, r 124(1).
4 LRA 2002, s 62(1).
5 LRA 2002, s 62(3).

6 LRR 2003, r 124(1) and (4).
7 LRA 2002, s 62(4).
8 LRA 2002, s 62(5).
9 LRA 2002, s 131.
10 LRA 2002, s 62(2).
11 LRR 2003, r 124(3).
12 LRA 2002, s 62(1).
13 LRA 2002, s 62(3).
14 LRA 2002, s 62(7).
15 LRA 2002, s 62(6).
16 LRA 2002, s 63.
17 LRR 2003, r 124(2).
18 LRR 2003, r 124(5).
19 LRR 2003, r 124(6).
20 See 67 Fees.
21 LRR 2003, r 124(2).
22 LRR 2003, r 124(5).
23 LRR 2003, r 124(6).
24 See 67 Fees.
25 LRR 2003, r 124(3)(a).
26 LRR 2003, r 124(3)(b).
27 LRR 2003, r 124(3)(c).
28 LRR 2003, r 124(5).
29 LRR 2003, r 124(6).
30 See 67 Fees.
31 LRR 2003, r 124(4).
32 LRR 2003, r 124(5).
33 LRR 2003, r 124(6).
34 See 67 Fees.

182 VENDOR'S LIENS

A vendor's lien arises when a binding contract for sale of the land is made, and subsists until the purchase money is paid. It can continue even though the vendor has executed a transfer of the land and given possession to the purchaser. If the vendor has agreed that he will take some other form of security for the purchase money, then the lien does not arise.

A vendor's lien is a type of equitable charge which arises automatically by operation of law. It gives the vendor the right to apply to court for an order for sale under which he will be paid the money due.[1]

If a registrable disposition of a registered estate is made for valuable consideration, completion of the disposition by registration has the effect of postponing to the interest under the disposition any interest affecting the estate immediately before the disposition the priority of which is not protected at the time of registration.[2] A vendor's lien is an interest affecting the estate *before* the transfer (as it arises on creation of the contract). Consequently, on registration of the transfer the purchaser of the registered estate takes free of the vendor's lien unless the vendor has already protected the lien before registration of the transfer. In that event, although the purchaser will still be obliged to honour his contractual obligations under the contract and the vendor may be able to sue the purchaser for the unpaid amount, if the purchaser does not pay him, the vendor cannot request the court to order that the property be sold to repay him. The vendor should therefore protect his lien by entering an agreed notice or a unilateral notice against his own title before completing the transfer.

If the vendor's lien has arisen on a sale of unregistered land, HMLR will, if it is apparent from its examination of the title that the lien has arisen, enter a notice of it in the register.[3]

If the vendor remains in actual occupation of the land, the vendor's lien may take effect as an interest falling within LRA 2002, Sch 1, para 2 or Sch 3, para 3 which overrides first registration or registered dispositions. An overriding interest of that nature is subject to the duty of disclosure under LRR 2003, rr 28 and 57.[4] For liens arising under LRHUDA 1993 s 32(2), see 34.6 Vendor's lien.

182.1 Agreed notice

In addition to the usual documents required,[5] the vendor should deliver to HMLR the contract or a certified copy of it.

The agreed notice in the register will give details of the interest protected.

The applicant may prefer to apply for entry of a unilateral notice where he does not wish the terms of the contract giving rise to the lien to be open to public inspection and copying.

182.2 Unilateral notice

The vendor should deliver to HMLR the usual documents required.[6]

The statement in panel 11 or conveyancer's certificate in panel 12 of form UN1 should be completed on the following lines to show the interest of the applicant:

person having the benefit of a vendor's lien arising under an agreement for sale dated [*date*] made between [*registered proprietor*] and [*purchaser*].

The unilateral notice in the register will give brief details of the interest protected and identify the beneficiary of that notice.

---

1 See *Barclays Bank plc v Estates & Commercial Ltd (In Liquidation)* [1997] 1 WLR 415.
2 LRA 2002, s 29.
3 LRR 2003, r 35.
4 See 128.4 Duty to disclose overriding interests.
5 See 119.1 Agreed notice.
6 See 119.3 Unilateral notice.

183 WRITS OR ORDERS AFFECTING LAND

A writ or order of the kind mentioned in Land Charges Act 1972, s 6(1)(a) is treated as an interest affecting an estate or charge for the purposes of the LRA 2002.[1] However, it cannot be an interest belonging to a person in actual occupation within LRA 2002, Sch 1, para 2 or Sch 3, para 2 which overrides first registration or registered dispositions.[2] Such a writ or order is:

(a) one affecting land issued; or
(b) one made by any court for the purposes of enforcing a judgment or recognisance.

A writ or order which relates to an undivided share under a trust of land, or which has the effect of creating an interest under a trust of land, is not an interest affecting land for this purpose, as it does not affect the legal estate.

A writ or order affecting land may be protected by application for the entry in the register of an agreed notice or a unilateral notice, and possibly a restriction. The application may be made by the person who has obtained such a writ or order, or his assignee or chargee.[3] In practice, an application for an agreed notice will be the usual course of action. The entitlement to apply for entry of a restriction and the form of restriction will depend on the nature of the writ or order; LRR 2003, r 93 specifies the form of restriction for which persons having the benefit of certain types of writ or order will be entitled to apply. A restriction does not confer any priority. However, it prevents an entry being made in the register relating to any disposition, or a disposition of a specified kind, unless the terms of the restriction have (where applicable) been complied with.

183.1 Agreed notice

In addition to the usual documents required,[4] an applicant should deliver to HMLR the writ or order or a certified copy of it. This should satisfy HMLR as to the validity of the applicant's claim in accordance with LRA 2002, s 34(3)(c).

The agreed notice in the register will give details of the interest protected.

183.2 Unilateral notice

An applicant should deliver to HMLR the usual documents required.[5]

The statement in panel 11 or conveyancer's certificate in panel 12 of form UN1 should be completed on the following lines to show details of the interest of the applicant:

> person having the benefit of a [*insert details of writ or order in question*] of the [*name* Division of the High Court] *or* [*name* County Court] dated [*date*] [*set out full court reference and parties*].

The unilateral notice in the register will give brief details of the interest protected and identify the beneficiary of that notice.

183.3 Restriction

An applicant should deliver to HMLR the usual documents required.[6]

Panel 9 of form RX1 should set out the required restriction(s). A restriction in a standard form contained in LRR 2003, Sch 4 does not require the approval of HMLR to the terms of the restriction under LRA 2002, s 43(3). The form of restriction sought will depend on the nature of the writ or order.

Where the writ or order relates to the legal estate in the registered title and imposes a limitation upon dispositions, an application may be made for entry of an appropriate form of restriction to reflect this limitation.[7]

Where the writ or order relates to an undivided share under a trust of land, or has the effect of creating an interest under a trust of land, the interest cannot be protected by the entry of a notice. Instead, application may be made for entry of a restriction in Form A, if such a restriction does not already appear in the register. The wording of Form A is set out in Appendix IV. In such a case, a person having a beneficial interest under a trust of land has a sufficient interest to apply for entry of a restriction in Form A, to ensure that a survivor of the joint proprietors (unless a trust corporation) will not be able to give a valid receipt for capital money.[8]

A beneficiary under a trust of land created by such a writ or order may, where appropriate, also have a sufficient interest to apply for entry of a restriction in Form II. The wording of Form II is set out in Appendix IV. For example, if the effect of the writ or order is that the registered proprietor holds the registered title on a trust of land for himself and the beneficiary. The purpose of the restriction is to ensure that the beneficiary receives notice of a disposition.

This restriction does not prevent a disposition, provided its terms are complied with. This is because the interest of the beneficiary will be overreached where the requirements of Form A have been met.[9]

HMLR must give notice of the application for a restriction to the proprietor of the registered estate or charge concerned, if it has not been made by or with his consent or a person entitled to be registered as such proprietor.[10]

---

1 LRA 2002, s 87(1).
2 LRA 2002, s 87(3).
3 LRR 2003, r 172.
4 See 119.1 Agreed notice.
5 See 119.3 Unilateral notice.
6 See 153.1 Application for entry of restriction.
7 See, for example, 76 Freezing Orders, Restraint Orders and Interim Receiving Orders.
8 LRR 2003, r 93(a).
9 LPA 1925, ss 2 and 27.
10 LRA 2002, s 45.

APPENDIX I
HMLR OFFICES AND ADDRESSES[1]

HMLR offices

- Birkenhead
- Coventry
- Croydon
- Durham
- Fylde
- Gloucester
- Hull
- Leicester
- Nottingham
- Peterborough
- Plymouth
- Swansea
- Telford
- Weymouth

HMLR addresses

Royal Mail address for business customers: HM Land Registry [*insert customer team's office name or, if none, name of customer's closest office*] PO Box 7803 Bilston WV1 9QN	DX address for business customers: HM Land Registry [*insert customer team's office name or, if none, name of customer's closest office*] DX 427301 Bilston 3	Hand-delivery address for business customers: HM Land Registry [*insert customer team's office name or, if none, name of customer's closest office*] HMLR Mailroom Restore Digital EDM House Village Way Bilston WV14 0UJ
Royal Mail address for members of the public: HM Land Registry Citizen Centre PO Box 7806 Bilston WV1 9QR	Hand-delivery address for members of the public: HM Land Registry Tŷ Cwm Tawe Phoenix Way Swansea Enterprise Park Swansea SA7 9FQ	
Royal Mail address for service of proceedings on HMLR: HM Land Registry Litigation and Indemnity Lawyers PO Box 2079 Trafalgar House 1 Bedford Park Croydon CR90 9NU	Royal Mail and DX addresses for agricultural credits applications: Agricultural Credits Department PO Box 292 Plymouth PL1 9JG Agricultural Credits Department DX8249 Plymouth 3	Royal Mail and DX addresses for bankruptcy applications: HM Land Registry Bankruptcy Unit PO Box 292 Plymouth PL1 9JG HM Land Registry Bankruptcy Unit DX8249 Plymouth 3

Royal Mail and DX addresses for land charges applications:	Royal Mail address for local land charges – light obstruction notice applications:	Royal Mail address for local land charges:
Land Charges Department PO Box 292 Plymouth PL1 9JG Land Charges Department DX8249 Plymouth 3	Light Obstruction Notices PO Box 3286 Twyver House Gloucester GL1 9HP	HMLR Local Land Charges PO Box 7804 Bilston WV1 9QP

1 Reproduced with kind permission of HMLR.

APPENDIX II
LIST OF FORMS[1]

Schedule 1 forms

ADV1	Application for registration of a person in adverse possession under LRA 2002, Sch 6
ADV2	Application to be registered as a person to be notified of an application for adverse possession
AN1	Application to enter an agreed notice
AP1	Application to change the register
AS1	Assent of whole of registered title(s)
AS2	Assent of charge
AS3	Assent of part of registered title(s)
CC	Entry of a note of consolidation of charges
CCD	Application to cancel a caution against dealings
CCT	Application to cancel a caution against first registration
CH1	Legal charge of a registered estate
CH2	Application to enter an obligation to make further advances
CH3	Application to note agreed maximum amount of security
CI	Certificate of inspection of title plan
CN1	Application to cancel a notice (other than a unilateral notice)
CS	Continuation sheet for use with application and disposition forms
CT1	Caution against first registration
DB	Application to determine the exact line of a boundary
DI	Disclosable overriding interests
DL	List of documents
DS1	Cancellation of entries relating to a registered charge
DS2	Application to cancel entries relating to a registered charge
DS3	Release of part of the land from a registered charge
EX1	Application for the registrar to designate a document as an exempt information document
EX1A	Reasons for exemption in support of an application to designate a document as an exempt information document

EX2	Application for official copy of an exempt information document
EX3	Application to remove the designation of a document as an exempt information document
FR1	First registration application
HC1	Application for copies of historical edition(s) of the register/title plan held in electronic form
HR1	Application for registration of a notice of home rights
HR2	Application for renewal of registration in respect of home rights
HR3	Application by mortgagee for official search in respect of home rights
HR4	Application for cancellation of a notice of home rights
NAP	Notice to the registrar in respect of an adverse possession application
OC1	Application for official copies of register/plan or certificate in form CI
OC2	Application for official copies of documents only
OS1	Application by purchaser for official search with priority of the whole of the land in a registered title or a pending first registration application
OS2	Application by purchaser for official search with priority of part of the land in a registered title or a pending first registration application
OS3	Application for official search without priority of the land in a registered title
PIC	Application for a personal inspection under LRA 2002, s 66
PN1	Application for a search in the index of proprietors' names
PRD1	Request for the production of documents
PRD2	Notice to produce a document, LRA 2002, s 75 and LRR 2003, r 201
RX1	Application to enter a restriction
RX2	Application for an order that a restriction be disapplied or modified
RX3	Application to cancel a restriction
RX4	Application to withdraw a restriction
SC	Application for noting the overriding priority of a statutory charge
SEV	Application to enter a restriction in Form A on severance of joint tenancy by agreement or notice
SIF	Application for an official search of the index of relating franchises and manors
SIM	Application for an official search of the index map
ST1	Statement of truth in support of application for registration based upon adverse possession

ST2	Statement of truth in support of application for registration based upon adverse possession of a rentcharge
ST3	Statement of truth in support of application for registration of land based upon lost or destroyed title deeds
ST4	Statement of truth in support of application for registration and/or noting of a prescriptive easement
TP1	Transfer of part of registered title(s)
TP2	Transfer of part of registered title(s) under power of sale
TR1	Transfer of whole of registered title(s)
TR2	Transfer of whole of registered title(s) under power of sale
TR4	Transfer of a charge or portfolio of charges
TR5	Transfer of portfolio of titles (whole or part)
UN1	Application to enter a unilateral notice
UN2	Application to remove a unilateral notice
UN3	Application to be registered as beneficiary of an existing unilateral notice
UN4	Application for the cancellation of a unilateral notice
UT1	Application for upgrading of title
WCT	Application to withdraw a caution

Schedule 3 forms

Form 1	Certificate as to execution of power of attorney (LRR 2003, r 61)
Form 2	Statutory declaration/certificate/statement of truth as to non-revocation for powers more than 12 months old at the date of the disposition for which they are used (LRR 2003, r 62)
Form 3	Statutory declaration/certificate/statement of truth in support of power delegating trustees' functions to a beneficiary (LRR 2003, r 63)
Form 4	Certificate as to vesting in an incumbent or other ecclesiastical corporation (LRR 2003, r 174)
Form 5	The like certificate under LRR 2003, r 175
Form 6	Transfer where the tenant for life is already registered as proprietor (LRR 2003, r 186 and Sch 7, para 5)
Form 7	Certificate of powers of overseas corporations (LRR 2003, r 183)
Form 8	Certificate of powers of corporations other than overseas corporations (LRR 2003, r 183)

Commonhold forms

CM1	Application to register a freehold estate in commonhold land
CM2	Application for the freehold estate to cease to be registered as a freehold estate in commonhold land during the transitional period
CM3	Application for the registration of an amended commonhold community statement and/or altered memorandum and articles of association
CM4	Application to add land to a commonhold registration
CM5	Application for the termination of a commonhold registration
CM6	Application for the registration of a successor commonhold association
COE	Notification of change of extent of a commonhold unit over which there is a registered charge
CON1	Consent to the registration of land as commonhold land
CON2	Consent to an application for the freehold estate to cease to be registered as a freehold estate in commonhold land during the transitional period
COV	Application for registration with unit holders
SR1	Notice of surrender of development right(s)

Economic Crime (Transparency and Enforcement) Act 2022 Certificates

OE1	Certificate to comply with a restriction that has been entered in the register under paragraph 3 of Schedule 4A to the Land Registration Act 2002 or paragraph 6 of Schedule 3 to the Economic Crime (Transparency and Enforcement) Act 2022
OE2	Certificate to support an application to register a disposition of a qualifying estate (a) by an overseas entity which became entitled to be registered as proprietor of that estate on or after 5 September 2022 (but was not so registered), or (b) where the application includes a disposition made by an overseas entity which became entitled to be registered as proprietor of that estate on or after 5 September 2022 (but was not so registered)

Other forms

ACD	Application for approval of a standard form of charge deed and allocation of official HM Land Registry reference
ADD	Standard form of deed of variation/priority/postponement of a charge
AMS1	Application for Application Management Service
CIT	Investigation or enforcement proceedings (court, insolvency, tax)
CNG	Change of name (transgender and non-binary)
COG1	Update registered owner's contact address
DJP	Application to remove from the register the name of a deceased registered proprietor
DS2E	Application to cancel entries relating to a registered charge
e-ACD	Digital mortgage: approval
ID1	Evidence of identity for a private individual
ID2	Evidence of identity for a corporate body
ID3	Evidence of identity for use with FR1 only
ID5	Certificate to be given by a conveyancer where a person's identity has been verified by way of an online video call
JO	Trust information
PN1ID	IOPN search: evidence of identity
PSS1	Application for Pre-submission Enquiry Service for complex commercial or infrastructure development enquiries
RD1	Request for the return of an original document(s)
RQ	Request for a restriction by owner(s) not living at the property
RQ(Co)	Request for a restriction by a company
RXC	Restriction: consent or certificate
ST5	Statement of truth in support of application for cancellation of a restriction in Form A

1 Reproduced with kind permission of HMLR.

APPENDIX III
LAND REGISTRATION RULES 2003, SCHEDULE 1A: PRESCRIBED CLAUSES LR1 TO LR14

- All words in italicised text and inapplicable alternative wording in a clause may be omitted or deleted.
- Clause LR13 may be omitted or deleted.
- Clause LR14 may be omitted or deleted where the Tenant is one person.
- Otherwise, do not omit or delete any words in bold text unless italicised.
- Side-headings may appear as headings if this is preferred.
- Vertical or horizontal lines, or both, may be omitted.

LR1. Date of lease	
LR2. Title number(s)	**LR2.1 Landlord's title number(s)** *Title number(s) out of which this lease is granted. Leave blank if not registered.*
	LR2.2 Other title numbers *Existing title number(s) against which entries of matters referred to in LR9, LR10, LR11 and LR13 are to be made.*

LR3. Parties to this lease *Give full names and addresses of each of the parties. For UK incorporated companies and limited liability partnerships, also give the registered number including any prefix.* *For overseas entities, give the following:* *(a) The territory of incorporation or formation;* *(b) The overseas entity ID issued by Companies House for the Landlord and/or the Tenant pursuant to the Economic Crime (Transparency and Enforcement) Act 2022. If the ID is not required, state 'overseas entity ID not required'.* *(c) Where the entity is a company with a place of business in the United Kingdom, the registered number, if any, issued by Companies House, including any prefix.* *Further details on overseas entities can be found in practice guide 78: overseas entities.*	**Landlord** **Tenant** ***Other parties*** *Specify capacity of each party, for example 'management company', 'guarantor', etc.*
LR4. Property *Insert a full description of the land being leased* *or* *Refer to the clause, schedule or paragraph of a schedule in this lease in which the land being leased is more fully described.* *Where there is a letting of part of a registered title, a plan must be attached to this lease and any floor levels must be specified.*	**In the case of a conflict between this clause and the remainder of this lease then, for the purposes of registration, this clause shall prevail.**

LR5. Prescribed statements etc. *If this lease includes a statement falling within LR5.1, insert under that sub-clause the relevant statement or refer to the clause, schedule or paragraph of a schedule in this lease which contains the statement.* *In LR5.2, omit or delete those Acts which do not apply to this lease.*	***LR5.1 Statements prescribed under rules 179 (dispositions in favour of a charity), 180 (dispositions by a charity) or 196 (leases under the Leasehold Reform, Housing and Urban Development Act 1993) of the Land Registration Rules 2003.*** ***LR5.2 This lease is made under, or by reference to, provisions of:*** Leasehold Reform Act 1967 Housing Act 1985 Housing Act 1988 Housing Act 1996
LR6. Term for which the Property is leased *Include only the appropriate statement (duly completed) from the three options.* *NOTE: The information you provide, or refer to, here will be used as part of the particulars to identify the lease under rule 6 of the Land Registration Rules 2003.*	From and including To and including *OR* The term as specified in this lease at clause/schedule/paragraph *OR* The term is as follows:
LR7. Premium *Specify the total premium, inclusive of any VAT where payable.*	

LR8. Prohibitions or restrictions on disposing of this lease *Include whichever of the two statements is appropriate.* *Do not set out here the wording of the provision.*	This lease does not contain a provision that prohibits or restricts dispositions. *OR* This lease contains a provision that prohibits or restricts dispositions.
LR9. Rights of acquisition etc. *Insert the relevant provisions in the sub-clauses or refer to the clause, schedule or paragraph of a schedule in this lease which contains the provisions.*	**LR9.1 Tenant's contractual rights to renew this lease, to acquire the reversion or another lease of the Property, or to acquire an interest in other land** **LR9.2 Tenant's covenant to (or offer to) surrender this lease** **LR9.3 Landlord's contractual rights to acquire this lease**
LR10. Restrictive covenants given in this lease by the Landlord in respect of land other than the Property *Insert the relevant provisions or refer to the clause, schedule or paragraph of a schedule in this lease which contains the provisions.*	
LR11. Easements *Refer here only to the clause, schedule or paragraph of a schedule in this lease which sets out the easements.*	**LR11.1 Easements granted by this lease for the benefit of the Property** **LR11.2 Easements granted or reserved by this lease over the Property for the benefit of other property**
LR12. Estate rentcharge burdening the Property *Refer here only to the clause, schedule or paragraph of a schedule in this lease which sets out the rentcharge.*	

LR13. Application for standard form of restriction *Set out the full text of the standard form of restriction and the title against which it is to be entered. If you wish to apply for more than one standard form of restriction use this clause to apply for each of them, tell us who is applying against which title and set out the full text of the restriction you are applying for.* *Standard forms of restriction are set out in Schedule 4 to the Land Registration Rules 2003.*	The Parties to this lease apply to enter the following standard form of restriction [against the title of the Property] *or* [against title number]
LR14. Declaration of trust where there is more than one person comprising the Tenant *If the Tenant is one person, omit or delete all the alternative statements.* *If the Tenant is more than one person, complete this clause by omitting or deleting all inapplicable alternative statements.*	The Tenant is more than one person. They are to hold the Property on trust for themselves as joint tenants *OR* The Tenant is more than one person. They are to hold the Property on trust for themselves as tenants in common in equal shares *OR* The Tenant is more than one person. They are to hold the Property on trust *Complete as necessary*

APPENDIX IV
LAND REGISTRATION RULES 2003, SCHEDULE 4: STANDARD FORMS OF RESTRICTION

In the forms in this Schedule—

(a) words in [square brackets] in ordinary type are optional parts of the form; the brackets are not to be included in the restriction,
(b) words in [square brackets] in italic type are instructions for completion of the form, and are not to be included in the restriction,
(c) where (round brackets) enclose one or more words, the brackets and all words in ordinary type enclosed in them are part of the form and, unless also enclosed in [square brackets], must be included in the restriction, and
(d) where a form includes a group of clauses introduced by bullets, only one of the clauses may be used; the bullets are not to be included in the restriction.

Rule 91A contains other permitted modifications of some forms.

Rule 91B contains provisions as to how a consent or certificate, required by the terms of a restriction to be given by a corporation aggregate, is to be signed on its behalf.

Form A (Restriction on dispositions by sole proprietor)

No disposition by a sole proprietor of the registered estate (except a trust corporation) under which capital money arises is to be registered unless authorised by an order of the court.

Form B (Dispositions by trustees of the legal estate – certificates required)

No [disposition *or specify type of disposition*] by the proprietors of the registered estate is to be registered unless one or more of them makes a statutory declaration or statement of truth, or their conveyancer gives a certificate, that the [disposition *or specify type of disposition*] is in accordance with [*specify the disposition creating the trust*] or some variation thereof referred to in the declaration, statement or certificate.

Form C (Dispositions by personal representatives – certificate required)

No disposition by the personal representative of [*name*] deceased, other than a transfer by way of assent, is to be registered unless such personal representative makes a statutory declaration or statement of truth, or their conveyancer gives a certificate, that the disposition is in accordance with the terms of
[*choose whichever bulleted clause is appropriate*]

- the will of the deceased [as varied by [*specify date of, and parties to, deed of variation or other appropriate details*]]
- the law relating to intestacy as varied by [*specify date of, and parties to, deed of variation or other appropriate details*]

or some [further] variation thereof referred to in the declaration, statement or certificate, or is necessary for the purposes of administration.

Form D (Parsonage, diocesan glebe, church or churchyard land)

No disposition of the registered estate is to be registered unless the instrument giving effect to the disposition contains either certificate (a) or certificate (b):

(a) the disposition [*choose one of the bulleted clauses*]

- [is made in accordance with Part 1 of the Church Property Measure 2018,
- is made in accordance with Part 2 of the Church Property Measure 2018,
- is made in accordance with section 29 of the Church Property Measure 2018,
- is made in accordance with section 29 of the Church Property Measure 2018 by virtue of section 4(9) of the Ecclesiastical Offices (Terms of Service) Measure 2009,
- is made in accordance with sections 33 and 34 of the Church Property Measure 2018,]
- falls within section 117(3)(a) of the Charities Act 2011;
- is made under the authority of a faculty granted under the common law power referred to in *In re St. Mary Magdalene's Paddington* 1980 Fam.99;
- is made in accordance with [*specify other Act, Measure or authority*];

(b) the Church Commissioners are a party to the instrument and have applied their seal to it.

Form E (Non-exempt charity – statement required)

No disposition by the proprietor of the registered estate to which sections 117 to 121 of the Charities Act 2011 apply, or section 124 of that Act applies, is to be registered unless the instrument contains a statement complying with section 122(2A) or section 125(1A) of that Act as appropriate.

Form F (Land vested in official custodian on trust for non-exempt charity – authority required)

No disposition executed by the trustees of [*name of charity*] in the name and on behalf of the proprietor is to be registered unless the transaction is authorised by an order of the court or of the Charity Commission, as required by section 91(4) of the Charities Act 2011.

Form G (Tenant for life as registered proprietor of settled land, where there are trustees of the settlement)

No disposition is to be registered unless authorised by the Settled Land Act 1925, or by any extension of those statutory powers in the settlement, and no disposition under which capital money arises is to be registered unless the money is paid to [*name*] of [*address*] and [*name*] of [*address*], (the trustees of the settlement, who may be a sole trust corporation or, if individuals, must number at least two but not more than four) or into court.

[*Note — If applicable under the terms of the settlement, a further provision may be added that no transfer of the mansion house [shown on an attached plan or otherwise adequately described to enable it to be fully identified on the Ordnance Survey map or title plan] is to be registered without the consent of the named trustees or an order of the court.*]

Form H (Statutory owners as trustees of the settlement and registered proprietors of settled land)

No disposition is to be registered unless authorised by the Settled Land Act 1925, or by any extension of those statutory powers in the settlement, and, except where the sole proprietor is a trust corporation, no disposition under which capital money arises is to be registered unless the money is paid to at least two proprietors.

[*Note — This restriction does not apply where the statutory owners are not the trustees of the settlement.*]

Form I (Tenant for life as registered proprietor of settled land – no trustees of the settlement)

No disposition under which capital money arises, or which is not authorised by the Settled Land Act 1925 or by any extension of those statutory powers in the settlement, is to be registered.

Form J (Trustee in bankruptcy and beneficial interest – certificate required)

No disposition of the

[*choose whichever bulleted clause is appropriate*]

- registered estate, other than a disposition by the proprietor of any registered charge registered before the entry of this restriction
- registered charge dated [*date*] referred to above, other than a disposition by the proprietor of any registered sub-charge of that charge registered before the entry of this restriction

is to be registered without a certificate signed by the applicant for registration or their conveyancer that written notice of the disposition was given to [name of trustee in bankruptcy] (the trustee in bankruptcy of [*name of bankrupt person*]) at [*address for service*].

Form K (Charging order affecting beneficial interest – certificate required)

No disposition of the

[*choose whichever bulleted clause is appropriate*]

- registered estate, other than a disposition by the proprietor of any registered charge registered before the entry of this restriction
- registered charge dated [*date*] referred to above, other than a disposition by the proprietor of any registered sub-charge of that charge registered before the entry of this restriction

is to be registered without a certificate signed by the applicant for registration or their conveyancer that written notice of the disposition was given to [*name of person with the benefit of the charging order*] at [*address for service*], being the person with the benefit of [an interim or a final] charging order on the beneficial interest of [*name of judgment debtor*] made by the [*name of court*] on [*date*] (Court reference [*insert reference*]).

Form L (Disposition by registered proprietor of a registered estate or proprietor of charge – certificate required)

No [disposition *or specify type of disposition*] of the registered estate [(other than a charge)] by the proprietor of the registered estate [, or by the proprietor of any registered charge, not being a charge registered before the entry of this restriction,] is to be registered without a certificate signed by

[*choose one of the bulleted clauses*]

- a conveyancer
- the applicant for registration [or their conveyancer]
- [*name*] of [*address*] [or their personal representatives] [or [their conveyancer *or specify appropriate details*]]
- [*name*] of [*address*] [or their personal representatives] and [*name*] of [*address*] [or their personal representatives] [or [their conveyancer *or specify appropriate details*]]
- [*name*] of [*address*] and [*name*] of [*address*] or the survivor of them [or by the personal representatives of the survivor] [or [their conveyancer *or specify appropriate details*]]
- [*name*] of [*address*] or [after that person's death] by [*name*] of [*address*] [or [their conveyancer *or specify appropriate details*]]

that the provisions of [*specify clause, paragraph or other particulars*] of [*specify details*] have been complied with [or that they do not apply to the disposition].

[*Author's note: LRR 2003, r 91A provides for alternative wording to be used at the start of this restriction. See 153.2 Forms of restriction.*]

Form M (Disposition by registered proprietor of registered estate or proprietor of charge – certificate of registered proprietor of specified title number required)

No [disposition *or specify type of disposition*] of the registered estate [(other than a charge)] by the proprietor of the registered estate [, or by the proprietor of any registered charge, not being a charge registered before the entry of this restriction,] is to be registered without a certificate signed by the proprietor for the time being of the estate registered under title number [*specify title number*] [or [their conveyancer *or specify appropriate details*]] that the provisions of [*specify clause, paragraph or other particulars*] of [*specify details*] have been complied with [or that they do not apply to the disposition].

[*Author's note: LRR 2003, r 91A provides for alternative wording to be used at the start of this restriction. See 153.2 Forms of restriction.*]

Form N (Disposition by registered proprietor of registered estate or proprietor of charge – consent required)

No [disposition *or specify type of disposition*] of the registered estate [(other than a charge)] by the proprietor of the registered estate [, or by the proprietor of any registered charge, not being a charge registered before the entry of this restriction,] is to be registered without a written consent signed by

[*choose one of the bulleted clauses*]

- [*name*] of [*address*] [or their personal representatives] [or [their conveyancer *or specify appropriate details*]]
- [*name*] of [*address*] [or their personal representatives] and [*name*] of [*address*] [or their personal representatives] [or [their conveyancer *or specify appropriate details*]]
- [*name*] of [*address*] and [*name*] of [*address*] or the survivor of them [or by the personal representatives of the survivor] [or [their conveyancer *or specify appropriate details*]]
- [*name*] of [*address*] or [after that person's death] by [*name*] of [*address*] [or [their conveyancer *or specify appropriate details*]]

[*Author's note: LRR 2003, r 91A provides for alternative wording to be used at the start of this restriction. See 153.2 Forms of restriction.*]

Form O (Disposition by registered proprietor of registered estate or proprietor of charge – consent of registered proprietor of specified title number or certificate required)

No [disposition *or specify type of disposition*] of the registered estate [(other than a charge)] by the proprietor of the registered estate [, or by the proprietor of any registered charge, not being a charge registered before the entry of this restriction,] is to be registered without a written consent signed by the proprietor for the time being of the estate registered under title number [*specify title number*] [or [their conveyancer *or specify appropriate details*]].

[*The text of the restriction may be continued as follows, to allow for the provision of a certificate as an alternative to the consent.*]

or without a certificate signed by

[*choose one of the bulleted clauses*]

- a conveyancer
- the applicant for registration [or their conveyancer]
- [*name*] of [*address*] [or [their conveyancer *or specify appropriate details*]]

that the provisions of [*specify clause, paragraph or other particulars*] of [*specify details*] have been complied with [or that they do not apply to the disposition].

[*Author's note: LRR 2003, r 91A provides for alternative wording to be used at the start of this restriction. See 153.2 Forms of restriction.*]

Form P: Disposition by registered proprietor of registered estate or proprietor of charge – consent of proprietor of specified charge or certificate required.

No [disposition *or specify type of disposition*] of the registered estate [(other than a charge)] by the proprietor of the registered estate [, or by the proprietor of any registered charge, not being a charge registered before the entry of this restriction,] is to be registered without a written consent signed by the proprietor for the time being of the charge dated [*date*] in favour of [*chargee*] referred to in the charges register [or [their conveyancer *or specify appropriate details*]].

[*The text of the restriction may be continued as follows, to allow for the provision of a certificate as an alternative to the consent.*]

or without a certificate signed by

[*choose one of the bulleted clauses*]

- a conveyancer
- the applicant for registration [or their conveyancer]
- [*name*] of [*address*] [or [their conveyancer *or specify appropriate details*]]

that the provisions of [*specify clause, paragraph or other particulars*] of [*specify details*] have been complied with [or that they do not apply to the disposition].

[*Author's note: LRR 2003, r 91A provides for alternative wording to be used at the start of this restriction. See 153.2 Forms of restriction.*]

Form Q (Disposition by registered proprietor of registered estate or proprietor of charge – consent of personal representatives required)

No [disposition *or specify type of disposition*] of the

[*choose whichever bulleted clause is appropriate*]

- registered estate by the proprietor of the registered estate
- registered charge dated [date] referred to above by the proprietor of that registered charge

is to be registered after the death of [*name of the current proprietor(s) whose personal representatives' consent will be required*] without the written consent of the personal representatives of the deceased.

Form R (Disposition by registered proprietor of registered estate or proprietor of charge – evidence of compliance with club rules required)

No [disposition *or specify type of disposition*] of the registered estate [(other than a charge)] by the proprietor of the registered estate [, or by the proprietor of any registered charge, not being a charge registered before the entry of this restriction,] is to be registered unless authorised by the rules of the [*name of club*] of [*address*] as evidenced by

[*choose whichever bulleted clause is appropriate*]

- a resolution of its members
- a certificate signed by its secretary or conveyancer
- [*specify appropriate details*]

Form S (Disposition by proprietor of charge – certificate of compliance required)

No [disposition *or specify type of disposition*] by the proprietor of the registered charge dated [*date*] referred to above is to be registered without a certificate signed by

[*choose one of the bulleted clauses*]

- a conveyancer
- the applicant for registration [or their conveyancer]
- [*name*] of [*address*] [or their personal representatives] [or [their conveyancer *or specify appropriate details*]]
- [*name*] of [*address*] [or their personal representatives] and [*name*] of [address] [or their personal representatives] [or [their conveyancer *or specify appropriate details*]]
- [*name*] of [*address*] and [*name*] of [*address*] or the survivor of them [or by the personal representatives of the survivor] [or [their conveyancer *or specify appropriate details*]]
- [*name*] of [*address*] or [after that person's death] by [*name*] of [*address*] [or [their conveyancer *or specify appropriate details*]]
- the proprietor for the time being of the sub-charge dated [*date*] in favour of [*sub-chargee*] [or [their conveyancer *or specify appropriate details*]]

that the provisions of [*specify clause, paragraph or other particulars*] *of* [*specify details*] have been complied with [or that they do not apply to the disposition].

[*Author's note: LRR 2003, r 91A provides for alternative wording to be used at the start of this restriction. See 153.2 Forms of restriction.*]

Form T (Disposition by proprietor of charge – consent required)

No [disposition *or specify type of disposition*] by the proprietor of the registered charge dated [*date*] referred to above is to be registered without a written consent signed by

[*choose one of the bulleted clauses*]

- [*name*] of [*address*] [or their personal representatives] [or [their conveyancer *or specify appropriate details*]]
- [*name*] of [*address*] [or their personal representatives] and [*name*] of [*address*] [or their personal representatives] [or [their conveyancer *or specify appropriate details*]]
- [*name*] of [*address*] and [*name*] of [*address*] or the survivor of them [or by the personal representatives of the survivor] [or [their conveyancer *or specify appropriate details*]]
- [*name*] of [*address*] or [after that person's death] by [*name*] of [address] [or [their conveyancer *or specify appropriate details*]]
- the proprietor for the time being of the sub-charge dated [*date*] in favour of [*sub-chargee*] [or [their conveyancer *or specify appropriate details*]]

[*Author's note: LRR 2003, r 91A provides for alternative wording to be used at the start of this restriction. See 153.2 Forms of restriction.*]

Form U (Section 37 of the Housing Act 1985)

No transfer or lease by the proprietor of the registered estate or by the proprietor of any registered charge is to be registered unless a certificate by [*specify relevant local authority*] is given that the transfer or lease is made in accordance with section 37 of the Housing Act 1985.

Form V (Section 157 of the Housing Act 1985)

No transfer or lease by the proprietor of the registered estate or by the proprietor of any registered charge is to be registered unless a certificate by [*specify relevant local authority or housing association etc*] is given that the transfer or lease is made in accordance with section 157 of the Housing Act 1985.

Form W (Paragraph 4 of Schedule 9A to the Housing Act 1985)

No disposition (except a transfer) of a qualifying dwelling-house (except to a qualifying person or persons) is to be registered without the consent of—

(a) in relation to a disposal of land in England, the Secretary of State, or
(b) in relation to a disposal of land in Wales, the Welsh Ministers,

where consent to that disposition is required by section 171D(2) of the Housing Act 1985 as it applies by virtue of the Housing (Preservation of Right to Buy) Regulations 1993.

Form X (Section 133 of the Housing Act 1988 or section 173 of the Local Government and Housing Act 1989)

No disposition by the proprietor of the registered estate or in exercise of the power of sale or leasing in any registered charge (except an exempt disposal as defined by section 133(11) of the Housing Act 1988) is to be registered without the consent of—

(a) in relation to a disposal of land in England, the Secretary of State, and
(b) in relation to a disposal of land in Wales, the Welsh Ministers,

where consent to that disposition is required by [*as appropriate* [section 133 of that Act] *or* [section 173 of the Local Government and Housing Act 1989].

Form Y (Section 13 of the Housing Act 1996)

No transfer or lease by the proprietor of the registered estate or by the proprietor of a registered charge is to be registered unless a certificate by [*specify relevant registered social landlord*] is given that the transfer or lease is made in accordance with section 13 of the Housing Act 1996.

Form AA (Freezing order on the registered estate)

Under an order of the [*name of court*] made on [*date*] (Court reference [*insert reference*]) no disposition by the proprietor of the registered estate is to be registered except with the consent of [*name*] of [*address*] or under a further order of the Court.

Form BB (Freezing order on charge)

Under an order of the [*name of court*] made on [*date*] (Court reference [*insert reference*]) no disposition by the proprietor of the registered charge dated [*date*] referred to above is to be registered except with the consent of [*name*] of [*address*] or under a further order of the Court.

Form CC (Application for freezing order on the registered estate)

Pursuant to an application made on [*date*] to the [*name of court*] for a freezing order to be made under [*statutory provision*] no disposition by the proprietor of the registered estate is to be registered except with the consent of [*name of the person applying*] of [*address*] or under a further order of the Court.

Form DD (Application for freezing order on charge)

Pursuant to an application made on [*date*] to the [*name of court*] for a freezing order to be made under [*statutory provision*] no disposition by the proprietor of the registered charge dated [*date*] referred to above is to be registered except with the consent of [*name of the person applying*] of [*address*] or under a further order of the Court.

Form EE (Restraint order or interim receiving order on the registered estate)

Under [a restraint order *or* an interim receiving order] made under [*statutory provision*] on [*date*] (Court reference [*insert reference*]) no disposition by the proprietor of the registered estate is to be registered except with the consent of [*name of prosecutor or other appropriate person*] of [*address*] or under a further order of the Court.

Form FF (Restraint order or interim receiving order on charge)

Under [a restraint order *or* an interim receiving order] made under [*statutory provision*] on [*date*] (Court reference [*insert reference*]) no disposition by the proprietor of the registered charge dated [*date*] referred to above is to be registered except with the consent of [*name of prosecutor or other appropriate person*] of [*address*] or under a further order of the Court.

Form GG (Application for restraint order or interim receiving order on the registered estate)

Pursuant to an application for [a restraint order *or* an interim receiving order] to be made under [*statutory provision*] and under any order made as a result of that application, no disposition by the proprietor of the registered estate is to be registered except with the consent of [*name of prosecutor or other appropriate person*] of [*address*] or under a further order of the Court.

Form HH (Application for restraint order or interim receiving order on charge)

Pursuant to an application for [a restraint order *or* an interim receiving order] to be made under [*statutory provision*] and under any order made as a result of that application no disposition by the proprietor of the registered charge dated [*date*] referred to above is to be registered except with the consent of [*name of prosecutor or other appropriate person*] of [*address*] or under a further order of the Court.

Form II (Beneficial interest that is a right or claim in relation to a registered estate)

No disposition of the registered estate, other than a disposition by the proprietor of any registered charge registered before the entry of this restriction, is to be registered without a certificate signed by the applicant for registration or their conveyancer that written notice of the disposition was given to [*name*] at [*address*].

[*Author's note: LRR 2003, r 91A provides for alternative wording to be used at the start of this restriction. See 153.2 Forms of restriction.*]

Form JJ (Statutory charge of beneficial interest in favour of the Lord Chancellor)

No disposition of the

[*choose whichever bulleted clause is appropriate*]

- registered estate, other than a disposition by the proprietor of any registered charge registered before the entry of this restriction
- registered charge dated [*date*] referred to above, other than a disposition by the proprietor of any registered sub-charge of that charge registered before the entry of this restriction

is to be registered without a certificate signed by the applicant for registration or their conveyancer that written notice of the disposition was given to the Lord Chancellor, at [*address and Lord Chancellor's reference number*].

Form KK (Lease of property in Wales by registered social landlord)

This restriction was revoked by the Regulation of Registered Social Landlords (Wales) Act 2018 (Consequential Amendments) Regulations 2018 which came into force on 15 August 2018.

Form LL (Restriction as to evidence of execution)

No disposition of the

[*choose whichever bulleted clause is appropriate*]

- registered estate by the proprietor of the registered estate
- registered charge dated [*date*] referred to above by the proprietor of that registered charge

is to be registered without a certificate signed by a conveyancer that that conveyancer is satisfied that the person who executed the document submitted for registration as disponor is the same person as the proprietor.

Form MM (Interest in beneficial joint tenancy subject to charge under section 22(1) of the Health and Social Services and Social Security Adjudications Act 1983 or section 71 of the Social Services and Well-being (Wales) Act 2014)

No disposition of the registered estate made after the death of [*specify the name of the person whose beneficial interest under a beneficial joint tenancy is subject to a charge under section 22(1) of the Health and Social Services and Social Security Adjudications Act 1983 or section 71 of the Social Services and Well-being (Wales) Act 2014*], or after that person has become the sole proprietor of the registered estate, is to be registered unless—

(1) the disposition is by two or more persons who were registered as proprietors of the legal estate at the time of that person's death,
(2) notice of a charge under section 22(1) or (6) of the Health and Social Services and Social Security Adjudications Act 1983 or section 71(1) or (5) of the Social Services and Well-being (Wales) Act 2014 for the benefit of [*name and address of the local authority*] has been entered in the register or, where appropriate, such charge has been registered, or
(3) it is shown to the registrar's satisfaction that no such charge is subsisting.

Form NN (Disposition by registered proprietor of registered estate or proprietor of charge – consent or certificate required)

No [disposition *or specify type of disposition*] of the registered estate [(other than a charge)] by the proprietor of the registered estate [, or by the proprietor of any registered charge, not being a charge registered before the entry of this restriction,] is to be registered without a written consent signed by

[*choose one of the bulleted clauses*]

- [*name*] of [*address*] [or their personal representatives] [or [their conveyancer *or specify appropriate details*]]
- [*name*] of [*address*] [or their personal representatives] and [*name*] of [*address*] [or their personal representatives] [or [their conveyancer *or specify appropriate details*]]
- [*name*] of [*address*] and [*name*] of [*address*] or the survivor of them [or by the personal representatives of the survivor] [or [their conveyancer *or specify appropriate details*]]
- [*name*] of [*address*] or [after that person's death] by [*name*] of [*address*] [or [their conveyancer *or specify appropriate details*]]

or a certificate signed by

[*choose one of the bulleted clauses*]

- a conveyancer
- the applicant for registration [or their conveyancer]
- [*name*] of [*address*] [or [their conveyancer *or specify appropriate details*]]

that the provisions of [*specify clause, paragraph or other particulars*] of [*specify details*] have been complied with [or that they do not apply to the disposition].

[*Author's note: LRR 2003, r 91A provides for alternative wording to be used at the start of this restriction. See 153.2 Forms of restriction.*]

Form OO (Disposition by proprietor of charge – consent or certificate required)

No [disposition *or specify type of disposition*] by the proprietor of the registered charge dated [*date*] referred to above is to be registered without a written consent signed by

[*choose one of the bulleted clauses*]

- [*name*] of [*address*] [or their personal representatives] [or [their conveyancer *or specify appropriate details*]]
- [*name*] of [*address*] [or their personal representatives] and [*name*] of [*address*] [or their personal representatives] [or [their conveyancer *or specify appropriate details*]]
- [*name*] of [*address*] and [*name*] of [*address*] or the survivor of them [or by the personal representatives of the survivor] [or [their conveyancer *or specify appropriate details*]]

- [*name*] of [*address*] or [after that person's death] by [*name*] of [*address*] [or [their conveyancer *or specify appropriate details*]]
- the proprietor for the time being of the sub-charge dated [*date*] in favour of [*sub-chargee*] [or [their conveyancer *or specify appropriate details*]]

or a certificate signed by

[*choose one of the bulleted clauses*]

- a conveyancer
- the applicant for registration [or their conveyancer]
- [*name*] of [*address*] [or [their conveyancer *or specify appropriate details*]]

that the provisions of [*specify clause, paragraph or other particulars*] of [*specify details*] have been complied with [or that they do not apply to the disposition].

[*Author's note: LRR 2003, r 91A provides for alternative wording to be used at the start of this restriction. See 153.2 Forms of restriction.*]

Form PP (Disposition by registered proprietor of registered estate or proprietor of charge – certificate of landlord or of a conveyancer, required)

No [disposition *or specify type of disposition*] of the registered estate [(other than a charge)] by the proprietor of the registered estate [, or by the proprietor of any registered charge, not being a charge registered before the entry of this restriction,] is to be registered without a certificate signed by

[*choose one of the bulleted clauses*]

- the proprietor for the time being of the registered estate comprising the reversion immediately expectant on the determination of the registered lease
- the proprietor for the time being of the estate registered under title number [*specify title number*]
- [*name*] of [*address*] [or by [*name*] of [*address*]]

or by a conveyancer, that the provisions of [*specify clause, paragraph or other particulars*] of [*specify details*] have been complied with [or that they do not apply to the disposition].

[*Author's note: LRR 2003, r 91A provides for alternative wording to be used at the start of this restriction. See 153.2 Forms of restriction.*]

Form QQ (Land included in a list of assets of community value maintained under section 87(1) of the Localism Act 2011)

No transfer or lease is to be registered without a certificate signed by a conveyancer that the transfer or lease did not contravene section 95(1) of the Localism Act 2011.

Form RR (Deputy appointed under section 16 of the Mental Capacity Act 2005 – solely owned property)

No disposition during the lifetime of [*name of person who lacks capacity*] of the [registered estate] [registered charge dated [*date*]] is to be completed by registration unless made pursuant to an order of the court under the Mental Capacity Act 2005.

Form SS (Trustee appointed in place of a person who lacks capacity – jointly owned property)

No disposition of the [registered estate] [registered charge dated [*date*]] made during the lifetime of [*name of person who lacks capacity*] is to be completed by registration without the written consent of the Court of Protection.

APPENDIX V
LAND REGISTRATION RULES 2003, SCHEDULE 3: FORMS REFERRED TO IN RULE 206

Form 1 – Certificate as to execution of power of attorney (rule 61)

Date of power of attorney: ....
Donor of power of attorney: ....
Donee of power of attorney: ....
I/We ....
of ....
....

certify that

- the power of attorney ('the power') is in existence [and is made and, where required, has been registered under (*state statutory provisions under which the power is made and, where required, has been registered, if applicable*)],
- the power is dated (*insert date*),
- I am/we are satisfied that the power is validly executed as a deed and authorises the attorney to execute the document on behalf of the donor of that power, and
- I/we hold [the instrument creating the power] *or* [a copy of the power by means of which its contents may be proved under section 3 of the Powers of Attorney Act 1971] *or* [a document which under section 4 of the Evidence and Powers of Attorney Act 1940, paragraph 16 of Part 2 of Schedule 1, or paragraph 15(3) of Part 5 of Schedule 4 to the Mental Capacity Act 2005] is sufficient evidence of the contents of the power.

Signature of conveyancer .... Date ....

Form 2 – Statutory declaration/certificate/statement of truth as to non-revocation for powers more than 12 months old at the date of the disposition for which they are used (rule 62)

Date of power of attorney: ....
Donor of power of attorney: ....
I/We ....
of ....

do [solemnly and sincerely declare] *or* [certify] *or* [state] that at the time of completion of the .... to me/my client I/my client had no knowledge—

- of a revocation of the power, or
- of the death or bankruptcy of the donor or, if the donor is a corporate body, its winding up or dissolution, or
- of any incapacity of the donor where the power is not a valid lasting or enduring power of attorney, or

Where the power is in the form prescribed for a lasting power of attorney—

- that a lasting power of attorney was not created, or
- of circumstances which, if the lasting power of attorney had been created, would have terminated the attorney's authority to act as an attorney, or

Where the power is in the form prescribed for an enduring power of attorney—

- that the power was not in fact a valid enduring power, or
- of an order or direction of the Court of Protection which revoked the power, or
- of the bankruptcy of the attorney, or

Where the power was given under section 9 of the Trusts of Land and Appointment of Trustees Act 1996—

- of an appointment of another trustee of the land in question, or
- of any other event which would have the effect of revoking the power, or
- of any lack of good faith on the part of the person(s) who dealt with the attorney, or
- that the attorney was not a person to whom the functions of the trustees could be delegated under section 9 of the Trusts of Land and Appointment of Trustees Act 1996, or

Where the power is expressed to be given by way of security—

- that the power was not in fact given by way of security, or
- of any revocation of the power with the consent of the attorney, or
- of any other event which would have had the effect of revoking the power.

Where a certificate is given—

Signature of conveyancer .... Date ....
Print name ....
Firm name or employer (if any) ....
Capacity (e.g. acting for ...) ....;

or

Where a Statutory Declaration is made—

And I make this solemn declaration conscientiously believing the same to be true and by virtue of the provisions of the Statutory Declarations Act 1835.
Signature of Declarant .... Date ....
DECLARED at .... before me, a person entitled to administer oaths.
Name ....
Address ....
Qualification ....
Signature ....;

or

Where a statement of truth is made—

I believe that the facts and matters contained in this statement are true.
Signature .... Date ....
Print name ....
Firm name or employer (if any) of any conveyancer signing ....
Capacity of any conveyancer signing (e.g. acting for ...) ....

WARNING
1. If you dishonestly make a statement which you know is, or might be, untrue or misleading, and intend by doing so to make a gain for yourself or another person, or to cause loss or the risk of loss to another person, you may commit the offence of fraud under section 1 of the Fraud Act 2006, the maximum penalty for which is 10 years' imprisonment or an unlimited fine, or both.

2. Failure to complete the form with proper care may result in a loss of protection under the Land Registration Act 2002 if, as a result, a mistake is made in the register.
3. Under section 66 of the Land Registration Act 2002 most documents (including this form) kept by the registrar relating to an application to the registrar or referred to in the register are open to public inspection and copying. If you believe a document contains prejudicial information, you may apply for that part of the document to be made exempt using form EX1, under rule 136 of the Land Registration Rules 2003.

Form 3 – Statutory declaration/certificate/statement of truth in support of power delegating trustees' functions to a beneficiary (rule 63)

Date of power of attorney: ....
Donor of power of attorney: ....
I ....
of ....

do [solemnly and sincerely declare] or [certify] or [state] that at the time of completion of the .... to me/my client I/my client had no knowledge—

- of any lack of good faith on the part of the person(s) who dealt with the attorney, or
- that the attorney was not a person to whom the functions of the trustees could be delegated under section 9 of the Trusts of Land and Appointment of Trustees Act 1996.

Where a certificate is given—

Signature of conveyancer .... Date ....
Print name ....
Firm name or employer (if any) ....
Capacity (e.g. acting for ...) ....;

or

Where a Statutory Declaration is made—

And I make this solemn declaration conscientiously believing the same to be true and by virtue of the provisions of the Statutory Declarations Act 1835.
Signature of Declarant .... Date ....
DECLARED at .... before me, a person entitled to administer oaths.
Name ....
Address ....
Qualification ....
Signature ....;

or

Where a statement of truth is made—

I believe that the facts and matters contained in this statement are true
Signature .... Date ....
Print name ....
Firm name or employer (if any) of any conveyancer signing ....
Capacity of any conveyancer signing (e.g. acting for ...) ....

WARNING

1. If you dishonestly make a statement which you know is, or might be, untrue or misleading, and intend by doing so to make a gain for yourself or another person, or to cause loss or the risk of loss to another person, you may commit the offence of fraud under section 1 of the Fraud Act 2006, the maximum penalty for which is 10 years' imprisonment or an unlimited fine, or both.
2. Failure to complete the form with proper care may result in a loss of protection under the Land Registration Act 2002 if, as a result, a mistake is made in the register.
3. Under section 66 of the Land Registration Act 2002 most documents (including this form) kept by the registrar relating to an application to the registrar or referred to in the register are open to public inspection and copying. If you believe a document contains prejudicial information, you may apply for that part of the document to be made exempt using form EX1, under rule 136 of the Land Registration Rules 2003.

Form 4 – Certificate as to vesting in an incumbent or other ecclesiastical corporation (rule 174)

(*Date*). This is to certify that the registered estate (*or* registered charge *or* that part of the registered estate) comprised in a [*describe the transfer*] under the provisions of [*state the Act or Measure*] (*if such transfer were a conveyance under such Act or Measure*), vests in the incumbent of .... (*or* the bishop of .... *as the case may be*) and his successors immediately (*or as the case may be*) upon the happening of the event following, namely, the [*state event*].

(To be sealed by the Church Commissioners)

Form 5 – The like certificate under rule 175

(*Date*). This is to certify that the [*describe scheme, instrument or transfer, &c.*] operates to vest immediately (*or*, on publication in the 'London Gazette', *or at some subsequent period, as the case may be*), the registered estate (*or* registered charge *or* that part of the registered estate [*include description by reference to a plan or to the register if possible*]) in the [*describe the corporation or person*].

(To be sealed by the Church Commissioners)

Form 6 – Transfer where the tenant for life is already registered as proprietor (rule 186 and paragraph 5 of Schedule 7)

(*Date*). Pursuant to a trust deed of even date herewith, [made between A.B. (*name of tenant for life*) and C.D. and E.F. (*names of trustees of the settlement*)], I, the said A.B., hereby declare as follows —

(a) The land is vested in me upon the trusts from time to time affecting it by virtue of the said trust deed.
[(b) The said C.D. and E.F. are the trustees of the Settlement.
(c) The following powers relating to land are expressly conferred by the said trust deed in extension of those conferred by the Settled Land Act 1925 (*fill in the powers, if any*).]
(d) I have the power to appoint new trustees of the settlement.

(To be executed as a deed)

Form 7 – Certificate of powers of overseas corporations (rule 183)

I ....
of ....
(*insert workplace address, including country*) certify that—

- I give this certificate in respect of .... (the corporation),
- I practise law in .... (*insert territory*) (the territory) and am entitled to do so as a qualified lawyer under the law of the territory,
- I have the requisite knowledge of the law of the territory and of the corporation to give this certificate,
- the corporation is incorporated in the territory with its own legal personality, and
- the corporation has no limitations on its powers to hold, mortgage, lease and otherwise deal with, or to lend money on a mortgage or charge of, land in England and Wales.

Signature .... Date ....

Form 8 – Certificate of powers of corporations other than overseas corporations (rule 183)

I ....
of ....
(*insert workplace address*) certify that—

- ....(the corporation) has its own legal personality, and
- the corporation has no limitations on its powers to hold, mortgage, lease and otherwise deal with, or to lend money on a mortgage or charge of, land.

Signature of conveyancer .... Date ....

APPENDIX VI
LAND REGISTRATION RULES 2003, SCHEDULE 9: FORMS OF EXECUTION

Note: All dispositions other than assents must be executed as a deed. In the case of an assent the words 'as a deed' may be omitted.

A. Where the instrument is to be executed personally by an individual —

Signed as a deed by (*full name of individual*) in the presence of:	*Signature*

Signature of witness ....
Name (in BLOCK CAPITALS) ....
Address ....
....
....
....

B. Where the instrument is to be executed by an individual directing another to sign on his behalf —

Signed as a deed by (*full name of person signing*) at the direction and on behalf of (*full name of individual*) in [his][her] presence and in the presence of:	*Sign here the name of the individual and your own name,* *eg:* John Smith by Jane Brown

Signature of first witness ....
Name (in BLOCK CAPITALS) ....
Address ....
....
....
....

Signature of second witness ....
Name (in BLOCK CAPITALS) ....
Address ....
....
....
....

C. Where the instrument is to be executed by a company registered under the Companies Acts, or an unregistered company, using its common seal

Executed as a deed by affixing the common seal of (*name of company*) in the presence of:	*Common seal of company*

Signature of director ....

Signature of [director] [secretary] ....

D(i). Where the instrument is to be executed by a company registered under the Companies Acts, or an unregistered company, without using a common seal, acting by a director and its secretary or by two directors —

Executed as a deed by (*name of company*) acting by [a director and its secretary] [two directors]	*Signature* Director *Signature* [Secretary][Director]

D(ii). Where the instrument is to be executed by a company registered under the Companies Acts, without using a common seal, acting by a director—

Executed as a deed by (*name of company*) acting by a director in the presence of:	*Signature* Director

Signature of witness ....
Name (in BLOCK CAPITALS) ....
Address ....
....
....
....

E. Where the instrument is to be executed on behalf of an overseas company without using a common seal —

Executed as a deed by (*name of company*), a company incorporated in (territory) acting by (*full name(s) of person(s) signing*), who, in accordance with the laws of that territory, [is][are] acting under the authority of the company.	*Signature in the name of the company* Signature of Authorised [signatory] [signatories]

Note: In the case of an overseas company having a common seal, the form of execution appropriate to a company registered under the Companies Acts may be used, with such adaptations as may be necessary, in place of execution by a person or persons acting under the authority of the company.

F(i). Where the instrument is to be executed by a limited liability partnership incorporated under the Limited Liability Partnerships Act 2000, without using a common seal, acting by two members—

Executed as a deed by (*name of limited liability partnership*) acting by two members	*Signature* Member *Signature* Member

F(ii). Where the instrument is to be executed by a limited liability partnership incorporated under the Limited liability Partnerships Act 2000, without using a common seal, acting by a single member—

Executed as a deed by (*name of limited liability partnership*) acting by a member in the presence of:	*Signature* Member

Signature of witness ....
Name (in BLOCK CAPITALS) ....
Address ....
....
....
....

APPENDIX VII
ECONOMIC CRIME (TRANSPARENCY AND ENFORCEMENT) ACT 2022 CERTIFICATES

Certificate OE1

Certificate to comply with a restriction that has been entered in the register under paragraph 3 of Schedule 4A to the Land Registration Act 2002 or paragraph 6 of Schedule 3 to the Economic Crime (Transparency and Enforcement) Act 2022

Note – a separate certificate is required for each disposition by an overseas entity.

Title number(s) ……………..

I/We …………………………… of ……………………………………………..
certify that the following provision under paragraph 3(2) of Schedule 4A to the Land Registration Act 2002 applies to the [*specify transfer, lease or charge*] ('the disposition') dated [*insert the date of the disposition*] made by [*insert the name of the overseas entity*] ('the overseas entity') to [*insert the name of transferee, lessee or chargee*]:

[Select and complete the relevant provision below. You may delete the words in italics and the provisions that do not apply.]

[ ] The disposition: [*select and complete the relevant statement*]

- was made in pursuance of a statutory obligation under [*specify the statutory provision under which the obligation arose*].
- was made in pursuance of an order of the [*specify which court*] court dated [*specify the date of the court order*], case number [*provide the proceedings number*].

- occurred by operation of law on the basis that [*explain how operation of law arose giving any relevant legislative provision*].

[ ] The disposition was made in pursuance of a contract made before the restriction was entered in the register, being a contract dated [*insert date*] made between [*give the names of the parties to the contract*] relating to [*give the details of the property to which the contract related*].

[ ] The disposition was made in the exercise of a power of sale or leasing conferred on the proprietor of a registered charge or a receiver appointed by such a proprietor, being a charge dated [*insert the date of the charge*] made between [*provide the parties to the charge*] and registered on [*provide the date of registration of the charge*].

[ ] The Secretary of State has given consent under paragraph 5 of Schedule 4A to the Land Registration Act 2002 to the registration of the disposition, by a consent dated [*insert date*].

[ ] The disposition has been made by an insolvency practitioner and in circumstances both specified in [*insert the title of the regulations made under paragraph 3(3) of Schedule 4A to the Land Registration Act 2002 and the specific provision relating to the circumstances*].

Signature……………………….

Name…………………………..

Status…………………………..

Firm……………………………

Date……………………………

> A certificate by an individually regulated conveyancer must be signed in their own name and their status given (e.g. solicitor, licensed conveyancer, CILEX Conveyancing Practitioner).
>
> Any other employee of a conveyancer must sign in their employer's name but must state their own name and their status (e.g. secretary, paralegal) as well as providing their employer's name.

Certificate OE2

Certificate to support an application to register a disposition of a qualifying estate

(a) by an overseas entity which became entitled to be registered as proprietor of that estate on or after 5 September 2022 (but was not so registered), or
(b) where the application includes a disposition made by an overseas entity which became entitled to be registered as proprietor of that estate on or after 5 September 2022 (but was not so registered).

Note – a separate certificate is required for each disposition by an overseas entity.

Title number(s) ....

I/We .... of .... certify that the following provision under paragraph 4(2) of Schedule 4A to the Land Registration Act 2002 applies to the [*specify transfer, lease or charge*] ('the disposition') dated [*insert the date of the disposition*] made by [*insert the name of the overseas entity*] ('the overseas entity') to [*insert the name of transferee, lessee or chargee*]:

[Select the relevant provision below. You may delete the words in italics and the provisions that do not apply.]

[ ] The disposition: [*select and complete the relevant statement*]

- was made in pursuance of a statutory obligation under [*specify the statutory provision under which the obligation arose*].
- was made in pursuance of an order of the [*specify which court*] court dated [*specify the date of the court order*], case number [*provide the proceedings number*].
- occurred by operation of law on the basis that [*explain how operation of law arose giving any relevant legislative provision*].

[ ] The disposition was made in pursuance of a contract made before the overseas entity became entitled to be registered, being a contract dated [*insert date*] made between [*give the names of the parties to the contract*] relating to [*give the details of the property to which the contract related*], and that the overseas entity became entitled to be registered on [*insert date*].

[ ] The disposition was made in the exercise of a power of sale or leasing conferred on the proprietor of a registered charge or a receiver appointed by such a proprietor, being a charge dated [*insert the date of the charge*] made between

[*provide the parties to the charge*] and registered on [*provide the date of registration of the charge*].

[ ] The Secretary of State has given consent under paragraph 5 of Schedule 4A to the Land Registration Act 2002 to the registration of the disposition, by a consent dated [*insert date*].

[ ] The disposition has been made by an insolvency practitioner and in circumstances both specified in [*insert the title of the regulations made under paragraph 3(3) of Schedule 4A to the Land Registration Act 2002 and the specific provision relating to the circumstances*].

Signature..........................

Name...............................

Status...............................

Firm................................

Date................................

A certificate by an individually regulated conveyancer must be signed in their own name and their status given (e.g. solicitor, licensed conveyancer, CILEX Conveyancing Practitioner).

Any other employee of a conveyancer must sign in their employer's name but must state their own name and their status (e.g. secretary, paralegal) as well as providing their employer's name.

Index

References are to page numbers.